We Have Not Been Moved
Resisting Racism and Militarism
in 21st Century America

Edited by Elizabeth "Betita" Martínez,
Matt Meyer, and Mandy Carter

With a Foreword by Cornel West and
AfterPoems by Sonia Sanchez and
Alice Walker

War Resisters League

We Have Not Been Moved: Resisting Racism and Militarism in 21st Century America
Edited by Elizabeth Martínez, Matt Meyer, and Mandy Carter © 2012

This edition © 2012 PM Press

ISBN: 978-1-60486-480-9
LCCN: 2011939675

PM Press
P.O. Box 23912
Oakland, CA 94623
pmpress.org

**973.
9**

War Resisters League
339 Lafayette Street
New York, NY 10012
www.warresisters.org

10 9 8 7 6 5 4 3 2 1

Cover by Josh MacPhee
Layout by Jonathan Rowland

Printed in the USA on recycled paper, by the Employee Owners of Thomson-Shore in Dexter, Michigan.
www.thomsonshore.com

Ultimately, there can be no peace without justice, and no justice without peace. The two great moral issues of our time, peace and human rights, are so closely related that we can say that they are one and the same.
  —Coretta Scott King, Madison Square Garden Anti-War Rally, June 8, 1965

A true revolution of values will soon look uneasily on the glaring contrast of poverty and wealth… A true revolution of values will lay hands on the world order and say of war: "This way of settling differences is not just." … A genuine revolution of values means in the final analysis that our loyalties must become ecumenical rather than sectional. Every nation must now develop an overriding loyalty to mankind as a whole in order to preserve the best in their individual societies. This call for a world-wide fellowship that lifts neighborly concern beyond one's tribe, race, class and nation is in reality a call for an all-embracing and unconditional love.
  —Rev. Dr. Martin Luther King Jr., "Beyond Vietnam" (1967)

Contents

II. (Re)Defining Racism and Militarism: What Qualifies? Who Decides?

III. Chickens and Eggs: War, Race, and Class

IV. The Roots and Routes of War: Patriarchy and Heterosexism

V. The Roots and Routes of War: Nationalism, Religion, Ageism

VI. Where Do We Go from Here? Organizing Against War and Racism

VII. AfterPoems

Foreword

King's Truth

Revolution and America's Crossroads

Cornel West

This historic book and monumental collection of many of the prophetic giants of our time could not appear at a more propitious moment. We are at a fundamental crossroad in the history of America—America as imperial power and America as democratic experiment. Elizabeth "Betita" Martínez, Matt Meyer, and Mandy Carter have given us this prophetic intervention to keep alive the grand legacy of Martin Luther King Jr. These three legendary freedom fighters bring together the best of the peace movement and the best of the anti-racist movement in our time. And Martin Luther King Jr. smiles from his grave—a precious gesture that acknowledges that his true work and witness have not been forgotten in the age of Obama.

But the words of Rabbi Abraham Joshua Heschel still haunt us: "The whole future of America depends on the impact and influence of Dr. King." Rabbi Heschel often spoke those words during the last years of King's life, when 72 percent of whites and 55 percent of Blacks disapproved of King's opposition to the Vietnam War and his efforts to eradicate poverty in America. King's dream of a more democratic America had become, in his own words, "a nightmare," owing to the persistence of "racism, poverty, militarism, and materialism" in oligarchic America. This is why in his last years, King called America a "sick society" and planned to preach a sermon entitled "Why America May Go to Hell" the Sunday after he was assassinated. King always acknowledged the many decent Americans, yet it seemed they "lack all conviction, while the worst are full of passionate intensity."

He did not think that America should or ought to go to hell, but rather that it may go to hell owing to its national decline, cultural decay, and political paralysis. King was not an American Gibbon telling the story of the decline and fall of the American empire, but rather a courageous and visionary Christian blues man, fighting with every fiber in his being to persevere and prevail with style and love in the face of the four great catastrophes of militarism, materialism, racism, and poverty.

For King, militarism was an imperial catastrophe that produced a military-industrial complex and national security state that warped the country's priorities and resulted in an unquestioned and high proportion of the U.S. budget. Smart weapons of mass destruction rule the world yet stunt our stature (as with the immoral drones dropping bombs every four days on innocent civilians). Materialism was a spiritual catastrophe, promoted now by a corporate media multiplex and culture industry that hardens the hearts of hardcore consumers and coarsens the consciences of would-be citizens. Clever gimmicks of mass distraction yield a cheap soul-craft of addicted and self-medicated narcissists. Racism was a moral catastrophe, most graphically seen in the prison industrial complex and targeted police surveillance in Black and brown ghettos, rendered invisible in public discourse. Arbitrary uses of the law—in the name of wars against drugs—have produced, in Michelle Alexander's apt phrase, a new Jim Crow of mass incarceration. Lastly, poverty was the economic catastrophe inseparable from the power of greedy oligarchs and avaricious plutocrats indifferent to the social misery of poor children, elderly citizens, and working people. For King, these four catastrophes constituted an iron cage for powerless citizens wedded to two corrupt political parties beholden to big money—liberal and conservative versions of oligarchic rule. At the top are golden cages for well-to-do citizens, inside gated communities on joyless quests for pleasure.

The age of Obama promised to build on King's legacy in the face of the monumental catastrophes of the Bush administration. And the financial catastrophe of 2008 provided a propitious moment to renew and revive the soul of America. We needed a King-like story to explain to ourselves why and how we drifted so far away from King's dream, the best of who and what we are. Yet no such narrative was forthcoming from our brilliant and charismatic president. There was no narrative about the greed of Wall Street oligarchs and avarice of corporate plutocrats in search of profits at any cost, with no allegiance to national interest, public life, or common good. No investigations, no prosecutions, no accountability of economic elites who engage in insider trading, market manipulation, and predatory lending, or of political elites who authorized torture or wiretapping. Yet law and order has been expanded and intensified for deported immigrants, evicted homeowners, unemployed and underemployed citizens, homeless veterans, public workers and teachers, and innocent poor children. In short, the Obama administration reinforced a reign of hypocrisy by remaining beholden to Wall Street oligarchs (as with Larry Summers and Tim Geithner as his chief economic advisors) and corporate plutocrats (as with Jeffrey Immelt, chairman of the Jobs Commission and CEO of no-tax-paying General Electric).

Just when the King legacy required democratic vision and strong fights for homeowners, workers, and poor people in the form of jobs, home relief, and investment in education, infrastructure, and housing, the Obama administration gave us bailouts for banks, record profits for Wall Street, and massive cuts against the vulnerable to balance the budget. As Tavis Smiley rightly noted on our 2011 Poverty Tour, the bipartisan budget deal of 2011 was itself a "war against the poor"—the last phase of a thirty-year, top-down, one-sided class war against poor and working people in the name of a morally bankrupt policy of deregulating markets, lowering taxes, and cutting spending for those already socially neglected and economically abandoned. The top 400 Americans own more wealth than the bottom 150 million Americans. Yet a wealth tax is inconceivable just as a fair income tax seems impossible. Still, we must fight back with a dramatic story and moral integrity.

The lack of a King-like narrative to reinvigorate poor and working people enabled right-wing populists to seize the moment with credible claims about government corruption and ridiculous claims about deregulated markets and lower taxes. They have draped themselves in nostalgia about slaveholding Founding Fathers. This right-wing threat to the Obama administration and the future of the country is real. It is a catastrophic response to King's four catastrophes, and would lead to hellish conditions for many, if not most, Americans. Yet the Obama administration continues to capitulate, cave in, or punt on second down. Oligarchic America still triumphs beneath the seductive smile of its neoliberal Black mascot—as was true for its white neoliberal and conservative mascots Bill Clinton and George W. Bush. And Martin Luther King Jr. weeps from the grave, and from the newly minted Memorial on the National Mall. King never confused substance with symbolism. He never conflated a flesh-and-blood sacrifice with a stone-and-mortar edifice. We rightly celebrate his substance and sacrifice, because he loved us all so deeply. But let us not remain satisfied with symbolism and edifice because we too often love the status quo even as it crumbles.

Our greatest writer, Herman Melville (a white, literary bluesman, who spent his life in love with America even as he was our fiercest critic of American exceptionalism), noted: "Truth uncompromisingly told will always have its ragged edges; hence the conclusion of such a narration is apt to be less finished than an architectural finial."

King's true response to our crisis can be put in one word: revolution. A revolution in our priorities, a reevaluation of our values, a reinvigoration of our public life and a fundamental transformation of our ways of thinking and living that promotes a transfer of power from oligarchs and plutocrats to everyday people and ordinary citizens who respond to catastrophes with style and love—like John Coltrane, Toni Morrison, Tennessee Williams, and Martin Luther King Jr. In concrete terms, this means support for King-like politicians such as Bernie Sanders, massive community and media organizing, civil disobedience, and life-and-death confrontations with the oligarchic powers that be. Like King, we need to put on our cemetery clothes and be coffin-ready for this next great democratic battle in the epic of American and world history. This text is a major step and weapon in that battle!

Resisting Racism and War

An Introduction;

or, What Will It Take to Move Forward?

Matt Meyer, Elizabeth "Betita" Martínez, and Mandy Carter

We are fighting for our freedom,
We shall not be moved;
Fighting for our children,
We shall not be moved;
Just like a tree that's planted by the water,
We shall not be moved.
—traditional folk/gospel song, origins unknown

She gathered her babies,
their tears slick as oil on black faces,
their young eyes canvassing mornings of madness.
Momma, is Master going to sell you from us tomorrow?
Yes.
Unless you keep walking more
and talking less.
Yes.
Unless the keeper of our lives
releases me from all commandments.
Yes.
And your lives,
never mine to live,
will be executed upon the killing floor of innocents.
Unless you match my heart and words,
saying with me,
I shall not be moved.
—excerpt from Maya Angelou's "Our Grandmothers" (1990)

It has become common knowledge that, when Dr. Martin Luther King Jr. was planning to make a strong statement against U.S. involvement in the Vietnam War and

1

intervention in Southeast Asia—effectively linking the anti-war movement to the massive civil rights and racial justice movements, many of his advisors urged him not to do it. Too much potential "mainstream" support, they argued, would be lost from such a linking of issues and communities. King, however, went ahead—well aware that true leadership was, as he put it, less a searching for consensus than a molding of consensus. Vincent Harding, a King advisor who helped draft the speech which would come to be known as "Beyond Vietnam," himself has strong words to say about leadership and the linking of issues. The movement King came to epitomize, Harding implores, was not primarily a movement for civil or race-based rights, but rather a Black-led movement for human freedom. Close to half a century later, however, it is no more common than it was in those heady but segregated days for freedom struggles and peace campaigns to be carefully and strategically connected.

In 2003, noted Chicana historian and activist Elizabeth "Betita" Martínez, writing about the post–September 11 coalitions against escalating conflict and war in the Gulf, raised the question: the War Resisters League resists *what*? This query, set forth in a larger piece on whether the anti-war movement had an obligation to be anti-racist as well, was aimed at problematic War Resisters League (WRL) practice in the years following 9/11, and controversies which took place within the eighty-plus-year-old organization about emphasis, direction, and resources. Many institutions with that long a history would have reacted defensively to such publically raised criticisms. Some may have drafted a letter in response, dealing point by point with issues brought up in the article, and which ones some WRLers agreed with, disagreed with, or were split about. The WRL, however, decided on a different approach altogether: they invited Martínez to fly out to New York City on the eve of their next national committee meeting. An open forum was held at a popular venue, free to anyone in the New York progressive community. The forum discussed issues of the connections between racism and militarism, Martínez had noted in her poignant article. One result of the discussions held at that public event, and at the subsequent WRL meetings held later that same weekend, is the book you now hold in your hands.

The significance of linking progressive and radical "people of color" and "white folk" based in the empire known as the United States of America has been a pressing one for well over a century. That intellectual giant W.E.B. Du Bois famously called the "problem of the color line" the most significant issue facing the United States in the twentieth century is no small indictment, and the problem shows few signs of improvement even in the era of an American president of African descent. The focus of this book is on connecting, in both theoretical and practical terms, our struggles in resistance to both racism and militarism. These two of the three "giant triplets" which must be overcome, mentioned (along with extreme materialism) by Dr. King in his 1967 speech, are reviewed here in historical and contemporary terms, from a diversity of activist and academic perspectives. We join together, however, just like Dr. King suggested, believing that a radical revolution of values is needed, to "conquer" the idea that "machines and computers, profit motives and property rights" are considered more important than people. True freedom, we believe, and the peace so many of us seek, can only come about when justice—political, judicial, social, economic, and cultural in form and content—is available to all. Resisting racism and militarism, for us, is a vital starting point at this moment in the development of our twenty-first century freedom movement.

Many of us took careful note when pioneering pacifist researcher Johan Galtung declared, in 2010, that the fall of the U.S. empire was at hand. Never one for flashy rhetoric, Galtung remains respected the world over for his intensive studies of social movements and what it takes to make social change. A founder of the International Peace Research Association, and of the global field of peace studies, he accurately predicted ten years in advance that the Soviet Union would come to an end, beginning with the fall of the Berlin Wall. Now, Galtung states that the U.S. empire is, itself, up "against a wall." It is, in his words, "an empire in despair; an empire, I would say, in its last phase. …It cannot last longer than till about 2020."

Reflecting on Galtung's dramatic analysis, it may be useful to think back ten years, or even twenty, to the changes witnessed by the last generation of radicals. Apartheid will never end, we were assured by astute observers, at least without a bloodbath. Many of us who came of age in the 1970s and 1980s seriously thought we might never see an end to the racist regime in our own lifetimes. Yet in 1994, with significantly less violence than anyone expected, Nelson Mandela was elected president, and a formal end to political apartheid came about. "You could hardly find a single white person, after the elections, who admitted to supporting apartheid!" noted South African poet and former political prisoner Dennis Brutus. "Like all revolutions," Brutus reminded us, "radical change seems impossible till very late in the struggle, when things begin to take place at a frighteningly furious fast pace. After that, all those radical changes appear to have been quite inevitable."

Closer to home, there was hardly a social scientist or grassroots campaigner in the United States at the turn of the twenty-first century who suggested—in even a cautious manner—that we'd have a Black president by the decade's end. In broad, historical terms, the election of Barack Hussein Obama should not have been such an unbelievable achievement. Should any of us have been so surprised that the U.S. empire would need to make accommodations, especially in the decades following the defeats in Southeast Asia, following the tumult of revolution in the Middle East and Latin America, following the Black liberation movements of the late 1960s through 1970s—which had to be violently and illegally (even by the minimal standards of U.S. law) repressed, following the ever-intensifying economic collapses of the 1980s and 2000s? Very few, if any, radicals believed or expected that Obama would lead us to a nation-state or world of justice and peace, or even to a time of full racial equality. But neither did we expect that a figure such as Obama could emerge from the smoking ashes of four decades of struggle and crisis, to help "fix" the status quo. We were woefully unprepared for the challenges and possibilities presented by the "Obama movement." We must do more than simply anticipate the "enormous changes at the last minute" (to borrow Grace Paley's poignant phrase), that will surely rock our world in the years to come.

We must use the best of our imaginations today to look forward ten years, toward 2020 and beyond. What events seem impossible today, which will appear inevitable and obvious in 2020? What projects do we need to take on now, what choices and decisions do we need to make, to put us in a position to shape positive social change over the next era of struggle? Johan Galtung suggests that, with the end of the U.S. empire, two options will be likely for the U.S. nation-state: there will either be a blossoming of people's rights and freedoms, or a clamped-down fascism with narrowly defined rights and increased repression. How can we build bridges that will make that first road the most appealing one to the broadest number of people? Certainly as editors of this volume we believe that one urgent task is to draw clear connections between the evils of militarism and racism, and provide inspiring examples of ways in which these evils have been and can be resisted.

In looking to provide a focused definition of the interconnected problems of racism and militarism, we must first be forthcoming about our own bias as editors. While we respectfully present articles that we feel are filled with essential truths, and while among the three of us there are differences in ideological background and occasionally tactical approach, we are firmly rooted in the tradition that has come to be known as revolutionary nonviolence. In taking obvious inspiration from the words and actions of Dr. King, going well beyond his 1963 "dreams" of a multiracial America, we are also aware of our apparently contradictory admiration of two other leaders of that period: Malcolm X and Bayard Rustin. While Minister Malcolm has been diminished by the catchphrase "by any means necessary," we understand that his true revolutionary reach is rooted in his deep economic and social analysis of the nature of white supremacy and the colonial subjugation of African peoples based in America. And while there is much to criticize about Bayard's shifts away from the peace movement in the late-1960s, we also recognize that this master strategist was dealing with his own contradictions—attempting to balance his pacifist and anti-segregationist politics with his own life as a gay man and his economic orientation regarding the nature of class and labor in building for longterm change.

For us, revolutionary nonviolence is an experiment, a methodology that has hardly been seriously explored (by radicals in the industrialized north at least). In the words of feminist Barbara Deming, this "nonviolence of the strong" is still "in the process of invention." We therefore also reject the false dichotomies which divide progressive peoples, such as the adherence to holier-than-thou pacifism which prevents some nonviolent reformists from entering into coalition or dialogue with revolutionaries engaged in armed struggle. We take our example from Pan-African pacifist Bill Sutherland, who spent his last fifty-seven years serving as a bridge between people on the continent and in the Diaspora, maintaining equally close and challengingly loving relationships with little-known local strikers and world famous leaders of guerilla liberation movements, with recognizable Nobel Peace Prize recipients and hardly known conscientious objectors. We believe that the greatest violence taking place today is not on the traditional battlefields of conflicting armies, but in the dizzying poverty and economic inequalities which destroy far more lives than any gun or bomb. For us, building alliances with those who profit from this greater violence—or those who make excuses for them—is much more difficult then breaking bread with people who believe that they must defend themselves if attacked.

We are moved by the words of South Carolina campaigner Kevin Alexander Gray, who wrote—in his Call for a New Anti-War Movement—that "no effort for social change starts in the mainstream." We must, Gray reminds us, be willing to take bold stands that will excite and incite people—drawing attention to the issues at hand such that politicians will be forced to listen. Gray's Call, which emphasizes the U.S. war on drugs and the massive and growing prison industrial complex as contemporary domestic flashpoints of violence perpetrated against communities of color, also understands that worthwhile reformists call for "reconciliation, repentance, and redemption" in dealing with racial inequality and the war mentality. A more radical approach, however, requires nothing short of justice. And justice, in turn, "means restitution—paying the debt."

We are aware that revolutionary nonviolence requires us to become disciplined, lifelong fighters for fundamental change: willing to take great risks and expecting the casualties that inevitably come in any revolutionary battle. And we accept the approach of Mohandas Gandhi, whose admonition to the Indian movement regarding the British imperialists—to "never let them rest"—was so inspiring to Martin Luther King. But we also understand that we must take great care in codifying "us" and "them" structures, or making any individual person become a permanent enemy. We are heartened by the words of feminist Zillah Eisenstein, who, in her essay "Mythic Enemies and Newest Races" in *The Audacity of Races and Genders*, suggests that "present-day conflicts deny and misrepresent important histories that would otherwise allow a common humanity" that would serve to unite broad groupings of people. As "the" Muslim becomes the favorite figure to hate and fear in the United States today, "new constructions of nations and races are continuously manufactured to assist in the 'othering' process that allows for the creation of necessary enemies." As adherents of revolutionary nonviolence, we maintain that our only true enemies are the institutions of white supremacy and racism, of materialism and corporate capitalism, of sexism and heterosexism, of militarism, war, and the root causes of war.

We cannot be shocked, but still we are horrified, at the unchecked U.S. military budget, which in Fiscal Year 2011 reached the highest point (in constant dollars) than since the last year of World War II. Now exceeding the combined total of the military budgets of the rest of the planet earth, the 2011 budget is an increase of over

100 percent from the amounts spent just twelve years earlier. We are heartened that some radical circles which previously did little to consider the implications of rampant militarism are now taking special note, as in the Socialist Register 2009 special focus on "Violence Today: Actually Existing Barbarism." An increase in the neoliberal agenda internationally requires an increase in the scope of the global policeman, even if that also means waging war against nature and the earth itself. And while we agree with political economist Samir Amin that the current crisis necessitates the radicalization and linking of popular struggles especially among what he terms "the periphery," we cannot agree that these struggles require armed resistance. We feel greater connection to recent writings of Horace Campbell, whose research on the mobilized networks to elect Barack Obama in the 2008 elections suggest the potential for a revolutionary moment in twenty-first century U.S. politics. Campbell's focus on "Ubuntu, self-organization, and self-mobilization," along with optimism as a political act, draws from both Gandhian and Guevara principles of love as a radicalizing force—and nonviolence as the key element in a future revolutionary project.

There are many grassroots examples of outstanding programs and groups that have worked to link racism and militarism, and to shine a light to a not-far-off day when we may be rid of these twin evils. There are even more words which have been written about why and how we may approach dealing with these interrelated "isms." This book seeks to take the reader on a course which spans several decades and numerous ideologies, collecting some of the most important voices on these subjects and campaigns. No single volume could hope to include all or most of the various thinking on these vital points. But we hope and believe that we have successfully collected an important cross-section: both of work that has received too little attention, and of thinking which is fundamental if we are to overcome the errors of our pasts.

It is not a coincidence of our peace-making ideals that we begin this book with an original poem from Indigenous Two Spirit activist Chrystos. Her words help to wonderfully set the context of U.S. history from multiple points of view. In our conversations about this work, written especially for this volume, she asked whether we were using the spelling "American" or "amerikan"? Throughout the book, each of six sections of essays is introduced by an original poem, including inspiring new work by Liz Roberts, Mary Jane Sullivan, Sarah Husein, Dylcia Pagán, and Malkia M'Buzi Moore. The poem "Wild Poppies," by anti-imperialist former political prisoner Marilyn Buck is also included; we had discussed its use with Marilyn before her untimely death at the end of 2010, just weeks after her release on parole.

We are proud to open with an insightful and overlooked dialogical exchange, which took place in the pages of *Liberation* magazine in the late 1950s. Monroe County NAACP leader Robert Franklin Williams had essentially been run out of town by the direct organizing of the Ku Klux Klan, and by the lack of support he received from the national office of his own organization when he called for self-defense against the Klan. Franklin asks whether Negroes can any longer afford to be pacifists, while *Liberation* editor Dave Dellinger asks, in a related article, whether pacifists are willing to "become" Negroes. Dr. Martin Luther King Jr., a frequent contributor to *Liberation*, responds to the discussion with a feature on "the social organization of nonviolence." Finally, Catholic Worker founder Dorothy Day reports on an interview and discussion she held with Mabel and Robert Williams, after they chose exile in revolutionary Cuba over constant flight from white supremacists and the FBI. This fascinating series of commentaries, with woven subtexts on race, war, solidarity, and resistance, helps set the stage for the nuanced articles which follow. No final definitive agreement is reached by the four authors in question, but it is clear that general respect and a willingness to work together pervade the conversations which took place. The movements that all four of those figures would help to build in the decade that followed must be eclipsed by the even more massive movement that we are called upon to build today.

The remaining essays of the first section of our book, "Connections, Contexts, and Challenges," also serve to set the stage for the questions that follow. Three pieces by Barbara Deming help reflect the deep convictions and innovative thinking taking place throughout the 1960s, infused with what would come to be understood as feminist approaches to self-determination and alliance-building. A never-published piece by War Resisters League member Ruth Reynolds follows. Reynolds—as a personal friend of Pedro Albizu Campos and stalwart campaigner for an end to U.S. colonialism in Puerto Rico—came to be known as the key link between the imprisoned island and the few "northamericans" willing to speak out against empire. Finally, three more recent pieces by our own Betita Martínez shine light on the ways the issues of racism and the modern peace movement continued to take shape throughout the 1990s and 2000s.

The second section of *We Have Not Been Moved* focuses upon perspective: who defines what racism is, and what are the debates over how racism and militarism are understood and fought against in the contemporary context. Both academic and activist voices strive to give life to working meanings. We search for answers that can begin to build the broad movement needed for radical change. An interview with civil rights pioneer Vincent Harding starts us out, visioning an America that lives up to the hopes and dreams of past movements. Plowshares cofounder Liz McAlister follows up, along with Muslim American Society leader Ibrahim Abdil-Mu'id Ramey and Fellowship of Reconciliation trainer Alejandra Cecilia Tobar Alatriz, looking at what might constitute an anti-racist, anti-militarist United States. An article on work within the often neglected "other America" by southern activist Anne Braden begins a reflection on what it means to be a good ally to "people of color," which also includes commentary by environmentalist Ted Glick and by Liz Walz. Several academic pieces on the construction and meaning of whiteness follow—authored by Peace and Justice Studies Association's Dean Johnson and by Susan B. Goldberg and Cameron Levin. An interview with veteran organizer Bob Brown of the All-African Peoples Revolutionary Party takes us into myth-busting history lessons, complimented by historian Dan Berger's article on civil rights and Black Power in contemporary perspective. The section is rounded out by an article on the challenges of the Obama era from Black Commentator Bill Fletcher.

"Chickens and Eggs: War, Race, and Class" helps us take the discussion of racism and militarism into a new arena in the third section of the book. Though no definitive agreement or single, incontrovertible "line" is presented or adhered to, a range of viewpoints are articulated to help guide stronger organizational ties and campaigns. We are challenged to reflect upon the most thoughtful and sometimes divergent critiques of how modern-day oppression and violence manifest themselves in our groups as well as our society. Dave Dellinger, former Southern Christian Leadership Council (SCLC) education director Dorothy Cotton, Veterans for Peace and WRL leader Ellen Barfield, and longtime WRL staff person and Socialist Party leader David McReynolds share their perspectives on the role of class, capital, and race in the work for lasting peace. They bring to the fore some sharp questions about how strong the connections between racism and militarism really are, and what role class plays in mediating or exacerbating these conflicts. An essay on economics by political prisoner David Gilbert challenges us to rethink the true nature of the U.S. nation-state. National Black United Front chair Conrad Worrill, "race traitor" Mab Segrest, and Critical Resistance cofounder Ruth Wilson Gilmore reflect on some current what-are-to-be-dones.

The sections of "The Roots and Routes of War," review the sticky and sometimes competitive struggles against between racism and militarism, sexism, heterosexism, nationalism, ageism, and religion. Starhawk leads off the first of these discussions in a piece on the importance of women-specific actions, followed by three classic pieces by Andrea Dworkin, John Stoltenberg, and Audre Lorde. The vital connections which those three had with the anti-war and pacifist movements is too often forgotten; these articles remind us of the challenging but necessary links we all need to make to fight patriarchy, racism, and war while maintaining a connection between our means and our ends. Coeditor Mandy Carter is also featured in this section, along with Kitty Mattes, Victor Lewis, Jon Cohen, Catalyst's Chris Crass, and INCITE!'s Andrea Smith, each pushing the boundaries of how we integrate a diversity of perspectives and radical analysis into our holistic agenda for change.

Matthew Lyons outlines the role of right-wing nationalism post-9/11 in consolidating twenty-first-century racism, while Fred Ho presents the perspective that examining "race" and white skin privilege is itself racist: national liberation is the real issue that must be emphasized. José López, director of Chicago's Juan Antonio Corretjer Puerto Rican Cultural Center and an international spokesperson for the Puerto Rican movement, discuses the contours of their work within the larger freedom struggle, and reflects upon the true meanings and power of principled solidarity. Gwendolyn Zoharah Simmons summons the spiritual to our militant struggles, as she recounts her own amazing history—from SNCC to the Nation of Islam to her work today—and reflects on the lessons we all need to learn. Rabbi Lynn Gottlieb looks at similar issues from different perspectives, as she "gazes into the mirror" of American racism. Joel Kovel, editor of the journal *Capitalism, Nature, Socialism*, helps frame the conundrums of traditional and nontraditional Christian thought with a very modern and new critique on the nature of war. Edward Hasbrouck takes a look at ageism and identity, while a dialogue between editor Matt Meyer and activist Jim Haber takes apart strategic problems and possibilities that come up when we try to make these links.

Finally, the closing section of *We Have Not Been Moved* centers on organizing. Presenting the experiences of those engaged in ongoing work to bring about a more just and humane society, it is no coincidence that many of the stories related in this conclusion come from young activists and organizers. Chris Knestrick's reflection on privilege opens the section, followed by Matt Meyer's essay "We Have Not Been Moved: How the Peace Movement Has Resisted Dealing with Racism in our Ranks." Though more optimistic than its title implies, the article chronicles concrete fault lines of the broad anti-war movements of the 1980s and 1990s; these are also the focus of Suzanne Ross's piece on solidarity organizing in the Central America solidarity movement of the same period. Meyer and U.S. Labor Against War activist and Vietnam veteran Greg Payton outline their internationalist reasons for hope in "To Live is to Resist." Kenyon Farrow, Nada Khader, Momo Chang, Daniel Hunter, Sylvanna Falcón, B. Loewe, and Frida Berrigan are among a new generation of front-line activists, represented in a series of articles on specific challenges and solutions faced in contemporary work. Reflections are also provided by Mumia Abu-Jamal, john a. powell, Tim Wise, Linda Burnham, David Billings, Jean Zwickel, and Meg Starr. A look at the tasks ahead, including some concrete reasons for hope, is provided in Francesca Fiorintini and Clare Bayard's closing article. And the "Anti-Racist Gandhi Manifesto," penned by local activist and former plowshares prisoner Sachio Ko-yin, is included as a practical means for carrying the work forward. We are also honored to end the book with the poetry of two figures whose lives have provided countless examples of tireless work resisting both racism and militarism. Both Sonia Sanchez and Alice Walker, after learning of this project, agreed to have their words close this volume. We have called these lyrical gifts "afterpoems" to signify their special status in helping us envision new tomorrows.

We have long tried to make practical connections between the struggles against racism and militarism. When whites in South Africa's anti-apartheid movement formed an anti-draft group to link those movements in the liberation movement, the WRL was one of the first organizations outside of the continent to provide support, with an eye toward making those links among our own movements here in the Americas. An educational packet that we created to accompany the 1984 U.S. End Conscription Campaign–United Democratic Front tour included the interview with Dorothy Cotton reprinted in this volume. In 2010, however, when Cotton—given her role as a close advisor to Martin Luther King Jr.—provided the Introduction to the reprint of King's book *Why We Can't Wait*, her words brought the need for those links into sharp, contemporary perspective: "We learned some important lessons in our Birmingham struggle, and we need to apply these lessons now. As Martin said, 'We can't wait.' We cannot wait, because the jails are full of young black men, including many who are fathers but unable to parent their children. We can't wait, because we know now that failing to make education a priority cheats the country of latent talent. We can't wait, because our young men and women are being programmed to ill (it's called 'serving our country')."

From the military to the schools, from the prison yard to neighborhood back yards, this book looks at the major venues of modern struggle—from a multiplicity of perspectives—to help tomorrow's revolutionaries begin building the future today. By highlighting the key issues which need to be addressed, we hope to provide some foundation for movements which can, must, and will win victories. If our hopes are for nonviolence and peace, it is clear that we can wait no longer to redouble our work for justice. It is time to step boldly together; it is time to make our move.

How the Moon Became a Stranger

Chrystos

In Honor of Clayton Arrow-Topknot, July 2011

Some came with rifles pointed at our hearts
We died as they decided
if we are human, have souls
The pope's court argued this point for years
We tried to point in another direction
as pointing is extremely rude in our cultures
They arrived with war hearts
We thought they were guests
This points to the continuing clash between us
Points which stab our hands
as we work to include in our place
strangers who hate us
instead of being grateful for our haven
They discovered we died
rather than be imprisoned or enslaved
Not as a point of honor
but because we could not comprehend
the point of cages & whips
mystified by their meaning
for when we live in Spirit
these are useless objects
which store no food for winter
offer no protection from rain
cook no meals
We didn't even use whips on our horses
Soon they stole darker people than ourselves
with hair like buffalo hide
They pointed whips at their hearts
forcing them to do work
the rifles were too lazy to do
Sometimes we were able

to hide & protect the ones who escaped
You can see their faces in old tribal sepias
All of us together were forced
to learn the deadly whip of english
this language of greed, dominance, rape & theft
so we'd no longer be able to speak to our ancestors
The point of this was to force us
to become slaves to buying things, more things
to fruitlessly attempt to fill the emptiness in our souls
& the pockets of the insatiable rich
who bulldoze their way into copying exactly
what they had supposedly fled
for freedom
which they used to incinerate women
demolish forests
create hierarchies of terror
build more prisons
All these lies bubble up burning
in the eyes of the young
who need to know what happened here
We, of the Indigenous light
adhere to our tribal names
not some race imposed by strangers who cannot see
the free colors of the snow
We are footsteps who'd never dare deface the moon
When we pray
safe in our lodges
this pointy, whipped world the rifles brought
       evaporates
We are reborn in our Grandmother's heart
no longer strangers to ourselves
This is why our ceremonies are outlawed
       Even as he kills, a man with a gun
       is a fool, not a god
Race is an advertising gimmick
Different colors of flowers
all of whom bear fruit
Watch stallions
red or black or brown or buff
fight each other
teeth flashing under the moon

12

over mares
not the colors of their hides
The point of all this crazy strangeness
was to appease the poor rifles
who do not understand
how to be human
& believe god to be a tyrant
instead of Creation
Perhaps time is bearing fruit
Let's bury these useless deadly rituals
  To be a rifle
  is to be a slave
When we come to courage
to abandon our prisons of race & war
  we become blessedly
  pointless.

By Any Means Necessary: Two Images

Carrie Mae Weems

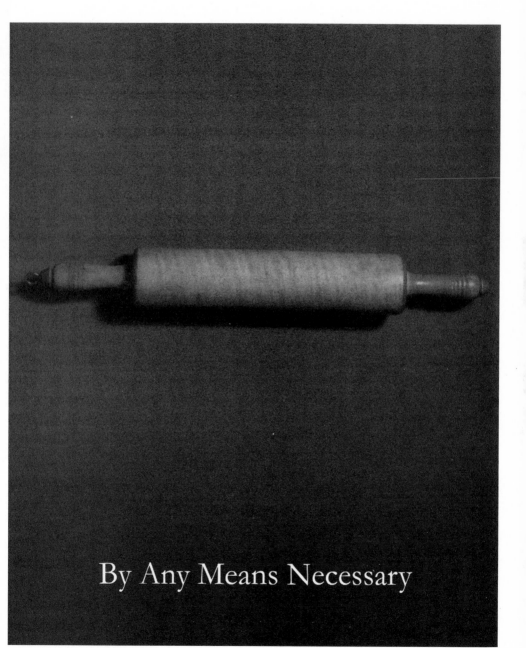

By Any Means Necessary

I. Connections, Contexts, and Challenges

Helping Hands

Karl Bissinger

Wild Poppies

Marilyn Buck

I remember red poppies, wild behind the school house
I didn't want to be there, but I loved to watch the poppies
I used to sit in the window of my room, sketching charcoal trees
what happened to those magnolia trees, to that girl?
I went off to college, escaped my father's thunderstorms
Berkeley. Rebellion. Exhilaration!
the Vietnam War, Black Power, Che took me to Chicago
midnight lights under Wacker Dr. Uptown. South Side. Slapped
by self-determination for taking Freedom Wall photos
without asking
on to California, driving at 3:00 in the morning in the mountains,
I got it: what self-determination means
A daunting task for a young white woman, I was humbled
practice is concrete… harder than crystal-dream concepts
San Francisco, on the front steps at Fulton St.
smoking reefer, drinking "bitterdog" with Black Panthers and white
hippie radicals, talking about when the revolution comes
the revolution did not come. Fred Bennett was missing
we learned he'd been found: ashes, bones, a wedding ring
but later there was Assata's freedom smile
then I was captured, locked into a cell of sewer water
spirit deflated. I survived, carried on, glad to be
like a weed, a wild red poppy,
rooted in life.

Are Pacifists Willing to Be Negroes?

A 1950s Dialogue on Fighting Racism and Militarism,

Using Nonviolence and Armed Struggle

Dave Dellinger, Robert Franklin Williams,

Rev. Dr. Martin Luther King Jr., and Dorothy Day

Founded in 1956 as a forum for debates on strategies and tactics, coalition and move-ment-building, Liberation *magazine came to be an important foundation of the growing civil rights, human rights, peace and anti-war movements of the 1960s and '70s. Edited by leading pacifists A.J. Muste, Dave Dellinger, and Bayard Rustin, the magazine—in part funded by the War Resisters League—was seen by many as part of the New Left, but had roots in the calls for revolutionary nonviolence coming from the radical conscientious objectors and resisters of World War II. The following 1959 excerpted exchange (between King, Williams, and Dellinger) is a case in point of how seemingly divergent peoples were respectfully discussing their points of ideological and practical differences, with an eye toward the greater unity which may be achieved. Williams's classic book* Negroes with Guns *had not yet been published, but he was already an iconic leader—as the NAACP local chapter president who was advocating armed self-defense against the KKK. Three years later, Catholic Worker founder Dorothy Day traveled to Cuba—where Williams was living in exile—and gave an update to the conversation.*

Because North Americans tend to look at famous figures and frozen moments of massive events, we have a harder time remembering or understanding the ways in which movements are built by small steps, overcoming obstacles all the way. Beyond the can-onization of King, the ways in which we remember Williams (as an early militant and, later, the first president of the Republic of New Afrika), Dellinger (as a member of the Chicago Eight and the center of the coalitions against the war in Vietnam), and Day (as the architect of the modern Catholic left), do not help us in holding onto the fact that each of the four of them were affected by and helped affect the tides of history which came their way. This dialogue, held in the pages of Liberation, *helps remind us of both their humanity as well as the force of those times. Looking at the tactical issues faced after the now-historic Montgomery bus boycott, and the increased lynching of Black activists in the South, Dellinger especially turns the question of whether the Black movement should embrace absolute nonviolence on its head, centering his argument on the responsibilities of anti-racist white peaceniks. Over fifty years later, with some of the same points creating challenges and divisions within our organizations and campaigns, we may do well to create greater spaces for respectful discussion in our quest for building more successful movements.*

Dave Dellinger: Robert F. Williams makes a strong case for a negative answer to the question many Negroes are asking these days: can Negroes afford to be nonviolent? The Montgomery bus protest, which was once hailed as a portent of greater victories to come, is fast becoming an icon for pacifist devotions. In Alabama and Mississippi, in North Carolina and Virginia, in Little Rock and Tallahassee, the organized movement for liberation is almost at a standstill. In almost any southern town, the individual Negro who dares to assert his dignity as a human being in concrete relationships of everyday life rather than in the sanctuary of the pulpit is in danger of meeting the fate of Mack Parker or Emmett Till.

In such a situation, it would be arrogant for us to criticize Robert Williams for arming in defense of himself and his neighbors. Gandhi once said that although nonviolence is the best method of resistance to evil, it is better for persons who have not yet attained the capacity for nonviolence to resist violently than not resist at all. Since we have failed to reach the level of effective resistance, we can hardly condemn those who have not embraced nonviolence. Nonviolence without resistance to evil is like a soul without a body. Perhaps it has some meaning in heaven but not in the world we live in. At this point, we should be more concerned with our own failure as pacifists to help spread the kind of action undertaken in Montgomery than with the failures of persons like Williams who, in many cases, are the only ones who stand between an individual Negro and a marauding Klan.

When nonviolence works, as it sometimes does against seemingly hopeless odds, it succeeds by disarming its opponents. It does this through intensive application of the insight that our worst enemy is actually a friend in disguise. The nonviolent resister identifies so closely with his opponent that he feels his problems as if they were his own, and is therefore unable to hate or hurt him, even in self-defense. This inability to injure an aggressor, even at the risk of one's own life, is based not on a denial of the self in obedience to some external ethical command, but on an extension of the self to include one's adversary. "Any man's death diminishes me."

But it is a perversion of nonviolence to identify only with the aggressor and not with his victims. The failure of pacifists with respect to the South has been our failure to identify with a "screaming Mack Parker" or with any of the oppressed and intimidated Negroes. Like the liberals, we have made a "token" identification to the point of feeling indignant at lynching and racist oppression, but we have not identified ourselves with the victims to the point where we feel the hurts as if they were our own. It is difficult to say what we would be doing now if Emmett Till had been our own son, or if other members of our family were presently living in the south under the daily humiliation suffered by Negroes. But it is a good bet that we would not be in our present state of lethargy. We would not find it so easy to ask them to be patient and long-suffering and nonviolent in the face of our own failure to launch a positive nonviolent campaign for protection and liberation. The real question today is not can Negroes afford to be pacifists, but are pacifists willing to be Negroes?

This question is particularly pointed in the South, and those of us who live in the North should not feel overconfident as to how we would act if we lived there. But the tragic fact is that in the South, the bulk of the members of the Society of Friends and of other pacifist groups live down to the rules of segregation much as other people do… So long as this pattern is maintained, a temporary absence of overt violence only means the appearance of peace when there is no peace. Human beings must love one another, or they will learn to hate one another. Segregation is incompatible with love. Sooner or later, segregation must erupt into violence, and those white persons who conform to the practice of segregation are as surely responsible as those of either color who bring out the guns.

Robert Williams makes a bad mistake when he implies that the only alternative to violence is the approach of the "cringing, begging Negro ministers," who appealed to the city for protection and then retired in defeat. The power of the police, as the power of the F.B.I., the courts, and the federal government is rooted in violence. The fact that the violence does not always come into bloody play does not alter the fact that the power of the government is not the integrating power of love but the disintegrating power of guns and prisons. Unfortunately, too many of those who hailed the precedent of the Montgomery bus protest have turned away from its example and have been carrying on the fight in the courts or by appeals to legislators and judges.

In Montgomery, it was Rosa Parks, Martin King and their comrades who went to jail, not the segregationists. The power of the action lay partly in the refusal of the participants to accept defeat when the power of the local government was stacked against them, partly in their refusal to cooperate with the evil practice (riding the segregated buses) and partly in the spirit of dignity and love expressed in the words and actions of King.

Those of us who are white will never experience the indignities that are imposed from birth to burial on our colored brothers. But the least we can do while working for another Montgomery is to refuse to conform to segregation wherever we are… These simple acts of identification and decency could turn out to be more revolutionary than we dare hope.

Robert Franklin Williams: In 1954, I was an enlisted man in the U.S. Marine Corps. As a Negro in an integrated unit that was overwhelmingly white, I shall never forget the evening we were lounging in the recreation room watching television as a news bulletin flashed on the screen. This was the historic Supreme Court decision that segregation in the public schools is unconstitutional. Because of the interracial atmosphere, there was no vocal comment. There was for a while complete silence. I never knew how the Southern white boys felt about this bulletin. Perhaps I never will, but for myself, my inner emotions must have been approximate to the Negro slaves' when they first heard about the Emancipation Proclamation. Elation took hold of me so strongly that I found it very difficult to refrain from yielding to an urge of jubilation. I learned later that night that other Negroes in my outfit had felt the same surge of elation.

On this momentous night of May 17, 1954, I felt that at last the government was willing to assert itself on behalf of first-class citizenship, even for Negroes. I experienced a sense of loyalty that I have never felt before. I was sure that this was the beginning of a new era of American democracy. At last, I felt that I was a part of America and that I belonged. That was what I had always wanted, even as a child.

I returned to civilian life in 1955 and the hope I had for Negro liberation faltered. I had returned to a South that was determined to stay the hand of progress at all cost. Acts of violence and words and deeds of hate and spite rose from every quarter. An attitude prevailed that Negroes had a court decree from the "Communist inspired court," but the local racist had the means to initiate the old law of the social jungle called Dixie. Since the first Negro slaves arrived in America, the white supremacists have relied on violence as a potent weapon of intimidation to deprive Negroes of their rights. The Southerner is not prone to easy change; therefore the same tactics that proved so successful against Negroes through the years are still being employed today. There is open defiance to law and order throughout the South today. Governor Faubus and the Little Rock campaign was a shining example of the Southern racists' respect for the law of the land and constituted authority.

The State of Virginia is in open defiance of federal authority. States like my native state of North Carolina are submitting to token integration and openly boasting that this is the solution to circumvention of the Supreme Court decisions. The officials of this state brazenly slap themselves on the back for being successful in depriving great numbers of their colored citizens of the rights of first-class citizenship. Yes, after having such short-lived hope, I have become disillusioned about the prospect of a just, democratic-minded government motivated by politicians with high moral standards enforcing the Fourteenth Amendment without the pressure of expediency.

Since my release from the Marine Corps, I could cite many cases of unprovoked violence that have been visited upon my people… The Southern brute respects only force. Nonviolence is a very potent weapon when the oppressed is civilized, but nonviolence is no match or repellent for a sadist. I have great respect for the pacifist, that is, for the pure pacifist. I think a pure pacifist is one who resents violence against nations as well as individuals and is courageous enough to speak out against jingoistic governments (including his own) without an air of self-righteousness and pious moral individuality. I am not a pacifist and I am sure that I may safely say that most of my people are not. Passive resistance is a powerful weapon in gaining concessions from oppressors, but I venture to say that if Mack Parker had had an automatic shotgun at his disposal, he could have served as a great deterrent against lynching.

Rev. Martin Luther King is a great and respected leader of our race. The Montgomery bus boycott was a great victory for American democracy. However, most people have confused the issues facing the race. In Montgomery the issue was a matter of struggle for human dignity. Nonviolence is made to order for that type of conflict. While praising the actions of those courageous Negroes who participated in the Montgomery affair, we must not allow the complete aspects of the Negro struggle throughout the South to be taken out of their proper perspective. In a great many localities in the South Negroes are faced with the necessity of combatting savage violence. The struggle is for mere existence. The Negro is in a position of begging for life. There is no lawful deterrent against those who would do him violence. An open declaration of nonviolence, or turn-the-other-cheekism is an invitation that the white racist brutes will certainly honor by brutal attack on cringing, submissive Negroes. It is time for the Negro in the South to reappraise his method of dealing with his ruthless oppressor.

In 1957, the Klan moved into Monroe and Union County (North Carolina). In the beginning we did not notice them much. Their numbers steadily increased to the point wherein the local press reported as many as seventy-five hundred racists massed at one rally. They became so brazen that mile-long motorcades started invading the Negro community. These hooded thugs fired pistols from car windows, screamed, and incessantly blew their automobile horns. On one occasion they caught a Negro woman on the street and tried to force her to dance for them at gun point. She escaped into the night, screaming and hysterical. They forced a Negro merchant to close down his business on direct orders from the Klan. Drivers of cars tried to run Negroes down when seen walking on the streets at night. Negro women were struck with missiles thrown from passing vehicles. Lawlessness was rampant. A Negro doctor was framed on a charge of performing an abortion on a white woman. This doctor, who was vice-president of the NAACP, was placed in a lonely cell in the basement of a jail, although men prisoners are usually confined upstairs. A crowd of white men started congregating around the jail. It is common knowledge that a lynching was averted. We have had the usual threats of the Klan here, but instead of cowing, we organized an armed guard and set up a defense force around the doctor's house. On one occasion, we had to exchange gunfire with the Klan. Each time the Klan came on a raid they were led by police cars. We appealed to the President of the United States to have the Justice Department investigate the police. We appealed to Governor Luther Hodges. All our appeals to constituted law were in vain. Governor Hodges, in an underhanded way, defended the Klan. He publically made a statement, to the press, that I had exaggerated Klan activity in Union County—despite the fact that they were operating openly and had gone so far as to build a Klan clubhouse and advertise meetings in the local press and on the radio.

A group of nonviolent ministers met the city Board of Aldermen and pleaded with them to restrict the Klan from the colored community. The city fathers advised these cringing, begging Negro ministers that the Klan had constitutional rights to meet and organize in the same way as the NAACP. Not having been infected by turn-the-other-cheekism, a group of Negroes who showed a willingness to fight caused the city officials to deprive the Klan of its constitutional rights after local papers told of dangerous incidents between Klansmen and armed Negroes. Klan motorcades have been legally banned from the City of Monroe.

The possibility of tragedy's striking both sides of the tracks has caused a mutual desire to have a peaceful coexistence. The fact that any racial brutality may cause white blood to flow as well as Negro is lessening racial tension. The white bigots are sparing Negroes from brutal attack, not because of a new sense of morality, but because Negroes have adopted a policy of meeting violence with violence.

I think there is enough latitude in the struggle for Negro liberation for the acceptance of diverse tactics and philosophies. There is need for pacifists and nonpacifists. I think each freedom fighter must unselfishly contribute what he has to offer. I have been a soldier and a Marine. I have been trained in the way of violence. Self-defense to a Marine is a reflex action. People like Rev. Martin Luther King have been trained for the pulpit. I think they would be as out of place in a conflict that demanded real violent action as I would be in a pulpit praying for an indifferent God to come down from Heaven and rescue a screaming Mack Parker or Emmett Till from an ungodly howling mob. I believe if we were going to pray, we ought to pass the ammunition while we pray. If we are too pious to kill in our own self-defense, how can we have the heart to ask the Holy God to come down to this violent fray and smite down our enemies?

As a race, we have been praying for three hundred years. The NAACP boasts that it has fought against lynching for fifty years. A fifty year fight without victory is not impressive to me. An unwritten anti-lynch law was written overnight in Monroe. It is strange that so-called Negro leaders have never stopped to think why a simple thing like an anti-lynch law in a supposedly democratic nation is next to impossible to get passed. Surely every citizen in a republic is entitled not to be lynched. To seek an anti-lynch law in the present situation is to seek charity. Individuals and governments are more inclined to do things that promote the general welfare and well-being of the populace. A prejudiced government and a prejudiced people are not going to throw a shield of protection around the very people in the South on whom they vent pent-up hatreds as scapegoats. When white people in the South start needing such a law, we will not even have to wait fifty days to get it.

On May 5, 1959, while president of the Union County branch of the NAACP, I made a statement to the United Press International … and I said then what I say now. I believe that Negroes must be willing to defend themselves, their women, their children, and their homes. They must be willing to die and to kill in repelling their assailants. There is no Fourteenth Amendment, no equal protection under the law. Negroes *must* protect themselves... The Negro on the street who suffers most is beginning to break out of the harness of the nonviolent race preachers. The fact that the NAACP had to issue a statement saying, "The NAACP has never condoned mob violence but it firmly supports the right of Negroes individually and collectively to defend their person, their homes and their property from attack" is a strong indication of the sentiment among the masses of Negroes. How can an individual defend his person and property without meeting violence with violence? What the NAACP is advocating now is no more than I had advocated in the first place. I could never advocate that Negroes attack white people indiscriminately. Our branch of the NAACP in Union County is an interracial branch.

It is obvious that the Negro leadership is caught in a terrible dilemma. It is trying to appease both white liberals who want to see Negro liberation given to us in eye-dropper doses and the Negro masses, who are growing inpatient and restive under brutal oppression. There is a new Negro coming into manhood on the American scene and an indifferent government must take cognizance of this fact. The Negro is becoming more militant, and pacifism will never be accepted wholeheartedly by the masses of Negroes so long as violence is rampant in Dixie. Even Negroes like King who profess to be pacifists are not pure pacifists and speak proudly of the Negro's role of violence in this violent nation's wars. In a speech at the NAACP convention, he said, "In spite of all our oppression, we have never turned to a foreign ideology to solve our problems. communism has never invaded our ranks. And now we are simply saying we want our freedom, we have stood with you in every crisis. For you, America, our sons died in the trenches of France, in the foxholes of Germany, on the beachheads of Italy and in the islands of Japan. And now, America, we are simply asking you to guarantee our freedom." King may not be willing to partake in expeditions of violence, but he has no compunction about cashing in on the spoils of war. There are too many Negro leaders who are afraid to talk violence against the violent racist and are too weak-kneed to protest the warmongering of the atom-crazed politicians of Washington.

Some Negro leaders have cautioned me that if Negroes fight back, the racist will have cause to exterminate the race. How asinine can one get? This government is in no position to allow mass violence to erupt, let alone allow twenty million Negroes to be exterminated. I am not half so worried about being exterminated as I am about my children growing up under oppression and being mentally twisted out of human proportions.

We live in perilous times in America, and especially in the South. Segregation is an expensive commodity, but liberty and democracy too have their price. So often the purchase check of democracy must be signed in blood. Someone must be willing to pay the price, despite the scoffs from the Uncle Toms. I am told that patience is commendable and that we must never tire of waiting, yet it is instilled at an early age that men who violently and swiftly rise to oppose tyranny are virtuous examples to emulate. I have been taught by my government to fight, and if I find it necessary I shall do just that. All Negroes must learn to fight back, for nowhere in the annals of history does the record show a people delivered from bondage by patience alone.

Rev. Dr. Martin Luther King Jr. on the Social Organization of Nonviolence: Paradoxically, the struggle for civil rights has reached a stage of profound crisis, although its outward aspect is distinctly less turbulent and victories of token integration have been won in the hard-resistance areas of Virginia and Arkansas.

The crisis has its origin in a decision rendered by the Supreme Court more than a year ago, which upheld the pupil placement law. Though little noticed then, this decision fundamentally weakened the historic 1954 ruling of the Court. It is imperceptibly becoming the basis of a *de facto* compromise between the powerful contending forces.

The 1954 decision required for effective implementation resolute federal action supported by mass action to undergird all necessary changes. It is obvious that federal action by the legislative and executive branches was half-hearted and inadequate. The activity of Negro forces, while heroic in some instances, and impressive in other sporadic situations, lacked consistency and militancy sufficient to fill the void left by government default. The segregationists were swift to seize these advantages, and unrestrained by moral or social conscience, defied the law boldly and brazenly.

The net effect of this social equation has led to the present situation, which is without clear-cut victory for either side. Token integration is a developing pattern. This type of integration is merely an affirmation of a principle without the substance of change.

It is, like the Supreme Court decision, a pronouncement of justice, but by itself does not insure that the millions of Negro children will be educated in conditions of equality. This is not to say that it is without value. It has substantial importance. However, it fundamentally changes the outlook for the whole movement, for it raises the prospect of long, slow change without a predictable end. As we have seen in Northern cities, token integration has become a pattern in many communities and remained frozen, even though environmental attitudes are substantially less hostile to full integration than in the South.

This then is the danger. Full integration can easily become a distant or mythical goal—major integration may long be postponed, and in the quest for social calm a compromise firmly implanted in which the real goals are merely token integration for a long period to come.

The Negro was the tragic victim of another compromise in 1878, when his full equality was bargained away by the Federal Government and a condition somewhat above slave status but short of genuine citizenship became his social and political existence for nearly a century.

There is reason to believe that the Negro of 1959 will not accept supinely any such compromise in the contemporary struggle for integration. His struggle will continue, but the obstacles will determine its specific nature. It is axiomatic in social life that the imposition of frustrations leads to two kinds of reactions. One is the development of a wholesome social organization to resist with effective, firm measures any efforts to impede progress. The other is a confused, anger-motivated drive to strike back violently, to inflict damage. Primarily, it seeks to cause injury to retaliate for wrongful suffering. Secondarily, it seeks real progress. It is punitive—not radical or constructive.

The current calls for violence have their roots in this latter tendency. Here one must be clear that there are three different views on the subject of violence. One is the approach of pure nonviolence, which cannot readily or easily attract large masses, for it requires extraordinary discipline and courage. The second is violence expressed in self-defense, which all societies, from the most primitive to the most cultured and civilized, accept as moral and legal. The principle of self-defense, even involving weapons and bloodshed, has never been condemned, even by Gandhi, who sanctioned it for those unable to master pure nonviolence. The third is the advocacy of violence as a tool of advancement, organized as in warfare, deliberately and consciously. To this tendency many Negroes are being tempted today. There are incalculable perils in this approach. It is not the danger of sacrifice of physical being which is primary, though it cannot be contemplated without a sense of deep concern for human life. The greatest danger is that it will fail to attract Negroes to a real collective struggle, and will confuse the large, uncommitted middle group, which as yet has not supported either side. Further, it will mislead Negroes into the belief that this is the only path and place them as a minority in a position where they confront a far larger adversary than it is possible to defeat in this form of combat. When the Negro uses force in self-defense he does not forfeit support—he may even win it, by the courage and self-respect it reflects. When he seeks to initiate violence he provokes questions about the necessity for it, and inevitably is blamed for its circumstances. It is unfortunately true that however a Negro acts, his struggle will not be free of violence initiated by his enemies, and he will need ample courage and willingness to sacrifice to defeat this manifestation of violence. But if he seeks it and organizes it, he cannot win. Does this leave the Negro without a positive method to advance? Mr. Robert Williams would have us believe that there is no effective and practical alternative. He argues that we must be cringing and submissive or take up arms. To so place the issue distorts the whole problem. There are other meaningful alternatives.

The Negro people can organize socially to initiate many forms of struggle, which can drive their enemies back without resorting to futile and harmful violence. In the history of the movement for racial advancement, many creative forms have been developed—the mass boycott, sit-down protests and strikes, sit-ins, refusal to pay fines and bail for unjust arrests, mass marches, mass meetings, prayer pilgrimages, etc. Indeed, in Mr. Williams's own community of Monroe, North Carolina, a striking example of collective community action won a significant victory without use of arms or threats of violence. When the police incarcerated a Negro doctor unjustly, the aroused people of Monroe marched to the police station, crowded into its halls and corridors, and refused to leave until their colleague was released. Unable to arrest everyone, the authorities released the doctor and neither side attempted to unleash violence. This experience was related by the doctor who was the intended victim.

There is more power in socially organized masses on the march than there is in guns in the hands of a few desperate men. Our enemies would prefer to deal with a small, armed group rather than with a huge, unarmed but resolute mass of people. However, it is necessary that the mass-action method be persistent and unyielding. Gandhi said the Indian people must "never let them rest," referring to the British. He urged them to keep protesting daily and weekly, in a variety of ways. This method inspired and organized the Indian masses and disorganized and demobilized the British. It educates its myriad participants, socially and morally. All history teaches us that like a turbulent ocean beating great cliffs into fragments of rock, the determined movement of people incessantly demanding their rights always disintegrates the old order.

In this form of struggle—noncooperation with evil through mass actions—"never letting them rest"—which offers the more effective road for those who have been tempted and goaded to violence. It needs the bold and the brave because it is not free of danger. It faces the vicious and evil enemies squarely. It requires dedicated people, because it is a backbreaking task to arouse, to organize, and to educate tens of thousands for disciplined, sustained action. From this form of struggle more emerges that is permanent and damaging to the enemy than from a few acts of organized violence.

Our present necessity is to cease our internal fighting and turn outward to the enemy, using every form of mass action yet known—create new forms—and resolve never to let them rest. This is the social lever, which will force open the door to freedom. Our powerful weapons are the voices, the feet, and the bodies of dedicated, united people, moving without rest toward a just goal. Greater tyrants than Southern segregationists have been subdued and defeated by this form of struggle. We have not yet used it, and it would be tragic if we spurn it because we have failed to perceive its dynamic strength and power.

I am reluctant to inject a personal defense against charges by Mr. Williams that I am inconsistent in my struggle against war and too weak-kneed to protest nuclear war. Merely to set the record straight, may I state that repeatedly, in public addresses and in my writings, I have unequivocally declared my hatred for this most colossal of all evils and I have condemned any organizer of war, regardless of his rank or nationality. I have signed numerous statements with other Americans condemning nuclear testing and have authorized publication of my name in advertisements appearing in the largest circulation newspapers in the country, without concern that it was then "unpopular" to so speak out.

Dorothy Day (writing in 1962): The first people who came to see me the day I arrived in Cuba were Robert and Mabel Williams, exiles from the United States, and wanted by the FBI... Robert Williams came to the attention of the public some years ago as local representative of the NAACP, when he urged that the Negroes arm themselves and use man's natural right to defend himself. His lawyer, Conrad Lynn, is an old friend of the *Catholic Worker* and well known in legal circles for his defense of the Puerto Rican Nationalists. Conrad was the first lawyer to come to our defense when the first twenty-eight pacifists were arrested in 1955 for refusing to take shelter during an air raid drill, on the grounds that such drills are acts of psychological warfare. In the late 1940s, he had defended a group that included Irene Mary Naughton, one of our editors, when they were arrested at Palisades Park, New Jersey, where Negroes were not permitted to use the swimming pool.

Williams's case has interested me from the beginning, because I have felt that he was merely advocating what the Catholic Church in its theology permitted: "the right of a man to defend his life," an argument which is used in all debates about pacifism. (But all Catholics as well as others become pacifists of a kind in regard to racial and class war and it is a false patriotism and nationalism, which plunge them into armed resistance.) Williams keeps pointing out that since the colored have armed themselves under his leadership in Union County, there has been no violence, no lynching, as there have been in other parts of the South.

While we talked, he showed me two news releases from the Southern Nonviolent Coordinating Committee of Atlanta, Georgia, distributed by the Southern Conference Educational Fund of Louisville, Kentucky. The first story was a protest against the killing of an unidentified Negro discovered in Goodman, Mississippi, on September 13 of this year in the Big Black River, his body in a sack weighted down with one hundred pounds of rocks... In Ruleville, Mississippi, the second news release told of two young Negro women active in registering Negroes to vote who were shot in the head, arms, and legs by bullets from a shotgun fired from a speeding car. (I was shot in this way at Koinonia Farm, Americus, Georgia in the mid-fifties, when a few editors of the *Catholic Worker* took turns going down to visit the Christian interracial community started by Clarence Jordan some years ago.)

Williams's contention is that a man has a right and a duty to defend himself, and that if it is known that a Negro will defend the life of his family and himself by shooting, there will be fewer attacks instigated by the White Citizens Council and the Ku Klux Klan...

There is no racial discrimination in Cuba, where 35 percent of the population is Negro and there has always been intermarriage. Negroes have held high political office and rank in the army, even when they were not accepted socially. There were kinds of discrimination, in the past, probably based on degree of color, education, and financial status. But with the revolution, the accent is on "all men are brothers."

The case of Williams became a *cause celebre* in the Negro press in the United States and also in the Cuban press, and the family was offered occupation and hospitality at the Hotel Capri, one of the largest hotels of Cuba, in the Vedado district. Here they have two big rooms, overlooking the ocean. On a clear day they can see on the horizon, four miles out, the American warship *Oxford*, and sometimes others. People are always gazing from stone walls that border the Malecon, which is the drive along the ocean, and pointing out to one another the ever present American threat four miles out of the harbor.

I talked to the Williams in their two-room apartment all one afternoon, on another occasion. He is a big man with a beard and he has a soft and gentle face. It was hard to think of him harboring hatred. But the present situation has been building up for many years. He has been in Havana now for more than one year. The Hotel Capri is an expensive place, but I am sure they long for their own home. The children are going to a special school, a boarding school that is run outside Havana for the children of repatriates born in the United States who speak English and have little knowledge of Spanish. Cuba is a paradise for children, where everyone is thinking of them and their needs. Mabel is studying Spanish, but Robert is finding it hard to learn a new tongue. He is filled with his own work besides, which takes a good deal of his time, getting out an exile's edition of the *Crusader*, a little paper which he used to mimeograph in Monroe, North Carolina, but is now printed in Havana and which he is having a hard time circulating in the United States.

William Worthy, the journalist from the *Baltimore Afro-American*, who was recently sentenced to three months in jail for visiting Cuba without a U.S. passport, and is currently out on bail, had given me a shopping bag filled with Afro-American papers and gifts of toilet articles, medicines and candy for his friend Williams. We exchanged news, mine being about Bill Worthy whom I had seen a few days before at dinner, the night before I sailed, and Williams telling me of his difficulties getting his paper out.

I have the greatest admiration for Robert Williams, the exile, forced out of his own country with threats against his life merely because he was asserting man's essential dignity, and his right to defend his life. It is a natural right, as taught by the Church, and it is only because of the life of grace, opened to us by the coming of Jesus, that we hold to our pacifist stand throughout race war, class war and every other type of war. As a pacifist, and my pacifism is based on the teachings of the Sermon on the Mount, I must accept the supernatural point of view and the idea that absolute pacifism is to be aimed at.

The teaching of the Church has always been that man has a natural right to defend his life. Many are called but few are chosen, one might say, to turn the other cheek in such a way that it mitigates wrath rather than increases it. Few can love even their brothers, their closest associates, without the help of grace. Everyone speaks of the ease with which we can love the masses, the people, and be hostile or indifferent to our neighbor, pass on the other side as the priest and Levite did. "And how can we love God whom we don't see if we do not love our brother whom we do see?" It seems to me that this is the whole teaching of the Church, and the working out of love of brother in the building up of a new social order.

We have long been confronted with the problem of pacifism in such a social order as the one we live in with its race prejudices. Certainly it does not work out unless we are getting down to the roots, trying to change all those things that make for war—poverty, class hatred, race hatred. Pacifism is impossible unless we are ready to give up our lives in order to save them. "For he who would save his life will lose it; but he who loses his life for my sake will save it. For what doth it profit a man if he gain the whole world, but ruin or lose himself?" (Luke 9.24.)

Williams is, or rather he was, a Unitarian; and his wife Mabel was a Catholic. Neither profess any religion now. Those who said "Lord, Lord" also had tried to kill them, and they have had a lifetime of seeing their brothers discriminated against, scorned, insulted, tortured.

The battle is still raging about integration, and from his exile Williams listens to the American broadcasts, publishes his little paper the *Crusader* which he tries to get into the States, writes for Cuban magazines and thinks of nothing but his life's battle. He is truly an exile, safe for the time, but his eyes always seem to be on his own country with love and hate and longing.

Revolutionary Democracy

A Speech Against the Vietnam War

Bayard Rustin

In this never-before-published essay written as the first draft of a speech delivered at a 1965 anti-war rally held in New York's Madison Square Garden, civil rights pioneer Bayard Rustin lays out a call for "revolutionary democracy" as prescient today as it was five decades ago. The rally, held less than one year after the infamous Tonkin Gulf resolution allowing U.S. military advisors into Vietnam, was an early mass expression, sponsored by the anti-nuclear group SANE. Also on the program was Coretta Scott King, who linked the anti-war and civil rights causes two years before her husband would publicly do so. As this speech demonstrates, popular perceptions that Rustin was an early advocate of the war are largely inaccurate. In fact, as with the Great March, the connections between international peace, racial equality, and worker's rights were always carefully articulated. As these issues continue to evade the U.S. empire-in-decline, at a time when progressives reminisce and celebrate the hundredth anniversary of Rustin's birth and the fiftieth commemoration of the March, Rustin's words ring out for militant action for a global economic and political democracy not yet obtained.

Though Congress refuses to admit it, we are at war. It is a useless, destructive, disgusting war. We must end the war in Vietnam. It harms people on both sides. It reveals the bankruptcy of America's foreign policy. The bombings, the torture, the harassment and the needless killings are abhorrent to me, and to all civilized men. Therefore, I am for supporting any and every proposal that is humane and relevant, that will end the war in Vietnam.

I am not a military strategist, I have never been one, and after observing the Pentagon mentality, I don't want to be. President Johnson has admitted this is a fruitless war, that no one can win—neither the Northern regime, nor the Southern regime. If that is true (and who here has reason not to believe him) then we must accept negotiations and not through the back door and not with any face saving devices. We must negotiate now! Period. If in order to negotiate, Hanoi insists that the Viet Cong must be part of those negotiations (and the United States says the Viet Cong is dominated by Hanoi) isn't it ridiculous to agree to sit down with Hanoi but not with the Viet

Cong? The United States cannot continue to insist on negotiations only with Hanoi and not the Viet Cong. We must sit down with all interested parties.

We must forget mutual recriminations and diplomatic hedging and arrogance—and we must negotiate now!

For years in Vietnam, the United States supported the Diem Government which was undemocratic and became increasingly unpopular. It was a government restricted to the backing of a religious minority. Diem was incapable of carrying out the social and economic reforms which were periodically announced (and just as periodically forgotten). And after fiasco after fiasco when we finally realized how catastrophic this American position was, the people of Vietnam were either sympathizing with the Viet Cong or else they were utterly demoralized. And the best that the United States could do was to govern by military fiat and by coup d'état.

We have not learned from this experience. Even now in the Dominican Republic we are repeating this sterile policy in even more tragic form. We did not have to seek out democratic forces in the Dominican Republic. They existed in the Government of Juan Bosch. Yet, we stood idly by when Bosch was overthrown by Rightist Generals. And then, when there was a popular movement in support of Bosch, and democracy, we intervened on the side of the Generals again and on the side of social reaction. The reason we gave was that there were Communists there—fifty-four or fifty-five or fifty-eight, the numbers game changed rapidly.

Do the so-called political realists say that wherever there are fifty or so Communists in the midst of a popular democratic revolution, those Communists must inevitably take over? If they say so, then the Pentagon and Mao are one in agreement.

In the Dominican Republic, in Vietnam, we must be on the side of revolutionary democracy. And, in addition to all the other arguments for a negotiated peace in Vietnam, there is this one: that it is immoral, impractical, unpolitical, and unrealistic for this nation to identify itself with a regime which does not have the confidence of its people. (And it is tragic for us, in effect, to allow communism to appear over and again as the defender of democracy and change).

Vietnam and the Dominican Republic show how America's war hawks have proven themselves as up-to-date as the dodo bird.

I say to the President: American cannot be the policeman of this globe! If we are going to send the marines into every Latin American country that has fifty or so Communists in the middle of a revolution, if we are going to move every time Communists take one side or another in revolts in Africa, if we are going to be the patron of all the right-wing generals in Asia, then we are damned to move tragically from disaster to disaster. We will not only have the wrong policy. We will have an overextended fatal policy all over the world.

I am not an isolationist. Let me say that America has the funds to give massive aid to Vietnam and Southeast Asia, and to carry on in the United States a vast program or social reconstruction. But the fact is that the present war psychology diverts planning and programs from what in fact will help people (in Vietnam or in Mississippi). This war psychology diverts creative energy to an infantile faith that biological agents, chemical warfare, and crude power can sustain freedom and democracy. The continuation of this fruitless war is the continuation of a psychology that will permit the American people to tolerate longer the suffering of America's 50 million poor. It will permit reaction to spread in the name of patriotism. And it will force us to seek military solutions to problems that are purely political (as is being done in Santo Domingo), and it will divert attention and energy from the struggle for racial equality in this country—America's first need, if we are to dare to speak of democracy abroad.

The civil right movement has double responsibility in this period. We must see to it that rightists do not use the threat of communism to begin another witch-hunt. We have seen that they will begin with SNCC, CORE, and Martin Luther King. We must continue to build up alliances of forces necessary for progressive social change. Moreover, we must apply the slogan of "one man, one vote" internationally—in Saigon, Hanoi, Formosa, in Spain and in Peking and Moscow and even Havana, as well as in Mississippi. And we must join with the progressive elements of this society to end the war in Vietnam.

Therefore, I advocate the following:

1. We must declare our willingness to negotiate with all parties;
2. We must lift the blockade;
3. We must immediately halt the bombings of North Vietnam;
4. On humanitarian grounds, we must send food, clothing and medicine to the people of North Vietnam—with only one string attached: that the food go to the underclothed, the unfed, and the sick.
5. We should repeat our willingness to invest funds in the economic development of South Vietnam and Southeast Asia, but we should add: we will do this through an international agency and under international control.

One hopes to God that before it is too late, this country will finally learn that in the year 1965 workers and peasants, whether they are in Mississippi or South Vietnam or North Vietnam, are searching for dignity and freedom from domination. Together, they are more powerful than American troops and the vast American arsenal. Today, the making of the peace—which was once an activity pondered only by utopian thinkers—has now become an urgent and practical political necessity.

The actor Ossie Davis recently pointed out that we must say to the President: "If you want us to be nonviolent in Selma, why can't you be nonviolent in Saigon?"

All the weapons of military power, chemical and biological warfare, cannot prevail against the desire of the people. We know that the Wagner Act, which gave labor the right to organize and bargain collectively was empty until workers went into the streets. The unions got off the ground because of sit-down strikes and social dislocation. When women wanted to vote, Congress ignored them until they went into the streets and into the White House, and created disorder of a nonviolent nature. I assure you that those women did things that, if the Negro movement had done them, they would have been sent back to Africa! The civil rights movement begged and begged for change, but finally learned this lesson—going into the streets. The time is so late, the danger so great, that I call upon all the forces which believe in peace to take a lesson from the labor movement, the women's movement, and the civil rights movement and stop staying indoors. Go into these streets until we get peace!

Southern Peace Walk

Two Issues or One?

Barbara Deming

The man took a leaflet and read a few lines. "This is the Nashville, Tennessee to Washington, D.C. Walk for Peace," it began; "Since 650 B.C. there have been 1,656 arms races, only sixteen of which have not ended in war. The remainder have ended in economic collapse." He looked up. "Are you walking with that nigger?" he asked.

This kind of discussion of our message had been anticipated by the committee for nonviolent action, when it decided that the walk should be integrated. "Token integrated," somebody later commented. Of thirteen young men and women committed to walk the whole distance, Robert Gore was the only Negro, though we hoped others might join before Washington. Whether they did or not, it was assumed that in the many talks about war and peace we would attempt to provoke along the way, we were sure to be asked a good many times whether we would be happy to see Robert married to our sisters. Before we headed south, we discussed the question of just how distracting our obvious attitude to race relations might be, and the proper way to cope with this. Events then proved our tentative conclusions to have been utterly inadequate.

Most of those advising us felt that battle on the two issues simply could not be combined. Of course we ought never to deny our belief in racial brotherhood; but Robert's presence was enough to confirm it. We should try to avoid talking about it; we were there to talk about peace. And it would be folly to seek to associate ourselves too closely with the people down there who were struggling for integration. Many people would then shy away from us. And they, the Negroes, could be harmed by it even more than we. They had enough of a burden to bear, already, without our giving their opponents added ammunition—the charge of their being "unpatriotic."

I supposed that the advice was practical, but it depressed me. I think we all left the meeting feeling unsatisfied—wondering a little why, then, the walk was to be integrated. We'd talked about the fact that this could lead us into danger. The South was unpredictable, it was stressed: we might not run into any trouble at all; on the other hand, we just might all get killed. In a cause we were not to appear to be battling for?

I had felt for a long time that the two struggles—for disarmament and for Negro rights—were properly parts of the one struggle. The same nonviolent tactic joined us, but more than this: our struggles were fundamentally one—to commit our country in act as well as in word to the extraordinary faith announced in our Declaration of Independence: that all men are endowed with certain rights that must not be denied them. All men, including those of darker skin, whom it has been convenient to exploit; including those in other countries, with whose policies we quarrel; among those rights which are not to be questioned, the right to be free to pursue happiness, and among them the right not to be deprived of life. In short, the Christian faith, still revolutionary, that men are brothers and that—no matter what—our actions must respect that fact. The only mode of battle that does, implicitly, respect this fact is that of nonviolence, and I have heard that for more and more of those in the civil rights as well as in the peace movement, the very attempt to practice it has implanted a corresponding faith, however tentative. But of course it is possible to hold a faith and yet not recognize all its implications, to be struggling side by side with others and yet be unaware of them. Perhaps it wasn't realistic to think of joining ranks.

We started out, in Nashville, with only a wistful look in the direction of the integration movement. We marched past a sit-in demonstration at a "Simple Simon's" and "smiled in." We didn't even picket for a few minutes; didn't pause in our marching. "There they are"—we turned our heads. We caught a glimpse of a row of young people at a counter—a glimpse, as in a flash photograph, of young heads held in a certain proud and patient fashion; and then we had marched past. A few steps away, in front of a movie theater, several adolescent toughs loitered—faces furtive, vacant. Did they plan trouble? In a minute, we were out of sight. It felt unnatural, I think, to all of us.

That afternoon we held a small open meeting at Scarritt College for Christian Workers. Two Negro leaders were among those present—James Lawson and Metz Rollins. Members of the group staging the sit-in—the Student Nonviolent Coordinating Committee—had been invited; but none came. Was this because they were shy of association with us? Or was it perhaps because, as one walker suggested, they felt that we should have done more to demonstrate solidarity with them? Rollins inclined his head, smiled. "It may well be."

Lawson spoke that afternoon. In the course of his talk, he remarked,

> There is a clear-cut relation between the peace walk and what some of us are seeking to do in the emerging nonviolent movement in the South. Some people have tried to classify our efforts here as one that is of and for and by the Negro. They have tried to define the struggle for integration as a struggle to gain the Negro more power. I maintain that it is not the case. Go among the common ordinary people ... for the "leading Negroes" are not the leaders of this movement. ... Listen to their prayers and to their speech. They are constantly thinking not in terms of civil rights but in terms of the kingdom of God on earth, the brotherhood of all men. ...What is behind it is an effort to build a community for all of us ..."the beloved community." I say that this

work is related to the work for peace. ... It might be a prototype to speak to the whole world. ... And the peace walk is related to the task of building community here. ... The movements are related to each other, in a sense are one and the same enterprise.

I took down the words he spoke, in my notebook, nodding, "Yes" and at the same time, disregarding them—perhaps because I was tired from the long drive south, and the process of breaking myself in again to group life, to sleeping on the floor, to packing up and moving each day; or perhaps because the meeting room was very nearly empty: the peace movement and the civil rights movement were certainly not visibly related here.

On Easter afternoon, we walked out of Nashville, heading out along Route 70N toward Knoxville. Two Fisk students, members of S.N.C.C., did appear just before starting time, to walk with us for a little while. Their presence was well noted. The signs we carried were unconventional: "If your conscience demands it, refuse to serve in the armed forces," "refuse to pay taxes for war," "Defend freedom with nonviolence"; but more conspicuous than our signs, quite obviously, were the Negro students—while they remained with us—and after a while the single figure of Robert Gore. Robert carried the "lollipop" sign that simply labeled the walk: NASHVILLE TO WASHINGTON; but he was in himself our most provocative, most instantly legible sign—walking along very quietly; dressed, carefully, not in hiking clothes but sober sports jacket and slacks; head held high, a quiet tension in his bearing.

We encountered a certain amount of southern courtesy—"Well, have a nice walk!" and now and then an expression of active sympathy—"God go with you!" "You mean you agree with us?" "I sure do!" But less friendly messages were of course more common—"Boo!" "Get out of here!" As we held out our leaflets, car windows were rolled up swiftly; some cars actually backed off from us in a rush; citizens on foot stepped quickly behind shop doors. Approaching a leaflet victim, one tried, by remaining very calm oneself, and looking him quietly in the eye, to prevent his flight, and infect him with corresponding calm; but the exercise was difficult. Soon the "hot rod gang" began to face us in the field. Parking their cars by the roadside, they would line up, leaning against them, waiting our approach, assuming looks that were meant to kill—expressions glowering and at the same time pathetically vacant. We would offer leaflets, walk past; they would hop into their cars, speed past us, line up again by the roadside. And now the first warnings began to be delivered to us. I handed a leaflet to the manager of a garage, and to the Negro employee who stood beside him. "I hear they're going to shoot you a little farther down the line," the white man told me softly. "They don't like niggers there, you see." He turned and smiled fixedly into the eyes of the black man by his side—"That's what I hear." The Negro made no answer, returning the stare but allowing nothing to come to the surface of his look—his shining eyes fathomless. The white man turned back to me. "I just hope you'll be all right," he said—not pretending not to pretend. I told him, as brightly as I could, "Keep hoping."

That first night we slept on the floors of a white church near Old Hickory; the next night our "advance worker" had arranged for us to stay in a Negro church in Lebanon. Lebanon was a small town that had lately seen much violence. Fifteen months before, a young Negro minister, Reverend Cordell Sloan, had been assigned to the town to try to build a Negro Presbyterian church. He had felt called, as well, to try to build a sit-in movement. This was the first small town in the South in which the struggle had been taken up; and it involved not college but high school students. Retaliation had been vigorous. Just recently the headquarters of the group had been demolished with rocks, while the Negroes themselves stood pressed against the walls inside, and the police looked on. This day, as we filed along the highway, a car slowed down in passing, a young man leaned his head out: "You walking into Lebanon?" "That's right." "Good place for you to be walking. We're going to hang you all there." It was a bright beautiful day. Fruit trees were coming into bloom; the purple redbud was out. Horses and goats and litters of many-colored pigs ran in mixed company through the long Tennessee fields. The fields were vivid with flowering mustard. We marched along, trying not to straggle out, but to keep fairly close together. Just before midday a car approaching us suddenly whizzed into a side road and stopped; the doors flew open, and several men leaped out. Well, here it is, I thought; may we all behave well. Then I saw that their faces were dark. They were students from Lebanon, two of them come to walk into town with us. More planned to join us later. They held out their hands for signs to carry.

We stopped by the side of the road and shared a picnic lunch. We bought a carton of milk at a nearby store, and in a shy ritual gesture passed it from hand to hand, each drinking from the spout. One the road again, we walked past and all-Negro primary school, set high on a hill. The entire school stood out in the yard, waving to us. I ran up the hill with leaflets. A sweet-faced teacher asked me—so softly that I could hardly catch the words: "How many colored are with you?" I told her that two of the young men she saw were from Lebanon. "I thought I recognized J.T.," she said; and in her voice, in her face, was a contained, tremulous pride and excitement. A few miles further on, more students waited by the road to join us; a littler further on, more; and at the town's edge, still more. As we stepped onto the sidewalks of the town, more of us were black than white.

A car sped by, an arm jerked out of the window and slung an empty coke bottle. The youngest of the team, Henry Wershaw, gave a little cry: he had been hit in the ankle. He was able soon to limp on. We kept close ranks, to be ready for worse than that; but everyone was stepping lightly; the mood among us was almost gay. One small boy, Sam, strode with us, eyes sparkling. A pretty young woman named Avis, in a light-colored summer dress, almost skipped along the street. The citizens of the town, as usual, stepped back from us in dread; withdrew behind their doors and peered out, through the glass panes, in amazement and dread, as the unarmed troop of us passed. There were several among us who bore the marks of violence at the hands of townspeople. The skill of one of the young Negroes showed, beneath his close-cropped hair, an intricate tracery of scars: he had been hit with a wrench during one of the sit-ins. There were others walking, too, who had suffered such blows; and none had ever struck back. They walked along the street now, lighthearted, as if secure, faces extraordinarily bright, while those who had, in one way or another condoned the blows struck, drew back, in the reflex of fear. Before we headed south, the women had been cautioned against walking in public next to a Negro man; it might make things dangerous for him. At any rate, we were told, best to take our cue from the man himself. I had carefully made no move to walk next to any of these students. But now one after another, as we moved through the town, stepped alongside me, to introduce himself, to exchange a few words—free of caution. They had made their choice, had entered a fight, and if one was in it, then one was in it—ready to take what might come. At lunch one of them talked about this a little: "When you see those hoodlums arriving, you just divorce yourself from your body—prepare your body for anything: spit, fists, sticks, anything."

Police cars had begun to drive past us at frequent intervals; but our friends remarked that we mustn't assume that they were there for our protection. During recent trouble, one woman had asked an officer whether the police intended to protect them from the mob. "We're hired to protect the city, not individuals," had been his reply. We headed for the town square now, preparing ourselves for "anything." We walked through uneventfully. Within our herding, an officer in a squad car pulled up next to a car full of young toughs and told the driver, "Not today, Hank, not today." We turned the corner and limped the final block to Picketts Chapel Methodist Church.

In the white churches were we had stayed so far, we had had the use of the church kitchen in which to fix our meals, from supplies we carried about with us; once the pastor's wife had kindly fixed us sandwiches and lemonade; and evenings, after supper, as many as five members of the congregations had sometimes dropped in to ask questions. This day, as we sat in the churchyard easing our feet, women began to appear from the four points of the compass, carrying bowls and platters; all who had walked were soon summoned into the room behind the church to a feast: fried chicken, garden peas, turnip greens, two kinds of potato salad, three kinds of pie. After we had sat down together to eat, we were invited into the church itself; word of a meeting had been spread through the community; the door kept opening, and soon the church had filled up.

The shape this meeting took swiftly dissolved any remaining anxieties about the harm we might do to the integrationists and to ourselves if we sought association with them. Reverend Sloan spoke first—a think, handsome man with gentle but stubborn demeanor, and the luminous wide eyes of a man who is almost blind but who sees what it is that he wants to do. "I hope the town never gets over what it saw today," he began. What the town had seen of course, as we walked through its streets together, was the first integrated gathering that had ever occurred in Lebanon. The white community had seen, and the Negro community had seen, too, the brotherhood of which Sloan preached made visible—turned fact. "I hope it gets into its system, I hope it gets to the bone," said Sloan. It was clear that he meant both white community and Negro. We learned, at the end of the meeting, that this was the largest audience he had ever had there. He had made great headway with students, but adults had been largely apathetic. Because of the drama of our arrival, any adults were present tonight, gazing about them in quiet astonishment, and he was addressing them particularly.

He spoke of the struggles in which he and his followers had been involved; he spoke of the opposition they had encountered—sprayed with insecticides, hit with ketchup bottles, threatened with pistols, run down with lawn mowers, "Name it, we've had it." "The proficient, efficient, sufficient police" had been on the scene. He smiled wryly. "We like to get killed." Many had been arrested. He asked those who had been to jail to stand. A large number stood. The leader of the peace walk, Bradford Lyttle, here interrupted to ask those among the peace walkers who had been to jail to stand, too; and an equal number rose. "Let no one be afraid of going to jail," the minister urged; "It has become an honor… It's easy to say, isn't it? But come and try it." They shouldn't be afraid, he repeated; they should be afraid of being slaves any longer. "The only think I'm afraid of is going back into the old way of living again. We've gone too far." He reminded those in the audience who had not been fighting that when freedom came, they, too, would enjoy it—unless perhaps they'd feel too guilty to enjoy it. They had better begin to get the feeling of it right now. Then he got very specific about the ways in which they could help, and the ways in which they had been doing the movement harm.

After he had spoken, Bradford Lyttle spoke about the work of the C.N.V.A. He spoke at ease, his words briefer than they often were—so much obviously could be assumed to be understood by this audience. He felt very strongly, he told them, that America was in a desperate situation today. Here were the most prosperous and happily situated people who had ever lived, on the verge of giving up their souls—for we were professing ourselves quite willing to murder hundreds of millions of other human beings to try to preserve our own standards of life. Many Americans were beginning to demonstrate in protest—to name themselves unwilling. He urged them to join the protest. C.N.V.A. believed in disarming unilaterally, and in training for defense through nonviolent resistance. Heads nodded. No one stood up to hurl the familiar challenge: Are we supposed to lie down and let the Russians walk right over us? Of all the signs we carry, the sign that usually remains the most abstract for those who read it is "defend freedom through nonviolent resistance"; but when the students of Lebanon walked through their town carrying that banner, the message could no remain abstract. If our walking beside them had made visible for the community the substance of what Reverend Sloan had been preaching, their walking beside us had made visible the substance of what Bradford Lyttle preached. Forty-five people in that audience came forward to put their names on C.N.V.A.'s mailing list.

Reverend Sloan called for a collection to be taken up for both causes. Many who had little enough to spare opened their purses. Some who had never given before gave this night. We stood and clasped hands and sang the hymn that has become the theme song of the movement in the South: "We shall overcome some day! …Black and white together… We shall live in peace!" The words seemed to belong to both our causes.

The next day we were scheduled to walk to the small town of Carthage, set on the bluffs of the Cumberland River. A number of the people who had walked into town with us the day before turned up to see us on our way. Reverend Sloan was among them, and the leader among the students, Bobby, and Sloan's right-hand man, a tall, very homely newspaper reporter, Finley, a man of wit and feeling; and quite a few others. We expected to be escorted to the town's edge and I rather think they had expected to walk only this far, themselves; but most of them ended by walking with us all the way to Carthage. Passing motorists again leaned out of their cars to shout threatening or vile remarks. "Let not your hearts be troubled," Reverend Sloan advised, in his soft, rather lilting voice. He and Finley left for a while to ride up ahead with Bradford and find a place for us to stay that night. They found it at Braden Methodist Church, where Sloan knew the assistant minister, Beulah Allen. "How could we turn you out?" she said to Bradford; "You can never tell when the stranger will be the Lord."

After we had entered Carthage with our banners, Sloan and Finley and Bobby took a little stroll about its streets. The walk had now linked them dramatically with that town; and who knows when their battle may not be taken up there?

Again, this evening, women of the community appeared, arms laden; a feast was spread for us in the church basement. Again, after dinner together, we moved into the "sanctuary"; and again the church filled up. It was the first integrated meeting that had ever taken place here, too. That night, the women in our group slept in the house of Beulah Allen's sister, Dona. As we tiptoed through her room, Dona's old mother woke, and Dona introduced us. "Honey, they look white," Dona's mother whispered to her. "Mama, they are," said Dona. "Lord bless us!" said the old lady.

Braden's Methodist Church was set up on a little rise just above the large town square, and as we gathered noisily first in the basement and then in the church proper, a good many of the white people of the town and of the country round the town gathered in the square and stood glaring up. A few of them had thrown some rotten fruit and vegetables, as we sat outside before dinner; a few had walked past, holding empty coke bottles—but not quite bringing themselves to throw those. During the meeting, the door would open and shut, open and shut, as more and more of the Negro community kept arriving; and one was never quite sure that some of the crowd below might not be arriving at last. But again there were a lot of cops around, and again they had decided to keep order. The crowd just stood, until past midnight, glaring up at the small frame building which resounded with our talk and laughter and singing and prayer. Dona reported to us afterward that she had gone outside one and found several white boys loitering and had asked them in. "They don't understand," she explained to us; "They've never even been outside the country." If the resistance movement had not yet taken root among the Negroes of Carthage, they hardly needed to be introduced to the idea of nonviolence. They had found it long ago in the New Testament.

This meeting was above all an old-fashioned prayer meeting. Bradford Lyttle talked again briefly—drawing a picture of the worldwide nonviolent movement. And he issued a rather shy invitation to them to walk with us the next day. Reverend Sloan then rose and declared that he would be less shy about it: he would simply tell them that they should walk with us. Robert Gore asked Beulah Allen if he could say a few words from the pulpit, and he spoke of how the message of Jesus—to love one's enemies—was a strange message, a revolutionary one. "That's right," came from the audience—"Amen!" But it was Beulah Allen who led the meeting, and who spoke the prayers. I think few of us had ever before this evening felt that we were being prayed for. These days we were now approaching on the walk promised to be the most trying. We were about to enter Cumberland County, where—we had been told by both friends and antagonists—no Negro was supposed to remain after nightfall. The last Negro family that had tried to build had been burned out; the last Negro who had tried to walk through the county had been found dead by the side of the road. Beulah Allen had heard these stories too. She stood solidly before the altar rail, spread out her arms, raised up her voice—have in a piercing should, half in a song—and addressing God as though he were indeed there just about us, just beyond the roof—"Heavenly FATHER! ... Heavenly FATHER!"—she asked Him to give us courage, and also a good night's sleep that night, asked Him to teach all of us, including the people out there in the square, and the people along the road we were going to walk, how best to behave. The words themselves vanish now in my memory, having entered too deeply that evening into my flash. I looked about me, and the other walkers, too, were sitting up, stock still. We had all of us heard, before, theatrical versions of such prayer—intended sometimes to be funny or sometimes to be endearing; and Beulah's prayer retained for us of course something of the extravagance of theatre; but now we were in the play; we were at the heart of it, amazed.

Again we sang together. Dona, accompanying us at the upright piano, hit the keys with a heavily pouncing, laboring but joyful, heartfelt emphasis of her own. The rhythm was always almost jazz, and as we nodded our heads, tapped our feet, our weariness and the nudging fears we'd kept down all the past days dissolved. Again, at Reverend Sloan's prompting, we sang the integration hymn—reaching out and taking hand: "We shall overcome some day!" "Now this is difficult," Reverend Sloan said, with a flickering smile, and prompted, "Black and white together some day." He prompted, "We are not afraid today." At the end of the meeting, Beulah Allen gave us a blessing, and exclaimed, "It's been so sweet!" At that moment, I recalled the words of James Lawson about "the beloved community." It seemed that we had been living in that community this past hour.

The next morning I learned to my astonishment that our evening's meeting had not caused the breach between us and the white community that might have been supposed. I entered one of the shops on the square to buy some things, expecting to be served with glum hostility. The young woman behind the counter—who clearly knew who I was—was full of both curiosity and warmth. She chattered eagerly about the peculiar weather they had been having this past year, and "It's the times, I think," she ventured. I asked whether she felt that atomic tests were disrupting the weather, and she nodded: "There's One who is more powerful; we forgot that." As I left, "I hope you come back and see us again," she said.

In the course of the next few days, we walked into mythical Cumberland County and walked out of it, unharmed. Two Quaker couples who bravely put us up received middle-of-the-night telephone calls, threatening "roast nigger for breakfast"; one night the fire department arrived in the yard, summoned by false alarm; one night local high school students swarmed up to the house—but when invited in, sat and talked until late, quietly enough, their curiosity about us obviously deeper than their hostility. (As they left, they were arrested by the police—as eager to protect them from us as to protect us from them.) It was actually at the edge of the county, the first night after we left Carthage, that we had our nearest brush with violence. Reverend Sloan and Finley and Bobby and other had walked with us again this third day, but had taken their final leave of us at a little one-room Negro church by the side of the road, way out "nowhere," between towns. No one was in the church, but we had been told that we could spend the night there. We had crawled into our sleeping bags, scattered out on the floor between the pews, and were listening sleepily to the small country noises in the air, when abruptly the ruder sound of rocks hitting the building brought us full awake. Two of the men stepped outside and called into the dark, inviting the besiegers to come and talk to us about it. The hail of rocks stopped and the people rustled off into the dark. We could hear the crickets again for a while and then the barrage began again; a rock came crashing through one of the windows. Another two stepped outside, this time carrying flashlights aimed at themselves. to show the strangers were they were and that they were unarmed. We could hear their voices and we could hear the stones still flying and suddenly we heard a small gasping cry. Eric Weinberger had been hit on the side of the head and knocked off his feet. He staggered up, and called to them again, "It's all right. You hit me in the head, but it's all right. But now why don't you come and talk with us?"—and seven or eight young men finally emerged out of the dark and consented to talk. They were young workingmen from around there. They talked for a good while, and finally they said that well, they might perhaps agree with some of the things we said about war and peace, but they couldn't understand our walking around with a nigger, and all sleeping in the same building with him. And then one of them asked the time-worn question: "Would you let a nigger marry your sister?" The question was posed to Sam Savage, who is a southerner himself. When he answered that yes, he would; the decision would, after all, be hers to make—they exclaimed in sudden anger and disgust: well, he was not real southerner then, and there was not use talking about anything further; and they stamped off into the dark. At which point, one might have said that the advice we had been given before starting out on the walk had now been proved to be correct: the two issues of race relations and of war and peace could not be discussed together. However, there is a final chapter to this story. After a short time, the young men returned, wanting to talk further. The talk this time went on until the one who had done the most arguing remarked that they must be up early to work and had better get some sleep. But would we be there the next evening, he wanted to know. (We had of course, unfortunately, to move on.) As they left, he shook hands with Sam, who had said that yes, he'd let his sister marry a black man. It is my own conviction that these men listened to us as they did, on the subject of peace, just because Robert Gore was traveling with us. It made it more difficult for them to listen, of course; it made the talk more painful; but it also snatched it from the realm of the merely abstract. For the issue of war and peace remains fundamentally the issue of whether or not one is going to be willing to respect one's fellow man.

Nonviolence and Radical Social Change

Barbara Deming

Is nonviolence a relevant—a practical—discipline for those who want to bring about radical social change? I believe that it is.

I believe it is the most practical discipline. What revolutionaries speak of bringing into being is a new world in which men will treat each other with true respect. Those who accept the discipline of nonviolence try to bring this world into being immediately, by acting out that respect now—even toward the men with whom we are struggling.

Some would object: that is all very fine, but can you actually win when you fight this way? Some would object that when we are nonviolent we may respect the enemy, but we don't respect ourselves—we don't stand up for ourselves. They would agree with Stokely Carmichael and with Carl Oglesby that nonviolence is essentially a kind of prayer—a humble petition to those who are in power to be good to us; and that by petitioning them, we actually reinforce their authority, when we should be challenging their authority. Our petition, they charge, is based on the naïve assumption that the powers that be victimize us only because they are not fully aware of how unhappy we are; and if we let them know this—in a nice way—they will of course do something to change things for us. As Carmichael put it to the white power structure: "We have found you out; you are not the nice guys you are supposed to be." And, he concludes, we have found out therefore that nonviolence does not work.

I agree very much that once cannot simply petition those in power for change—expect to touch the consciences of men. It is not that easy to do. One has to confront those in power with power on our part. But here I differ with Carmichael and others because I believe that in nonviolent struggle one can do just this—can confront them with such power. Too often those who believe in nonviolence have limited their actions to petition, but we needn't limit ourselves in this way. We can go very much further—and must.

What is the power of nonviolence? Radical nonviolence, if it is really employed as it can be, relies on the application of two kinds of pressure—two pressures which are particularly effective in combination.

The pressure that those describing nonviolence tend always to omit from the description is the pressure of our refusal to cooperate with a system which denies us our freedom—but which exploits us, that is to say which relies on our cooperation. This is how we stand up for ourselves nonviolently: we refuse the authorities our labor, we refuse them our money (our taxes), we refuse them our bodies (to fight in their wars). We strike. We go even beyond this and block and obstruct and disrupt the operation of that system in which we cannot feel like free men. Those who are committed to nonviolence have simply never gone as far as they could in this direction. (Though they went furthest perhaps under Gandhi—went far enough to enable them to throw the British out of India without killing a single Englishman. One can make life as usual, business as usual, simply impossible for our antagonists.

But I have spoken of a combination of pressures. And this is crucial in defining the power of nonviolence. Noncooperation, disruption, can be nonviolent or violent. When it is nonviolent I believe it is immensely more powerful in the long run. Because one has then, as it were, two hands upon the adversary. With on hand on shakes up his life drastically, makes it impossible for him simply to continue as he has been. With the other hand we calm him, we control his response to us. Because we respect this rights as well as ours, his real, his human rights—because we reassure him that it is not his destruction that we want, merely justice—we keep him from responding to our actions as men respond to violence, mechanically, blindly. We force him to think—to ask all kinds of questions of himself, about the nature of our actions and our grievance, about the real issues involved, abut what others watching the struggle will think, about where his own real long-term interests lie—whether they don't lie in adjusting himself to change.

When we fight this way, we can count on suffering, in the long run, many fewer casualties. Though it may not feel that way at first, because we are suffering all of them and the other side none. The antagonist cannot, beyond a point, escalate violence against us when we are using none. Conscience quite aside, it won't look right to others.

If he does continue to escalate violence, unreasonably, he will begin to lose the sympathy of allies and supporters on whom he depends. We will being to gain them. The genius of guerilla warfare is to make it impossible for the other side to make full use of its weaponry. We carry this principle even further.

In brief, men have barely begun to experiment with the power there is in noncooperation and disruption; and they have barely begun to experiment with the control they can wield over an antagonist's response to this if one remains strictly nonviolent, treating the other always with basic respect.

Of course, I had better stress, in struggle of this sort, though one can expect fewer casualties finally than in violent struggle, one has, nevertheless, to expect them—one has to take the psychological step of entering real battle. One cannot withdraw when one does begin to get hurt. One has to learn that if we are taking casualties—even though we are not hurting anyone on the other side—it does not mean that something is going wrong.

Experiment with nonviolent struggle has barely begun. But in a world in which traditional violent battle can escalate into nuclear warfare, it is an experiment that is absolutely necessary to push to its furthest limits.

On Revolution and Equilibrium (Excerpt)

Barbara Deming

The challenge to those who believe in nonviolent struggle is to learn to be aggressive enough. Nonviolence has for too long been connected in men's minds with the notion of passivity.

"Aggressive" is an ambiguous word, of course, and my statement needs qualifying. In this connection I recommend to all the book *On Aggression* by the Austrian naturalist Konrad Lorenz. I have quoted Bradford Lyttle's reference to it: "Lorenz studies [the unniceness of people] as aggressiveness and argues convincingly that it's instinctive with men." Actually, though Lorenz does argue that aggressiveness is instinctive—in men as in animals—he challenges the view that there is anything basically "unnice" about that instinct. The correct translation of his original title, *Das Sogennante Bose*, would be *The So-Called Evil Instinct*. He argues that this instinct plays a very positive, life-*promoting* role among animals. Just to give one example: the instinct of each member of a species to fight for its own bit of territory "gives an ideal solution to the problem of the distribution of animals"—so that they don't all crowd into one place and eat up all the food available there and then starve. "The environment is divided between the members of the species in such a way that, within the potentialities offered, everyone can exist." "What a peaceful issue of the evil principle." Aggressiveness may "function in the wrong way" sometimes, by accident, he writes, and cause destruction, but "we have never found that the aim of aggression was the extermination of fellow members of the species." He writes of another, a very special instinct that has been developed in the process of evolution "to oppose aggression ... and inhibit those of its actions that [could be] injurious to the survival of the species." He describes various ritualized "appeasing" gestures that are made by the weaker animal of the species at a certain point in any conflict, and describes how the stronger animal is then automatically restrained from taking advantage of the other and inflicting real injury upon him. He points out the "strangely moving paradox that the most blood-thirsty predators, particularly the Wolf ... are among the animals with the most reliable killing inhibitions" (toward their own species, that is). For this "built-in safety device" was developed specifically in those creatures who were born heavily armed. And he points out the special dilemma of Man. He is born "harmless" and so "no selection pressure arose in the prehistory of mankind to breed inhibitory mechanisms preventing the killing of his" fellows—and then he invented artificial weapons! Fortunately, Lorenz comments, "Inventions and responsibility are both the achievements of the same specifically human faculty of asking questions." Clearly the questions he has asked have, to date, resulted in a more rapid development of invention than of self-discipline, but Lorenz remains optimistic about Man, and sees him as still capable of evolving. "I assert," he writes, "that the long-sought missing link between animals and the really humane being is ourselves"—a hypothesis that I find persuasive.

What has very clearly worked, in the evolution of animals, to preserve and advance the life of each species, has been a particular *balance* of two instincts. The one, as it were, asserts the individual's right to exist. This is the so-called evil instinct. Lorenz names it "aggression." But just as I would substitute another word for Fanon's "violence," I would substitute another word here—and rename aggression" "self-assertion." The second instinct restrains the first when it endangers *another's* right to exist. In human terms, the first amounts to respecting one's own person, the second to respecting the person of the other. Lorenz points out, by the way, that the only animals capable of love are those that are "aggressive." One can, it seems, *only* another "as one loves oneself."

This lifesaving balance—this equilibrium between self-assertion and respect for other—has evolved among animals on the physiological plane. In human beings it can be gained only on the plane of consciousness. And the pleas this essay makes is precisely that we make the disciplined effort to gain it—all those of us who hope really to change men's lives, who, in Frantz Fanon's words, "want humanity to advance a step further," want to "set afoot a new man," lies in discovering within ourselves this poise. But it calls equally for the strengthening of *two* impulses—calls both for assertion (for speaking, for acting out "aggressively" the truth, as we see it, of what our rights are) and for restraint toward others (for the acting out of love for them, which is to say of respect for their human rights). May those who say that they believe in nonviolence learn to challenge more boldly those institutions of violence that constrict and cripple our humanity. And may those who have questioned nonviolence come to see that one's rights to life and happiness can only be claimed as inalienable if one grants, in action, that they belong to all.

Responsible Pacifism and the Puerto Rican Conflict

Ruth M. Reynolds

This never-before-published essay outlines some of Reynolds's thoughts, written in 1954 at the height of one of the most significant twentieth-century uprisings on the island, about the role of peace activists in the struggle against racism and imperialism.

In my youthful debate with Conscience, over whether or not I should become a pacifist, the point at issue was not whether or not violence was wrong—I knew it was—but whether pacifism was not an irresponsible withdrawal from conflict situations. I felt that the citizen has the obligation to confront and deal with civic problems, and that one cannot purchase immunity from responsibility by saying, "I want to keep my hands clean."

Knowledge of Gandhian techniques in the liberation struggle in India was for me a beam of white light. The pacifist could enter conflict situations, participate in them, accept voluntarily whatever suffering was imposed by military or civil foes of justice. He could risk his own life for the good of society, without threatening the life of his enemy. He could be a responsible citizen and be a pacifist.

Adult life is much more complicated than we believe when we are young, and circumstances draw us into areas not of our own choosing. Call it Providence or call it Fate, we do not shape our destinies in broad outline, but only in fine details. I did not decide, upon reaching maturity, to spend my life in seeking to remedy the ills we have inflicted on Puerto Rico. I was drawn gradually into the struggle between Puerto Rico's determination to be free and my own government's determination to hold her. That I am wedged between these two determinations in their struggle, respecting the first and trying to destroy the second, seems as inevitable as being born, although I suppose could have prevented it had I tried.

Whenever any Puerto Rican patriot out of desperation, fires a gun, the cry goes up that I am not a pacifist or I would not know people who fire guns, I would not associate with members of the political group to which they belong, I would stay out of situations pregnant with violence. I promptly add to suspicions that I am not a pacifist by losing my patience, and spouting off, "A pacifist need not necessarily be a sissy."

On March 1, 1954, four Puerto Ricans fired on our House of Representatives, wounding five Congressmen. If anyone was shocked by this event, it was I, for they were all my friends. Two were nodding and dancing acquaintances, always respectful;

one, Lolita, I had seen many times, but never but for a passing moment alone; the fourth and youngest—Rafael Cancel Miranda—I had watched grow from sheltered youth to responsible fatherhood, and had entertained hopes that his fine mind and patriotic dedication might make a decisive contribution to the emancipation of his people. Now all these hopes were shattered—shattered by his own act—and prison seems his only future, at least for a long time.

Of course I knew what would follow, and tried to resign myself to it. One job I lost before I even knew that anything had happened. Then started the FBI inquiries—more jobs begun and lost, subpoenas ad infinitum, insinuations, guilt by association charges, visits from the city police. The press is not the independence of Puerto Rico, but the murder of all top United States public officials, and the District Attorneys search busily for a plot to such effect. We who know better go to "confession" before the Grand Jury, although there's nothing to confess; we lose our jobs and look for others; we are frustrated in our efforts to squeeze a word of truth into the mass of lies that fill the public mind. We fight the resentment that mounts in our own hearts, and try to remember that even the District Attorney is our brother.

And all the while the Law is searching legalistically for clues that are not there, we too are seeking a way to reconcile this latest shock with all our past experience. The microscope of the detective cannot find what lies behind it, but the heart that shares with Puerto Rican patriots the anguish of their status knows the pressures borne with patient hope, so long is that hope and the brave to folly. We cannot condone, but we can comprehend; we cannot justify, but we can feel compassion.

We can do more than that, for no act can be understood apart from this environment. We must not join the District Attorneys concentrating on minutiae but ignoring the cosmos. We must probe behind the deed into its setting. What quenched the Dawn in young men's eyes—that they should think that one dramatic gesture, followed by death or years of living death, was all that they could do? Why did a poet's breath become a fiery bullet direct at the men who make our laws? We do not know, and yet we do know, we whose souls are tortured by the same grief and whose spirits are stretched brittle by the same tensions. We too have felt the heels of Wealth and Power crushing our noblest efforts into obliteration. We too have seen Albizu Campos, the Puerto Rico paschal lamb of sacrifice, suffering in agony from what physicians call "burns of unknown cause" but which he believes result from atomic radiation directed at him by our government. We too are overwhelmed at times by the indifference and cynicism that we meet, and by a sense of dark futility.

Yes it is our own sense of guilt that saves us from like desperation. For we are yankees, and, although our government honors us by treating us like Puerto Ricans who oppose its practices, we know that we are born and bred in this land, and that whatever the United States Government does, good or bad, we share in its responsibility. If anyone must be killed in expiation for our sins, well, here am I, my friends, shoot me! I'm planning to die someday, anyway!

What does the pacifist do when he finds himself set down in No Man's Land, with bitter battle raging all around? Well, if he's not a coward, he doesn't run, but stays and faces the issue. He keeps his sense of values, and, while he condemns violence on either side, he realizes that Empire is in itself the basic violence, and that to oppress with violence is worse than to resist oppression with violence. He tries to play his own role in compassion and understanding, demonstrating in practice, not in theory, that there is a better way. Thus and only thus can he show that pacifism is not irresponsible withdrawal from conflict, but rather a saner, more constructive way of fighting.

Where Was the Color in Seattle?

Looking for Reasons Why the

Great Battle Was So White

Elizabeth "Betita" Martínez

The final three pieces of this section are modern-day classics, penned by coeditor Elizabeth "Betita" Martínez at three key junctions of the contemporary justice struggles. The so-called "Battle of Seattle" during the 1999 Washington-based meetings of the World Trade Organization was an historic protest against globalization and neoliberalism. With an impressive coming-together of labor, anti-war, and economic justice activists, Martínez publically questioned why radicals of color were essentially omitted from the coalitions developed around the anti-IMF/World Bank demonstrations. Ten years later, following the coalitions which developed against President Bush's pro-war, anti-constitutional reactions to 9/11, Martínez again wrote a widely distributed article, originally appearing in Z Magazine. "Looking for Color in the Anti-war Movement" asserted that anti-war work had to be anti-racist in order to achieve any manner of success, and targeted actual organizations (spotlighting the War Resisters League) who seemed to be resisting making the changes needed to thrive and grow. Finally, "Combatting Oppression Inside and Out" reviews contemporary successes at forging anti-racist practice.

> I was at the jail where a lot of protesters were being held and a big crowd of people was chanting "This Is What Democracy Looks Like!" At first it sounded kind of nice. But then I thought: is this really what democracy looks like? Nobody here looks like me.
> —Jinee Kim, Bay Area youth organizer

In the vast acreage of published analysis about the splendid victory over the World Trade Organization (WTO) last November 29–December 3, it is almost impossible to find anyone wondering why the 40–50,000 demonstrators were overwhelmingly Anglo. How can that be, when the WTO's main victims around the world are people of color? Understanding the reasons for the low level of color, and what can be learned from it, is absolutely crucial if we are to make Seattle's promise of a new, international movement against imperialist globalization come true.

Among those who did come for the WTO meeting were some highly informative third world panelists who spoke Monday, November 29 about the effects of WTO on health care and on the environment. They included activist-experts from Mexico, Malaysia, the Philippines, Ghana, and Pakistan. On Tuesday, at the huge rally on November 30 before the march, labor leaders from Mexico, the Caribbean, South Africa, Malaysia, India, and China spoke along with every major U.S. union leader (all white).

Rank-and-file U.S. workers of color also attended, from certain unions and locals in certain geographic areas. There were young African Americans in the building trades; blacks from Local 10 of the ILWU in San Francisco and Latinos from its Los Angeles local; Asian Americans from SEIU; Teamsters of color from eastern Washington state; members of the painters' union and the union of Hotel Employees and Restaurant Employees (H.E.R.E.). Latino/a farmworkers from the UFW and PCUN (Pineros and Campesinos del Noroeste) of Oregon also attended. At one point a miner from the South Africa Labor Network cried, "In the words of Karl Marx, 'Workers of the world, unite!'" The crowd of some 25,000 people cheered.

Among community activists of color, the Indigenous Environmental Network (IEN) delegation led by Tom Goldtooth conducted an impressive program of events with Native peoples from all over the United States and the world. A fifteen-member multistate delegation represented the Southwest Network for Environmental and Economic Justice based in Albuquerque, which embraces eighty-four organizations primarily of color in the United States and Mexico; their activities in Seattle were binational.

Many activist youth groups of color came from California, especially the Bay Area, where they have been working on such issues as Free Mumia, affirmative action, ethnic studies, and rightwing laws like the current Proposition 21 "youth crime" initiative. Seattle-based forces of color that participated actively included the Filipino Community Center and the international People's Assembly, which led a march on Tuesday despite being the only one denied a permit. The predominantly white Direct Action Network (DAN), a huge coalition, brought thousands to the protest. But Jia Ching Chen of the Bay Area's Third Eye Movement was the only young person of color involved in DAN's central planning.

Seattle's twenty-seven-year-old Centro de la Raza organized a Latino contingent in the labor march and local university groups, including MEChA (Movimiento Estudiantil Chicano de Aztlan), hooked up with visiting activists of color. Black activists who have been fighting for an African American Heritage Museum and Cultural Center in Seattle were there. Hop Hopkins, an AIDS activist in Seattle, also black, made constant personal efforts to draw in people of color.

Still, the overall turnout of color from the United States remained around five percent of the total. In personal interviews, activists from the Bay Area and the Southwest gave me several reasons for this. Some mentioned concern about the likelihood of brutal police repression. Other obstacles: lack of funds for the trip, inability to be absent from work during the week, and problems in finding childcare.

Yet several experienced activists of color in the Bay Area who had even been offered full scholarships chose not to go. A major reason for not participating, and the reason given by many others, was lack of knowledge about the WTO. As one Filipina said, "I didn't see the political significance of it how the protest would be anti-imperialist. We didn't know anything about the WTO except that lots of people were going to the meeting." One of the few groups that did feel informed, and did participate, was the hip-hop group Company of Prophets. According to African American member Rashidi Omari of Oakland, this happened as a result of their attending teach-ins by predominantly white groups like Art and Revolution. Company of Prophets, rapping from a big white van, was in the front ranks of the 6 a.m. march that closed down the WTO on November 30.

The problem of unfamiliarity with the WTO was aggravated by the fact that black and Latino communities across the United States lack Internet access compared to many white communities. A July 1999 federal survey showed that among Americans earning $15,000–$35,000 a year, more than 32 percent of white families owned computers but only 19 percent of black and Latino families. In that same income range, only 9 percent of African American and Latino homes had Internet access compared to 27 percent of white families. So information about WTO and all the plans for Seattle did not reach many people of color.

Limited knowledge meant a failure to see how the WTO affected the daily lives of U.S. communities of color. "Activists of color felt they had more immediate issues," said Rashidi. "Also, when we returned people told me of being worried that family and peers would say they were neglecting their own communities, if they went to Seattle. They would be asked, 'Why are you going? You should stay here and help your people.'"

Along with such concerns about linkage came the assumption that the protest would be overwhelmingly white as it was. Coumba Touré, a Bay Area activist originally from Mali, West Africa, said she had originally thought, "the whites will take care of the WTO, I don't need to go." Others were more openly apprehensive. For example, Carlos ("Los" for short) Windham of Company of Prophets told me, "I think even Bay Area activists of color who understood the linkage didn't want to go to a protest dominated by 50,000 white hippies."

People of color had reason to expect the protest to be white-dominated. Roberto Maestas, director of Seattle's Centro de la Raza, told me that in the massive local press coverage before the WTO meeting, not a single person of color appeared as a spokesperson for the opposition. "Day after day, you saw only white faces in the news. The publicity was a real deterrent to people of color. I think some of the unions or church groups should have had representatives of color, to encourage people of color to participate."

Four protesters of color from different Bay Area organizations talked about the "culture shock" they experienced when they first visited the "Convergence," the protest center set up by the Direct Action Network, a coalition of many organizations. Said one: "When we walked in, the room was filled with young whites calling themselves anarchists. There was a pungent smell, many had not showered. We just couldn't relate to the scene, so our whole group left right away." Another told me, "They sounded dogmatic and paranoid." "I just freaked and left," said another. "It wasn't just race, it was also culture, although race was key."

In retrospect, observed Van Jones of STORM (Standing Together to Organize a Revolutionary Movement) in the Bay Area, "We should have stayed. We didn't see that we had a lot to learn from them. And they had a lot of materials for making banners, signs, puppets." "Later I went back and talked to people," recalled Rashidi, "and they were discussing tactics, very smart. Those folks were really ready for action. It was limiting for people of color to let that one experience affect their whole picture of white activists." Jinee Kim, a Korean American with the Third Eye Movement in the Bay Area, also thought it was a mistake. "We realized we didn't know how to do a blockade. We had no gas masks. They made sure everybody had food and water, they took care of people. We could have learned from them."

Reflecting the more positive evaluation of white protesters in general, Richard Moore, coordinator of the Southwest Network for Environmental and Economic Justice, told me "the white activists were very disciplined." "We sat down with whites, we didn't take the attitude that 'we can't work with white folks,'" concluded Rashidi. "It was a liberating experience."

Few predominantly white groups in the Bay Area made a serious effort to get people of color to Seattle. Juliette Beck of Global Exchange worked hard with others to help people from developing (third world) countries to come. But for U.S. people of color, the main organizations that made a serious effort to do so were Just Act (Youth ACTion for Global JUSTice), formerly the Overseas Development Network, and Art and Revolution, which mostly helped artists. Many activists of color have mentioned Alli Chaggi-Starr of Art and Revolution, who not only helped people come but for the big march in Seattle she obtained a van with a sound system that was used by musicians and rappers.

In Just Act, Coumba Touré and two other members of color—Raj Jayadev and Malachi Larabee—pushed hard for support from the group. As a result, about forty people of color were enabled to go thanks to special fundraising and whites staying at people's homes in Seattle so their hotel money could be used instead on plane tickets for people of color. Reflecting on the whole issue of working with whites, Coumba talked not only about pushing Just Act but also pushing people of color to apply for the help that became available.

One of the problems Coumba said she encountered in doing this was "a legacy of distrust of middle-class white activists that has emerged from experiences of 'being used.' Or not having our issues taken seriously. Involving people of color must be done in a way that gives them real space. Whites must understand a whole new approach is needed that includes respect (if you go to people of color thinking you know more, it creates a barrier). Also, you cannot approach people simply in terms of numbers, like 'let's give two scholarships.' People of color must be central to the project."

Jia Ching Chen recalled that once during the week of protest, in a jail holding cell, he was one of only two people of color among many Anglos. He tried to discuss with some of them the need to involve more activists of color and the importance of white support in this. "Some would say, 'We want to diversify,' but didn't understand the dynamics of this." In other words, they didn't understand the kinds of problems described by Coumba Touré. "Other personal conversations were more productive," he said, "and some white people started to recognize why people of color could view the process of developing working relations with whites as oppressive."

Unfortunately the heritage of distrust was intensified by some of the AFL-CIO leadership of labor on the November 30 march. They chose to take a different route through downtown rather than marching with others to the Convention Center and helping to block the WTO. Also, on the march to downtown they reportedly had a conflict with the Third World People's Assembly contingent when they rudely told the people of color to move aside so they could be in the lead.

Yet if only a small number of people of color went to Seattle, all those with whom I spoke found the experience extraordinary. They spoke of being changed forever. "I saw the future." "I saw the possibility of people working together." They called the giant mobilization "a shot in the arm," if you had been feeling stagnant. "Being there was an incredible awakening." Naomi, a Filipina dancer and musician, recalled how "at first a lot of my group were tired, grumpy, wanting to go home. That really changed. One of the artists with us, who never considered herself a political activist, now wants to get involved back in Oakland. Seattle created a lot of strong bonds in my small community of coworkers and friends."

They seem to feel they had seen why, as the chant popularized by the Chicano/a students of MEChA goes, "Ain't no power like the power of the people, 'Cause the power of the people don't stop!"

There must be effective follow-up and increased communication between people of color across the nation: grassroots organizers, activists, cultural workers, and educators. We need to build on the contacts made (or that need to be made) from Seattle. Even within the Bay Area, activists who could form working alliances still do not know of each other's existence.

With mass protests planned for April 16–17 in Washington, D.C., at the meeting of the World Bank and the International Monetary Fund (IMF), the opportunity to build on the WTO victory shines brightly. More than ever, we need to work on our ignorance about global issues with study groups, youth workshops, conferences. We need to draw specific links between WTO and our close-to-home struggles in communities of color, as has been emphasized by Raj Jayadev and Lisa Juachon in *The Silicon Valley Reader: Localizing the Effects of the Global Economy* (1999), which they edited.

Many examples of how WTO has hurt poor people in third world countries were given during the protest. For example, a Pakistani told one panel how, for years, South Africans grew medicinal herbs to treat AIDS at very little cost. The WTO ruled that this was "unfair" competition with pharmaceutical companies seeking to sell their expensive AIDS medications. "People are dying because they cannot afford those products," he said. A Filipino reported on Indigenous farmers being compelled to use fertilizers containing poisonous chemicals in order to compete with cheap, imported potatoes. Ruined, they often left the land seeking survival elsewhere.

But there are many powerful examples right here in the United States. For starters, consider:

- WTO policies encourage sub-livable wages for youth of color everywhere including right here.
- WTO policies encourage privatization of health care, education, welfare, and other crucial public services, as well as cutbacks in those services, so private industry can take them over and run them at a profit. This, along with sub-livable wages, leads to jeopardizing the lives of working class people and criminalizing youth in particular.
- Workers in Silicon Valley are being chemically poisoned by the chips they work on that make such wealth for others. WTO doesn't want to limit those profits with protection for workers.
- WTO has said it is "unfair trade" to ban the import of gasoline in which certain cancer-causing chemicals have been used. This could have a devastating effect on people in the United States, including those of color, who buy that gas.
- Overall, WTO is controlled by U.S. corporations. It is secretly run by a few advanced industrialized countries for the benefit of the rich and aspiring rich. WTO serves to further impoverish the poor of all countries.

Armed with such knowledge, we can educate and organize people of color. As Jinee Kim said at a San Francisco report-back by youth of color, "We have to work with people who may not know the word 'globalization' but they live globalization."

Looking for Color in the
Anti-War Movement

Elizabeth "Betita" Martínez

Part I: Why "Anti-War" Has to Be "Anti-Racist" Too

As a speaker at a San Francisco anti-war rally last fall, I tried to emphasize the importance of seeing the threatened war on Iraq in terms of this country's racism here and
around the world. In that spirit, I ended my comments with a chant by some activists
of color marching to the rally: "One, two, three, four/We don't want your racist war!"

Few people in that mostly white crowd of some 15,000 chanted with me or
clapped. I was troubled, but later that day a Bay Area anti-war movement leader told
me, "You got off easy. In the 1970s, Black Panther leaders like Bobby Seale and Dave
Hilliard were booed when they mentioned racism at early anti–Vietnam War rallies."

Seeing racism as a separate, secondary issue is an old problem in the U.S. peace
movement, which does not always realize that it must be anti-racist as well as anti-war.
Today, with the "Permanent War" becoming all too permanent, that realization is all
the more crucial. Do people really think the expanding U.S. empire will be stopped
by white folks alone?

The education, mobilization, organization, participation, and leadership of people
of color in the anti-war movement have been recognized as important far more today
than previously. More people of color can be seen at demonstrations than during the
Vietnam War. We sometimes find people of color in the leadership of anti-war organizations. For example, they compose half of the Steering Committee of the national
coalition United for Peace and Justice, which also voted to make people of color half
of UPJ's co-chairs and half of its Administrative Committee. Anti-war teach-ins in
Spanish and bilingual publications are being produced.

Such changes are good but questions persist. Why, for example, is there not more
color in today's anti-war movement when the troops who fight and die are disproportionately black, brown, and red? Why isn't there more color when those who pay
such a heavy price for cutbacks in vital social services due to military spending are
often people of color?

The first answer is the way that racism conditions the attitudes and conduct of
many anti-war activists, often without their realizing it. There are also obstacles within
communities of color, frequently rooted in experiences of racism, that impede their

own anti-war organizing. We can begin with some thoughts about the first problem—how racist ideas and practice among white activists hold back building the strongest possible anti-war movement.

"Diversity Is Not Our Job"

Throughout history, U.S. peace groups have been primarily composed of and led by whites, mostly middle-class men. On one level, this happens because anti-war whites usually reach out first to friends or acquaintances and this means other whites. That still holds true today for the anti-war movement and its frequent partner, the anti-corporate globalization or global justice movement. It has often held true for the white-led solidarity movements of recent years, like the main organizations supporting popular struggles in Central America, for example.

It also holds true today even in racially diverse cities like San Francisco. The problem became obvious to this writer when four coalitions put on the big February 16, 2003, demonstration (February 15 elsewhere). At meetings I attended of their coordinating committee, out of twenty-five representatives you might find a half dozen of color and an even smaller proportion under forty years of age (few of whom played a leading role in the discussion).

Far too many cases have occurred across the country of white activists showing ignorance, indifference, or arrogance toward people of color. Incidents might be as major as the Washington, D.C., protest against the World Bank and the IMF on April 16, 2000, when no Black or Latino leaders were asked to speak at the main event—an amazing omission, given the colors of Washington, D.C. Or they might be as minor as when a Chicano in Sacramento, California, encountered a peace activist leafleting at a food co-op. He asked if there would be speakers of color at the event she was promoting, and the activist replied, "Diversity is not our job."

Cases of whites refusing to acknowledge and accept leadership from activists and organizations of color head the list of structural problems. Not calling on activists of color at meetings or favoring those deemed "the most articulate" has been noted. White activists starting coalitions without input from or serious outreach to people of color and then calling the coalition "citywide" have occurred, in places such as New York. White activists have used their greater resources to dominate a coalition.

Sometimes the conflict concerns tactics. For example, whites planning civil disobedience may forget that immigrants and others of color risk jail, deportation and special police violence for participating. As a Chicano organizer commented, "there are young white activists who do not think beyond the fact that they can get arrested and be out of jail overnight with no serious problems. They do not recognize that white privilege—combined with class privilege—can make this happen."

Often the problem is culture clash. It might be marginalizing non-English-speaking immigrants and rarely thinking of the need for translation of literature, meetings, or slogans. There can also be conflicts about style of work as basic as how a meeting is chaired. Participants of color may end up feeling that a meeting had a very "white style"—meaning a tendency to move in a strictly linear direction, with no time allowed for building trust and new leadership.

The problem can be hard to finger at times. A person of color at a mostly white meeting may feel that veiled power relations are in operation, but be unable to identify just how. One Chicano student activist commented that while white-dominated meetings may be supposedly "leaderless," actually informal and therefore unaccountable leaders are calling the shots. Those same dynamics can be observed in all-white meetings, but the feeling of exclusion usually intensifies for a person of color.

Such problems led to sharp criticism on a KPFA (Pacifica) "Hard-Knock Radio" program, in which hip hop activists discussed whether the anti-war movement was a whites-only mission. One person said that organizers will call for peace around the world but "when it comes to people of color here, they just want Peace on the Plantation."

There's a War at Home, Too

The racist practices described here are symptomatic of stubbornly held ideas that include, first, denying there is a war at home along with today's wars abroad, and the two are intimately connected. Second, denying that both are racist wars (as well as apparently forgetting that U.S. foreign policy is fundamentally rooted in racism).

Angela Davis once noted that the black community did not join the anti–Vietnam War movement in great numbers (even though blacks have been largely anti-war, one could add). One reason, she said, was that it did not see white peace activists energetically defending the Black Panthers, who were fighting a war for survival at the time.

In the same spirit, David Graham Du Bois, stepson of the revered scholar, recently wrote in an "Open Letter to the U.S. Peace Movement" that, confronted by the Iraq war, Black Americans "are generally silent largely because there has been so little evidence that those who call us into the streets to demonstrate for peace understand how color racism and white supremacy are used in the United States against the interests of peace, justice and the pursuit of happiness for all peoples. It is not enough to call up the peace legacy of Martin Luther King, in speeches and slogans... You must organize to end racism with the same enthusiasm and determination as you organize to stop the war."

Similarly, Earl Ofari Hutchinson wrote in 1991, soon after the Rodney King beating in L.A., "How is it that thousands of white activists can wage passionate campaigns against oppression and human rights abuses in Chile, El Salvador, South Africa... but not in the ghettos and barrios of their own cities?"

As these African Americans affirm, peace activists have often failed to recognize that there is a "war at home" along with the wars abroad, and that the war at home includes an unending struggle with racism as shown in the criminalization of youth, the expanding prison industrial complex, ongoing inequality in social institutions like schools and housing, and a constant stream of actions to take back the gains of the 1960s like affirmative action and bilingual education.

Today the war at home has intensified. People of color suffer severely from its effects, as seen in massive new attacks in the name of Homeland Security. Under the Special Registration program, over 13,000 Arab, Muslim, South Asian, and North African males who complied with the program face deportation, almost all for minor immigration violations. This represents a huge increase in racial profiling and criminalizing immigrants, especially those of color. Another direct connection between the wars abroad and at home can be seen in the deadly cuts in funding education, health care, child care, and low-cost housing for the sake of gigantic military spending.

These and other realities carry a stark message: the same capitalist, empire-building forces that impose the wars abroad also impose the war at home. The main victims of both are peoples of color. Both are racist wars. We cannot oppose one and not the other.

Although white anti-war activists may recognize that communities of color are engaged in longstanding struggles against white supremacy and for self-determination, most do not see (or want to see) the linkage between those struggles and building the anti-war movement. That blindness underlies many of the problems we have seen in building anti-war unity across color lines. One simple example: lack of respect for leadership by people of color, in many situations.

The drive for self-determination is also ignored in the way many white activists look at Palestine's struggle against the Israeli occupation and fail to see its relationship to the whole U.S. empire-building project. Instead of solidarity, Arab American activists have noted, some whites say those who support Palestine's struggle are anti-Semitic; some fear alienating Jews if they do support Palestine; some dismiss that struggle out of total ignorance about Israeli, Arab, and Islamic history, or they think Islam oppresses women across the board so too bad for Palestine.

War Resisters League Resists What?

A major example of resistance to defining the anti-war struggle as anti-racist can be found in the War Resisters League, which has been almost entirely white for eighty years. Last February David McReynolds of its Executive Committee, widely admired for his work against the Vietnam War, resigned from all posts. The immediate cause named by McReynolds was the vote by the WRL's National Committee to retain a project called ROOTS (originally Youth Peace), which had been created several years earlier to increase the League's young membership. ROOTS is staffed by people of color. In explaining his resignation, McReynolds wrote that by voting to retain ROOTS, the majority had set the League "on a course which … [could] result in the end of the organization. That course was to shift our primary focus from being a peace and disarmament organization…to a 'broader focus' in which the League would be not only an 'anti-war' organization, but also an 'anti-racist' organization."

McReynolds commented that the causes of war "sometimes—though not as often as the 'politically correct caucus' thinks—[include] racism… I have seen Clergy and Laity Concerned, once a voice for peace and social change, vanish after it capitulated to its own 'politically correct' group which insisted that if CALC was serious about racism it had to turn over a majority of its board to members of color. It did so." McReynolds also stated very briefly and without examples that "almost none" of ROOTS's material (primarily a youth-oriented newsletter) is pacifist, contrary to WRL basic principles.

Some WRL members have questioned why being officially anti-racist is so controversial when the WRL had no great problem agreeing to declare itself anti-sexist. Today upheaval continues within the WRL, with hopes of positive change. ROOTS continues and WRL remains in the United for Peace and Justice (UFPJ) coalition

The Open Letter about Racism

With many problems of racism in the movement surfacing during 2002–2003, the position taken by McReynolds and others in the WRL became "the straw that broke the back of silence concerning those problems," as a national UFPJ leader told me. The result: an "Open Letter About Racism in the Movement" circulated among thousands of activists shortly after the February 15–16, 2003 rallies. Issued by a multiracial group in New York City, the Open Letter discussed white supremacy as experienced by its authors over a one-year period. It listed many of the problems already mentioned in this article.

That Open Letter was an encouraging move, especially when compared to other events. For example, in April 2003 in the Boston area, the popular white anti-racist speaker Tim Wise was scheduled to speak on the topic "Racism and White Privilege in the Peace Movement." Somehow his title was changed to "Race and the Peace Movement."

White Efforts to Combat Racism

As that Open Letter confirmed, anti-war white activists have been critical of racism in the movement. On a minimal level, they often express regret that their meetings include too few people of color. This regret can lead to no concrete action or tokenism. Alternately, they will agree, "Yes, we must get more people of color involved," but as Tonto might have said to the Lone Ranger, "Who is 'we,' white man?" In other words, they aim to "diversify" what continues to be their movement in their eyes, rather than seeking to build alliances between equals.

More serious efforts by white anti-war activists to combat racist tendencies can be dated back decades. Anne Braden, the longtime white southern anti-racist leader, wrote a groundbreaking article in 1987, "Undoing Racism: Lessons for the Peace Movement," offering analysis and concrete recommendations that work for today.

An unusual example of whites collaborating to solve such problems with people of color as equals developed in September 2001 in the Albany, New York area. The Stand for Peace Anti-Racism Committee (SPARC) was formed "to build an anti-racist, multi-racial movement for justice and peace." SPARC organized a forum held last August 13 for people of color "to discuss our involvement and leadership in working for peace and justice" and strategies for "how we can make connections" in combatting the wars at home and around the globe.

The forum drew a diverse group of thirty or more people, about one-third of whom had not been politically active in the past. Thus "it turned out to be more of a speak-out than an in-depth discussion of strategic questions," said African American scholar/activist Barbara Smith. But the spirit of the meeting was enthusiastic and participants expressed strong interest in continuing the dialogue at a follow-up meeting that same month.

In November 2001, New York City (70 percent people of color) saw a group of ten young(ish) white organizers and activists put out a powerful letter called "An Anti-Racist Coalition? We have a long way to go." They included members of mostly local groups working for the rights of welfare recipients, workers (UNITE), gay, lesbian, bisexual, and transgender people (FIERCE) and others who had attended meetings to plan for an October 7 march. Their letter sharply criticized those meetings for marginalizing people of color as well as youth and working class participants. It also presented many practical suggestions for improvement.

Other ideas and actions have come from white anti-racist groups like Active Solidarity and Heads Up in the Bay Area, and AWARE in Philadelphia. Direct Action to Stop War, also of the Bay Area, which shut down San Francisco's financial district the day after war was declared, saw positive efforts in anti-racist organizing.

San Francisco's Chris Crass, of the Challenging White Supremacy (CWS) Workshops, has put together an informal "toolbox" for whites. It begins with a broad political recommendation: develop an analysis of war that connects U.S. empire-building abroad to the war at home. Understand that demands for peace without justice ring hollow in communities that face structural violence every day, whether the United States is dropping bombs elsewhere or not.

The list includes what Sharon Martinas, creator of CWS programs, has called "anti-racist toilet training," for whites. For example:

- Attend an anti-racist training and encourage other white activists to do so. Recognize how white privilege consistently socializes white activists to think of themselves as superior.
- Instead of that Eurocentric "come join us" approach, check in with organizations of color working against war at home and abroad.

- Respect the leadership of people of color. Be accountable; do what you say you will do.
- Prioritize reading books by radical people of color, especially feminists. Learn more about the struggles of communities of color.
- Set concrete goals for yourself that can be measured, such as: in one month, will talk with two white anti-racist activists in my community and two of color.
- Remember that it is not your intentions or motives that count but the impact of your actions as a white person in a white supremacist society.

The Black civil rights movement of the 1960s shows it is possible for vast numbers of white people in this land to say a loud "no" to actions and policies that exclude, demean, or marginalize people of color. Everyone should remember William Moore, Mickey Schwerner, Andy Goodman, Jonathan Daniels, Viola Liuzzo, and other white activists killed in the southern freedom struggle. Their lives were not worth more than any black life lost in that movement, but their commitment set an inspiring contemporary example for anti-racist whites.

The time is more than ripe to show that commitment again. Whites should not only say "no" to racism but also carry out energetic campaigns of "yes" to any action that advances genuine collaboration. This is no simple or easy task, but what could be more worthwhile?

A young white friend wrote last year, "Wouldn't it be beautiful if we could get thousands of white organizers all over the country to reject those old racist habits? To stop thinking of their work as the center of everything and educate other white folks too? To see why they have to fight racism along with militarism so the solidarity we talk about is real? Then we could truly say: another world is possible."

Part II: Anti-War Organizing among People of Color

"An Emergency Summit Conference of Asian, Black, Brown, Puerto Rican, and Red people against the war was held in Gary, Indiana, on June 3–4, the first such meeting ever held in the United States … over 300 delegates attended the historic conference," said the article in the newspaper *El Grito del Norte*.

The year was 1971. The war was in Vietnam. Today people of color do not yet have the collective strength of those years and there are major obstacles to anti-war organizing in our communities. We cannot just blame racism from whites for blocking our participation if we are not doing everything possible to build effectively among ourselves. People of color need to be so strong, so numerous, and so effective that they cannot be ignored.

The obstacles start with class issues. A widespread feeling exists in communities of color that anti-war activism can't be a priority when folks are struggling with daily problems of survival—paying the rent, doctors' bills, bad schools, drugs in the 'hood—as well as direct racist attacks. Along with job and family, where's the time? Poor and working class African Americans may say, "We can't be protesting the war, we've got to be defending ourselves ... anti-war stuff is for white middle-class kids."

Immigrants, especially the undocumented, often keep quiet for fear of losing their livelihood or being deported if they speak out or sound "un-American." Older immigrants may say they feel gratitude or debt to the United States for their improved economic condition and their children's. Low-income youth of color may be attracted to the military as the only road to college, a good job, and U.S. citizenship.

Middle-class activists of color (as well as whites) sometimes say that grassroots people just don't grasp foreign policy or don't want to be bothered. Actually those activists may really be blaming "the masses" for a supposed lack of intelligence as a way of hiding their own unwillingness to struggle with complex international issues. When a brother says with well-founded cynicism, "This war stuff is the same old crap"—does that really mean he would never understand or care about the stakes?

Anti-war organizing can be impeded by middle-class, conservative, often intensely anti-Communist organizations of color. They may oppose going against the war because it could undermine their work on what they call "more important issues," not to mention their financial support. Among Latinos, we find the League of United Latin American Citizens (LULAC) not wanting Mexicano anti-war activists in this year's Cinco de Mayo parade in Houston, Texas. Blacks have similar organizations as do South Vietnamese people in northern California.

For African Americans, seeing Colin Powell and Condoleezza Rice at the top adds a complicating perspective. If they had opposed the wars, their rare success as Blacks making it into the halls of power would have been impossible.

These examples leave us asking not just where is the color in the anti-war movement but also "where is the working class?"—a question for white activists also. Other obstacles to our anti-war organizing include:

- The U.S. mass media with their lies, distortions and omissions of reality. Unlike white society, few people of color have access to alternative media (especially not in Chinese or other Asian languages). A Pew poll last April found that support for the Iraq war was far lower from immigrant Latinos—who often came from countries with direct knowledge of United States imperialism—than from Latinos born here, who had been barraged by mainstream media all their lives.
- The feeling that there are no leaders and ordinary people cannot take the action needed without strong leaders (failing to think of themselves as leaders).
- Among Blacks and Latinos, the contradiction of anger at U.S. racism existing alongside a desire for respect from the white-dominated society, and

especially the opportunity to win that respect in wartime. Black poet Brian Gilmore, in the *Progressive*, quoted W.E.B. Du Bois referring to these feelings as that tragic state of "double consciousness."

- Identification with the United States as a nation, especially in relation to other countries: not nationalism, but nation-ism.
- Fear of attending anti-war demonstrations because of repression by police, who target people of color.
- A general dread of any contact with the INS (Immigration and Naturalization Service), especially since 9/11. Thousands of Arab, Islamic people and South Asians in particular have suffered mass roundups, indefinite imprisonment without cause under brutal conditions, and deportation. The recent expulsion of many Cambodians, and the threatened expulsion of hundreds more, has intensified that dread. Earlier, under "Operation Tarmac," came the raids and subsequent firing of Latino immigrant airport workers, first in Salt Lake City in December 2001 and then Seattle in April 2002, none on criminal charges.
- For Latinos as for Asians, difficulty in unifying all their different nationalities against the war, given the diversity of class, language, politics, religion, attitudes about gender and sexuality, and others.
- Dislike of working within the white-dominated anti-war movement, given its racist tendencies. A single meeting can turn you off.
- Fear of conflict with pro-war family or friends.

Hany Kahlil, of the United for Peace and Justice staff based in New York, has added several other very concrete problems, summarized as:

1. When you haven't experienced your own power to keep a health clinic open or get a stop-sign on a street, for example, you have difficulty imagining you can take on something huge like a war, so why try?
2. It's hard to sustain energy and hope if we don't have measurable benchmarks for progress. For example, we need to see where our campaigns fall far short of stopping a war but are steps that strengthen our base and win allies.
3. Many groups have shied away from taking on the war in part because they are afraid of dividing their organization's membership. We need to be prepared to struggle with our own people if necessary. That fear overlaps with the problem that much of our work is concentrated in the nonprofit sector, which can make funding the priority.
4. Lack of capacity and resources.
5. In the case of Black Americans, Bill Fletcher of TransAfrica Forum has said that, as a society, they are economically and psychologically depressed

today. "Worn down by all the deprivation and attacks of recent years, they are a battered people. Such a state of being leads many to think struggle is not worthwhile."

Overcoming the Obstacles

Many individuals of color are opposed to the wars and empire-building even if they don't participate in demonstrations or join anti-war organizations. What might overcome the obstacles and make them more ready to get involved?

Anti-war organizers of color will say: education is key. That process must include drawing out the connections between people's immediate concerns—the bread-and-butter issues—and the war. An obvious example is the brutal cutbacks in education, health care, child care, and other social services to finance the biggest military budget seen in years. Another is the vast increase in racial profiling and criminalizing immigrants of color by such means as the "Special Registration" program.

People of color have sometimes become active against the war in places where organizations already exist that have won respect for their work on an issue important to local residents. In New York and Chicago, for example, organized Latino opposition to United States militarism against Vieques, Puerto Rico made it natural to take on Bush's wars and empire-building. The result has been one of the strongest pockets of Latino organizing in the United States. Also in New York, anti-war activism has been launched by people of color already organized around such issues as welfare rights, reparations, and immigrant rights, like CAAAV: Organizing Asian Communities. A group in Los Angeles, Centro (CSO), had a Latino base for years that enabled it to help Latinos Against the War win support.

In these cases, the existence of trust together with education about how the foreign and domestic wars are connected helped pave the way for involvement. Monami Maulik, director of Desis Rising Up and Moving (DRUM) in New York has pointed out that the current war on terrorism criminalizes immigrant communities much as the "war on drugs" criminalized African American and Latino communities for years. That kind of historical comparison helps advance the educational process.

Immediate connections also exist. Korean Americans constantly hear U.S. threats to attack their homeland because of its nuclear weapons. To them, the war abroad and the war at home are inseparable; recently they have energetically organized educational events and protests in the United States. Filipinos have similar connections. Even before the war, many were engaged, directly or indirectly, in opposing U.S. militarism and its puppets in the Philippines. Their anti-war organizing has been intensified by the firing of over 1,000 baggage screeners at airports in the Bay Area, the vast majority Filipino, for being noncitizens.

A subtle linkage between U.S. wars abroad and the war at home can be found in the way African American activists often say they will join a struggle defined as "against imperialism" rather than "for peace." Fighting U.S. imperialism echoes their own historical struggle, dating back to slavery. Black Workers for Justice in North Carolina issued a statement in late 2002 taking that anti-imperialist perspective even further. It emphasized the importance of "concretely linking the struggles of all People of Color and the oppressed internationally for a better world."

From all this organizing experience, one message emerges: perhaps the most effective way to build anti-war activism in communities of color is first to establish a base within each community, to begin where the people are, and grow. Organized activists of color then come to the table with white groups much more ready to form coalitions or alliances. At the same time, we can hope that the Anglo activists have developed anti-racist views and practices among themselves. We should also affirm the value of organizing according to communities other than those defined by color, such as women, gays, students, elders, the disabled, artists, and others.

Learning from Our Histories

Among the tools useful in advancing our anti-war organizing today is teaching our own histories of anti-war work. Martin Luther King spoke out against the Vietnam War in 1967 despite being strongly advised that he should "stick to civil rights issues" or lose support. Julian Bond of the Student Nonviolent Coordinating Committee (SNCC) in the 1960s (more recently Chair of the NAACP) opposed the Vietnam War. That cost him the seat he had won in the Georgia state legislature. In Harlem, thousands of African Americans marched against the draft. One sign carried the unforgettable words of Vietnam War resister Mohammad Ali: "No Vietcong ever call me nigger!"

Among Asian Pacific Islanders, intense organizing took place from coast to coast. It included the Bay Area Asian Coalition Against the War, the Asian Coalition Against the War in New York, and the Van Troi Anti-Imperialist Youth Brigade of Vietnamese people in Los Angeles. Japanese Americans organized in San Francisco's J-Town, and Filipinos also in that city. At times activists in the three cities demonstrated simultaneously.

One of the best-kept secrets about the anti–Vietnam War movement is the Chicano protests during 1970 in various parts of California. They even included Fresno, in the conservative Valley area, and culminated in the August 29, 1970, Chicano Moratorium against the war in Los Angeles. Some 20,000 people marched that day. In the middle of a peaceful rally we were tear-gassed, chased, and sometimes beaten by hundreds of police. Repression by police that afternoon left three Chicanos dead. Rubén Salazar, a *Los Angeles Times* reporter whose articles had criticized the police, was shot to death as he sat inside a bar after the attack.

As these stories reveal, standing against war is not new or alien to communities of color. We have our heroes and martyrs; we can be inspired by them.

That heritage should be made known, especially to youth of color, some of whom have been very active in anti-war work. Education about the war, demonstrating against the cutbacks in spending on schools while more prisons are built, and opposition to military recruitment are three major issues or youth organizers.

In Oakland, Youth Together has worked intensely in five high schools with school-wide teach-ins, workshops connecting the war with budget cuts, and mobilizing for major demonstrations.

Other groups doing similar work in Oakland include the Youth Empowerment Center and the East Side Arts Alliance. Bojil (formerly Olin) has done leafleting and made flags, along with Conscious Roots and San Francisco City College students, as part of the Schools Not Jails Coalition. These youth, who include many Latinos, also do media work.

In LA, Youth Organizing Communities with its Students Not Soldiers campaign has made military recruiters know they are unwelcome at two high schools including Roosevelt, the nation's largest. YOC has also worked to make students aware that their parents must register with school authorities that they do not want personal information about their children given to the military. In Chicago the SW Youth Collaborative-Generation Y Project, with a strong base with Arab and Palestinian residents, has also done educational work on Palestine, Iraq, and other key issues. They will launch a Still We Rise campaign this fall.

The educational and organizing work that can bring more people of color to oppose the Bush wars and empire-building must emphasize the connections with people's daily lives and how they are hurt in material ways. Self-interest exists and must be shown. But there is another kind of consciousness to be raised.

Let us remember the anger and sense of injustice people of color in this land can and do feel when they learn of what the United States has done to millions of people around the world, mostly people who look and struggle and suffer like them. The killing of up to 8,000 civilians in Iraq during the bombings last spring should be personally unacceptable to us all. It is a moral imperative that we affirm their humanity and thus our own. Never has there been a more important time to stand and shout at this nation's rulers: No, no, not in our name.

Go to Church Already

Another crucial and often neglected constituency is churchgoers. Anti-war organizing grew in Williamsburg, New York, as a result of El Puente's building a base in local Catholic churches. On Good Friday this year some 5,000 Latinos in Williamsburg participated in a march combining the message of Good Friday with anti-war spirit. In Chicago, a community Methodist church brought together 100 other churches—mostly of Latinos and Blacks—in a coalition that held demonstrations and other anti-war activities.

In Washington, D.C., last May, more than 1,000 grassroots Black people attended a peace rally at the Plymouth Congregational Church. Talk about the war and domestic evils such as police brutality and denial of health care stirred the crowd. Damu Smith, who heads Black Voices for Peace, emphasized that the event was "coming out of the Black experience."

As anti-war organizers often ask, why aren't people of color (as well as whites) doing more in the churches, especially since the leaders of all major denominations have spoken out against the U.S. wars?

Women, Raise Your Voices

In anti-war organizing by people of color, women are always a dynamic force—and the number keeps growing. Women of Arab origin head the list wherever they are found. Oakland's Women of Color Resource Center listed 10 reasons why women should oppose the war in its Women, Raise Your Voices! Campaign. Last spring, the WCRC held a conference of leaders of women's organizations across the country and continues to build on its belief that women are key to the anti-war movement.

Anti-war groups of color have been working to join forces and form alliances. Nationally there is RJ911 (Racial Justice 911, meaning September 11, 2001), a network that has held two national meetings of people of color. It is still being built. In the Bay Area RJ911 was the main sponsor of an inspiring day when Bay Area activists formed and marched together for the first time as a contingent of color on February 16, 2003. Korean drummers banged out Mexican rhythms while Puerto Ricans danced salsa with blacks and Filipinos, and a sizeable number of Chinese marched with Latinos, thanks to having organized together for low-cost housing.

San Francisco's Institute for Multiracial Justice held meetings in April and June bringing together activists from various groups who wanted to develop new tactics for anti-war work. From Los Angeles, Strategic Action for a Just Economy (SAJE), the tenants' rights group of families, and others of color brought members to the Bay Area to join in and learn from local anti-war activities.

Across the land, activists of color are working to develop the right strategy and tactics for organizing a movement that will grow beyond its initial, semispontaneous stage. They know, as do many white activists, that building a multiracial, multinational, multilingual, multiclass movement is our best hope ... for preventing illegal and inhuman assaults on the world's most vulnerable people. For holding back the most powerful, most frightening empire ever seen. For transforming society into a world of peace with justice for all living creatures.

Combating Oppression Inside and Outside

Elizabeth "Betita" Martínez

There is a promising new development among social justice activists aimed at overcoming racism, a longtime barrier to unity. In the anti-war and global justice movements, activists from mostly white organizations have been challenging oppression politics in their own practice. That means racism, in particular, but also sexism, homophobia, and other destructive forces.

Professional anti-racist training projects for whites have long existed. There is the twenty-five-year-old People's Institute for Survival and Beyond, based in New Orleans, which offers intensive sessions conducted by experienced activists and organizers of color. There are church—sponsored projects like Crossroads, born in 1986. In San Francisco, the twelve-year-old Challenging White Supremacy (CWS) workshop has regularly offered anti-racist training to thousands of primarily white social justice activists and others who want to get involved.

The new efforts are different. Most importantly, they emerged out of movements. The successful mass actions against the WTO in 1999, followed by the widely read article "Where Was the Color in Seattle?," opened up movement debates about white privilege and organizing on a scale that had not existed in decades. The CWS workshop recruited younger generation global justice organizers to develop an anti-racism training program—the Catalyst Project, in the Bay Area—specifically for this new upsurge. Catalyst Project joined with thousands of white global justice, and later anti-war, activists around the country. Together they were struggling to understand white supremacy and bring anti-racism into the structure, strategy, and vision of their groups.

The Colours of Resistance network, formed in 2000 in the United States and Canada, brought together activists of color and white anti-racists in the global justice movement to advance multiracial, anti-imperialist politics in their movement. The COR website has became an important tool, collecting essays and perspectives from what they refer to as "a collective liberation tendency."

Over the past five years, dozens of organizations and networks have made commitments to anti-racist work. These efforts have often included training and support from groups like Catalyst Project, CWS, and People's Institute. But activists within the groups have formed the organizing cores to lead the internal change process. Frequently people of color have played leading roles in the process.

Some examples—and dozens now exist across the United States—include the Ruckus Society, United Students Against Sweatshops, and Young Religious Unitarian

Universalists—all national organizations. Even some long-established organizations led by mostly older people have been moving to challenge oppression politics within their midst, like the War Resisters League. What is critical to understand is that for most of the activists leading these efforts, anti-racism isn't just consciousness-raising. It's an important step in developing a multiracial left movement in this country.

SOA Watch offers one of the most recent examples of an organization incorporating anti-racist politics. For fifteen years it has worked to close the U.S. School of the Americas in Ft. Benning, Georgia, which trains the Latin American military in all forms of brutal repression against their own people. Its graduates have directed and conducted torture sessions, assassinations, and massacres, with thousands of victims. SOAW's annual protest at the School, which included 16,000 people last November, always attracts a wide range of people in terms of age, gender, geography, ableness, and, to some degree, sexual orientation. But it has always been almost totally white.

SOA Watch Combats Oppression Politics

Since the organization's goal is to abolish a powerful instrument of monstrous oppression, SOAW realized it had to look at any oppressiveness within its own policies and action. It had to develop an institutional analysis rather than just focusing on individual behavior. Failure to do so would prevent evolution of an anti-oppressive organizing practice. That, in turn, would not only be a violation of the commitment to social justice but also a strategic error, undermining the alliance building so vital to victory.

SOA Watch, therefore, launched its Anti-Oppression Working Group three years ago, with a booklet, Compilation of Anti-Oppression Resources, a sexual assault team, and work on physical accessibility. Since the beginning, it has hosted anti-racism training at every major fall and spring event.

It was then decided to host an open forum where eighty SOAW people came together as a multiracial, multigenerational group for a wide-open discussion. Participants raised many problems such as arrogant leadership, favoritism toward those who had done SOA jail time, women of color saying they felt marginalized, people of color wanting respect for different communication styles, and frequent disagreement about SOAW's strict nonviolence guidelines.

The forum had great impact. For the first time, it was not just the working group raising the issues. Suddenly there were way more people calling for support of the group's anti-racist and anti-oppression initiatives. Now called the Anti-Oppression and Accessibility Working Group, it has published educational reading materials bilingually along with programs in Braille, in large print, and sign language (ASL) at all major events.

Anti-oppression work was a centerpiece and a priority of the November 2004 SOAW gathering, with the usual agenda modified to make time for its various activities.

The first day featured training in resisting sexual assault. Emphasis was then placed on whites learning to understand white privilege and other aspects of white supremacy, no matter how uncomfortable it might be.

With that goal, the program included showing the documentary *The Color of Fear* and then a discussion led by Darren Parker, a Black activist and intellectual from Philadelphia. At least 350 mostly white participants attended.

Near the end of the discussion, an important and universal message came from Rev. Graylan Hagler, senior black minister at two Washington, D.C., churches, who gave a fiery speech blasting the failure of many churches to educate their congregations about horrors like the SOA and take a stand against the repressive forces that prevail today (including "Christian Supremacy"). Given the strong religious presence in SOAW, why aren't church leaders doing more and what should be done to get them going? His message needs to be heard by churches everywhere.

Later came a paired presentation by this writer and Chris Crass, again to a primarily white audience, but smaller in number. After emphasizing that our goals were not what the "diversity industry" of corporate origin promotes, I offered a historical, systemic review of white supremacy and the militarism it has sustained as seen at the SOA. Then Chris Crass, a longtime white anti-racist trainer and Catalyst Project coordinator, stood on a chair and demonstrated vividly how white supremacy upholds white privilege. He placed his experience growing up with white privilege in a historical and institutional analysis and explained that while white people are structurally positioned to maintain their privilege, they also have a responsibility to end supremacy and join multiracial movements to build a just society.

None of the presentations drew signs of defensiveness from whites and some twenty people expressed appreciation after the second set. The smaller workshop seemed more productive in terms of interaction.

People of Color Caucus

At the end of the evening until almost midnight, some forty people of color came together. There were twice as many women as men and participants' backgrounds included China, Korea, India, Kenya, Argentina, Ecuador, three U.S. Blacks, five or six Latinos mostly from Chicago, and a Jewish-Mexican. At least six to eight were undergraduate students.

Topics they wanted to discuss included internalized racism, identity issues, coalition building, and relations between Puerto Ricans and Mexicans/Chicanos. Individual recommendations to the Working Group included:

- better outreach with more information to people of color about upcoming SOAW events including this gathering
- better Spanish translation

- having more grassroots Latin Americans come to speak about conditions in their country rather than U.S. visitors
- scheduling more times for people of color to get together
- a policy change that would mean "less of a we are saving them and more of a working together"

One suggestion was to set up an Anti-Oppression People of Color Working Group to collaborate with organizations of color to close the SOA.

Later a Latin American urged that SOAW build closer relations with organizations in Latin America—let's not forget they are the primary victims of the SOA and imperialist oppression. Latinos in the United States, he said, can be doing much more in that direction. We could, for example, be supporting efforts to pressure Latin American governments to stop sending anyone for training at the SOA, a step that Venezuela's President Hugo Chávez recently took.

The weekend saw small but important steps forward in the Working Group's activity. You could feel a solid sense of commitment from dedicated white organizers, like Jackie Downing in the Bay Area, to mention only one person whose work sets a great example.

Future work will move the struggle against internal oppression forward and bigger steps can be predicted. It won't be easy or quick. There are few models or blueprints for this work. There is a lot of commitment and some good analysis out there, but not a lot of tried and proven strategies for transforming organizations. Those advocating it, as in SOAW, remain a minority. More dialogue between groups trying to do this difficult but important work could be a big help. Darren Parker's comments make clear what are some of the other problems facing us all. But there is a new awareness, among white activists in SOAW and other organizations across the country, that the job must be done.

II. (Re)Defining Racism and Militarism: What Qualifies? Who Decides?

Continental Walk, 1976—Washington, D.C.

Janet Charles

river of a different truth

Liz Roberts

a poem in itself
a small phrase of lani guineer's
tucked away in a tome of passion
for justice
she was another black woman
thrown under the proverbial bus
and i realize it doesn't matter
that i don't know much
in the way of details
i know what's right
it's right to struggle
it's right to risk everything
for the work of an actuated democracy
it's right to let steel pulse,
soaring with righteous beauty,
into my heart
pounding
it's right to feel uncomfortable,
pushing through my own racism
to a place of understanding
of how i've been carefully shaped
into a well intentioned but
pernicious gatekeeper
of my own privilege
and the power and privilege
of those who came to name
themselves white
it's right to feel awkward,
stumbling, as i reject
the benefits and challenge myself
to use the trappings only as an insurgent
as a double agent for parity

it's right to throw off the artifice of race,
a deadening construct authored by those who own,
intimidate, silence, lie and exploit
upheld by those who tacitly comply
to reap their pittance or fortunes
at the expense of others
it's right to practice a dance
of radical resistance
it's right to let my drop of the water
of conviction
rain deep into the river of change,
flooding itself towards
the inevitable oceans
of community

Nonviolent Change of Revolutionary Depth

A Conversation with

Vincent Harding

In June 2011, the Applied Research Center—publisher of ColorLines *magazine and website—issued a special report on young people's ("the millenials") attitudes on race, racism, and social systems. The report, "Don't Call Them 'Post-Racial,'" asserted that the question of defining race and racism might be more complicated than in the past—but that racism itself is sadly alive and well. In this section of the book, we bring together authors who attempt to clarify the contours of race and racism, and their intersections with war, militarism, and violence. In addition to some basic descriptions of movement experiences, several articles define the history of whiteness and white supremacy, and examine the peoples and methods used to develop an effective fight back.*

Dr. Vincent Harding insists that we call what has popularly been termed the "civil rights" movement the more accurate and descriptive "Black-led freedom" movement. He understands and constantly argues that the legacy of that struggle and its leaders—including but hardly limited to the man whom Harding served as a close advisor, Rev. Dr. Martin Luther King Jr.—is "a true revolution of values," and justice for all. As the key drafter of King's 1967 "Beyond Vietnam" speech, Harding helped outline the sickness which, then and now, eats at the soul of "America": the giant triplets of racism, extreme materialism, and militarism. Speaking about the need to build a new society and renewed education systems at the 2010 U.S. Social Forum held in ravaged Detroit, Harding asserted that those still working for radical, multiracial change were "citizens of a society which does not yet exist." This interview with Harding, conducted by the Boston Research Center for the Twenty-First Century (BRC, now named the Ikeda Center), reviews some of the main connections needed to overcome the "sickness" and make that still-needed revolution come about.

Boston Research Center: In your book *Martin Luther King: The Inconvenient Hero,* you pay a lot of attention to the last years of King's life. You say he was trying to develop a "more militant form of nonviolence" that would appeal to the increasingly alienated urban black youth of America. Could you describe how this "more militant" nonviolent movement might have evolved, had it taken shape, and how it might have differed from other nonviolent movements today?

Vincent Harding: I'm not sure, and I'm fairly certain he wasn't sure either. But he was very clear about the fact that when he left the South and moved to places like Chicago, Los Angeles, Newark, or Detroit, he was moving into another environment—one in which there were, in many ways, deeper expressions of frustration and rage than there were in the South. It's not that those things didn't exist in the South, but there was a difference. Part of this difference simply derives from the urban experience as opposed to small city, small town, rural experience. Part is essentially the experience of people who are essentially migrants in a new setting, and who, therefore more off-balance spiritually and psychologically than those who, almost literally, know their place, have a grounding. Those who are grounded in a given situation are less likely to fly into a rage, and more likely to find substantive ways of fighting their battles.

King was trying to deal with the fact that there was a younger generation that needed outlets for its rage, that needed to know that its anger was being taken seriously and being addressed. In the direction he was headed, I think there would have been a much more conscious attempt to open up the movement to the whole other community—to folks who had not had the quieting effects of traditional black religion in their lives, who did not necessarily feel they were a part of the tradition that had produced the Birminghams and the Selma to Montgomery marches.

One of his major concerns would have been to find more creative uses for mass civil disobedience, to find ways in which people could engage the system by clogging it, stopping it—challenging the system with their very being. I remember him talking about what it might mean to have people go on one of Chicago's major highways—the Dan Ryan Expressway which runs right through the city from north to south—and block it with their bodies as a way of protesting the terrible conditions under which black people and poor people were living in Chicago. He was trying to work these things out not as a solitary figure, but in consultation with his staff, with people in the local communities, and with advisors and friends from all over the country and all over the world.

What he was clear about was that change of a revolutionary depth was necessary in America. The other thing he as clear about was that if it was going to be real change, and not simply cosmetic, it had to be accomplished nonviolently. These two things, which to many people, maybe most people, seem in total contradiction, were what he was trying to think through and work through—a way of creating nonviolent revolutionary change.

A Revolution of Values

BRC: One implication of the last statement is that violence can lead to cosmetic change rather than real change. Could you explain more about Dr. King's thinking concerning nonviolent revolution? Did he believe that social change brought about force could never last?

VH: Part of his concern was to move us away from an environment in which we believed violence was necessary for change. If your goal is to find alternatives to violence, then you can't build violence into your process of change. If you do, that makes the results cosmetic, since you're not really changing anything about the values that you hold most strongly.

Toward the end of his life King was constantly talking about a revolution of values in American society. He focused on our dependence on militarism to solve problems, our deep engagement with materialism and what that did to us, and he was concerned about what he saw as a dangerous anti-communism, an almost religious ideology that kept us from seeing the truly revolutionary claims made by human beings all over the world. And then, of course, there was the issue that he started with—racism and white supremacy in American society. All of these were value issues that had to be addressed, but he was wise enough to know that you can't get at values just by saying you are going to get at values. You've got to get at the structures that support the values, so he raised questions about the structural transformation of American society as well.

BRC: In your writings, you suggest this "revolution of values" frees us from the barriers and institutions that hold us in bondage to "our worst selves." How does personal transformation relate to this process of social change?

VH: They're fundamentally related. One of the things that Martin saw from the beginning of his Montgomery bus boycott days, for instance, was that a black community that was controlled by fear or by a lack of confidence in its own capacities to work and stand together for change, or by some kind of subliminal belief in white superiority, could not break through the barriers of legal segregation. In Montgomery he saw a kind of magnificent dialectic going on, as people decided step-by-step that they had to challenge what was going on, that it was wrong, that they could not take it. At that same moment, they were changing themselves and their assumptions; they were finding mechanisms for overcoming their fears. It was clear to him then that you can't change institutions if you don't have people who are at least in the process of changing themselves. I don't stand with those who feel you first have to change people and then you can change institutions. The two are constantly moving, dialectical activities—as we challenge institutions we discover new resources in ourselves, and as we discover these new resources, we are able to mount more effective challenges.

One of King's greatest concerns was how to keep the issue of values at the forefront of this process. This is why, especially in the last three or four years of his life, he kept saying, "We don't want to be integrated into the kind of mainstream that is America today. We need to change the mainstream, to create a new mainstream, because this mainstream is not good for people's spirits or people's lives." King was really calling for a redemptive movement among black people themselves and among all black people's allies, so that as we rethought our own values, our own vision, our own hope, as we asked ourselves, "What is the kind of America that we are really committed to? What do we want?" we could shape weapons of struggle that would be consistent with the vision we're trying to create? I think it's absolutely clear that the relationship between personal transformation and the transformation of society was inextricable for him. How, especially in the midst of the dynamics of a mass movement, which is very powerful, very beautiful, but also very uncontrollable in many ways, do you get people to focus on what should go on inside at the same time that something is going on outside? He was dealing with this in his own life, in the lives of his coworkers, and in the life of his nation.

Deep Aspirations Beneath Diverse Revolutions

BRC: Martin Luther King during his last years said repeatedly that the United States was "on the wrong side of a world revolution." What did he mean by this, and would you say it is still the case today?

VH: I think he was focusing on two or three kinds of revolutionary activity. One was the process that had begun shaking the foundations of white, Western control of the world during World War I, and that had accelerated incrementally during World War II. King was very conscious of the anti-colonial movement, which at times used the resources of Marxist ideology and the strategies of Marxist liberation struggles, but was not the same as "world communism." King believed that it was an authentic movement of nonwhite people throughout the world to stand up and demand liberation from the control and arrogance of the white West. By simply labeling it Communist, we would miss a great deal of what was going on.

He also focused on the revolution going on among peoples of the producer countries—the countries that provided raw materials and that were also, in many cases, the poorest countries in the world. These peoples had begun raising questions about their relationship to the wealth of the West. In some cases they simply asked, "How can we get some of that wealth?" But in other, more significant instances, people asked, "Why is this wealth so unfairly distributed?" King said that these were profoundly revolutionary questions. But he also felt they were profoundly spiritual questions, because he believed in the fundamental oneness of humankind. There was something absolutely wrong about one part of humankind devaluing another part, something wrong in failing to recognize that, in the long run, we are all going to have to pay for that treatment of our sisters and brothers.

And he focused on several specific geographic areas: South Africa, where for a long time the United States had supported the apartheid government; Vietnam, where we stood behind those who opposed the best aspirations of the ordinary people of that country; and the rest of the Americas—we assumed we had the right to control the resources and the politics of the southern part of this hemisphere. He saw people rising up in all of those places, calling for change, sometimes in language that other people found too Marxist, but he knew those people were asking for something that went beyond Marxism or capitalism. They were asking for a new life for themselves. He believed that is we denied them that because it threatened the white West and the capitalist centers of the world, we were on the wrong side of the revolution.

BRC: In your book *Hope and History*, you describe the African-American freedom movement not as simply a civil rights movement, but as a struggle to "expand" democracy in America, and as such, unique in its contribution to the prodemocracy struggles around the globe. Since 1990, when you published that book, much of the hope for peace and freedom that emerged around the world after the end of the Cold War has been dashed. What do you see as the source of hope for democracy movements today, including our own in America?

VH: The human experience is such that, if I am deeply involved in a struggle for democracy in the former Czechoslovakia, or in Tiananmen Square, or in Johannesburg, or in Birmingham, I am profoundly affected by it. The fact that a particular movement may not "succeed," does not mean that it has been wiped from my memory. My life has been affected; I have tasted something very real. I have learned that certain possibilities for human relationships exist that I didn't know about before. The fact that people experienced these things in very palpable and profound ways means that these truths now exist permanently in the universe. Energy does not go out of existence. Truth is an energy that will find its manifestation and expression in some other way, in some other place, in other people. That is one of my major sources of hope.

Another comes from the time I spend with children and young people. Even in the midst of all the difficulties they face being young in America today, I see great possibilities in them. As long as the capacity to see new possibilities exists, then there can be hope. Because, as you know, we come to new situations politically and economically and socially only insofar as people are willing to dream them first. And young people still have the capacity to dream. I find that a source of hope.

Pluralism, Trust, and Hope

BRC: Pluralism makes a consensus on core values difficult, especially religious pluralism—which is why many people are calling for more interfaith, interreligious, and intercultural dialogue. What advice do you have for us at the Center for pursuing such dialogue?

VH: My daughter, who is both a scholar and a poet, regularly fusses with me about our work on these kinds of things. She says, "Daddy, you people talk too much, you're too word-oriented. You've got to find some way to get at these things through the arts."

I think that all of us who are concerned about such things need to hear that message. Having logical discussions about our similarities and differences only opens one level of our being, but religion operates at many levels of our being, so that we may respond to the any levels of the divine. All of us who want to find meeting points and places of joint engagement have to open up to a variety of possibilities. I would think, especially in an academic community like this, that we need to break out of the linear explication of our similarities and our differences. We've got to find a way to bring our spirits together.

BRC: In your book *There Is a River* you say, "there will be no hope for a truly just society on these shores until we address the issue of the human spirit and its role in our struggle for political transformation." Can you comment on this idea?

VH: In America today, it seems one of our major difficulties is lack of trust. Ultimately, you cannot have a democratic community, you cannot have a human, creative community, without trust in yourself, trust in each other, and trust that there is something beyond the self and others. This leads to hope—and involves issues of human spirit. One of our great challenges at this point is to figure out what we can bring into our industrialized society from the best insights of the other traditions of the world. We've got to be very intentional about a recognition of our need for healing. Part of that healing, of course, is related to racial and gender issues. Part of it is the fact that you can't live in a society that keeps cutting up things and people and situations without feeling cut up inside yourself. We have to have some understanding of the people who wrote about creating a more perfect Union. There were all kinds of messy intentions there, but the best intentions are beautiful ones. The idea that the American people are to create a more perfect Union—that is really a spiritual calling. You can't talk about it without talking about issues of the spirit.

Toward "A More Perfect Union"

BRC: In your writings you explore the delicate, interdependent relationship of student and teacher as well as that of follower and political leader. The Commission on Global Governance, whose ideas on UN reform formed the basis for some of the Center's past dialogues, pointed to "a poverty of leadership" at all levels in the world today, and to an "ethical vacuum." How do you think these two problems relate? Will the leadership appear, in other words, only when the people are ready?

VH: Again, I go back to King as an example. It's very important to recognize that he was not operating in a vacuum, that he was operating in a situation of ferment. In Montgomery, leadership was being taken by women—ordinary, marvelous African-American women. It was those women who were prepared to respond to Rosa Parks's personal initiative. When she refused to move to the rear of the bus, women who had been involved in various kinds of political activism were ready. One of those women ran off 35,000 copies of a stencil by herself the night after Mrs. Parks's arrest in order to let people know about it. And she saw to it that her students passed it out in important places. King came out of that ferment—people decided they were going to let Mrs. Parks's arrest become a catalyst for their movement as a community and they knew they needed a spokesperson.

Our difficulty with leadership today, in part, is that we have not figured out where we need to go and what is necessary to get there. We haven't figured out what kind of "more perfect Union" we would like to move toward. Part of the difficulty here is that we have gotten so enmeshed in individualistic thinking that even the concept of a more perfect Union is elusive. Yesterday, the television was on, and I heard, "Are you dissatisfied with the quality of your drinking water?" I was only half-listening, but what I unconsciously expected to hear next was, "Get together with your neighbors and find out why the drinking water is like that." But it was a commercial for an individual filter you could buy to solve the drinking water problem for the seven people or the two people in your family. That seems to me to be a perfect example of what happens when community breaks down—we all opt for our own personal solutions to what are clearly community-wide problems.

BRC: There's a debate going on right now in America over the proper role of journalism, or rather about whether it ought to have any role, in the cultivation of civic virtues. What are your views on this question of "public journalism"?

VH: Journalists have a major responsibility for the creation of a context of democratic engagement. Hannah Arendt said that we become most human in the process of conversation. Journalism offers a way of opening up the conversation space for the community—offering ideas, information, stimulation for the community to get involved in always richer, deeper, more informed levels of conversation about what it means to create a more perfect Union. I think journalists have this tremendous responsibility because they have access to folks in ways that many other people don't. How this is affected by the world of the Internet I'm not quite sure, but clearly it changes the way space is made for the engagement of the public.

BRC: Do you think there's an awareness of that today among journalists?

VH: Let me take it beyond journalism. One of our major challenges today is that relatively few people are even thinking about what has to be done to create democratic space, to develop democratic spirit, to create appreciation for democratic values. We are supposedly a democracy, but very little in our educational, commercial, or community processes intentionally deals with what it means to live in a democracy. We simply feel that we were given one in 1776 (perhaps we returned to the issue in the 1940s or '50s or '60s) and that everything should go on its democratic way automatically. We need to know enough history to realize that democracy has to be fought for, maybe in every generation now. We don't have a mechanism for that.

If we look around at this bastion of higher education, where is the advanced study center for the development of democracy in America? We've got advanced computer centers, advanced business centers, and advanced political centers—which usually do not take up issues related to democracy. One of our major challenges is to figure out how to build structures that will help us understand what democracy is supposed to be about, and to help create new democratic structures with which to continue building our society. There are so many forces at work in society that run counter to democratic responsibility that unless there is an intentional effort to teach democracy, we'll find ourselves in a situation—maybe we're already there—where most people in this democratic nation know almost nothing about the meaning of democracy.

Regaining a Moral Compass

The Ongoing Truth of King's Vision

Elizabeth McAlister

In this short article written for Sojourners *magazine, McAlister outlines the continuing lessons to be learned from the teachings of Martin Luther King and the Black-led freedom movement.*

From 1963 to 1966, while teaching art history at Marymount College in Tarrytown, N.Y., I was in a Catholic religious community blessed with questioning and concerned women. I was already convinced the Vietnam War was wrong—a conviction born of morality and scripture, but with little political analysis. Martin Luther King's words in spring 1967 expressed some of my consciousness: "I was a clergyman … and … I accepted as a commission to … bring the ethical insights of our Judeo-Christian heritage to bear on the social evils of our day. War is one of the major evils facing humankind."

How profoundly our lives today are molded by the racism, materialism, and militarism about which Martin spoke so powerfully. How do we hold ourselves, each other, our communities, our churches, and our nation accountable? Perhaps it is the same way we carry forward King's idea that our national identity is secondary to our spiritual identity. How do we speak to an imperial nation that assumes it is entitled to dominate and control not only the earth and seas but all of outer space? We know that it has the intention and it has the means—nuclear stockpiles with world-destroying capacity.

King's insight has been realized in the United States. Our nation's "war on terror" is but the latest example: an epidemic of violence in the service of the rich and powerful. President Bush continued the war of the powerful against the powerless, with new excuses, new imperatives, new lies. The war has cost upwards of a trillion dollars. We have experienced the hostility of the Islamic world, the anger of our allies, the diminishment of our system of government, the complicity of the media, the silence of Congress, and the apathy of citizens. War has not made us more secure; it has made us less free.

With King, I see our government possessing "power without compassion, might without morality and strength without sight." Along with others, I struggle to reclaim a moral compass, to remind our leaders and military of the need to lay aside the pursuit of domination in our world. We have no right to kill. And neither do we have the power, nor insight, nor ability, to control history.

Four Vignettes on the Road of the Broken Rifle

Reflections on War and Resistance

Ibrahim Abdil-Mu'id Ramey

This article, which originally appeared in Fellowship *magazine, charts his thoughts and experiences on war, resistance, and change across national and cultural borders.*

Vignette 1: The Kitchen Table and the Bomb

I'm ten years old. I sit at a kitchen table in a very small house in the segregated Black community of Norfolk, Virginia with my parents, Cleo and Addie Ramey, and an older cousin, Addie Lee Mason. We are in the most militarized city in the United States, but it is a city with jobs. All of the family have migrated from the deep South to the up South, and my parents have settled in Norfolk.

The conversation turns to the issue of the atomic bombings of Hiroshima and Nagasaki. My people are not educated, and they don't know anything about the physics of nuclear explosions. But they do know that atomic bombs killed a whole lot of people in Japan.

Daddy mentions that Japanese people were put into special camps during the war, but German and Italian-Americans were allowed to be free. "They dropped the bombs on Japan because they're a colored nation," he says. "Why didn't they bomb them Germans?"

I remember family conversations about white racism and segregation in the household, but never one about racism and war.

"Why did America bomb all those people? They said that most of them weren't even soldiers."

Ten years later, I was still struggling with my father's question.

Vignette 2: A Wannabe Soldier Looks at Killing and Says "No"

It's the early spring of 1968, and I'm seated in the first-year Military Science class at the University of Pennsylvania with twenty other ROTC wannabe soldiers: academic, unbolted, and thoroughly untested. The closest we've come to real weapons is the ancient M-1 rifles that we're learning to field-strip and reassemble.

We're paying attention, more or less, to the instructor, Major Chandler, who, with Sergeant Major Tedeschi, preps the young men on the art of killing for God and country. We're young and incredibly naïve, but even in an Ivy League college, the cold realities of Vietnam and the draft loom large in our futures. The rage of the Tet Offensive makes all of us think even more about our futures after Penn.

I, for one, think that the Vietnam adventure is stupid and unjust, but the residual Boy Scout and love-your-country programming kicks in hard, too hard to allow me to join the protest movements that rise up fiercely against the war. I figure that not everybody goes to Vietnam, but if I have to, it's better to go in as a Second Lieutenant. Maybe I'll be in some unit away from the fighting and mass killing.

So the Major, a combat vet, is explaining some tactical combat ideas and he starts talking about a firefight in Vietnam. "We put eighteen of those dirty yellow bastards in the ground forever," he says, with the smug confidence of a man who has killed many.

The bravado clearly impresses some of the kids in the class, but I think back to the atom bomb talked about around the kitchen table years before. Are the Vietnamese "yellow bastards" anything like the "niggers" murdered by the KKK and their friends in the South? And I remember Muhammad Ali's question, what Vietnamese ever called me by that name?

Later that evening I revisit a book that someone gave me, an autobiography of Ho Chi Minh, the North Vietnamese leader. I don't tell people in the unit that I'm reading this, but I pay attention to Ho's chronicle of visiting the United States as a young cabin boy working on a French cruise ship, and later, his writing about the horror of Black racial lynchings in the South.

In an instant, something crystallizes, and everything changes. Someone is demanding that I prepare to make war against a people who not only have not made war against my own people, but who sympathize with our condition. And I realize that Ho Chi Minh and the people of Vietnam are not my enemies, and that Muhammad Ali was right. Daddy's question floats up again, but this time, I have an answer.

This is another war against colored people. Fought, in part, by colored people in America who aren't really free themselves.

I don't have a "political analysis" or "worldview" at this point, but I decide to turn in the uniform. I return it with a nasty note to the ROTC commander about protesting "imperialism." I finished the book about Ho a few days before April 4th, 1968 [the day that Dr. King was killed].

Two of my high school classmates and Boy Scout friends from Norfolk—Richard Lassiter and Johnny Johnson—will take my place in Vietnam and die within the year.

Vignette 3: Standing at the Gates of Hell, but Smiling

It's a cold, deserted New Year's Eve, on the edge of a new year and a new millennium. (It will certainly be a new year for me, as I'm getting married in exactly seven days.)

A hundred or so of us are in the little town of Mercury, Nevada, to gather in protest at the nuclear test site with friends from the Western Shoshone nation who pray with us and brief us before we move out across the desert floor to the gates of the test site, where, we know, we'll be arrested for federal trespass by the U.S. government.

Of course, the land is the ancestral land of native people. It doesn't "belong" to a nation that stole it, any more than anything stolen really belongs to thieves. But the Shoshone people and their leader, Corbin Harney, are patient and resolute, and they have given us, mostly Anglos, permission to be on their sacred land for the action.

As we walk across a desolate desert floor, the explosions over Hiroshima and Nagasaki come to mind again. Two weapons, made in the United States, were detonated over cities containing "enemy" populations, but hundreds more were exploded deep within the earth of Nevada. The native people, more than any others, feel the deep wounds of this defilement: their soil and water and animals have been poisoned, and disproportionately, they suffer from cancer and birth defects. In fact, the entire cycle of mining, uranium refinement, and nuclear testing continues to kill the earth and those who live on it. This is a Hiroshima that is not so far away.

That night, a few dozen of us are arrested—including ebullient Martin Sheen, who sits with other men in a makeshift detention cage and even signs a few autographs.

The police who process the arrestees are more tired and bored than truculent, and after a few statements, we're released to go back to Las Vegas and, in my case, eventually home.

The Shoshone people, however, are not released. The half-life of the plutonium that poisons their earth and water is thousands of years.

Vignette 4: A Small Boy in a War Zone

In March of 2000, the United States is not "officially" at war with Iraq, but the war against the people of Iraq does not need to be official in order to be brutal and ugly and terribly lethal. A small group of us, Jewish and Christian and Muslim, has journeyed to Iraq to see what the war is like, knowing that perhaps 1.5 million Iraqis have died since 1990 from the effects of devastating economic sanctions.

But the warfare has been more than economic.

In the southern part of Iraq, near the city of Al-Nasiriyyah, American military aircraft have launched periodic attacks against Iraqi ground radar sites in a prolonged cat-and-mouse game of radar targeting and counterstrikes. Sometimes the attaching planes hit their targets. Sometimes, they hit neighborhoods.

We are in the home of an Iraqi woman, a schoolteacher who taught English to secondary students. She was at home one day, grading papers, as her two children played in the narrow street outside with other kids. An air-launched missile fired against an Iraqi military target went off course, veered into the street, and exploded. Her little girl was killed instantly. Her son had most of his left hand blown off.

She weeps as she tells the story to her North American visitors. The son with the mangled hand looks sad, but resigned our Iraqi handlers, from Saddam's state apparatus, are bored and impatient; they've heard all of this before.

But what can we say to the mother of a dead daughter and a wounded son? Only that we are responsible, too, for her loss, and for the political and economic system that inflicts death on so many millions in this world?

My journey, like that of so many others, began with a question that stuck in my conscience like a small rock in the sole of a shoe. I did not personally experience Hiroshima, or Vietnam, or the Nevada Test Site, or a missile attack in Iraq. But others did. And their stories and their suffering would not go away.

War is not an event, but a system, that has polluted and engulfed all of us who live on this earth. Those of us who are not called to fight wares, or who to refuse to do so, are nonetheless morally compelled to resist this system, to refuse to pay for it or rationalize it. We must also give comfort to those who have been victims of war.

I give thanks that my journey on the path of the broken rifle began as a child in that small kitchen in Norfolk so long ago, surrounded by people who refused to let an inconvenient question go unasked.

Questioning Our Reality

Alejandra Cecilia Tobar Alatriz

The following article originally appeared in Fellowship *magazine, published by the Fellowship of Reconciliation. At the time of its writing, Chilean-born Alatriz was a nonviolence trainer with FOR's Peacemakers Program. She remains an activist and performing artist based in Minneapolis.*

> Black and white.
> Young and old.
> Rich and poor.
> Straight and gay.

The wonders of dichotomous thinking deeply ingrained in our western culture do not cease to amaze me. "So, what's behind the name?" a young man asked me in a theatre one night. "I mean, you look pretty white."

I remember pausing to let the anger welling up inside me pass through my body and be released in a long and deep exhalation. Seeing his curiosity, i softened. In a world where we allow our realities to fit into boxes that limit our possibilities of experience, someone with my name—Alejandra—is supposed to look darker.

Indeed, because of the lightness of my skin, i have access to privileges within most institutions that my darker friends do not. If i shorten my name (or change it to something easier to pronounce) and speak solely in English, i am heard just the same as the next light-skinned person, most of the time. If i tie back my locks, wear a pretty skirt, and resist the urge to greet folks with a hug and a kiss, no one gets uncomfortable, In fact, if i choose not to disclose my language, culture, and most of what i cherish about my identity, i rarely experience racism.

It is very interesting to me when i meet individuals who actually question my identity as a person of color. One white minister once asked me why i would put myself in such small terms. He wondered why we could not just look at each other as human beings. He said he believed in Dr. King's vision of a man being judged by his character and not by the color of his skin.

I struggled with this. It is difficult for me to be critical of well-intentioned white folks who present simple solutions that deny the complexity of our present racial and class structures.

Assuming a position of colorblindness without first actively dismantling the racism deeply ingrained in our economic, social, political, and educational institutions is a white man's luxury. I can only assume this minister was not wondering why so many people of color are poor, in prison, or on death row. It was easy for him to ask me to let go of being Latina and put myself in the human category with him. He doesn't introduce himself as a white male: for him, being white and being human are the same thing. As i keep breathing out my frustration, questions come to mind.

Why do those who commit crimes against white persons get, on average, higher prison sentences than those who commit crimes against black persons? Why are under-resourced schools mostly populated with children of color? Why is the history of the United States heavy with instances of death, oppression, and denial of land and basic human rights for people of color?

How can i keep challenging unearned white privilege at the personal, institutional, and cultural level?

Because i am blessed to have white allies who constantly support me and use their privilege to allow my voice to come forward.

Because these same white allies believe my pain and my joys. Though admitting to not fully understanding what it means to be a person of color, they say they are willing to keep learning and struggling, for life.

Because i look at the United States foreign policy and see it dripping with racist strategy that assumes that most have to lose in order for the few in power to win.

Because i know that all of us are dying from this in various ways.

Because mi familia loves and supports me in my work.

Racism is complex, incredibly painful, and at times seemingly indestructible. There are days when i want to reject all expectations that i should educate white people on racism because i am a person of color. There are times when i say no more will i share my pain so that others will understand that it is real. There are moments when i feel so empty and invalidated that all i want to do is sleep. Then i look outside my window and notice weeds growing through cracks on the cement blocks. I see the trees swaying and bending—holding their ground in the face of the bitter cold wind. I realize that today black, brown, tan, yellow, olive, and white little boys and girls are able to hold hands, when forty years ago this was not their reality.

I have hope. I have a vision of justice that i am willing to die for. I have the understanding that issues of oppression are complex and interrelated. I believe in the transformative power of our humanity.

Things are rarely as dichotomous as we have been taught to believe. Knowing this gives me the freedom to claim all aspects of my identity that fall in the areas in between. This freedom gives me the strength i need to survive.

I invite you in this struggle for mutual survival.

Revolution is coming. Let it begin from within.

Finding the Other America

Anne Braden

An early version of this article was featured as part of a War Resisters League organizing packet on the connection between racism and militarism.

I f we are serious about the challenge of the unfinished business of racism, we must start by realizing that this is not a task we must complete. It is one we must begin. It is the basic contradiction in our entire history as a nation. The first European settlers who landed on these shores saw themselves as creating a great new experiment in democratic government. Yet they were enslaving a whole population of human beings, Africans, and committing genocide against the Indigenous peoples of North America. As a nation, we have never really dealt with this contradiction. We've only picked around the edges of it. So our first step is to turn ourselves inside out and our institutions upside down. I grew up seven decades ago in a society (Alabama) that was totally racially segregated. In my young adulthood I was fortunate enough to have to face the painful fact that this society that had nurtured me and been good to me was just plain wrong. And I was able to change sides in the racial divide. I was just one of many people of my generation and those that followed who went through this experience. I think what we went through at that time is, in microcosm, what this whole country must go through. I can testify that although this is a very painful experience it is not destructive, because once we have done it we are free. We are not really free of the racism within us because we will always see the world through white eyes, but we are free to struggle consciously against it, so it no longer shapes our lives without our even knowing it.

In recent years, across the country, there has been a wave of initiatives to look back at history, especially in the South—efforts to bring to justice criminals from the past. The crimes include the brutal lynching of Emmett Till in 1955; the 1963 murder of civil rights leader Medgar Evers in Jackson, Mississippi; the terrible bombing of a black church in Birmingham, Alabama, later the same year, which killed four young girls; the slaying of three civil rights workers in Philadelphia, Mississippi, in 1964; and tragedies in many other communities. It is a good thing that this is happening. An individual, a community, and a nation must face past evil to move on to a better future. In 1979, in Greensboro, North Carolina, five anti-racist labor organizers were murdered by avowed Nazis and members of the Ku Klux Klan. In the wake of this tragedy, the Greensboro Justice Fund was set up by widows of the victims and survivors to support ongoing movements against racism. It is a remarkable example of people transforming personal heartbreak into a creative movement. We have just celebrated the Fund's 25th anniversary. People in Greensboro have now set up a Truth and Reconciliation Commission modeled on the one in South Africa. The purpose is to bring together those who have been on opposite sides of the issue that divided the city twenty-five years ago. It is surely a worthy objective. But there is also a danger. We can all become quite self-righteous in assuring ourselves that we would not have done what those people did. And maybe we would not have pulled the trigger or set the bombs. But would we have spoken out? There were huge pressures not to do so.

People establishing structures to examine a community's past want to establish communication across the racial divide. In Louisville, Kentucky, where I have lived and worked for 60 years, well-intentioned white people intermittently have set up meetings between representatives of the black and white communities. It never works. Why? The median income of black families in our community is less than 50 percent that of whites. How can you have communication when that kind of gap exists? Instead, people who want a change in relationships must work for living wage legislation, more low-income housing, and health insurance for everyone. In 1964, I interviewed Bob Moses, organizer of the voting-rights drive that ultimately changed Mississippi and the nation. He said, "The job of white people is not to prepare the Negro [the terminology at that time] for entrance into the larger society, but to prepare society for the changes that must be made to include room for Negroes." That is what this society has never done—before, then, or since. We have not made "room" for African Americans. Thus today, if there do not seem to be enough jobs or housing or health care for everyone, blacks can do without. The problem is that the assumption that the good things of life are for whites first was built into our institutions from the beginning so firmly that we accept it as part of the scenery. Given this framework, whites must make a very conscious decision and take concerted action to "change sides" on the issue of race.

But once we make that decision, we can feel overwhelmed. This problem is so massive, what can we possibly do to change it? The Kentucky Alliance Against Racist and Political Repression, with which I work in Louisville, has an approach to this problem. We say we have to grab hold of something specific, some specific manifestation of racism in our local institutions—for example the police force, the court system, our educational institutions, or job discrimination. Joint struggles around these specific issues actually do bring people together. (We also link local issues to global ones, pointing out that this same issue of racism has shaped our foreign policy and consigned huge populations—as in Iraq—to a subhuman status. And then it becomes all right to drop bombs on them.) The first task of whites in these struggles is to be vocal and visible. Often those of us who think we have seen the light on race tend to sit and examine our own souls. That may be a good thing for us to do and it may make us feel better, but it is not going to bring one iota of change in the conditions under which most people of color live or do anything to bring people together across the divide. We must speak out and act publicly and thereby break through what seems to be a solid wall of white resistance. Today there is an added challenge. Many white people have the illusion that race is not a problem anymore. They say we can now move on to "other" issues. I call these people the colorblind crowd. It is certainly true that our society faces many life-and-death issues. But we can't deal effectively with any of these problems until we mount an aggressive offense against racism. This is not only morally right; it's a practical matter. As long as our society can dump its problems on people of color it will not seek or find real solutions. Once we realize that, we must act publicly; we must reach out to people we don't know. We have a tendency to spend all our time with people who agree with us. But our challenge is to go to people who don't agree with us. We must knock on their doors—or call them on the phone—because they won't come to us, and they won't respond to e-mail or snail mail. They must hear a human voice, and, if possible, see us. And when we reach them, our approach should not be to make them feel guilty. Guilt is not a productive emotion; rather, it can be paralyzing. We should see ourselves as offering them a great opportunity, the possibility of finding a whole "other world" or other community to live in.

I call what I joined "the other America." This other America has always existed, even before the slave ships arrived. African Americans have always fought against their oppression, and many died rather than endure slavery. And at least some whites have joined these struggles—in the early resistance to slavery, the Abolitionist movement, the Reconstruction period after the Civil War, the upsurges of people's movements in the 1930s, the civil rights activities of the 1950s and '60s, and beyond to today in the twenty-first century. And this resistance actually has roots that stretch back to the beginning of the human race. In every age, no matter how cruel the oppression carried on by those in power, there have been those who struggled for a different world. I believe this is the genius of humankind, the thing that makes us half divine: the fact that some human beings can envision a world that has never existed. Perhaps no one living today will see a major change. But it will come. And living in that world that is working to make it happen lets us know that our lives are worthwhile. Meantime, there are things we can do right now to reform our domestic situation and—critically important—to change our foreign policy. Our nation and the planet are teetering on the brink of destruction. Some people think there is nothing that can be done because those who want to turn time backward are so firmly in control of the government. But we must stop acting as if history started two years ago. Things have not always been as they are now. In the South, for instance, our greatest change happened when we lived under a literal police state. And it does not take a mass movement to begin. Every mass movement has started because a few people came together and began to talk to others. Today there are huge new possibilities of real communication because Hurricane Katrina opened the eyes of masses of people to the reality of racism and poverty in this country. Our job is to talk with them. And we must do it *now*.

On Being a Good Anti-Racist Ally

Ted Glick

This article first appeared as part of Glick's regular column, "Future Hope."

> *"Political leadership is a matter of program, strategy and tactics, and not the color of those who lead it, their oneness of origin with their people, nor the services they have rendered."*
> —C.L.R. James, *The Black Jacobins*

Probably the most educational year of my life was the year that I spent in the U.S. prison system following a conviction for a nonviolent raid on Selective Service and FBI offices in Rochester, N.Y., in the fall of 1970. This was during the height of the peace movement against the war in Vietnam. Over the course of eleven months I spent time in three federal prisons and five county jails.

In every joint I spent time in, the majority of my fellow inmates were African American and Latino. This was a new experience for me. I was twenty or twenty-one at the time, and growing up I had had almost no close social contact with those of another culture or color.

I can still remember some of the individuals I met and the strength that they gave me by their kindness and interest in my life. There were very few whom I interacted with who seemed like "criminals" to me. The more I got to know them, the more I came to realize that racism and a class system which kept many people poor were, without question, the real reasons for why they were there.

I also learned that if you treat others with respect they will virtually always treat you with respect. Since getting out of prison thirty-three years ago I have tried to keep faith with those brothers from whom I learned so much.

I have made a conscious effort to be a good anti-racist ally as I go about the work of helping to build a popular movement for fundamental social transformation in the United States.

There are many things that go into being such a good ally: serious study, learning to be humble, building friendships with those from other cultures, following leadership from people of color especially on issues most important to them, and being willing to risk damaged relationships, conflict, or worse by being outspoken about racist statements or actions when among people of European descent.

But perhaps the hardest thing is to reject liberal paternalism when interacting with other activists of color.

Liberal paternalism is keeping quiet when a person of color says something that you strongly disagree with or proposes a course of action you feel is wrong. It is "going along to get along," being afraid to engage in frank and upfront, while respectful, discussion over important issues, instead deferring too easily to the viewpoint of the person(s) of color you are talking with out of fear of being thought of as too pushy or arrogant.

I find this the hardest, because I am totally aware of the personal experiences that most people of color have had with too many white people who interact with them arrogantly or dishonestly. I try very hard to function differently, and this can make it harder to openly disagree because of the fear that the disagreement will be taken in a wrong way.

I do think there is the need for what someone once called a "bending of the stick." That is, when there is such a long history of white supremacy in our society, to get us back to a situation of equality and straight-up-ness, there does need to be some bending of the stick back past the midpoint for a time so that social and personal relations can then straighten themselves out.

But C.L.R. James's words above cannot be forgotten. There are far too many examples of progressive activists of color (and whites) becoming corrupted and bought off. Those who come from backgrounds of oppression and exploitation can raise themselves up to become oppressors and exploiters themselves. And those who have once given freely of themselves for the cause of human liberation can lose their courage and go backwards.

Sound "program, strategy, tactic." Yes, those are critical.

As critical is the continuing development of a humane and truly alternative, multiracial, resistance culture that can help all of us grow and learn, keep grounded, become better people in all aspects of our lives. We can't function in our personal and political interactions in ways similar to those of the corrupt and inhuman capitalist system that is literally destroying our ecosystem, many of its life forms and many of its people. We must be known as people who can deal with differences and disagreements in a way, which is affirming and constructive, not dishonest and destructive.

In the words of the late Fred Rogers (Mr. Rogers): "At the center of the universe is a loving heart that continues to beat and that wants the best for every person. Anything we can do to help foster the intellect and spirit and emotional growth of our fellow human beings: that is our job. Those of us who have this particular vision must continue against all odds. Life is for service."

The Culture of White Privilege
Is to Remain Silent

Liz Walz

This 2008 article from Fellowship *magazine portrays an individual's process in dealing with personal and institutional racism within the peace movement.*

Several years ago, during a community meal in my home at the time, Darren, the fiancé of one of my housemates, suggested that our anti-war activism and organizing was racist. I couldn't believe it: I'd recently been released from serving a year in jail because of the analysis that the United States was making war on brown-skinned people. I'd lived in a cellblock with black, white, and Asian women—helping create an ethos of sisterhood—how could I be racist?

The very suggestion raised feelings of humiliation and anger in me, and I reacted defensively. I don't remember the details of that conversation—but I'm sure I was invested in silencing this black man. Our relationship eventually fractured painfully after a series of charged e-mails.

In the years since that dinner conversation, I have come to agree with his perspective. Layers of self-justification and ego have been peeled—sometimes ripped—away in my ongoing process of dealing with racism as a white person working in predominantly white peace and faith communities.

Mentors in the Mennonite-rooted Damascus Road program articulate three stages of conversion that whites typically go through:

- Realizing that racism is not a historical problem, it continues today. Although the Civil Rights movement made tremendous strides in legally ending segregation, systemic racialized discrimination and violence still are common occurrences;
- Recognizing that white people carry unearned benefits based on our skin color, "white privilege," and that perpetuating white privilege is the purpose of racism;
- Understanding that the receipt of those white privileges shapes us in damaging ways—and out of that recognition, being motivated to act out of self-interest rather than paternalism.

At one time, at about this point in the conversation, I would point out other forms of institutionalized violence which exist in addition to racism: sexism, homophobia, ageism, ableism, classism, and so on. A graduate of the Challenging White Supremacy workshop wondered aloud to me whether I was bringing up these issues to avoid my discomfort with talking about institutionalized power systems based on race. After all, she pointed out, in many circles white people frame the dialogues on class, gender and ability—focusing on racism requires white people like me to sit firmly in the learner's seat—rather than taking control of the conversation. This role reversal is uncomfortable—and part of my growing edge has been learning to live with discomfort as I increasingly recognize the situations in which I'm on the "wrong" side of injustice.

In my formation as a Catholic Worker and as a Plowshares activist, I was encouraged and inspired to take personal responsibility for the ills in society and the misdeeds of my government. Socialized as a woman, I've spent no small amount of time and energy learning to claim my voice—*especially* when it differs from the charismatic male leader(s) whom I've put on a pedestal.

These lessons have been hard won and I've made many mistakes along the way. There have been costs—alienating friends, family, and community members, and losing access to job and social opportunities as a consequence of voicing different and unpopular opinions about "American values."

Yet, I have emerged as a woman with a certain social and political analysis, the propensity to take initiative, and a stronger personality. Confronting-racism work has challenged me at this deep level of identity, revealing assumptions I had about the power of white people (and the white peace movement) to have any relevance at all in the lives of brown and black-skinned people throughout the world, much less in my own (predominantly black) neighborhood.

The Jena 6

In mid-October, I was talking with a white friend about the visible absence of white activists at the Jena gathering this past September. She had learned about the Jena march but had not gone; she confessed disappointment at having "missed the boat." During that conversation, we together made a commitment to be more responsive in the future—to move from analysis to action in regards to racism.

Just days later, we learned of another march to be held in Jena on the Dr. Martin Luther King Jr. holiday in January 2008: white supremacists and the KKK have announced their intent to promote "the views of the majority." My friend and I recognized this as an opportunity to stand as white allies in support of the Jena families and community and we started brainstorming organizing possibilities.

We learned that the current phase and slogan of the Jena 6 campaign is, "We are all Jena." That is, the experience of racism and legalized injustice in Jena are not social anomalies in this one small southern town. Racialized oppression and violence occur in every state, city, and town of these United States.

The message we received from the Jena families is, "Don't come to Jena—organize in your own back yard." This information put an end to the visions in my head of contacting friends and allies across the nation with a call to travel to Jena. Instead, I am putting out this invitation to whites in the Fellowship of Reconciliation (FOR) community and other predominantly white peace and justice groups: break the silence—find the organizers of color who are working on issues in your community and get behind them, following and supporting, not taking over.

Vocabulary: Various organizations use terms differently. This is how terms are used in this article:

Racism: prejudice or bias, plus (the systemic misuse of) power

Racialized groups: denotes racial categories imposed on certain groups on the basis of superficial attributes such as skin color.

White supremacy or white superiority: the belief that people with white skin are more competent, capable, savvy and intelligent, etc. than people of color and that white cultural values are "normal." This is the dominant socialization in the United States and is internalized by both whites and people of color.

Racial inferiority: the internalized belief, held by white people or people of color, that racialized groups are inferior, and which denigrates (or artificially romanticizes) cultural differences.

White privilege: the "benefit of the doubt" that white people typically enjoy in situations where they are otherwise anonymous—in public, the marketplace, when interacting with strangers, etc. Historically, this has played out in wage differentials, access to mortgages and loans, unequal distribution of tax dollars among neighborhoods and school districts, access to housing, etc.

Anti-racist or anti-oppression organizational identity: An organization (1) which has moved past symbolic or tokenized representation of people of color to creating an organizational cultural identity reflective of the backgrounds of participants; and (2) where the group with access to structural power—decision-making and resource deployment—has people of color in the majority.

Doing Our Own Work

Another guiding principle for whites working for racial justice is also the title of a training program: *Doing Our Own Work*. This refers to whites taking responsibility for our own education and growth in learning about racism. One temptation I struggled with in cultivating relationships of accountability was turning first to people of color to provide me with relevant information, advice, and emotional support in my struggles. Mentors quickly cautioned me against using people of color to ease my conscience. Asking people already burdened by racism to add "taking care of me" to their plate can be an expression of entitlement. Instead, I first seek out other white anti-racist allies for my regular conversation and brainstorming partners, people I am connected to through several fine education and training organizations, a few of which are listed in the adjacent sidebar.

I do sometimes talk with a few friends of color about my journey—for example, soliciting feedback about this article. Darren and I were eventually able to begin a new relationship—a gift from him which I was not entitled to, but which I deeply value. Darren has given permission for me to approach him as a sounding board—while retaining the full right to say "no" to me. But for most of the people of color with whom I am in relationship, my primary aim is to simply be in relationship, to listen. I lean against the temptation to turn every conversation into a process about my anti-racism work. As trust deepens, I am intentional about when and why I approach the topic of racism. None of these relationships would have been possible with the quality I enjoy had I not taken steps to unlearn white assumptions and behaviors, making mistakes and being open to correction along the way.

For me, making the commitment to break the silence around racism in predominantly white social change groups has meant practicing addressing racism in the places where my relationships are strongest—among friends and family. When engaging with anyone about situations that I now understand to be offensive or injurious, I have learned to support and respect the dignity of the person I'm interacting with while identifying damaging comments and behaviors.

It is a shock for my friends and family members, like most white social change activists, to realize they are perpetuating racism and white supremacy. They don't believe they *intend* to behave in racist ways—and I am learning to be both careful and direct when confronting them with the information that the *impact* of their actions perpetuates white supremacy.

This is not easy feedback to offer and it is not easy feedback to receive. As a person socialized to be nice and "if you can't say anything nice, don't say anything at all," I've had to strengthen the muscle of interrupting racist dynamics when my preference would be to simply avoid the conflict. In these cases, Darren's voice offers clarity that calls me to greater integrity:

On a philosophical level I would challenge your assertion that folk aren't intentionally behaving in racist ways. I've found that there are varying degrees of willful ignorance and a good deal of folk behaving with a level of paternalism and cruelty which they would very much not tolerate if it were directed toward themselves. For instance, let me go to the 'burbs and tell them the way they raise their children is the great problem of the world and so I and others need to go there and educate them since they are being raised so poorly... as opposed to suburban whites coming to the city to "help" and see how fast they find it offensive and ridiculous.

Whiteness and Silence

I'm sharing this around the theme of silencing, because it is the silence of white people that allows racism to injure people of color day in and day out—in personal and systemic ways. I am trying to grow in my ability to sit in the discomfort of interrupting a conversation or meeting, to the risk of offending the speaker and receiving backlash—rather than maintaining silence.

When white people stay silent—especially in all-white groups—we protect the egos of those who are ignorant of or who don't care about their impact. I was afraid to hurt the feelings of those who were speaking; now I see that if I remain quiet, people of color are doubly injured: first by the comments and actions themselves, and second by the silence of those of us who could take the risk to name the dynamic. It is the fear of losing privilege that keeps me and other whites silent in the face of the violence of racism: in our homes and families, faith communities, schools, workplaces, in the media and legal systems—and in our own hearts.

In this journey of recognizing the ways I carry whiteness and the impacts of white privilege and white superiority today, I have discovered greater compassion for the parts of myself I don't like to acknowledge. This is the beginning of change. In this space of compassion, I have felt the false ego that white-socialization creates melt away into some identity that is more human. In some situations, I have been able to sit in curiosity and to actually hear those whose ideas and values that radically differ from my own. Along with this has come a capacity to sit in the fire of criticism without either falling apart or lashing back. All of this contributes to a humility from which I am more readily able to apologize—when I recognize the impact of my words or actions or silence has contributed to the injury or diminishment of another—and greater courage to intervene in racist dynamics, for example by writing this article.

I still have a long way to go in breaking the silence and moving from *understanding* to *action*. This is my perception about most white peace activists as well. Simply feeling better about my listening skills or my understanding of the history of American racism is not the goal—these are intermediate steps along the way. There are ample opportunities for me to be active on behalf of racial justice, just as I am active in international peace work. My current efforts are to join allies in affecting the predominantly white peace groups of which I am a part.

A mentor cautioned me to be realistic about the pace of changing this deep and abiding social construct—for a small nonprofit to demonstrably own an anti-racist/anti-oppression identity, the transition optimistically takes eight years of ongoing work. For one single church or worship community, twenty years. Groups like the Christian Peacemaker Teams, Pax Christi, the Atlantic Life Community, and the War Resisters League have begun to engage an anti-racist lens. None are "there" yet in terms of organizational accountability, a shift in access to power, economic, and staff resources. How long will it take our predominantly white peace communities to transform? And what is your next step in breaking the silence?

Towards a Radical White Identity

Susan B. Goldberg and Cameron Levin

The Alliance of White Anti-Racists Everywhere (AWARE)–Los Angeles work to collectively develop an anti-racist practice, and tools for nurturing anti-racist practice among white people and working in transformative alliance with people of color. This article, by two AWARE members writing for their online "toolbox," outlines their basic beliefs, definitions, and methodology.

> *Our attempts to dismantle dominance and oppression must follow a path*
> *other than that of either vilifying or obliterating whiteness... Whites need*
> *to acknowledge and work through the negative historical implications*
> *of "whiteness" and create for ourselves a transformed identity as White*
> *people committed to equality and social change. Our goal is neither to*
> *deify nor denigrate whiteness, but to diffuse its destructive power. To teach*
> *my White students and my own children that they are "not White" is to*
> *do them a disservice. To teach them that there are different ways of being*
> *White, and that they have a choice as White people to become champions*
> *of justice and social healing, is to provide them a positive direction for*
> *growth and to grant them the dignity of their being.*
> —Gary Howard, *Why We Can't Teach What We Don't Know: White*
>   *Teachers, Multicultural Schools*

With these words Gary Howard captures the challenge for white people who struggle to stand against racism.[1] In this paper we endeavor to share the work we do to "teach different ways of being white," by offering the idea of a Radical White Identity. This identity offers white people a racial and cultural identity that directly addresses white supremacist history in this country. We center our work in racial identity development and from this foundation we build a clear analysis and practice for creating radical white culture. Our aim is twofold: 1) To create an alternative to the dominant white culture through building a community of white anti-racist people who represent a subculture of whiteness; and 2) to offer a form of white identity that is explicitly anti-racist and allows white people to acknowledge and embrace our histories and cultures. Through this evolving cultural/racial identity we will create our

---

1   For the purpose of this article we will use the term "white" to describe a socially constructed racial group made up of European Americans living in the United States.

anti-racist practice, our racial identity model, and our role in the process of creating radical social transformation.

In our work, we hope to put forward an analysis that looks at the dynamics of race, power, privilege and the white supremacist system, the historical origins of whiteness, the diversity of experience of white people as it is impacted by class, geography, gender, sexual orientation, family of origin, and the historical and contemporary work of white anti-racist organizing and action. We offer this analysis in the hopes of fostering and nurturing a viable identity for white people: a radical white identity.

Introduction

We are continuously struck by the power and legacy of white supremacy and racism on every aspect of United States culture and history. It is a legacy that continues to fester and bleed because truths are not told, reparations are not made, and racism, rather than being eradicated, has been embraced as a vital tool shaping our nation's history and present day realities. The historical examples of racism from many different peoples in this land are overwhelming and endless. We have come to see and believe that until the legacy of the white supremacist system is fully addressed, all people living in the United States will be unable to move forward with our humanity intact.

It is in the interest of facilitating change in white people, both those conscious and unconscious of racism, that we do the work we aim to summarize in this article. We address this community because it is our community. We have struggled with the painful realities of racism all around us and have searched for the most effective way to be involved in a movement for change. In our personal journey to come to terms with the realities of racism we have been told time and again by our friends of color that a critical piece of the work is to engage white communities to create change.

We were compelled to write this article as an attempt to coalesce the work against racism in which we have been fortunate to be immersed for the past several years. As children, one of us was raised by radical parents with a long history of struggle and the other was awakened to injustice based on his early experience in the educational system. We began our initial formal exploration of whiteness with the National Conference of Christians and Jews (now the National Conference for Community and Justice) Brotherhood Sisterhood Camp and in Children of War, a group that worked with refugees from war-torn countries, in 1990. These groups offered us a series of unique and invaluable experiences in beginning to discover our identities. The programs emphasized that we had a racial identity as white people, we had absolute responsibility for actively addressing racism, and based on race we had privileges that gave us advantages over every other group of people. We continued in different parts of the country to actively struggle against racism through community organizing and social justice campaigns and to help articulate and define an identity and process for white people to be effective allies in the struggle for racial justice.

We have been very fortunate to learn from and work with mentors and teachers including the NCCJ Los Angeles community, Sharon Martinas and the Challenging White Supremacy Workshop, The Peoples Institute, and many other individuals who have taught and continue to teach us about white identity and racism. The articulation and practice of the radical white identity is our effort to contribute to and build upon the foundation we stand. Our framework is rooted in our belief in the importance of a racial identity model for white people. We recognize that racial identity is a social construct, and yet we cannot deny that racial identity is meaningful as it impacts and shapes every person's experience in this country. The progression and development of white identity has not moved along the same lines as identity development in oppressed communities. We recognize the emergence of a critique of politics based solely on identity. Many progressive people in oppressed groups are moving beyond an identity politics framework to an integrated analysis based on understanding the interlocking nature of oppressions.

Contrary to an in-depth dialogue in progressive communities of color about the realities of racism and white supremacy, white progressives, as a large community, have not struggled with the contradictions of being white in a white supremacist system. While we fully appreciate the limitations of identity politics, our intention is not to replicate the model other oppressed groups have created but to develop a specific model in the context of whiteness.

In our time spent working against racism, we have often come across overly simplistic analyses of racism, from liberal whites and from movements for change. Some of these analyses include:

1. Seeing racism as the problem in itself rather than a tool of a greater system
2. Seeing white people's experience as monolithic and creating a group identity solely based on racism
3. Seeing white people as having no real stake in changing the system
4. Failing to offer any alternative anti-racist white racial identity

We believe that too many anti-racist models for white people are constructed out of guilt. We recognize that feelings of guilt, as one begins to fully realize the extent of the realities of racism are an important part of a heartfelt process of conscious development. Guilt is a place to visit, not a place to live. When guilt becomes the operating force of a white person involved in anti-racist work, their work and relationships are negatively impacted. Some examples of this are placing people of color on an unrealistic pedestal, and a disassociation from whiteness and white people. Disassociation from whiteness can lead to cultural tourism, rejection and judgment of white people, and the inability to fully embrace all parts of oneself. White people driven by guilt (consciously or unconsciously) are limited in their ability to be effective allies in multiracial movements and in building radical white communities of resistance.

Systemic Analysis

In a traditional liberal analysis, racism is seen as the source of racial oppression. This means that in the liberal model there are two roles: the oppressor and the oppressed. This model tells white people that they are only in the role of oppressor and have no common bonds with people of color and no stake in changing a racist system. We see racism as a *tool* of the larger white supremacist system. The white ruling elite has power and class interests in keeping white people and people of color divided. For example, one of the very early formations of racism in law and custom in our country was motivated by the desire to break any potential bonds between poor European indentured servants and African slaves. When the system is hidden, it obscures the role of the white ruling elite, the complexity of difference among white people, and the power of white people and people of color uniting to create a road to fundamental change. With an understanding of the white supremacist system a white person can also see that ending the system's control allows for the fullness of their humanity, because in denying the humanity of another we also deny our own.

Forging a Radical White Identity

With this analysis as our foundation we can begin to create an alternative identity for white people. All human beings must develop and sustain a healthy self-identity in order to thrive. This is particularly important for people who commit to a life struggling against the injustices of the White supremacist system. Often we have witnessed conscious white people who are aware of and understand racism but deny that they are white because of the guilt and shame associated with what it means to be white in the United States. As we discussed above, the problem with this denial is that white people are white, and when this is denied it creates an often confusing internal conflict which affects both one's work against racism and one's relationships. It is important for white people who challenge and fight the injustices of racism to have an honest sense of themselves without hiding, dismissing or subjugating any of their realities. It has been our experience that white people who have developed this holistic radical white identity have the ability to sustain the struggle against racism, to challenge, connect, and bring more white people into the struggle and to create and maintain honest relationships with people of color. The liberation movements of the 1960s are examples of the power of radical racial identities to transform communities. During this movement era many communities of color developed radical racial identities such as the Black Power, Asian American, and Chicano identities.

These identities challenged the dominant socially constructed oppressive identities that had been forced on them by a white supremacist system. These racial identities stressed reconnecting with ones stolen cultural roots, resisting the white supremacist system through political and social struggle, and creating an identity based on self-expression and creation of culture. These identities offered people of color a way to resist the white supremacist system, take control of their communities, and claim their own culture. The creation of a radical white identity offers white people a way to resist the white supremacist system by having a positive racial identity. This radical racial identity can lead to the creation of an alternative white culture. Culture is an integral part of racial identity. It is our culture/cultures that allow us to define who we are, our values, and what makes us distinct and unique from one another. Some elements of an alternative white culture include redefining social relationships, the creation of art that embraces a new vision of whiteness, and the participation in rituals of celebration and community.

Components of Radical White Identity Model

The development of the radical white identity is an ongoing process that is based on the following core pieces—understanding white privilege, ethnic/cultural roots, multiple identities, history of multiracial struggle and white anti-racist resistance, and white anti-racist practice.

Privilege: all white people raised in this society are granted fundamental privilege in all institutions and aspects of U.S. culture. This white skin privilege is granted differently based on one's socioeconomic class, gender, sexual orientation, physical ability, and age. The white privilege we receive shapes our whole lives and how we experience our racial selves. White culture and racial identity are made invisible to white people. We are like fish who don't know what water is—it is everywhere and yet we do not know how to see it or name it. It is difficult to understand how our actions, and behaviors, which are not intentionally racist, in many cases, can be oppressive to people of color.

Through uncovering these "cultural norms" of white privilege we can begin to change and modify them so we are not acting out our ignorant racism, cultural racism, or institutional white supremacy. It is important to be continuously engaged in a process of uncovering how white skin privilege shapes who we are and how we relate to the world around us. We also need to explore how we can use privilege to undermine the larger white supremacist system. In our work we have found that for many white people the process of uncovering our privilege is a challenging and transformative process. For many, this is the beginning of a journey to awareness and fundamental change.

Ethnic/religious/cultural roots: as white people we have tremendous privilege, but it has not been without a price. When we came to this country we were not "white." We were Irish, Jewish, Russian, Italian, etc. Our ethnic identity was our primary identity, and it linked us to our community and culture. The dominant white racial identity was created through the process of assimilation. This meant people from European countries would be allowed access in this country as long as they would leave their customs, traditions, cultural practices, and social norms behind and assimilate to become (white) "Americans." When European immigrants came to the United States there was immediate pressure to change their cultural practices and act "American." There were many "educational" services offered by churches and charity organizations that "taught" these immigrants how to assimilate into being white.

More blatant measures were expressed in news stories in papers like the *New York Times, Harpers, Atlantic Monthly*, and many other publications. In 1877, the *New York Tribune* identified the Irish as "a race with more wholesome and probably unreasonable terror of law than any other... Is there no other way [besides violence] to civilize them? This editorialist wanted to know."[2] In her book *Learning to Be White*, Thandeka writes that in the 1870s the Chicago Times "characterized the city's Slavic inhabitants as descendants of Scythians, "eaters of raw animal food, fond of drinking blood of their enemies... Let us whip these Slavic wolves back to the European dens from which they issue, or in some way exterminate them."[3] One of the primary ways of becoming "American" and erasing one's ethnic culture was to become a consumer. European immigrants were told to act "American" by becoming consumers of "basic necessities." Immigrants were actively discouraged from their own cultural practices such as making clothes or home remedies—these were to be replaced with consumable goods and services. The market, butcher, or tailor, were all offered to replace our ability to provide the needs that we once knew how to provide for ourselves. Today most white people think of themselves as having no real culture. We look at communities of color and see culture lacking in our own lives. These feelings leave a void in white people that causes us to develop oppressive solutions for filling this void. Sometimes white people appropriate the cultures of people of color, for example embracing Native American spiritual practice without reflection or consideration, or we deny any sense of racial identity, focusing on everyone being a colorless human or part of a nondistinct colorful rainbow.

It is up to each individual to decide how we want to connect to our ethnic roots. But all white people need to understand the history of assimilation into the dominant white race. It is important to understand that the primary way to assimilate people is to sever them from their ethnic/cultural roots and that this process has a profound impact on the humanity of a community.

Multiple Identities: our whiteness always exists in relationship to other aspects of our identity. It is tempting to oversimplify for the sake of clarity when exploring our white identity. However, when we do this we are not telling the whole story. While we must strive to understand our whiteness, we have to be aware of all the different identities that make up who we are. Whether it is one's class, gender, sexual orientation, or age, they all interact with racial identity and white privilege. We need to better

---

2   Matthew Frye Jacobson, *Whiteness of a Different Color* (Cambridge, MA: Harvard University Press, 1998), 34.
3   Thandeka, *Learning to Be White* (New York: Continuum Publishing Group, 2001), 67.

understand how our identities are interconnected. When we see our overlapping identities we can recognize the interlocking nature of oppressions and privilege. A poor white lesbian living in the South is very different from a CEO who runs a Fortune 500 company. Both of these people are white and share racial privilege, yet society treats them very differently because of the realities of their other identities. Ultimately all systems of oppression are constructed around supremacy of one group exercising power over another. We must challenge and understand the interlocking nature of how these identities interact and shape one another.

History of multiracial struggle and radical white anti racists: for any culture to exist it must have a history. Radical white people have a history of resistance to white supremacy from the founding of this country. Millions of white people have stood against racism and white supremacy throughout the 400-year history of the United States. The history of white people actively resisting the white supremacist system has been covered over and lost. We never read in a standard high school history text about how white people imposed a white supremacist system on people of color. We also do not learn the history of how some white people have actively resisted racism or about multiracial efforts to come together to fight white supremacy. These individuals and groups serve as role models for white people and shining examples of resistance. The history of resistance in this country also includes countless examples of effective multiracial coalitions. Whole multiracial societies such as the Maroon societies, consisting of escaped slaves, poor white indentured servants, and Indigenous peoples of the Americas existed throughout the Americas. Learning our history gives us the ability to imagine and create new possibilities.

Anti-Racist Practice: at the core of our model is a white anti-racist practice that grows from a holistic foundation. As white people we need to develop a conscious practice that provides meaningful tools to stand against systemic racism and that teaches how to participate in a multiracial society in ways that do not perpetuate oppression. An anti-racist practice involves becoming active white people who work to build alliances with other white people against racism in our homes, schools, workplaces, and communities. We need to continuously practice the skills and tools for challenging personal and interpersonal racism and engaging in crosscultural communication. In addition we need to work collectively with people of color and white allies to think critically and work collectively towards a radical systemic change that addresses the root systems of supremacy. In our work with white people we integrate the above core pieces into a model for developing a radical white community. Most training models that work with white people either focus primarily on giving a space for white people to talk about being white or on the practice of being anti-racist.

We are interested in integrating both, the power of meaningful personal discovery and the importance of a viable active anti-racist practice. Again, we believe that a model that holds a positive radical identity at its core is essential to this integration. The workshops we facilitate create a dynamic learning environment based on experiential learning models. We create exercises to facilitate a process of self-discovery and deep exploration of the realities of the larger social systems and institutions in a safe and supportive environment. At the foundation of this work is a model of active dialogue. This model of dialogue allows for personal growth in a context of collective learning. In addition, we use tools from the world of theater and movement, popular education techniques, readings from radical writers, and visual and written expression. We believe strongly that this work is ongoing. We also understand that many people are not able to commit to an ongoing process of meetings so we offer a six-workshop series to introduce white people to this process. Within each workshop we explore white racial identity, historical analysis, and building practical anti-racist skills. Each workshop is organized around a specific theme that builds the development of the radical white identity. The workshops are created in such a way to be inclusive and meaningful, both for white people who are new to a racial consciousness and for those who are engaged and committed to anti-racist work. In addition to the workshops there is a group of white people in Los Angeles meeting regularly to engage in the development and practice of the radical white identity model. This group is calling itself AWARE—Alliance of White Anti-Racists Everywhere. There are now several projects initiated by this group, including study groups to explore the literature and theoretical basis for the identity model and a history project to collect the history of white people working together, as individuals or with people of color, to end the racist system. In addition, this group has initiated a multiracial dialogue that is beginning to look deeply at how we talk about race and racism and how to further the work of racial justice. The work of struggling against racism is life-long. The work of deepening one's clarity of her/his role in the struggle is also life-long. In order to sustain this journey conscious workshop.

A Never-Ending Journey

White people need to have a process of understanding, challenging, growing, and developing a healthy radical white identity. An identity that is not about arriving at a fixed destination but rather one that shifts and changes with time, knowledge, experience and history. An identity that claims the multiple truths of white people's experiences, the racial skin privileges, the history of resistance to white supremacy, and a role in the process of social transformation. The radical white identity is about the practice of anti-racist work and the practice of building and sustaining authentic relationships. It is important that white people develop the skills to engage with people of color in truly respectful and accountable ways. It is also important that white people develop the skills to connect and build community with other white people, continuously growing the ranks of conscious white people, ready to work for racial justice. A racial identity based on the inherent valuable and complex humanity of each person involved will lay the foundation for this important work. "The work of dismantling systematic racism and building new institutions that are not based on white power and privilege needs to be infused with a deep love for and among all of us who are working together. Antiracism work can quickly become warped if it involves white people who fundamentally do not love themselves."[4] We hope that the model laid out in this article will help in some way to develop and sustain white people who are able to contribute fully to the incredible task of radical racial transformation.

---

4   Tobin Shearer, "White Spaces," *The Other Side Online* 28, no. 2 (March–April 2002).

Weaving Narratives

The Construction of Whiteness

Dean Johnson

This academic paper, an edited version of Johnson's introduction to his dissertation "Critiquing the Soul of White Supremacy," provides intensive insights into the origins of racism in U.S. society.

In order to understand how the theologies of whiteness function to reinforce systems of domination and oppression it is necessary to first examine how and when the socially constructed qualifier "whiteness" came into being and how it functions in U.S. society. I will argue that whiteness developed out of a social and theological crisis during colonial history that resulted in the creation of social boundaries based on skin color. These new social boundaries of whiteness were reinforced by theology and colluded with preexisting binary oppositions of superiority, such as male/female, light/dark, and Christian/infidel. As the colonial endeavors of Christian Europe continued and intersected with the Enlightenment ideas of the autonomous individual and scientific reasoning, rational justifications were created along with racialized categories based on European standards. In what has become the United States, European standards were utilized to create racial, gender, political, and social hierarchies that were reinforced by social practices and laws. The creation or re-creation of these hierarchies has continued throughout U.S. history.

Assumptions and Definitions

There are two primary assumptions that undergird this work. First, white privilege exists. White privileges are advantages afforded to whites, or those assumed to be white, and denied to other racial groups simply because of the color of their skin. These advantages or "unearned entitlements" come at the price of disadvantages for those outside the privileged group. Statistically proving the existence of white privilege is very easy. Being born white or to a white mother is the foundation of a better chance at life from conception, better access to education, health insurance, and employment throughout young adulthood, and an overall greater chance of not living in poverty. However, given my emphasis on the everyday practices of whites it is necessary to name some of the less visible privileges. Consider the following examples:

- Whites can choose to be aware of or to ignore their racial heritage.
- Whites can choose to have little contact with people of color.
- It is unlikely a white person will be stopped in an airport just for looking Muslim.
- Groups of white youth are allowed to gather in public without being harassed by the police.
- When the media and educators talk about U.S. history and "civilization," white people are always credited with making it happen.
- A white person can turn on the television or open to the front page of the paper and see white people widely and positively represented.
- A white person does not wonder if he/she is being stopped by the police because of his/her race.
- Whites can go to the mall or a restaurant without questioning the kind of service they may receive.

White privilege exists as measurable forms of social status granted by government regulations and laws. It also exists as a set social arrangements or veiled assurances for whites as they go throughout their daily lives.

The second assumption is that humans are sociocultural beings who produce or construct their collective social realities. A person learns the rules of society and the language of culture through the processes of socialization. "Appropriate" behaviors, or the norms of society, are determined through social relationships (family and friends), social groups (churches and clubs), and the societies (countries and towns) to which a person belongs. More importantly, the way a person learns the rules, norms, and behaviors of society is accomplished by personally adopting the dominant cultural narratives and communal narratives as one's own. As will be discussed in Chapter Two, dominant cultural narratives help to create a framework of meaning or interpretative lens that helps individuals decipher information and make decisions. For Christians, the dominant cultural narratives inform their theological narratives.

How terms are understood and used has a profound impact on any work; therefore it will prove helpful to have a general overview of how several terms will be used. Race, racism, white superiority, and whiteness are all interconnected terms, but they still have distinct meanings. The modern concept of *race* originated within the efforts of western science to classify humans founded on biological characteristics. Stuart Hall has described race as a "floating signifier," that is, race is a socially constructed classification of difference with sociohistorical significance structured in language and ascribed privilege within a given context. Race is a signifier that has meaning in a specific culture and that meaning is rooted in a set of demarcations of which biological difference is crucial. For the purpose of this dissertation it is important to note that not all cultures give race the same social weight or significance. This was true in Europe prior to the fifteenth century. As will be argued, race only gained significance in European and Amero-European society as a result of colonial expansion. It will also be shown that racial classifications, especially the classification of "white," change over time. For example, in precolonial Europe the Irish were not seen as white. It was only after several decades of colonial expansion that the Irish, the Italians and other "fair-skinned" European groups became white and gained access to the rights and privileges that come with being white in the contemporary United States.

Racism is a dominant cultural narrative; in other words, it is a framework of meaning, constructed around race and constituted by claims that whites are superior to nonwhites. Racism carries the power to exclude or include based on socially defined differences assigned to biology. As will be argued below, white postcolonial societies have created systems of power premised on the claim that nonwhites and poor whites are inferior.

Many white people believe that racism ended after the Civil Rights Movement because overt bigotry and hatred are no longer deemed publicly acceptable; indeed, in the post–Civil Rights era it has become politically correct to be "colorblind." Colorblindness, in this context, entails not overt discrimination or use of racist speech. Racism is then relegated to a few ignorant whites, and thereby eliminating from serious consideration institutions and systems of power which are based in, or informed by, white privilege. In addition, most whites believe that race problems in the United States are due to minority groups being stuck in the past or because individuals within these groups do not take enough personal responsibility for improving their lot in life. From this perspective, even the few ignorant whites are not the problem; rather it is individuals in communities of color who make poor choices and then resort to using the race card as the excuse for their inability to succeed. In this dissertation racism refers to both group and individual behaviors. Collectively, racism exists in the privileges afforded to whites by political, legal, and social systems based solely on their skin color and physical features. For the individual, the perpetuation of racism develops as he or she acquires a set of beliefs from society, groups, friends, and family. For several of the whites I interviewed racism was still very much a part of their memory. Twenty percent of those interviewed reported that on occasion he or she could still "hear" the voice of his or her father, or another male relative, in his or her head uttering racial slurs when in tenuous or conflict situations with a person of color.

White superiority is a term that may cause discomfort to white readers. It likely conjures images of white hate groups like the Ku Klux Klan, Aryan Nations, or National Socialists (also known as the neo-Nazis). It will be argued throughout this dissertation that white superiority is something that pervades and shapes all European and Amero-European history since colonialism. Attitudes of white superiority (re)create a racialized, superior, and privileged "us," and a racialized, inferior, disadvantaged "them." White superiority is not the sole property of white hate groups, but is a part of the everyday dominant cultural narratives out of which most of Amero-European society operates. White superiority is what allows whites to ignore the sociopolitical systems that grant them privilege. Misty Greene, an interviewee, provides a good example of white superiority. Greene shared during the course of our interview that her step-daughter dated black men because she was "not pretty enough to date a white man." The implicit meaning in Greene's statement is that white men are superior to black men. Another example can be seen in the subtle ways that white superiority operates in the lives of congregations and individuals when those groups and individuals are never in the situation of having to address issues of privilege and race. Being in the normative group means a person never has to talk about the racialized status quo. Eighty percent of those interviewed for this dissertation shared that they rarely engaged in conversations about race, racism, or privilege while growing up. The same number of subjects also related that their faith communities rarely engaged in dialogue about these same issues. The reason that they gave for not having had these discussions was the relative absence of persons of color in the midst in their midst. Furthermore, the great majority of my research subjects believed race and privilege would have been addressed had people of color been present to "make it an issue."

Whiteness, like other racial labels, is difficult to define because the definition is contingent on the syntax or social context and upon who is making the determination about its meaning. For the purposes of my dissertation whiteness is both a "category of analysis and a mode of lived experience." As a category of analysis whiteness is a cultural narrative, a social framework, and system of boundaries that allows white superiority to be maintained in U.S. society through shifting systems, practices, and histories that culminate in privileges, resources, and power for whites. As a model of lived experience narratives of whiteness reinforce conscious and unconscious attitudes of white superiority, arrogance, and privilege. As a dominant cultural narrative and a system of boundaries whiteness comes to represent interlocking hierarchical structures found in and maintained by the sociocultural institutions of whites.

Theology is a human construct, an attempt to put into words an understanding of God, or Ultimate Reality. Theology (literally, God-talk) is a task that is done by every Christian. As it is with all human endeavors to articulate the metaphysical, theology has never been apart from the vicissitudes of a historical cultural reality; theology is created within a particular historical and political context. For much of the history of Christianity, theology has served as the voice of the powerful and is dictated in doctrines or theological geographies. According to the Workgroup on Constructive Christian Theology, these theological geographies represent the "collectively rendered maps that Christians have drawn over the years in order to help them find their way around this complex terrain of faith." Theological geographies, or doctrines, are the teachings/foundations of the church that ideally influence the decisions made by the members of the church. Historically, normative/dominant/white theology has been constructed and handed down from the Church hierarchy to the laity. In much of this work, theologians and Church leaders have practiced proof-texting, the selective use of decontextualized biblical passages to make a theological argument.

Although there has always been an official theology of the Church, there have also always been theologies of resistance that challenge or deny the sociopolitical status quo. These theologies of resistance are inevitably heretical to a greater or lesser degree. Beginning with the various reform movements of the early fifteenth century, and especially during the twentieth century, theological doctrines have been highly contested by those outside the normative group. Many of the disagreements have taken place as protests to church authority, abuse, and domination. Since theology is contextual and church leaders make use of selective biblical passages to make their arguments, theologies are always political; such theologies create the boundary lines which determine what is considered acceptable at the time the statements are made. Those who are part of the power structure of any society establish the dominant cultural narratives, including the accepted theology. In Europe and the United States, the dominant theological narrative has been established by whites.

The theologies of whiteness are the theologies out of which white Christians implicitly operate. Not all white theology is bad but within white Christianity there exist narratives, themes, and practices of white superiority and privilege. Like other types of theology white theologies are constructed in a context. If European and Amero-European history consists of dominant cultural narratives of white superiority, then it follows white theology is deeply rooted in white superiority. The focus of this dissertation will be on those exclusivist theologies of whiteness that maintain the oppression and domination of those who are not granted the status of whiteness.

Boundary Theory and Durable Inequality

Now that some basic definitions have been established let us return to the task of establishing how whiteness has been constructed over the past five-hundred years and how it continues to operate today. There are two ways of analyzing the construction of whiteness: boundary theory and durable inequality. Matt Wray has charged those who do whiteness studies to focus their attention, "on the processes and agents that generate symbolic boundaries and grant them social power." As noted above, one of the assumptions of this dissertation is that societies are socially constructed and individuals learn how to function within the society through rules, both spoken and unspoken, that are passed on through social relationships such as family, school, and church. People not only learn the rules of behavior but also how to perceive and understand that world. Guided by these social rules and prescribed understandings of reality, each person also learns how to identify and categorize persons and objects. The way a person learns how to perceive and classify the world has a direct impact on how he or she goes about daily life.

One way to organize people is through social boundaries that are enacted through social practices of exclusion or inclusion. Boundaries are a tool for bringing about social solidarity. One example of boundaries used to set groups apart in the Christian celebrations known variously as communion, the Eucharist, or the Lord's Supper. Within most congregations, there are specific qualifications to determine who is allowed to participate. Catholicism requires that a person be a full member of the Catholic Church in order to receive communion, while the United Methodist Church allows everyone, even those who are not Methodist and those who are not baptized to receive communion.

Charles Tilly refers to another type of social boundary, "durable inequality." Tilly argues, "Significant inequalities in advantages among human beings correspond mainly to categorical differences such as black/white, male/female, citizen/foreigner, or Muslim/Jew rather than to individual differences in attributes, propensities, or performances." These inequalities persist because of social organization, which is reinforced by institutions that "control access to value-producing resources."

Colonial Expansion and the Social and Theological Crises of Race

All social boundaries are produced by a particular set of political and social concerns that assist in maintaining the dominant group's power. In the case of whiteness, the roots of these boundaries are found in the abysmal situation in Europe in the fourteenth and fifteenth centuries. This was a time when Europe was devastated by wars, plagues, poverty, and disease. It was out of this context, on a quest for economic leverage, that mariners left their homes in search of resources and commodities: gold, cocoa, and coffee.

Europe, prior to the late fifteenth century colonial contact, existed in a system of stark binaries of domination that served as social boundaries, such as: utopia/apocalypse, light/dark, civilized (British)/savage (Irish), Christian/heretic (or infidel), and landowner/landless. The dichotomies in Europe were due in large part to church doctrines rooted in a specific interpretation of the genesis of humanity and the Creation in Christian scripture.

Europe's contact with darker skinned people of the Americas and Africa caused questions for the church and legal authorities regarding the origins of humans; indeed it was perceived as a threat to biblical authority. David Theo Goldberg notes that the "Western metaphysics of evil as black and good as white is as old at least as Pythagoras." European Christian interactions with the Moors and Muslims (who were considered "non-Christian infidels") throughout the Middle Ages (400–1400 CE) started to shape anti-black sentiments of non-Christians. However, in relationship to contemporary understandings of the racialized other interactions to this point had focused primarily on religious practices and orthodox belief. Race was not a category of durable inequality prior to colonial contact.

What is notable about European contacts with other peoples is the degree to which these new peoples were different from any previously encountered. These people organized themselves fundamentally differently than Europeans. While European institutions and values created boundaries around personal property, personal piety, personal salvation and the biblically elect, Indigenous cultures in the Americas and Africa based their existence on community, relational interdependence, and reciprocity. The new encounters represent a "turning point in reality" for European society, as well as a breach in the Euro-Christian worldview. This turning point in European culture is made even more acute by theological crisis.

One of the salient markers of fifteenth and sixteenth century Europe is an obsession with how the origins and causes of dark skin can be reconciled with the belief every human is a descendent of the original parents found in the biblical narrative of Creation. This then is the theological crisis: if human beings evolved from one set of parents, how can the reality of people with different skin tones be explained? Monogenesis is this idea that one couple was responsible for all humanity, and this belief serves as a foundation for much of Christian theology. Colin Kidd notes that, "the whole Christian scheme of Fall, transmission of original sin and the redemption of Christ, if it has a valid claim to universality, seems logically to require all humans are descended from the first parents Adam and Eve." For Europeans of the time the question of who was worthy of receiving salvation was invalidated if the origins of humanity could no longer be assured. Salvation as a social boundary began to come apart, creating a crisis.

As noted earlier, an individuals' understanding of the origins of humanity shapes that individuals' understanding of the redeem-ability of human beings. Dwight Hopkins observed that, "Christianity privileges the story of the Garden [of Eden] because the entire religious understanding of God's revelation to humankind hinges on the origins of the human race coming directly from divine manufacturing." European Christians believed themselves to be the overseers of creation. This was the environment in which Columbus made his decisions to leave and exploit the paradise of the Orient and then mistakenly landed in the Americas.

There was a logistical paradox and potential problem for would be conquerors and plunders leaving Europe. They were told that this new paradise was a place of harmony and peace (Eden) while at the same time the Satanic ran free. These conflicting stories led Europeans to believe in a paradise that was populated by savages who did not make appropriate use of God-given resources. The conquistadors, colonizers, and eventually the settlers were unable, or perhaps unwilling, to acknowledge the existence of civilizations based on models different than their own.

To review briefly, the theological crisis of genesis raised by colonial expansion called into question the very foundation of European Christianity. If not everyone was a child of Adam and Eve, who were they? If monogenesis was not true, then the tenets of salvation must also be questioned. If some were not descendants of the primordial parents, were they saved? Rooted in notions of being the chosen people and having been given dominion over creation, the European church-states initiated the creation of white superiority based on skin color and purity/goodness.

According to Aime Cesaire: The chief culprit in this domain is Christian pedantry, which laid down the dishonest equations *Christianity=civilization, paganism=savagery*, from which there could not but ensue abominable colonialist and racist consequences, whose victims were to be the Indians, the Yellow peoples, and the Negroes [italics in original].

As the "Age of Discovery" continued, travel writings reinforced Europe's self-understanding they were the children of God and the children of light; those outside of Europe were then by definition "outside of the light, so that Africa, for example, was considered the Dark Continent." It is this setting codified in religious and theological language that eventually gave rise to Enlightenment notions of Otherness.

The Creation of Whiteness

As the sixteenth century came to a close, notions of white Christian superiority were paramount in the dominant cultural narratives so that social boundaries were created and justified with theological arguments. Whiteness became codified with religious purity and eventually led to the conflation of "white," "European," and "Christian." Social boundaries take different shapes in different contexts. During colonial expansion, notions of race and racism were a function of context. Christians understood the peoples of Africa and the Americas to be descendants of Adam and Eve but also in need of conversion and salvation from their "monstrous," "hethanistic," and "savage" ways.

In the British mind, a person's skin color not only represented biological characteristics but also her or his intelligence and behavioral traits. It is these claims that forever fixed behavior and biology in the dominant cultural narratives of the West, and created the durable inequality binary of white/Other. Africans were considered inferior and tainted due to their dark complexion, and Africa was seen as a place of great misery for Europeans; to wit, fifteenth century images such as that of the Cape of Bojador, beyond which, "lay the mouth of Hell where the seas boiled and people turned black because of the intense heat," remained popular in the seventeenth century and served to (re)enforce the Curse of Ham. As representative of all things evil and sinful, Africans were unredeemable. In contrast, the Americas were a land of endless possibilities, a land of plenty and plenty of land, a new Eden. Europeans understood themselves to be "the divine gardener" of the new Eden found on the Atlantic frontier cultivating Christianity and civilization. However, in the minds of Europeans there was an obstacle to creating a new Eden in the Americans: the "red savage," the loiterers of the land. Ideas of Indigenous peoples as savage, heathen, uncivilized, and childlike were created upon contact and fueled by religious language. From the time of the first encounter with Indigenous Americans and Africans, Europeans were simultaneously attracted and appalled by these "exotic" and "barbarous peoples."

The above examples demonstrate the construction of whiteness and how it was applied to nonwhites in order to serve the purposes of the white colonizer. The treatment of nonwhites by white Christians led to tens of millions of Indigenous Americans being infected by European diseases, maimed, tortured, killed, exploited, forcibly removed from their homelands, confined in strange surroundings and on reservations, and treated as wards of the United States. Tens of millions of Africans were sold or stolen from their families, pushed from their lands, forced into slavery, beaten, molested, abused, murdered, and otherwise treated as property. Identifying and examining how Indigenous peoples were treated by white colonizers illustrates the construction of whiteness and the roots of the Enlightenment thinking, namely, the arrogance of white European superiority.

The Creation of Whiteness and the Conflation of Race and Gender

Whiteness as a fluid system can also be seen in the relationship between race and gender. Race and gender are inseparable in that both have been used in interchangeable ways to give white men privilege and to disenfranchise women and people of color. The relationship between race and gender is rooted in the white Christian interpretation that women and nature are things to be dominated. In precolonial Europe, at least two major streams of thought developed as a result of the belief in the biblical mandate for dominion: the authority of men over women *and* over nature. As European men interpreted Genesis: man does not find a helper or an equal among the animals, so God creates woman (2:23). European Christian men convinced themselves that they were the rulers of all women and Others. During the fifteenth and sixteenth centuries, women and children were sold as slaves or abandoned. In addition, there were almost daily occurrences of violence against those who were accused of being witches. Columbus, when describing the earth, compared it to a woman's breast: Columbus's image feminizes the earth as a cosmic breast, in relation to which the epic male hero is a tiny, lost infant, yearning for the Edenic nipple. The image of the earth-breast here is redolent not with the male bravura of the explorer, invested with his conquering mission, but with an uneasy sense of male anxiety, infantilization and longing for the female body. At the same time, the female body is figured as marking the boundary of the cosmos and the limits of the known world, enclosing the ragged men, with their dreams of pepper and pearls, in her indefinite, oceanic body.

Out of the yearning for the forbidden, the exciting, and the utopia of comfort, the explorers were not only seeking conquest, but imaging a heaven or a paradise on earth. The exotic and the forbidden became one and the same. Anne McClintock writes, "The gendering of America as simultaneously naked and passive and riotously violent and cannibalistic represents a doubling within the conqueror, disavowed and displaced onto a feminized scene." Given the patriarchal structures influenced by biblical dominion developed in Europe, the process of exploration became one of domestication. While the geographic locations of colonial exploration were being gendered, the Indigenous peoples of those locations were being racialized.

The ongoing binaries of dominator/dominated as characterized by the male/female relationship, the man/nature relationship, and pure/impure relations allowed for the European domestic scene to develop as the pure (white) while the poor, sick, and colonized were feminized and impure (color). These binary relationships helped inform the thinking of seventeenth and eighteenth centuries. The result was European expansionism that led to the commodification of the colonial Other. McClintock has argued that, "Gender here, then, is not simply a question of sexuality but also a question of subdued labor and imperial plunder; race is not simply a question of skin color but also a question of labor power, cross-hatched by gender." Her argument continues with an explanation of how race became gendered and gender became racialized.

The linking of gender and race found in contemporary whiteness and white superiority began to occur during colonialism because of the dominator/dominated relationship. The Christian superiority of the previous centuries merged with Enlightenment rationalizations of white male superiority and the subjugation of women, people of color, and nature.

Race and Racism: Whiteness and the Enlightenment

The use of whiteness as a social boundary began with the theological crisis resulting from European colonial expansion and encounters with Indigenous Africans and Americans. The processes of Modernity and, eventually the Enlightenment (eighteenth century) solidify whiteness through the creation of a model against which all people would be measured. The white, male, heterosexual, educated, elite became the beacons of "the light of reason." These men, many of whom had a love-hate relationship with Christianity and a disdain for the Church as the repository of all knowledge, expanded the notions of male Christian superiority. Forsaking monogenesis, they developed ways to explain the differences of biological race through reason and science. In the process of developing rational/scientific ways of explaining racial difference they built upon the durable inequalities of men over women, educated over imbecile, and even Christian over heathen. The white, heterosexual, educated, elite male became the model against which societies and their members were judged. As an ideal model, whiteness influenced the arrangement of such categories as race, gender, class, religion, and sexual identity.

The Enlightenment was manifest in the continued search for the cause(s) of blackness as well as the development of the family of man, also called "the great chain of racial being." Goldberg writes, "Enlightenment thinkers were concerned to map the physical and cultural transformations from prehistoric savagery in the state of nature to their present state of civilization of which they took themselves to be the highest representation." In other words, the various populations of the world were constructed as a "natural" evolutionary hierarchy with western European at the apex.

Whiteness became a social boundary and category of durable inequality when non-European men are declared deviations from the white European elite male norm. Natural-law theorists argued that for systems of social hierarchy to be maintained scientific proof in the form of equivalencies in nature must be found. Although seen as a system based on rational scientific thought, some Enlightenment thinkers believed that hierarchical systems found both in nature and in societies were ordained by God.

The scientific proof solidifying racial hierarchies in the dominant cultural narratives of the time comes in 1776 with the publication of Johann Friedrich Blumenbach's *On the Natural Varieties of Mankind.* Although there had been other writings on the animal species and the species of *man* by Linnaeus and Comte de Buffon, Blumenbach's five-degree division of mankind was influential into the late nineteenth century. Blumenbach argued that human beings are of one species but are represented in five different degenerations: Caucasian, Mongolian, Ethiopian, American, and Malaysian, and he has been credited with creating the classification of *Caucasian.* The term comes from the Caucasus Mountains/Caucasus region between the Black Sea and the Caspian Sea and has biblical significance. Due to the presence of sea shells, the Caucasus Mountains were believed by some biblical geographers to be the final resting place of Noah's Ark and thus the possible point of origin for post-flood humankind. Fixing this as an origin point also assisted in naturalizing Blumenbach's ultimate theory.

In Blumenbach's theory Caucasian served as a reference for both white and Christian superiority. Caucasian designates white superiority by making whites the model against which all other peoples are measured. It also makes claim to Christian superiority by attaching the highest form of humankind (whites) to the Hebrew Bible's story of the flood. In the twenty-first century Caucasian is now a taken-for-granted categorization and lives on in the dominant cultural narratives, representing a category of durable inequality and white superiority.

Gender and Class: White Superiority and Whiteness Beyond Race

Pre-eighteenth-century conceptions of the inferiority of women informed the scientific thinking and work of the Enlightenment. Enlightenment thinkers not only assumed that their communities represented the zenith of civilization, they also considered themselves the model of rational and aesthetic being. The intelligence attributed to women and nonwhite men, by contrast, approximated that of a white male child.

By expanding on Blumenbach's ideas, a number of theories were developed in the natural and social sciences to support white superiority and the inferiority of all others. The academy created systems of biology and medicine to explain white superiority. Polygenesis, the theory that the races originated in a number of distinct and diverse contexts, gained adherents in the mid-nineteenth century through the 1930s. Pieter Camper was the first to use human skulls and cranial measurements to support polygenesis and the superiority of whites. Charles Darwin's *Origin of Species* raised questions about the evolutionary development of humanity, and prompted the creation of two camps. The first believed that some species of human beings were moving backward due to inbreeding, miscegenation, and certain environmental factors. The second camp believed that some human species had reached a high level of evolution due to cultural, political, and technical abilities found globally.

The relationship among whites of different classes was just as complex during and following the Enlightenment as the relationships between whites and the differentiated other. According to Matt Wray, there were four groups of whites in colonial America: white servants, former servants and slaves, yeomen or small landowners, and the elites or those who held large estates and public offices. Due to economic hardships created by white elites, the number of poor, landless freemen had increased in size during the late eighteenth century and they were often forced to live outside the territories. In 1728, William Byrd surveyed the land between Virginia and North Carolina where he observed freemen whom he labeled *lubbers*. Lubbers was a derogatory term derived from Lubberland, "an imaginary place of plenty without labor, a land of laziness were the inhabitants lolled about without purpose." Lubbers represented a threat to the social order: they were considered lawless, lazy, and immoral. Byrd believed the lubbers to be backward and lazy in part because the men made the women do all the work. Wray wrote, "[for elites] lubbers occupied an ambiguous place: their dirt-encrusted skin was white, but their behavior and attitudes were not."

After the French and Indian War ended in 1763, poor whites were struggling to move out of poverty. Many of these poor whites moved into the western frontier. A new class, the *Cracker*, of whites was created. According to documents written by military officer Gavin Cochrane, crackers were nothing more than "boasters" and "horse thieves." While degrading members of the lower classes for not being white enough, the government often used the poor white groups to do dangerous, dirty and otherwise difficult jobs, such as putting down slave revolts. By delineating these internal others, I have attempted to further argue here for fluidity of whiteness as a social boundary. Whiteness as represented by elite, white males is created out of the narratives of fifteenth century Christianity and later fortified in the science narratives of the Enlightenment.

The Early United States and Whiteness as the Unifier

In 1776, the same year Blumenbach published *On the Natural Varieties of Mankind*, the United States of America was established. It was clear to those in power since the first colonial contact with the Americas and Africa, that nonwhites and poor whites were inferior. The framers of the *Declaration of Independence*, of whom Thomas Jefferson is a prime example, were influenced greatly by the Enlightenment project. In 1776 Thomas Jefferson wrote the following regarding the local Indians: "Nothing would reduce those wretches so soon as pushing the war into the heart of their country. But I would not stop there. I would never cease pursuing them while one of them remained on this side of [the] Mississippi… We would never cease pursuing them with war while one remained on the face of the earth."

He believed that the Indians should be civilized or annihilated from the earth, and his position on Africans was not any better. Although there are examples of Jefferson's ambivalence with the institution of slavery, there is substantial evidence that he believed in the moral, aesthetic, and intellectual inferiority of persons of color. A decade later he wrote: "I advance it therefore as suspicion only, that blacks, whether originally a distinct race, or made distinct by time and circumstances, are inferior to the whites in the endowments both of body and mind."

Heavily influenced by the tide of Enlightenment thinking, the framers of the U.S. Constitution bound racial and gender hierarchies into law. The legal implications can be seen in the Constitutional Convention and later meetings of the new Congress. At the Constitutional Convention in 1787, it was determined that slaves would be counted as three-fifths of a person for the sake of representation and taxation, white women would not be allowed to vote, and Indians would be excluded completely from representation and taxation. In 1790, naturalization into the United States was limited to "any alien, being a free white person who shall have resided within the limits and under the jurisdiction of the United States for a term of two years." In addition, the interactions between whites and native peoples were further restricted in laws which limited trade and intercourse. The end of the eighteenth century was marked not only by sociopolitical strictures, but also by the enactment of race and gender laws that served as what Charles Mills has called the "Racial Contract." This racial contract is a "set of formal or informal agreements or meta-agreements" between an ever shifting but distinct population of human beings who are considered white, and an inferior population of human beings who are considered nonwhite. It is a contract from which every white person benefits, albeit the benefit varies according to factors such as sex/gender, class, and religion. It is out of the racial contract, grounded in Enlightenment science, economics, religion, legal codes, and Constitutional law that the nineteenth-century narrative of Manifest Destiny emerges.

Whiteness and Manifest Destiny

Manifest Destiny was established under the guise of bringing order to the lives of savages by civilizing/Christianizing them as well as subduing nature for the betterment of society. The following quote from a pastor refers to both the biblical belief in domination and economic lust: "Humanity must not, cannot allow the incompetence, negligence, and laziness of the uncivilized peoples to leave idle indefinitely the wealth which God has confided to them." The dominant cultural narratives of the nineteenth century held close to the "religious myth of a pure English Anglo-Saxon church."

The Anglo-Saxon race of people could be found in Northern Europe. The Anglo-Saxon church myth, then, represented Europeans as the pure white race and as God's chosen and providential people. Manifest Destiny, an essentially colonial idea, was based on the theory of Anglo-Saxon superiority. The people, especially the men, of European linage believed it was their divine right and biblical calling and duty to civilize the savage other of the world. Just as the man was the head of the household in Eurocentric culture, the Europeans and Americans represented the authority in world order. They were destined to subdue and domesticate those whom they considered inferior, all in the name of God. This was especially true with regard to the Western expansion of the United States.

To civilize the savage Other meant the ongoing subduing, conversion/assimilation, relocation, or eradication of native populations. The programs of assimilation and conversation often involved missionaries and church institutions working in partnership with the U.S. government, indeed, the federal government often preferred to use Christian missions to "pacify" the Indigenous Peoples of America in order to ease the way for U.S. expansion.

The military-style residential school system was created to completely assimilate American Indians into U.S. culture through the eradication of Indian identity, traditions, and cultures. Children were taken from their families and communities often by force in order to be converted to Christianity and indoctrinated in Amero-European ways.

White superiority is secured in the nineteenth century by means of the combined influence of religion and science as expressed in the narratives of the Enlightenment and Manifest Destiny. The elite male remains the model of normalcy, while Americans Indians, Mexican Americans, African slaves, and African Americans, immigrants, women, poor white working class, and the queer community each define whiteness by representing what it is not. The economic success of the United States could not have happened if not for the backs of slaves or the lands of aboriginal Americans. Yet the dominant cultural narratives carry forward an understanding of the innate inferiority of anyone who is not white, male, and a landowner.

Contemporary Whiteness and White Superiority

White theological anthropology of the early-to-mid-twentieth century is driven by the ideas of the previous three hundred-plus years of Amero-European dominant cultural narratives. Whiteness, maleness, Christianity, heterosexuality, Americanism, and upper-and-middle-class status become the signifiers of normalcy and common sense. In other words, whiteness is not just biology, but access to a place in the system that creates normalcy and common sense. As a system of inclusion and exclusion, whiteness in the twentieth century can be epitomized by the continual struggle by whites to hold onto power.

During the early 1900s immigrants and poor whites faced several struggles as they tried to become more American. Jews, Italians, and Poles struggled to make ends meet as low wage laborers and were not considered white until the 1920s and 1930s. Indeed, until this time they were considered to have the same status as blacks and were therefore low on the social Darwinist scale of whiteness. Immigrants of color faced a more fierce set of limitations. Anti-Asian sentiments in the United States led to the 1924 Immigration Act, which prevented the immigration Eastern Asians and Asian Indians. In 1942, most Japanese persons, including lawful citizens, residing in the United States were forced into internment camps (prisons) and remained there until 1945. Poor whites, especially in the South, were considered backward and subjects of eugenics testing. They were also considered degenerates and subjected to forced sterilization in order to not contaminate the white gene pool.

Sexual minorities in the first half of the twentieth century were seen as perversions of nature on the level of interracial relationships. In an article published in 1913, Margret Otis discussed relationships among girls in all-girl institutions. She noted not only the number of same-sex relationships among the girls but also how many of these which were interracial. Based on the gender preferences of the interracial couple in her study, she concluded that the difference in skin color served as a substitute for the lack of difference in sex, that is, white is to masculine as black is to feminine. Although it is difficult to determine just how widely her work was read, her work was an expression of the popular sentiments conflating race, sex, and sexuality that began with colonialism.

Also during the first twenty years of the twentieth century, women made certain political gains. After decades of struggle they won the right to vote when the Nineteenth Amendment was passed in 1920. During World War I, women had become part of the U.S. military as nurses and during World War II were indispensable to manufacturing and production and the overall economy. Still, the role of women was one of subordination as they remained in the popular mind merely mothers and wives. The demise of modern society was blamed in part on the changing roles of women within society. It was understood that with the increase of the social, political, and economic roles played by women there came a cost to the family and therefore society. The privileges women received were based upon the needs of the time as deemed appropriate by the dominant culture.

African Americans and blacks were treated differently depending on where they resided in the United States. Blacks who lived in large cities in the north were confined to particular neighborhoods or sections of the city that, more often than not, had substandard housing and received substandard services. Blacks who lived outside major cities in the north were confined to "their side of town," and subjected to the town's sundown code, which meant "Whites Only After Dark." Blacks in the American south were subject to Jim Crow laws and customs and, even worse, lynching. Lynching is the murder of a person generally a man who is of African dissent, for an alleged crime without any due process. As a result of the ongoing violation of black civil and human rights, the National Association for the Advancement of Colored People (NAACP) was created just prior to World War I. It spent a great amount of time working against lynching.

The relationship of blacks to the dominant culture is complex and yet very simple. Blacks were and continue to be used by the powers that be when it benefits them. A series of laws known as the "One Drop Rule" were enacted in southern states starting in 1910. The laws declared that anyone who had even a drop of black blood in their ancestry was legally black. During the World Wars black soldiers were asked to fight on behalf of the United States and democracy, while at home President Woodrow Wilson simultaneously (re)created segregation in federal offices. It was these tensions that eventually led to the height of the black Civil Rights struggle.

Blacks have always struggled against white superiority and domination since their first contact with whites. After a lengthy organized resistance to white domination between 1950 and to the mid-1970s, their sacrifices, persistence, and hope were to some degree rewarded. With the strength drawn from the sacrifice of generations of freedom fighters, and sparked by crucial political events—*Brown v. Board of Education of Topeka* in 1954 and the 1955 murder of Emmett Till, for example—the Civil Rights Movement slowly gained momentum. The Movement eventually caught the attention of the national media with the Montgomery Bus Boycott (1955). Inspired and informed by other independence movements, particularly in Africa, this epic social change movement won blacks the right of equal access to education, government, business, jobs, and political structures with the passing of the Civil Rights Acts (1964 & 1968) and the Voting Rights Act (1965). The ban on interracial marriage was erased (by *Loving v. Virginia*, 1967), and racial restrictions were also removed from immigration quotas (1965). These legal victories resulted, at least in part, from the pressure of social protests.

The Civil Rights Movement highlighted the inconsistencies found in the ideals of the U.S. Constitution and Declaration of Independence and the realities of everyday life for people of color. The movement not only made visible the immorality of racism in the United States, but framed it in terms of white ignorance. The arguments made during the Civil Rights Movement were steeped in reason; in other words, no reasonable person would be intentionally racist. It would be several years before Martin Luther King Jr. and other Civil Rights activists acknowledged that racism, and whiteness, were sociopolitical systems.

In the post–Civil Rights era liberal notions of colorblindness, claims by whites that they do not see color, have kept inequality functioning. If everyone is to be treated as equal under the laws of the land, and if the inferiority of nonwhites and women result from the ignorance of some individuals, then, in the mind of whites, racism and sexism must no longer be issues.

Some Conclusions

I have argued that whiteness came into being through more than five hundred years of dominant cultural narratives undergirded by Christianity, laws and sciences which have proclaimed the innate inferiority of those outside dominant white culture. Currently, systematic discrimination remains hidden to most whites because they believe that everyone achieved equality after the Civil Rights movement. Although the binary structures of the past are still alive and well, the structures have become more fluid constantly redefining the boundaries of whiteness.

In order to analyze the theologies of whiteness found in the contemporary United States, it is necessary to identify the measurements of whiteness that comprise the matrix of white superiority. Whiteness is visible through skin privilege often granted to those who appear to have white or light skin. Whiteness is also invisible when whites do not have to think about their race. Frances Kendall writes, "Many of us who are white have little sense of what that means for our lives, and we are not particularly interested in finding out. It doesn't seem relevant... Because we are in the dominant power group racially, we are able to define how we are seen by other white people."

Whiteness is both individual and social. Most whites see themselves as individuals and not members of a racial group. Since not all whites receive the same amount of privilege, there is no clear identification with others who belong to the white racial group. Many whites believe that they are not privileged due to their life's circumstances and therefore do not acknowledge whiteness as something which gives them status.

Whiteness is law. Most of the laws and legal structures in the United States were created by whites for whites. Interactions between whites and nonwhites have been regulated and legislated since contact. It is the U.S. legal system since the writing of the Constitution that has deemed the worth of individuals and groups, be they American Indians, slaves, women, or immigrants. The legal system has helped maintain white dominance to such a degree that today there is a disproportionate amount of nonwhites imprisoned and disenfranchised by the U.S. legal system.

Whiteness is sex and gender. Laurel Schneider argued that, "race affects one's experience and even the embodiment of one's gender, and gender affects one's experience and even the embodiment of race. White men have used race and gender in interchangeable ways to gain privilege and to disenfranchise women and nonwhites. This can be demonstrated by the feminization of people of color." Schneider writes, "the white race is thus gendered male by virtue of its dominance, and the nonwhite races are gendered female, indicating their need for supervision."

Whiteness is class. Elizabeth Bounds observes that to be white is to be at least middle-class. Race has been made into a class and class has been racialized. An example of how class and race have been aligned can be found in a study of elite, white men as conducted by Joe Feagin and Eileen O'Brien. One study participant stated, "So the blacks we met there were really 'white blacks.' When I moved to another state, though, the experiences were totally different, because these were more, should we say, 'urban blacks.'" The blacks that this person labeled as "white blacks" were similar to his own socioeconomic status as a white, middle-upper-class male. Due to their proximity in status, the blacks were more white than "urban blacks" whom he assumed were poor.

Whiteness is heterosexual. For centuries Christians have grounded moral society in a heterosexual marriage and it is no different today. Organizations such as Focus on the Family repeatedly address the issue of gay marriage by arguing, for instance, that society will collapse if queer communities are given the same marriage rights as heterosexuals. This argument is not significantly different than those arguments made about interracial marriage over the course of U.S. history.

Whiteness is Christian. Since the fourteenth century Christianity and whiteness have been one and the same. In contemporary culture this can be seen in statements like "God Bless America," or the motto on the state of Indiana's license plates: "In God We Trust." The arguments for the Pledge of Allegiance and school prayer are all undergirded by arguments about the faith of the so-called "Founding Fathers."

White superiority is represented by the characteristics and boundaries of whiteness that have been invented and fostered over time in the dominant cultural narratives of white society. As a system, it is like a lizard that will sacrifice its tail in order to avoid capture or escape becoming a larger animal's next meal. In doing so, the lizard is no less a lizard, and its tail does grow back. White superiority can sacrifice a part of the system and be no less than it was before because it, too, can regenerate its lost pieces. A system such as this can only be dismantled by clearly identifying all of its parts and dealing with each one.

The Pan-Africanization of Black Power

True History, Coalition-Building, and the All-African People's Revolutionary Party: An Interview with Bob Brown, Organizer for the All-African People's Revolutionary Party (GC)

Matt Meyer and Dan Berger

A firm and informed grasp of the development of the modern Black liberation movement is as important as understanding the origins of "white" as a designation for human beings. Though no single volume can adequately express the complexities and diversity of this movement, the following two pieces help bring to light some little-known behind-the-scenes realities of that movement, and dispel some common myths as well.

Matt & Dan: Many people look to Stokely Carmichael's 1966 call for "Black Power" as a great turning point in the U.S. movement for social change. Embraced by some and criticized by others, there seems little doubt—but much mythologizing—about what that moment meant, and where its roots came from. What is your perspective on this?

Bob Brown: The struggle for Black Power did not begin on June 16, 1966, in Greenwood, Mississippi, with the Student Nonviolent Coordinating Committee (SNCC) and Kwame Ture (then known as Stokely Carmichael), as some activists and scholars incorrectly claim. Black Power's sociopolitical ancestors can be traced to the thousands of communal, tribal and territorial states, kingdoms, empires and civilizations that were produced, through mass struggle, over millenniums of Africa's sociopolitical and economic development. The modern expression of revolutionary Black Power was the mass struggles and movements culminating in the Egyptian, Ghanaian, and Guinean revolutions, in the order of their independence. They intensified, inspired and nurtured a tidal wave of revolutionary mass struggle that swept Africa and the African Diaspora from 1951 through 1994, when Azania (South Africa) became independent. Black Power has as its essence a Pan-African and international dimension, a consequence of Africa's continental size and location; the Indigenous struggle for socioeconomic advancement, continental unity and development; the waves of invasions and colonization that the mark the successive phases of her history; and the dispersion of People of African descent to every corner of the world.

[Former Ghanaian president] Kwame Nkrumah's and [former Guinean president] Sékou Touré's contact with the movement in the United States predate their contact with Kwame Ture or SNCC. These contacts were developed and maintained through two decades of study, work, and struggle, of resistance and repression. They spanned the entire spectrum of the movement, Nationalist and Pan-Africanist, Socialist and Communist, Civil Rights, Pacifist and Peace. These contacts ebbed and flowed according to the dialectical growth and development of the African and World Revolutionary Process, and blossomed once again, in 1966 and '67.

Matt & Dan: How did Kwame Ture and you first develop direct ties to Osagefyo Kwame Nkrumah and Sékou Touré?

Bob: In January 1966, SNCC publicly denounced the War in Vietnam, the first Civil Rights organization in the United States to do so. On February 21, 1966, Osagefyo left Accra to travel to Hanoi to meet with Ho Chi Minh and to offer a proposal to end the illegal, immoral, and racist United States war against Vietnam. When Nkrumah arrived in Peking en route to Hanoi on February 24, the Chinese government informed him that Ghana's armed forces and national police had overthrown him in a coup d'état called "Operation Cold Chop." This coup was organized and financed by Western governments. Several members of the top and middle leadership of the Convention Peoples Party, which Nkrumah founded, and members of his government, were active participants in this coup. On May 14, Black Nationalism seized power within SNCC, through Kwame's election as chairman. Thirty-two days later, during the "Mississippi March Against Fear," Kwame, the twenty-five-year-old chairman of SNCC, re-echoed the cry for Black Power, and thanks/no thanks, to the media, was catapulted onto the world's political stage.

Kwame spent much of 1967 traveling the world, meeting revolutionary leaders at gatherings in Puerto Rico, England, Cuba, Vietnam, Algeria, Guinea, Tanzania, etc. While in Hanoi, Kwame had dinner with Ho Chi Minh and Pham van Dong, the then Prime Minister of North Vietnam from 1955 through 1976, and Prime Minister of reunified Vietnam from 1976 until his retirement in 1987. SNCC and Kwame were invited, because of their position against the Vietnam War, and their role in helping spread the Anti-Draft and Anti-War Movement into the African community. (Kwame had helped develop and popularize the rallying cry "Hell No, We Won't Go!). Uncle Ho told Kwame about his experiences in Harlem during the 1920s, and his interaction with the Garvey Movement. He asked Kwame: "When will African People in the United States go back to Africa?" This was the first time Kwame had thought about it. Before he left Hanoi, Kwame received a telegram inviting him to attend the Eighth Congress of the Democratic Party of Guinea and to meet Sékou Touré and Kwame Nkrumah—an invitation made possible by Madame Du Bois. Thanks to her, Kwame also met, and later married, Miriam Makeba. He moved to Guinea in 1968, to work, study and struggle under the tutelage and direction of Nkrumah and Touré.

Matt & Dan: SNCC and the Black Panther Party had a close relationship in the late 1960s. What were Stokely (Kwame) and your contributions to the early Panthers? How did this work lead to the development of the All-African People's Revolutionary Party (A-APRP) in the United States?

Bob: From 1962 to 1966, Kwame Ture spent most of his political energy struggling to register people to vote, especially in Mississippi and Alabama, and helping to build the Mississippi Freedom Democratic Party (MFDP), and the Lowndes County Freedom Organization (LCFO), which was the first Black Panther Party. In August of 1966, Kwame, Muhammad Ahmad (formerly known as Max Stanford) of the Revolutionary Action Movement (RAM) and Bill Epton of the Progressive Labor Party (PLP) announced the formation of the Black Panther Party in New York, the first chapter outside of Alabama. Between August of 1966 and the summer of 1967, RAM cadre and former cadre struggled to build Panther Chapters from New York to San Francisco. In October 1966, Huey Newton, Bobby Seale and Lil' Bobby Hutton announced, with Kwame's permission, the formation of the Black Panther Party for Self-Defense in Oakland, California. Bobby and Huey were former members of RAM.

I founded the Illinois Chapter of the Black Panther Party (BPP) July/August of 1968, in response to Kwame's request, and was one of its Midwest organizers. I was a member for less than eight months, the last three of which I spent in ideological and organizational isolation, a victim of one of the first Counter-Intelligence Program (COINTELPRO) efforts against the Panthers in Chicago. On bail for refusing to be drafted into the United States Army, I was prohibited from traveling outside of northern Illinois, under ruthless attack from the police, FBI, and their informants and provocateurs within the Party and larger movement. Sekou (Chico) Neblett, the East Coast Field Marshall of the BPP, and the Boston Chapter, were purged in May of 1969. Kwame officially resigned, for ideological reasons, in July, and our faction within the Panther Party severed all remaining relationships with them. This faction included Sekou and Renee Neblett in Boston; David Brothers and Bill "Winky" Hall in New York; Ethel Minor, Jan Bailey, Koko and Steve Farrow, Helen Colbert, and Paul and Evelyn Monroe in D.C., Frank Hughes in Richmond; Cleve Sellers in Greensboro; Mukasa (Willie Ricks) in Atlanta. We licked our political wounds, and kept organizing, despite twenty-four-hour surveillance and harassment, and for some of us, imprisonment or the threat of imprisonment. All of us were former SNCC organizers, and all of us, except Renee and Frank, were members of the first Central Committee of the All-African People's Revolutionary Party (A-APRP) when it was formed in October 1972.

Nkrumah called for the formation of the A-APRP in the *Handbook of Revolutionary Warfare*, which he wrote while he was still in power in Ghana. The unpublished manuscript was stolen by the CIA during the 1966 coup. Nkrumah rewrote the *Handbook* in Guinea. He gave Kwame a copy of the draft when they met in 1967. It was published in 1968. Nkrumah founded the first A-APRP Work-Study Circle in Conakry in 1968, with Kwame Ture, Franz Tagoe, and Lamin Jangha its first members. The first chapter of the A-APRP in the United States was formally launched in October 1972.

I first heard about the *Handbook* in 1967, before it was published, through Ethel Minor and Christine Johnson. Ethel was a member of SNCC, and later, the Panthers and the A-APRP. She also served as one of Kwame's secretaries and the editor of *Stokely Speaks*, Kwame's second book. Sister Christine, as we called her, was a friend of Nkrumah's during his student days at Lincoln University in Pennsylvania. She founded and was the Director of the Nation of Islam's University in the early 1960s, and a mentor of Malcolm X. I bought a copy as soon as it was published from Ishmael Flory's bookstore. Ishmael was the chairperson of the Communist Party of Illinois, Indiana, Wisconsin, and Iowa.

Kwame left the United States in January 1969, to live, work, study, and struggle in Conakry, Guinea, with Kwame Nkrumah and Sékou Touré, who served as co-presidents of the Government of Guinea and co-responsibles of the Democratic Party of Guinea (PDG). Between 1969, when I resigned from the Chicago Panthers, and 1971, our local cadre organized a network of organizations and institutions that included *Pan-African Roots*, our newspaper; student organizations on many of the major campuses; the Organization of Young West Indians; the Chicago Chapter of the Pan-African Student Organization in the Americas (PASOA); the Chicago Chapter of the Student Organization for Black Unity (SOBU); the Kwame Nkrumah Center, an independent school and community center in Chicago Heights; a food-buying club with welfare mothers on Chicago's Westside; a network of schools that taught African Martial Arts. We also continued SNCC's work with the youth gangs in Chicago and its suburbs; our efforts to help build the Black Consortium, a united front of organizations, churches, and gangs in Chicago; and our work with the student, Puerto Rican, Chicano, peace, and other movements.

Kwame returned to the United States in 1970. About a half dozen of us met with him and South African cultural icon Miriam Makeba [his then wife] at his mother's house in New York. We decided to organize a political education and fundraising drive in the United States and Canada. I volunteered to coordinate it. I was the youngest, newest, and most eager cadre at the meeting, and they unanimously agreed to let me try. Kwame came to the United States again, in 1971, for our annual political education and fundraising drive, which I coordinated. Random House had just published *Stokely Speaks: From Black Power Back to Pan-Africanism*. I also coordinated a concert tour for Miriam Makeba. At the end of this drive, Kwame convened a meeting in Greensboro of about twenty-three organizers who were part of our loose network. We reported on our work and accomplishments, and discussed and agreed upon a strategy to move forward. I represented a network of organizers in Chicago who had been working together since the Spring of 1969 when I resigned from the Panthers. This network included Tommy Carter, Banbose Shango, Ron and Vivian Patterson, Arthur "Top Cat," Brumfield, Ruwa Cheri, Eugene Love, Roy and Grace Walker, Roy Brown, and others. Tommy, Top Cat and I had worked with SNCC, and Tommy and I were former Panthers. I was elected to the Administration and Program Committees, with Ethel and Cleve Sellers as my "responsibles."

The Chicago Chapter of the Black Panther Party still existed, on paper at least, having been destroyed by the murder of Fred Hampton and Mark Clark in December of 1969, and the tidal wave of arrests, resignations and purges that preceded and followed their death. The split in 1971 between Huey Newton and Eldridge Cleaver was the final nail in its coffin. Scholars and activists falsely believe and claim that Fred Hampton pioneered the development of relations with the Young Lords, the Young Patriots, the Blackstone Rangers, and other organizations that became known as the "Rainbow Coalition." We respect Fred's contributions and achievements, but we also respect ours as well. History properly records that Fred's and the Chicago Panthers' work in this area continued SNCC's work in Chicago—Monroe Sharp's, Joyce Brown's, Yaree Amir's, Kwame Ture's, and mine.

Before the Greensboro meeting, several of our key cadre in Chicago, but not all of the ones listed above, announced the formation of the first Work-Study Circle of the A-APRP in the United States. Other study groups existed in Boston, New York, Baltimore, D.C., Richmond, Greensboro, Atlanta, Houston, Toronto, Halifax, and other cities in North America and the Caribbean, but they were not formally affiliated with or called A-APRP. At the Greensboro meeting, Kwame told me that our announcement of an A-APRP Work-Study Circle in Chicago, and our call to build such circles in every corner of the Western Hemisphere, was premature. He asked me to disband it immediately. I reluctantly, but without question, accepted his request. I never fully understood his reasoning, and never asked why. Unfortunately, this decision precipitated a split in our ranks in Chicago.

Matt & Dan: What were some of your differences with the Panthers?

Bob: Kwame and I were draft resisters, uncompromisingly opposed to the top-down, command structure and culture that militaries impose, too often at the point of a gun. Many of the Panther's key leadership were former military men, several of whom held top security clearances while they were in the military. Some of the Panther's leaders were former gang members at the highest level, or ex-cons who dreamed of, tried to, and/or committed rape, burglary, and murder. There was nothing unusual or abnormal about their joining the movement at that time. We wanted them, recruited them, and got them, with all of the strengths and weaknesses they brought. We also wanted and recruited students, and former students, like Kwame and me, but the students were outnumbered and outgunned.

The culture of the Black Panther Party, like the culture of the ghetto and a sector of the movement then and now, was anti-intellectual, anti-ideological. The Panthers' form of political education, in Chicago at least, was forcing its members to stand at attention and recite quotations from Chairman Mao's *Red Book*, lessons which could not be applied to our situation, and did not work when we tried. The Panthers, with the exception of a few isolated members here and there, were anti-Africa, and never saw Africa as their home, like we did. Many of them called Kwame a "punk for running from the struggle in Babylon to hide in Africa." And when Huey denounced Kwame, falsely accused him of being a CIA agent (a lie that was created by the FBI), and declared him the "enemy," there was nothing more we could do for the Black Panther Party, or with it.

We have no regrets, remorse or recriminations. We gave the Panthers all we had and did all that we could, despite receiving little or nothing in return. We simply moved on, learning, as best we could, from our, from SNCC's, the Panthers', Nkrumah's, and Touré's mistakes. We made many mistakes, and those of us who worked the hardest made the worst and most mistakes! But it is time to exhale, time for closure, time to tell the truth, and thereby enable and empower a new generation of youth to take up from where SNCC and the Panthers left off.

Matt & Dan: The question of land seems central to any revolutionary process. As a Pan-Africanist, what is your perspective on the "land question" for those in what is now the United States?

Bob: I had the privilege to spend about ninety days in jail in 1987–88 with WaBun-Inini (Vernon Bellecourt) of the American Indian Movement (AIM), for refusing to testify at a federal grand jury that investigated Libyan students in the United States, and their efforts to build solidarity and support for the Libyan revolution in North America. WaBun-Inini and I spent one week together in the "hole" at the Metropolitan Correctional Center in New York. Dr. Mutulu Shakur of the Black Liberation Army, Filiberto Ojeda Rios of Los Macheteros, Joe Doherty of the Provisional Irish Republican Army, Yu Kikumura of the Japanese Red Army, and Larry Davis, a brother born in New York who was accused of killing several cops, were there when we arrived and when we left. We were locked down in our cells for twenty-three hours each day, and could only talk through the walls, or quickly as we passed each other's cell. Of course, the guards and the FBI were listening and recording twenty-four hours per day, so there was very little of substance that we could say.

Mutulu, Tupac Shakur's stepfather, was in the next cell. He and I discussed very briefly his position and mine on this land issue. I told him, frankly and honestly, that my position was simple: anyone who wants to own or live on any inch of this land, including in the White House, must talk to and pay rent to the Indigenous People, the Original Caretakers. I had the honor and privilege to introduce him to Wabun-Inini, whose position was also simple and clear. His land is what is called Minnesota, other states in the region and Canada, and he did not have the authority or the right to give Indian land in Louisiana, Mississippi, Alabama, Georgia or South Carolina to anyone. My position on this issue has not changed, and I have taken every opportunity to facilitate contacts and dialogue between AIM and the Republic of New Afrika (RNA, which calls for the creation of a New Afrikan nation in the five states of the "Black belt" south), and will continue to do so for the rest of my life.

"Free the Land!" is RNA's slogan, but I often shout it as well. When they say it, they refer to the Black Belt South in the United States. When I say "Free the Land," I refer to Africa, our ancestral and just Homeland. I support any and all People, from Zimbabwe to Palestine to Ireland to the Americas, who are struggling to return to, reclaim, and rehabilitate their ancestral and just national homes.

Matt & Dan: What was the A-APRP presence and work in Africa? How did developments there impact the A-APRP's work in the United States and vice versa? How did the A-APRP relate to other organizations doing similar work at the time?

Bob: From 1968 to 1972, our primary work focused on helping to take Nkrumah back to Ghana, and to introduce him to a generation of students and activists in Africa and the world, who knew little or nothing about him. Kwame traveled throughout Africa and the African Diaspora, on assignments given to him by President Nkrumah and President Touré. Kwame Ture also traveled extensively with Miriam on her concert tours. These travels afforded him the opportunity to meet a host of progressive and revolutionary forces—political and cultural, and lay the foundation for future alliances and relationships. In April of 1972, Nkrumah died in Bucharest, from cancer. Amílcar Cabral, in his speech at Nkrumah's funeral in Conakry, declared that he had really died from the "cancer of betrayal."

On May 25, a broad-based coalition of forces organized African Liberation Day (ALD) demonstrations in Washington, D.C., and San Francisco. ALD was dedicated to Nkrumah. More than 30,000 people demonstrated in D.C. and at least 10,000 in San Francisco. ALD manifestations were held throughout the world. I participated in the ALD demonstration in D.C., but my role was consciously limited to support for [former SNCC organizer] Cleve Seller's work. He represented Kwame and us in the African Liberation Day Coordinating Committee. ALD 1972 was the largest and most militant African demonstration in the United States since the assassination of Dr. King in 1968. Kwame sent a message, through Cleve, to the ALD demonstration in D.C., but did not attend. Representatives of Liberation Movements and progressive and revolutionary Embassies throughout Africa and the African Diaspora participated in the ALD activities. Our work had finally born fruit, and the climate was ripe for the launching of the A-APRP.

Kwame came to the United States in the fall of 1972, for another political education and fund raising drive, which I again coordinated. This time however, we recruited new cadre, and organized A-APRP Work-Study Circles in more than twenty-five cities throughout North America. Kwame was banned from traveling to most of the countries in the British Commonwealth and French Community; and he was not welcomed in a number of countries supported or controlled by Moscow and Peking. This ban made it difficult, if not impossible, to recruit and build the A-APRP in the Caribbean, Central and South America, Europe, and Africa. On late October 17, 1972, Kwame publicly announced the formation of the All-African People's Revolutionary Party at a press conference at Howard University. We held our first Central Committee meeting with seventeen key cadres present, sixteen of whom were former organizers/members of SNCC and the BPP.

By 1976, through our hard work, study and struggle, through our mass political education and mass propaganda campaigns, the A-APRP had introduced a new generation of students, youth, and women in North America to Africa, Pan-Africanism, Kwame Nkrumah, and Sékou Touré. We had recruited hundreds of supporters and dozens of members in key cities and on key campuses across North America, and key countries in Africa and the African Diaspora. We had also reconnected with many of our old allies, and linked up with new ones, Pan-African and International.[1]

---

1 These included: the Afar & Issas Liberation Movement, African Awareness Association, African Kung-Fu and Karate School, the African National Congress of South Africa, the African Party for the Independence of Guinea and the Cape Verde Islands, the African United Front of Canada, the Alliance for Global Justice, the American Indian Movement, the Anguilla Independence Movement, the Antigua & Caribbean Liberation Movement, the Antigua-Barbuda Caribbean Liberation Movement, the Arab Ba'ath Socialist Party of Iraq, the Arab Information Center, the Arab-American University Graduates, ASCRIA, the Azanian People's Organization, the Ba'ath Arab Socialist Party of Syria, the Black Consciousness Movement of Azania, the Black Consciousness Movement of Brazil, the Black Liberation Army, Cham Cha Mapinduzi of Tanzania, the Committee in Solidarity with the People of El Salvador, the Communist Party of Cuba, the Communist Party of Vietnam, the Crusade for Justice, the Democratic Party of Guinea, the Emancipation Support Committee of Trinidad, the Eritrean People's Liberation Front, Farabundo Martí National Liberation Front (FMLN), Fatah, the Friends of the Congo, the Front for the Liberation of Mozambique, the Front for the Liberation of the Congo, the Gambian Anti-Apartheid Movement, the General Union of Palestinian Students, the General Union of Palestinian Women, the Hackney Black Peoples Association, Hands Off Assata!, the International Indian Treaty Council, the Iran People's Fedayin Guerrilla, the Iranian Students Association, the Irish Civil Rights Movement, the Irish Republican Socialist Party, the Islamic Student Association, Julienne Lumumba (Patrice Lumumba's daughter), the June 12 Disarmament Committee, the June 4th Movement of Ghana, the La Raza Unida Party, Lavalas, the Libyan Students Committee, the Mathaba, the MELS Study Movement of Botswana, the Mobilization for Survival, the Movement for Global Justice, the Movement for Justice in Africa (Liberia), the Movement for Justice in Gambia (Gambia), the Movement for the Independence of Puerto Rico, the Nation of Islam, the National Black United Front, the National Coalition to Smash the FBI-CIA, the National Coalition to Smash Zionism, the National Association of Arab-Americans, the National Joint Action Committee, the National Liberation Front of Algeria, the National Liberation Front of Vietnam, the National Union for Democracy and Progress of

The African Liberation Support Committee (ALSC)—the coalition of Democratic, Nationalist, Marxist and Maoist forces that organized ALD in 1973 and 1974, had abandoned it by the fall of 1974, and did not attempt to organize it in 1975 (not in D.C. at least). By 1976, ALD in the United States had been destroyed and abandoned by fights and splits within the ALSC. For the overwhelming majority of the forces in ALSC, Africa was a temporary issue, not a principled or permanent concern; a local concern, not a Pan-African one. Most were reluctant, and many were openly opposed, to linking Palestine Day to African Liberation Day, despite the fact that they are commemorated only ten days apart, May 15 and May 25, respectively, and share common enemies, a common history, and common aspirations.

In May of 1976, the A-APRP organized ALD to *Take ALD Back to Africa*, in order to institutionalize it as a permanent institution within the worldwide African Revolution, and in order to use it as a vehicle to help build the A-APRP. More than 3,000 people attended our ALD 1976 in D.C., and by the 1980s, we jointly commemorated ALD and Palestine Day, and have done so every year since. We have organized ALD manifestations in dozens of cities around the world every year since 1976. Most of the organizations mentioned above, and a virtual who's who of revolutionary Pan-African cultural artists have participated in our ALD events, including: Amafuju, the Awareness Art Ensemble, Bishop Janice Hollis and Her Gospel Body

---

Cameroon, the National Union of Eritrean Students, the National Union of Eritrean Women, the National Union of Ethiopian Students, the New Afrikan People's Organization, the New Forces, the New Jewel Movement, Nicaragua Network, No War on Cuba, the Organization of Arab Students, the Oromo National Liberation Front, the Palestine Information Center, the Palestine Liberation Organization, the Pan-African Congress Movement of England, Pan-African Liberation Organization, the Pan-African Movement of Barbados, the Pan-African Student & Youth Front, the Pan-African Student & Youth Movement, the Pan-African Students Organization in the Americas, the Pan-African Union for Social Democracy, the Pan-African Union of Sierra Leone, the Pan-Africanist Congress of Azania, the People's Action Committee for Liberty & Democracy (CAP-Liberte), the People's Fedayin Organization of Iran, the People's National Party of Jamaica, the Popular Front for the Liberation of Saghia el Hamra and Rio de Ore, the Popular Movement for the Liberation of Angola, Pro-Libertados, the Provisional Government of the Republic of New Africa, the Puerto Rican Socialist Party, the Rastafarian Brotherhood Organization in Jamaica, the Rastafarian Improvement Association of the Virgin Islands, the Revolutionary Committee Movement of Senegal, the Revolutionary Committees Movement of Libya, the Revolutionary Theory and Action Collective, the Sandinista Front for National Liberation, Sein Fein, the Society for the Promotion of Education Research of Belize, the Somali National Alliance, the Somali Students Association, that Somalian National Movement, the South West African People's Organization, the Southern Sudan National Movement, the Student Organization of Black Unity, the Sudanese People's Liberation Movement, the Tigrean People's Liberation Front, the United Caribbean Association of the Virgin Islands, the Universal African American People's Organization, the Universal African Improvement Association—African Community League, the Venezuela Solidarity Network, the Virgin Islands Unity Movement, the War Resisters League, the Workers and Peasant Party of the Congo, the Workers Party of Korea, the Worldwide African Anti-Zionist Front, the Zimbabwe African People's Union (ZANU), and the Zumbi Foundation.

& Spirit, Charles Thompson, Dele Ojo, English Man, Gil Scott-Heron, Honey Boy Martin, Letta Mubulu, Lucy Murphy, Mutabaruka, the Sensational Nightingales, Nina Simone, Peter Tosh, Plunky and the Oneness of Juju, and the Uhuru Sasa Dancers.

From 1970 to 1984, Kwame spoke on at least 100 college campuses in North America yearly, reaching a conservative estimate of 50,000 to 100,000 students and activists. He also traveled, when permitted, to a host of countries in the Caribbean, Central and South America, Europe, Asia, the Middle East, and Africa. When Sékou Touré died in 1984, we cancelled our drive, a decision that we have not yet recovered from, financially or politically. The military in Guinea seized power, banned the PDG, and imprisoned, tortured and murdered hundreds of Sékou Touré's family members and PDG cadre. We decided to cut back on our drive, so that Kwame could spend more time on the ground in Guinea. From 1984 until 1996, when Kwame became too sick to travel, he spoke on no fewer than fifty campuses in North America yearly, to audiences averaging 500 to 1,000 students. He also spoke where ever in the world he was invited and permitted to enter, thanks to the victories of the heroic struggle to lift the travel ban against him.

The primary sources of the A-APRP's alliances at its formation were those that we had developed through our more than a decade of work with SNCC and the Black Panthers, and those we gained through our linkages with Nkrumah, Touré, Fidel, and Uncle Ho. They were part of a larger, interlocking, and sometimes conflicting network of progressive and revolutionary forces across the United States, Africa and the world. To the extent our limited resources allowed, their allies became our allies, and their enemies our enemies, more or less. Our primary goals included: (1) consolidating and defending liberated countries—revolutionary and progressive countries that were in varying stages of political and economic transformation; (2) assisting national liberation movements in varying stages of their struggle for political independence, against colonialism and neocolonialism; (3) working with forces who were struggling against war, repression, racism, Zionism, and apartheid; and (4) working with revolutionary and progressive student, youth and women's movements and organizations.

By the 1980s the A-APRP had relationships with more than 100 progressive and revolutionary movements, parties and governments throughout Africa, the African Diaspora, the Middle East, the Americas, and the world. The A-APRP supported, and the A-APRP (GC) continues to support, the struggles to free all political prisoners, prisoners of war, and prisoners of conscience in the United States, Azania (South Africa), occupied Palestine, Ireland, and the world.

Matt & Dan: What has been the A-APRP's relationship to Indigenous movements in the Americas and Palestine, including the American Indian Movement and the Palestine Liberation Organization? How has working with these groups related to building an international African party?

Bob: Marx and Lenin declared that the most important national question for the British working class is the Irish National Question. We dialectically and creatively applied this axiom to our Pan-African situation. We proclaimed that the three most important national questions for African people were national questions of the Palestinian people, the Indigenous peoples of the Western Hemisphere, and that of the Irish. Since the formation of the A-APRP, we have made this position a core principal of our strategy to build and consolidate international relationships.

When SNCC was founded in 1960, Jewish groups and individuals, most of whom were pro-Zionist, proved to be one of its major allies and bases of financial support. In June 1967, SNCC announced its support for the Palestinian People and Revolution, and for their just struggle to return to, liberate and reclaim their land. When SNCC announced its support for the Palestinians, a heroic act of international solidarity, for an oppressed people, the Zionist organizations and individuals withdrew their financial support, and dramatically weakening SNCC. One of the fundamental issues that split both SNCC and the BPP was the question of coalitions—especially the national and class basis of coalition work. One of the myths of history, created by Bayard Rustin and perpetuated by Eldridge Cleaver and Huey Newton, was that Kwame categorically opposed any and all coalitions, especially with people of European descent. This was never true; Kwame's position—that Europeans should take principled responsibility for organizing primarily in their own communities—is clearly stated in his book *Black Power*. The A-APRP (GC), the inheritor of this legacy, is principled, revolutionary, independent and anti-Zionist. We are very much for coalition-building, but we are not for sale. No retreat, no compromise, no surrender!

Kwame and I were red, black, green, and gold babies: Nkrumah-ists, Touré-ists. From our high school and college days we have had principled and positive contacts and relationships with Marxist and Marxist-Leninist cadre, especially with their red diaper babies. We have had, and continue to have, positive and principled ties with pacifists, anarchists, democratic socialists, and other revolutionaries from every corner of the world.

During the period of the A-APRP's founding, the movement in the United States was wracked with ideological chaos and organization confusion. It remains, unfortunately, chaotic and confused today. The overarching struggle in the movement was, and remains, a nation (including, race, ethnicity, and religion), class, and gender struggle. What is our identity, as African People worldwide? Where is our national home? What is our class interest? What is the role of women, and youth in the revolutionary struggle? Who are our nation, class and gender allies, or enemies? The A-APRP's support, and the A-APRP (GC)'s continuing support, for the Indigenous Peoples of the Americas, and the Palestinian people, addresses these interrelated principles and concerns. It also enables and empowers us to satisfy our nationalist, internationalist, moral, and ethical duty to fight, as Dr. King called us to, against injustice anywhere and everywhere we find it.

Rescuing Civil Rights from Black Power

Collective Memory and Saving the State in Twenty-First-Century Prosecutions of 1960s-Era Cases

Dan Berger

This article, a slightly different version of which originally published in the Journal for the Study of Radicalism *(Spring 2009), helps connect the civil rights and Black Power movements of the 1960s and 1970s to the current struggles to free U.S. political prisoners and build militant movements that can the withstand the ongoing realities of state repression.*

> *History, I contend, is the present—we, with every breath we take, every move we make, are History—and what goes around, comes around.*
> —James Baldwin

Recent historical studies have shown that the movement for black power significantly predated its 1966 emergence as a slogan during a protest march in Mississippi. Scholarly texts and memoirs have excavated numerous projects to show that radical perspectives of black power—politically, culturally, strategically—defined the post–World War II war period in multiple ways. These monographs discuss the movement as always being a national phenomenon, rather than one distinctly Southern and then discretely Northern. The explicit articulation of "Black power" in the late 1960s and early 1970s is thus presented as a more explicitly militant iteration of the Black freedom struggle rather than as a deviation from the civil rights movement. Such a presentation further challenges the dichotomous view of civil rights as noble and nonviolent, Black power as vicious and violent. These contributions trace a constantly evolving movement targeting deeply entrenched structures of white supremacy in the politics, culture, economics, and values of the United States writ large. The manifestations of the black freedom struggle, its goals and strategies, shifted over time, and several of these studies have documented the nuances of these ebbs and flows. But this more fluid view of the black freedom struggle eschews rigid periodization in favor of an approach emphasizing change along a continuum of repression, imagination, and resistance.

This historical intervention comes at a critical time, as the civil rights movement becomes enshrined in U.S. popular memory through films, monuments, museums, street names, and cultural kitsch. Although memory is always a terrain of struggle, the current moment is a pivotal one in shaping how society perceives the history and impact of the black freedom struggle and postwar race relations at a time when participants in and out of authority positions join scholars and others in shaping the collective memory of a recent yet bygone period.

As an era still shaping U.S. policy and culture, the post–World War II movement for racial and economic justice is being debated in the academy as it is being memorialized and mobilized in daily life. That many veterans of the movement are still alive and active participants in these processes imbues both the history and memory of the time with excitement and urgency. This urgency finds itself in court in the early twenty-first century, with the legal apparatus constituting a vital mechanism of state efforts to shape collective memory through trials, incarceration, and the discourse these legal endeavors generate. These trials express struggles with and by the state over what attributes of that era will be officially embraced in this one. Several Sixties veterans, of both the left and right, now find themselves at the center of legal cases on thirty-plus-year-old charges emanating from their activism at the time. These courtroom battles are particularly bringing the civil rights—black power movement(s) back into focus—and putting some key figures of that time, now in their sixties and seventies, in prison. Occurring simultaneously, these trials of white supremacists and black militants constitute a vital part of memorializing the period; these retroactive trials are the clearest state intervention in collective memory of the 1960s era. Various officials, from judges and state attorneys general up to Alberto Gonzalez and FBI head Robert Mueller, have said that these trials serve to punish long-ago crimes and right the wrongs of yesterday—the eternal truth of justice making itself known. These proclamations are echoed by the families of the deceased and, in the cases of ex-Klansmen, various civil rights organizations.

Theorists of collective memory insist that the past is invoked to shape the present; collective memory, writes Barbie Zelizer, is "a graphing of the past as it is used for present aims, a vision in bold relief of the past as it is woven into the present and future." As a result, the prosecution of former Klansmen and ex-Black Panthers is discussed here with an eye toward what such trials mean—both for remembering the 1960s and for the current period. Indeed, these cases present a clear invocation of "the sixties as a political metaphor." Whereas studies of and struggles over memory often take shape amid material (particularly popular) culture, these cases add a legal and discursive component. These high-profile cases from a volatile, and recent, time provide the raw material relied on to construct a usable past. Triumph and tragedy present fertile territory for exploring the shaping and significance of collective memory, and digging up old murder cases uses the court system in an attempt to make triumph out of tragedy. Although it is not often seen as such, the legal system—including laws, trials, and prisons—is a premier site by which the state makes official distinctions of both memory and value. Subsequently, the discourse of such memory is transmitted to society at large, at least partially, through news stories, thereby affixing media to the process of representing and amplifying memory. Indeed, though courtrooms are sites where history is told, sometimes most honestly, most of the public learns, at best, only of the existence and verdict of trials. As such, mediated discourse reduces trials to stories that can be transmitted as public knowledge.

Through the arrest and prosecution of white racists and (mostly) Black militants in the past fifteen (but especially the past five) years, the government has taken an active role in periodizing and classifying the civil rights—black power movements. These trials and the surrounding discourse enforce the exact rigid demarcation between civil rights and Black power that scholars have sought to deconstruct. Among other things, these cases valorize a noble civil rights movement while demonizing a misguided Black power movement—presenting each one as geographically and tactically discrete, opposed, and immutable. The civil rights movement is presented as noble, nonviolent, and limited to the South, where its greatest enemy was vigilante white violence rather than an entrenched state system of white supremacy.[1] Indeed, individual white terror, protected by backward Southern sheriffs, is presented as the main enemy of African Americans and the movement in general. Such a paradigm, played out discursively and judicially, implicates Black power as the antithesis of civil rights—a violent and unnecessary overreaction.

These proceedings reify the nobility of the civil rights movement on the grave of the Black power movement. The federal government, in this narrative, emerges as a subtle hero—its best efforts thwarted by an antiquated Southern system at the time, the federal government succeeds decades later as a result of what is cast as its dogged perseverance. Through both trials and discourse, the federal government's attacks against Black power are minimally part of the memory terrain.

---

1   Although describing the civil rights movement as nonviolent is hardly new, it does present one of the more obvious cleavages between scholarship and popular discourse. A handful of books demonstrate the extent to which self-defense, and even armed struggle, characterized black activism in both North and South before 1966. To give but one example, the well-known Mississippi organizer Medgar Evers contemplated launching an armed guerrilla war, despite the invocation of him as a pacifist in popular culture, such as the movie *Ghosts of Mississippi*. See also, among others, Muhammad Ahmad, *We Will Return in the Whirlwind: Black Radical Organizations 1960–1975* (Chicago: Charles Kerr Publishers, 2007); Lance Hill, *Deacons for Defense: Armed Resistance and the Civil Rights Movement* (Chapel Hill: University of North Carolina, 2004); Charles Payne, *I've Got the Light of Freedom: The Organizing Tradition and the Mississippi Freedom Struggle* (Berkeley: University of California Press, 1997); Christopher Strain, *Pure Fire: Self-Defense as Activism in the Civil Rights Era* (Athens: University of Georgia Press, 2005); Timothy Tyson, *Radio-Free Dixie: Robert F. Williams and the Roots of Black Power* (Chapel Hill: University of North Carolina, 1999); and Simon Wendt, *The Spirit and the Shotgun: Armed Resistance and the Struggle for Civil Rights* (Gainesville: University Press of Florida, 2007). Of course, in challenging the assumed tactical splits, these texts also challenge any neat geographic divider in conceptualizing the Black freedom struggle.

Ultimately, these trials suggest that the goals of the civil rights movement have been met—these cases being the last unfinished business of the time—while deriding Black power demands as inherently criminal and violent. But it remains largely at the level of abstraction and intimation, given that discourse of the revived court cases remains fairly separate between the right- and left-wing radicals. Still, as the below discussion aims to make clear through an examination of these trials, these court cases present a triumphant narrative affirming a liberal racial order and the ultimate authority of the state, as white terrorists and black militants find themselves on trial decades later.

Right-Wing Radicals: The Ku Klux Klan and Civil Rights Murders

On 24 January 2007, police arrested James Ford Seale, a seventy-one-year-old former Klansman and Mississippi sheriff's deputy, for the murder of two Black teenagers in 1964. Less than a month later, news stories reported on the attempts to pass a law establishing a Justice Department unit to prosecute other white supremacist murderers. After decades of passivity, the federal government and various Southern states have gone after their racist past by going after those who terrorized the civil rights movement and Black communities in general. Between 1989 and 2007, twenty-nine cases were reopened, leading to twenty-eight arrests and twenty-two convictions of "civil rights era crime." (There have been, more recently, calls to reopen rape cases involving white men sexually attacking black women; as of summer 2011 no such thing has occurred.) The first target was Byron de la Beckwith, who for years bragged of assassinating Mississippi civil rights leader Medgar Evers in 1963. Like many of his fellow Klansmen now being tried, Beckwith's trials resulted (twice) in hung juries in brief show trials. The case was reopened in 1989, resulting in his 1994 conviction.

Other prosecutions followed, mainly in Mississippi and Alabama, especially since the turn of the century. These cases have targeted both obscure and well-known murders of African Americans, activists and otherwise, as well as white civil rights activists. In 1998, former White Knight of the Ku Klux Klan, Sam Bowers, was convicted for ordering the death of civil rights activist Vernon Dahmer. Thomas Blanton (in 2001) and Bobby Frank Cherry (in 2002) were convicted for their roles in the infamous 1963 Birmingham Sixteenth Street Baptist Church bombing that killed four young girls. In Mississippi Ernest Avants was convicted in 2003 for the 1966 death of sharecropper Ben Chester White, and Klan leader Edgar Ray Killen was convicted in 2005 for orchestrating the notorious murders of James Chaney, Andy Goodman, and Mickey Schwerner. Most recently, retired Alabama state trooper James Bonard Fowler pleaded guilty in November 2010 for the shooting death of twenty-six-year-old Jimmie Lee Jackson during a 1965 demonstration—a murder that helped catalyze the well-known Selma-to-Montgomery march. Fowler has always admitted to shooting Jackson, though he maintains it was in self-defense. In exchange for his plea, he was sentenced to six months in prison.

These cases are fighting against time. The culture of post–World War II white supremacist violence among everyday white people was most visible before 1965. Several key participants have passed away—for instance, two coconspirators in the Birmingham church bombing died before Blanton and Cherry were indicted—and the memory of witnesses is fleeting. The attempt to reopen one of the most notorious examples of white terrorism demonstrates this difficulty. The 1955 murder of fourteen-year-old Emmett Till for whistling at a white woman in Mississippi helped focus international attention on the routine violence of Southern white supremacy. All the more so when the two men tried for the heinous crime were acquitted by an all-white jury but still bragged of their deeds. Yet with all other known suspects dead, a 2007 Mississippi grand jury refused to indict Carolyn Bryant, the white woman who Till allegedly whistled at, for any wrongdoing in Till's murder. (Prosecutors alleged that Bryant, whose then-husband participated in the murder, was a coconspirator in the killing.)

With a little prodding from modern civil rights organizations, the federal government has joined some Southern states in trying to establish the infrastructure to continue prosecuting these so-called cold cases of white supremacist terror. Around the time a grand jury let Bryant go, Georgia Congressman and civil rights veteran John Lewis introduced the Unsolved Civil Rights Crimes Act to "create a cold cases unit within the Justice Department to track down evidence in the unpunished killings." The law has been dubbed the Till Act for short, paying homage both to the slain black teenager and the Emmett Till Justice Campaign created to pursue such a law.

Although the House of Representatives allocated $100 million for the creation of the unit by a vote of 422 to 2, the bill has, at least temporarily, been stalled in the Senate. Still, with passage of the act seemingly imminent, then–Attorney General Gonzalez and FBI Director Mueller announced in June 2007 that they were reopening a hundred cases with a priority given to about a dozen of them. It is, said one news article, a prosecutorial attempt "in the South to close the books on crimes from the civil rights era."

The official involvement of the federal government extends from investigation to prosecution. Some of the recent civil rights cases have been reopened on technicalities, and various news stories described as a "sudden realization" that the deceased was killed or found on federal property. This fact has allowed the government to try these ex-Klansmen on federal charges of kidnapping or manslaughter. Although tried in the Deep South states in which the murders occurred, the use of federal charges adds an extra layer of gravitas to the cases: this is the full force of the government being brought to bear on the history of Southern injustice.

And yet, the specter of white supremacist terrorism haunts these trials in ways that make clear the living history and breathing memory of the era. One of the most recent defendants, James Ford Seale, was tried in the James O. Eastland Federal Courthouse: the very edifice where justice was said to be delivered was named after the arch segregationist Mississippi Senator who urged the people and institutions of his state to resist and reject Supreme Court rulings on all civil rights matters. Further, the defendants in these trials are not the only ex-Klansmen being brought out of the woodwork. Several witnesses at trial, themselves former Klan members, implicated the attorney for Klan leader Sam Bowers as himself an active participant in Klan activity at the time. That witnesses remember attorney Travis Buckley's Klan involvement, including his participation in the meeting during which Bowers ordered the death for which he stood trial in 1998, testifies to the elusive nature of trying to hold unreconstructed and unrepentant racists accountable for a pervasive system of white supremacy. Despite the noble intent and do-gooder discourse surrounding these cases, they are inherently individual. Whether out of legal expediency, political belief, or both, the trials focus on the involvement of individuals separate from any organization or broader context. At Bowers's 1998 trial, for instance, the district attorney said that the Klansmen who killed Vernon Dahmer in 1966 "did it because one person told them to do so." Although such rhetoric may be successful in securing the conviction of an unabashed white supremacist leader, it also exposes the limitations of shaping collective memory or crafting historical narratives rooted in individual legal cases. These trials can be seen as the juridical equivalent of the Rosa Parks myth: the simplistic notion that history is created by individuals acting alone and without any social or institutional framework.

The Till Act codifies some of these problems. With the picayune details common to legislation, the bill specifies its targets in ways that define what counts as the civil rights activism and opposition. The Act only covers murders that occurred prior to December 31, 1969. Because perpetrators of racist murders in the 1940s are likely deceased, the law functionally applies to those killings that occurred in the 1950s and 1960s. And though the act itself does not limit investigations to the South, such a belief, opined historian David Garrow, "is voiced repeatedly in the House Judiciary Committee report that accompanied the bill, so it is quite possible that the Department of Justice would apply the bill only to the South ... By encouraging cold case prosecutions only in the South and by focusing only on murders committed in the 1960s, the bill effectively limits itself to the kinds of easy cases that fit our expectations and that everyone can agree on—while ignoring the cases that cut against our wistful, nostalgic desire to see civil rights history as just a Deep South morality play featuring drooling racists versus Gandhian victims."

As such, the law, and by extension the cases carried out ostensibly under its mandate, institutionalize a rigid legal and political memory in contrast to a much more nuanced set of emerging historical narratives.

Left-Wing Radicals: Black Power Militants and Anti-State Violence

The day before James Seale was arrested, eight former Panthers were arrested for the 1971 murder of San Francisco police Sergeant James Young in an attack on the

Ingleside police station. This shooting occurred eight days after the murder of Black Panther Party field marshal and prison organizer George Jackson at San Quentin. Police say the shadowy Black Liberation Army (BLA), a clandestine offshoot of the Black Panthers, was responsible for the attack. Three Panthers were arrested in New Orleans in 1973 for the attack and gave confessions that they later said were false and obtained through torture. A court agreed in 1975, declaring that "when the two San Francisco police investigators who came to Louisiana to interview the three men were out of the room, New Orleans officers stripped the men, blindfolded them, beat them and covered them in blankets soaked in boiling water," according to a story in the *San Francisco Chronicle*. "They also used electric prods on their genitals, court records show. The men were freed after a court found their rights had been violated and they were not allowed to have counsel." Of the three men arrested and tortured in New Orleans, one, John Bowman, passed away one month before the 2007 arrests. Another, Harold Taylor is one of the eight who were arrested. The last man, Rueben Scott, was the prosecution's star witness in 1975 and is believed still to be the main witness in the current case, despite having recanted his confession as coerced.

The same two San Francisco police investigators came out of retirement in 1999 to continue prosecuting the case. Although denying any link to the BLA in general or this crime in particular, four of the eight and Bowman spent a few weeks in jail in 2005 for refusing to testify in front of a grand jury investigating the case. The men stated their moral and ethical opposition to the proceedings, arguing that attempting to reinstate old charges based on tortured confessions was an attempt to use post-9/11 legal shifts to legitimize barbarous investigatory practices. The grand jury did not pass down any indictments, and the men were left alone until their arrest. Joining Richard Brown, Ray Boudreaux, Henry Jones, and Harold Taylor are four other ex-Panthers—two of whom, Herman Bell and Jalil Muntaqim, have been in prison for more than thirty years on separate charges emerging from other suspected BLA attacks on police officers. Muntaqim, whose given name is Anthony Bottom, was arrested the day before the attack in which Young was killed. His inclusion in the case testifies to its most chilling aspect—although most newspaper accounts of the arrests have focused on the killing of Sgt. Young as impetus for the arrests, the eight initially faced a broader, nebulous charge of conspiracy. This conspiracy charge, according to a story in the *San Francisco Chronicle*, alleges that the eight "carried out a 'terror and chaos' campaign aimed at 'assassinating law enforcement officers' that began in 1968 and ended in 1973, Deputy Police Chief Morris Tabak said."

In response to a defense motion, the presiding judge dismissed the conspiracy charge against five of the men in February 2008, stating that the statute of limitations for this charge had long ago passed. This move released Richard O'Neal from the case entirely. The judge refused to dismiss the conspiracy charges against Bell, Muntaqim, and Torres because they had not lived in California since the mid-1970s. Thus they were, according to the judge, not subject to California's statutory limits. However, in July 2009, Bell and Muntaqim pleaded guilty to lesser charges in exchange for the state dropping all charges against four of the men and returning Bell and Muntaqim to New York, where they continue to fight for parole. That leaves only Francisco Torres left in the case, which continues to drag on at the expense of California taxpayers into its seventh year.

Though mostly dismissed, such a sweeping charge of conspiracy also indicts a whole era of black power militancy. Historically, the government has had greater success garnering convictions on conspiracy charges since the burden of proof with such allegations has a lower standard of evidence than a given criminal act itself. (If recent political trials are anything of a guide, conspiracy charges are based at least in part on guilt by association). The five-year period claimed by the conspiracy charge was a time of articulated warfare between sectors of the radical left and the political/repressive arms of the state; the FBI's counterintelligence program (COINTELPRO) was at its height, leading to the deaths of dozens of Black Panthers—overtly by police as well as in internecine warfare, some of which was later shown to have been provoked by law enforcement. The level of repression sparked armed groups such as the BLA—as well as the Weather Underground and a range of other expressions of militancy that targeted state and corporate entities through protests, bombings, and a general culture of fierce opposition to the U.S. government and its ability to police the world or its racially oppressed communities at home. The complexity of this period in particular has been, so far, among the most understudied aspects of the black power era, in large part because it is so difficult to record. But the case of the "San Francisco 8" brings it into focus through the courtroom, embodied in the fates of these men. Thus, out of the memory emerges a battle over history and context.

Although the most dramatic, the San Francisco 8 case is not the only recent legal challenge based on dormant charges to have raised the specter of black power. The twenty-first century has seen some celebrities and many foot soldiers in the black liberation movement being targeted. In 2005, the state of New Jersey raised its bounty from $50,000 to $1 million for the capture of Assata Shakur, the former Panther and BLA member who escaped from prison in 1979 and has been living in political exile in Cuba since the 1980s. Kamau Sadiki, the father of Shakur's child and himself a former member of the Black Panther Party who served five years in prison in the mid-1970s for a BLA robbery, was sentenced to life in prison in 2003 for the 1971 death of a police officer in Georgia. Sadiki was arrested in New York in early 2001 on separate, but contemporary, charges that were subsequently dismissed. Once in custody, though, police officers tried to get his help in solving other BLA-suspected cases. That proved futile, but FBI files listed him as a suspect in the Atlanta killing and he was transferred to Georgia. The timing was a bit odd: the District Attorney refused to prosecute the case in 1972 for insufficient evidence, there was no new evidence, and Sadiki had been living a quiet life working for the phone company in New York City.

Two other such cold cases bear mentioning. Gary Freeman, born Joseph Pannell, was arrested in Canada in 2004 after living there for thirty-five years. He was wanted in the United States for the 1969 shooting of a white police officer in Chicago. The officer survived, but police claim Freeman was a Black Panther carrying out a politically motivated attack. After fighting extradition for four years, during which time he denied any involvement in either the Panthers or the attack, Freeman pled guilty to the shooting in a deal that saw him serve 30 days in Cook County Jail (to be followed by two years probation) and pay $250,000 in restitution to a fund that supports the spouses and children of police officers, paramedics, and fire fighters who die in the line of duty. And five members of the enigmatic Symbionese Liberation Army, whose most famous action was the kidnapping of newspaper heiress Patty Hearst but whose rap sheet also includes two shooting deaths and at least two bank robberies, have also found themselves in court in recent years for charges emanating from their 1970s activities. The SLA arrests include the extradition of James Kilgore from South Africa, where he had been living and working as a well-respected academic for years, and the arrest and trial of Kathy Soliah, who had been living a quiet life in Minnesota as Sara Jane Olson.

To these cases could be added other examples that don't quite fit the cold-case formula but still implicate the legal system in remembering and historicizing the black power movement. H. Rap Brown, who famously declared violence to be "as American as cherry pie," was sentenced to life in prison in 2002 for the shooting death of a Fulton County sheriff's deputy two years earlier. The former leader of the Student Nonviolent Coordinating Committee had become imam of a Muslim community in Atlanta, changing his name to Jamil Al-Amin. As with many of the Black power cold cases, Al-Amin denied any involvement in the shooting for which he was charged; he and his supporters allege the case to be the culmination of decades of harassment made possible by a climate of anti-Muslim hysteria, carried out by the courts, in the wake of the 9/11 attacks.

Less visible but equally significant, several ex-Panthers who have been incarcerated for decades on politically motivated charges of that era, including Bell and Muntaqim, have been denied parole in recent years. Each time, the parole board has declared their opposition to the men's release due to the severity of the original charges rather than any egregious behavior since their incarceration. But the parole process is supposed to judge prison behavior and rehabilitation, rather than the severity of the sentencing charge, which cannot change. In the most extreme case, ex-Panther Veronza Bower has been held more than five years past his mandatory release date after serving all of a thirty-year sentence. In the parole denial, as in the retroactive trials, Black power is treated as a heinous violation of the law, not a political movement and or even a cultural phenomenon. With this framework, the state becomes not only the mechanism for securing justice, as it would seem in the prosecution of ex-Klansmen, but the victim utilizing its own apparatus to secure redress for itself. Whereas the former set of trials champions the federal government's ability to foster a black-white national unity, the latter grouping makes clear that such harmony is possible only through a bolstered and unchallenged security apparatus.

Justice for Whom? The FBI, the Klan, and the Black Freedom Struggle

Underpinning these trials is a curious but familiar geographic division in how the political struggles of the time period are discussed: the civil rights movement was located in the South, where Southern officials upheld an antiquated system that died with them. White supremacy, in this discourse, is so strictly embodied that it lacks any significant structural or historical dimension. The enlightened North, including the federal government, tried its best to bring the wayward South into the fold—and these prosecutions do now what they were somehow unable to do at the time. As several people involved in the prosecution of ex-Klansmen have noted, these trials rest on the cooperation of once resistant Southern states. Yet such a claim elevates state power over federal in suggesting that it is only with the involvement of the individual, now enlightened Southern states that the federal government of the United States is able to prosecute criminals. Such rhetoric, furthermore, does not accompany the trials of leftists, who never boasted of any state protection and in which the collaboration of local and national law enforcement has long been a familiar phenomenon.

This position implies that racial oppression was a Southern phenomenon, rendering incomprehensible the politics and militancy of black power as a nihilistic and misanthropic enterprise—a gang more than an idea or movement. These trials obfuscate a more fluid approach to the civil rights—black power era and use geography to reinforce firm political (and tactical) divisions: between a noble Southern movement that had violence done to it and a misguided Northern movement that was itself violent. Indicting individuals obscures the broader movements from which people came and the material and ideological structures that they put forth or responded to and that still pervade. Such trials also ignore the role of law enforcement in fostering white supremacist violence by both commission and omission—that is, by either participating in it or turning a blind eye—as well as the role such state-sponsored suppression played in catalyzing black militancy. Removing the specter of state violence serves to separate history from memory.

Each prosecution, whether of right-wing or left-wing radicals, involves a particular narrative about the role of law enforcement at both federal and local levels. Trials of ex-Klansmen often call into question the reactionary caliber of Southern cops, just as black power cases valorize the police departments once under attack by the BLA. This process can be neatly traced in news stories of the respective cases, whereby police officers or their representatives are often sources in decrying Black Power violence but rarely quoted or mentioned in explaining violence against civil rights activists. The role of local police departments in persecuting the Panthers is generally unexamined, as is the large number of unarmed black citizens murdered by the 1970s police culture of trigger-happy racial profiling. Historian Akinyele O. Umoja notes that nearly 1,000 black people were killed by American police between 1971 and 1973. By the end of the decade, there was also a significant rise in white supremacist organizing by neo-Nazi groups.

More troubling is the depiction and representation of the FBI. Despite the heroic role afforded the FBI in the film *Mississippi Burning* (alluded to in several news stories about the Klan arrests), historians generally agree that the FBI failed to protect civil rights workers adequately from white supremacists and waged an illegal counterinsurgency campaign targeting the black power movement. Although how damaging the FBI was at any given moment and whether its repressive activities were aberrant or inherent qualities are still debated, the agency nonetheless comes in for deserved criticism in scholarly debates of the Sixties. Yet the state recasts the FBI as heroic in and through these trials. It is a clash of memory versus history. This version of a heroic FBI is particularly evident in regards to the Till Act and the civil rights murders. In this telling, the FBI did its best to investigate and prosecute these murders when they occurred—only to be stymied by backward Southern officials. Supporters of the Panthers, however, charge that the FBI was particularly involved in attempting to crush black militancy—including in the pre-1966 South—by any means necessary. They point to the FBI's COINTELPRO, the vanguard of Sixties-era state repression, which saw law enforcement infiltrate organizations, make false accusations against key members, pit groups against each other, arrest organizers, and create a general environment of fear and distrust.

The Klan was not immune from FBI attention. The FBI had infiltrators in several Klan chapters throughout the South. To protect the identity of its informers, the FBI allowed its men to beat, harass, and intimidate civil rights workers; one informer was an accessory to the murder of activist Viola Liuzzo, a white woman from Michigan who went South to help the movement. But beyond the active role of such men, which only became known later, the FBI's approach to the Southern civil rights movement can generally—and generously—be described as one of ambivalence. The bureau did little to prevent attacks against civil rights workers, and only when facing presidential pressure did it prosecute anyone involved in the "white hate groups" the bureau was monitoring. And yet, news stories such as those profiling agent Jim Ingram, who joined the FBI in the 1950s and came out of retirement to help investigate the civil rights cold cases, give the impression that the bureau is continuing a time-honored tradition of upholding racial justice. Such stories are consistent with what communication scholars have identified as the uplift tendency of American journalism, which may criticize aspects of the state but is always oriented to its maintenance and well-being.

The FBI's voluminous files on Klan activity are now being used in investigating civil rights cold cases. But this is a new development. As recently as 2001, it was revealed that the FBI had withheld evidence from Alabama officials that could have been used to prosecute all of the Birmingham church bombers at the time the attack occurred. Contrast this not only to the black power movement, where the history of duplicitous and malicious activity is well documented, but also to the recent trials of Black radicals, where the FBI has taken its own initiative in offering evidence and forensic experts to prosecute former members of the Black Panther Party—the organization J. Edgar Hoover once defined as the "greatest threat to the internal security of the United States."

The role of FBI as savior or villain begs the question: on whose behalf is justice being pursued in prosecuting these cold cases? With both white supremacists and black militants, the official discourse, as presented in news reports, has depicted both groups of defendants as violent, thuggish vigilantes pursuing a bankrupt vision. But there are deep differences—not only in the race of the defendants but also in the application and politics of retroactive justice. The victims in need of retribution are vastly different: individuals harmed or the state, the ability of black people to vote or the role of the police in marginalized communities. Indeed, even though individuals were killed in the cases involving suspected BLA members, the victims are embraced and invoked only as representatives of and for the state. The main organizations invoked in the trials are the Ku Klux Klan, the century-old robed defenders of white supremacy, and the Black Liberation Army, a decade-long group known specifically for attacking police officers as the "occupying army" of Black communities. Whereas the former has often enjoyed the protection of the federal government, the latter emerged from the shell of an organization, the Black Panther Party, targeted for destruction by the federal government. It was, in fact, the functional destruction of the Panthers that led some of its members to pursue a clandestine approach. As a right-wing populist organization making use of terrorism to uphold a strict racial hierarchy, the Klan primarily targeted African Americans and their white allies, especially Jews and communists. As a left-wing splinter group trying to wage "armed struggle" as a way to continue Black nationalist revolt in a climate of intense repression, the BLA attacked law enforcement (as representatives of the state—an argument equally voiced by the government in retroactively prosecuting suspected BLA members) and drug dealers (for sapping the vitality of Black communities).

The simultaneous prosecutions afford the government a heroic role of moderation against extremism of the left or right. And yet, pursuing a politics of moderation through garnering lengthy convictions of senior citizens presents a troubling moral equivocation that rescues the state from both its own inaction and its own overaction. In one set of cases, prosecutions uphold a liberal narrative of racial tolerance; in the other, prosecutions advance a claim of justice for the state itself. According to Tom Niery, a New York police detective who worked on BLA cases in the 1970s, "There are a lot of people who ambushed police officers still walking around today. We're looking for justice, wherever justice can be had." Such justice is accomplished physically through the incarceration of those deemed responsible for the shooting deaths of police officers and symbolically in the discourse and presentation of former radicals being captured all these years later. Meanwhile, no state official has ever been punished for attacking civil rights or black power activists, including for the murders carried out under COINTELPRO. Thus, the state cements its power to delineate right from wrong in the politics of race, violence, and collective action.

Truth, Reconciliation, and Collective Memory

History and memory are intimately related but hardly interchangeable. Where they intersect and depart provides the raw material out of which the past becomes mobilized in the present. These cases are being reopened in a post–civil rights world that has seen an immense retreat from racial justice and the affirmation of a putatively post-racial society. Yet these cases constitute a spectacular intervention by the state in how the black freedom struggle is remembered in its historic context and its impact on the contemporary political landscape, especially concerning the lived realities of race. The state—specifically, the political establishment and legal apparatus—is always implicated in the rise, fall, and memorialization of social movements. Such official involvement occurs both behind closed doors, where trials are decided and policy established, and at the center of public debate. The highly visible nature of certain acts of statecraft delineates official priorities and sanctioned values.

Emphasizing the spectacular role of such proceedings does not negate the impact of the state's gaining its pound of flesh from those allegedly guilty of murder long ago, but at least with the white defendants, people have lived the prime of their lives free and without consequences. That the situation is more complicated for the black defendants, several of whom have already served time in prison in the intervening years, testifies to the pitfalls of equivocating on the different cases, contexts, charges, and consequences. And yet at a certain level, the spectacle of hauling senior citizens to court transcends race to make clear the state's ability to serve as final arbiter of people's fate, no matter the time frame. It is worth noting that few of those tried in recent years have lived in hiding. Outside of Freeman and two former SLA members, no one arrested was living under an assumed name and presumably could have been arrested at any point in the past three or four decades (although several reports on Seale's arrest quoted people saying they thought that he had died years earlier). That none of them was prosecuted before now is curious, given that success in these cases has been based almost entirely on new consciousness and new jury pools—not new evidence.

It is hard to say definitively why these cases crop up now, though they can certainly be mapped against the current terrain of the federal government and racial politics. These prosecutions, like all invocations of collective memory, speak more to the political landscape in which they emerge than to the historic one about which they comment. The trials are symbolic rituals organized by and through the state to intervene in the contemporary politics of black citizenship and political mobilization. Several incidents stand out in this regard: criticism of the catastrophic response to Hurricane Katrina, which destroyed predominantly black areas throughout the Gulf Coast and saw the government widely critiqued for what many called race-based neglect; contentious debates around immigration (including the rise of the Minutemen, a White Citizen's Council for the globalization era); and challenges to the unpopular war in Iraq, which includes record low enlistment rates among African Americans. All of these phenomena, of course, transpire in a post-9/11 environment in which the government must live up to its pledged promise to stamp out terrorists, including domestic ones—and, it would seem, regardless of the time frame in which they occurred. Even before the contextual shifts enabled by the September 11 attacks, the start of these cold case prosecutions must also be mapped against the twinned realities of a growing black middle class and the fact that poverty and incarceration remain concentrated in black communities, as they have since the 1960s.

Evaluating the contemporary racial landscape for institutional racism must also include the continued presence of openly white supremacist organizations. The Southern Poverty Law Center, a civil rights organization at the heart of helping prosecute former and current Klansmen, said that the Klan experienced a 60 percent membership increase between 2000 and 2005, mostly among younger people. These numbers fly in the face of assertions, including those of prosecutors involved in these cases, that the trials "symbolize the shedding of the past, the healing of old wounds and the death of an underground army of thugs that once ruled [the South] with torment and terror." And it weakens the claim Senator Christopher Dodd and Congressman John Lewis put forth defending the Till Act as a bold step toward removing "a great stain on our justice system."

These cases not only rewrite the memory of racial justice struggles in the mid-twentieth century, they also attempt to redraw the alliances of contemporary struggles for racial justice and the continuities joining yesterday's struggles with today's. Going after former Klansmen has brought together the U.S. Congress, families of the deceased, and civil rights organizations that have long been trying to reopen these cases. These prosecutions join the NAACP, the Urban League, and the Southern Poverty Law Center to the federal government. The Till Act would institutionalize this partnership by giving millions of dollars to federal and state governments to prosecute former Klansmen based on investigations often led by these civil rights groups. To prosecute aging racists as if individual terrorism was the greatest enemy of the civil rights movement is to forget the economic and social goals and demands of the movement—and at a time when many of the gains, including political enfranchisement and equal access to education, are under attack.

With the black power cases, however, prosecutions emerge out of preexisting cooperation between state and federal law enforcement agencies. There does not seem to be any visible social movement clamoring for these men to be incarcerated. And there is no need to institutionalize the black power movement through federal legislation—even legislation aimed at capturing lawbreakers attached to the black power movement. The civil rights movement is thus given official recognition denied to the black power movement, even if in a negative way. The public display of reopening old civil rights murders, together with the Till Act, provide the (federal but also certain individual state) government's legitimation to the civil rights movement as a valued attribute of our national history by acknowledging the crimes committed against its participants.

In the prosecution of black radicals, however, black power emerges only as villain. It is, therefore, being remembered so that it can be forgotten. Paradoxical as this may seem, it is a common case in collective memory, where forgetting "also serves to establish collectivity" by delineating the boundaries of acceptable memory. These cases invoke black power for the precise purpose of incarcerating its adherents and burying its appeal. Black power is a recent enough phenomenon, one inextricably linked to the positively remembered civil rights movement and one still holding significant enough purchase among African American communities that its forgetting can only be accomplished by publicly revoking its tenets.

The San Francisco 8 and other retroactive black power cases receive no mention in coverage of the cold cases, and the Till Act is clearly designed to prosecute white supremacist murders—cases where both the moral and evidentiary arguments are far more self-evident than many of the black power cases. That is, crimes of the radical left are always crimes worth pursuing; they don't need special laws to be "reopened." Of course, these cases are being reopened to the extent that people have been actively prosecuted in the past ten years in ways they have not been in the twenty years before then. But these cases are not being officially reopened in the sense of requiring federal legislation, nor are they being discussed as "cold" or reopened cases. Rather, the surrounding discourse and the underlying framework cast them first and foremost as old criminal cases, rather than, as with the prosecution of former Klansmen, as political trials aiming to correct historical wrongs through the legal system. One set of trials is historically specific—the civil rights movement had a beginning and end, and certain acts of violence occurring in those parameters are now being prosecuted for the maintenance of an almost postracial national unity. In the other set, however, justice is framed as transhistorical: if a police officer dies, there is no limit in time or space at which the state will stop in pursuing justice for its representatives. This transhistoric approach would seem a vital ingredient in criminalizing and therefore forgetting black power while reifying civil rights through its specificity. That is, we can value the civil rights movement because we know precisely when it was, what it did, and crucially, when it was over. Black power, meanwhile, becomes an elusive phenomenon palpable only in relation to acts of violence.

This historic positioning has multiple implications. Even though they were ultimately dropped, the use of conspiracy charges against the San Francisco 8 defendants provides one such example. Conspiracy charges have been used more sparingly with the former Klansmen and only when more serious charges have not panned out—rather than, as with the San Francisco 8, to amplify the severity of the charges. Trials of Klansmen have not featured multiple defendants; even the Birmingham church bombers were tried separately. White supremacy remains prosecuted at the level of individual violence, whereas Black power is a criminal conspiracy. There is also a sentence disparity. It may seem strange to quibble over charges and sentence length; given the age of these men, it is likely that a long sentence is functionally a death sentence. But precisely because these cases convey a message of official importance, there is a significant difference between Edgar Ray Killen getting sixty years on triple manslaughter charges for the deaths of three civil rights workers versus Kamau Sadiki being sentenced to life in prison plus ten years for first degree murder of a police officer.

From start to finish, such prosecutions are more than, as Dodd and Lewis said of the Till Act, "a hopeful *postscript*" to the country's "struggle for racial equality" (emphasis added). Several commentators have criticized the sudden interest in elderly Klansmen while African Americans disproportionately fill the prisons and the worst schools, among other examples of injustice. "If past is prologue, we can look for the record on Katrina and voting rights and racial profiling and sentencing disparities to be set right around 2050," Deborah Mathis tersely wrote on BlackAmericaWeb.com of these cold cases. Thus far, historian David Garrow has been among the few to appear in print calling for the state to show as much interest in prosecuting the murderers of Black Panthers—outside of the South and after 1968—as it has in going after Southern white supremacists of the early 1960s.

Garrow's suggestion is a worthy one. Likewise, Gary Freeman's plea agreement, a brief symbolic incarceration accompanied by restitution, takes a step toward restorative rather than retributive justice. But we might build off these examples to look for models of justice beyond and instead of the courtroom. Memory is a process of struggle, a constantly shifting and competing set of narratives, rather than something imposed and accepted without question. So the state is not the only actor in this struggle over memory. The first public statement of the San Francisco 8, distributed online and published on its support website, offers an interesting counterproposal. Although making no mention of the prosecution of ex-Klansmen, the 2007 statement (released on May 19, the birthday of Malcolm X) makes three concrete policy proposals that cast their case as a struggle over memory and policy alike. They call for anti-torture legislation, reopened hearings on COINTELPRO, and perhaps most significantly, the creation of a Truth and Reconciliation Commission. "We believe such a Commission could serve as a catalyst to forge substantial resolutions to heal America's racial trauma," the ex-Panthers wrote.

Such an entity would not resolve all the myriad issues raised by such a tumultuous period. But it is a model that, unlike the courtroom trials, has the power to indict both individuals and institutions for their wrongdoing. Amnesty has been a precondition for existing Truth and Reconciliation Commissions. Freeing people from legal consequences is designed to encourage the full disclosure of wrongdoing—from all sides, and in a way that at least theoretically enables a complicated narrative allowing for the varying positions of power for each aggrieved party. In forfeiting a legal-based approach, Truth and Reconciliation forefronts politics and situates individual responsibility against the broader structures of state authority. It also attempts to develop a new model of justice beyond the state and rooted in acknowledging the unfortunate choices many people make in unequal societies. Such an approach, therefore, seems better suited to address the subject positions of race, class, and gender than a courtroom setting. The Truth and Reconciliation Commission established to investigate the 1979 Klan murders of communist activists in Greensboro provides an example of this model applied to the United States. (See http://www.greensborotrc.org/ for more information on this process).

Independent of the state, such bodies not only pass judgment but interpret the past in a way that eludes narrow and equivocating legalistic applications that define political movements through the lens of law and individual crime. It is this attempt to reconcile history with memory and equality with justice that might best serve society's ability to address the enduring problem of the color line.

Author's note: This article benefited greatly from conversations with or feedback from Alan Berger, Andy Cornell, John Jackson, B. Loewe, Claude Marks, Barbara Savage, Heather Thompson, Timothy Tyson, Laura Whitehorn, and Barbie Zelizer, as well as the editorial support of Zoe Trodd, Timothy Patrick McCarthy, and the Journal for the Study of Radicalism *reviewer. Citations were removed from this edition for space reasons. To receive the citations or for other correspondence, contact the author c/o Annenberg School for Communication, 3620 Walnut Street, Philadelphia PA 19104, or to danberger81@gmail.com.*

The Unacceptability of Truth

Of National Lies and Racial America

Tim Wise

This short excerpt from an essay written following the break between Obama and Rev. Jeremiah Wright originally appeared in LiP *magazine.*

9/11 was neither the first, nor worst act of terrorism on American soil. The history of this nation for folks of color, was for generations, nothing less than an intergenerational hate crime, one in which 9/11s were woven into the fabric of everyday life: hundreds of thousands of the enslaved who died from the conditions of their bondage; thousands more who were lynched (as many as 10,000 in the first few years after the Civil War, according to testimony in the Congressional Record at the time); millions of Indigenous persons wiped off the face of the Earth. No, to some, the horror of 9/11 was not new. To some it was not on that day that "everything changed." To some, everything changed four hundred years ago, when that first ship landed at what would become Jamestown. To some, everything changed when their ancestors were forced into the hulls of slave ships at Goree Island and brought to a strange land as chattel. To some, everything changed when they were run out of Northern Mexico, only to watch it become the Southwest United States, thanks to a war of annihilation initiated by the U.S. government. To some, being on the receiving end of terrorism has been a way of life. Until recently it was absolutely normal, in fact.

But white folks have a hard time hearing these simple truths. We find it almost impossible to listen to an alternative version of reality. Indeed, what seems to bother white people more than anything... is being confronted with the recognition that black people do not, by and large, see the world like we do; that Black people, by and large, do not view America as white people view it. We are, in fact, shocked that this should be so, having come to believe, apparently, that the falsehoods to which we cling like a kidney patient clings to a dialysis machine, are equally shared by our darker-skinned compatriots.

This is what James Baldwin was talking about in his classic 1972 work, *No Name in the Street*, wherein he noted: "White children, in the main, and whether they are rich or poor, grow up with a grasp of reality so feeble that they can very accurately be described as deluded—about themselves and the world they live in. White people have managed to get through their entire lifetimes in this euphoric state, but Black people have not been so lucky: a Black man who sees the world the way John Wayne, for example, sees it would not be an eccentric patriot, but a raving maniac."

And so we were shocked in 1987, when Supreme Court Justice Thurgood Marshall declined to celebrate the bicentennial of the Constitution, because, as he noted, most of that history had been one of overt racism and injustice, and to his way of thinking, the only history worth celebrating had been that of the past three or four decades... We're shocked to learn that lots of black folks still perceive the United States as a racist nation—we're literally stunned that people who say they experience discrimination regularly (and who have the social science research to back them up) actually think that those experiences and that data might actually say something about the nation in which they reside. Imagine... It is the historic leadership of the nation that has cast aspersions upon it; it is they who have cheapened it, who have made gaudy and vile the promise of American democracy by defiling it with lies. They engage in a patriotism that is pathological in its implications, that asks of those who adhere to it not merely a love of country but the turning of one's nation into an idol to be worshipped, if not literally, then at least in terms of consequence.

Race, History, and "A Nation of Cowards"

Bill Fletcher Jr.

A version of this article originally appeared on BlackCommentator.com.

U.S. Attorney General Eric Holder's 2009 remarks to the effect that when it comes to race, the United States is a nation of cowards brought forth immediate condemnation by right-wing talk radio. This was to be expected. The more mainstream media also reacted, albeit more mildly. Nevertheless, they have tended to focus on Holder's wording, suggesting that he would be more likely to be heard if he used other language, such as that the people of the United States need to be more sensitive to race.

The problem that Holder encountered was not simply the attitude of the people of the United States toward race, but more fundamentally, the prevailing attitude toward history. The United States has the distinction of being one of the few countries on the planet that has little interest in history as such, and when it is forced to address history, it tends to view history in terms of myth(s). As such, there are few useful lessons, often making history a boring subject in school, not to mention something that is ignored when it is time to develop policy.

Let's take the example of the American Revolution. Most of what passes for the history of the War of Independence either falls into the realm of myth or the selective use of facts. Rarely are we presented with the significant fact that the colonies probably would not have won had it not been for the intervention of the French and Spanish (not to mention Haitian volunteers who are often completely overlooked). Ignoring these facts, except perhaps to acknowledge the Marquis de Lafayette, gives one a completely inaccurate sense of what it took to win independence from Britain, not to mention the impact the American Revolution had on bringing a revolution to France.

We also fail to acknowledge in most histories of the Revolution the mighty contradiction in the middle of the entire process: all men are created equal…vs. slavery.

In the United States, the prevailing approach toward history, then, is to set it aside and assume that we can march forward, ignoring the past and any lessons it has to offer. In a recent speech, I suggested that in other spheres, such an approach would be ridiculed. Consider the horrible bridge collapse in Minneapolis in 2008. Could anyone ever imagine the Minneapolis–St. Paul authorities proposing to ignore the causes of the collapse; failing to investigate anyone or anything responsible, and not taking appropriate action prior to building a new bridge? Such an approach would defy imagination.

Holder's comments were attempting to highlight just that point, specifically in the realm of history and race relations. With all the excitement in connection with the election of the first African American president, there have been too many mainstream white Americans who believe that we have now entered a postracial era where we can all march forward, hand in hand, with the past behind us.

Holder's comments, much more than Obama's March 2008 speech on race, acknowledge that race and racism remains a problem deeply embedded in the fabric of the United States, a problem that must be understood in order for it to be fully eradicated. Although Holder did not indicate specifically how this should happen, he should be loudly applauded for calling the attention of the United States to the necessity for this dialogue.

If we are to build on Holder's comments, what could it mean to confront the "cowardice" when it comes to race? Here are a few ideas:

The Bill Clinton "Race Initiative" was poorly focused. A real dialogue would need to happen at several levels simultaneously. A "Truth and Reconciliation Commission" model might be a good framework. There would need to be, in other words, a commission that directs the work of a multi-year study and dialogue.

The Commission would sponsor studies on different aspects of race and racism in U.S. history, going back to the colonial era and running through the present. Such studies would be published and be the basis for local discussions, available to all, but also targeted at key opinion-makers and political leaders.

A curriculum would be developed that would be introduced in the public school system and that would be made available for private schools, as well as colleges and universities. The U.S. Department of Education would sponsor a special training program for teachers to use the curriculum.

Hearings would be held across the United States, looking at different aspects of race. This would not simply focus on what is happening to people of color, but would also look at the impact of race and racism on the lives of white Americans.

Through vehicles established at the time of the 2001 United Nations World Conference Against Racism, further hemispheric discussions would be encouraged, with the full and constructive participation of the United States, examining race in the Western Hemisphere.

Specific policy recommendations would be put before the President of the United States with the intention of translating them into legislative action items. Such proposals would aim to repair the damage which resulted from the hundreds of years of racist oppression we have experienced in North America.

The question remains as to whether there is the political will—what Holder described as "courage"—for the United States to come to grips with its history. After all, that history is not as Pollyanna-ish as the myth we have been taught, but it is nevertheless more exciting, challenging, and true.

III.   Chickens and Eggs:
War, Race, and Class

Amache: Japanese-American Relocation Center, 1942–1945—Post Office

Mary Jane Sullivan

Amache

Mary Jane Sullivan

What walks with me in this fallow field?
Heifers and crows retrieve the wild within the space
of physical sight, the surface one starts on.
The frame of human presence that once created gardens
hides in the finite remains of concrete,
a landscape of witness.

A voice comes, recedes and disappears.
Perhaps I can chance its reappearance.
Why do I come here?
Amache, Indian Princess of the Great Plains,
the aquifers cracked, the air dried out
and the soil rose into clouds falling like rain.
Amache, human beings categorize nature
turn seeing into tyranny

I am not sure of the tree that catches my eye
but I hear catalpa.
Does it find its form or is empty of it?
Naming can build walls.
Calling people names defines identity,
denies the other that is within.
Over trails of sweated labor, grasslands of brown thrasher and lark bunting
a solitary trucker high gears it towards Kansas,
a highway frontier of the transcendental drift,
a marketplace of products.
Amache, what is untold sidles its own becoming.
I am entering this forgotten city where perhaps the earth will speak
for our living is the common thread.
The silence resembles the escape of the wind born catalpa
points to the threshing of cantaloupe, squash, watermelon
by the hands of immigrants who skirted the edges of this camp;
tied memory into a knot of produce.

How fertile the compost of memory.
Back then we were called, japs, yellow devils,
taken from the cool downwind of Pacific air
taken from home stepping down from orange blood-lit skies
into custody, hands gripping suitcases.
So many faces that no idea can contain the expanse
the face of nature, the face of the universe
an infinite within and then the eye of a lens
where in a shutter the breath expires.

Amache, I, mother to no one,
wears the threatened face for the jailor's
barbed wire fences, guard towers
one mess hall per unit, dirt floors, damp, cold walls.
Stories of home fused with the turning of soil
become remnants. We boarded transports
The measured traces of the rail beds syncopated our journey.
Backtracking along the paths of immigrants, the trails of the Indian,
changing lives, precarious lives
in a stateless state of exception.
In the crackling heat of August I again see
A young woman grasp a letter outside the post office,
boys play touch football, watch towers in the background.
An elderly man at the table with a cup of tea looks up
offers a wildflower to his grandson. The boy smiles.
He is awake in the now where the past and future meet.

To simply be without fear in this experience of loss
determines my love for what I have yet to hold.
Perhaps this moment occupies the wordless.
Perhaps I am here to understand that the world is saturated
with feeding a frenzied body.
Perhaps in the absence of place and the forgoing of pleasure
the seed that does not take root becomes a field of relics
A hearing of the land itself waits on unfinished surfaces.
If I were to only to love this world.
But here is the presence of the no more
underfoot to the presence of the not yet
I cannot really measure the ground of barrack markers.
There are narratives, outside these frames, often in opposition:
Faces that erase the memory of love.

The distortion of a face is the messenger
for the original face and the unkillable human core.
Even when burned into a concrete wall, evaporated at the moment
when struck, mere flames cannot destroy the human rising from ashes,
from containment, from relocation.
The unkillable human does not border on fiction.
Amache, it is something otherwise, something other than being here.
Something that runs against borders, beyond color lines
into the fragments of dirt and the updraft of the wind.

The Antiwar Campaign

More on Force without Violence

Dave Dellinger

The question of economics, the fundamental issue of class and capital, has long plagued progressive movements in the United States. In the struggle to build organizations, political parties, and campaigns which would inspire and include the working class, the peace movement has too often been confused about how best to deal with uniting broad, mainstream sectors of society which may be selectively anti-war while simultaneously mute about class issues which cause war. In addition, the ties between race and class have too often been neglected by a U.S. left that is, in itself, an "undeveloped" state. This section seeks to shed light on the connections between race, class, and militarism, not answering the "chicken and egg" question but accepting that different points of view will be necessary if we are to build principled unity across lines of difference.

This selection is from Dave Dellinger's essential book More Power than We Know, *published in 1975 just as the massive movement he helped lead was beginning to wane. Though long out of print, the book continues to inspire new generations looking for nitty-gritty how-to examples of dealing with war, the causes of war, and the diverse peoples confronting the evils of everyday life.*

We all wish that the movement had been more successful than it was, that its activities had been more sustained and less erratic. We wish the movement had been more resolute and less susceptible to co-optation by hypocritical negotiations, partial bombing halts, and electoral promises by dishonest or impotent peace candidates. We wish the war had ended sooner and with far less victims. We wish that it had ended more completely instead of in the current fuzzy way that allows the government to continue the politics of war by other means. But the lesson of the sixties and early seventies is not that we should abandon the methods that were applied with limited resolution and limited but real success. The lesson is that we must build on these methods, must extend and supplement them, must experiment with ways of making them even more effective.

To complicate matters, we have to put an end not only to war but to the causes of war, not only to imperialist war abroad but to class, race, and sex war at home. For this we need more love, not less; more participatory democracy, not less; more respect for human life, not less; we need less concentration of power, not more; less groups and organizations playing god, not more. In a word, we need more force and less violence.

I

Movement experience since 1956 teaches us that it is necessary to define and resist our own special forms of oppression, to define and refuse our own conventional roles as oppressors (whether as men, whites, adults, achievers, or leaders), and to crystallize and pursue our spiritual as well as material needs. In the absence of any one of these endeavors, our liberation will be more limited than necessary both before and after the end of capitalism.

It also teaches us that it is important for each group to work in conjunction with other groups to bring about an all-inclusive revolution that will do away with the institutional and cultural absurdities that constrict and repress everyone. The spirit and material arrangements of capitalism accentuate all other forms of oppression and disunity, fracturing both human solidarity and universal solidarity (that is, universe-al solidarity or unity with the universe). No one can be fully free or whole so long as society is organized around the drive to get more profits, power, status, or privilege (even wages or wisdom) than someone else—not even those who have renounced those drives but still must relate to a society that has not. We can never completely escape its pollution of the spirit and of human interrelationships any more than we can totally escape from air, sky, water, and the vegetable and animal worlds. We cannot be fully human so long as the media; the legislative, executive, and judicial branches; and the economic, cultural, and educational institutions are dominated and corrupted by antisocial drives. It is not enough that individuals or groups within some or all of these institutions try to modify or compensate for the most glaring antisocial results and sometimes succeed. It is as if we were riding in a bus headed up the wrong side of a divided highway. From time to time the good-hearted driver may swerve to avoid a collision, turn on the stereo, hand out goodies to the passengers, or remind us to fasten our seat belts. But unless we discover that we are going the wrong way, and insist on reversing directions, we are doomed.

II

The idea that the "working class" will be the agent of the saving anti-capitalist revolution has lost all meaning in today's world, unless we extend the definition of "working class" to include the 51 percent of the population who are women and the more than 95 percent who do not own or control the banks and major corporations. (Having a few shares of stock or participating in profit-sharing devices does not confer ownership or control, any more than it gets rid of the antisocial motivations and functions of the economy.) Once we have done this necessary updating of the working class, the term has lost any useful precision of meaning, and its constant reiteration as a link to the revolutionary analyses and programs of the past (as a sign of one's Marxist orthodoxy) is a form of fetishism. On the one hand, the compulsion to prove one's revolutionary orthodoxy and one's devotion to "the working class" can be compared to the need of unfulfilled and insecure men (including many who are sexually impotent) to assert and exalt their maleness. It tends to be a neurotic way of trying to deny and overcompensate for grievous lacks and inadequacies in one's own revolutionary activity. On the other hand, confining revolutionary dynamism to "the workers" is a form of romanticism and crippling self-abnegation that has interesting parallels with the phenomena of men ascribing qualities of intuition and compassion to women, whites at sexuality and rhythm to black, or colonizers lauding the "noble savage" (natives). In each case, there is an element of ascribing to the romanticized group qualities we suppress or fear to assert in our own lives. In each case, the relationship is oppressive. Usually those who insist on the "leadership" or "revolutionary agency" of the "working class" have abandoned their own attempts to be fully active revolutionary agents themselves. Usually they have little association with members of that important section of the population that was once meaningfully referred to as the working class. Or if they do, they have failed to achieve creative alliances and are trying to manipulate or control workers in the interests of their own paternalistic notions of what is good for "workers" and the rest of society. There is another pattern, "tailism," that is also encouraged by working-class fetishism. In tailism, the disoriented and insecure revolutionary initially tries to adopt or imitate the workers' life style, mannerisms, or patterns of behavior, as conceived (usually inaccurately) by the revolutionary. At one stage of their development in the sixties, the Weather-people, RYM II (Revolutionary Youth Movement II), Rising Up Angry, the White Panthers, the Worker-Student Alliance, Progressive Labor Party, Venceremos and the National Caucus of Labor Committees all stressed the daily violence of working class life and dutifully set out to overcome their own "bourgeois" aversion to fist fights and strong-arm tactics today and armed struggle tomorrow.

On the surface tailism appears to renounce manipulation, but in the end it usually does not. Healthy relationships of equality are not established, and sooner or later the tail resents its subservience and tries to wag the unfortunate dog to which it has attached itself; either that or it abandons the struggle and withdraws to its more privileged environs, disillusioned with the human imperfections of the chosen revolutionary agents.

Tailism also often extends to accepting uncritically proposals put forward by whatever workers the "revolutionary vanguard" has joined forces with or attracted into its ranks—although the process usually ends with the idolaters overcompensating at some other point "worker" advancing the proposal is apt to be and agent provocateur sent in by the FBI or the police department, the results can be doubly disastrous. Many whites and white organizations go through at least a stage of tailism in their relations with Blacks, Native Americans, and other oppressed ethnic groups.

The problem of tailism is complicated by the fact that it often represents a genuine but poorly applied effort to compensate for previous isolation or prejudice and to learn from the formerly disdained group. Whites and members of the more privileged sectors of society do need to listen to blacks and "workers," just as men need to listen to women. Sometimes we need to listen, reflect, and absorb for quite a while, resisting the temptation to frame a ready answer (mental or verbal) to each argument or assault, perhaps even postponing a response until a future occasion. The delay may make it possible to develop new understandings and syntheses freed from the frozen patterns of the past. But an automatic, uncritical acceptance of the challenger's view usually prevents genuine absorption and growth as surely as automatic resistance or rejection.

Tailism is demeaning to both parties—and unhealthy attempts to compromise a fact usually recognized by serious blacks, workers, etc. It deprives both of the spirited dialogue and mutual growth they need, on which sound revolutionary organizations and alliances are based. Genuine Marxism has always condemned the practice. The more one's own practice and the practice of one's organization is rooted in serious revolutionary study and protracted struggle, the less apt one is to succumb to it. One is less likely to slip into either fetishism or tailism if one's life as a revolutionary involves some of the risks, dangers, privations, and insecurities imposed on blacks and workers. One doesn't have to seek them out artificially, if one is engaged in serious struggle. The government or other authorities will take care of that for you. Even so, clinging to luxury living, private fortunes, and other middle- or upper-class privileges denied to most of society can contribute to guilty, unequal relationships with whatever prime victims of society one works with whatever prime victims of society one works with—and unhealthy attempts to compensate.

Gandhi used to say that everyone should do her or his share of the "bread labor" of society—the daily work necessary to produce the necessities of life. The current emphasis in movement families, communes, collectives, and projects on sharing the shit work is a step in the same direction. Sharing society's necessary work does not necessarily mean working an a capitalist factory or on an assembly line, though doing so for a year or more is probably as basic to one's education as time spent in college or prison. It can lead to a great understanding of the real strengths and weaknesses of the "working class" and help prevent the fetishes that come from theory without practice and form absurd attempts to act as if Marx in 1848 (*The Communist Manifesto*) or 1883 (the year of his death) could predict the dynamics of revolution in the United States in the 1970s and 1980s. To insist that is to deny the validity of Marxist methodology. Fifteen years before his death, Marx decried such idolatry: "All I know is that I am no Marxist." (Quoted by Wolfgang Leonhard in *Three Faces of Marxism*, Holt, Rinehart, Winston, from *Collected Works of Marx and Engels* vol. XXII [69]).

III

Material and technological conditions have changed drastically since Marx's day. In addition, we have learned a great deal about the dynamics of social change since then (from the women's and nonwhite movements, from the experience of the Soviet and other revolutions) and about nonmaterial human needs. There may have been a time when it would have taken the steelworkers, autoworkers, dock-workers, and other blue-collar workers to supply the motor power for a certain type of revolution, though not necessarily the own we now want, or even the one capable of fulfilling Marx's goal of "the free development of one in the free development of all." There may have been such a time, although to think so may involve a bit of genuflection to orthodoxy even there, since this was not the way revolution came about in Russia, China, North Vietnam, Yugoslavia, Korea, or Cuba, none of which had a sizable industrial working class. Today, postal workers, airplane mechanics, network technicians, computer repairmen and operators, government workers, and countless other members of the "new working class" are at least as strategically located as the "old" working class. For many of them, the gap between their social vision and material expectations, on the one hand, and what capitalist society provides at least as great as that of the workers in heavy industry and what used to be called basic production. Revolution in the technocratic society is not apt to be sparked by old-fashioned economic misery, though the inexcusable poverty and degradation of many can be an important contributing factor. Breakdowns in the ability of the profit-oriented, overmilitarized corporate society to provide almost everyone with the goods and services to which they have become accustomed (as I write, gasoline, fuel oil, meat at reasonable prices, etc.) or which they know are technologically possible (high-grade public transportation; an unpolluted environment; low-rent, livable housing) or humanly possible (privacy, safety, non-Watergate-type government) will play a more important part than some of the considerations that were (or seem) dominant in Marx's day.

This is not to say that any of these factors will produce an apocalyptic moment when capitalist society is no longer able to function at all and everyone, led by important sectors of either the new or the old working class, will insist on alternate values and institutions for themselves and society. History may proceed, on the surface at least, by fits and starts, but not in once-and-for-all apocalypses. And the periods of vast energies and climactic changes usually come when we least expect them—often as delayed reactions to events that the society seemed to take in stride or adapt to with minimal adjustments such as the energy crisis and the Watergate disclosures, or to events that we hardly noticed at the time (such as the changes in agriculture, mores, and psychic tolerance that followed World War II and led to the unexpected eruption of the civil-rights movement ten years later). But even as many activists and their younger brothers and sisters are resting, contemplating, absorbing the lessons from the sixties, or engaging in important fragments of the total struggle, the society is proving itself unable to fulfill its promises, win back the loyalty of its subjects, or prevent the disgust and disillusionment of millions of others, opening them to at least the possibility of new visions and struggles. We shall have to wait to see what is going to happen—weighing, however, not as spectators but as participants in some of the current struggles. The work done by those who opposed the Korean war, when mass meetings usually consisted of fifty of a hundred persons, was as important to the country's political development as the work done in the late sixties, when mass protests often swelled to several hundred thousand. Some of the work being done today should be viewed in that perspective. Without it, the large-scale actions will not return, or will be unnecessarily flawed.

But there is more. We have learned that revolution does not necessarily flow from seizing the power and repressive machinery of the state and using it for the benefit of the people (at least theoretically for their benefit). It may provide some beneficial reforms for a time, gains in the Soviet Union, beginning in 1929 if not before, and the growing gap in Soviet income differentials. (As far back as 1939, at the New York World's Fair, a worker in the Soviet exhibit assured me that "people with special talents can become rich in the Soviet Union"—this at a time when most of the population was still extremely poor. In the early 1950s a Soviet diplomat told a small group of us, whose revolutionary aspirations he underestimated, that "Americans don't understand the Soviet Union. We have our millionaires."

Oppressed people and groups have to make the revolution for themselves. There is no other way—no shortcut to be provided by the "revolutionary workers" or a dedicated band of professional revolutionaries. Eugene Debs once said: I would not be a Moses to lead you into the Promised Land, because if I could lead you into it someone else could lead you out of it.

Political parties that scheme, maneuver, and prepare (with the best of intentions) to take advantage of the strikes and dissatisfactions of workers in heavy industry (or any other "key" segment of society) to lead them into the promised land are apt to have a less than desirable understanding of what the promised land looks like and a less than honorable relationship to those for whom they manipulate and administer the revolution. They are apt to be the first to frustrate its promised by delaying fulfill-ment until…until a new revolution deposes the revolution's guardians. The people who have been "liberated" may not have been liberated at all, even though some crushing burdens may have been removed, as the people of France and Czechoslovakia were rescued but not liberated by the triumphant U.S. and Soviet armies. Unless the people have exercised their own powers of self-reliance and human solidarity before and during the revolution, they are not apt to be in a position (spiritually or materially) to exercise them after it. And then where are they? Representative communism is as debilitating as representative democracy.

We had better aim not at seizing power but at eroding, undermining, dissolving. Democratizing, decentralizing, and distributing it. But when this becomes our goal, it becomes clear that there can be no single sector of society that will make the revolution and no single form of oppression or privation that will motivate it, though some group may take the lead at the particular point in history when the triumph of the revolution, which has been taking place all along, becomes manifest in the release of new energies and the accelerated passing of old forms of power and of inegalitarian relationships. The most we can do to speed up the revolution is to encourage, embody, and express through concrete resistance activities a new attitude toward the material and spiritual relationships of production and distribution, a new spirit of egalitarianism and new respect for the dignity, selfhood, freedom, and inviolability of all human beings, including ourselves, other sections of the working class, and those who currently oppress all of us.

IV

A.J. Muste used to say (after Teresa of Avila, I believe) that there is no way to peace, peace is the way. (The difference between revolutionary word-mongering and serious work is that he usually said so after carefully and precisely proving it.) Similarly there is no way to revolution, revolution is the way—revolution in our own lives, revolution in the organizations and methods through which we struggle, and revolution in our conceptions of what revolution means for both the spiritual and material fulfillment of all human beings. If freedom is one of our goals, we must include in our conception of revolution the freedom of everyone to choose or reject any aspect of what seems revolutionary to us, with the exception that we must be prepared to act to prevent them from interfering with the equally choices of others.

Insofar as I can tell, the revolution, the struggle, and the fulfillment begin now, and in one form or another last forever. Still, it is inspiriting to anticipate and work for the time when no one will be in prison, no one in a bombing plane or under a bomb, no one working as boss or flunky, no one scheming or manipulating to rise above rather than with one's fellows—time when none of the institutions or beliefs of the society assumes that some human beings are less valuable than any others. At that time, the very words "material," "spiritual," "personal," and "political" may conceivably drop out of usage, or at least have very different connotations than today, as it becomes increasingly clear that these interrelated aspects of reality cannot usefully be separated.

Let's Talk about Green Beans

An Interview with Dorothy Cotton

Matt Meyer and Iris Marie Bloom

This essay originally appeared as part of the War Resisters League organizing packet The Violence of Racism and Militarism: South Africa and the United States.

Matt Meyer and Iris Marie Bloom: What have been some of the more positive memories you've had about Black and white organizing together? What have been the lessons learned from the civil rights campaigns?

Dorothy Cotton: Initially, in the places where I've lived and worked in the South it was all Black people working together. I was in Petersburg, Virginia, when I got involved in the civil rights movement, in demonstrations, and it was all black. I do remember that in Montgomery, where the Montgomery bus boycott was going on, there were two or three outstanding examples of whites who really stuck their necks out at a time when whites were really brutalized for relating to the black struggle.

But the kind of organizing that we did at a very grassroots level, starting in my case in Petersburg, was Black. I don't ever remember white people getting involved in Petersburg. When I went to Atlanta, Georgia, to become a staff member with Dr. Martin Luther King we inherited the Citizenship Education Program that you may know about. Again, in the first years, the people who came to those workshops that were run by Andrew Young and myself were all black. Eventually we got a white person on our staff working directly with the training program and it became his job to go into Appalachia to do some recruiting, to talk about Dr. King and his work. A few whites, in fear and trembling, started to relate to us. You could tell they were very nervous about it, but they did begin.

In the Citizenship Education Program, which was the training program for SCLC (Southern Christian Leadership Conference), thirty, four, fifty, sometimes sixty or more people would come together every single month and we'd stay together for five days. The whole point was that these people would learn to think in new ways about themselves, about who they were, and about what they could do. They would come to feel that they could assume some responsibility for their lot in life.

We had run this program for a few years when we started reaching out to whites and eventually had a group of whites come to one of the training sessions. That was a very dramatic event because it was sort of a dream that we could actually be in these sessions together. I remember having tears in my eyes when white people sat in those workshops and started to tell some of the same kinds of stories that black people had told about their suffering, their oppression, their brutalization by police—not because they were black but because they were poor. I do remember crying at a workshop because I was so struck, I was so shaken by that realization and by my own not knowing that white people too suffered. I think one of the scars left by segregation is that we all develop misconceptions of each other. So many whites in the South felt that all white people were doing just fine. They were white, they were affluent, they had plenty, and there was just not this sense that they suffered too. I remember learning that lesson and started to open my heart, open myself, to them and realize that we were all in this together.

MM and IMB: Those whites who were part of the Citizenship Education Program were not organizers. When did Black and white activists start working together?

Dorothy: We could point to Mississippi Summer, when the Freedom Party in Mississippi—which was blacks working for change, trying to get black people involved in the political process and understanding why they ought to register to vote—decided to have what they called Mississippi Summer or Freedom Summer. They brought in hundreds and hundreds of students from places north. That's one group of people who came down to help organize.

MM and IMB: What were the relationships going on there? Were they basically very cooperative or were there some tensions?

Dorothy: Both. There was a real opening of arms and hearts and houses to the whites who came down to help with the voter registration drive. Many of these whites got really turned on by the movement and felt that they were involved in something real. But what also happened was that they came down with greater skills. Some of these people worked in the SNCC office—Student Nonviolent Coordinating Committee— and they were skilled in using electric typewriters, for example. I remember some-body being really upset and feeling intimidated that some of the whites coming down had these greater skills than the poor blacks, some of whom had not even seen an elec-tric typewriter. Some of them began to feel that they didn't want these people around with the greater skills taking over their struggle.

There was sort of a love-hate relationship in a number of quarters that I picked up more from SNCC than SCLC. At SCLC there was a recognition that blacks needed to see some black role models in leadership positions. That was the dynamic in both SNCC and SCLC. Tensions did rise when whites assumed leadership roles. Eventually that became a reason to ask whites to leave some sections in SNCC. Blacks realized that they needed to do it for themselves.

MM and IMB: Aside from making clear who should take public leadership roles and the other extreme, which is asking folks to leave, what were other ways that folks in SCLC or SNCC dealt with these issues?

Dorothy: We were great discussants. People who organized in the movement just about lived together. We were together all the time and we dealt with it simply by raising it. Sometimes there were healthy discussions and sometimes they were angry discussions. But there was an attempt in some quarters to work it through. There were few whites who were strong enough to stick it out while Black folks I'd say grew strong enough to have them there as colleagues in the struggle.

MM and IMB: How do you think that that history has impacted on the movement today?

Dorothy: On the one hand I think that students, younger people, do talk. There's not a lot of organizing going on among the student population that I touch. I'm at Cornell University and, when students were involved in anti-apartheid divestment protest activities on campus, there were many, many more whites involved in that than Blacks. I felt very badly about that, but there were more whites giving leadership to that effort on campus. We were always surprised when we saw Blacks in the groups because it was so rare to see Blacks involved.

I traveled to about eight cities during the King birthday celebrations and I heard students pleading and asking, "What can we do?" I didn't see a lot of organizing—or any organizing going on—among students. But in organizations where there are older people involved, my sense is that in all of these there is a desire to be more broadly representative of the population. Most of the predominantly white organizations often articulate their wish for blacks and other minorities to be involved, I had a fairly dramatic experience recently when I went to the Soviet Union in October with a group from the FOR (Fellowship of Reconciliation) and I was the one Black person in that group of seven. I realized that there's still a great deep-seated discomfort of whites around blacks. I think that I realized what a large piece of work that we still need to do. The question is which came first, the chicken or the egg. Do Blacks not involve themselves in large numbers because they pick up certain vibrations from whites, which suggest that whites cannot relate to them as persons. But somehow you sort of stand out as some sort of special entity requiring a special kind of reaction, and so we are never persons together?

I'm very conscious of a piece of work that we need to do, and that is to create a lot of forums where people can bring their feelings out; to create a lot of projects where we in facts do things together across racial lines; and to have incorporated in those projects intentional moments when we dialogue about how we are being together. How are we as persons together; let's stop and check out feelings.

Julius Lester, who teaches at Amherst, was talking about whites who come up to him and who want to talk about some of the grave and profound issues of the world. He said something like he was rather turned off by that and I realized I can relate to that, to be turned off by that. He said, "Why can't we just talk about green beans? First." If we can talk about green beans first, then maybe we can go on later and talk about how to do some other things—how to end the war, and how to build an organization, how to do a lot of things. What he's saying is be a person with me first. If you're too afraid and uncomfortable to be a person with me first, we can't organize anything together.

I Beg to Differ

Ellen Barfield

I have always felt disagreement with the phrase at the end of WRL's expanded website membership statement that racism is a *cause* of war (and to strive nonviolently for the removal of the causes of war, including racism, sexism, and all forms of human exploitation). This book's preparation finally created the push I needed to articulate it. I do *not* agree that racism, or any of the other societal ills of discrimination, *cause* war. I mean, I cannot recall a war created by the attackers simply saying, "We hate their skin color. Let's wipe them out."

In my estimation it is nearly always greed that is the underlying cause of war, be the putative reason the desire for territory or resources (in that case perceived need, which is greed) the revolutionary urge to be in control of a people's own social and economic governance (less clearly greed, but certainly the desire to keep more of the profits of a people's effort to themselves), or struggles over power—and power allows the exploitation of resources, religious, or political differences—which, like nearly all wars, include taking territory and spoils, the hope for which often encourages differences of opinion to amplify to war.

Tribal and dynastic struggles are clearly about power to control territory and resources, as are colonial and imperialistic ones. The U.S. Revolution is an excellent example of the wealthy colonists persuading others to fight to wrest control of the economy from the former leader. Even the Crusades, apparently about European Christians "freeing" the "Holy Land" from its resident Muslims, were also about opening trade routes through an area whose common designation by Western Europeans, the "Middle East," refers to its location between them and the Asian source of tea, porcelain, and other desired trade goods.

Though I do not think racism a *cause* of war, I do consider it one of the primary *enablers* of war. Spurring racism is an easy way to persuade often otherwise reluctant regular folks to embrace the war. Sadly, a very common human tendency is to designate in-group and out-group, who is us, and who is them. Racial differences, differences in skin color, hair texture, shape of features, are rapidly noticed and often feared and hated. Along with the physical differences usually go cultural differences, religious, philosophical, political.

Different appearances and beliefs are primary ways people develop attitudes of better than and worse than. A common emotional trick is for a group to bolster its feelings of worth by denigrating another group's characteristics. The racism simmers along in relatively calm circumstances, with isolated instances of abuse, until a need is dimly perceived which can be met by stealing the land and resources of the different looking and thinking people. Then war fever is stirred by demagogues, fearmongering ensues about the evil of the new enemy, and relatively respectable cover stories are created to justify the war.

With the European colonialist impulse to explore, conquer, and take, the resident natives in the new lands had darker skins and fewer weapons, but mouth-watering resources, so invasion and oppression became widespread. More classical racism, not just prejudice but the power to enforce discrimination, justified the massive thievery of natural resources and the labor of the native people. Later, under the circumstances of existing racist oppression and exploitation when revolutionary sentiment arose, understandable race-based hatred and revenge inspired anti-colonial wars, and, wonderfully, overthrow of colonialism without war.

So I certainly do agree that racism and war are closely related, just not as cause and effect. And I think it is really important to avoid the easy throwaway line that discrimination *causes* war. Unfortunately, ignorant westerners fed on myths of exceptionalism are too often oblivious to the historical atrocities of empire, so that when oppressed people rise up, violently or not, it is common to hear again the racist assumptions of backwardness and inherent viciousness, blaming the longtime victims. The whine, "Why do they hate us?"

Militarism and Racism: A Connection?

David McReynolds

I t is likely that my own contribution to this project may be a minority view, but if so it can help to sharpen the discussion. I say a "minority view" because I'm not convinced that there is any direct link between war and racism.

That the United States is haunted by racism is true enough. And it is true, as applies to our own country, that "deeply as Americans love peace, there has never been a war they didn't feel they ought to fight." If one thinks of the Spanish-American War or the First World War we have two examples of wars into which the country stumbled, in the first case because of William Randolph Hearst (but what a grand Empire it gave us!), in the second case because the Germans had made the mistake of sinking an American passenger ship (not widely known is that Woodrow Wilson was so angry about British interference with U.S. ships at sea that he had contemplated asking Congress for a declaration of war against Great Britain!).

Even in the case of our Civil War, one of the most terrible wars of the nineteenth century, race was not the primary cause. That was, in my view, the matter of the high tariffs which hurt the South, opened the door to secession and accounted for the support Britain gave the Confederacy. The issue of slavery was always in the background, but I don't feel it was the main reason. (And, while it may be heresy to suggest it, the Civil War did not result in anything more than the nominal freeing of Southern Blacks. They remained under profound oppression, forced into share cropping, unable to vote, unable to count on the courts for justice—the true "beginning of the end" of the fact of slavery in the Southern states came with the Civil Rights movement a century after the end of the Civil War).

Racism is a problem for Northern Europeans (and for those they encountered as they expanded their empire!). In North America, Africa, and India, the Northern Europeans sought to keep the races separate and frowned on intermarriage. Southern Europeans, while every bit as brutal in their dealings with the natives of the New World or Asia, were much more likely to accept intermarriage. I do not want to gloss over the degree of racism in colonial Cuba, Brazil, etc. but the only place in North America where I think the lines of color wavered, at least after the sun went down, was New Orleans.

But on the matter of war, there are very few links that I can think of between racism and war. In the terrible case of the conflict between the Hutu and the Tutsi, the conflict was not racial but tribal. There were many roots to the Burundi Genocide, but I don't think race is one.

The massive murders in Cambodia by the Khmer Rouge were so terrible that one is tempted to look for some logical explanation—such as, possibly, the hostility between the urban and the rural populations. But in these cases of mass violence what stands out is how little real difference there was between the murderers and the murdered.

If we look to Germany and the Nazis, we think we see, as we peer back into history, separations between the Jews and the non-Jews in Germany that, in fact, did not exist. What remains most shocking about the mass murder of the Jews was that they had integrated so well into German life that for the most part German Jews took few precautions. (The Nazi murders of the Roma, and the Slavs, was different, in that these were never part of Germany in 1930, and could be seen as "the other.")

I've given three cases where terrible outbreaks of violence took place that were not wars, and were not rooted in race. But there is one aspect of these killings—and of war itself—which is linked to racism, and that is the degree to which racism makes it possible for one group to see those of a differing color or religion as "the other." Once any ideology is able to define another group as "the other," violence is much easier, whether it is war, some form of genocide, or the unspoken crime of the mass imprisonment of so many of the American underclass.

If we look to Northern Ireland, racial differences do not exist. While there are class differences between the Catholics and the Protestants, the religious differences drove Northern Ireland into the long darkness of the "troubles." In the Middle East it is not racism that drives the Israelis and Palestinians against each other but the fact that the Israelis are—for the most part—a European transplant into an Arab world. It is colonialism, not racism, which explains the tensions there.

War seems to me very distinct from racism. One can have a deeply racist society (such as the United States) and yet not have a war. And one can have wars between peoples who have virtually no significant racial differences. World Wars I and II were for the most part between nations and people who had far more in common than they had that separated them. The alliances we saw in both wars owed more to traditional power blocs than to race. (In both the First and Second World Wars France and Britain allied with Russia.)

Where race might have played a role—though I doubt it—would be the question of whether the United States would have dropped nuclear bombs on Germany. Certainly American racism was there for all to see—going back to the efforts to curb "Oriental" immigration to the United States, the second class category of the Chinese brought in as laborers on the West Coast, to the sending of the Japanese on the West Coast to concentration camps, the record is clear. I've no question it made it easier to drop nuclear weapons on the Japanese. But I'm not sure how much easier.

What we may not understand from our position in 2009 is how savage the feelings were in the 1940s toward the Germans (as they had been, incidentally, during the First World War). The Germans were "Huns." When thinking about postwar plans, the American fury with the "Huns" who had been the enemy twice in thirty years, led to very serious consideration of plans to dismember Germany, to prevent it from rebuilding heavy industry, so that the "German enemy" could not rise yet a third time. I am afraid it is only too possible to believe that, if the tide of war had not changed by 1944, if the Nazis forces threatened the Allied armies with defeat, a nuclear bomb would not have been used in Germany.

If we can, for the moment, leave racism behind and just think about the nature of mass violence directed against whole populations, it is remarkable how irrational it is, how "limitless" it becomes once started. The recent Israeli attack on Gaza, which was so out of proportion to the Palestinian rockets fired into Israel, is a contemporary example of the deliberate use of massive violence against largely civilian targets. There was nothing particularly "racial" about the Japanese rape of Nanking. The Allied bombing of civilian targets in World War II was horrendous—the virtually unrestrained, and very deliberate targeting of civilians. This was, painfully, true also in the Korean War, which the United States has never properly reexamined, and the Vietnam War. Does one need to look at the mass killing in former Yugoslavia to see that race was not the key factor?

War generally has some economic basis, some effort to control resources. But that hardly explains why Alexander the Great marched through India. As I indicated earlier, the United States nearly went to war against Great Britain rather than Kaiser's Germany. The Japanese thrust into China and the Pacific cost them, economically, far more than it could have gained them.

It was, I think, the glory of an expanded Japanese Empire which drove that war. Certainly the U.S. wars in the Gulf area have no racial basis that I can think of, but rather, and rather obviously, the desire to control the oil. But even that has always seemed to me not quite rational. The money needed to maintain U.S. control over that area is a vast hidden subsidy to the price of gasoline—we not only pay a certain amount per gallon for the gasoline, but we pay a huge fee in taxes to maintain the military. When, ironically, oil is a "fungible commodity," always available on the world market to those with the dollars. The Japanese, who have virtually no natural energy resources, have built their own industrial empire by buying the oil on that world market.

Which leads me to suggest that war is not as rational a means of gaining access to needed supplies as it may seem. And that would lead us into a deeper discussion of why the institution of war remains so powerful, so acceptable to virtually all nations. And that would be a different and longer discussion.

On the matter of the links between racism and war, I just don't see them.

Looking at the White Working Class Historically

David Gilbert

O ne of the supreme issues for our movement is summed-up in the contradictions of the term "white working class." On one hand there is the class designation that should imply, along with all other workers of the world, a fundamental role in the overthrow of capitalism. On the other hand, there is the identification of being part of a "white" oppressor nation.

Historically, we must admit that the identity with the oppressor nation has been primary. There have been times of fierce struggle around economic issues but precious little in the way of a revolutionary challenge to the system itself. There have been moments of uniting with Black and other Third World workers in union struggles, but more often than not an opposition to full equality and disrespect for the self-determination of other oppressed peoples. These negative trends have been particularly pronounced within the current era of history (since WWII). White labor has been either a legal opposition within or an active component of the U.S. imperial system.

There have been two basic responses to this reality by the white left:

1. The main position by far has been opportunism. This has entailed an unwillingness to recognize the leading role within the United States of national liberation struggles, a failure to make the fight against white supremacy a conscious and prime element of all organizing, and, related to the above, a general lack of revolutionary combativeness against the imperial state. More specifically, opportunism either justifies the generally racist history of the white working class and our left or romanticizes that history by presenting it as much more anti-racist than reality merits.

2. Our own tendency, at its best moments, has recognized the leading role of national liberation and the essential position of solidarity to building any revolutionary consciousness among whites. We have often, however, fallen into an elitist or perhaps defeatist view that dismisses the possibility of organizing significant numbers of white people particularly working class whites.

There is very little analysis, and even less practice, that is both real about the nature and consciousness of the white working class and yet holds out the prospect of organizing a large number on a revolutionary basis. This fissure will not be joined by some magical leap of abstract thought—either by evoking classical theories of class or by lapsing into cultural or biological determinism. We must use our tools of analysis (materialism) to understand concretely how this contradiction developed (historically). But an historical view cannot be static. In seeing how certain forces developed, we must also look (dialectically) at under what conditions and through what means the contradiction can be transformed.

In this review, I want to look at three historical studies that contribute to the needed discussion:

1. Ted Allen's two essays in *White Supremacy* (a collection printed by Sojourner Truth Organization);
2. W.E.B. Du Bois, *Black Reconstruction* (New York: 1933);
3. J. Sakai, *Settlers: The Mythology of the White Proletariat* (Chicago: 1983)

Ted Allen's "White Supremacy in U.S. History" and "Slavery and the Origins of Racism"

Allen's two essays provide us with a very cogent and useful account of the development of the structure of white supremacy in the United States. He shows both how this system was consciously constructed by the colonial ("Plantation Bourgeoisie") ruling class and what was the initial impact on the development of the white laborers. Contrary to the cynical view that racism is a basic to human nature and that there always have been (and therefore always will be) a fundamental racial antagonism, Allen show that systematic white supremacy developed in a particular historical period, for specific material reasons.

"Up to the 1680's little distinction was made in the status of Blacks and English and other Europeans held in involuntary servitude. Contrary to common belief the status of Blacks in the first seventy years of Virginia colony was not that of racial, lifelong, hereditary slavery, and the majority of the whites who came were not free." Black and white servants intermarried, escaped together, and rebelled together" (3).

A rapidly developing plantation system required an expanding labor supply. The solution was both to have more servants and to employ them for longer terms. A move from fixed-term servitude (e.g., seven years) to perpetual slavery would be valuable to the ruling class of the new plantation economy. The question for analysis is not so much why there was a transition to chattel slavery but why it was not imposed on the white servants as well as on the Blacks. To analyze this development we need to understand that any method of exploiting labor requires a system of social control.

There were a series of servile rebellions that threatened the plantation system in the period preceding the transition to racially designated chattel slavery and white supremacy. Allen cites numerous examples. In 1661, Black and Irish servants joined in an insurrectionary plot in Bermuda. In 1663, in Virginia, there was an insurrection for the common freedom of Blacks, whites and Indian servants. In the next twenty years, there were no fewer than ten popular and servile revolts and plots in Virginia. Also many Black and white servants successfully escaped (to Indian territories) and established free societies.

Allen places particular emphasis on Bacon's Rebellion that began in April 1676. This was a struggle within the ruling class over "Indian policy," but Bacon resorted to arming white and Black servants, promising them freedom. Allen says "the transcendent importance" of this revolt is that "the armed working class, Black and white, fought side by side for the abolition of slavery." He mentions, but doesn't deal with the reality, that Bacon's cause was to exterminate the Indians. Allen's focus is on the formation of chattel slavery, but it is a problem that he doesn't analyze the other major foundation of white supremacy: the theft of Native lands through genocide.

The twenty year period of servile rebellions made the issue of social control urgent for the plantation bourgeoisie, at the same time as they economically needed to move to a system of perpetual slavery. The purpose of creating a basic White/Black division was in order to have one section of labor police and control the other. As Allen says, "The non-slavery of white labor was the indispensable condition for the slavery of black labor."[1]

A series of laws were passed and practices imposed that forged a qualitative distinction between white and Black labor. In 1661, a Virginia law imposed twice the penalty time for escaped English bond-servants who ran away in the company of an African life-time bond-servant. Heavy penalties were imposed on white women servants who bore children fathered by Africans. One of the very first white slave privileges was the exemption of white servant women from work in the fields and the requirements through taxes to force Black children to go to work at twelve, while white servant children were excused until they were fourteen. In 1680, Negroes were forbidden to carry arms, defensive or offensive. At the same time, it was made legal to kill a Negro fugitive bond-servant who resisted recapture.

What followed 1680 was a twenty-five-year period of laws that systematically drew the color line as the limit on various economic, social, and political rights. By 1705, "the distinction between white servants and Black slavery were fixed: Black slaves were to be held in life long hereditary slavery and whites for five years, with many rights and protections afforded to them by law" (6).

---

[1]   There were several reasons why Blacks were the planters' choice for perpetual slavery. 1) After the English revolution of 1640–1666, the demand for labor expanded in England and limited the supply of English labor available to the colonies. 2) The alliance against feudalism that the English bourgeoisie had by necessity forged with the lower classes limited their ability to impose wholesale slavery. 3) In the colonies, it would be harder for escaped Black slaves to blend in with the dominant white settler population.

We can infer from these series of laws that white laborers were not "innately racist" before the material and social distinctions were drawn. This is evidenced by the rulers' need to impose very harsh penalties against white servants who escaped with Blacks or who bore them children. As historian Philip Bruce observed of this period, many white servants "had only recently arrived from England, and were therefore comparatively free from ... race prejudice."

The white bond-servants now could achieve freedom after five years service: the white women and children, at least, were freed from the most arduous labor. The white bond servant, once freed, had the prospect of the right to vote and to own land (at the Indians' expense).

These privileges did not come from the kindness of the planters' hearts nor from some form of racial solidarity. (Scottish coal miners were held in slavery in the same period of time.) Quite simply, the poor whites were needed and used as a force to suppress the main labor force: the African chattel slaves. The poor white men constituted the rank and file of the militias and later (beginning in 1727) the slave patrols. They were given added benefits, such as tax exemptions to do so. By 1705, after Blacks had been stripped of the legal right to self-defense, the white bond servant was given a musket upon completion of servitude. There was such a clear and conscious strategy that by 1698 there were even "deficiency laws" that required the plantation owners to maintain a certain ratio of white to African servants. The English Parliament, in 1717, passed a law making transportation to bond-servitude in the plantation colonies a legal punishment for crime. Another example of this conscious design is revealed in the Council of Trade and Plantation report to the king in 1721 saying that in South Carolina "Black slaves have lately attempted and were very nearly succeeding in a new revolution—and therefore, it may be necessary to propose some new law for encouraging the entertainment of more white servants in the future."

It would be important to have a concomitant analysis of the role of the theft of Indian land and of the impact of the slave trade itself. Allen's analysis of early plantation labor, however, provides an invaluable service.[2]

When Black and white labor were in the same conditions of servitude, there was a good deal of solidarity. A system of white supremacy was consciously constructed in order to extend and intensify exploitation (through chattel slavery) and have shock troops (poor, but now privileged, whites) to suppress slave rebellions.

Thus the 1680–1705 period is a critical benchmark essential to understanding all subsequent North American history.[3] As Allen tells us, "It was the bourgeoisie's deliberately contrived policy of differentiation between white and Black labor through

---

2   He notes that Black historian Lerone Bennett Jr. also developed the same basic analysis.

3   Many Black nationalists cite this period as when an oppressed Black (or New Afrikan) Nation was within North America. This set of laws and color restrictions clearly went beyond the class exploitation of laborers to the systematic oppression of Afrikans as a people.

the system of white skin privileges for white labor that allowed the bourgeoisie to use the poor whites as an instrument of social control over the Black workers" (5).

Allen refers to, but doesn't fully develop, the impact of white supremacy on the white laborers. His general analysis is that by strengthening capitalist rule it reinforced exploitation of whites too: "white supremacy [was] the keystone of capitalist rule which left white labor poor, exploited and increasingly powerless with respect to their rulers and exploiters." But since "the mass of poor whites was alienated from the black proletariat and enlisted as enforcers of bourgeois power" (40), it would be useful to have more analysis of the interplay of these two contradictory roles: exploited/enforcers. In any case, the overall effect was to break the white workers from their proletarian class struggle alongside Blacks and to bind them more tightly to their own ruling class.

W.E.B. Du Bois's *Black Reconstruction, 1860–1880*

Du Bois's work is a classic study, an absolutely essential reading to understanding U.S. history. The book deals not only with the Reconstruction period that followed the Civil War but also with the War itself and the period of slavery preceding it. This review will only focus on the insights about the relationship of white labor to Black people and their struggles. There are, however, two essential theses that Du Bois puts forward that should be pointed out here:

1. The slaves were not freed by Lincoln's or by the Union's benevolence. The slaves essentially freed themselves. First they fled the plantations in great numbers, depleting the South of labor for its wartime economy. Secondly, they volunteered to fight with the Union to defeat the slavocracies. The Emancipation Proclamation of 1863 came only when Lincoln realized that he needed to use Black troops in order to win the war. (It applied only to states at war with the Union.) 200,000 Black troops made the decisive difference in the war.

2. Reconstruction was not this period of unbridled corruption and of heartless oppression of the noble (white) South that has since been depicted by the propaganda of history. Not only did Reconstruction see the active role of Black people in the government, but also, based on that, it was an era of democratic reform that brought such things as free public education, public works, and advances in women's rights to the South. At the same time, Du Bois shows how Reconstruction was defeated by a systematic campaign of terror, with the complicity of the capitalist North.

Du Bois's analysis of the prewar south, starts with the basic structures (whose origins Allen described) in place and well developed. The system of slavery demanded a special police force and such a force was made possible and unusually effective by the presence of poor whites. By this time there were "more white people to police the slaves than there were slaves" (12).

Still, there were very important class differentiations within the white population. 7 percent of the total white Southern population owned three-quarter of the slaves. Seventy percent owned no slaves at all. To Du Bois, a basic issue is why the poor whites would agree to police the slaves. Since slavery competed with and thereby undercut the wages of white labor in the North, wouldn't it seem natural for poor whites in general to oppose slavery?

Du Bois presents two main reasons:

1. Poor whites were provided with nonlaboring jobs as overseers, slave-drivers, members of slave patrols. (Du Bois doesn't indicate what percentage of whites held jobs like this).

2. There was the "vanity" of feeling associated with the master and the dislike of "negro" toil. The poor white never considered himself a laborer, rather he aspired to himself own slaves. These aspirations were not without some basis. (About a quarter of the Southern white population were petty bourgeois, small slave-owners). "The result was that the system was held stable and intact by the poor white... Gradually the whole white South became an armed and commissioned camp to keep Negroes in slavery and to kill the black rebel" (12).

There was another factor that had heavy impact on both poor whites in the South and the Northern working class. In early America, land was free (based on genocide of the Indians) and thus acquiring property was a possibility for nearly every thrifty worker. This access to property not only created a new petty bourgeoisie emerging out of the white working class, it also created an ideology of individual advancement rather than collective class struggle as the answer to exploitation.

The Northern working class tended to oppose the *spread* of slavery but not oppose slavery itself. If slavery came to the North it would compete with and undercut free labor. If the plantation system spread to the West, it would monopolize the land that white workers aspired to settle as small farmers. But there was very little proabolition sentiment in the white labor movement. Northern white labor saw the threat of competition for jobs from the fugitive slaves and the potentially millions behind them if abolition prevailed in the South. There was considerable racism toward freed Blacks in the North.

The most downtrodden sector of white workers—the immigrants—might seem to have had the least stake in white supremacy. But the racism had its strongest expression among these sections because at the bottom layer of white labor, they felt most intensely the competition from Blacks for jobs, and blamed Blacks for their low wages.[4] During the Civil War, the Irish and other immigrant workers were the base for the "anti-draft" riots in the Northern cities. These were really straight out murderous race riots against the local Black population.

For Du Bois, the position of the Northern working class, appears somewhat irrational. Freed slaves did represent, its true, potential competition for jobs. However, Du Bois argues, "What they (white workers) failed to comprehend was that the black man enslaved was an even more formidable and fatal competition than the black man free" (20).

This analysis seems inadequate. As materialists we have to wonder why such a formidable consensus of a class and its organizations would hold a position over a long period of time that was opposed to their interests.[5] In addition to the issue of competition, we must ask if the super-exploitation of black labor was used to provide some additional benefits for white labor—in a way, did the formation of the U.S. empire anticipate some of the basic oppressor/oppressed worker relations described by Lenin with the development of imperialism? Certainly the issue in relationship to the Native Americans is clear: genocide provided the land, which allowed many white workers to "rise" out of their class (which also strengthened the bargaining power of remaining laborers). This reality firmly implanted one of the main pillars of white supremacy. There were undoubtedly also some direct benefits from the super-exploitation of slave labor for the white working class that Du Bois does not analyze. Data presented in *Settlers* indicates that white American workers earned much higher wages than their British counterparts.

Du Bois sees the material basis of white labor antagonism to Blacks as based in competition for jobs and its impact on wage levels. On the other hand he sees the existence of a slave strata as even worse competition. But how did this second aspect play itself out? Perhaps as direct competition only for the white working class in the South. But here there was the counterforce of slavery being the direct basis for a large section of whites to become petty bourgeois, while others got jobs overseeing and controlling Black labor. It isn't clear how slavery in the South would directly compete with Northern labor—and on the contrary some benefits might be passed on as a result of the super exploitation of Black labor. Certainly first the wealth generated by King Cotton and then the availability of the cheap raw materials were cornerstones of the Northern industrialization that provided and expanded jobs.

Further, this issue cannot be treated in isolation from the other main pillar of white supremacy—the availability of land based on genocide of the Native Americans.

---

4   The most frequently cited examples of "competition" are Black workers lowering wages or, in later years, being used as strike breakers. But in reality the role of the white immigrants wasn't that passive. Before 1850, Black workers predominated in many trades in both Northern and Southern cities. A huge influx of white foreigners, particularly after the Irish famine in 1846, caused a radical change. The unskilled Irish, in particular, pushed Blacks out of these occupations (Philip Foner, *Organized Labor & The Black Worker, 1619-1981* [New York: International Publishers: 1982], 6).

5   Even prominent European Marxists who came here soon dropped the demand for abolition.

It is doubtful that the capitalist class would have opened up the West for settlement without a guarantee of still having an adequate supply of cheap labor for industrialization. Earlier in England, to prepare the way for manufacture, there had been the brutal enclosure movements, which forced peasants off the land in order to create a large supply of cheap labor. In North America, the movement was in the opposite direction: people were actually settling the land, becoming peasants, while manufacture was developing. It is unlikely this would have been allowed without slavery to guarantee cheap labor for the main cash crops and raw materials, and an influx of immigrant labor into the Northern cities.

In any case, the predominant position among Northern labor opposed the spread of slavery but did not favor abolition; these positions were punctuated by occasional race riots with a white working class base. In addition to the aspiration to rise to the petty bourgeoisie, a labor aristocracy began to develop in the prewar period, usually based in longer established white settlers as opposed to the immigrant workers. After 1850 unions of skilled labor began to separate from common labor. These skilled unions established closed shops that excluded Blacks and farmers.

After the Civil War the defeat of the slavocracy, the presence of the Union Army, the reality of thousands of armed Black troops, all should have created radically new conditions and possibilities for Black/poor white alliance in the South. Du Bois, in his very positive view of Reconstruction, goes so far as to describe it as "a dictatorship of labor" in the South (187). Reconstruction with the important Black role in Southern politics, did mean a lot of democratic reforms while it lasted. There are some significant indications of poor whites allying. For example, early on in Reconstruction, Mississippi and South Carolina had popular conventions with significant poor white involvement. The Jim Crow laws, later passed in Mississippi, found it necessary to place severe strictures against whites associating with Blacks. But there isn't much evidence of a solid alliance from any large sector of poor whites.

The basis for an alliance seems clear. The basic problem of Reconstruction was economic; the kernel of the economy was land. Both freed slaves and poor whites had an interest in acquiring land. It would seem logical to have an alliance to expropriate the old plantation owners.

Du Bois gives several reasons why this alliance didn't come to fruition:

1. Poor whites were determined to keep Blacks from access to the better land from which slavery had driven the white peasants (i.e., if people took over ownership of land they had worked, the ex-slaves would get the choice plantation land).
2. Poor whites were afraid that the planters would control the Black vote and thus be able to politically defeat the poor white's class aspirations.
3. Petty bourgeois whites still wanted to have cheap Black labor to exploit.

4. White labor was determined to keep Blacks from work that competed with them; poor whites were desperately afraid of losing their jobs.
5. White labor, while given low wages, were compensated with social status, such as access to public parks, schools, etc.; the police were drawn from their ranks; the courts treated them leniently. In short, white labor saw a threat to their racial prerogatives in every advance of the Blacks.

These reasons were all very real. However, it is not clear on the face of it, why they should override the potential for joint expropriation of the plantation owners. We also must look at a factor that Du Bois mentions but does not develop sufficiently, the power backing up Reconstruction was the Union Army. Despite the importance of Black troops, there is no indication that the Union Army as a structured institution was ever anything over than an instrument of Northern capital. Northern capital wanted to break the national political power of the old plantation owners (hence the Black vote) but they certainly didn't want to support the liquidation of private property, even in the South. In fact, by 1868 the Union Army had forcibly retaken almost all the plantation land seized and worked by communities of freed slaves (See Vincent Harding, *There Is a River*). Thus died the promise of "40 acres and a mule."

Thus, Du Bois's characterization of Reconstruction as a "dictatorship of labor" backed by the Union Army seems overdrawn. He is much more on the mark when he says "It was inconceivable, therefore, that the masters of Northern industry through their growing control of American government, were going to allow the laborers of the South any more real control of wealth and industry than was necessary to curb the political power of the planters" (345).

It seems to me that with the presence and dominance of Union troops, the joint expropriation of the old plantations did not appear as a very tangible possibility. It is in that context, that the poor whites' overwhelming choice was to try to reconsolidate their old white privileges. (This would also be the natural spontaneous choice given the history and culture.) The power context also reflects on the question of alignments on a national scale.

Looking nationwide, Du Bois reasons, "there *should* have been [emphasis added]...a union between the champions of universal suffrage and the rights of the freedmen, together with the leaders of labor, the small landholders of the West, and logically, the poor whites of the South" against the Northern industrial oligarchy and the former Southern oligarchy (239). This union never took place. Du Bois cites two main reasons:

1. The old anti-Black labor rivalry.
2. The old dream of becoming small farmers in the West becoming a dream of labor-exploiting farmers and land speculation.

Here again Du Bois's explanation, while helpful, does not seem to be sufficiently materialist; the implication seems to be white workers going against their more basic material interest. We need to also specify some of the concrete benefits that accrued to white labor at the expense of Black (and Indian) subjugation. Also to reiterate, these choices took place in the context of a vigorous and rising U.S. capitalism. The prospect of white supremacist rewards that capitalists could offer must have seemed very real and immediate while the prospect of overthrowing private property (which would necessitate alliance with Blacks) must have seemed difficult and distant.

By the 1870s, the labor movement in the North saw the growth of craft and race unions. "Skilled labor proceeded to share in the exploitation of the reservoir of low-paid common labor" (597). The position of common labor was greatly weakened since their strikes and violence could not succeed with skilled labor and engineers to keep the machinery going.

In the South, the poor whites became the shock troops for the mass terror that destroyed the gains of Black Reconstruction. Du Bois explains that the overthrow of Reconstruction was a property—not a race—war. Still, the poor whites involved were not simply tools of property. They perceived their own interests in attacking the Black advances. In fact, some of the early examples of Klan-style violence that Du Bois provides show such bands attacking the old-planters as well as the freed slaves.

Du Bois documents, state by state, the war of terror that defeated Reconstruction. Here, I will indicate it with one example: in Texas, during the height of the war, there were an average of sixty homicides per month. Black Reconstruction was also defeated with the complicity of Northern capital which was sealed with the withdrawal of Union troops in 1877. The defeat of Reconstruction meant that the color line had been used to establish a new dictatorship of property in the South. For Black labor, this meant a move back toward slavery in the form of sharecropping, Jim Crow laws, and violent repression. For white labor, their active support of the "color caste" (white supremacy) immeasurably strengthened the power of capital, which ruled over them.

J. Sakai's *Settlers: The Mythology of the White Proletariat*

While Allen and Du Bois focus on specific periods, Sakai sketches the whole time from the first European settlement to the current time. Also, Sakai examines the relationship of the white proletariat to Native Americans, Mexicanos, and Asians, as well as to the Black nation.

This, of course, is quite a scope to cover in one book. Sakai starts from an explicit political perspective: what is called the "United States"…"is really a Euroamerican settler empire, built on colonially oppressed nations and peoples." In this light, a lot is revealed about U.S. history that is not only quite different from what we learned in school but that also debunks interpretations generally put out by the white left.

Even for those of us who think we understand the white supremacist core of U.S. history, reading *Settlers* is still quite an education. To take one stark example, when the Europeans first arrived there were an estimated 10 million Natives in North America. By 1900, there were only 300,000. Sakai also critiques the white supremacist nature of movements mythologized by the left such as Bacon's Rebellion, Jacksonian Democracy, and the struggle for the eight-hour workday. Sakai shows that integral to most advances of "democratic" reform for white workers was an active consolidation of privileges at the expense of colonized Third World peoples.

In covering such a range, there are some points of interpretations that could be questioned. Overall it is a very revealing and useful look at U.S. history. For this review, I just want to look at one period, the 1930s. Then we also will examine the overall political conclusions that Sakai draws.

The Depression of the 1930s was a time of intensified class struggle, the building of the CIO, the famed sit-down strikes such as Flint, the height of the Communist Party USA.[6] The CIO of this period has often been praised by leftists as exemplary in including Black workers in its organizing drive.

Sakai sees the essence of the period as the integration of the various European immigrant minorities into the privileges of the settler nation (white Amerika). In return, as U.S. imperialism launched its drive for world hegemony, it could depend upon the armies of solidly united settlers (including the whole white working class) serving imperialism at home and on the battlefield. The New Deal ended industrial serfdom and gave the European "ethnic" national minorities integration as Amerikans by sharply raising their privileges—but only in the settler way: in government regulated unions loyal to U.S. imperialism.

Where the CIO organized Black workers it was utilitarian rather than principled. By the 1930s, Black labor had come to play a strategic role in five industries (usually performing the dirtiest and most hazardous jobs at lower pay): automotive, steel, meatpacking, coal, railroads. Thus, in a number of industrial centers, the CIO unions could not be secure without controlling Afrikan (Black) labor. "The CIO's policy, then, became to promote integration under settler leadership where Afrikan labor was numerous and strong (such as the foundries, the meat packing plants, etc.) and to maintain segregation and Jim Crow in situations where Afrikan labor was numerically lesser and weak. Integration and segregation were but two aspects of the same settler hegemony" (86).

At the same time, it was CIO practice to reserve the skilled crafts and more desirable production jobs for white (male) workers. For example, the first UAW/GM contract that resulted from the great Flint sit-down strike contained a "noninterchangibility" clause, which in essence made it illegal for Black workers to move up from being janitors or foundry workers. Such policy came on the heels of Depression trends

---

6   Initially "Committee for Industrial Organization," then "Congress of Industrial Organizations."

that had forced Blacks out of the better jobs. Between 1930–1936 some 50 percent of all Afrikan skilled workers were pushed out of their jobs.

Roosevelt's support of the CIO came from a strategy to control and channel the class struggle. A significant factor in the success of the 1930s union organizing drives was the government's refusal to use armed repression. No *U.S.* armed forces were used against Euro-Amerikan workers from 1933–1941.[7]

This policy was in marked contrast to, for example, the attack on the Nationalist party in Puerto Rico. In 1937, one month after President Roosevelt refused to use force against the Flint sit-down strike, U.S. police opened fire on a peaceful nationalist parade in Ponce, Puerto Rico. Nineteen Puerto Rican citizens were killed and over a hundred were wounded. While leftists committed to organizing of the '30s might want to bring in different examples and argue Sakai's interpretations, I think that overall subsequent history of the CIO has been clear: it has both reinforced white monopolies on preferred jobs and has been a loyal component of U.S. imperial policy abroad.[8]

What conclusions about the white working class can we draw from this history? Sakai takes a definite and challenging position. *Settlers* is addressed, internally, for discussion among Third World revolutionaries. Still, it is important for us to grapple with its politics and to apply those lessons to our own situation and responsibilities.

Sakai's general view of the history is that the masses of whites have advanced themselves primarily by oppressing Third World people—not by any means of class struggle. Also that for most of U.S. history the proletariat has been a colonial proletariat, made up only of oppressed Afrikan, Indian, Latino and Asian workers.[9] On top of this basic history, U.S. imperial hegemony after WWII raised privileges to another level. "Those expansionist years of 1945–1965 … saw the final promotion of the white proletariat. This was an en masse promotion so profound that it eliminated not only consciousness, but the class itself" (147).

Thus, for Sakai, there is an oppressor nation but it doesn't have a worker class, at least not in any politically meaningful sense of the term. To buttress this position Sakai,

---

7   This point could be misleading. There were several bloody clashes between workers and local or state police forces—e.g., at Flint, and during the general strike in San Francisco. Here, though, Sakai is emphasizing the role of the Federal Government and the broader ruling class strategy led by Roosevelt.

8   For a version of the same history that emphasizes the CIO's commitment to organizing Black workers see Philip Foner, chapter 16. Foner emphasizes that after five years of the CIO's organizing (1935–1940), the number of Black trade union members rose from 100,000 to 500,000 with many trade union benefits for those workers. He admits, however, that "such militant activities made no real dent in Negro joblessness," and that "the CIO also did little to break down the discriminatory lines in industries where blacks were employed" (233).

9   For certain periods, immigrant Europeans were genuine workers … until they, too, were integrated into the settler privileged.

1. discusses the supra-class cultural and ideological unification in the white community;
2. points to the much higher standard of living for white-Americans; and
3. presents census statistics to indicate that whites are predominantly (over 60 percent) bourgeois, middle class and labor aristocracy.

Here, Sakai enumerates class based solely on white male jobs in order to correct for situations where the woman's lower status job is a second income for the family involved. This method, however, fails to take account of the growing number of families where the woman's wages are the primary income. The methodological question also relates to the potential for women's oppression to be a source for a progressive current within the white working class.

In a way, Sakai puts forward a direct negation of the opportunist "Marxist" position that makes class designation everything and liquidates the distinction between oppressed and oppressor nation.

Sakai's survey of U.S. history understates the examples of fierce class struggle within the oppressor nation, which imply at least some basis for dissatisfaction and disloyalty by working whites. Still, these examples—defined primarily around economic demands and usually resolved by consolidation of privileges relative to Third World workers—can not be parlayed into a history of "revolutionary class struggle."

Class consciousness can not be defined solely by economic demands. At its heart, it is a movement toward the revolutionary overthrow of capitalism. "Proletariat internationalism"—solidarity with all other peoples oppressed and exploited by imperialism—is a necessary and essential feature of revolutionary class consciousness. In our condition, this requires up front support for and alliance with the oppressed nations, particularly those within the United States (Black, Mexicano, Native). Thus white supremacy and class-consciousness can not peacefully coexist with each other. One chokes off the other. An honest view of the 350-year history clearly shows that the alignment with white supremacy has predominated over the revolutionary class consciousness.

Furthermore, the culture of a more or less unified, supra-class, white supremacist outlook is also a very important factor. That culture is a reflection of a common history as part of an oppressor nation; it also becomes a material force in perpetuating that outlook and those choices. Common culture is a format to organize even those whites with the least material stake in white supremacy.

All the above considerations, however, do not provide a complete class analysis. There are other aspects of people's relationship to the mode of production, which are important. A central distinction is between those who own or control the means of production (e.g., corporations, banks, real estate) and families who live by wages or salaries, i.e., by working for someone else. Those who live by the sale of labor power have little control or access to the basic power that determines the purpose of production and the direction of society as a whole. In the best of times, most white workers may feel comfortable; in periods of crisis, the stress might be felt and resolved on qualitatively different lines within the oppressor nation (e.g., which class bears the costs of an imperialist war or feels the brunt of economic decline). Even among whites, those who aren't in control have a basic interest in a transformation of society. It may not be expressed in "standard of living" (goods that can be purchased) as much as in the quality of life (e.g., war, environment, health, and the impact of racism, sexism, decadence). Crises can bring these contradictions more to the surface, expressing the necessity to reorganize society.

In my view there definitely is a white working class. It is closely tied to imperialism; the labor aristocracy is the dominant sector, the class as a whole has been corrupted by white supremacy; but, the class within the oppressor nation that lives by the sale of their labor power has not disappeared. This is not just an academic distinction; under certain historical conditions it can have important meaning.

A dialectical analysis goes beyond description to look at both the process of development and the potential for transformation. This is the great value of the Ted Allen essays. They show how white supremacy was a conscious construction by the ruling class under specific historical conditions. This implies that, under different historical conditions, there also can be a conscious deconstruction by oppressed nations, women, and the working class. Our analysis has to look for potential historical changes and movement activity that could promote revolutionary consciousness within the white working class.

In approaching such an analysis, we must guard against the mechanical notion that economic decline will in itself lessen racism. The lessons from Du Bois's description of the "anti-draft" riots of the 1860s (as well as our experience over the last twenty years) shows the opposite to be true. Under economic pressure, the spontaneous tendency is to fight harder for white supremacy. While the absolute value of privilege might decrease, the relative value is usually increasing as Third World people abroad and within the United States bear the worst hardships of the crisis. The white workers closest to the level of Third World workers can be the most virulent and violent in fighting for white supremacy.

Rarely have major sectors of the white working class been won over to revolutionary consciousness based on a reform interest. Imperialism in ascendancy has been able to offer them more bread and butter than the abstraction of international solidarity. But a more fundamental interest could emerge in a situation where imperialism in crisis can't deliver and where the possibility of replacing imperialism with a more humane system becomes tangible.

Some Lessons from the '60s

In the '60s and '70s, it appeared as though the rapid advance of national liberation was remaking the world in the direction of socialism. In the past twelve years, the painful setbacks have shown just how difficult it is to create a viable alternative to underdevelopment in the Third World. Today we are in an historical juncture of crisis in social practice and theory. Nonetheless, given prevailing conditions, the contradictions and social struggles are likely to continue to be most intense in the Third World. Now, however, we have no clear guidelines as to when, how, or even if these struggles can lead to socialism in the world.

While it is discouraging to no longer have a defined outline for the triumph of world revolution, the human stake in the outcome of the social crises and struggles does not allow us the luxury of demoralization. We have to make our most intelligent and concerted effort to maximize the potential for humanitarian and liberatory change.

Solidarity with the Third World struggles has to become our top priority for both humanitarian and strategic reasons—the more we can do to get imperialism off their backs, the better the chances for their potential for leadership toward world transformation to bloom. But solidarity cannot be ethereal, it cannot be developed and sustained with any scope without some sort of social base within the oppressor nation. Class may very well not be a primary form for such a social base, but we still need to establish more realistic and useful terms for the role class can play in the next period of social upheaval and motion. The historical lessons we examined make it clear that it would be unreal to talk about the white working class "as a whole," or even the majority of it, as a revolutionary force. But, on the other hand, the predominance of white supremacy is not genetically determined nor is it carved in stone historically. We need to look for what conditions and movement activity can promote anti-imperialist organizing within the white working class—both to build solidarity forces and to point the direction toward a genuine long-term emancipation of working people from a system based on exploitation, dehumanization, and war.

The movement of the 1960s showed the potential for positive response from whites to the rise of national liberation struggles, along with a desire for a more humane and cooperative society. It is true that this response came first from elite students, the children of the petty bourgeoisie and professionals. These sectors felt more secure in their privilege and felt less immediately threatened by advances for Black people than did the poorer sectors of whites. Also, students and intellectuals are frequently the group that early on, albeit subjectively, responds to emerging contradictions in a given society. The movement was a real reflection of the objective advance of national liberation and the need to transform U.S. society. As the war in Vietnam dragged on, increasing numbers of working class youth became involved in the movement.

This fledgling success and glimmer of potential of the '60s also provided some historical lessons that we have not done nearly enough to analyze and codify. The movement involved more than the traditional unrest of students. Broader cultural identification played a major role in generating a larger youth movement. First and foremost it was the impact of Black culture, with its more humane values of social consciousness, emotional expressiveness, and sense of community—primarily through the genesis of rock 'n' roll. The cultural rebellion also importantly involved an opening of sexual expression that challenged the prevailing straitjacket of repression. Paradoxically, to the grim realities we've come to understand, at that time drugs (particularly marijuana and LSD) were seen as liberation from repressive control and promoting anti-authoritarianism.

Civil rights and anti-war activity among whites started mainly on the campuses, and the student movement was a spearhead for political consciousness throughout the '60s. Most white working class youth were initially indifferent if not downright hostile to these initial stirrings. But over the years there were increasing cultural links that laid the basis for a broader movement. For example, white working class youths, who dropped out of the daily work grind and were often into drugs, gravitated to communities near campuses. Anti-draft counselling offices brought many into more direct, political contact with the movement. The burgeoning of community colleges meant that more working class youth were themselves students. By the late 1960s, the growing disenchantment and anger about the war in Vietnam provided a unifying focus and sense of identity for all the disaffected. When soldiers in Vietnam started to turn against the war, that added a new dimension to the movement, as well as significantly deepening its class composition.

The main base for the anti-imperialist movement of the '60s was a social movement of youth, heavily impacted and in many ways generated by Black culture. As the movement developed, it involved increasing numbers of working class youth, who played a major role in the movement's growth and heightened militancy. This extension showed,

1.   the ability of culture to be a bridge to deepening the class base of a social movement;
2.   the increasing ways the draft, in the context of a bloody and losing war, made the interests of some working class people intersect with those of national liberation;
3.   the contagious effect of victorious revolutions and liberatory vision.

The New Left did have an intelligent strategy for extending the movement and deepening it's class base, but abandoned it at the very moment it was achieving stunning success. The Revolutionary Youth Movement (RYM) strategy called for the extension of what had started as a primarily elite student base to a broader, particularly working class, youth base by doing more work around the draft, with G.I.s, in community colleges, and among youth in working class neighborhoods. The movement, still heavily male supremist, had little sense of the role of women and often lapsed into very negative sexist posturing. However even here the freedom energy and rhetoric of the movement provided a new opening for women's liberation. Women active in the Civil Rights Movement and in SDS (Students for a Democratic Society) provided a major impetus for the new wave of feminism that emerged in 1967. Unfortunately the reaction of men within the movement was so sexist that it led to what has become an ongoing and destructive stasis that pits anti-imperialism and women's liberation against each other. But RYM did offer a vision extending the movement to involve broader working class sectors without losing the political focus on anti-war, anti-racism and militancy.

Large numbers of working class youth did get involved in the movement. At the high point, millions took to the streets in the wake of the 1971 invasion of Cambodia and the killing of students at Kent State. This movement was of course not magically free of racism, as painfully illustrated by the failure to make issues of the killings at Jackson State and of Chicano anti-war activists in Los Angeles. But it was a movement that could, with political leadership, have strong anti-imperialist potential.

SDS, which correctly formulated the RYM strategy in December of 1968, was already splintered apart by May 1971. The dissolution of SDS shortly before the triumph of its strategy was not simply a question of stupidity or even just a matter of the pervasive power of opportunism. The student movement had reached a crisis in 1969 because its very successes had moved it from simply "shocking the moral consciousness of America" to realizing it was in fundamental opposition to the most powerful and ruthless ruling class ever. The murderous attacks on the Black movements we supported (dozens of Black activists were killed and a couple of thousand incarcerated from 1968 through 1971) drove the point home graphically at the same time that the dictates of solidarity urgently pressed us to qualitatively raise our level of struggle. The movement went into a crisis in 1968 because it came face to face with the terrifying reality of imperialism's power.

RYM was a creative and realistic strategy to extend the base and power of the movement, although it needed to be joined by an equally strong politics on women's liberation. But for all of its value as a transitional strategy, RYM was of course in itself nowhere near an adequate basis for overthrowing bourgeois power. So, looking for immediate answers in the crisis, the left floundered on the perennial dilemma in white supremist society. The majority looked for a magic solution to the problem of power by mythicizing the white working class (the majority in the United States) as "revolutionary"—in reality this position meant a retreat into white supremacy and away from confronting imperialism. The minority tried to maintain purity around racism and the war by seeing ourselves as exceptional whites, separated from any social base—in reality this position meant abandoning responsibility for building a movement that could sustain militant struggle against imperialism.

While a youth movement in itself can't be sufficient, the promising success of RYM within its realm does suggest some lessons:

1.   the role culture can play in building cross-class movements;
2.   the value of looking for potential points of intersection of interests of whites with the advance of national liberation (e.g. costs of imperialist

wars, G.I.s, draft, taxes, social priorities; situations of common oppression where there is third world leadership such as welfare, prisons, and some labor struggles; situations where a vision of a revolutionary alternative can be most readily perceived, such as with youth, and women;

3. the likelihood that social movements can play more of a role in involving white working people in a progressive struggle than traditional, direct forms of class organizing.

The social movements though—youth, Lesbian-Gay-AIDS, anti-war and anti-nuclear, ecology, and potentially around housing, health, and education—have typically had a "middle class" leadership and a primarily middle class base. ("Middle class" meaning people from college educated backgrounds—mainly professionals and petty bourgeois.)

While the Women's movement is usually labeled as a social movement because it is not one of the traditional struggles for state power, it should be more appropriately grouped with national liberation and class as responding to one of the three most fundamental structures of oppression. No movement can be revolutionary and successful without paying full attention to national liberation, class content, and the liberation of women. After the collapse of the anti-war and youth movements in the '70s the women's movement provided the most sustained and extensive impetus for social change within white America. Like the social movements, the leadership and main active base was middle class. With the ebbing of the radical women's liberation tendency that identified with national liberation, the apparent leadership of contemporary feminism has a more pronounced middle class character—at the same time that many more working class women, while eschewing the name "feminism," have actively adopted and adapted the goals and struggles of the movement.

We would argue that the women's movement and the social movements, to be revolutionary, must relate to racism, national liberation, and Third World leadership. But we should add that, as with the youth movement, each should be looking for ways to extend its base into the working class on an anti-racist and pro–women's liberation basis.

The Lesbian-Gay-AIDS movement has been of particular urgency, militancy and importance in this period. The struggle around AIDS has pushed the radical sector toward the need to ally with Third World and poor white communities impacted by intravenous drugs and poor health care. The AIDS movement has also provided leadership in breaking through the sterile conservative (cut back services to the poor) versus liberal (defend state bureaucracy) definition of political debate. ACT-UP and others have provided an excellent example of mobilization and empowerment from below for self-help while at the same time demanding a redistribution of social resources to meet these social needs.

Peace, ecology, the homeless, health care, education all speak to important pieces that express the inhumanity and ineffectiveness of the whole system. Of course these movements have been, almost by definition, reformist. But that doesn't mean that they have to be under all circumstances: e.g.,

1. a deeper crisis in imperialism where it has less cushion from which to offer reforms,
2. a situation where revolutionary alternatives are strong enough to be tangible,
3. a political leadership that pushes these movements to ally with national liberation, promote women's liberation, and deepen their class base, while at the same time drawing out the connections among the different social movements into a more coherent and overall critique of the whole system.

Under such circumstances and leadership, the social movements could not only involve far more white working class people in anti-systemic struggles, but would also serve to redefine and revitalize class issues and class struggle itself.

Lessons from the '60s certainly don't offer a blueprint for the '90s, which are a very different decade. Clearly we are not now in a period of progressive social upheaval. Economic dislocation, at least initially, provides fertile ground for white supremacist organizing. National liberation struggles are not at this point achieving a clear path to socialism.

What is certain is that there will be changes, and, at points, crises. We can't afford to repeat the old errors of once again floundering on the dilemma of either "joining" the working class's white supremacy or of abandoning our responsibility to organize a broader movement. While there is no blueprint, the basis for a real starting point is an analysis of actual historical experience.

In sum, revolutionaries must be realistic about the history of white supremacy, the impact of material wealth and dominance, and the mushrooming of job and status differentials among workers, both nationally and internationally. There is nothing approximating the Marxist revolutionary proletariat within white America. At the same time, the distinction between those who control the means of production and those who live by the sale of labor power has not been completely obliterated.

A system of white supremacy that was historically constructed can be historically deconstructed. A key factor for whites is the tangibility of a revolutionary alternative as opposed to the more immediate relative privileges that imperialism has had to offer. In this regard we have no map of what the future will bring. The experience of the '60s does offer some possible lessons for when the system is under stress.

1. Anti-imperialist politics are more important than initial class composition.
2. Culture, especially with ties to Third World people, can be an important force for building progressive cross-class movements.

3. In seeking to extend such movements, revolutionaries should look for intersection points of white working class interests with the advance of national liberation, such as the draft.

4. Women's liberation must play a central role in all movements we build.

5. The various social movements, if we can fight for an alliance with the national liberation and the presence of women's politics and leadership, can be important arenas for extending base to include working class people, mutually redefine class and social issues, and make the connections to an overall anti-systemic perspective.

Chinweizu, War, and Reparations

Dr. Conrad W. Worrill

As the Houston Chapter of the National Black United Front has so eloquently stated, we must stand against the war, because "we understand that Global White Supremacy is the driving force behind much of America's foreign and domestic policy."

As the Houston Chapter of NBUF proclaims, we must say "No To War! YES TO REPARATIONS!" We should listen to the wisdom of our great ancestor, the Honorable Marcus Mosiah Garvey on the question of war. Garvey said, "If the war is not yours... Never go into war foolishly. Never sacrifice your life without good results for your cause. War is the best time to take advantage of your transgressor, whoever he may be. Whenever he is engaged in war and he promises you nothing, you will never get anything from him in time of peace."

All of the forces that represent the world of white supremacy that oppose the just demands of African people for reparations will not prevail in their efforts to disrupt, diminish, or stifle the mass momentum that we are witnessing by African people in America, and throughout the world, who are organizing, day-by-day and block-by-block, around the issue of reparations just because they are involved and obsessed in an unjust war in Iraq.

On April 27, 1993, the great African scholar and thinker Chinweizu, presented a paper at the second plenary session of the First Pan-African Conference on Reparations in Abuja, Nigeria. I think it is timely in the face of the attacks on the Reparations Movement and U.S. involvement in the War on Iraq, to refer to the keen insights that Chinweizu presented in this paper. Chinweizu put forth the following historical background: "Contemplating the condition of the Black World is vexatious to the spirit: that is probably the strongest impetus which has brought us all here today."

For many centuries, and especially in the last five, the Black skin has been a badge of contempt. For instance, it used to be said in Brazil that if you are white and running down the street, you are an athlete, but if you are Black and running down the street, you are a thief! And in most parts of the world today, if you are white and rich, you are honored and celebrated, and all doors fly open as you approach; but if you are Black and rich, you are under suspicion, and handcuffs and guard dogs stand ready to take you away.

Yes, the Black skin is still the badge of contempt in the world today, as it has been for nearly 2,000 years. To make sure it does not remain so in the twenty-first century is perhaps the overall purpose of our search for reparations.

We are gathered here today, thinkers and activists who want to change Black People's condition in the world. What things do we need to change, both in the world and in ourselves, if we are to accomplish the mission of reparations? What changes must we make in structures, in psychology, in historical consciousness and much else?

We might begin by noting that Blacks are not the only people in the world who are seeking, or who have sought, reparations. In fact, by only now pressing our claim for reparations, we are latecomers to a varied company of peoples in the Americas, in Asia, and in Europe. Here is a partial catalogue of reparations, paid and pending, which are twentieth century precedents for reparations to the Black World.

In the Americas, from Southern Chile to the Arctic north of Canada, reparations are being sought and being made. The Mapuche, an aboriginal people of Southern Chile, are pressing for the return of their lands, some 30 million hectares of which were, bit by bit, taken away and given to European immigrants since 1540. The Inuit of Arctic Canada, more commonly known as the Eskimo, were in 1992 offered restitution of some 850,000 sq. miles of their ancestral lands, their home range for millennia before European invaders arrived there.

In the United States, claims by the Sioux to the Black Lands of South Dakota are now in the courts. And the U.S. Government is attempting to give some 400,000 acres of grazing land to the Navaho, and some other lands to the Hopi in the southwest of the United States.

In 1988, the U.S. Government admitted wrongdoing in interning some 120,000 Japanese-Americans under Executive Order 9066 of 1942, during WWII, and awarded each internee $20,000.

In Europe, after WWII, the victors demanded reparations from Germany for all damages to civilians and their dependents, for losses caused by the maltreatment of prisoners of war, and for all nonmilitary property that was destroyed in the war. In 1921, Germany's reparations liability was fixed at 132 billion gold marks. After WWII, the victorious Allies filed reparations claims against Germany for $320 billion. Reparations were also levied on Italy and Finland. The items for which these claims were made included bodily loss, loss of liberty, loss of property, injury to professional careers, dislocation and forced emigration, time spent in concentration camps because of racial, religious and political persecution. Others were the social cost of war, as represented by the burden from loss of life, social disorder, and institutional disorder; and the economic cost of war, as represented by the capital destroyed and the value of civilian goods and services foregone to make war goods. Payments were made in cash and kind, goods, services, capital equipment, land, farm and forest products; and penalties were added for late deliveries.

Perhaps the most famous case of reparations was that paid by Germany to the Jews. Reparations were paid by West Germany to Israel for crimes against Jews in territories controlled by Hitler's Germany, and to individuals to indemnify them for persecution. In the initial phase, these included $2 billion to make amends to victims of

Nazi persecution; $952 million in personal indemnities; $35.70 per month per inmate of concentration camps; pensions for the survivors; $820 million to Israel to resettle 50,000 Jewish emigrants from lands formerly controlled by Hitler. All that was just the beginning. Other, and largely undisclosed, payments followed. And even in 1992, the World Jewish Congress in New York announced that the newly unified Germany would pay compensation, totaling $63 million for 1993, to 50,000 Jews who suffered Nazi persecution but had not been paid reparations because they lived in East Germany.

On Being White and Other Lies

A History of Racism in the United States

Mab Segrest

An excerpt from Memoirs of a Race Traitor.

Four years of full-time anti-Klan organizing and I began to get sick. First it hit my stomach, and I was up all night puking. That was the week after Eddie and Tim, Tuscarora Indians, walked into the local newspaper office in Robeson County with sawed-off shotguns and held twenty people hostage for most of the day. While I and a host of others waited outside, they finally released everyone after the Governor promised to investigate racist violence, drug trafficking and law enforcement complicity in both. I got home and got well, then it hit my throat and came and went for another three months. The first time, I was back in Robeson County, after Lumbee Indian leader Julian Pierce was killed the month before he would have beat the white power structure in a fair election for District Attorney by consolidating Black, Indian and poor white votes. Later it hit me in a motel in Shelby, where we were trying to build up local support for a case against neo-Nazis who murdered three young men in an adult bookstore, "to avenge Yahweh on homosexuals."

I slowed down then and started tracking another way; my roadmap was not the spidery backroads of North Carolina, but history. I knew I needed to understand the genesis of the violence that was sickening me.

A year or so into the process, I found James Baldwin's piece "On Being White and Other Lies" on microfiche in the Duke University library. Baldwin's face watched from the opposite page, light off his features showing as whiteness on the duotone, his intelligent eye emerging from the blackness like a galaxy, Andromeda perhaps. But in his universe it was definitely I who was under observation:

> America became white—the people who, as they claim, "settled" the country became white—because of the necessity of denying the Black presence and justifying the Black subjugation. No community can be based on such a principle—in other words, no community can be established on so genocidal a lie. White men—from Norway, for example, where they were Norwegians—became white by slaughtering the cattle, poisoning the wells, torching the houses, massacring

214

Native Americans, raping Black women. This moral erosion has made it impossible for those who think of themselves as white to have any moral authority… It is the Black condition, and only that, which informs the consciousness of white people. It is a terrible paradox, but those who believed that they could control and define Black people divested themselves of the power to control and define themselves.[1]

Baldwin's words resonated with my own sense of whiteness. I could see the country was going backwards, and I understood instinctively from my childhood in the Jim Crow South what that meant. This knowledge had brought me to anti-Klan organizing, and it also fed my deepening sense of crisis. But I also came to suspect that these changes, the bloody effects of which I had experienced so intimately working for North Carolinians Against Racist and Religious Violence, might involve more than just the roll-backs of the civil rights movement I had lived through in my adolescence. What was the larger historical framework, and what did it mean?

I was convinced that most white progressives hugely underestimate the power of race in U.S. history as well as the degree to which racial struggles have shaped other political struggles in this country. I suspected that both feminism and the gay and lesbian organizing I had done for over a decade had been as profoundly shaped by race as by gender, but with far less acknowledgement. I had spent many of my years in these movements trying to ensure that my new women's community would not replicate the segregation of my Alabama childhood, but I often felt my head bloody from beating it up against a familiar wall of what felt like willed ignorance, or disoriented from wandering in fogs of personalization and guilt. If racism equals "power plus prejudice," as the anti-racist formula states, how do we really go about explaining this "power" to people in ways that help them to understand what a huge force it is we are up against, how inevitably we all have been shaped by it, and how much we need to do beyond "fixing" ourselves?

A Bridge, Not a Wedge

This essay was originally delivered as a keynote at the National Gay and Lesbian Task Force's Creating Change Conference in Durham, North Carolina, in November 1993. I have elaborated the remarks to conclude this book. The reflections on the economy in the 1980s and 1990s complete the assessment of capitalism undertaken in "On Being White and Other Lies" and show the emergence of what I believe is a fourth stage, beyond commerce, industrial and finance capitalism, driven by the technological advances of the information age. The remarks on racism, while targeted to white gay and lesbian organizers, are relevant to other predominantly white movements within

---

1   James Baldwin, "On Being White and Other Lies," *Essence* (April 1984), 90–92.

the United States. I have also expanded my reflections on the ways that homophobia hurts heterosexuals, especially the way that the right is attempting to seed homophobia in communities of color. I certainly hope that homophobia will not prevent heterosexuals reading this piece from seeing its relevance to their lives.

Good morning, and welcome to Durham. Those of you making your first trip South may already be disoriented by our peculiar blend of hospitality and repression, which comes from having spent 246 of the last 374 years as a slave culture. But it's important for all of us to the history of racism in the United States—in which the South has played a particularly visible but by no means singular role. If coming South reminds us of this, so much the better. If the South is the cradle of the Confederacy and of many subsequent right-wing movements, it is also the mother of all resistance, the heir to generations of Africans' determination to be free, from the moment they set foot on the slave ships, all across the Middle Passage, to the long, cold, white nightmare on this continent. The South is the heir to their creativity. For however destructively white supremacist culture has defined them, African Americans have continually re-created themselves, have known in their songs and in their hearts before I'll be a slave, I'll be buried in my grave. I call some of their names, a verbal libation: Harriet Tubman, Frederick Douglass, Ida B. Wells, Ella Baker, Martin Luther King, Rosa Parks, Fannie Lou Hamer. We meet on their ground, and on the ground of Tuscaroras, Algonquins, Cherokee, Lumbee, Sioux, who fought their own wars with the U.S. Army, the long and brutal history of which should remind our movement what it means to take on the U.S. military, arguably the most repressive force in the world.

I feel honored to address you this morning, but I also feel urgent. I am afraid that I will not explain clearly enough my conviction that the gay and lesbian liberation movement must understand racism more fully if we are to survive, and that we cannot understand racism if we do not understand the anti-human virulence of capitalism. If we did understand these two great barriers to human liberation, we would behave differently—position our movement differently, structure our organizations differently, develop and respect our leaders differently. In this regard, I think we are similar to many progressive movements in the United States. The gay movement has more visibility, more access to corridors of power, than we have ever had. But, our failure to understand racism is killing us. Maybe twenty years ago, our movement and institutions had the luxury of stupidity.

Maybe twenty years ago, white queers could approach issues of racism out of guilt, or a desire to be liked, or to be "good." Maybe then we could offer token jobs and token recognition to people of color, saving the decision-making, the real power, for the folks who looked like the President, or the Chief Justice, or the CEO of Exxon. But the right has called our diversity bluff. Their most recent and effective propaganda, such as the video "Gay Rights, Civil Rights," uses African American spokespeople to proclaim that we are not a "genuine" minority in the tradition of Martin Luther King but a privileged group after "special rights." Many Black people have no illusions that the producers of this propaganda have their best interests at heart. However, these divisive strategies become most apparent as the lies they are where our movement has relationships with people of color (including those in our own midst). In all those towns and cities where there are few links between visible gay organizations and people of color, such strategies are dangerously effective among both people of color and straight whites. The wildfire of the right's insurgent fascism is sweeping down the canyons that divide us, and we must respond to racism now for our own survival—to save our little white asses. And we should be thankful for the opportunity.

When we don't get race, it kills us. When we don't understand capitalism, not only are we more confused about race, not only do we confuse power with money, not only do we deny our clearest voices—we also fail to understand the forces driving the history of our times. We won't have successful strategies if we don't understand our times. If we don't understand why things are happening to us now, we will never have the vision and the strategy to seize the future and shape it.

Last year, as part of my new job for the Urban-Rural Mission of the World Council of Churches, I traveled to Juárez, Mexico, to visit the *maquiladoras*. Fortune 500 companies built these "twin plant" factories along the U.S.-Mexico border in the 1970s when the Mexican President, faced with mounting pressure from his country's international debt, developed "free trade zones." (Many other Third World countries were saddled with similar huge debts when the International Monetary Fund and the world Bank encouraged them to borrow too much money. The consequence has been to keep those poor countries' people and resources at the disposal of richer countries and under the control of domestic authoritarian regimes, since democracies are less inclined to starve their people.)

In Juárez, first we toured the industrial districts, driving past rows of seemingly innocuous factories. Then we went behind one of the *maquilas*. On the other side of a drainage ditch, Mexican families lived in houses made from cardboard and scrap lumber. There was an acrid smell rising from ditch water the bright green color of astroturf. A pipe from the plant fed unprocessed waste the color and consistency of breast milk into the water. Families washed and dried their laundry in the polluted water. Our guide later showed us pictures of babies born to women *maquila* workers in Brownsville, Texas—babies who had no brains. The workers in these factories are 70 percent women.

Then we went to visit a *colonia*, a poor neighborhood that feeds workers into the *maquilas*. As we rounded the hill, I looked out to the horizon, and all I could see were scores of the same cardboard houses. They stretched from mesa to mesa for acres, the pattern broken only by an occasional power line or by water brought in in old chemical barrels.

There on the hill outside of Juárez, the taste of its dust in my mouth, I found myself face to face with the latest manifestation of a virulent capitalism in which masses of humanity become pawns for massive profits for a few.

What does this mean, I thought, to gay people?

While the New Right's "family values" campaigns of the 1970s and 1980s pumped up hostility against gay men and lesbians, the forces that eventually brought Reagan and Bush to the White House stole this country. Corporate profits from the postwar boom peaked in the mid-1960s, then began to decline, squeezed by increasing foreign competition from both established and newly industrializing countries. In the 1960s and 1970s, the men who run the multinationals responded with mergers and hostile takeovers to try for fast profits, rather than using the money to retool basic industries and maintain our infrastructure. They did not improve our products—how many of you began driving Volkswagens or Hondas rather than American cars in the 1970s and 1980s? Rather, they cut labor costs—by attacking unions and by sending our basic industries to Third World countries, where people work for one tenth the wages (*maquila* workers make $4 a day).[2]

New computer technologies have allowed this rearrangement of the global assembly line because now production and assembly of particular products can be dispersed to countries with the "comparative advantage" of cheap labor costs and lax labor and environmental standards. "Money" is reduced to electronic impulses, both highly concentrated and rapidly deployed.

Between 1970 and 1990 conservative administrations and Congress restructured our federal tax policy to provide incentives for corporations to invest overseas, decreasing the percentage of corporate taxes that constitute the total federal budget from 23.4 percent to 9.7 percent. Reagan gave so many corporations "tax expenditures"—deductions and credits—that many Fortune 500 companies stopped paying taxes altogether and even got money back from previous years. IBM paid virtually no U.S. taxes between 1986 and 1988 with U.S. assets of $39 billion and a worldwide profit of $26 billion.[3]

The people in control of our economy "de-industrialized" the United States, leaving us a service economy with lower-paying jobs. These corporate and governmental decision makers "feminized" the work force, because the way they could save the most money was by eliminating the unionized, higher salaried, white men's jobs. By 1973, the standard of living from the postwar expansion peaked, and wages began to fall. In the 1970s for the first time since World War II, the standard of living for white workers began to decline.

The New Right, which would mobilize a racist, sexist and homophobic backlash to the justice movements of the 1960s, was born just at this moment of declining white living standards. In 1973, Kevin Phillips had articulated in The Emerging Republican

---

2   Thanks especially to Jacqui Alexander for many careful readings of drafts and for her confidence that I would, indeed, someday, finish the essay in a useable form. Thanks also to Barbara Smith for close editing and encouragement and to Tobi Lippin and Peter Barnes for feedback and support.

3   Howard Zinn, *A People's History of the United States* (New York: Harper & Row, 1980), 24. The most recurrent explanations for the psychology of white racism (in distinction to its material base) draw heavily on Freudian theories of repression and projection, as do Rawick, Roediger, Takaki, and Jordan.

Majority the formula for forging a right-wing populism based on racist backlash to issues such as busing and affirmative action. The "New Right" movement had been brewing since Barry Goldwater's 1964 Presidential campaign brought conservatives together and generated a mailing list. It was fed by the success of George Wallace's populist racist presidential campaigns, which garnered 10 million votes in 1968 and showed the "old Right" a way to break up the Democratic coalition that had dominated U.S. politics since the Depression. At the same time, ultraconservative strategists Howard Phillips and Paul Weyrich recruited televangelists Jerry Falwell and Pat Robertson to shape the national organizations that formed the basis for a Religious Right politicized by issues of prayer in schools, feminism and the new gay liberation movement. These two thrusts—one racist, the other based on gender and sexuality—took separate courses but sprang from the same impulse and the same ultraconservative strategy.[4]

While the ideologues blamed feminists, people of color, poor people and gay people for the national decline, the stage was set for business moguls to siphon off billions. In 1980, Barry Goldwater's disciple Ronald Reagan was elected President on a platform of deficit reduction. Then his administration pumped up the deficit from $79 billion to $155 billion and the national debt from $1 trillion to $2.6 trillion with inflated military spending. In 1986, 63 percent of the tax dollar (not counting trust funds such as Social Security) went to pay for past, present or future wars.[5]

While Reaganites inflated the war budget, they slashed the "safety net" that was put in place in the 1930s and 1960s to protect us from the ravages of unrestrained capitalism. The federal government cut federal social spending and passed on insufficient bloc grants to the states. Cities cut taxes to draw investments and concentrated on service, not manufacturing jobs, then, many went bankrupt in the 1980s under the double pressure of increased responsibility for social services and a reduced tax base. States became the managers of social spending and in the 1990s will increasingly face bankruptcy under this pressure. In 1991, New York carried a $6 billion deficit, California $10 billion. Then there is the savings and loan scam, which is costing us $100 billion a year. The United States in the 1990s is facing the kind of "structural adjustment" economic policies that we have long foisted on Third World countries, likely with the attendant volatile social movements and beefed up police state to repress them.[6]

---

4   For more on the precapitalist "tendency to seize upon physical differences as the badge of innate mental and temporal differences" see Thomas Gossett, *Race: The History of an Idea in America* (Dallas: Southern Methodist University Press, 1975), 3–16. "Prior to 1500 differential valorization of human races is hardly noticeable," historian Magnus Morner comments of "the hierarchic classification of human races dictated by European ethnocentricity," *Race Mixture in the History of Latin America* (Boston: Little Brown, 1967), 6. Michael Omi and Howard Winant agree: "Race consciousness, and its articulation in theories of race, is largely a modern phenomenon" dating to European explorers' "discoveries," *Racial Formation in the United States* (New York: Routledge, 1989), 58.

5   T. Walter Wallbank, Alastair M. Taylor, and George Barr Carson Jr., eds. *Civilization Past and Present*, vol. 2 (Chicago: Scott, Foresman & Company, 1965), 280.

6   Zinn, *A People's History*, 23.

The collapse of the Soviet bloc in the late 1980s (due in part to its own massive military spending) has left capitalism without the counterforce that the U.S.S.R. offered for the past seventy years, speeding up the process of economic integration of global markets as three huge trading blocs have emerged: in the Pacific Rim (dominated by Japan), in Europe (dominated by Germany) and in the Americas (dominated by the United States). The situation in the *maquilas* is one result of the policy of deindustrialization and hemispheric economic integration that U.S. economic elites helped to put in place with the political support of the same white workers they have begun to dislocate; and with the passage of the North American Free Trade Act, the *maquila* economy will spread to all of Mexico, and eventually all of Latin America and back north.

With the communist threat suddenly diminished, the Bush administration dropped a lot of its military hardware on the unfortunate people of Iraq in half-million dollar smart bombs over Baghdad—with every bomb, BAM! another school, BAM! another AIDS research project, BAM! BAM! bridges and sewer systems, BAM! low-income housing complexes. We also killed 200,000 people.

The demographics of the United States win shift radically over the next half-century, fed by Latino immigrants from war-torn and economically ravaged Central American countries; Asians who began to immigrate in greater numbers when Congress repealed racist immigration quotas during the Viet Nam War; and declining white birth rates. By the middle of the next century, there will be as many people of color in this country as white people. We lesbians and gay men will have a chance to build a potentially new kind of power base at the local, state and national level with progressive people of color, marginalized workers both within and outside of unions and progressive feminists. Will our racism allow us to make that choice? (Feminists will face similar decisions, and we are already seeing the emergence of a right-wing feminism as well as the cultivation of right-wing Black leadership such as Clarence Thomas and General Colin Powell.) As we walk the corridors of power, it may be not our lobbyists, our congresspeople, the queer members of a Democratic administration who carry our hopes of success. It may be the unseen lesbian secretaries and gay janitors, the Black Congressional Caucus and the National Conference of Mayors who are as much the source of our power.

Many of these people know that no movement or person in this country can escape the repression and dehumanization that was required for the genocide of Native peoples and the enslavement of Africans. That's what we fight when we "Fight the Right." Let our presence in the South this weekend remind us of that. The only "special right" that the United States gives to minorities is the right to be the target of genocidal policies. We have only to look at AIDS policy to confirm this truth. Just as we do not want people of color buying the right's homophobic argument that we are after "special rights," not civil rights, it is also vital that our movement does not buy the racist backlash to affirmative action propagated over the last two decades by the same Republican forces. When we put both parts of their strategy together, it's clear that, to them, all civil rights are "special rights" that victimize privileged white men.[7] When any "minority," whether racial, ethnic, gendered or sexual, buys into these wedge strategies, we play ourselves for fools and disrupt the possibility of a transformative political majority in the next century.

It's my belief that racism shapes all political movements in the United States, for better and for worse, but because white people so seldom talk about how we are affected by racism, we don't understand how to counter it. We just act it out. In the lesbian and gay movement, much of our analysis has flowed from an understanding of gender, leaving race and class at two removes from our analysis. But approaches to racism have shaped the debates within our own community on issues such as passing and assimilation, radical transformation versus reform, legal strategies versus empowerment of the grassroots. One of the dominant paradigms for dealing with race in the twentieth century emerged from the University of Chicago in the 1920s. It was called the ethnicity model, and it theorized that immigrants to the United States go through cycles of contact and conflict then assimilation.[8] Now this theory, on the one hand, was an improvement over the dominant paradigm it replaced, which was the biological approach to race, that saw racial differences as inherited and that justified slavery and colonialism. (This context should make us beware of the biological theories of homosexuality now being advanced.)

But the ethnicity paradigm was based on European experience, not the experiences of people of color. At the same time that European immigrants were being assimilated—if painfully—into our economy, Jim Crow reigned in the South for African Americans, Asians were kept out of the country altogether by immigration quotas, Native Americans were suffering record rates of poverty on a land base once again decimated by white theft, and Chicanas were forming their own mutualistas in the Southwest in the face of racist white unions. So this business of assimilation operates differently above and below the color lines, as do most manifestations of American "democracy." If we generic gay and lesbian white-folks set as our movement's goal being assimilated into American culture, getting "our piece of the pie," we ignore or deny the reality that gay and lesbian people of color will never be assimilated in the same way within this system because it was constituted to exclude them. And, as Derrick Bell has argued in reference to African-American liberation, and as Colorado proved

---

7   Winthrop Jordan, *The White Man's Burden: Historical Origins of Racism in the United States* (London: Oxford University Press, 1974), 33. *White over Black: American Attitudes Toward the Negro 1550–1812* (Baltimore: Penguin, 1969), is a longer version of this excellent book, which was abbreviated in *The White Man's Burden* to make it more accessible to students. References are to *The White Man's Burden* unless otherwise specified.

8   Zinn, *A People's History of the United States*, 26–28; "African slavery is hardly to be praised. But it was far different from plantation or mining slavery in the Americas, which was lifelong, morally crippling, destructive of family ties, without hope of any future" (27).

in regard to gay civil rights, wherever assimilation goals may become enshrined in law, they can just as easily be overturned.[9]

If we follow the ethnicity theory, we perpetuate the belief that the issue of "homophobia" is mainly a matter of personal prejudice, which contact with us will diffuse. We ignore the extent to which the most powerful political and economic forces in this country have an investment in our degradation. Literally, right-wing groups invest millions in slandering us, knowing that these efforts will build up their grassroots base and their funding chests. In the Oregon Citizen's Alliance campaign, they put back into their vicious homophobic ballot initiative campaign only one dollar out of every three raised. The rest of the money, according to the Task Force's Fight the Right organizer Scot Nakagawa, went into a range of regressive causes. Such campaigns also distract people from the corporate theft that may beggar us all.

The assimilation model leads us to try to smooth the rough edges of our community, putting limits on visible leadership by people of color, working class white gay men and lesbians and anyone else who doesn't look and act like most lobbyists. It leads to "outing" powerful, rich people to show that they, too, are gay. It leads to surveys that tout the marketing power of the gay dollar and position us as a movement of the middle to upper class, with higher than average spending power. This dynamic sets us up to be a "buffer class," in a similar way that Jews were portrayed in Europe, to draw off class anger from the economic elite who are really making the decisions and reaping the rewards in a period of national economic crisis and decline. It makes us appear narrow and selfish (which I do not think we are) and cuts us off from allies, increasing our vulnerability to insurgent right-wing populist movements agitated by economic unrest. This is classic fascism, and its foundation has already been laid in our time and our nation.[10]

The two models of race thinking that emerged to counter the ethnicity model were nationalism and socialism. I would argue that we have opted for the wrong model. We don't need a queer nationalism—as powerful as the militancy and anti-assimilationist stances of Queer Nation have been. We need a queer socialism that is by necessity anti-racist, feminist and democratic; a politic that does not cut us off from other people, but that unites us with them in the broadest possible movement. Now I live in a state where folks shoot both "commies" and "queers," so I had better explain first what I do not mean by socialism: I don't mean the KGB or the Berlin Wall or Stalin's gulags or the repression of spirituality or creativity or initiative. What I really mean is a more genuine democracy, where the citizens of our country have more direct access to all the decisions that affect us, not only in the political but also in the economic arena. (The NAFTA vote was important because it offered a rare occasion where the U.S. Congress got to vote on what multinational corporations do.) What I mean is a less lonely society, where we think collectively about resources for the common good,

---

9   Marvin Harris, *Patterns of Race in the Americas* (New York: W.W. Norton, 1974), 12.
10   Quoted in Gilberto Freyre, *The Masters and the Slaves* (New York: Knopf, 1956), 178.

rather than struggling individually against each other for material and psychic survival. What I mean is a more humane society, where our driving motive is abundant life for all rather than increasing extravagance for a few and suffering for many more. Nor do I think there is presently any complete blueprint for how this political and economic democracy would occur in the United States. We are called on to invent it, as the "New Left" set out to do thirty years ago.

With the collapse of socialist governments around the world, we are called on to reinvent the movements for a society, in Margaret Randall's words, where "everyone contributes and everyone is cared for." Randall feels that many of these socialist movements failed because they would not develop a feminist agenda. Queer socialism would occur within a profoundly feminist revolutionary context, defined by Randall as "a feminist discourse based on an ideology embracing democratic relations of power, a redefinition of history and of memory, and a world view that favors life over the signs of imminent death that we experience on so many fronts."[11]

This Queer Socialism of a "newer left" would recognize the damage done by 500 years of colonial rule. People of color have suffered for 500 years from the European/Christian war between mind and body, soul and body, projected onto all women and onto cultures that often had more holistic worldviews and darker skins. The mind/body split allows the hundred white men owning poultry plants in Mississippi to tell the Black women workers, "we only want your bodies, not your minds" as those men lock the women into plants where twenty-seven out of thirty in one factory acquired carpal-tunnel syndrome.[12] It generates rape and devastating physical and psychological violence against women. It also defines gay men and lesbians in this period as only perverse bodies engaged in sinful/sick/illegal physical acts, as "abominations." And it discards the old and the disabled. When we lesbians and gay men see that Black women in Mississippi poultry plants and Mexican women in *maquilas* are also defined as only bodies, to be used and discarded, machines without feelings and souls, we can understand more fully how our fates are implicated in theirs. When we don't respond to others being hurt by similar forces, how can we expect them to respond to our crises and pains? As Rabbi Hillel taught 2,000 years ago, "If we are not for ourselves, who will be for us? [But] if we are not for others, who are we?"

As Queer Socialists we would bring our insights and strengths to a range of progressive struggles. A Queer Socialism would be inevitably inflected for gender, would have our anger and our militancy, our humor and our flair, and would shape a movement that includes gay and lesbian homeless people, many of them cross-dressers and many, people of color. We know that in some cultures that do not hate the body, the male and female principles are not so much at war as they are in this culture, and that gender-transgressive people like the berdache in American Indian societies are considered holy

---

11   Eduardo Galeano, *Open Veins of Latin America: Five Centuries of the Pillage of a Continent*, trans. Cedric Belfrage (New York: Monthly Review Press, 1973), 50.

12   Zinn, *A People's History of the United States*, 29.

people—as we are holy people. A Queer Socialism would clarify our roles as workers, as "means of production." But we gay people also bring the knowledge that humans are not only "means of production," however much capitalism seeks to define us that way. We know and insist that our needs include not only the survival needs of food, shelter, health care and clothing, but also dignity, pleasure, intimacy and love.

In adding our lavender stripe to the rainbow, we bring our grief and our creativity in the too-familiar face of death. I have watched my gay brothers care for one another to the grave, joined in their care, of course, by lesbians and heterosexuals. I've been around a good bit, and I have not witnessed this particular tender brotherhood in the face of disease and death in other places in the same way. Many of these are white men, middle-class men, who have taught me about courage and compassion. None of what I urge here is about categories we cannot escape. It is about who we choose to be.

Gay men and lesbians also bring the ability to create familial love that does not depend on biology, on the worship of our own gene pools. Those nonbiological parents among us know that we can love and parent any child—it mainly requires our rapt attention to an unfolding wonder—and that the children in the inner cities, the babies born in the *maquilas*, are also our children. As an African proverb teaches, "It takes a whole village to raise a child." These days, it must take a whole country unwilling to write off any of its young.

A Queer Socialism would not be provincially urban. It would recognize that the most crucial battles for gay/lesbian politics in the next decade will not be in the cities where we have our power base, where most of our people are concentrated. The right has finally figured out to take us on their turf, not ours. These battles will be in areas that are more rural and historically more conservative. In those areas, we will develop new models not dependent on a critical gay mass and gay infrastructure. We will create broad-based movements against homophobia and all forms of social injustice rather than movements only for gay and lesbian rights. These movements will hold heterosexuals accountable for heterosexism, generating heterosexual allies, then trusting them to do their jobs. The trust we will gain through this process is one of the opportunities within the crisis. Heterosexuals will increasingly learn how their fates are implicated in ours, how homophobia erodes their most intimate relationships and corrupts their institutions, building repression into our military, fear into our schools' quest for understanding and knowledge, and mean-spiritedness into proclamations of love from churches, mosques and synagogues. If the Religious Right has its way, they will use homophobia as an ax against the very taproot of this country's democratic potential, the revolutionary concept of human dignity and equality.

In my vision of a reinvigorated movement, the National Gay & Lesbian Task Force would take a stand on major issues of our time, such as the North American Free Trade Act: against NAFTA and in solidarity with working people, who are most of our people; in recognition that unemployed people (whose numbers NAFTA will increase) are six times more likely to commit acts of violence than people who are employed, and some of that will be hate violence; and in recognition that NAFTA will override our national and local laws on labor and environmental standards (as "unfair labor practices"), constricting once again this country's democratic possibilities.

In my movement, the Task Force would call up Ben Chavis, the new NAACP Director, and say, "Rev. Chavis, thank you for your support of the March on Washington"—for which he came under serious attack from within his own organization—"and we'd like to return the favor." We'd say, "The next time a big vote on racism comes up in Congress, we'll be there with you, with our 100,000 members and $4 million budget, because we appreciate your help and because that's about our people, too." My movement would not avoid these stands for fear it would divide our constituency—which is already divided; it would take leadership stands to unite us around broader principles.

In our movement, we see the opportunity in the crisis to do what we should have done twenty-five years ago: increase our determination to keep faith with one another by not tolerating racism, sexism, anti-Semitism, ageism, the fear and neglect of the disabled or class divisions in ourselves or in our organizations.

In our movement we don't panic or blame ourselves, we stay accountable and take the long view. The Quincentenary of Columbus's arrival in the Americas gave us the opportunity to reflect on 500 years of resistance. The people of color among us let us know that this is not a decade's or even a lifetime's struggle. If we sacrifice our relationships to immediate victories, we will lose in the long haul. How we treat one another matters more than any particular "win" because our goal is a transformed culture, which also requires transformed human relationships.

In our movement, we seize the opportunity to face our own self-destructive fears and isolations in the messages of the right, and to stare them down. As Creek poet Joy Harjo wrote: "Oh, you have choked me, but I gave you the leash, You have gutted me, but I gave you the knife, You have devoured me, but I gave you the heated thing. I take myself back, fear."[13]

In our movement, we claim no more or less than our human place among the creatures on the planet. Queer Socialism moves us to the post-Queer.

This reenergized movement will be, in Suzanne Pharr's eloquent terms, "not a wedge, but a bridge"; not a point of division, but of expansion and connection. To those who insist on denying us our full humanity, we will insist on the sacred humanity of all people. A bridge, not a wedge. A bridge, not a wedge. It has a nice ring to it. We can say it like a mantra when we feel the right getting too hot. Folks from San Francisco can help us in this imaging—all those bays, all that steel hanging up in the air and people got the nerve to drive across it. How does it stay up there, anyway, across the blue expanse?

Yes, the fires are burning. But think of all that water.

And, even in a hot wind, bridges will sing.

---

13 "The Columbus Letter of March 14th, 1493," quoted in Virgil J. Vogel, *This Country Was Ours: A Documentary History of the American Indian* (New York: Harper & Row, 1972), 34.

Race, Prisons, and War

Scenes from the History of U.S. Violence

Ruth Wilson Gilmore

When editors Leo Panitch and Colin Leys selected a 2009 theme for the annual Socialist Register, they could not help but focus in upon the rampant nature of "violence today." Utilizing a famous dichotomy set forth by Engels and oft-referred to by Rosa Luxemburg, which suggested that if capitalism were allowed to continue the world would see a new level of what can only be understood as "barbarism," the '09 Register chronicled the "actually existing barbarism" of continued racism and sexism, endless war, and intensified oppression. Looking at the U.S. manifestations of our barbaric moment in time, noted professor and president of the American Studies Association Ruth Wilson Gilmore focused upon the connecting point between war and racism: the U.S. prison system. Gilmore's important essay follows from her work in Golden Gulag: Prisons, Surplus, Crisis, and Opposition in Globalizing California. *We are proud to reprint that vital essay here.*

> *Moreover, the important question for the future in this case is not "can it happen again?" Rather, it is "can it be stopped?"*
> —David Stannard, *American Holocaust: The Conquest of the New World*

What can be said about a political culture in search of "infinite prosperity" that is dependent on a perpetual enemy who must always be fought but can never be vanquished? The United States ranks first in military power, wealth, war-making, murder rates, and incarceration rates. At the time of this writing in the summer of 2008, one in one hundred U.S. adults was locked in a cage, and an additional two percent were under the direct supervision of the criminal justice system. While the vast majority of people in custody did not kill or violently harm anybody, the centrality of violence to all aspects of U.S. life helps explain the continuum from policing and prisons to war. Rather than rehearse well-known critical histories of stolen land, stolen labor, gender domination, and iron-fisted capital expansion, this essay uses them to historicize current events. It constructs a series of scenes from various periods that, in sum, are designed to demonstrate the persistence and convergence of patterns and systems. The resulting narrative arc is more cumulative than teleological, even though I believe with all my heart there's an end to violence in both senses of "end": violence produces power, which under the grow-or-die culture of capitalism seems like a slightly erratic expression of self-interest; but violence does not produce *all* power, which means perhaps that its effectiveness might come to a finish.

Southern Louisiana: Armed White Men

The violence wrought by Hurricane Katrina in September 2005 focused singularly shocked global attention on the naked, official, and organized depth of U.S. racism. A global chorus—including many residents of the United States—insisted they had not really known how bad it still is to be poor and of color in the richest and most militarily powerful nation-state in the history of the world. The views of dead Black people floating in the floodwater, and living Black people huddled on roofs or in rowboats, or crammed into the hold of a troop transport ship in dry-dock, or into the vastness of the Sugar Bowl football stadium, either taught or reminded the world what it used to know about the United States: it is difficult and dangerous to be Black in this country. One particularly outstanding image, shot on both still and motion film from hovering helicopters, demonstrated in stark terms how the disaster was—and remains—a political rather than natural phenomenon. Picture: a line of armed white men pointing their Winchester rifles at a group of mostly Black people to keep them from walking across an interstate highway bridge from New Orleans onto the dryer ground of neighboring Gretna. Professional and amateur pundits marveled at this scene's explicitness. OK, they reasoned, perhaps unorganized neglect had allowed the levees to crumble, and perhaps the cumulative effects of flooding Black neighborhoods to save white ones during previous hurricanes and floods stretching back across the century had increased the vulnerability of those locations. But how could anybody explain officers of the law stopping, rather than helping, people in obvious danger of dying? What is the continuity that produces and exploits group-differentiated vulnerability to premature death so casually, without fear of political consequence or moral shame?

Armed white men of Gretna figured in the media a century earlier, when a ready-to-lynch mob hit the streets one afternoon in the year 1900. A New Orleans newspaper account of the hunt concluded, "The shots brought out almost everybody-white in town, and though there was nothing to show for the exciting work, except the arrest of the Negro, who doesn't answer the description of the man wanted, Gretna's male population had its little fun and felt amply repaid for all the trouble it was put to, and all the ammunition it wasted."[1] This was a story of a nonlynching (although the "man wanted" and others were slain that day) during the long period of Jim Crow rule committed to destroying Black self-determination. Had the 1900 Gretna gang caught its quarry everybody would still have had "fun"—and used even more ammunition, since one favorite pastime of lynchers was to empty their Winchesters into the victim's *dead* body, to watch the bullets destroy whatever human form remained after burning,

---

1   Ida B. Wells-Barnett, *On Lynchings* (Amherst: Humanity Books, 2002).

cutting, tying, dragging, flaying, disemboweling, dismembering had, in Ida B. Wells's words, "hurled men [and women] into eternity on supposition."[2]

Wells, whose *On Lynchings* was first published in 1892, used the pulpits of international organizations and the press to argue precisely how lynching combined the forces of both violence and ideology—or coercion and consent—to produce and consolidate power. She showed that this combination particularly provided the capacity to stifle association and competition, minimize ownership, and independence of thought and action, and therefore guarantee the extraction from Black communities of cheap labor (including sex) and profits from the sale of consumer goods. Her aim was not only to bear witness to the fact of each event—that someone died or nearly died—but also to testify to its context, to trace out the event's underlying or true cause. To achieve her end, she examined not only what people did, but also how the stories of their actions were narrated and used. Her exposition and analysis demonstrated the role of lynching in renovating racist hierarchy, gender subordination, and regional accumulation strategies. To do all this hard work every lynching was exemplary, which means it wasn't quick. Lynch mobs did not just take off after somebody with the intent of killing them extra-legally—albeit in most cases with the sanction of sworn state agents from sheriffs to governors to juries. Lynching was public torture, and both press and posse elites encouraged "everybody white" to get in on the fun. Mobs thrilled to participate in the victim's slow death, to hear agonized cries for pity and smell roasting human flesh, to shoot dead bodies to smithereens, to keep body parts—ears, penises, breasts, testicles, charred bones—as souvenirs, and to read detailed descriptions of torture in the newspapers. Mobs South, North, and West could usually count on the press to explain away the kidnapping, torture, and murder by invoking the naturalness of human sacrifice—particularly through the repetitive ascription of subhumanity to the victim—and thereby to vindicate the torturers ("everybody white") via the contradictory claim of supremacy.

If "everybody-white" in Gretna were also the "males" of Gretna, their violence ("fun"—in other words, its distance from "criminality") cannot be legitimated in the same way for all males. But that's not an end but a beginning, because a dynamic society in which the victors present themselves as the pattern of human nature (in which *homo economicus* strips off his bourgeois haberdashery and becomes the imperially naked human nature in action), invites mighty struggles to establish who counts as masculine. Moreover, Ida Wells spelled out clearly that the "usual crime" of rape pinned on lynch victims was a fiction, a lie known by everybody in the South. By publishing the open secret that white women had consensual, intimate, illegal sex with Black men, Wells dared name, in black-and-white, a persistent weakness in the hierarchy of entitlements and exclusions organizing white supremacy.

People then and now think race is natural because of the biology of reproduction, even though the biology of reproduction proves race is made of the social and political

---

2   Ibid., 48, 53.

meanings assigned to it. And to complicate the issue, sex is not reproduction, while reproduction is always differentiation.

That's a lot to keep under control, and torture helped to perpetuate the normative view that there *should be* control. Thus it made no difference that most of the people tortured did not have illegal sex, consensually or not, with anybody. The convolution here is indicative of the paroxysms of thought and argument that stunningly establish a threshold of sanctioned torture (should nonconsensual sex be so punished?) and thereby evade the question of how "criminality" is naturalized by presenting it as the origin of the explosive horror of violence (the illegal sex) that then must be fought with the explosive horror of violence (the torture and lynching).

Enshrouding this necessary convolution are the constantly renovated gender relations that give coherence to the rhetoric of vulnerability and perpetration. The rape of women of color, and the pervasiveness of domestic violence in all kinds of households, speak both to the gendered hierarchy of racism and to the notion that masculinity is constituted through differentially legitimated force. Thus the spasmodically systematic application of violence to secure material and ideological domination over "infinite prosperity" is a consistent practice of, rather than a rude eruption in, everyday life.

Representatives of and advocates for Black and poor people doomed, displaced or disappeared in the 2005 events in Gretna and New Orleans followed in Wells's footsteps, and carried grievances and demands for remedy before international bodies. When the United States showed up for its regularly scheduled interview at the United Nations Human Rights Commission in Geneva in 2006, commissioners asked questions about the usually suspect aspects of U.S. life: Why are there so many poor people?

Why are there so many prisoners? Why does racism persist in what Wells termed "the organized life of the country"?[3] And in particular, why hasn't the devastation that slammed Black and poor communities where the Mississippi flows into the Gulf of Mexico been redressed?

Members of the Human Rights Commission struggled to understand how the United States could be lax in living up to the terms of treaties that it had helped to write, but even though Article VI of the U.S. constitution specifies that Treaties are part of "the supreme Law of the Land," Native Americans do not puzzle over the question that (perhaps just for show) seemed to mystify the Geneva commissioners.[4] The United States has in fact consistently broken every treaty ever written with Indigenous peoples, a habit of disregard unmodulated by a single wrinkle of official remorse, much less by redress for the slash-and-burn movement of white people across North America, from Virginia and New England in the seventeenth century, through coast-to-coast horrors of extermination committed in the name of god, lawgiving, freedom,

---

3   Ibid., 48.
4   Rev. Daniel Buford, Untitled Report, CITY: Peoples Institute for Survival and Beyond, 2006.

and accumulation. Puritans described the screams of Indians being burned alive in torched villages as "God laughing at his enemies."[5]

Indian-killers wore the body parts of those they had killed as jewelry, and made other useful and decorative objects from human remains. Through the violent dialectics of murder, dislocation, and disease, more than 95 percent of Indigenous Americans were hurled into eternity within the first few generations after contact with European colonizers.[6] The rest were removed, relocated, or "terminated"—an astonishing word, meant to describe dispersal of people from reservations to cities. Weapons of various types, constantly improved to become like the rifles wielded in Gretna in 1900 and again in 2005, enforced Indigenous agreement to treaties that consigned first nation peoples to places and life-ways not their own, the alternative being straightforward extermination.

Southern New England: The Military-Industrial Complex

I was born and raised in New Haven, Connecticut, a small city dominated at first by tightfisted Puritans but then, over the centuries, shaped by Native Americans (many of whom passed as, or into, white or Black), free Black people, Southern and Eastern Europeans, and Puerto Ricans, Dominicans and most lately Chicana/os and Mexicans. It became a Catholic city with a significant Jewish population sometime in the early twentieth century, during the height of the biggest immigration boom, in absolute numbers, in the history of the United States. New Haven was ruled, first overtly and then behind-the-scenes, by WASPs, until they didn't care about it anymore, when it ceased being a prosperous polity around 1980. The principle of "dispersed inequality" that Robert Dahl famously and erroneously concluded in 1957 would be the future of the United States multiethnic republic appeared to work well enough to warrant his book on New Haven politics during the post–World War II period, when the Elm City's two principal products of economic activity, guns and students, were being turned out in high quality and at high cost. But when things started to get bad, in New Haven and throughout the United States, Dahl wisely repudiated his signature concept (even though U.S.-trained political science doctoral candidates must, to this day, commit its error to heart).

Every New Haven schoolchild of the long twentieth century learned about the political and material marvels achieved by the white men whose names mark many of the city's major streets: Judges Goffe, Dixwell, and Whalley, who signed the death warrant for Charles I and fled to New Haven when Charles II took the throne; Eli Whitney, interchangeable parts innovator, wartime profiteer, and cotton gin engineer; and Oliver Fisher Winchester, developer and manufacturer of the repeating rifle—the gun that "won" the west. Youngsters toured their monuments, reported to each other

---

5   Michael Mann, *The Dark Side of Democracy: Explaining Ethnic Cleansing* (Cambridge: Cambridge University Press, 2005), 84.

6   Stannard, *American Holocaust*, ix–x.

on their accomplishments, and sang and danced their praise in dead-serious amateur musicals performed for elected and other elites.

Killing kings, mass-producing weapons, and framing accumulation as an inalienable right coalesced into white supremacy—the modern theory and practice that explains how, over the past few centuries, authority devolved from the person of the monarch to one, and only one, sovereign race. That race's divinely conferred and energetically exercised freedom to have, to take, to kill, to rule, and to judge when any of these actions is right or wrong—individually and in the aggregate—kept institutions like Winchester's arms factory and Yale University humming day and night.

Killing *somebody* has always been on the American agenda, and avoiding being caught in American crosshairs an ontological priority. For example, the lessons white supremacists violently offered to Black GIs after World War I can be summed up in a couple of imperatives: expect nothing, and don't wear your uniform. Lynching, which had minimally abated during the brief engagement in the war, heated up in the aftermath. There is always an increase in murder in the United States after the country goes off to war and wins—just as there is always a sudden spike after executions—which together form strong evidence that the "state models behavior for the polity."[7] The bloody "red summer" of 1911, best known for the Palmer raids against leftist political and labor organizers, was simultaneously a time of intense racist lynching in the name of white supremacy. The class and race wars were related rather than coincidental. Not surprisingly, J. Edgar Hoover began his rise to power as the chief engineer of capitalist white supremacist policing by serving as technocratic overseer for many of the 1919 actions.

He was still around as head of the FBI when over an 18-month period in 1969–71 federal and local police destroyed the Black Panther Party. In 1969, no less than in 1919, rhetoric about violence and violent action brought into view a perpetual enemy who must always be fought but can never be vanquished, presented as simultaneously criminal (acting outside the law) and alien (not belonging to the polity). But when Black GIs came back after World War II they were not about to "expect nothing" or hide their uniforms in the bottom of a trunk. Having heard from wives and fathers, sisters and friends, about the work radicals were doing stateside to advance the double-victory cause—the fight against U.S. racism as part of the fight against fascism—many decided to fight to get well-paying blue collar jobs in factories. In New Haven, it was making guns. Winchester's was the biggest factory in the New England gun belt, and the rifles used to kill Indigenous people were still being produced long after the theft of the continent had been completed. Winchester's became the place where Black men went to work after doing their two or three or four years in the armed service—"protecting" Berlin, South Korea, Okinawa, Thailand, Laos, South Vietnam. They knew how to shoot. They

---

7   Dane Archer and Rosemary Gartner, *Violence and Crime in Cross-National Perspective*, (New Haven: Yale University Press, 1984).

worked overtime on the assembly line. The wives worked at Yale in low-paying jobs. Their children sang and danced: when they were not rehearsing "Jump Jim Crow" they warbled about superior inventions and modern points of view. The modern point of view that sustained the social order was the relentless industrialization of killing, requiring fewer exertions of human physical and mental strength per person hurled into eternity. This was the military-industrial complex: the set of workers, intellectuals, bosses, boosters, places, materials, relationships, ideas, and political-economic capacity to organize these factors of production into the machinery of death. Eventually, President General Dwight David Eisenhower got nervous enough about the military-industrial complex to give it its name. He revered war; he loved capitalism. But did not like how war-making and profit-making had become so thoroughly intermeshed during the Cold War that, he argued, both entrepreneurial innovation and industrial policy would be shaped (and perhaps squeezed) by their might. His anxiety was about 185 years too late, though perhaps it is never too late to say you're sorry. The United States has never had an industrial policy other than the one cohering around warfare, although it became most fully operationalized with the establishment of the Pentagon and consolidated power of the Department of Defense's many constituents in the post-1945 era.

Winchester's New Haven arms factory was taken over by the Olin-Matheson corporation in 1963. After an employee buyout to forestall the factory's closure in 1981 failed, the factory was first acquired by a French holding company, then sold to a Belgian arms-making cartel. By the time the factory was completely shut down in 2006, prosperity had long since exited the city—along with nearly 25 percent of its population. What was left in its wake were poor Black and Brown people, a spatially segregated arc of extremely well-to-do white households, and a shrunken middle-income stratum struggling to make public schools and services respond as they had in the earlier period. As has been the case across the United States, especially in places where wide gaps between rich and poor coincided with declining local economies, criminalization became the preferred public response to the problems created by poverty. Young people from households which had been supported by guns produced and exported to kill other people's children now got their hands on imported guns to kill neighbors, family, and friends. Mostly, however, they were busy being poor.

The expansion of criminalization is always explained away by reference to a secular rise in violent activity—rape, murder, child molestation are the unholy trinity. Highly rationalized, interpersonal violence did not account for the kinds of laws and techniques used to lock people up. But it served as an excuse, throughout the United States, to shift infrastructural investment from schools and hospitals to jails and prisons. The same family that bought and later dumped Winchester's funds, the Olin Foundation, is among the principal sponsors of intellectual hacks who churn out racist reports and soundbites proving that prison expansion is good for society. The war against the poor has thus oscillated between modes of incorporation (a job in a gun factory or a cot in a cage) that maintain the central force of racial capitalism.

From the Greyhound Station to Abu Ghraib: Prisons as Manifest Destiny

"Criminal" has long been on the rise in the lexicon of putatively transparent or self-explanatory terms—like race or gender—used to designate fundamental (whether fixed or mutable) differences between kinds of people. Ida B. Wells saw the active connection between race-making and outlaw-making when she wrote: "To lynch for a certain crime not only concedes the right to lynch any person for any crime but it is in a fair way to stamp us a race of rapists and desperadoes."[8] The first public infrastructural accomplishment in post-Katrina New Orleans was to convert the city's Greyhound station into a jail; Burl Cain, the warden of the notorious Angola State prison—a post civil war plantation where 85 percent of prisoners are Black and an equal percentage serving sentences for the rest of their natural lives—was put in charge. In other words, the elites didn't start by burying the dead or feeding the living, but they did close a port—the bus station—in order to lock up as many as possible whose exit from the city had not yet been accomplished through dispersal or death. Of all sites, the bus station! In the United States, buses are symbolic of working class mobility, and also—especially in the South—of the struggle, organized during the height of the long twentieth century civil rights movement, to desegregate transportation no less than schools.

The conversion of the bus station into a jail occurred not long after Gretna's police blocked the public bridge, whose very existence symbolized the disinvestment in city centers in favor of the suburbanization of the 1950s and 1960s. The failed levees of New Orleans themselves were, in their disintegration, symbolic not simply of urban abandonment but rather of a recalibration of (as opposed to a wholesale withdrawal from) the wealthRACE, producing urban landscapes of the Big Easy, as New Orleans is familiarly called.

In the twenty-five or so years leading up to Katrina, a massive expansion of prisons and criminalization spread across the United States, driven by different, but connected, processes of displacement, abandonment, and control. As was the case with kidnapped African labor and stolen Indigenous land, a completely involuntary migration—this time around via conviction and incarceration—has once again resulted in the mysterious disappearance of millions of people. This ongoing disappearance is apparently not fully grasped, even in its accomplishment, to judge from the calmness with which most people in the United States of all races receive the news that one out of every hundred of the country's adults is locked up in a prison or jail.

The rise of the cage as a large-scale all-purpose solution to problems is a relatively recent phenomenon in world history. Modern prisons were born and grew up with the United States, as impersonal but individualized sites of large-scale social control, in the long historical turn marked by the consolidation of the bourgeois nation-state

---

8   Wells, *On Lynching*, 41.

as the world's fundamental political economic unit, the normalization of capitalism, and the development of racist science and philosophy to explain it all. Although the reformist purpose of prisons was to end bodily torture, in the United States prison did not replace torture but rather complemented its role in securing social order.

In the case of slavery prison was beside the point: there was no purpose in locking up a tool with life in it, while there was plenty of purposefulness in demonstrating to that and other living tools the imminence of premature death as the likeliest respite from endless suffering.[9] And in the case of land theft, there was no point in locking people up at public expense when those Indigenous people who had not been slaughtered could be deported to reservations to fend for themselves. But what of others?

By the late 1840s, when various U.S. political factions were debating the merits of permanently grabbing part or all of Mexico, the most clear-eyed proponents of "Manifest Destiny" hesitated at the prospect of bringing into the union millions of Mexicans who, whatever they were, were not white. Supremacists claimed they had coaxed from (rather than forced into) the landscape a set of nearly identical, locally controlled governmental institutions run by enfranchised white men. They were determined to maintain the absolute dominion of the sovereign race. Thus the anxiety was not just about having more not-white folks on U.S. territory, but dealing with the problem of the vote—itself symbolic of their material delusion concerning local governance. If the Mexican-become-American men voted, then what of the union of free white men? The master-race republic sought to expand its wealth without diluting its distribution scheme. As we have seen, in the post–Civil War period, public torture was pervasively used, even as the modern prison increasingly became part of rural no less than urban landscapes. Jim Crow, then, did not only work to suppress Black people; it was both template and caution for all who were not members of the sovereign race. That century's globalizing contradictions, characterized by Indigenous extermination, wars of territorial expansion, socio-spatial segregation, racist science and eugenics, the redrawing of the world's imperial contours, and the spread of democratized blood-and-soil nationalism, coalesced at the time of the 1898 Spanish-American war, and these forces in sum gave both political and theoretical shape to the twentieth century's continuing human-sacrifice rampage.

The end of the nineteenth century was also defined by the development of the modern business corporation and the rise of engineering and a technocratic view of how to manage systems and structures—whether the DuPont Corporation, the city of Los Angeles, or the State of Mississippi.

This combination of "what" and "how" formed the basis of "Progressivism"—a movement misunderstood as an opening through which common people might democratically overcome racial capitalism and white supremacist imperialism. Rather, Progressives developed large-scale complex public and private institutions in order to

---

9   Saidiya Hartman, *Scenes of Subjection* (Oxford: Oxford University Press, 1997).

guarantee the privatized extraction of value from land and other factors of production. As a result, it should not be surprising that Progressivism developed in the South and that Jim Crow was part of its original structure. Under the aegis of Progressivism, prisons became regulated by specialists and segregated by age and gender. This might not sound so bad—except for the fact that before the Progressive period few youngsters and few women were in any prisons anywhere.

Reform, then as now, opened the door to expanding prison under the guise of social improvement. At the same time, in the South the official end to the convict lease system took uncompensated labor (prisoners) out of competition with unemployed free labor; the struggle to end that system was resolved, in racist terms, by the formation of prison plantations for men (mostly Black) so that free workers (profiled white) could be assured of exclusive right to jobs, whether or not the work actually existed. In the late twentieth and early twenty-first century, prison expansion has proceeded along these two fronts—as the necessary response to "criminality," and as a reform of that response. The disfranchisement of prisoners gave George W. Bush the 2000 election.

The rationality underlying prison growth uses both rhetoric and practices of violence to make mass incarceration seem other than what it is—a machine for producing and exploiting group-differentiated vulnerability to premature death. The intellectuals who have figured out how to exercise racism without naming race have to work extremely hard to realize their goals, and they draw on a template and legacy of thought developed from and for the kinds of wars they imagine the United States is fighting when it sends troops and materiel abroad. War and incarceration are supposed to bring good things to the places destroyed in the name of being saved; the devastation wrought overseas in Iraq and Afghanistan is both prefigured and shadowed by the history and current experience of life in the United States itself. The convergence of theory and technique come into view in the construction of the perpetual enemy who must always be fought but can never be vanquished.

For the past twenty-five years, the militarization of everyday domestic life in the United States is acted out, in full dress, through, for example, the intensified criminalization of kids, who in California in 1988 were officially named "street terrorists." Another example is the way that people in the United States have gotten into the habit of wearing photo identification as though it were jewelry. Everyone expects to be stopped, but the expectation of what happens afterward diverges wildly. In such a milieu of battle-readiness and checkpoint-cheeriness it was remarkably easy for the lawyers defending the Los Angeles policemen who beat up Rodney King to argue, in spite of the visual evidence, that King was "in control" of the situation. A millisecond of the globally circulated film of his beating shows King trying to get up as he is kicked and pummeled. This effort made King a violent desperado; and while the jury that acquitted the four cops probably would have let them go anyway, because the jurors came from a community of retired police and military and had a narrative of events on which to hang the cops' plea.

"Criminality" worked too well to fail in the courtroom.

The 1992 multicultural uprising against the verdict brought forth both spontaneous and systematic radical understandings of the internal racist logic of U.S. institutions. It also gave a boost to the top-down development of legal and other machinery designed to suppress such opposition to racist policing.

Although the Los Angeles police chief at the time was run out of his job, he has been replaced by a series of men for whom policing people of color is the number one priority (Gretna in 1900 had a "Black detective" to help in that work, just as apartheid South Africa had Black police). Each has demanded a larger police force, arguing that every time something happens like Rodney King being beating up, or thirteen-year-old Devin Brown being shot dead because a policeman said he thought the kid, driving a stolen car, was "a drunk" (which King was), the city will go up in flames if there isn't enough police power to keep it under control. They shop their techniques and demands around the world (getting rich as consultants along the way). Like the military, they want to surge. And as with contemporary warfare, they claim that what they do benefits the assaulted as well as the assaulter. The triggerman is safer and the target is precise. However, just as the outcome of what is called "surgical strikes" in the era of increasingly capitalized warfare has meant that more civilians than ever die in each conflict, so it is the case with policing "the war on the streets" at home.

The police and the military also act to guarantee their institutional role in the apparatus and activities of the state. On the one hand, for a nation conceived in the violence of Indigenous extermination and chattel slavery, one might think that the governmental agents charged with "defense" and "internal pacification" would have nothing to worry about. But they do have things to worry about—ranging from the technical capacity to capitalize a lot of their individual human labor, to the fact that their opponents work around the clock to abolish policing, prisons, the military, and capitalism.

The constant agitation produces constant effort to shape both thought and action, and those in uniform use bodily violence as both rhetorical pretext and as disciplining practice in order to reproduce power.

The torture of prisoners by U.S. military jailers at Abu Ghraib in Iraq in 2004 focused singularly shocked global attention on the naked and official depth of U.S. racism. The revelation of the hidden spectacle that soldiers staged for themselves and the various audiences they sent pictures to, occurred a year before Katrina, and in retrospect the similarity of press and pundit reactions to the two outrages is rather compelling evidence of how successfully the production of power through violence works. Once the pictures came to light, one phrase, invoking a physical action, came up several times in English, French and Spanish language newspapers of varying political persuasions in both the "first" and "third" worlds: "when Americans look away." I can't tell you whether the phrase emerged in one place and then travelled, or whether it is a phrase commonly used to describe Americans' ADHD, or something else.[10] What does the phrase assume about "Americans" and where they look? Were these newspapers right in assuming the real audience for the hidden spectacle, who happened to stumble onto it, could, as has happened historically, look and then look away—not out of denial, much less pity or shame, but rather with a deep and perhaps empathetic shrug for the *torturer*? The fact of torture consigns the tortured to a category of undifferentiated difference, an alien-ness underscored by religious or citizenship distinctions, but not reducible to them since both religion and citizenship can be changed. This suggests that the torture of prisoners today is about constructing racial categories no less than when white supremacy was being secured a hundred years ago.

Once the evidence of the outrage at Abu Ghraib was paraded before Congressional committees (and in art shows inviting "public" comment in elegant books), the perpetrators were plucked out of the "chain of command" and sent to prison. A lot was made of the fact that two or three of them had been stateside prison guards, and so what could one expect? Analytically, one could expect at least some critics to understand that what the guards did in both the United States and Iraq was to help consolidate policing and prisons' institutional dominance. These institutions aspire to the same degree of security for their existence at the state and local level that the Pentagon enjoys at the federal level. This reduces questions of institutional reform to marginal squabbles over cost-benefits and better practices.

Such a devolution of criticism makes reformist reform very powerful in the way that neoliberalism operates.[11] But it is not only the current set of institutions structured in dominance that matter—though they do. The culture of capitalism—not the culture of *consumption* but of *capitalism*—informs all the tendencies laid out in the scenes depicted in this essay. "Grow or die" works hand-in-hand with structural inequality to keep producing an outcome that people keep being shocked by. And yet, while being shocked, many are also persuaded of the naturalness of the system and are therefore vulnerable to accepting the proposition advanced by the man who coined "manifest destiny" to describe Anglo Saxons' right to control the planet. As Charles Kingsley, the author of *Westward Ho* wrote in a letter to a friend in 1849: "It *is* expedient that one man die for the people. One tribe exterminated if need be to save a whole continent. 'Sacrifice of human life?' Prove that it is *human* life."[12]

Abolition Now

In the dream of advocates for people locked up in Guantanamo and other known and unknown U.S. military-controlled prisons around the planet, the prisoners should be

10 Attention Deficit Hyperactivity Disorder, a condition so commonly attributed to children "acting up."

11 Ruth Wilson Gilmore, *Golden Gulag: Prison, Surplus, Crisis, and Opposition in Globalizing Capitalism* (Berkeley: University of California Press, 2006).

12 Quoted in Reginald Horsman, *Race and Manifest Destiny: The Origins of American Racial Anglo-Saxonism* (Cambridge, MA: Harvard University Press, 2002), 77.

brought into the U.S. criminal justice system where they can be charged, face their accusers, and be judged by their peers. This seems unlikely as a remedy for the real problem, which is violence, prisons, and warfare. It also proposes that things will cure things—better buildings (Bush's promise to remedy Abu Ghraib), training sessions (what U.S. professional has not taken a harassment training session in the past two years?), handbooks, and new laws. Yet in regular U.S. prisons and jails, where one out of every hundred U.S. adults lives, torture and terror happen every day. In California, every week a prisoner dies from medical neglect of easily treatable maladies.

Throughout the United States, the households of prison guards, along with police and military, are more likely to experience domestic violence than households whose income is not organized around the willingness to use bodily violence.

The proliferation of new prisons in the United States was followed by the proliferation of laws to guarantee their present size. And contemporaneously with domestic prison growth, there has occurred a U.S.-led global production of a criminal class without rights, designed to evade rather than fulfill the terms of treaties—including the global prohibition against torture. The concept of a rights-less person is an indirect legacy of the 1857 Dred Scott Supreme Court decision that used race to define who counts as human and therefore who bears human rights. Today the world is full of activists who try to practice human rights as a science, bringing before courts and the "organized life" of the planet claims of injury and demands for redress. Given the power that violence produces, it is perhaps time to pause and consider how the unfinished work of radical abolition might help us in practical as well as theoretical ways to get out of the trap of reformist reform. The violence of torture and official murder, toward the end of stealing labor, land, and reproductive capacity, has driven the history of the United States. If reform within that history is the pattern for change, it can only result in a "changing same."[13]

---

13   LeRoi Jones, "The Changing Same (R&B and New Black Music)," in Jones, *Black Music* (New York: William Morrow & Co., 1967), 180–211.

IV. The Roots and Routes of War: Patriarchy and Heterosexism

Dean of Students Ann Marie Penzkover and Her Niece Mariah, Wisconsin

Andrea Modica

From *Real Indians: Portraits of Contemporary Native Americans and America's Tribal Colleges*

Genocide: remembering Bengal, 1971

Sarah Husein

Who are men that bleed the bones of infants?
Guns in hand keep marching forward?
Line up other men by eight and ten
on the edge of river banks
then hide behind trees to shoot them?

Who are these men that suck
on bones
of infants?
Command death by hundreds
show up at doorsteps
with light in hand
turning villages
into mass graves?

Who are these men
that sleep amidst bodies raw,
and howling dogs
lay by the dying hills
and the bloodied rivers?

Who are these men that place flags
in other's soil
and claim its flesh to feed their own children?

Who are these men
that don't know their skin
their uniform's history?
Kill fathers along with their babies
allow mothers to go on living
disembody the elderly and still breathe
to witness their own victory?

Who are these men
that bleed the bones of children
take eight year old girls into bed
and rip them?

Who are these men that look upon the moon
and not bleed, fuck one woman 80 times a night
and still cum?

How do these men
these heads of Nations
keep on building
breathing?

Why We Need Women's Actions and Feminist Voices for Peace

Starhawk

This section, the first of two related parts, looks at the "Roots and Routes" of modern war-fare: the interplay between war and oppression based on gender, sexuality, and sexual orientation. Understanding that male supremacy and white supremacy are, at very least, intertwined, we have tried to take good care not to imply any hierarchy regarding which form of oppression—if any—is "worse," "more fundamental," or deserving of greater attention than any other. While recognizing that this book is focused upon the specific connections between racism and militarism, we include in this section the voices of leaders of the movements against heterosexism. The articles selected have special emphasis on the correlations between heterosexism, racism, and violence, but do not conform to any single or simple line regarding how these social evils interact. It seems clear, at very least, that any successful and long-lasting struggle for justice will have to include parts of all of these perspectives.

Among the hundreds of groups and actions being mounted against the war on Iraq are a significant number called and organized by women. Code Pink: Unreasonable Women for Peace has disrupted Congressional hearings and mounted an ongoing women's peace vigil at the White House since the beginning of the Iraq war. Women in Black hold vigils in hundreds of communities around the world on a regular basis. Women Rising for Peace and Justice, the women's caucus of United for Peace, has issued numerous calls for women's actions against the war.

Women are deeply impacted by war, racism and poverty—the three evils named by Martin Luther King. But when we stand for peace as women, it is not to make a case for our special victimhood, but to represent a different vision of strength. Women-initiated and women-led actions have a special energy and power. That power comes not from excluding men—most of these actions welcome men as participants—but because of the joy and visionary potential that arise when we come together as women to defend the values of life and caring that we hold dear.

To defend those values, we need not just women's voices against the war, but specifically feminist voices. For feminism allows us to analyze patriarchy, the constellation of values, ideas and beliefs that reinforces male control over women.

No set of qualities is innately or exclusively "female" or "male." Men can be compassionate, loving and kind, as women can be tough, brave, or callous. But patriarchy assigns the qualities associated with aggression and competition to men, and relegates to women the devalued roles of nurturing and service. Patriarchy values the hard over the soft, the tough over the tender; punishment, vengeance, and vindictiveness over compassion, negotiation, and reconciliation. The "hard" qualities are identified with power, success and masculinity, and exalted. The "soft" qualities are identified with weakness, powerlessness, and femininity, and denigrated.

Under patriarchy, men are shamed and considered weak if they exhibit qualities associated with women. Politicians win elections by being tough—tough on terror, tough on crime, tough on drugs, tough on welfare mothers. Calls for cooperation, negotiation, compassion or recognition of our mutual interdependence are equated with womanly weakness. In the name of "toughness," the power holders deprive the poor of the means of life, the troubled and the ill of treatment and care, the ordinary citizen of our privacy and civil rights. Force, punishment, and violence are patriarchy's answer to conflicts and social problems.

Patriarchy finds its ultimate expression in war. War is the field in which the tough can prove their toughness and the winners triumph over the losers. Soldiers can be coerced into dying or killing when their fear of being called womanlike or cowardly overrides their reluctance to face or deal death. War removes every argument for tenderness and dissolves all strictures on violence. War is the justification for the clampdown that lets the rulers impose control on every aspect of life.

Wise feminists do not claim that women are innately kinder, gentler, more compassionate than men per se. If we did, the Margaret Thatchers and Condoleezza Rices of the world would soon prove us wrong. We do claim that patriarchy encourages and rewards behavior that is brutal and stupid. We need raucous, incautious feminist voices to puncture the pomposity, the arrogance, the hypocrisy of the war mongers, to point out that gorilla chest-beating does not constitute diplomacy, that having the world's largest collection of phallic projectile weapons does not constitute moral authority, that invasion and penetration are not acts of liberation.

And we need to remind the world that modern warfare never spares the civilian population. Rape is always a weapon of war, and women's bodies are used as prizes for the conquerors. Women and children and men, too, who have no say in the policies of their rulers face death, maiming, wounding, and the loss of their homes, livelihoods, and loved ones in a war.

Patriarchy is the brother of racism, which sets one group of people above another, dehumanizing and devaluing the "other," who is seen as deserving of punishment, fair game for violence and annihilation.

We need feminist voices for peace because the issues of women's freedom and autonomy are being used cynically to justify anti-Arab racism and military takeovers of Arab countries.

The United States and its allies, who now pose as the liberators of women in the Muslim world, are the same powers which gave the Taliban, Saddam Hussein, and Al

Qaeda their start-up funds, supported them and put them in power, with no consideration for their impact on women. The "liberators" of Afghan women ignored the grassroots women's organizations such as RAWA, the Revolutionary Association of the Women of Afghanistan, installed a new government almost equally as oppressive as the Taliban., and excluded the heroic women who have risked their lives to educate their daughters and maintain some sense of freedom under oppressive rule.

We protest the hypocrisy which trumpets the oppression of women in Arab societies while the oppression of women in the West is never raised as an issue. Nor is the racism, economic oppression and endemic violence of Western culture acknowledged when the West is hailed as the flag bearer of freedom. Women cannot walk safely through the streets of the West, nor can we be assured of the means of life for our children, of health care in our illnesses, of care and support in our old age. The ongoing daily violence against women and children worldwide, the violence of battering, sexual assault, poverty, and lack of opportunity, the global traffic in women's bodies, is ignored. And the vast global inequalities which benefit the West are also not acknowledged. Nor is the history, that Western exploitation of the East and South generated the wealth that allowed our greater "development" and "enlightenment."

Oppression of women is real, in Muslim societies and non-Muslim societies, around the globe. But women cannot be liberated by the tanks and bombs of those who are continuing centuries-old policies of exploitation, commandeering resources for themselves, and fomenting prejudice against the culture and heritage which is also a deep part of a woman's being.

We need a feminist voice for peace to say that those who truly care about life and freedom will work to support, not conquer, those women in every culture who are struggling for liberation and social justice.

The war against Iraq is not about safety, security, or liberation. The war's real aims include gaining control of Iraq's rich oil reserves and establishing U.S. hegemony over the Middle East. Racism is the ideology of empire, the set of beliefs that tell us we deserve to rule because we are superior to some other group.

Racism and patriarchy are the recruitment tools for the legions of enforcers: the soldiers, police, judges, bureaucrats and officials who protect institutions of power. Patriarchy, racism, homophobia, discrimination against Arabs and Muslims, anti-Semitism, ageism and all forms of prejudice keep our eyes trained downward, looking at those we see as beneath us, instead of looking upward and seeing clearly how we are being manipulated.

We need strong feminist voices to cry out that there is no hierarchy of human value, that every child must be cherished, that we claim common ground with women, children, and men around the world.

Oil is the lifeblood, and the military is the ultimate enforcer of economic policies which disenfranchise the poor and undercut the livelihoods of working people around the globe, consolidating wealth and power in fewer and fewer hands, devouring the family farm, the vibrant neighborhood, the old growth forest and the last remaining wilderness, eroding the soil, poisoning the atmosphere, disrupting the earth's climate and threatening every life support system of the planet. The global corporate capitalist system also exalts toughness and ruthless competition, and exhibits utter disdain for caring, compassion, and nurturing values. Women staff the *maquiladoras* and the sweatshops that produce the cheap goods of the global economy. The vast majority of the world's poor are women and children. A feminist voice for peace must identify and address the root causes of war. "Peace" cannot be separated from justice, including economic justice. And real security can only come when we weave a new global web of mutual aid and support.

We need women's actions, to make these larger connections, to assert that compassion is not weakness and brutality is not strength, to dramatize our support for nurturing and life affirming values. And ultimately, we need women and men both to join our voices and roar like a mother tiger in defense of our interconnectedness with all of life, the true ground of peace.

Terror, Torture, and Resistance

Andrea Dworkin

The first selection is excerpted from "Terror, Torture, and Resistance" in Life and Death *by Andrea Dworkin (New York: The Free Press, 1997) and reprinted by permission of the Estate of Andrea Dworkin. It was originally delivered as the keynote speech at the 1991 Canadian Mental Health Association's "Women and Mental Health Conference— Women in a Violent Society."*

We're here because of an emergency. You all know that. We want to speak about the progress we've made, but we know that women are not any safer from rape now than when we started out. I'm glad that the Canadian Mental Health Association is concerned with our health—because I for one am sick to death. I am sick from the numbers of women who are being brutalized and raped and sodomized, who are being killed, who are missing, who in a women's culture of nonviolence don't hurt the people who are hurting us. We take our own lives. We commit suicide.

So many women I have known have spent every day of their lives fighting to stay alive, because of the despair they carry around with them from the sexual abuse that they have experienced in their lives. And these are brave, creative women. These are women who thought that they had a right to dignity, to individuality, to freedom—but in fact they couldn't walk down a city block in freedom. Many of them were raped as children in their own homes, by relatives—by fathers, uncles, brothers—before they were "women." Many of them were beaten by the men who loved them—their husbands, lovers. Many of them were tortured by those men. When you look at what happened to these women, you want to say, "Amnesty International, where are you?"— because the prisons for women are our homes. We live under martial law. We live in a rape culture. Men have to be sent to prison to live in a culture that is as rapist as the normal home in North America. We live under what amounts to a military curfew, enforced by rapists. We say we're free citizens in a free society. But we lie. We lie about it every day.

Race, Sex, and Speech in Amerika

Andrea Dworkin

This selection is excerpted from "Race, Sex, and Speech in Amerika" in Life and Death *by Andrea Dworkin (New York: The Free Press, 1997) and also reprinted by permission of the Estate of Andrea Dworkin. It was first published in a slightly altered form as "Thomas Jefferson, Sally Hemings, and the Real Bill of Rights," in* On the Issues *(Fall 1995).*

Amerika Now: The Eternal Present

The mental geography of Amerika is a landscape of forgetfulness, useful in a country saturated with sexual abuse; a flat nothingness—no history, no yesterday with facts and details; a desert lit up by the blinding glare of a relentless, empty optimism. The past is obliterated, because the past is burdened by bad news.

Slavery is a rumor, except that some black folk seem extremely pissed off about it. Rape is a lie, useful once for persecuting black men haunted by the rumor of slavery but now taken up with malignant intent by fanatic, angry women, traitors to forgetting. Free speech is bigger than a right; it is a theme park in which pimps and esteemed writers alternate "Discourse" with Spin-the-Bottle: one-handed art, one-handed sex—the sound of one hand typing. It's like a Utopian summer camp for spoiled brats: once you enter Free Speech Park you can go on all the rides you want and nobody can stop you; so there.

My colleagues—writers and feminists—proudly call themselves First Amendment fundamentalists or absolutists, in self-proclaimed philosophical and pragmatic accord with those who learn rules by rote, recite dogma without deviation, and will not think. History moves and society changes but forgetfulness is both blissful and patriotic. In Amerika, optimism and amnesia are forms of nationalism; and so is First Amendment fundamentalism—a happy loyalty to the status quo; we live in the best of all possible worlds. A country devoted to the eternal present is, of course, a perpetrator's dream come true; and Amerika does spawn perpetrators. Memory means accusation, recognition, discontent. In the Free Speech playground, one might rebel against being the pimp's ride, or even the esteemed writer's: don't fuck with me, one might say, spoiling the fun. The players, certain of their right to bang at will, might feel really bad: like, "censored."

At Amerika's best it produced Emerson, Whitman, Thoreau—they hated slavery; Elizabeth Cady Stanton, Susan B. Anthony, Margaret Fuller—they hated slavery;

Frederick Douglass, Sojourner Truth, Harriet Tubman—they hated slavery. Each and every one of them embodied an honest Amerikan optimism in intellect and activism that was not based on forgetting. They thought; they acted; they were citizens no matter what the law said; and they did not hide from life, reality, and responsibility by hiding behind the law—oh, well, slavery is constitutional, enough said. They were also Victorians and moralists—current swearwords.

The Founding Patriarchs Were Tyrants

George Washington was the richest man in Amerika. He freed all his slaves when he died, unlike Thomas Jefferson, who did not.

James Madison made an annual profit of $257 on each slave he owned and spent $12 or $13 on maintenance.

In 1619, the first black slaves were imported and the Virginia House of Burgesses, the first representative assembly in Amerika, was established. The Virginia House set up a mechanism for recording and enforcing contracts, which made the exploitation of indentured servants easier and more secure, backed by local, not British, law and force.

By 1700, fifty Virginia families controlled most of the region's money and owned most of the land, slaves, indentured servants (to be precise: owned the contracts of the indentured servants). The males of those families seemed to rotate being governor, advisers to the governor, and local magistrates.

In 1787, fifty-five white men met in Philadelphia to create a constitution, currently treated by both the political right and left as a divinely revealed text. Not much resembling Moses, most of them were lawyers; owned slaves and land or were rich from manufacturing or shipping (which implicated them in slave trafficking); owned white women—wives and daughters—who were not persons under the law. Half loaned money for profit. Forty had government bonds, thus a special interest in having a government that could redeem those bonds. Slaves, indentured servants, women, men who did not own property, and Indians were not invited to the party. It was a rich-white-guy thing.

The framers' idea was to form a republican central government that (1) could facilitate commerce among the states, internationally for the new union, and (if you are credulous) with the Indian nations; and (2) was too weak to interfere with slavery. Slavery was the basis for the agrarian economy of the South and the linchpin of what its ruling elite regarded as their "civilization." Slavery was still legal in the North, but the economy was industrial with a manufacturing and shipping base. This meant that the North profited handsomely from the transport and sale of kidnapped Africans.

The framers did protect slavery: outright in the body of the text ratified in 1787 for a twenty-year period and by creating a legal framework that kept the federal government anemic while giving the states virtually all the authority and powers of governance. The federal government had only the powers explicitly designated in the Constitution.

For instance, it got to regulate commerce, create a navy, coin money, tax, go to war, all with the famous checks and balances that made each exercise purposefully difficult; and, with its two representative assemblies standing in for white men with money, the federal government could provide the appearance of democracy, though never the substance.

The Bill of Rights, which is the first ten amendments to the 1787 Constitution, was ratified in 1791 largely because the rabble, having defeated the British in the name of equality as well as independence, demanded a legal guarantee of democratic rights—as in "We hold these truths to be self-evident, that all men are created equal." The framers gave in after protracted and stubborn resistance. Not by accident, they saw to it that equality—as an idea, an ideal, a right, a principle, an element of liberty or law—disappeared from the Amerikan political vocabulary and was lost to constitutional law. But in fact the framers went even further: they created a trick bill of rights. Rather than guaranteeing democratic rights that were inalienable, inviolable, and affirmative—the states be damned—they used the Bill of Rights as yet another means of restricting federal power. No citizen had a straight-out right to speak, to assemble, to bear arms, such that the government was obligated to uphold the right for the sake of the citizen. The Bill of Rights applied only to the central government, not to the states; so that when the First Amendment said, "Congress shall make no law," only the U.S. Congress was restricted.

The problem—from the point of view of those who value rights—is both structural and purposeful. James Madison—brilliant and cunning, contemptuous of ordinary (not elite) men, and an enemy of direct democracy—engineered the faux Bill of Rights so that it gave *freedom from*, not *freedom to*. The Second Amendment right "to keep and bear arms" suggested that all those guns vouchsafed to white men could be mobilized by the states to fend off illegitimate federal power, which was the elite definition of tyranny. *Freedom from* protected an armed, landed, moneyed, white-male ruling class from the projected incursions of a potentially bigger power, a central government. Speech and guns need to be thought of as forms of wealth analogous to land, slaves, money, women. If you had them, the federal government could not interfere; if you did not, Madison's faux Bill of Rights did not give you the right to them.

The system appeared to work as a democracy for white men because land was bountiful and could be acquired: taken from Indians. There were many efforts to turn Indians into slaves, but these failed; so the white guys killed the Indians instead. At first the conflict might have passed for a classic imperialist war with two armed if unequal sides; but it soon became an intentional, organized genocide.

State governments maintained supremacy over the federal government, even after the Civil War. The Thirteenth, Fourteenth, and Fifteenth Amendments were designed to stop slavery—to supersede all state slave laws and to stop the actual practice—as well as to enfranchise men, not women, who had been slaves. Their enactment—in 1865, 1868, and 1870—amounted to a huge federal power grab, successful because the South lay ruined, in defeat. These amendments were victor's justice, the Union's dignifying its dead through, finally, abolition and a new assertion of domestic federal power. But the idea was still to restrict government, this time state government, not to give affirmative rights to citizens. Under the Fourteenth and Fifteenth Amendments, the state could not stand in the way of a black man's due process or voting rights, but a mob sure could. Only the Thirteenth Amendment, which prohibited "slavery" and "involuntary servitude," restricted both states and individual citizens.

Congress still represented white men; and the states were still able, despite these new amendments, to enact despotic laws that contravened every value symbolized by the Bill of Rights to Amerikans, who were dazzled by the symbolism but indifferent to the substance. Without fear of challenge, southern states created complicated Jim Crow laws, a legal system of apartheid, enforced by police power, state courts, force of arms, and vigilante terrorism. States were able to determine which citizens had which rights until the defeat of de jure (legal) segregation, which could not have been possible without a triumph of federal power and the near-total destruction of states' rights as such. Empirically speaking, this happened sometime in the mid-1960s. Even then, the authority of the federal government to pass the 1964 Civil Rights Act did not reside in the Bill of Rights—the government could not expand a right to speak or assemble to blacks, for instance, because no such right existed. The federal government's civil rights authority resided in the commerce clause of the U.S. Constitution, the so-called spending power of Congress (you take federal money, you do what the feds say), in the power of the federal government to organize its own agencies (e.g., to create a civil rights commission), and in the Fourteenth and Fifteenth Amendments. The segregationists tried to use the Bill of Rights (for instance, the First Amendment freedom of association right) as a shield; consequently the Bill of Rights had to be ignored—informally suspended, as it were—in order to enable the federal government to protect black lives and liberty: to extend the simplest rights of human civil society to blacks.

Women got the vote in 1920 by constitutional amendment, but it was not until 1971 that the U.S. Supreme Court deigned to recognize the civil existence of women by holding that, under the Fourteenth Amendment, Idaho could not favor males over women as administrators of wills and estates "solely on the basis of sex." Idaho, said the Supreme Court, had to have other good reasons, too. The decision (*Reed v. Reed*) is appallingly narrow and condescending; but sex discrimination became litigable and women litigious.

Fortunately in 1965, in *Griswold v. Connecticut,* the justices had found in the Bill of Rights "penumbras" (shadows) and "emanations" in the First, Third, Fourth, Fifth, and Ninth Amendments—take that, Madison, you old fart—allowing them to strike down a state law criminalizing contraception. The justices were specifically protecting marital privacy, gender-neutral, by giving it constitutional legitimacy. By 1973 the penumbras and emanations joined with the Fourteenth Amendment in *Roe v. Wade* to strike down a Texas law criminalizing abortion; but this time the privacy, gender-specific, "cannot be said to be absolute." His is; the married couple's (his) is; hers ain't.

So, every time African Americans or women have needed a right in order to exercise liberty, we have needed an affirmative right—backed up by federal power: the opposite of what the Bill of Rights allows. Each time, we go against the way the Constitution was framed and freedom was conceived. For blacks and women, the states have been the tyrant; but both groups have needed affirmative rights that no government could trump. And although I myself have never met a penumbra I didn't like, it is wrong for women to continue to live in the shadows—of law or life. I want rights so affirmative they are lit up from inside: all flame, all fire, no shadow, no faux.

For these reasons—and more—each time I hear a colleague—writer or feminist—express adoration and obeisance to "the Founding Fathers" and their sacred founding texts, I get physically ill. I've been fluish a lot lately.

Disarmament and Masculinity

John Stoltenberg

John Stoltenberg originally wrote an outline for what would become the following essay—on the links between sexism and militarism—for the War Resisters League initiated Continental Walk for Disarmament and Social Justice in 1975. WRL rejected its use, as did WIN magazine, leaving the piece to find its first publication in a small California-based press in 1978. It is reprinted here, from Refusing to Be a Man, *with the author's enthusiastic permission.*

A meditation on war

If we could see more clearly how and why wars are waged, could we see more clearly how to end them? If we knew more about why men experience combat as the ultimate test of their masculinity, would we know more about how to resolve conflicts in nonviolent ways? If we did not hold on so desperately to masculinity, might we not also then be able to let go of warfare?

> *Sons or fathers, poor men or rich men, sacred or secular: all are homosexual in their worship of everything phallic. A sexual revolution might destroy what men do so well together, away from women: the making of His-story, the making of war, the triumph of phallic will.*
> —Phyllis Chesler[1]

> *It should require no great imaginative leap to perceive a deep relationship between the mentality of rape and genocide. The socialization of male sexual violence in our culture forms the basis for corporate and military interests to train a vicious military force.*
> —Mary Daly[2]

The politics of male sexual domination define not only the waging of wars but also the protesting of wars. After the U.S. military finally got out of Vietnam, this bitter lesson became clear. Women had put their bodies on the line in the movement against that genocidal war. Women had put their bodies on the line alongside young men who were

---

1   *About Men* (New York: Simon and Schuster, 1978), 103.
2   "Transvaluation of Values: The End of Phallic Morality," in *Beyond God the Father* (Boston: Beacon Press, 1973), 98–131.

being sent to fight it. But once the war ended, men in the antiwar movement revealed themselves to be completely uninterested in ending gynocide, men's eroticized aggression against the gender class women. For these men, rape was merely "a women's issue," whereas ending the war had been "a real radical's issue."

> *As a woman totally committed to the feminist cause I received several requests ... to march, speak and "bring out my sisters" to antiwar demonstrations "to show women's liberation solidarity with the peace movement," and my response was that if the peace movement cared to raise the issue of rape and prostitution in Vietnam, I would certainly join in. This was met with stony silence on the part of antiwar activists whose catchwords of the day were "anti-imperialism" and "American aggression," and for whom the slogan—it appeared on buttons—"Stop the Rape of Vietnam" meant the defoliation of crops, not the abuse of women.*
> —Susan Brownmiller[3]

> *Movement men are generally interested in women occasionally as bed partners, as domestic-servants—mother-surrogates, and constantly as economic producers: as in other patriarchal societies, one's wealth in the Movement can be measured in terms of the people whose labor one can possess and direct on one's projects.*
> —Marge Piercy[4]

The fact that wars are waged and rapes are committed by "normal" men—who experience aggression against other life as a paradigm of "manhood"—was entirely ignored by the men who had dominated the antiwar left. Men ostensibly committed to nonviolence refused even to entertain the notion that war and militarism were functions of male sexual violence—and that male sexual violence is a function of male supremacy. Though they espoused nonviolent, equitable, and nonhierarchical forms of social organization, they continued to act toward women in male-supremacist ways. It became clear that they were interested only in rearrangements of men's power over other men, not in any fundamental change in men's relationships with women. And many women who had been prominent in the movement for peace in Vietnam saw that in giving over their lives to a social-change movement based on terms defined by men, they had been deceived and betrayed.

> *Pornography is the theory, and rape the practice. And what a practice.*
> *The violation of an individual woman is the metaphor for man's forcing*

---

3   "War," in *Against Our Will: Men, Women and Rape* (New York: Simon and Schuster, 1975), 112–13.
4   "The Grand Coolie Damn," in *Sisterhood Is Powerful,* ed. Robin Morgan (New York: Vintage Books, 1970), 421–38.

himself on whole nations (rape as the crux of war), on nonhuman creatures (rape as the lust behind hunting and related carnage), and on the planet itself.
—Robin Morgan[5]

Any commitment to nonviolence which is real, which is authentic, must begin in the recognition of the forms and degrees of violence perpetrated against women by the gender class men.
—Andrea Dworkin[6]

White males are most responsible for the destruction of human life and environment on the planet today. Yet who is controlling the supposed revolution to change all that? White males… It seems obvious that a legitimate revolution must be led by, made by those who have been most oppressed: black, brown and white women—with men relating to that as best they can.
—Robin Morgan[7]

The post–Vietnam War era reverberated with a betrayal of women by "progressive" men—a betrayal that may be said to be the very essence of whatever political progressivism in this country has ever meant. At no time has an objection to tyranny been couched in terms that even hinted at an objection to men's tyranny over women.

I cannot say that I think you very generous to the Ladies, for whilst you are proclaiming peace and good will to Men, Emancipating all Nations, you insist upon retaining an absolute power over wives.
—Abigail Adams to John Adams in 1776[8]

Long before Vietnam, in the movement against slavery in the United States, women, black and white, also put their bodies on the line. But once the slavery of blacks was outlawed, men in the Abolition Movement opposed ending the ownership of women's bodies, black and white, by men—as breeders, as domestic servants, as carnal chattel, and as idiots under the law.

---

5 "Theory and Practice: Pornography and Rape," in *Going Too Far: The Personal Chronicle of a Feminist* (New York: Random House, 1977), 163–69.

6 "Redefining Nonviolence," in *Our Blood: Prophecies and Discourses on Sexual Politics* (New York: Harper & Row, 1976), 66–72.

7 "Goodbye to All That," in *Going Too Far*, 121–30.

8 From her letters in *The Feminist Papers: From Adams to de Beauvoir*, ed. Alice S. Rossi (New York: Bantam, 1973), 13.

In the abolition movement as in most movements for social change, then as now, women were the committed; women did the work that had to be done; women were the backbone and muscle that supported the whole body. But when women made claims for their own rights, they were dismissed contemptuously, ridiculed, or told that their own struggle was self-indulgent, secondary to the real struggle.
   —Andrea Dworkin[9]

It was, again, a bitter lesson. And many women who had been prominent in the movement for abolition saw that they had been deceived and betrayed.

During the late nineteen fifties and early sixties, women put their bodies on the line again in the movement against segregation and racial discrimination. But once the law guaranteed equal rights under the law for black men, men in the Civil Rights Movement opposed the right of women to absolute control over their own bodies and to absolute equality under the law. The right to decide whether and when to birth a child is the bottom line of freedom for women as a class—yet most birth control methods are ineffective or harmful, and the right to choose abortion is under massive attack. Without the absolute right to true reproductive self-determination, women as a class will continue to be exploited and manipulated in service to the economic, sexual, and psychological priorities of men. In addition, the Equal Rights Amendment has still not passed—over half a century after it was first introduced—and it is in serious danger of not passing ever. Opponents of the ERA are funded by the life insurance industry, which earns billions in profits based directly on women's inequality under the law, and also by various right-wing religious groups. ERA's most powerful opponents perceive accurately that the amendment will force a redistribution of wealth. Yet so-called radical men continued to ignore these issues as "reformist," even as, during the seventies, they established closer and closer economic, ideological, and sexual ties to the pornography industry.

To put it bluntly, feminism is a movement that "radical" men and "the left" seem only too willing to trash, to ridicule, to put in its "place," or to destroy if they can't control it.
   —Gary Mitchell Wandachild[10]

And many women who had been prominent in the movement for civil rights saw that they had been deceived and betrayed.

Now the nuclear arms race is a clear and present emergency, and in response to that emergency, there has been a growing national and international movement

---

9   "Our Blood: The Slavery of Women in Amerika," in *Our Blood: Prophecies and Discourses on Sexual Politics* (New York: Harper & Row, 1976), 76–95.
10   "Complacency in the Face of Patriarchy," in *For Men Against Sexism: A Book of Readings,* ed. Jon Snodgrass (Albion, California: Times Change Press, 1977), 83–97.

calling for disarmament. But though disarmament now seems as urgent as abolition once did, or as black male civil rights once did, or as peace in Vietnam once did, is there not again deception built into the goals and strategy and political theory of this movement for nuclear disarmament? If our political consciences respond solely to the "doomsday" rhetoric of the nuclear-arms emergency, isn't the betrayal of women again inevitable? Again, we are being told, there is a higher, more pressing cause, one that makes "women's issues" pale by comparison. Thus the threat of nuclear destruction is used by political "progressives" to silence women's demands for civil rights, freedom, and dignity and for an end to sexual violence. And thus the threat of nuclear war is used to manipulate women's guilt in order to maintain the political power of men over women.

> *Therefore if you insist upon fighting to protect me, or "our" country, let it be understood, soberly and rationally between us, that you are fighting to gratify a sex instinct which I cannot share; to procure benefits which I have not shared and probably will not share; but not to gratify my instincts, or to protect myself or my country. For… in fact, as a woman, I have no country.*
> —Virginia Woolf[11]

During the Vietnam War, for the first time in U.S. history, young males in large numbers rejected soldiership. Prior to that time, to heed the call of his country and to be a soldier was to be a real man (as the tales of World War II and Korean War veterans still tell us). But during the Vietnam War, a significant cultural adjustment occurred. Large numbers of mothers endorsed their sons' refusal to be cannon fodder. Large numbers of women who were the same age as draftable males identified with those who refused to fight that war. Large numbers of women, across the country, stood by those young males who refused to go to Vietnam and tirelessly labored to bring that war to an end. Large numbers of older men, too—rather than reject those who had rejected military service—admired those young men and encouraged them to resist.

It was very nearly a new moment in the history of men and war: There might then have developed a general consciousness among males that *militarism* is immoral, not simply that particular war in that particular country. There might then have emerged an awareness of the sexual politics of war, the relationship between manhood and violence and the global sex-class system. But that of course was not what happened. Instead, for young males, resistance to military service came to be viewed culturally as being consistent with conventional masculinity: if a young man refused to fight, his power and prerogative in the culture over women was completely intact—in the eyes of himself and in the eyes of enormous numbers of others ("Girls say yes to men

---

11   *Three Guineas* (New York: Harcourt, Brace & World, 1966).

who say no" and "Make love not war" were two popular slogans of the time). Thus male resistance to the war in Vietnam became a new and acceptable option for being a real man, instead of an occasion for examining the fundamental relationship between militarism and male supremacy.

> *Then Abraham lifted up the boy, he walked with him by his side, and his talk was full of comfort and exhortation. But Isaac could not understand him. He climbed Mount Moriah, but Isaac understood him not. Then for an instant he turned away from him, and when Isaac again saw Abraham's face it was changed, his glance was wild, his form was horror. He seized Isaac by the throat, threw him to the ground, and said, "Stupid boy, dost thou then suppose that I am thy father? I am an idolater. Dost thou suppose that this is God's bidding? No, it is my desire."*
> —Søren Kierkegaard[12]

> *Georg shrank into a corner, as far away from his father as possible. A long time ago he had firmly made up his mind to watch closely every least movement so that he should not be surprised by any indirect attack, a pounce from behind or above.*
> —Franz Kafka[13]

Why, historically, have fathers wanted sons so much—and then why have fathers wanted sons to go to war to be killed?

> *It is also true that you hardly ever gave me a whipping. But the shouting, the way your face got red, the hasty undoing of the braces and laying them ready over the back of the chair, all that was almost worse for me.*
> —Franz Kafka[14]

In every patriarchal family, there comes a time when the emerging manliness of the son pitches the father into a crisis of ambivalence: This young man is the masculine progeny the father wanted, yet this young man is a youthful physical rival he wanted not at all. Violence is frequently a father's futile attempt to bridge this distance between desire and dread. In the United States, as in other patriarchal nation-states, there exists a class of "superfathers"—the military brass, men who declare and manage wars—who act in other fathers' behalf to keep sons mindful of the power of the father by threatening sons

---

12   "Prelude," in *Fear and Trembling*, trans. Walter Lowrie (Garden City, New York: Doubleday & Company, Inc., 1954), 26–29.

13   "The Judgment," in *The Penal Colony*, trans. Willa and Edwin Muir (New York: Schocken Books, 1963), 49–63.

14   *Letter to His Father,* trans. Ernst Kaiser and Eithne Wilkins (New York: Schocken Books, 1966).

with extinction. It is boys who are sent to war. It is aging, adult men who send them. Their mothers and biological fathers may mourn when they die. But the setup—the war machine—keeps father power in place. This is, at root, the psychosexual function of militarism among fathers and sons: The superfathers reinforce a cultural exaggeration of father power over life (progenitation, done by penis) through maintaining the cultural obscenity of father power over death (annihilation, done by weapons—and by sons as extensions of weapons/penises).

When young males refused to fight in Vietnam, they feebly rebelled against male power over their own lives only to ascertain dominance over the lives of women. They did not have the courage and the vision—or perhaps, indeed, the desire—to renounce militarism completely by questioning the institution of patriarchy and by disavowing the cultural power attributed to fathers, in particular fathers' power over sons obtained through the ownership of women's bodies. Instead the sons made a deal—that they would not confront father power head on.

> [T]he only way that the Oedipus Complex can make full sense is in terms of power… The male child, in order to save his own hide, has had to abandon and betray his mother and join ranks with her oppressor. He feels guilty. His emotions toward women in general are affected. Most men have made an all-too-beautiful transition into power over others; some are still trying.
> —Shulamith Firestone[15]

In war, the fathers castrate the sons by killing them. In war, the fathers overwhelm the penises of the surviving sons by having terrorized them, having tried to drown them in blood.

> But this is not enough, for the fathers truly fear the potency of the sons. Knowing fully the torture chambers of male imagination, they see themselves, legs splayed, rectum split, torn, shredded by the saber they have enshrined. Do it to her, they whisper; do it to her, they command.
> —Andrea Dworkin[16]

No woman is ever guaranteed the right to be secure in her own person against forcible violation of her body rights. "Domestic security" within the United States applies only to men; it is a concept that has no real meaning in the lives of women. It does not mean, for instance, freedom for women from male predators who live here—or safety

---

15   "Freudianism: The Misguided Feminism," in *The Dialectic of Sex* (New York: Bantam Books, 1970), 41–71.

16   "Why So-Called Radical Men Love and Need Pornography," in *Take Back the Night: Women on Pornography,* ed. Laura Lederer (New York: William Morrow and Company, Inc., 1980), 148–54.

for women even inside their own homes. Unless a woman is visibly in the proprietorship of a male, she is likely to be the victim of heterosexual assault (for example, on any city street). That likelihood is legitimized by male-supremacist law, custom, and habit, which every normal American man has memorized in his flesh. Many women contract their bodies into marriage for safety (and because, economically, they have no alternative). But the institution of marriage legally sanctions the prerogative of husbands to aggress against their private property, the bodies of their wives.

> *Each man, knowing his own deep-rooted impulse to savagery, presupposes this same impulse in other men and seeks to protect himself from it. The rituals of male sadism over and against the bodies of women are the means by which male aggression is socialized so that a man can associate with other men without the imminent danger of male aggression against his own person.*
> —Andrea Dworkin[17]

When the superfathers of America speak of "national security," they take for granted that the body rights of men extend to territorial rights and property rights over the bodies of women and children. Defending these body rights is the basis of all relations between groups of men. Under patriarchy, males learn in their own bodies to eroticize aggression—that is, their impulse to act in a way that owns, dominates, and violates another person's body rights has been indelibly conditioned according to a cultural norm of how male eroticism is supposed to feel. Under patriarchy, normally acculturated males assume—correctly—that the same impulse to sexual violence exists in other males. They therefore endeavor to enter into homoerotic truces—nonaggression pacts contracted between men who tacitly agree to aggress against "others" (women, and sometimes weaker men, or men of other races) instead of one another. When a group of men shares power over "their" constituency of women, that sharing assuages their fears of one another's potential for aggression. In their hearts, men grow up terrified of giving offense to, and being attacked by, more violent males. Between men of different nations, armed (phallic) deterrence against forcible violation of the territory they own (the country they own) is men's first line of defense against assault by other men. The military postures of patriarchal nations are modeled exactly on the psychosexual needs of men to defend themselves against personal assault by other men, which can be understood as eroticized violence between males exclusively, and therefore homosexual. When male combat troops do aggress against the territorial rights of other men, their actual military strategy often involves heterosexual rape of the women belonging to those men

---

17   "The Root Cause," in *Our Blood: Prophecies and Discourses on Sexual Politics* (New York: Harper & Row, 1976), 96–111.

(for example, American soldiers in Vietnam). But the aggression men fear, and the fear upon which their "national defense" is predicated, is aggression from other men—that is, homosexual attack.

This country's superfathers want to make certain that the United States will have the biggest cock in the world—that is, the greatest potency for sadism, euphemistically referred to as "deterrent" capability—but America faces stiff competition, preeminently from the Soviet Union. Nuclear arms are an extension of men's potency for sadism. Nuclear arms are the capability for the ultimate, masculinity-confirming fuck. That capability fills the imaginations of those who have it and those who don't. As cock power is reckoned, it is in "lethality," the maximum threat that men can imagine wielding against one another. To be perceived as militarily "weak" is by definition to be feminized—vulnerable to attack. To be perceived as having the greatest potency for sadism is, as men imagine, to be "secure"—hence the arms race and the obsession with the quantity of bombs prepared to be dropped.

At present, the superfathers of the U.S. and the U.S.S.R. are parties to a precarious, tenuous homoerotic truce whereby the two supercocks:

- endeavor to keep stockpiles of bombs (cock power) balanced;
- agree not to aggress against each other's satellite nations (the male owners of which are themselves in homoerotic alliances with a supercock for protection);
- agree to respect each other's right, within their respective boundaries, to aggress against racial and ethnic minorities; and
- agree to respect any and all national policies prescribing the subjugation of women to men.

The values that inhere on a "small" scale in homoerotic transactions between men are the same values that inhere on a grander scale in all transactions between male-owned and male-supremacist nation-states. The "all-male pack" is essentially contemptuous of anyone who is female or who is construed as feminized, or not really manly. Between all-male packs, their respective commitment to perpetuate violence against women is a token between them of trustworthiness and truce. A male with a greater investment in eroticized aggression can enlist the loyalty of a male with a lesser investment in it simply by offering a promise of "protection" from his sadism. The arms race cannot be dismantled without dismantling the psychosexual structures of masculinity itself.

The stated reason for nuclear threat and counter-threat between the supercocks is to preserve and protect the political alignment of satellite nation-states. But the real reason is the need for global allegiance to the existing political alignment of the sexes—and the need for an irrefutable imperative for the maintenance of the sex-class system. Imagine: the superfathers and supercocks of the world locked in nuclear threat and counter-threat as an ultimate deterrent to sex-class rebellion. To advocate nuclear disarmament without an end to male supremacy is simply to ratify the rights of men and nations to enter into nonaggression pacts among themselves based upon their continued aggression against all women.

> *Nothing is more political to a feminist than fucking—nothing is less an act of love and more an act of ownership, violation; nothing is less an instrument of ecstasy and more an instrument of oppression than the penis; nothing is less an expression of love and more an expression of dominance and control than conventional heterosexual relation. Here the war mentality makes a visitation on our bodies and the phallic values of aggression, dominance and conquest are affirmed.*
> —Andrea Dworkin[18]

> *As the formula of "fucking as conquest" holds true, the conquest is not only over the female, but over the male's own fears for his masculinity, his courage, his dominance, the test of erection.*
> —Kate Millett[19]

What is disarmament if it is not the end of male sadism altogether, the end of male eroticized violence, the end of male eroticized aggression? What is disarmament if it is not the end of patriarchy, the end of father right, the end of male supremacy? What do males mean when they say they want disarmament if they have not made a commitment to lay down the dominance they wield over and against women? What, for a male, is nonviolent resistance to the superfathers of patriarchy if it is not repudiating and divesting himself of his birthright to bear arms over and against women's lives?

---

18   *Marx and Gandhi Were Liberals: Feminism and the "Radical" Left*, pamphlet (San Francisco: Frog in the Well, 1973).
19   "Norman Mailer," in *Sexual Politics* (New York: Avon Books, 1970), 314–35.

The Master's Tools Will Never Dismantle the Master's House

Audre Lorde

I agreed to take part in a New York University Institute for the Humanities conference a year ago, with the understanding that I would be commenting upon papers dealing with the role of difference within the lives of American women: difference of race, sexuality, class, and age. The absence of these considerations weakens any feminist discussion of the personal and the political.

It is a particular academic arrogance to assume any discussion of feminist theory without examining our many differences, and without a significant input from poor women, Black and Third World women, and lesbians. And yet, I stand here as a Black lesbian feminist, having been invited to comment within the only panel at this conference where the input of Black feminists and lesbians is represented. What this says about the vision of this conference is sad, in a country where racism, sexism, and homophobia are inseparable. To read this program is to assume that lesbian and Black women have nothing to say about existentialism, the erotic, women's culture and silence, developing feminist theory, or heterosexuality and power. And what does it mean in personal and political terms when even the two Black women who did present here were literally found at the last hour? What does it mean when the tools of a racist patriarchy are used to examine the fruits of that same patriarchy? It means that only the most narrow perimeters of change are possible and allowable.

The absence of any consideration of lesbian consciousness or the consciousness of Third World women leaves a serious gap within this conference and within the papers presented here. For example, in a paper on material relationships between women, I was conscious of an either/or model of nurturing which totally dismissed my knowledge as a Black lesbian. In this paper there was no examination of mutuality between women, no systems of shared support, no interdependence as exists between lesbians and women-identified women. Yet it is only in the patriarchal model of nurturance that women "who attempt to emancipate themselves pay perhaps too high a price for the results," as this paper states.

For women, the need and desire to nurture each other is not pathological but redemptive, and it is within that knowledge that our real power is rediscovered. It is this real connection that is so feared by a patriarchal world. Only within a patriarchal structure is maternity the only social power open to women.

Interdependency between women is the way to a freedom, which allows the I to be, not in order to be used, but in order to be creative. This is a difference between the passive be and the active being.

Advocating the mere tolerance of difference between women is the grossest reformism. It is a total denial of the creative function of difference in our lives. Difference must be not merely tolerated, but seen as a fund of necessary polarities between which our creativity can spark like a dialectic. Only then does the necessity for interdependency become unthreatening. Only within that interdependency of different strengths, acknowledged and equal, can the power to seek new ways of being in the world generate, as well as the courage and sustenance to act where there are no charters.

Within the interdependence of mutual (nondominant) differences lies that security which enables us to descend into the chaos of knowledge and return with true visions of our future, along with the concomitant power to effect those changes which can bring that future into being. Difference is that raw and powerful connection from which our personal power is forged.

As women, we have been taught either to ignore our differences, or to view them as causes for separation and suspicion rather than as forces for change. Without community there is no liberation, only the most vulnerable and temporary armistice between an individual and her oppression. But community must not mean a shedding of our differences, nor the pathetic pretense that these differences do not exist.

Those of us who stand outside the circle of this society's definition of acceptable women; those of us who have been forged in the crucibles of difference—those of us who are poor, who are lesbians, who are Black, who are older—know that survival is not an academic skill. It is learning how to stand alone, unpopular and sometimes reviled, and how to make common cause with those others identified as outside the structures in order to define and seek a world in which we can all flourish. It is learning how to take our differences and make them strengths. For the master's tools will never dismantle the master's house. They may allow us temporarily to beat him at his own game, but they will never enable us to bring about genuine change. And this fact is only threatening to those women who still define the master's house as their only source of support.

Poor women and women of Color know there is a difference between the daily manifestations of marital slavery and prostitution because it is our daughters who line 42nd Street. If white American feminist theory need not deal with the differences between us, and the resulting difference in our oppressions, then how do you deal with the fact that the women who clean your houses and tend your children while you attend conferences on feminist theory are, for the most part, poor women and women of Color? What is the theory behind racist feminism?

In a world of possibility for us all, our personal visions help lay the groundwork for political action. The failure of academic feminists to recognize difference as a crucial strength is a failure to reach beyond the first patriarchal lesson. In our world, divide and conquer must become define and empower.

Why weren't other women of Color found to participate in this conference? Why were two phone calls to me considered a consultation? Am I the only possible source of names of Black feminists? And although the Black panelist's paper ends on an important and powerful connection of love between women, what about interracial cooperation between feminists who don't love each other?

In academic feminist circles, the answer to these questions is often, "We did not know who to ask." But that is the same evasion of responsibility, the same cop-out, that keeps Black women's art out of women's exhibitions, Black women's work out of most feminist publications except for the occasional "Special Third World Women's Issue," and Black women's texts off your reading lists. But as Adrienne Rich pointed out in a recent talk, white feminists have educated themselves about such an enormous amount over the past ten years, how come you haven't also educated yourselves about Black women and the differences between us—white and Black—when it is key to our survival as a movement?

Women of today are still being called upon to stretch across the gap of male ignorance and to educate men as to our existence and our needs. This is an old and primary tool of all oppressors to keep the oppressed occupied with the master's concerns. Now we hear that it is the task of women of Color to educate white women—in the face of tremendous resistance—as to our existence, our differences, our relative roles in our joint survival. This is a diversion of energies and a tragic repetition of racist patriarchal thought.

Simone de Beauvoir once said: "It is in the knowledge of the genuine conditions of our lives that we must draw our strength to live and our reasons for acting."

Racism and homophobia are real conditions of all our lives in this place and time. I urge each one of us here to reach down into that deep place of knowledge inside herself and touch that terror and loathing of any difference that lives there. See whose face it wears. Then the personal as the political can begin to illuminate all our choices.

> Prospero, you are the master of illusion.
> Lying is your trademark.
> And you have lied so much to me
> (lied about the world, lied about me)
> that you have ended by imposing on me
> an image of myself.
> Underdeveloped, you brand me, inferior,
> That's the way you have forced me to see myself
> I detest that image! What's more, it's a lie!
> But now I know you, you old cancer,
> and I know myself as well.
> —Caliban, in Aimé Césaire's *A Tempest*

Practical, Common Sense, Day-to-Day Stuff

An Interview with Mandy Carter

Matt Meyer

Mandy Carter: For the last year I've been thinking a lot about why we don't have better working relationships between black and white organizers, activists, and just people. I've been working in the movement since 1969, so it's not a big surprise that there are not more blacks involved in the anti-war movement, and it's not a big surprise that there's not more white people involved in, I guess you might call it, grassroots organizing—housing rights, welfare rights, bread and butter stuff. I don't think it's going to be easy to overcome these barriers but I think there are real concrete things that we can do, from both sides, to deal with the question and get on with some cooperative organizing.

Matt Meyer: What kind of concrete things?

Mandy: Sometimes I think people look too hard to figure out what the problem is. It's real practical, common-sense, day-to-day stuff. For instance, language: we all have ways we talk to each other. For instance I went to a meeting recently and there were some black people and white people in the room and the white person was going on about how we needed to work better together. He had all this highfalutin language, big words, big concepts and finally a black person in the room said, "Oh, you mean we just need to figure out a way to work better with each other?" "Oh yeah, that's what I meant," he said. Well why didn't he just come out and say that? Why did he need to go through all this stuff and go through this whole theoretical things, rather than down to earth—what are we gonna do to get on with getting on?

Then on the other hand you've got black fold who have language that they feel like is within their own community and sometimes they feel that white people think that they're either ignorant or not bright because they don't speak in these big long words.

Another real practical thing is rather than trying to figure out how you're going to work together in terms of organizing, why can't friendships be established and get to know people as friends? We tend to forget that, even within our own movement, within the peace movement we don't do that enough. We don't stop long enough to enjoy and have fun, go out for a couple of beers, get unserious for a while.

Matt: I want to throw out two words that come up often when predominantly white groups talk about organizing multiracial constituencies. Those words are out "outreach" and "leadership."

Mandy: In terms of outreach, you always hear this line about "How can we get more black people involved in what we're doing?" Maybe the question should be more like. "How can the peace movement get more involved with what the black folk get involved with?" For instance, here in Durham (NC), every single week there is a meeting of the tenants' steering committee. We have a number of public housing projects in the city of Durham and each one of them has their own built-in system of meetings. I wonder how many of the folks from the peace movement would be willing to make a commitment that every single week, or at least minimally once a month, they would go to those meetings. Don't expect everyone to come running to our meetings. If someone were to make a commitment, that would go a long, long way in helping with outreach because it would show that there's a real sense of interest and concern, and most importantly, consistency and duration.

In terms of leadership, hopefully whenever there is a group being formed right from the very beginning there would be equal sharing of black/white responsibilities or leadership. It's important for brand new groups, or coalitions, or campaigns to not have a lot of white people getting together saying. "Let's go ahead and form this and then we'll go out and see where we can get black people to come in." If there's a serious attempt to make it a real multiracial effort, it has to happen right from the very beginning. I just don't see people doing that. They always do the other. They always get it formed then the go out and try and find people to fit in.

Matt: Have there been lessons from the anti-apartheid movement of the last few years?

Mandy: I have to be honest with you. I have the feeling that the South Africa organizing, at least for the black folks I'm aware of who are involved in it, it's like people come out of their respective corners and they come together and then they go back to their respective corners. For a long time a lot of people didn't want to deal with the South African issue. Central America became the next big issue after Vietnam, nuclear power, nuclear disarmament, and now Central America. Yet, Central America wasn't able to get people of color out, they're a brown race. Then you've got South Africa and of course black people feel more connected to it because that's where we came from. But it sure does make you wonder why aren't we getting this racial stuff happening in all of our issues and why does it take something like South Africa to really bring the black people out? What's going to happen in another year or two when

South Africa is no longer the "hot" issue of the time? Are we going to build anything from the multiracial stuff that we're doing right now? What happened after the civil rights struggle was over? Did people sort of drift off into their own little corners and say we'll get back together again when we need to?

Matt: What has been your most memorable experience with a multiracial effort?

Mandy: The one that left a huge impact on my life was 1968, right after King had been killed. Before his death he had decided to organize a Poor People's March from the south into Washington, D.C., and set up a tent city to focus attention on poverty and the desperate needs of poor people—not just blacks. I went to that when I was eighteen or nineteen and I stayed in Resurrection City for about two weeks. It really turned my head around. It was the first time I realized that there was a difference between blacks who live in the city—like Chicago, New York, Detroit—and blacks who were coming from the south. Within a short period of time you had people getting real territorial about—well this is the California area, or this is the Detroit area. People were out protecting their perimeters because there were some robberies going on and some people were getting beaten up. I think it made everyone realize that what we've got to live with—the violence and desperate stuff that come with it—happens, even within a two-week period in this little city that had been created. A lot of the leadership of the Southern Christian Leadership Conference didn't stay at the camp. They had erected this tent and no one slept in it, they were all sleeping in this fancy hotel. That was a real rude awakening. These were our people yet they weren't willing to wallow in the mud with the rest of us. I'll never forget that. That two week period really turned me around. There were a lot of positive things that happened too, I'm not knocking that, but it sure made me realize that no matter where you go, no matter what color you are, no matter what your organizing experience is, you've got the plus side and you've got the down side. You've got to decide what you're going to take away from it.

Matt: What sorts of efforts are going on today regarding black organizers? For example, how did the Conference of Black Organizers come about?

Mandy: The Conference of Black Organizers mainly came out of a meeting that I had with a woman from Atlanta's Jobs With Peace and a man who was working with AFSC (American Friends Service Committee). We had gone to a big meeting in Washington, D.C., where they were trying to form this nation-wide organization of black folks to deal with the issues of jobs, peace, and justice. They had two meetings in Washington, D.C., and a lot of us were very unhappy because it was definitely geared toward Congressional stuff. People in the room included the mayor of Washington, D.C., and people from the Congressional Black Caucus. You got the feeling that whatever this group was going to be, even though they would include grassroots organizers and those working on disarmament issues, most of the energy would go into electoral stuff. This was when Jesse Jackson was thinking about running for the '84 elections. That'll give you a sense of the kind of people who got attracted to this meeting.

Out of that meeting the three of us met and said there's a real need for people like us who work in predominantly white organizations to find a way to network, to talk with one another, to share ideas or frustrations. Out of that one time we met, the three of us decided to form a group, which we called the Conference of Black Organizers, and we'll get the word out all across the area, which basically meant Florida up to New York. We organized a conference and brought the first group of people together.

Once we had that conference, all of a sudden it became better, in a way, because it included a lot of black folk who were working only in black organizations. It got to be much broader.

The Rise of Eco-Feminism

The Goddess Revived

Kitty Mattes

This article by Kitty Mattes, an environmental activist from upstate New York, originally appeared in the Fall 1990 issue of the Amicus Journal. *It remains an important contribution to the linking of peace, environmental, feminist, and anti-racist movements.*

*A*rachnophobia, a movie in which a community battles evil spiders with heroic tides of pesticides, was a major hit at theaters this summer; in the end, chemical-wielding man wins out over web-weaving spider. While reinforcing people's fears of the natural world, the movie glorifies the technological fix, and crudely illustrates the mentality environmentalists are up against. Humans increasingly control and stand apart from other forms of life. Among environmentalists, the deepening global crisis is leading to new modes of thought. Recent movements such as Green philosophy, bioregionalism, and deep ecology all seek to rearrange and reharmonize humankind's relationship to nature.

Ecofeminism, an intriguing manifestation of this quest, is rooted equally in environmentalism and women's liberation—two powerful movements that flowered in the 1970s. Combining the feminist and ecological perspectives, ecofeminism makes the woman/nature connection: the domination, exploitation, and fear of both women and nature are characteristic of patriarchal thinking. In other words, pollution of the planet and oppression of women are caused by the same set of attitudes.

"Nature-hating and woman-hating are particularly related and associated," says Ynestra King, "and are mutually reinforcing." King has become the major spokesperson for ecofeminism through her activism, writing and teaching over the last fifteen years. Currently, she teaches at the New School for Social Research in New York; her forthcoming book is titled, *Women and the Reenactment of the World.* Ecofeminism links human liberation and respect for nonhuman nature, explains King. Ecology is incomplete without feminism, she says, because it does not recognize the necessity of ending the oppression of women; and feminism is disembodied without the ecological perspective, which "asserts the interdependence of living things."

"Ecofeminism is a holistic way of thinking," says King, "a way of continuously connecting issues like violence against women, military violence, degradation of the planet. You can take any issue and see how these relationships work together." Everything on the feminist agenda—equal rights, quality of work, child care, reproductive choice, and domestic violence—is interconnected, just as the feminist agenda is connected to the environmental agenda.

Charlene Spretnak, whose books include *The Lost Goddesses of Early Greece and The Politics of Spirituality*, sees ecofeminism as one of the "new ecologies" that include Green politics, deep ecology, bioregionalism, "creation-oriented spirituality," and animal rights.

While mid-1970s feminist studies of domination are seminal to ecofeminism, Spretnak particularly emphasizes the impetus and inspiration of recent work on ancient goddess cultures.

Archaeologists studying graves and temples in Eastern Europe and the Middle East ("Old Europe"), have uncovered flourishing, unstratified farming societies where females and males had equal power, according to Marija Gimbutas, professor of archeology at the University of California. Religion centered on goddess figures; the female principle was conceived as creative and eternal, the male as spontaneous and ephemeral. This culture reigned until about 3500 BC, Gimbutas claims, when incursions by nomads gradually succeeded in destroying it.

Nomad society was based on the grazing of large herds and on small patrilineal units, with the hero as horseman and warrior. "In contrast to the sacred myths of pre-Indo-European peoples, which centered around the moon, water, and the female," Gimbutas has written, the religion of Indo-European peoples was "oriented toward the rotating sky, the sun, starts, planets, and other sky phenomena, such as thunder and lightening." Eventually the holistic, earth-oriented goddess cultures were displaced by the hierarchy and domination of patriarchy. Some ecofeminists even date the beginning of our cultural history from 8000 BC, the midpoint of the period when agriculture was first developed.

The ecofeminists view also claims some notable male voices. In his book, *The Dream of the Earth*, environmental philosopher Thomas Berry shows how the values and attitudes that emerged after the historical shift to patriarchy underpin our four central modern institutions: empire, church, nation, and corporation, all of which are hierarchical and male-dominated. Kirkpatrick Sale, a prominent spokesperson for Green values, whose latest book is *The Conquest of Paradise*, hails ecofeminism, especially as he sees it establishing a direct political link between men and women that is lacking in the traditional feminist movement.

But among ecofeminism's most obvious allies, there is also serious criticism of the movement. The ecofeminist stance on international population control programs—that they are tainted by racist and coercive overtones—puts them at odds with those environmentalists who consider curbing world population an urgent priority. Greens claim that ecofeminism does not exist as a separate philosophy at all, because their own philosophy incorporates the goals of ecofeminism. The "Ten Key Values" that form the basis of Green politics include "postpatriarchal values" which some see as an accurate description of the ecofeminist view.

Traditional feminists decry the woman/nature connection at the very core of ecofeminism, calling it a throwback to biological determinism. The identification of women with nature reinforces the Earth Mother stereotype, say feminists, and revives the "essentialism" and romanticization of women they have fought so hard to discredit. From nurturer on a pedestal to tramp in the gutter, the patriarchal woman is defined by her relationship with males, and feminists have always condemned such stereotypes. In this light, ecofeminists risk perpetuating women's marginality and "otherness."

Reromanticizing women does carry risks, including the potential for images of "the good feminist" (Earth Mother) and "the bad feminist" (militant), says Ynestra King. But she argues that all feminists—and indeed EVERYONE—should question the "ideal of human freedom and liberation over and against the natural and biological."

Biology as destiny is not just a threat to women, it is an excuse for all forms of oppression, she points out. But in deflating the concept of biological determinism, biology's role may be made irrelevant altogether. Instead, King says, "everyone needs to recover some awareness of the earthiness, the fleshiness of human life."

Irene Diamond, professor of political science at the University of Oregon, views the reshaping of the women/nature connection as part of a more general shift among feminists to "difference feminism" (also called cultural feminism), which spring from studies revaluing motherhood and women's culture in the early eighties. Diamond's recent book is *Reweaving the World: The Emergence of Ecofeminism,* coedited with Gloria Orenstein. Diamond believes that an identification with the biological has been assigned to women by western culture; men have chosen to dissociate themselves from nature and to associate women with it.

The ecofeminist viewpoint has informed a valuable critique of some of the directions taken by mainstream feminists, Diamond says. Women are now looking beyond the goal of integrating themselves into the work force, for example, and questioning the nature of work and the structure of the workplace itself. Day-care is no longer the more appealing alternative to mothering, as women and men are revaluing childcare, and questioning the role the state plays in it.

Ecofeminism simultaneously celebrates interconnectedness and diversity. Life is a web, not a hierarchy; within it diversity is essential for both healthy ecosystems and healthy societies. We are all different, but no one's difference is more important than another's. Since our very differences are valuable, all forms of domination are unhealthy. On a political level this stand can be linked to the recognition of the intrinsic worth of nonhuman life (hence animal rights), of Indigenous peoples (cultural survival), and of the integrity of minority cultures (as opposed to assimilation).

The celebration of differences may explain why more women of color are to be found in the ranks of the ecofeminists than among the traditional feminists. Rachel Bagby, associate director of the Martin Luther King Papers Project at Stanford University, praises the racial parity at ecofeminist gatherings. As she has put it, "None of us are tokens at someone else's party."

Third World women, most of whom find themselves within status in their cultures, also gain empowerment in ecofeminism. Their health and livelihoods are directly linked with environmental quality. Vandana Shiva, a physicist and ecofeminist in Delhi, India, maintains that "maldevelopment"—a model of progress based on the colonizing, modern West—means destruction for women, nature, and subjugated cultures. She calls for reinstatement of precolonial standards of productivity as the basis for a development based on conservation and ecology.

In Brazil, ecofeminism began to take shape in 1984 as people protested against the testing of experimental contraceptive drugs on poor women. Thais Corral, a journalist for Interpress Service in Rio de Janeiro, told *The Amicus Journal* that women quickly made the connections between this incident and other forms of ecological manipulation that also affect women and children, such as biotechnology and the use of chemicals in agriculture. "Women living in the country knew how to control their fertility," says Corral. When they had to move to the city, "they lost that knowledge." Now, the right wing want to control poor women's childbearing choices instead of dealing with the wider reasons for environmental collapse, such as destructive development, she believes. An ecofeminist group has emerged in Brazil, called the Network of Defense of the Human Species; the group plans an international conference next year in Salvador, Brazil.

Corral's concern—that the costs of a deteriorating environment fall hardest on those who can least afford it—is shared by all ecofeminists. "You can't just put the responsibility [for the crises] on women" says Ynestra King. The population issue must be looked at in the context of other issues, she believes. The United States, with 5 percent of the world's population, produced 25 percent of global warming gases, for example. "Let's face it," says King, "it's the rich, white people who pollute." Studies have repeatedly documented the relationship between rising economic and social opportunities for women and declining birthrates, so given the power, King maintains, women "will do it themselves."

Feminist and Green philosophers meet in ecofeminism, especially in its focus on "the value and integrity of not only women, but all creatures with whom we share the earth," says Irene Diamond. The ecofeminist celebration of diversity and sense of place is shared by Greens and is basic to bioregionalism. Calling ecofeminism "a new term for an ancient wisdom," Diamond believes that "ecofeminism is the philosophy and Green is the politics." In Germany, ecofeminists such as well-known leader Petra Kelly consider themselves Greens, Diamond points out, and as Greens, they hold political power.

Right now, it is a bit too soon to speak for true environmental politics in the United States. A tiny fraction of the American people has made meaningful life-style changes, but the national agenda consists mainly of approaching environmental problems through the legal system. The gap between philosophy and action keeps American environmentalism tenuous and peripheral. Western European countries are taking far more significant steps—in farm policy, recycling, pollution reduction, and family planning—due to cohesive political pressure. The danger in all "isms" is that they can be reduced to academic bombast or pop-press prattle. Ecofeminism may well inform a future solution to the planetary crises—and may even play a significant role. But at this time and in this place, it is still only a good idea.

Beyond the Color of Fear

An Interview with Victor Lewis (Excerpt)

Peggy McIntosh

Lee Mun Wah's 1994 documentary The Color of Fear *was hailed as a breakthrough film, one which, in the words of one commentator, "put in plain light the pain caused by racism in North America." Organized as a dialogue on racism and sexism, it brought together eight men to discuss the roots and remedies of injustice and violence in contemporary U.S. society. Victor Lewis, projected and seen by many as the quintessential "angry Black man" character, came across as a particularly powerful and transformational figure. These interview excerpts originally appeared in a longer booklet,* Beyond the Color of Fear, *one of the four SpeakOut!-published volumes.*

Victor Lewis: I think it's important to honor every bit of change and transformation that there is. Every bit of growth that you got has meant the world to at least thousands of people that you may well never meet, and certainly dozens of people that you're relatively close to, and some very close. And so that to me is part of the hope in making the building blocks of the new world, each changed self.

You know, I think it's no accident, in some ways, that it's easy for a group to fall into a path of benign or unconscious offensiveness or evil, but your turning away from it is something we sort of have to do soul-by-soul, individually, remembering the Bible story of the woman who was about to be stoned for adultery, and some of the upstanding people in the community decide to trap Jesus, by either getting him to say that the law that [says] we should stone adulteresses is wrong, in which case Jesus would be shown-up to be a phony, or he would have to endorse her killing, which they knew he didn't want to do. So they're like, "He's d***ed if he does; he's d***ed if he doesn't." And he says, "Sure go ahead and do what you've got to do relative to the law. I'm fully in support of that, but let whoever has not sinned cast the first stone."

That's a simple morality play in itself, but if you look at what happens afterward, the eldest member of that crowd got up and walked away. And then the next eldest got up and walked away, and the story says one by one, from the eldest to the youngest, they all disappeared. It wasn't a mass conversion, it was a something, clicking one by one by one by one with each of the persons, but so in a sense converting from a culture of, what did bell hooks call it, "a mass ethic of domination" toward a love ethic.

It's hard to fully realize, for example, the humanity of a person who seems—in the case of sexism—to symbolize the oppressor. You see all this male violence, and domination and exclusion, and it's like: what does it take to move you to moral outrage about sexism if you happen to have a male body?

This is something that I think requires the conversion of the individual soul as a part of a general cultural conversion. I think that we can have a much kinder society than we've got, but the individual members of that society have to become kind in order for that to be a reality. And I believe that we're on our way, and that those of us who are in *The Color of Fear* were selected to advance that cause somehow.

Peggy McIntosh: There's a place in the film where David Christianson (a white participant) tells Victor that his fear is unfounded. Victor assures that his fear has a foundation that's as secure as the rising and the setting of the sun. You mention that it may rest on his relationship to others, but that the two of you have "no relationship except what we have this weekend." That's that piece of my earlier thinking too, that unless I know somebody, and have been in direct relationship to them, there's nothing at all about race that would connect the two of us in one system. But structural systems relate us all to each other, whether we have met or not. I picked up on the respect of the group for David's stamina and heart, David. So I sometimes describe *The Color of Fear* as a film in which a large group of men of color love into awareness a white man, and then reveal the difficulties within themselves under a system of white privilege, to love each other. Victor, I'm curious about why, when you felt this really surprising affinity with David, you were also pretty sure you did not want that to show.

Victor: Because I thought it might be experienced as a betrayal of my solidarity with Black people, or other people of color, that we have a story that needs to be told, and we have some realities that need to be honored, and it's my job to represent those realities and to make sure that those stories get told and honored, and if I try to do that in the context of having my heart just sort of pouring out with affinity and compassion for this white man of relative privilege to me, then it could be misconstrued as me being a sell-out, or a wimp, or a milquetoast, not really taking the kinds of stands that need to be taken.

Peggy: And how do you cope with this accusation? I'm your friend; David is your friend. How do you cope with the accusation that you have sold out by becoming friends with us white people?

Victor: It's not my problem anymore. I used to feel that I owed it to somebody, either my community or to some abstract principle, to not let my personal feelings of love or affection or communion or kinship with, you know, the oppressor, or the world, the big human family... I used to feel that I shouldn't let that take precedence over some of the important identity politics agendas that I've sort of been exposed to, and come to accept to a certain extent. One of the things that being in this film has done for me is it has completely laid to rest my ambivalence about where to put myself on the identity politics spectrum. I'm very much over it. And I don't care really who it makes mad at this point.

I feel a deep sense of urgency to change the world, but that urgency is inseparably tied to the belief that the thing that is urgently needed is a more profound love that has direct implications on daily life, on social life, in business, in government, in public policy. That it's really about the depth of caring that's possible in the human spirit, and that it not only manifests with our children, and with our spouses, and with our close friends and relatives, but it begins to be the foundation for a new kind of society. And you know, as a Christian I've come to speak and think of this type of thing as the kingdom of God, meaning that I'm not in charge, David's not in charge, God is in charge; and if we're smart, the person, if you will, that I want to please is God. And if there's anybody's agenda that I want to endorse and give lip service to, or be the yes-man about, it's this great spirit-power that is at the foundation of the universe, certainly the foundation of our little lives. And I really feel that God wants the human family to recognize itself as one body, and that any other agendas—as far I'm concerned, if I'm able to, if I have the strength, if I have the courage, the imagination, the love to do it—should be subordinated to the affirmation of our common life.

Regarding your other question about the aftermath of the film: The late aftermath is that I do not want to do anything that will confuse the urgency of my message, which is that the world needs to conjure up a much more widespread and profound love, and a love that does not just affect our private lives, but affects our public life.

And I want people to know that I'm a pacifist, that, you know, I feel that it may be necessary to guide a cause of justice, but that it is antithetical to kill in the cause of justice. And this is a conviction that I've had for my entire adult life, twenty years at least. But because I can yell, it's very easy for people to presume that my politics are Black power and affirmation of one identity group over another, and that my views also include making allowance for the fact that some people may kill other people to move forward their agendas, and I don't endorse that.

The Politics of Accountability

Jon Cohen

This piece, appearing here for the first time in print, was lovingly edited by Phyllis B. Frank and Liz Roberts.

> *Without accountability, we are not only ineffective and unproductive, we end up violating our own ethical and political principles.*
> —Jon Cohen in an unpublished internal document critiquing the War Resisters League as a "closed" system (1994)

Accountability has become a watchword in the movement to end domestic violence. It is almost impossible to be involved in any work related to ending domestic violence without hearing the word accountability bandied about. But, while some might glaze over at its mention, for battered women, their advocates and allies, it is an essential tenet in the movement for freedom.

Accountability, as it relates to domestic violence work, is a commonly misunderstood term. Conventionally, accountability refers to people with less power and authority being answerable to those who have more power and authority. We see this in the workplace—employees are accountable to their employers.

But in movements for social justice and freedom, the meaning and practice of accountability is quite different. In fact, it is the converse of the traditional meaning and best understood in the context of the politics of oppression theory.

Oppression persists all over the world. It has often been constructed into the very development and culture of a nation. It is not just a theoretical concept; it is a reality with tangible basis and conditions, including a power differential and the use or threat of violence. Oppression most often operates as a dynamic between groups. In sexism, racism, classism, etc., one group, the dominating or more powerful group, marginalizes and violates the other. Dominating group members are often totally unaware of this dynamic. On the other hand, members of the marginalized group are hurt, discriminated against, and denied their basic human rights and are almost always aware of and clear about the oppression that is occurring.

Another important aspect of oppression is that whenever people have been oppressed in human history, they have resisted that oppression. It is an intrinsic truth of human nature that we yearn for freedom and fight and struggle to attain it. In every corner of the globe where people are being oppressed, they are resisting their oppression and organizing political and social movements to end it.

The meaning of accountability that we offer, in the context of political and social movements for justice and freedom, is as follows: members of dominating groups, those with greater power, privilege and authority, must be accountable to those who are members of the oppressed or marginalized groups—in the work toward ending all oppressions. Oppressed or marginalized people, being the targets of discrimination, marginalization and violence, are the experts because they face oppression (racism, sexism, homophobia, etc.) each and every day. The nature of oppression is to make the privileges and advantages that members of dominating groups receive invisible to them. As such they are not confronted with the harm they inflict on the oppressed group.

On the other hand, the realities of oppression are quite evident to the oppressed. Their very survival requires an intimate knowledge of the dynamics of the oppression against them. It is our perspective therefore that they must be seen as the leaders of the movements to end the oppression. They know best what it means to be the targets of the oppression and they know best what strategies will be most effective in ending the oppression.

Being accountable, then, means that those who are not members of the marginalized group must listen to the voices of, be answerable to, and accept leadership from the oppressed. Those who do are referred to as allies in the struggle for justice.

In the work to end domestic violence, it is critical to listen to the voices of women, particularly to battered women and their advocates. Mistakes and errors in judgment or strategy by allies, regardless of how well intentioned, could have devastating consequences for battered women and their children. It is a very real possibility that those not vigilant about this practice of accountability can endanger the lives of others.

"Listening to the voices" doesn't mean listening to this woman over here or that one over there, or trying to figure out which group of women to listen to. Rather it is figuring out how to hear the collective voice of battered women and the battered women's movement. Done properly, that will provide a body of thought, experience, theory and analysis from thousands of women over decades of work and struggle. With attention and diligence, it is not that hard to figure out what the collective voices of battered women are saying.

In many community coalition efforts there is a council working to build and improve a coordinated community response to domestic violence. The council is typically composed of community organizations and institutions such as, police, probation officers, prosecutors, judges, therapists, nurses, teachers, batterer programs, religious figures, etc.[1] As an example of putting this accountability concept into practice, decision-making among the various representatives would work as follows. Every

---

1   It's important to note that the author, a longtime anti-racist activist, had to negotiate very complicated feelings about the contradictions inherent in working with the criminal "injustice" system in the process of holding men accountable for their violence against women. He had a full

representative gets an equal vote or "say" with one exception: representatives of battered women, battered women's advocates, or their organizations. They alone would have veto power over any and all decisions of the coalition or council.

All of us who do domestic violence work (meaning everyone in every sector of the community—the criminal justice system, the social service system, faith communities, etc.) should be accountable to battered women and their advocates. That means that leadership from battered women and their advocates is central to all community efforts to end domestic violence. It doesn't mean simply that battered women's advocates get a seat at the table, but that everyone else follows their direction. It's worth noting that our definition of accountability is profoundly challenging to a system in which the conventional model is for those with less power to be answerable to those with more power.

Implementing and practicing such a policy in every community would be a powerful step forward in the effort to be accountable to battered women, to shift power in our struggle, to lift up and empower battered women, and to build the movement to end domestic violence.

awareness of the pervasive, discriminatory ways this system disproportionately metes out punishment on people of color and is one of the most atrocious institutional manifestations of white supremacy. This was a challenge he struggled with up until the end of his life.

Tools for White Guys Who Are Working for Social Change

Chris Crass

1. Practice noticing who's in the room at meetings—how many gender-privileged men (biological men), how many women, how many transgendered people, how many white people, how many people of color, is it majority heterosexual, are there out queers, what are people's class backgrounds. Don't assume to know people, but also work at being more aware—listening to what people say and talking with people one on one who you work with.

2a. Count how many times you speak and keep track of how long you speak.

2b. Count how many times other people speak and keep track of how long they speak.

3. Be conscious of how often you are actively listening to what other people are saying as opposed to just waiting your turn thinking about what you'll say next. Keep a notebook so that you can write down your thoughts and then focus on what other people are saying. As a white guy who talks a lot, I've found it helpful to writing down my thoughts and wait to hear what others have to say (frequently others will be thinking something similar and then you can support their initiative).

4. Practice going to meetings or hanging out with people focused on listening and learning—not to get caught in the paralysis of whether or not you have anything useful to say, but acting from a place of valuing other people's knowledge and experiences.

5a. Pay attention to how many times you put ideas out to the group you work with.

5b. Notice how often you support other people's ideas for the group.

6. Practice supporting people by asking them to expand on ideas and get more in-depth.

7a. Think about whose work and what contributions to the group get recognized.

7b. Practice recognizing more people for the work they do and try to do it more often. This also includes men offering support to other men who aren't recognized and actively challenging competitive dynamics that men are socialized to act out with each other.

8. Practice asking more people what they think about events, ideas, actions, strategy and vision. White guys tend to talk amongst themselves and develop strong bonds that manifest in organizing. These informal support structures often help reinforce informal leadership structures as well. Asking people what they think and really listening is a core ingredient to healthy group dynamics, think about who you ask and who you really listen to. Developing respect and solidarity across race, class, gender and sexuality is complex and difficult, but absolutely critical—and liberating. Those most negatively impacted by systems of oppression have and will play leading roles in the struggle for collective liberation.

9. Be aware of how often you ask people to do something as opposed to asking other people "what needs to be done": logistics, child care, making phone calls, cooking, providing emotional support and following up with people are often undervalued responsibilities performed by people who are gender oppressed (biological women and trans folks).

10. Struggle with the saying "you will be needed in the movement when you realize that you are not needed in the movement."

11. Struggle with and work with the model of group leadership that says that the responsibility of leaders is to help develop more leaders, and think about what this means to you: how do you support others and what support do you need from others.

This includes men providing emotional and political support to other men. How can men work to be allies to each other in the struggle to develop radical models of anti-racist, class-conscious, proqueer, feminist manhood that challenges strict binary gender roles and categories. This is also about struggling to recognize leadership roles while also redefining leadership as actively working to build power with others rather than power over others.

12. Remember that social change is a process, and that our individual transformation and individual liberation is intimately interconnected with social transformation and social liberation. Life is profoundly complex and there are many contradictions. Remember that the path we travel is guided by love, dignity and respect—even when it brings us to tears and is difficult to navigate. As we struggle let us also love ourselves.

13. This list is not limited to white guys, nor is it intended to reduce all white guys into one category. This list is intended to disrupt patterns of domination that hurt our movement and hurt each other. White guys have a lot of work to do, but if we white guys support and challenge each other, while also building trust and compassion we can heal ourselves in the process.

14. Day-to-day patterns of domination are the glue that maintain systems of domination. The struggle against capitalism, white supremacy, patriarchy, heterosexism and the state is also the struggle towards collective liberation.

15. No one is free until we are all free.

Heteropatriarchy and the Three Pillars of White Supremacy

Rethinking Women of Color Organizing

Andrea Smith

INCITE! Women of Color Against Violence is a national activist organization of radical feminists of color advancing a movement to end violence against women of color and our communities through direct action, critical dialogue and grassroots organizing. In a few short years since its original publication, Andrea Smith's essay has become a much-used classic for anti-racist study groups, direct action trainings, and social change course work. The version presented here contains a supplement from Smith's Heteropatriarchy: A Building Block for Empire *and appeared in modified form in* Against the Current *130 (2007).*

Scenario #1

A group of women of color come together to organize. An argument ensues about whether or not Arab women should be included. Some argue that Arab women are "white" since they have been classified as such in the U.S. census. Another argument erupts over whether or not Latinas qualify as "women of color," since some may be classified as "white" in their Latin American countries of origin or "pass" as white in the United States.

Scenario #2

In a discussion on racism, some people argue that Native peoples suffer from less racism than other people of color because they generally do not reside in segregated neighborhoods within the United States. In addition, some argue that since tribes now have gaming, Native peoples are no longer "oppressed."

Scenario #3

A multiracial campaign develops involving diverse communities of color in which some participants charge that we must stop the black/white binary, and end Black hegemony over people of color politics to develop a more "multicultural" framework.

However, this campaign continues to rely on strategies and cultural motifs developed by the Black Civil Rights struggle in the United States.

These incidents, which happen quite frequently in "women of color" or "people of color" political organizing struggles, are often explained as a consequence of "oppression olympics." That is to say, one problem we have is that we are too busy fighting over who is more oppressed. In this essay, I want to argue that these incidents are not so much the result of "oppression olympics" but are more about how we have inadequately framed "women of color" or "people of color" politics. That is, the premise behind much "women of color" organizing is that women from communities victimized by white supremacy should unite together around their shared oppression. This framework might be represented by a diagram of five overlapping circles, each marked Native women, Black women, Arab/Muslim women, Latinas, and Asian American women, overlapping like a Venn diagram.

This framework has proven to be limited for women of color and people of color organizing. First, it tends to presume that our communities have been impacted by white supremacy in the same way. Consequently, we often assume that all of our communities will share similar strategies for liberation. In fact, however, our strategies often run into conflict. For example, one strategy that many people in U.S.-born communities of color adopt, in order to advance economically out of impoverished communities, is to join the military. We then become complicit in oppressing and colonizing communities from other countries. Meanwhile, people from other countries often adopt the strategy of moving to the United States to advance economically, without considering their complicity in settling on the lands of Indigenous peoples that are being colonized by the United States.

Consequently, it may be more helpful to adopt an alternative framework for women of color and people of color organizing. I call one such framework the "Three Pillars of White Supremacy." This framework does not assume that racism and white supremacy is enacted in a singular fashion; rather, white supremacy is constituted by separate and distinct, but still interrelated, logics. Envision three pillars, one labeled Slavery/Capitalism, another labeled Genocide/Capitalism, and the last one labeled Orientalism/War, as well as arrows connecting each of the pillars together.

Slavery/Capitalism

One pillar of white supremacy is the logic of slavery. As Sora Han, Jared Sexton, and Angela P. Harris note, this logic renders Black people as inherently slaveable—as nothing more than property. That is, in this logic of white supremacy, Blackness becomes equated with slaveability. The forms of slavery may change whether it is through the formal system of slavery, sharecropping, or through the current prison industrial complex—but the logic itself has remained consistent. This logic is the anchor of capitalism. That is, the capitalist system ultimately commodifies all workers; one's own person becomes a commodity that one must sell in the labor market while the profits of one's work are taken by someone else. To keep this capitalist system in place—which ultimately commodifies most people—the logic of slavery applies a racial hierarchy to this system. This racial hierarchy tells people that as long as you are not Black, you have the opportunity to escape the commodification of capitalism. This helps people who are not Black to accept their lot in life, because they can feel that at least they are not at the very bottom of the racial hierarchy—at least they are not property; at least they are not slaveable.

The logic of slavery can be seen clearly in the current prison industrial complex (PIC). While the PIC generally incarcerates communities of color, it seems to be structured primarily on an anti-Black racism. That is, prior to the Civil War, most people in prison were white. However, after the thirteenth amendment was passed—which banned slavery, except for those in prison—Black people previously enslaved through the slavery system were reenslaved through the prison system. Black people who had been the property of slave owners became state property, through the conflict leasing system. Thus, we can actually look at the criminalization of Blackness as a logical extension of Blackness as property.

Genocide/Colonialism

A second pillar of white supremacy is the logic of genocide. This logic holds that Indigenous peoples must disappear. In fact, they must *always* be disappearing, in order to allow non-Indigenous peoples rightful claim over this land. Through this logic of genocide, non-Native peoples then become the rightful inheritors of all that was Indigenous-land, resources, Indigenous spirituality, or culture. As Kate Shanley notes, Native peoples are a permanent "present absence" in the U.S. colonial imagination, an "absence" that reinforces, at every turn, the conviction that Native peoples are indeed vanishing and that the conquest of Native lands is justified. Ella Shoat and Robert Stam describe this absence as "an ambivalently repressive mechanism [which] dispels the anxiety in the face of the Indian, whose very presence is a reminder of the initially precarious grounding of the American nation-state itself.... In a temporal paradox, living Indians were induced to 'play dead,' as it were, in order to perform a narrative of manifest destiny in which their role, ultimately, was to disappear."

Rayna Green further elaborates that the current Indian "wannabe" phenomenon is based on a logic of genocide: non-Native peoples imagine themselves as the rightful inheritors of all that previously belonged to "vanished" Indians, thus entitling them to ownership of this land. "The living performance of 'playing Indian' by non-Indian peoples depends upon the physical and psychological removal, even the death, of real Indians. In that sense, the performance, purportedly often done out of a stated and implicit love for Indians, is really the obverse of another well-known cultural phenomenon, 'Indian hating,' as most often expressed in another, deadly performance genre called genocide. After all, why would non-Native peoples need to play Indian—which often includes acts of spiritual appropriation and land theft—if they thought Indians were still alive and perfectly capable of being Indian themselves? The pillar of genocide serves as the anchor for colonialism—it is what allows non-Native peoples to feel they can rightfully own Indigenous peoples' land. It is okay to take land from Indigenous peoples, because Indigenous peoples have disappeared.

Orientalism/War

A third pillar of white supremacy is the logic of Orientalism. Orientalism was defined by Edward Said as the process of the West defining itself as a superior civilization by constructing itself in opposition to an "exotic" but inferior "Orient." (Here I am using the term "Orientalism" more broadly than to solely signify what has been historically named as the Orient or Asia.) The logic of Orientalism marks certain peoples or nations as inferior and as posing a constant threat to the well-being of empire. These peoples are still seen as "civilizations"—they are not property or "disappeared"—however, they will always be imaged as permanent foreign threats to empire. This logic is evident in the anti-immigration movement within the United States that targets immigrants of color. It does not matter how long immigrants of color reside in the United States, they generally become targeted as foreign threats, particularly during wartime. Consequently, orientalism serves as the anchor for war, because it allows the United States to justify being in a constant state of war to protect itself from its enemies.

For example, the United States feels entitled to use Orientalist logic to justify racial profiling of Arab Americans so that it can be strong enough to fight the "war on terror." Orientalism also allows the United States to defend the logics of slavery and genocide, as these practices enable the United States to stay "strong enough" to fight these constant wars. What becomes clear then is what Sora Han states—the United States is not at war; the United States *is* war. For the system of white supremacy to stay in place, the United States must always be at war.

Because we are situated within different logics of white supremacy, we may misunderstand a racial dynamic if we simplistically try to explain one logic of white supremacy with another logic. For instance, think about the first scenario that opens this essay: if we simply dismiss Latino/as or Arab peoples as "white," we fail to understand how a racial logic of Orientalism is in operation. That is, Latino/as and Arabs are often situated in a racial hierarchy that privileges them over Black people. However, while Orientalist logic may bestow them some racial privilege, they are still cast as inferior yet threatening "civilizations" in the United States. Their privilege is not a signal that they will be assimilated, but that they will be marked as perpetual foreign threats to the U.S. world order.

Organizing Implications

Under the old but still potent and dominant model, people of color organizing was based on the notion of organizing around shared victimhood. In this model, however, we see that we are victims of white supremacy, but complicit in it as well. Our survival strategies and resistance to white supremacy are set by the system of white supremacy itself. What keeps us trapped within our particular pillars of white supremacy is that we are seduced with the prospect of being able to participate in the other pillars. For example, all non-Native peoples are promised the ability to join in the colonial project of settling Indigenous lands. All non-Black peoples are promised that if they comply, they will not be at the bottom of the racial hierarchy. And Black, Native, Latino, and Asian peoples are promised that they will economically and politically advance if they join U.S. wars to spread "democracy." Thus, people of color organizing must be premised on making strategic alliances with each other, based on where we are situated within the larger political economy. Thus, for example, Native peoples who are organizing against the colonial and genocidal practices committed by the U.S. government will be more effective in their struggle if they also organize against U.S. militarism, particularly the military recruitment of Indigenous peoples to support U.S. imperial wars. If we try to end U.S. colonial practices at home, but support U.S. empire by joining the military, we are strengthening the state's ability to carry out genocidal policies against people of color here and all over the world.

This way, our alliances would not be solely based on shared victimization, but where we are complicit in the victimization of others. These approaches might help us to develop resistance strategies that do not inadvertently keep the system in place for all of us, and keep all of us accountable. In all of these cases, we would check our aspirations against the aspirations of other communities to ensure that our model of liberation does not become the model of oppression for others.

These practices require us to be more vigilant in how we may have internalized some of these logics in our own organizing practice. For instance, much racial justice organizing within the United States has rested on a civil rights framework that fights for equality under the law. An assumption behind this organizing is that the United States is a democracy with some flaws, but is otherwise admirable. Despite the fact that it rendered slaves three-fifths of a person, the U.S. Constitution is presented as the model document from which to build a flourishing democracy.

However, as Luana Ross notes, it has never been against U.S. law to commit genocide against Indigenous peoples-in fact, genocide *is* the law of the country. The United States could not exist without it. In the United States, democracy is actually the alibi for genocide—it is the practice that covers up United States colonial control over Indigenous lands.

Our organizing can also reflect anti-Black racism. Recently, with the outgrowth of "multiculturalism" there have been calls to "go beyond the black/white binary" and include other communities of color in our analysis, as presented in the third scenario. There are a number of flaws with this analysis. First, it replaces an analysis of white supremacy with a politics of multicultural representation; if we just *include* more people, then our practice will be less racist. Not true. This model does not address the nuanced structure of white supremacy, such as through these distinct logics of slavery, genocide, and Orientalism. Second, it obscures the centrality of the slavery logic in the system of white supremacy, which is *based on* a *black/white binary*. The black/white binary is not the *only* binary that characterizes white supremacy, but it is still a central one that we cannot "go beyond" in our racial justice organizing efforts.

If we do not look at how the logic of slaveability inflects our society and our thinking, it will be evident in our work as well. For example, other communities of color often appropriate the cultural work and organizing strategies of African American civil rights or Black Power movements without corresponding assumptions that we should also be in solidarity with Black communities. We assume that this work is the common "property" of all oppressed groups, and we can appropriate it without being accountable.

Angela P. Harris and Juan Perea debate the usefulness of the black/white binary in the book, *Critical Race Theory*. Perea complains that the black/white binary fails to *include* the experiences of other people of color. However, he fails to identify alternative racializing logics to the black/white paradigm. Meanwhile, Angela P. Harris argues that "the story of 'race' itself is that of the construction of Blackness and whiteness. In this story, Indians, Asian Americans, and Latinos/as do exist. But their roles are subsidiary to the fundamental binary national drama. As a political claim, Black exceptionalism exposes the deep mistrust and tensions among American ethnic groups racialized as 'nonwhite.'"

Let's examine these statements in conversation with each other. Simply saying we need to move beyond the black/white binary (or perhaps, the "black/nonblack" binary) in U.S. racism obfuscates the racializing logic of slavery, and prevents us from seeing that this binary constitutes Blackness as the bottom of a color hierarchy. However, this is not the *only* binary that fundamentally constitutes white supremacy. There is also an Indigenous/settler binary, where Native genocide is central to the logic of white supremacy and other non-Indigenous people of color also form "a subsidiary" role. We also face another Orientalist logic that fundamentally constitutes Asians, Arabs, and Latino/as as foreign threats, requiring the United States to be at permanent war with these peoples. In this construction, Black and Native peoples play subsidiary roles.

Clearly the black/white binary is central to racial and political thought and practice in the United States, and any understanding of white supremacy must take it into consideration. However, if we look at only this binary, we may misread the dynamics of white supremacy in different contexts. For example, critical race theorist Cheryl Harris's analysis of whiteness as property reveals this weakness. In *Critical Race Theory*, Harris contends that whites have a property interest in the preservation of whiteness, and seek to deprive those who are "tainted" by Black or Indian blood from these same white property interests. Harris simply assumes that the positions of African Americans and American Indians are the same, failing to consider U.S. policies of forced assimilation and forced whiteness on American Indians. These policies have become so entrenched that when Native peoples make political claims, they have been accused of being white. When Andrew Jackson removed the Cherokee along the Trail of Tears, he argued that those who did not want removal were really white. In contemporary times, when I was a nonviolent witness for the Chippewa spear-fishers in the late 1980s, one of the more frequent slurs whites hurled when the Chippewa attempted to exercise their treaty-protected rights to fish was that they had white parents, or they were really white.

Status differences between Blacks and Natives are informed by the different economic positions African Americans and American Indians have in U.S. society. African Americans have been traditionally valued for their labor, hence it is in the interest of the dominant society to have as many people marked "Black," as possible, thereby maintaining a cheap labor pool; by contrast, American Indians have been valued for the land base they occupy, so it is in the interest of dominant society to have as few people marked "Indian" as possible, facilitating access to Native Lands. "Whiteness" operates differently under a logic of genocide than it does from logic of slavery.

Another failure of U.S.-based people of color in organizing is that we often fall back on a "U.S.-centricism," believing that what is happening "over there" is as important as what is happening here. We fail to see how the United States maintains the system of oppression here precisely by tying our allegiances to the interests of U.S. empire "over there."

Heteropatriarchy and White Supremacy

Heteropatriarchy is the building block of U.S. empire. In fact, it is the building block of the nation-state form of governance. Christian Right authors make these links in their analysis of imperialism and empire. For example, Christian Right activist and founder of Prison Fellowship Charles Colson makes the connection between homosexuality and the nation-state in his analysis of the war on terror, explaining that one of the causes of terrorism is same-sex marriage:

> Marriage is the traditional building block of human society, intended both to unite couples and bring children into the world… There is a natural moral order for the family… the family, led by a married mother and father, is the best available structure for both childrearing and cultural health. Marriage is not a private institution designed solely for the individual gratification of its participants. If we fail to enact a Federal Marriage Amendment, we can expect not just more family breakdown, but also more criminals behind bars and more chaos in our streets.

Colson is linking the well-being of U.S. empire to the well-being of the heteropatriarchal family. He continues: "When radical Islamists see American women abusing Muslim men, as they did in the Abu Ghraib prison, and when they see news coverage of same-sex couples being "married" in U.S. towns, we make this kind of freedom abhorrent—the kind they see as a blot on Allah's creation. We must preserve traditional marriage in order to protect the United States from those who would use our depravity to destroy us?"

As Ann Burlein argues in *Lift High the Cross*, it may be a mistake to argue that the goal of Christian Right politics is to create a theocracy in the United States. Rather, Christian Right politics work through the private family (which is coded as white, patriarchal, and middle class) to create a "Christian America." She notes that the investment in the private family makes it difficult for people to invest in more public forms of social connection. In addition, investment in the suburban private family serves to mask the public disinvestment in urban areas that makes the suburban lifestyle possible. The social decay in urban areas that results from this disinvestment is then construed as the result of deviance from the Christian family ideal rather than as the result of political and economic forces. As former head of the Christian Coalition, Ralph Reed, states: "The only true solution to crime is to restore the family," and "Family break-up causes poverty." Concludes Burlein, "'The family' is no mere metaphor but a crucial technology by which modern power is produced and exercised."

As I have argued elsewhere, in order to colonize peoples whose societies are not based on social hierarchy, colonizers must first naturalize hierarchy through instituting patriarchy. In turn, patriarchy rests on a gender binary system in which only two genders exist, one dominating the other. Consequently, Charles Colson *is* correct when he says that the colonial world order depends on heteronormativity. Just as the patriarchs rule the family, the elites of the nation-state rule their citizens. Any liberation struggle that does not challenge heteronormativity cannot substantially challenge colonialism or white supremacy. Rather, as Cathy Cohen contends, such struggles will maintain colonialism based on a politics of secondary marginalization where the most elite class of these groups will further their aspirations on the backs of those most marginalized within the community.

Through this process of secondary marginalization, the national or racial justice struggle takes on either implicitly or explicitly a nation-state model as the end point of its struggle—a model of governance in which the elites govern the rest through violence and domination, as well as exclude those who are not members of "the nation." Thus, national liberation politics become less vulnerable to being coopted by the right when we base them on a model of liberation that fundamentally challenges right-wing conceptions of the nation. We need a model based on community relationships and on mutual respect.

Conclusions

Women of color–centered organizing points to the centrality of gender politics within antiracist, anticolonial struggles. Unfortunately, in our efforts to organize against white, Christian America, racial justice struggles often articulate an equally heteropatriarchal racial nationalism. This model of organizing either hopes to assimilate into white America, or to replicate it within an equally hierarchical and oppressive racial nationalism in which the elites of the community rule everyone else. Such struggles often call on the importance of preserving the "Black family" or the "Native family" as the bulwark of this nationalist project, the family being conceived of in capitalist and heteropatriarchal terms. The response is often increased homophobia, with lesbian and gay community members construed as "threats" to the family. But, perhaps we should challenge the "concept" of the family itself. Perhaps, instead, we can reconstitute alternative ways of living together in which "families" are not seen as islands on their own. Certainly, Indigenous communities were not ordered on the basis of a nuclear family structure. This structure is the result of colonialism, not the antidote to it.

In proposing this model, I am speaking from my particular position in Indigenous struggles. Other peoples might flesh out these logics more fully from different vantage points. Others might argue that some other logics of white supremacy are missing. Still others might complicate how these concepts relate to one other. But I see this as a starting point for women of color organizers that will allow us to reenvision a politics of solidarity that goes beyond multiculturalism, and develops more complicated strategies that can really transform the political and economic status quo.

Our Movements' Failures

Unfortunately it is not only the Christian Right, but our own progressive movements that often fail to critique heteropatriarchy. The issue is not simply how women are treated in the movement; heteropatriarchy fundamentally shapes how we think to resist and organize in countless ways.

First, because we have not challenged heteropatriarchy, we have deeply internalized the notion that social hierarchy is natural and inevitable, thus undermining our ability to create movements for social change that do not replicate the structures of domination that we seek to eradicate. Whether it is the neocolonial middle managers of the nonprofit industrial complex or the revolutionary vanguard elite, the assumption is that patriarchs of any gender are required to manage and police the revolutionary family.

Any liberation struggle that does not challenge heteronormativity cannot substantially challenge colonialism or white supremacy. Rather, as Cathy Cohen contends, such struggles will maintain colonialism based on a politics of secondary marginalization where the most elite class of these groups will further their aspiration on the backs of those most marginalized within the community.

Second, our sense of social hierarchy as natural then limits our revolutionary imagination. For instance, the theme of the U.S. Social Forum is "Another World is Possible: Another U.S. is Necessary." But the critical question we must ask ourselves is, if another world is possible, then is the United States itself necessary? If we put all our revolutionary imaginations together, is the best we can come up with a kinder, gentler settler colonial nation-state based on slavery and genocide?

This is where we should be informed by Indigenous peoples' (particularly Indigenous women's) struggles to reimagine nationhood without nation-states. The Indigenous models of nationhood are based on nations as inclusive rather than exclusive, based on respect and responsibility for land rather than control over territory, and are governed on principles of mutual respect, interrelatedness and responsibility for a larger world, rather than governed through violence, domination, and social hierarchy.

Third, our organizing often follows a gendered model that is based on a split between private and public spheres. That is, in the public sphere of social protest, we are supposed to be completely together people who have no problems. However, when it turns out we do have problems, we are supposed to address those problems in the private sphere—at home, or through social services. Because we cannot bring our whole selves to the movement, we then end up undermining our work through personal dysfunctionality that cannot be publicly addressed.

In addition, when we think to work collectively, our collective action is confined to the public spheres of protests and other actions. But our movements do not think to collectivize the work that is seen as part of the private sphere, such as daycare, cooking and tending to our basic needs. Consequently, we build movements that are accessible to very few people and which are particularly burdensome for women who often are responsible for caretaking in the private sphere.

Bombing for Women's Liberation?

Finally, because we lack an intersectional analysis of how heteropatriarchy structures white supremacy and colonialism, we end up developing organizing strategies that are problematic to say the least. To name but a few examples: We have anti-violence groups supporting the bombing of Afghanistan in order save women from the Taliban, and we have these same groups supporting the buildup of the prison industrial complex by relying on criminalization as the primary strategy for ending domestic and sexual violence.

These groups fail to see how the state itself is the primary perpetrator of violence against women, particularly women of color, and that state violence in the form of either the military or prison industrial complex is not going to liberate anyone.

We have racial and antiwar groups meanwhile organizing against state violence in Iraq and elsewhere, but cannot seem to do anything about ending violence against women in their own organizations. These groups fail to see that it is primarily through sexual violence that colonialism and white supremacy work.

And then we have mainstream reproductive rights and environmental groups supporting population control policies in order to save the world from poverty and environmental destruction, thus blaming women of color for the policies wrought by corporate and government elites, thus letting these elites off the hook.

In all these cases and many more, activists fail to recognize that if we do not address heteropatriarchy, we do not just undermine the status of women, but we fundamentally undermine our struggles for social justice for everyone.

Thus, if we are not serious about dismantling heteropatriarchy, then we are not serious about ending colonialism or white supremacy.

V. The Roots and Routes of War: Nationalism, Religion, Ageism

Kafka's Amerika

William P. Starr

Ten Years in Freedom

Dylcia Pagán

Freedom comes from our souls,
It is a part of our essence.

FREEDOM!

At times, we suffer for freedom and the end result is always beneficial.
FREEDOM!

Once I arrived to Borinquen, I felt freedom immediately in my heart
because our people received me from all walks of life with heartfelt
embraces.
FREEDOM!

One thing I have realized is that I have always been free, even while
incarcerated under the worst of conditions.
FREEDOM!

Personal freedom comes from within, when one is clear about what one
believes in. I believe in the freedom of my homeland, Puerto Rico.
FREEDOM!

People say that I have a way of being that is strong yet tender. I try to allow
my heart to always guide me.
FREEDOM!

I have walked the streets of San Juan, Guanica, Yauco, Jayuya, Adjuntas,
Las Marias; I have seen every day the need for freedom.
FREEDOM!

Puerto Rico appears to be free: Our people smile, dance, party, and share.
Yet our country is still not free. We remain a colony of the USA, never
being able to have self-determination.
FREEDOM!

In ten years, I have witnessed many beautiful awakenings:
The Victory of Vieques, The outburst of support for Comandante Filiberto
Ojeda Ríos after his assassination by the FBI.
FREEDOM!

The streets were filled with children, elders, government workers, even the
police saluted his funeral entourage.
FREEDOM!

As time passes, the victims are forgotten,

Reality sets in, nothing truly happens or has changed.

Conditions of poverty, poor housing, mis-education, corruption prevail,

But repression is alive and well.

We must continue forward, Never losing our spirit to be free.

FREEDOM!

I reside in Lioza, where the Cimarrones lived and the essences of our
African roots are from.

Young people here don't know who Lolita Lebrón or Adolfina Villanueva
are. They have no knowledge of the struggles their ancestors have endured.
FREEDOM!

Bomba and Plenas are heard on the streets every weekend. Once a year,
everyone hits the streets to celebrate 'Las Fiesta de Loiza.'
FREEDOM!

I wish we could celebrate the beauty of Mother Africa every day.

I wish we could show our children the beauty of freedom every day—in
the schools, the streets, the library, in our plazas.
FREEDOM!

A freedom that encompasses why they are so beautiful and alive,
Why their bodies move to unknown rhythm,
Why their skin is in luscious shades of chocolate,

Why the Veigigantes should be their heroes,
Why the Veigigantes should be called love,
Why every female should know that she is a Casica.
FREEDOM!

Freedom is something that comes from one's soul.
My soul tells that our battle has not been won.
We must make freedom a priority in our lives.
FREEDOM!

Yes, a freedom of spirit to change what surrounds us.
A change that incorporates all of our being—Mind, Body, and Soul,
Without fears.
FREEDOM!

Everything we need to accomplish in life has a consequence.
We live, We love, We work, We care, We fight for what is real and just
with dignity and commitment.
FREEDOM!

Let us begin to walk the freedom walk
With heads held high committed to humanity, self-determination, and
self-love.

LET US WALK AND FIGHT FOR A FREE PUERTO RICO!

FREEDOM!

Filiberto Ojeda Ríos Lives!

Lolita Lebrón Lives!

Free Oscar López Rivera!

Fragmented Nationalism

Right-Wing Responses to September 11

in Historical Context

Matthew Lyons

This section's review of the Roots and Routes of War focuses on the interplay between war, racism, and the violence produced by modern manifestations of nationalism, religious fundamentalism, ageism, and cultural intolerance. In putting together this section, we are strikingly aware that not all nationalisms, just like the many manifestations of religion, are created equal. Philosopher/poet Amiri Baraka, in his review of Manning Marable's 2011 book Malcolm X: A Life of Reinvention, *poignantly wrote that the essential "disconnect" in that work is the failure to understand "the revolutionary aspects of Black nationalism" so typified by Minister Malcolm's life. Both Malcolm and Martin, Baraka wrote, "were more objectively revolutionary on those Harlem streets or in those southern marches than any of the social democratic formations" of the modern liberal, reformist paradigm. Nonviolent activists, both reformist and radical, are not the only ones who too often carelessly dismiss what has come to be called revolutionary nationalism, in favor of a false internationalism which is, in practice, Eurocentric. The essays in this section attempt to correct some of these misperceptions. In addition, despite the fact that many among us are secular activists, basing resistance on a sense of political outrage or a general moral or spiritual calling, we must recognize that religion itself—while too often a cause of great violence and injustice—is also the motivating force for many people's anti-racist, anti-war work. We present essays that attempt to explain those perspectives. Reviews of issues regarding age, culture, and identity are also found here, as we try to frame and expose the strategic questions we need to hone in on as we strive to build new movements.*

In the wake of the 9/11 attacks, a movement long-building but barely considered seriously by the left came to greater prominence. Right-wing populism goes well beyond a minority fringe; its organizations, spokespeople, and ideology has played a dominant role in mainstream U.S. politics for at least the last decade. Though white nationalist beliefs come dangerously close to direct fascist principles, this movement continues to grow—sometimes organizing in spaces otherwise accepted as progressive strongholds: among anarchists, workers, anti-war protesters, and others. Their vehement proclamations, for a United States "still safe for white people," have only intensified with a U.S. commander-in-chief of part-African descent.

Nationalism has always been a central theme for the U.S. political right, but different rightists have expressed and interpreted nationalism in sharply different ways. Right-wing movements have disagreed on key questions about nationhood: who does the nation include and exclude? Who or what threatens it? How should the United States relate to the rest of the world? What is the state's role in building or protecting the nation?

The U.S. right's complex, divided response to the September 11, 2001, attacks embodied all of these disagreements. Neoconservatives and paleoconservatives, Christian rightists and far-rightists disagreed about what caused the attacks, how the federal government should respond at home and abroad, even about the legitimacy of the attacks themselves. Rooted in the distinct histories and nationalist philosophies of these varied right-wing movements, the debate reflected, above all, the U.S. right's fragmentation brought on by the end of the Cold War, and the diverse ways rightists attempted to replace anticommunism as an overarching principle.

The September 11 attacks on the World Trade Center and the Pentagon violently opened a new chapter in U.S. history and the history of American nationalism. Within days, President George W. Bush identified the attackers as members of al Qaeda, an underground Islamic right organization headed by exiled Saudi Arabian millionaire Osama bin Laden, and proclaimed a far-reaching, open-ended "War on Terrorism." U.S. troops soon invaded Afghanistan and overthrew the Taliban, Afghanistan's Islamic rightist rulers who had provided al Qaeda with a home base. In January of 2002, President Bush shifted focus by proclaiming Iraq, Iran, and North Korea to be an "axis of evil" that sponsored terrorism and possessed or sought weapons of mass destruction with which to threaten the United States and its allies.

Reactions to September 11 within the United States included pervasive patriotic displays and a general upsurge in nationalism and nativism. Over the following months, human rights groups reported hundreds of incidents of physical violence, harassment, and threats against Arab Americans, South Asians, Sikhs, and other people perceived to be Arab. President Bush and other officials repeatedly spoke out against ethnic and religious scapegoating. Bush declared that "the enemy of America is not our many Muslim friends; it is not our many Arab friends" and that "the terrorists are traitors to their own faith, trying, in effect, to hijack Islam itself."

At the same time, the Bush administration began a series of roundups of people from Middle Eastern and Muslim countries, many of whom were held secretly and under conditions that Amnesty International described as harshly punitive and a violation of basic rights. Most of the 1,200 detainees in the first group were deported; almost none were charged with any crimes connected with terrorism. The federal government also instituted a series of new security measures that critics across the political spectrum denounced as serious infringements on civil liberties. For example, the USA PATRIOT Act, passed in October 2001, created a vague new crime of "domestic terrorism" and gave the executive branch unprecedented latitude to conduct surveillance, share information between criminal and intelligence operations, and detain and deport noncitizens without due process. To many opponents, these measures evoked the mass imprisonment of Japanese Americans during World War II and the political witch-hunts of the early Cold War.

Cold War themes echoed loudly in the dominant right-wing response to September 11. As John Fousek argues, the U.S. Cold War foreign policy doctrine embodied a combination of three themes: national greatness, global responsibility, and anticommunism. President Bush's speech of September 20, 2001, which summarized the case for a War on Terrorism and set the stage for the invasion of Afghanistan, presented almost the same ideological package.

In his televised address to Congress, Bush expressed pride in his country's greatness: "America is successful because of the hard work, and creativity, and enterprise of our people." He asserted that the United States had been targeted for attack because of its democratic system and freedoms of religion, expression, and assembly. Invoking a U.S. responsibility to lead "civilization's fight," Bush declared that through the War on Terror "we have found our mission" and that "the advance of human freedom ... now depends on us." Echoing language once used against communism, he condemned the September 11 attackers as heirs to fascism and totalitarianism who "sacrific[ed] life to serve their radical visions" and "abandon[ed] every value except the will to power." Just as Cold Warriors had once divided the globe starkly between the Free World and the Red Menace, Bush now told the nations of the world: "Either you are with us, or you are with the terrorists."

Many rightists embraced President Bush's resurrected Cold War vision. It expressed, above all, ideas formulated by the neoconservatives, who played key roles in shaping Bush administration foreign and military policy. Yet other rightists diverged from Bush's line to varying degrees. Christian rightists generally supported the War on Terrorism but condemned America's sinfulness in terms that called into question the concept of national greatness. Paleoconservatives denounced the War on Terrorism and criticized claims of global responsibility as a cover for U.S. expansionism; at the same time, they demonized non-European immigrants as an immediate threat to U.S. security. Far-rightists rejected loyalty to the United States altogether and, in many cases, applauded the September 11 attacks as righteous blows against an evil Jewish elite. In place of Cold War ideology, these various factions offered alternative nationalist doctrines, all of which drew on themes older than the Cold War itself.

This article traces the origins and dimensions of the U.S. right's fragmented nationalist response to the September 11 attacks. Part I explores the debate's roots, showing how rightists gravitated toward three overlapping forms of nationalist ideology in the twentieth century: first racial nationalism, then business nationalism, and finally Cold War nationalism, which largely subsumed the other two and gave the U.S. right a degree of unity for several decades. Part II examines the development of four major right-wing factions after the Cold War, emphasizing the different ways in which they reworked right-wing nationalist themes to address post–Cold War circumstances in general and the September 11 attacks in particular.

At issue here are not only the varied fortunes of different rightist factions in shaping public policy, but also especially the tensions and interplay between them. If the neoconservative response was dominant after September 11, what prospects did the neoconservatives have to reunify the right behind their version of nationalism? To what extent did the dissenters address weaknesses or contradictions in the dominant rightist viewpoint, or dissatisfaction and grievances among important constituencies? Answering these questions highlights both the fragility and the adaptability of right-wing nationalism as a central force in U.S. political history.

I

U.S. nationalism has never been a unified ideology. Gary Gerstle argues that U.S. history in the twentieth century was radically shaped by the interplay between civic nationalism, which defined the United States in terms of philosophical ideals of political freedom and economic opportunity, and racial nationalism, which conceived of America as "a people held together by common blood and skin color and by an inherited fitness for self-government." Both of these traditions, Gerstle emphasizes, were complex: racial nationalism could demand narrow Anglo-Saxon purity or celebrate a degree of (European) ethnic melding; civic nationalism could encompass struggles for social justice or campaigns to isolate and suppress those regarded as politically disloyal.

Following a related approach, Cecilia Elizabeth O'Leary traces half a century of conflict over the meaning of "true patriotism" following the Civil War. "It was not until World War I, when the government joined forces with right-wing organizations and vigilante groups, that a racially exclusive, culturally conformist, militaristic patriotism finally triumphed over more progressive, egalitarian visions of the nation." This triumph, she adds, was soon contested once again by feminist, Black, labor, and leftist movements, although some radical groups, such as the Industrial Workers of the World, rejected patriotism altogether in favor of working class internationalism.

When we look at nationalism specifically within U.S. right-wing movements of the twentieth century, three major ideological currents stand out: racial nationalism, business nationalism, and Cold War nationalism. Often interconnected, these three political strands grew or changed, and gained or lost prominence, in distinct ways over the course of the century.

Racial nationalism held explicitly or implicitly that the United States was a nation of and for White people, i.e., those of exclusively European descent. In this view, America's national health required the defense of White people's physical and cultural purity against racial "pollution," and the subjugation, expulsion, or annihilation of non-European peoples, who were defined as racially distinct from and inferior to Whites. Racial nationalism was often an expansionist ideology, and often portrayed the United

States as a Christian nation sanctioned by God. These themes came together in the doctrine of Manifest Destiny, the nineteenth century belief that the United States had a God-given right to seize all of North America.

Racial nationalism was rooted in the system of racial oppression that originated in the seventeenth century with the first expulsions and mass killings of American Indians and the enslavement of African people. This system was periodically changed—notably with the abolition of slavery—and expanded to include White dominance over Mexicans, Asians, and other peoples of color, but remained a central facet of U.S. society. Beginning in the nineteenth century, as first Irish and then southern and eastern Europeans temporarily held subordinate and racially ambiguous status, some versions of racial nationalism defined the privileged group more narrowly, e.g., as White Protestants or northern Europeans.

Racial conceptions of American nationhood have shaped political forces and institutions across the spectrum. Among twentieth century right-wing movements, racial nationalism's high point was the Knights of the Ku Klux Klan in the early 1920s. Glorifying the original Ku Klux Klan of the Reconstruction era, the refounded Klan attracted millions of supporters in all regions of the country, behind its ideology of White Protestant supremacy. The Klan vilified and sometimes physically attacked Blacks, Mexicans, Catholics, Jews, and immigrants if they were not subservient enough. It supported the 1924 Immigration Act, which shut out most Asians and southern and eastern Europeans. Within White Protestant society, the Klan championed religious piety and "traditional values" against the growing independence of young men and women and the rising commercialization of sexuality in popular culture.

Like many right-wing movements, the 1920s Klan not only defended traditional hierarchies but also spoke to its members' sense of disempowerment and real grievances against elites. Often it promoted civic reform and challenged local elites in the name of "the plain people." At a time when racism and nativism pervaded the White labor movement, the Klan sometimes aided strikes by White workers and even Socialist Party electoral campaigns. In addition, the Klan movement included an autonomous women's organization, whose half-million members interwove racial and religious bigotry with calls to expand White Protestant women's social, economic, and political rights.

Internal conflicts, leadership scandals, and lack of a clear program weakened the Klan and it quickly collapsed as a national movement. It continued in the South, without its anti-elite tendencies, as a vigilante wing of the local power structure, using threats and violence to enforce Jim Crow segregation and stifle political dissent.

The Great Depression of the 1930s saw a new array of racial nationalist organizations that were influenced by European fascism. Some groups, such as Gerald Winrod's Defenders of the Christian Faith, added fascist trappings to an essentially conservative program of old-style racism, Protestant fundamentalism, and laissez-faire capitalism. In contrast, Father Charles Coughlin's National Union for Social Justice moved from liberal, pro–New Deal populism in 1934–1935 to full-blown fascism by the end of the decade. Initially, Coughlin presented himself as a friend of workers and advocated currency reform as a way to reduce economic inequality. At the same time, he was bitterly anti-leftist and targeted "parasitic" bankers while praising industrialists as "producers of real wealth"—a phony distinction historically linked to anti-Semitism. By the late 1930s, Coughlin was attacking Jews openly and defending German Nazi policies. He envisioned a strong authoritarian state to stifle class conflict and enforce a new racial order.

Even as he helped intensify right-wing anti-Semitism, Coughlin rejected Klan-style anti-Catholicism and nativism. Coughlin was himself a Catholic priest and his movement welcomed Whites of many different ethnic backgrounds.

In 1940–1941, U.S. fascists and fascist sympathizers were active in the broad coalition that opposed U.S. entry into World War II, including the America First Committee and other groups. This movement collapsed after the Japanese attack on Pearl Harbor that brought the United States into the war.

After World War II, open anti-Semitism and, to a lesser extent, White supremacy were discredited by their association with Nazism. During the 1950s and 1960s, as the civil rights movement gathered strength, Citizens' Councils and various Klan factions helped lead a racist backlash that championed Southern regional pride and defense of "states' rights" against federal interference. This movement echoed themes from the Confederacy, when proslavery southerners had rejected the United States entirely in favor of secession.

After the 1960s, some White supremacist groups on the Far Right concentrated on physical violence, while others focused on electoral activism and propaganda. Far-rightists were only intermittently able to build larger coalitions, but they emboldened more moderate political forces to scapegoat oppressed groups. Beginning in the 1980s, neo-Nazi doctrines pervaded and dramatically transformed the Far Right, as discussed below.

The civil rights movement and related anti-racist initiatives of the 1950s–1970s did not end racial oppression in the United States, but they broke the back of open, legally sanctioned racial discrimination. As a result, much of the U.S. right moved away from open racial nationalism with its explicit claims of racial superiority and inferiority. Many rightists turned to coded racism, scapegoating people of color implicitly through symbols such as welfare, crime, and immigration. Governor George Wallace of Alabama, a major champion of segregation, pioneered this tactic in his 1968 and 1972 presidential campaigns, each of which attracted millions of votes. In addition, many rightists shifted away from biological racism toward a more sophisticated cultural racism, which meant including a few people of color as long as they were loyal to dominant White values and beliefs. At the same time, explicit biological White supremacy and anti-Semitism remained strong in the paramilitary Far Right and related circles.

The second right-wing nationalist current, business nationalism, was rooted in capitalist opposition to the New Deal of the 1930s. In 1935–1936, after two years of temporary relief measures to soften the Great Depression's impact, the federal government began to establish a permanent system of welfare state policies, including unemployment and disability insurance, retirement benefits, minimum wage laws, tax reform, and limited support for labor unions' right to organize. Along with this "second" New Deal, President Franklin Roosevelt's administration also abandoned the U.S. government's traditional policy of high tariffs to protect U.S. industries against foreign competition, and initiated a series of reciprocal agreements with other countries to reduce trade barriers.

As Thomas Ferguson has shown, a new "historical bloc" of capital-intensive firms, investment banks, and internationally oriented commercial banks rallied to Roosevelt's combination of welfare state and free trade policies. This "multinationalist" business bloc included firms that were internationally competitive, and thus wanted low tariffs to boost trade, as well as companies with relatively low labor costs, which were willing to cut a deal with the increasingly militant labor movement. The multinationalists began as the cutting edge minority within the business community, grew in numbers after World War II, and played a dominant role in U.S. politics for forty years.

Multinationalists included a few Jews and Catholics, but most of them belonged to the White Protestant "Eastern Establishment" that dominated the most prestigious universities, foundations, and newspapers, as well as the foreign service. The multinationalists were oriented toward Europe; the British Empire was their model for a globally managed economy. They controlled both the national Democratic Party and the moderate wing of the Republican Party.

Business nationalists, based mainly in the Republican right, bitterly opposed the multinationalists and the New Deal. The nationalist bloc within the business community included labor-intensive manufacturing industries, which were especially vulnerable to labor unions, and large numbers of private or family-controlled firms, committed to laissez-faire individualism and hostile to the federal government. The bloc also included companies oriented toward domestic markets or U.S. dominated regions such as Central America, and firms that wanted high tariffs to protect them against stronger foreign competitors.

For most business nationalists, national independence meant economic self-reliance. They wanted a free hand to exploit the home market; cheap, minimal government; and high tariffs to keep out foreign competition. They hated labor unions and government regulators; they hated Britain, the main foreign competitor, and the Anglophile Eastern Establishment that advocated free trade and international alliances. Isolationist with regard to Europe, business nationalists favored unilateral U.S. expansion into Latin America and across the Pacific into Asia. Franz Schurmann describes some of the business nationalist worldview:

> The big bankers of Wall Street were internationalist—so were the communists with their Marxist doctrines, and so were the British with their empire. Moreover, the growing alliance between the Roosevelt-led administration and the unions seemed to indicate a

real alliance between the forces of international capital and their ostensible enemies, the revolutionary proletarians.... When Hitler began to preach that an international conspiracy of capitalists, Jews, and Bolsheviks was trying to crush the expansionist drive of the German nation, many in the United States understood and sympathized.

Business nationalism was initially centered in the Midwest, later in the Sun Belt. It won support from Midwesterners and Westerners who resented the dominance of Eastern politicians and banks, and from ethnic groups disproportionately hostile to Britain or sympathetic to the Axis, particularly German, Irish, and Italian Americans. In 1940–1941, Midwestern business nationalists spearheaded the America First Committee, the most prominent organization working to keep the United States out of World War II.

Like racial nationalism, right-wing isolationism was partly discredited by World War II, and it declined further as the United States entered the Cold War against the Soviet bloc. After the 1949 Chinese Revolution, business nationalists turned toward a "rollback" military strategy of unilateral attack against communism, while multinationalists favored Truman's more moderate "containment" strategy. Both factions supported the Cold War crusade against leftists at home and abroad. But nationalist-affiliated politicians such as Joseph McCarthy and Richard Nixon also used the charge of communist conspiracy against representatives of the Eastern Establishment, particularly in the Anglophile State Department and related agencies. McCarthy denounced as communists "the whole group of twisted-thinking New Dealers [who] have led America near to ruin at home and abroad."

After McCarthy's effort to purge Eastern elite figures from government was defeated, business nationalists in and around the National Association of Manufacturers provided core support for an array of ultraconservative organizations that moved from McCarthyism into even more grandiose conspiracy theories. The John Birch Society, for example, attacked the United Nations, the income tax, and all incursions by the welfare state or "world government" and alternated between isolationism and rollback in military affairs. Business nationalism also strongly influenced Barry Goldwater's 1964 presidential campaign, which denounced the Rockefellers, low tariffs, and federal government efforts to end segregation. Goldwater's business backing was confined almost exclusively to nationalists concentrated in the Sun Belt and the Midwest.

The third major strand of right-wing nationalism centered on the Cold War itself. As noted previously, the Cold War foreign policy consensus that emerged in the late 1940s rested, in John Fousek's words, on a synthesis of "three main constructs: national greatness, global responsibility, and anticommunism." According to this doctrine, not only was the United States the greatest country in the world, but it stood for universal values of freedom, and it had a global responsibility to uphold these values and spread them to the rest of the world. This mission, furthermore, pitted the United States in a global struggle against what many regarded as the expansionist, totalitarian menace of international communism.

Fousek calls this hybrid doctrine "American globalist nationalism." For our purposes here, the term "Cold War nationalism" more clearly emphasizes its ties to a specific historical period. From 1947 until the collapse of the Soviet bloc in 1989–1991, it served as the overarching rationale for U.S. geostrategy under both major parties.

President Harry Truman's Democratic administration—not the political right—first formulated and promoted Cold War nationalism. In his 1947 speech proclaiming the anti-Soviet strategy of containment, the president declared, "The free peoples of the world look to us for support in maintaining their freedoms. If we falter in our leadership, we may endanger the peace of the world—and we shall surely endanger the welfare of our Nation." The idea of America's global responsibility reflected the multinationalist Eastern Establishment's vision of the United States as leader of a global system. Yet by the 1950s, many former anti-interventionists on the right, too, had embraced Cold War nationalism. Given the Soviet threat, they argued, the United States could no longer avoid international alliances and overseas commitments.

The concept of America's global responsibility to uphold freedom gained broad support, in part, because it tapped into deeply rooted ideas of national mission that reached back to Manifest Destiny and ultimately to the New England Puritans. Manifest Destiny sanctified the conquest of Mexico's northern half and the systematic extermination of Native peoples. Similarly, Cold War nationalism provided a justification for the expansion of U.S. military, economic, and political dominance worldwide.

In the name of protecting freedom, the United States supported or installed brutal dictatorships in numerous countries, mostly in Asia, Africa, and Latin America. In Indonesia, for example, the U.S. government halted the Communist Party's growing popularity by backing a 1965 military coup that murdered close to 500,000 people, according to the Indonesian government's own conservative estimates. In this and other instances, the persistence of U.S. racial nationalism, and the assumption that people of color's lives were more expendable than European lives, reinforced Cold War doctrine in shaping U.S. foreign policy.

Sara Diamond draws a distinction between *anti-communism*, meaning "opposition to Communist bloc states and real live Communists," and *anticommunism*, which involved "a package of beliefs about the moral superiority of the United States, about the importance of protecting American lives above all others, and about the necessity of ensuring international order through military force." Anticommunism, which tended to reduce all progressive movements to Soviet plots, involved viewing the world dualistically: "good guys versus bad guys; bright, true Americans versus dark, suspicious aliens and criminal elements." These beliefs were central to Cold War nationalism.

Cold War circumstances contributed to the decline of older nationalist doctrines. In the 1950s and 1960s, economic and political elites became more willing to accept growing popular demands for civil rights reform, in part because the United States was competing with the Soviet Union for support and influence among Africa and Asia's newly independent countries. At the same time, the U.S. dominant position in the post–World War II capitalist world strengthened the multinationalist faction within the business community and weakened capitalist support for protectionism and other business nationalist themes.

As we have seen, however, both racial nationalism and business nationalism continued during the Cold War, notably in the anti–civil rights backlash, the John Birch Society and related conspiracist groups, and the Goldwater and Wallace presidential campaigns. All of these initiatives bolstered their arguments with Cold War themes, portraying anti-racist groups and welfare state reformers as communist tools or dupes.

Conversely, the right-wing version of Cold War nationalism incorporated themes from both business nationalism and racial nationalism. It rejected the New Deal legacy of social programs and government regulation, as well as newer civil rights reforms, as socialistic and un-American. Although often avoiding explicit racism, it treated cultural diversity as something that must be contained or suppressed. With a vision of America threatened by enemies within and without, right-wing Cold War nationalists promoted political and social conformism and the scapegoating of anyone they considered to be disloyal.

Cold War anticommunism brought together conflicting conservative factions and ideological tendencies. Economic libertarians emphasized individualism, market forces, and a sharply limited role for the state, while social traditionalists called for a strong state to enforce traditional morality and preserve existing social hierarchies. Anticommunism, which stood for both the capitalist market and obedience to authority, did not obliterate the differences between libertarians and traditionalists, but enabled them to join forces and see themselves as part of one movement. This conservative synthesis was known as "fusionism."

Right-wing ideological unity, fostered by fusionism and the Cold War, powered both the Old Right of the 1950s and 1960s and the New Right of the 1970s and 1980s. The Old Right emphasized anticommunism in both foreign and domestic policy and treated welfare state policies as a major target. New rightists retained these concerns. But rather than target popular New Deal programs such as Social Security, they focused on social issues such as abortion, education, homosexuality, and crime. With an aggressive mobilizing style, skillful organizing, and big increases in funding from a rightward-moving business community, the New Right helped send Ronald Reagan to the White House in 1980 and 1984 and gained direct access to the highest levels of government.

Michael Omi and Howard Winant argue that the New Right gained mass support because it spoke to a far-reaching sense of national crisis that many people experienced in this period. This crisis reflected the emergence of "new social movements" in the 1960s, the resulting transformation of political culture (especially racial politics), economic dislocations of the 1970s and 1980s, and the erosion of U.S. global hegemony highlighted by the Vietnam War. Omi and Winant argue that these changes "portended the collapse of the 'American Dream'—the apolitical, perpetually prosperous, militarily invincible, and deeply self-absorbed and self-righteous 'mainstream' American culture was, we think, shaken to its foundations by developments over this period."

The New Right addressed this crisis, in part, by reasserting so-called traditional values such as western European culture, private property, and the nuclear family. This involved explicit or implicit attacks on efforts by subordinate groups such as women, gay men and lesbians, and people of color to win equal rights and status. The New Right also employed populist scapegoating, blaming supposed liberal elites for a host of social problems. And the New Right's aggressive foreign policy appealed to many who feared a decline in U.S. global power.

Changes in the business community contributed to the New Right's rise. During the 1960s and 1970s, rapid growth of the Sun Belt economy fostered a new crop of right-wing entrepreneurs deeply hostile to the Eastern elite, concentrated in independent oil, real estate, finances, and other industries. Meanwhile, due to a variety of economic and political changes, many business multinationalists became increasingly hostile to the New Deal legacy. They began to call for cutbacks in government regulation and social programs, lower taxes, a rollback of labor union gains, and a more aggressive foreign and military policy.

The New Right represented a coalition of secular anticommunists, newly mobilized evangelical Christians, militarists, libertarians, tax cutters, nativists, and other factions. The New Right was also allied with the neoconservatives, a group of former Cold War liberal intellectuals who were alienated by 1960s social activism and George McGovern's 1972 presidential candidacy.

Cold War nationalism held these various forces together. The Reagan administration disappointed some libertarians by enacting big new subsidies for corporations, angered militarists who wanted an even more aggressive foreign policy, and increasingly frustrated Christian Right traditionalists by failing to outlaw abortion or restore prayer in public schools. But as a bloc, New rightists and neoconservatives supported the administration as it reintensified the Cold War and sharply increased military spending. Members of different conservative factions worked closely with the Reagan administration to bolster anti-leftist military and paramilitary forces around the world, from Salvadoran and Philippine death squads to Nicaraguan contras and Angolan UNITA rebels.

Cold War nationalist unity did not survive the Cold War. The U.S. right had sought to roll back communism for decades. In 1989, when the Soviet bloc actually began to disintegrate (and President Reagan left office), the conservative coalition fell apart. The debates included domestic policy issues and turf battles but centered on the U.S. role in a post–Cold War world. As the Reagan coalition splintered, three main poles of right-wing ideology emerged: neoconservatives, paleoconservatives, and the Christian Right. These forces, along with a resurgent Far Right, do not encompass all of the right, but they illustrate the range of right-wing approaches to nationalism in the post–Cold War period. The second half of this essay will examine the recent history of these four factions in turn, focusing on each faction's response to the September 11 attacks and how this embodied a distinct interpretation of nationalism.

II

In some ways, neoconservatives seemed unlikely candidates to become the leading voice of right-wing foreign policy. For much of their history, neoconservatives coexisted uneasily with older rightist factions. Many neocons were former liberal Democrats who only gradually abandoned their support for the welfare state. Many were former Socialists or Trotskyists who brought an Old Left polemical style to conservative politics. Most were Jews or Catholics—both groups with not-so-distant memories of discrimination. While much of the Old Right had leaned toward nativism and coolness toward Israel, neocons were staunchly pro-Zionist and often favored open immigration policies. Contrasting neoconservatism with other rightist currents, Gary Dorrien describes it as "a vehemently conservative ideology that accepts no guilt for reactionary movements of the past. [Neoconservatives] oppose feminism, affirmative action, and multiculturalism without the baggage of a racist and nativist past." Neoconservatism's roots were Cold War nationalist—not racial nationalist or business nationalist.

Neocons celebrated the United States as a land of individual opportunity and meritocratic fairness. They praised American capitalism as a system culturally and spiritually superior to all other systems. During the Cold War, they promoted anticommunism as a transcendent moral crusade, a world-historical struggle between freedom and totalitarianism. After the Soviet bloc's collapse, they looked for other targets with which to revive the U.S. sense of national mission and global responsibility.

The neoconservatives were a small network of professional intellectuals, not a political movement. Their influence depended on winning elite patronage, not on organizing a popular base. In the 1970s, the neocons forged links with national security elites and, along with the emerging New Right, profited from overall growing business support for conservative activism. In the 1980s, neoconservatives such as Jeane Kirkpatrick, Elliott Abrams, and William Bennett held important positions in the Reagan administration. In addition to their own publications such as *Commentary* and later the Rupert Murdoch–owned *Weekly Standard*, neocons built influential roles within older conservative bastions such as the American Enterprise Institute, the Hoover Institution, the *National Review*, and the *Wall Street Journal*. They also gained leading positions in the Olin Foundation and the Bradley Foundation, two important conservative funding sources.

During the 1990s, neocons developed strategic proposals for asserting U.S. global dominance. A 1992 Pentagon paper coauthored by neocons Paul Wolfowitz and Lewis Libby argued that the United States should use its military power to "deter… potential competitors from ever aspiring to a larger regional or global role" and to preempt other countries from acquiring weapons of mass destruction. In 1997, neocons William Kristol and Robert Kagan cofounded the Project for the New American Century (PNAC) to "promote American global leadership." Criticizing the Clinton administration's "incoherent policies," PNAC's founding document urged a return to "a Reaganite policy of military strength and moral clarity" and proclaimed "America's unique role in preserving and extending an international order friendly to our security, our prosperity, and our principles."

PNAC embodied the neoconservatives' close ties with economic, political, and military elites. In addition to neocons such as Abrams, Bennett, Libby, Wolfowitz, and Midge Decter, signers of the PNAC founding statement included Florida governor Jeb Bush, media mogul Steve Forbes, and two hawkish former defense secretaries: Dick Cheney, CEO of the oil services firm Halliburton Company, and Donald Rumsfeld, also in private industry. Another signer was Christian Right leader Gary Bauer. PNAC project directors included investment banker Lewis Lehrman and Bruce Jackson, a vice president at defense contractor Lockheed Martin and a former military intelligence officer.

Despite their elite connections, the neoconservatives' aggressive vision placed them at odds with much of the foreign policy and military establishment, which wanted the United States to exert world power through a pragmatic, managerial approach in collaboration with other industrialized countries. Both George Bush senior and Bill Clinton mostly followed the establishment foreign policy line. Bush's 1991 war against Iraq over its invasion of Kuwait raised neocons' hopes. But rather than overthrow Saddam Hussein's government, as neocons urged, both Bush and Clinton pursued a policy of "containment" against Iraq, including air strikes and economic sanctions that resulted in hundreds of thousands of civilian deaths but left the Iraqi government in place. In 1999, neocons supported Clinton's war against Yugoslavia, even in the face of Republican congressional opposition, but criticized his conduct of the war as half-hearted and inept.

The neoconservatives' political fortunes improved dramatically after the 2000 presidential election. George W. Bush's choice of Cheney as vice president and Rumsfeld as secretary of defense placed two close allies of the neocons in top patronage positions. Neocons in Bush's administration included Wolfowitz as deputy defense secretary, Libby as Cheney's chief of staff, Douglas Feith as undersecretary of defense for policy, and David Frum as Bush's speechwriter. The attacks of September 11 helped the neocons and their allies overpower the foreign policy pragmatists within the administration, represented above all by Secretary of State Colin Powell.

To neoconservatives, the War on Terrorism filled the void left by the end of the Cold War. "On September 11," wrote Charles Krauthammer, "American foreign policy acquired seriousness. It acquired a new organizing principle: We have an enemy, radical Islam … and its defeat is our supreme national objective, as overriding a necessity as were the defeats of fascism and Soviet communism."

In the wake of September 11, neocons presented an idealized portrait of the United States: united, determined, virtuous, and strong. "At the moment," wrote David Tell in the *Weekly Standard*, "America fairly vibrates with an almost tribal sense of identity, a fraternal concern that can barely be contained. We know exactly who we are. And we love ourselves as we should and must… We are all thinking the same things, and reaching the same conclusions." America's strength, neocons argued, was rooted in its commercial values of individual initiative, hard work, ambition, and reward for merit. "Never mistake our prosperity for sloth," warned Richard Poe, a columnist for neocon David Horowitz's *FrontPage Magazine*. "The zeal with which we peddle Big Macs can be a dreadful thing when turned to the bloody business of war."

Despite their own role as professional intellectuals with privileged access to the circles of power, neocons castigated U.S. critics of the War on Terrorism as elitist intellectuals who sneered at ordinary Americans. To the neocons, any effort to contextualize the September 11 attacks in relation to the U.S. long history of military intervention and support for oppressive regimes was simply an expression of hatred for America. They dismissed as groundless any concern about the human costs of bombing Afghanistan, nativist attacks against Middle Easterners and South Asians in the United States, or growing domestic repression associated with the War on Terror.

From the beginning, neoconservative aims for the War on Terrorism went far beyond the destruction of al Qaeda. In October 2001, Max Boot argued that the United States should depose Iraqi dictator Saddam Hussein, regardless of whether the Iraqi government was implicated in the September 11 attacks, since he was "currently working to acquire weapons of mass destruction" that would eventually be used against America. A PNAC open letter signed by many leading neocons (along with Christian Right leader Gary Bauer) shortly after the attacks urged President Bush to bring military pressure against Iraq, Iran, and Syria, and cut off all aid to the Palestinian Authority unless it immediately stopped all anti-Israeli terrorism based in its territory.

As during the Cold War, neocons argued that the United States had a mission to spread capitalist democracy across the globe. Michael Ledeen urged, "We must wage revolutionary war against all the terrorist regimes, and gradually replace them with governments that turn to their own people's freely expressed desires as the basis of their political legitimacy." Some neocons openly presented this as a program of imperial conquest, such as Max Boot in an article entitled "The Case for American Empire": "Afghanistan and other troubled lands today cry out for the sort of enlightened foreign administration once provided by self-confident Englishmen in jodhpurs and pith helmets."

Despite such visions of a new White Man's Burden modeled after the European example, neocon comments about Europe were generally negative, based on a perception that many current-day European intellectuals were critical of the U.S. role in the world. "Europeans," wrote David Brooks, "simply can't remember what it's like to be imperially confident, to feel the forces of history blowing at one's back, to have heroic and even eschatological aspirations." Once, multinationalists had looked to Europeans as partners in enforcing collective security; now, to neoconservatives, Europeans were has-beens who should stay out of America's (unilateralist) way.

Brooks's words evoke Gary Dorrien's comment that one of neoconservatism's distinctive features is a "tendency to invest its political beliefs with absolute ideological or even religious significance." Neocons celebrated the War on Terrorism as a cosmic struggle between Good and Evil—in Charles Krauthammer's words, "a transcendent conflict between those who love life and those who love death." True to their disavowal of ethnic and religious bigotry, neocons endorsed President Bush's repeated statements that Islam and Muslims were not the enemy. Yet they demonized "radical Islam" as the embodiment of pure evil, and described the War on Terrorism as a Manichean struggle between the civilized West and Middle Eastern barbarians.

David Brooks presented one of the most extraordinary elaborations of this type of demonization in his portrait of "bourgeoisophobes": those who hated America and Israel as the chief exemplars of commercial success. Bourgeoisophobia, Brooks argued, was rooted in a mixture of snobbery, envy, pessimism, anti-Semitism, and nihilism. Its adherents included Islamic terrorists and European intellectuals, leftists such as Karl Marx and W.E.B. Du Bois, liberals such as Arthur Miller and Michael Moore, race theorists such as Houston Chamberlain and Arthur de Gobineau, and even conservative pessimists such as Robert Bork and Allan Bloom, both of whom were often grouped with the neocons. In other words, bourgeoisophobes included virtually everyone who disagreed with Brooks's celebration of America, all supposedly linked in a shared belief system. This type of sweeping guilt-by-association logic was reminiscent of Senator Joseph McCarthy, whose 1950s smear campaigns had threatened neoconservatism's own forebears among Cold War liberals.

The neoconservatives' hawkish rhetoric resonated with many other conservatives. The Heritage Foundation, one of the core New Right institutions founded in the early 1970s, and one of the earliest to forge ties with the neocons, continued to support an interventionist foreign policy after the end of the Cold War. In the fall of 2001, Heritage Foundation policy analyst Kim Holmes urged "a systematic and comprehensive war against all forms of international terrorism," including the overthrow of the Afghan and Iraqi governments and threats of force against Iran, Syria, Sudan, and Libya. The Heritage Foundation also called for looser restrictions on cooperation between the military, intelligence agencies, and law enforcement; and investigation of immigrants who overstayed their visas for possible terrorist activity. Yet Heritage warned that to stop all immigration, as some rightists urged, "contradicts the free and open nature of America's democracy."

Other rightists, too, echoed neoconservative themes. William F. Buckley, *National Review* editor-at-large and one of the founders of conservative fusionism, responded to the World Trade Center attacks by urging the United States to invade Iraq and seize Baghdad. Buckley commented that "From now on, enemies who are associated with terrorist activity will not cohabit the globe with the United States of America." Columnist Ann Coulter declared that "This is no time to be precious about locating the exact individuals directly involved in this particular terrorist attack," and that those responsible included "anyone anywhere in the world who smiled" in response to the mass killings. To deal with such enemies, Coulter urged, "We should invade their countries, kill their leaders and convert them to Christianity." Jeffrey Hart wrote of the War on Terrorism, "A lot of people are going to die. We should make sure that most of them are not Americans."

If the neoconservatives and their allies responded to the Soviet bloc's collapse by trying to recreate Cold War nationalism, the paleoconservatives took the opposite approach. "All the institutions of the Cold War," Patrick Buchanan declared, "from vast permanent U.S. armies on foreign soil, to old alliances against Communist enemies that no longer exist, to billions in foreign aid, must be re-examined." Paleoconservatives wanted, instead, to revive business nationalism and a semiveiled racial nationalism. Evoking conservative positions going back to the 1930s, they promoted a non-interventionist foreign policy, ethnic monoculturalism, traditionalist Christian morality, and a complete end to government social programs. They called for protectionist trade barriers and attacked President George Bush senior as a representative of the globalist Eastern elite. While disavowing ethnic bigotry, paleocons portrayed dark-skinned immigrants as a threat to American civilization and denounced the power of a Zionist lobby in terms that played into classic stereotypes of Jews as a hidden, super-powerful presence.

Paleocon bastions included the Ludwig von Mises Institute, the Rockford Institute, the Independent Institute, and the journal *Chronicles*. Some paleoconservatives were veterans of the Old Right whose core beliefs had never changed. Others were New Right activists whose politics shifted under post–Cold War circumstances. Former Heritage Foundation policy analyst Samuel Francis reversed his aggressive interventionism when African and Latin American national insurgencies no longer loomed as "Soviet-sponsored terrorists"—and when he began to see non-European immigration and racial mixing as greater threats to U.S. security. Buchanan, a journalist who worked in both the Nixon and Reagan White Houses, abandoned his longtime support for free trade when he confronted Bush senior in the 1992 Republican primaries.

Paleocons resented neoconservatives' influence within the federal government and decried a neocon "takeover" of rightist think-tanks and foundations. Neocons, many of whom were Jewish, accused the paleocons of anti-Semitism and xenophobia. In 1990, when Iraq invaded Kuwait and President Bush massed troops in Saudi Arabia, the staunchly pro-Zionist neocons loudly supported war with Iraq. Paleocons portrayed the drive toward war as a Zionist plot. Buchanan, for example, charged that "the Israeli Defense Ministry and its amen corner in the United States" were the only groups pushing for war. He opposed military preparations until actual combat began in January, 1991.

Despite its roots in the 1930s right, paleoconservatism was not simply a throwback to a dead political era. It spoke to current-day fears and resentments among a broad sector of White Americans, who were angered both by the power of economic and political elites above and the erosion of their own privileges over traditionally oppressed groups below. The paleocons—and related movements such as the Patriot movement—expressed a backlash against several developments: recent social liberation movements (especially anti-racist, feminist, and lesbian and gay rights), growing state power, and economic dislocations connected to globalization, such as declining real wages and the shift of industrial jobs from the United States to the Third World.

Tapping these resentments, paleoconservatives contributed to several important post–Cold War political initiatives. In the 1990s, paleocons such as Sam Francis and *Chronicles* editor Thomas Fleming helped lead a resurgence of mass-based racial nationalism in the form of anti-immigrant campaigns and a neo-Confederate movement. Buchanan's 1992 and 1996 presidential campaigns garnered a third of the vote in many Republican primaries. Mixing anti-corporate rhetoric with scapegoating of immigrant and foreign workers, Buchanan and his supporters forged ties with the anti-globalization movement's liberal wing, including labor union leaders and Public Citizen founder Ralph Nader.

Paleocons (along with neo-Nazis, Christian rightists, John Birchers, gun control opponents, and anti-environmentalists) also influenced the rise of the Patriot movement, which feared that secret elites behind the federal government were plotting to impose tyrannical world government on the United States. Sections of the movement organized armed militias to thwart the expected crackdown and formed so-called common law courts that claimed legal authority and dismissed U.S. courts as corrupt and unconstitutional. Although spurred partly by genuine government repression, such as the 1993 destruction of the Branch Davidian compound in Waco, Texas, the Patriot movement was pervaded by apocalyptic conspiracy theories and specious constitutional arguments. Many Patriot activists claimed that all constitutional amendments after the Bill of Rights were invalid, including those that abolished slavery and gave women the right to vote.

The Patriot movement was strongest in the Midwest and West and appealed particularly to White working class and middle-class men hurt by corporate restructuring. The movement peaked in 1996, when 858 identified groups were active, militia members were estimated in the tens of thousands, and supporters and sympathizers, by one estimate, numbered up to five million. After that the movement declined rapidly: by 2000, only 194 units were active.

Several factors contributed to the Patriot movement's collapse. The militias were widely blamed for the 1995 bombing of the Oklahoma City federal building, which killed 168 people, although convicted bomber Timothy McVeigh was a neo-Nazi with no direct ties to the militias. After the Oklahoma City bombing, fear of violence and increased law enforcement pressure drove many moderate activists out of the Patriot movement, even as far-rightists provided new recruits. Factional clashes between moderates and neo-Nazi sympathizers tore apart some Patriot groups. Many activists were diverted into Republican electoral politics or other initiatives such as the campaign to impeach Bill Clinton. With a core constituency that was largely rural and downwardly mobile, and no significant elite support, the Patriot movement's access to funds and other political resources was limited. The movement failed to build durable institutions and could not sustain the apocalyptic fervor that fueled its explosive growth, when the expected dramatic confrontation with federal tyranny failed to take place.

Buchanan's presidential campaigns rode much the same wave of populist nationalism that buoyed the Patriot movement. In 1992, he criticized Bush senior's vision of a New World Order and condemned "the predatory traders of Europe and Asia" who threatened American industry and jobs. In the 1996 primaries, Buchanan intensified his populist rhetoric against "unfettered capitalism": "What's good for General Motors is not good for American if General Motors has become a transnational corporation that sees its future in low-wage countries and in abandoning its American factories." Buchanan's effort to build a power base for paleoconservatism suffered with the Patriot movement's collapse. In addition, most Christian Right leaders, who shared Buchanan's positions on many social issues, did not support his campaigns, because they were building their own base within the Republican Party and did not want to alienate the party's establishment.

At the same, Buchanan's economic protectionism, military anti-interventionism, and to some extent his anti-Zionism alienated most potential business support. Some capitalists, such as arch conservative textile magnate Roger Milliken and the protectionist U.S. Business and Industrial Council, still endorsed business nationalist policies. But in an era of globalization and free trade orthodoxy, such support was far more limited and sporadic than it had been in the 1930s.

In 2000, Buchanan left the Republican Party and won the Reform Party presidential nomination after a bitter struggle with other party factions. Racial nationalist groups such as the Liberty Lobby rallied to Buchanan, who tried to deflect charges of racism by expelling a number of campaign staffers and choosing Ezola Foster, a Black conservative activist, as his vice-presidential running mate. Buchanan received only 400,000 votes (0.43 percent) in the general election, sparking infighting among paleocons over whether he had betrayed the cause.

Thus, at the time of the September 11 attacks, paleoconservatives were in an isolated position. They held no significant positions in George W. Bush's administration. Yet their influence could be felt indirectly: President Bush sometimes played to economic nationalist constituencies with rhetoric about protecting U.S. "food security" and "industrial security" against foreign imports, and even imposed new tariffs on imported steel. And the paleoconservatives' anti-interventionism was echoed by several related sectors of the right, such as the John Birch Society, the Libertarian Party, and groups focused on promoting White racial identity.

Unlike most conservatives, paleocons regarded the September 11 attacks as a predictable response to the U.S. own brutal crimes overseas. To protect itself against future terrorist attacks, they argued, the United States must end its policy of global military intervention. "Who has reason to hate this country?" asked Joseph Sobran rhetorically. "Only a few hundred million people—Arabs, Muslims, Serbs, and numerous others whose countries have been hit by U.S. bombers."

Paleoconservatives portrayed the September 11 attackers as rational enemies, not evil nihilists, and they ridiculed claims by President Bush and neoconservatives that the United States was targeted because it stood for freedom and democracy. Buchanan retorted, "Osama bin Laden did not convince 19 educated young men to simultaneously commit suicide in defiance of freedom of assembly." The issue, he stressed, was U.S. foreign policy, not our system of government. "As Osama bin Laden said, they want us to stop propping up the Saudi regime they hate, and to get off the sacred Saudi soil on which sit the holiest shrines of Islam."

Paleocons wanted the United States to be (as Buchanan titled one of his books) "a republic, not an empire." They were horrified by neoconservative rationalizations for imperialism, such as occupying other countries in order to win them to democracy. Joseph Sobran wrote, "the United States is now a global empire that wants to think of itself as a universal benefactor, and is nonplussed when foreigners don't see it that way." Buchanan commented that "only naiveté would expect an occupied country to thank rather than revile us." Imperialism is a disastrous course, paleocons argued, because colonized peoples will inevitably use violence to throw off their colonizers, and because imperialism means the growth of big government, militaristic repression of the home population, and a flood of foreign immigrants.

In their denunciations of U.S. militarism and imperialist expansion, paleoconservatives sometimes resembled leftist critics of the War on Terrorism. Such resonances were evident, for example, on the paleocon-sponsored Antiwar.com website. A few war opponents, such as left-wing columnist Alexander Cockburn, even called for an alliance between leftist and rightist anti-interventionists. Yet most leftists were deeply hostile to the paleoconservatives' racial nationalism, anti-feminist and anti-gay politics, and authoritarian tendencies.

Like many rightists less critical of Bush's war, paleoconservatives opposed the expansion of federal authority to spy on U.S. citizens. They saw serious threats to civil liberties in such measures as the USA PATRIOT Act and the short-lived TIPS program (Terrorism Information and Prevention System), which would have recruited millions of civilians to report on "suspicious" activities.

At the same time, paleoconservatives tended to support repressive security measures against *non*-U.S. citizens. They called for the racial profiling of Middle Eastern men to screen potential terrorists and endorsed President Bush's plan to try non-citizens suspected of terrorism in special military tribunals where basic constitutional protections would be absent. Looking far beyond the government's mass round-ups of Middle Easterners and South Asians, paleocons demanded an immediate halt to all immigration and deportation of all undocumented immigrants. Sam Francis warned that "a vast subculture of non-Western immigrants" allowed terrorists to move freely within the United States. He declared that "Islam, a great and in many respects admirable faith, simply is not part of [the West], and those who subscribe to Islam and its civilization are aliens."

The paleocon-neocon debate involved strange reversals. Paleocons expressed open ethnoreligious bigotry yet portrayed Islamic militants as having legitimate grievances against the United States, while neocons, supposedly free of a nativist heritage, painted these militants as demonic, irrational killers. Similarly, while paleocons have usually been identified with isolationism or unilateralism, after September 11 it was neoconservatives who urged unilateral action while paleocons stressed the need to build alliances with Arab and European states and warned that war with Iraq could leave the United States truly isolated.

To varying degrees, other sectors of the conservative right echoed paleoconservative arguments after September 11. Some shared the paleocons' critique of U.S. foreign policy. A larger number supported or were silent about U.S. interventionism but agreed with the paleoconservatives about the expansion of police powers within the United States.

Anti-immigrant groups thrived on the upsurge of nativism and racism that followed September 11. The neo-Confederate League of the South, cofounded by paleoconservative Thomas Fleming, lost members after its president, Michael Hill, issued a statement calling the attacks "the natural fruits of a regime committed to multiculturalism and diversity" and urging Americans "not to fall prey to a false sense of patriotism." But overall the neo-Confederate movement, too, benefited from the post–September 11 climate.

The Libertarian Party and the John Birch Society, both relatively isolated factions within the right, supported focused military retaliation against the al Qaeda network but urged an overall shift to non-interventionism. The Birch Society argued that the United States must not become "further enmeshed in entangling alliances abroad" and that the Bush administration undermined U.S. sovereignty by seeking United Nations approval before bombing Afghanistan, rather than getting a congressional declaration of war as the Constitution required.

Libertarian Party commentator Mary Ruwart traced the 9/11 attacks to U.S. policies such as stationing troops in the Middle East, giving aid to Israel, blockading Iraq at the cost of hundreds of thousands of children's lives, and funding and training Osama bin Laden to fight the Soviet Union in Afghanistan in the 1980s. Harry Browne, the Libertarian Party's 2000 presidential candidate, asked on the day after the attacks, "When will we learn that we can't allow our politicians to bully the world without someone bullying back eventually?" He predicted that the government's response to the attacks would include a loss of freedoms for Americans. In response to those who would call his criticisms unpatriotic and un-American, Browne asked, "When will we learn that without freedom and sanity, there is no reason to be patriotic?"

Phyllis Schlafly's Eagle Forum, an important New Right group, applauded the Bush administration's military operations in Afghanistan and elsewhere, as well as Bush's demand that other countries choose sides in the U.S. War on Terror. But like the paleoconservatives, the Eagle Forum warned that the administration's domestic anti-terrorism measures were too harsh on U.S. citizens and too lenient on non-citizens. Schlafly's organization denounced plans to create a national I.D. card, use army troops in domestic police work, or give police broad new powers to spy on citizens, such as those enacted in the USA PATRIOT Act. "Only totalitarian regimes monitor the private actions of law-abiding citizens," declared Eagle Forum executive director Lori Cole. Instead, Schlafly urged, the United States should immediately halt all immigration for at least one year, deport all "illegal aliens," expand the Border Patrol and back it up with soldiers, require all non-citizens to carry an I.D. card, and sanction airlines to use racial profiling when boarding passengers, among other anti-immigrant measures. Schlafly denounced the growing numbers of documented immigrants as "mostly people from non-Western countries who don't share our respect for the Rule of Law and don't learn how to speak English."

Schlafly, best known for leading the fight to defeat the Equal Rights Amendment in the 1970s and 1980s, shared the paleoconservatives' business nationalist roots. In 1964 she aided Barry Goldwater's presidential campaign with her widely distributed book, *A Choice, Not an Echo*, which charged that Eastern elite "kingmakers" secretly controlled both major parties. The Free Congress Foundation (FCF) also agreed with the paleoconservatives in part. FCF (originally the Committee for the Survival of a Free Congress) was one of the core New Right think-tanks founded in the early 1970s and was headed by Paul Weyrich, arguably the number one architect of New Right political strategy in the 1970s and 1980s. Shortly after the September 11 attacks, FCF officer William Lind urged the United States to reduce its international commitments, arguing that, especially since the end of the Cold War, the United States had "given more and more countries and peoples reason to attack us." Lind called, however, for massive retaliation in response to the attacks themselves: a nuclear assault on Afghanistan to "wipe that nation and its people off the face of the earth." This contradictory mix of anti-interventionism and genocidal militarism evoked early Cold War rhetoric from the unilateralist right.

Weyrich criticized the USA PATRIOT Act as a dangerous expansion of the police state and an unconstitutional attack on citizens' rights, and FCF compared it to past civil liberties abuses such as the World War II mass internment of Japanese Americans. At the same time, FCF warned that the United States faced a "real war" along its southern border: a Mexican "war of reconquest" waged by "millions of illegal immigrants flooding into California and other states. ... Remember, an invading army eventually goes home. Immigrants stay, and unless they assimilate to their new country's culture, they replace that culture with their own." Like the paleocons, the Free Congress Foundation considered it a top priority to restore the dominance of traditional Western (White Anglo) culture against the threats of multiculturalism and moral decadence.

While the paleoconservatives stressed social traditionalism, the Christian Right successfully used it to build a mass movement. Conservative evangelical Christians formed the bulk of the New Right's activist base in the 1970s, and over the following two decades Christian Right groups mobilized an ever-widening circle of religious activists, from Baptist fundamentalists to Pentecostals and charismatics to right-wing Catholics. Christian rightists warned that liberal and morally corrupt elites were engaged in a secular humanist conspiracy to destroy traditional values. They tended to demonize their opponents as servants of Satan and envisioned a swift approach of the End Times, when Christ would return. Their core agenda was to reassert rigid gender roles, male dominance, and compulsory heterosexuality.

For Christian rightists, questions of nationalism were grounded in their belief that the United States was a Christian nation. This idea had been a component of racial nationalism, business nationalism, and some versions of Cold War nationalism; the Christian Right made it central and elaborated it in the doctrine of dominionism, which said that Christian men were called by God to assert control over a sinful secular society. Dominionist ideology was pioneered and disseminated by hardline groups such as the Chalcedon Institute, who advocated comprehensive theocratic rule. For a pragmatic majority of Christian rightists, represented by big organizations such as Focus on the Family, the Christian Coalition, Concerned Women of America, and the Family Research Council, dominionism meant gaining a measure of power within the existing political order.

Of the four post–Cold War right-wing factions examined in this article, the Christian Right was one of only two to achieve major political influence, and the only one to build a sustained mass movement. Several factors contributed to this success. The Christian Right primarily drew in prosperous Sun Belt suburbanites, who—unlike the economically distressed rural dwellers on whom many Patriot groups depended—were relatively well positioned to attract sympathetic media attention and exert political pressure. With financial help particularly from rightist Sun Belt entrepreneurs, Christian Right leaders built a large, well-rooted infrastructure of local, state, and national organizations, think tanks, and lobbying groups, as well as international media empires that were both powerful and lucrative. In addition, leading Christian Right groups carefully tailored their politics to channel popular grievances without cutting themselves off from elite support.

The Christian Coalition, founded by televangelist Pat Robertson in 1989, illustrates the movement's success at organizing. In 1987–1988, the Christian Right was rocked by highly publicized sex scandals involving leading televangelists Jim Bakker and Jimmy Swaggart, followed by Robertson's loss to George Bush in the 1988 Republican presidential primaries. Many predicted that the movement was finished. But building on Robertson's campaign organization and media empire and the huge grassroots constituency of conservative Christians, the Christian Coalition enrolled hundreds of thousands of members within a few years. Unlike the earlier Moral Majority's national direct-mail approach, the Christian Coalition focused on local organizing, and by 1995, it claimed 1,425 local chapters. And while the Moral Majority appealed mainly to Baptists, the Christian Coalition also recruited many charismatics, Catholics, and others.

Following the New Right coalition's breakup in the late 1980s, the Christian Coalition leadership pursued an ideological balancing act between the paleoconservatives and other factions. They echoed paleocon rhetoric about an elite globalist conspiracy threatening U.S. sovereignty, but, at least at the leadership level, sided with the neocons on issues of trade and military intervention. In the 1992 and 1996 Republican presidential primaries, Robertson supported moderate conservatives George Bush senior and Robert Dole, respectively—not paleocon Pat Buchanan.

As a rule, Christian rightists saw non-Christian belief systems as illegitimate if not downright evil, and they tended to promote Western civilization as superior to all other cultures. But Christian rightists worked harder than paleocons to protect themselves against charges of ethnoreligious bigotry, reaching out to politically conservative Jews and calling for "racial reconciliation" with people of color.

Unlike the anti-Zionist paleoconservatives, most Christian Right organizations strongly supported the Israeli state and especially Israel's political Right. This stance was rooted in apocalyptic theology, not concern for Jews. Most Christian rightists believed that a strong Israel hastened the millennial End Times in which all except true followers of Christ would be destroyed. Nevertheless, pro-Zionist politics helped draw the Christian Right and the neoconservatives closer together, and the latter generally tolerated anti-Semitism among their Christian Right allies.

The Christian Right encompassed a range of doctrines and strategies. Starting in the 1980s, a clandestine wing of the movement targeted abortion providers with threats, vandalism, arson, bombings, and several assassinations. Some members of this wing, which was rooted in hardline theocratic doctrines, also supported or helped to build the Patriot movement and armed militias in the 1990s. A much larger section of the Christian Right was active in electoral politics, lobbying, and grassroots propaganda work. Christian rightists did not seize control of the Republican Party, as the Christian Coalition tried to do in the 1990s, but became a large and powerful faction within it. In 2001, the Christian Right's most prominent and powerful representative in the Bush administration was Attorney General John Ashcroft, the son of a Pentecostal minister. Their influence was also reflected in the administration's strong opposition to abortion rights and sexual health education, and in President Bush's frequent use of religious language to explain his policies.

In the wake of September 11, many Christian rightists declared that the attacks happened because the United States had turned away from God. They pointed to various examples of national immorality, especially abortion, homosexuality, feminism, and the Supreme Court's ban on prayer in public schools. The anti-abortion rights group Operation Save America (formerly Operation Rescue) asked, "How much more of our heavenly Father's wrath must we experience before we turn to our offended Lord and confess and repent of the sin of shedding innocent blood (abortion)." Televangelist Jerry Falwell, best known as head of the Moral Majority in the 1980s, said that gays and lesbians, abortion providers, and liberal advocacy groups helped to secularize America and thereby helped let the attacks happen. The implication was that such groups were essentially treasonous—internal enemies of the United States. Other

Christian Right leaders criticized Falwell for being divisive but implicitly agreed with him. Robertson, for example, backed away from Falwell's comments but still asserted that groups that "strip religious values from our public square" helped to "take away the mantle of divine protection" that keeps America from harm. Embarrassment caused by these remarks helped lead Robertson to resign as president of the Christian Coalition in December, 2001.

Most Christian Right groups supported President Bush's call for a War on Terrorism. But while Bush spoke unambiguously of America as a bastion of freedom, justice, and moral strength, Christian rightist rhetoric shifted uneasily between America the virtuous and America the sinful. Family Research Council president Ken Connor declared that "Our courageous fighting men stand ready to defend America, to preserve the freedom bequeathed to us by the sacrifices of so many who have gone before us" and that "family, faith, and freedom ... are the eternal verities, the bedrock virtues on which our American civilization stands." But in the same article he warned that "We cannot ask the nation's young men and women to go forth into danger merely to defend a grasping consumerism [or] the right of pornographers to exploit women and children [or] so that the innocent unborn can continue to be slaughtered in abortion clinics."

Some Christian rightists took advantage of the post–September 11 climate of fear to intensify their harassment of abortion providers. In October and November 2001, when anonymous mailings of anthrax spores to federal officials caused widespread fear of bioterrorism, women's health clinics received hundreds of hate letters that contained an unknown powdery substance. Many of these letters were signed by the "Army of God." Anti-abortion activist Clayton Waagner, who had publicly threatened to kill abortion providers, later admitted to sending more than 550 of the letters and was indicted on federal charges.

On the issue of state repression, Christian rightists were divided. The American Center for Law and Justice, founded by Robertson, supported the USA PATRIOT Act and military tribunals, and Falwell's *National Liberty Journal* published an article endorsing looser rules on FBI surveillance. However, the Rutherford Institute, a Christian Right legal advocacy group, declared that the USA PATRIOT Act "pushes aside the Bill of Rights in favor of granting the federal government sweeping new powers to investigate and detain anyone deemed a threat to national security." A *Chalcedon Report* columnist wrote that the act "in essence, makes us a police state." Many Christian rightists, such as Ken Connor, expressed dismay that one of their own, Attorney General John Ashcroft, was helping to lead the expansion of federal police power. These tensions reflected the conservative Right's longstanding ambivalence about government repression.

There was also a degree of complexity in Christian Right statements regarding Islam. Some movement groups condemned Islam without hesitation. The American Center for Law and Justice declared simply that "if Christianity is true then Islam cannot be." The Chalcedon Institute's Mark R. Rushdoony warned that "Islam is a dangerous religion primarily because it is a false one ... It is not the great evil, but it is one manifestation of the evil of men in rebellion against God." Rushdoony claimed that Islam (unlike Christianity) had promoted forced conversion, slavery, prostitution, sexual debauchery, treachery, despotism, oppression, and murder. President Bush was "avoiding the root of the problem" when he praised Islam and denounced only its radical adherents, Rushdoony argued. Another Chalcedon writer warned, "if our leaders continue to sell Islam as a peaceful, wonderful faith, we may begin to see large numbers of conversions..."

Other Christian Right groups took a more nuanced approach to Islam. Focus on the Family's *Citizen* magazine published a series of relatively informative articles by Mark Hartwig about Islam and Osama bin Laden. Hartwig noted that "Muslim opinion is not uniformly in favor of bin Laden—nor is it uniformly anti-American," and quoted a fatwa by the grand mufti of Saudi Arabia condemning the September 11 attacks. Summing up an analysis of the concept of jihad, Hartwig concluded, "Christians should not accept the sweeping claim that Islam is a religion of peace. There's just too much contrary evidence. On the other hand, Christians shouldn't jump to the conclusion that their Muslim neighbors are bomb-toting fanatics: Even Muslims who believe in militant jihad don't necessarily like violence. Instead of fearing or hating Muslims, Christians should view them in light of our duty to preach the gospel."

A few Christian Right commentators recognized similarities between their own critiques of American society and those of Islamic militants. A Focus on the Family article entitled "Understanding Islamic Fundamentalism" observed: "Citing pornography, materialism, and a high divorce rate, radical Muslims see the United States as a failed Christian nation. One scholar observed that Muslims 'would respect the United States much more if we did not separate God from governance.'"

Joel Belz, in an article in the Protestant fundamentalist magazine *World*, condemned the September 11 attacks as "a monstrous kind of evil" far beyond America's own sins. Yet he quoted an Islamic fundamentalist, an embassy driver in New York City, as applauding the attacks with the words, "The Americans have forgotten that God exists." Belz commented, "How strange that an Islamic fundamentalist might explain the problem with the very same diagnosis by a typical American evangelical—but still mean something so very different." Belz himself described the World Trade Center as a symbol of America's "false deities," including materialism secularism, and pluralism, which he linked with the banking, media, and entertainment industries. "Babel needed just one tower; New York built two."

Christian rightists such as Belz might hint that the World Trade Center deserved to be destroyed, but many far-rightists declared it openly. This position traced back to major changes in the Far Right that began shortly before the end of the Cold War. Starting in the early 1980s, most White supremacist groups abandoned Ku Klux Klan–style segregationism in favor of neo-Nazi doctrines that called for a racially pure New Order. Before, the Far Right had blended racial nationalist and Cold War nationalist themes and sought to return to America's Jim Crow past. Now, with segregationism permanently defeated and a powerful New Right distancing itself from open racism, far-rightists increasingly abandoned loyalty to the United States, arguing that the country was hopelessly controlled by a secret Jewish elite. The Far Right remained small and politically marginalized, yet its doctrines and creative tactics influenced a much larger array of rightist initiatives.

Two main branches of the Far Right emerged. Cryptofascists such as Willis Carto of the Liberty Lobby and political cult leader Lyndon LaRouche pioneered electoral strategies that used a veneer of anti-elite conservatism to mask their authoritarian agendas. The most successful practitioner of this approach was former Klan leader David Duke, who won a seat in the Louisiana state legislature and the Republican nominations for U.S. senator in 1990 and governor in 1991. Although Duke lost both the Senate and governor's races, he received a majority of White votes statewide in both campaigns. Paleocons Sam Francis and Pat Buchanan, in turn, heralded Duke's opposition to affirmative action, welfare, school busing, and immigrants of color as a model for conservatives, and shaped their own political work partly after his example.

At the same time, more militant groups such as Aryan Nations, Posse Comitatus, and White Aryan Resistance openly rejected the legitimacy of the U.S. political system and promoted paramilitary strategies. They called for the creation of a racially pure White homeland in the Pacific Northwest or the complete overthrow of the "Zionist Occupation Government" (or "ZOG") in Washington. In the 1980s, federal agencies cracked down hard on the Order, an armed offshoot of Aryan Nations that "declared war" on the U.S. government, and the Justice Department brought conspiracy indictments against a number of neo-Nazi leaders. This marked a sharp turnaround from the 1970s, when the FBI had helped certain Far Right groups bomb, kidnap, and assassinate leftist activists.

The Far Right's big advance came in the 1990s, with the brief explosion of the Patriot movement and its paramilitary wing, the armed citizens militias. Fascists did not control the Patriot movement, but the movement allowed them to break out of political isolation more than any development since the America First anti-intervention campaign of 1940–1941. Neo-Nazi ideas circulated widely among Patriot groups, helping to frame the discussion for large numbers of politically engaged people alienated from the established order.

In the late 1990s, the Patriot movement shrank into a small, hardened core. This increased neo-Nazis' role within the movement but cut them off once again from the more moderate activists who abandoned Patriot groups. The Far Right suffered more setbacks in 2001. In July of that year, the Liberty Lobby, a leading disseminator of anti-Semitic conspiracy theories since its founding in the late 1950s, dissolved itself as a result of financial mismanagement. Also in 2001, Aryan Nations, a major center of the 1980s neo-Nazi revival, was forced to sell its Idaho compound and headquarters after being ordered to pay millions of dollars in damages to a woman and her son attacked by the group's security guards. Aryan Nations promoted Christian Identity, a neo-Nazi religious doctrine which claimed that White Christians were God's true chosen people and modern-day Jews were Asiatic imposters in league with Satan.

Neo-Nazi groups benefited from the outpouring of conspiracy theories and anti-immigrant racism that followed the September 11 attacks. The Southern Poverty Law Center, a human rights group, reported increases in the number of active neo-Nazi groups and websites from 2000 to 2001, as well as a big jump in shortwave radio programming by hate groups.

Unlike many of those who scapegoated immigrants, however, neo-Nazis refused to rally behind the U.S. government or embrace American patriotism. Their loyalty was not to the United States but to the Aryan race (roughly, non-Jews of European descent). Edgar Steele, former attorney for the Aryan Nations, wrote: "America is Jewish controlled now, at all levels. America IS the Jews." Posse Comitatus called on far-rightists to "sit back and watch the death throws [sic] of this Babylonian beast system..." Posse Comitatus was a self-appointed "law enforcement" group that repudiated all government authority above the county level, reflecting many neo-Nazis' rejection of the traditional nation-state.

Far-rightists were hostile to patriotic displays and calls for national unity. A.V. Schaerffenberg in the NS [National Socialist] News Bulletin commented, "No amount of chauvinistic cheers, jingoistic rhetoric or solemn vows to rebuild the obliterated buildings can bring back their dead, sacrificed on the altar of America's self-defeating Near East policy." Schaerffenberg was disgusted by media images of Whites and people of color, Jews and non-Jews coming together in a time of crisis: "'We're all Americans now!' Ugh!" Through such coverage, he claimed, the media was promoting "the racial poisoning of White America" and thereby serving Jewish interests. Responding to calls for ethnic and religious tolerance from President Bush and other leaders, Christian Identity minister and former Klan leader Thomas Robb commented, "Remember tolerance is an act of Satanic worship because Satan is the god of tolerance. He has no absolutes of right and wrong. Satan loves everybody!... But we are taught by Jesus Christ to be intolerant."

Far-rightists were split between opponents and supporters of the September 11 attacks. Some neo-Nazis condemned the hijackings, which they blamed on the U.S. "slavishly pro-Israeli foreign policy" coupled with supposedly lax immigration rules. Matt Hale, leader of the neo-pagan World Church of the Creator, declared: "4000 people died because Israel uses America as a 'human shield'... September 11th wouldn't have happened if the corrupt traitors in Washington D.C. didn't bankroll the terrorist state of Israel and didn't allow Arabs into the country in the first place." Posse Comitatus urged, "It is time to make those strangers in the land know under no uncertain terms that they are not welcome here. BOYCOTT ALL business's [sic] not owned and operated by White Europeans! Let's let them know that we DO NOT want them in our Christian Republic."

Some far-rightists saw an Israeli plot behind the September 11 attacks. Aryan Nations blamed the World Trade Center attack on "the Ruling Elite, the Jews: i.e.,

Mossad, the so-called New World Order," and called it a move "to further enslave us in a total police state." David Duke claimed that Israeli intelligence had "deeply penetrated" al Qaeda and helped engineer the attacks in order to win more U.S. support against Arab and Muslim opponents. He repeated a widely circulated fiction that thousands of Israelis working at the World Trade Center received prior warning of the September 11 attack and stayed away from work that day. Duke wrote that 9-11 was only the latest in a series of Israeli-instigated terror attacks against the United States. U.S. officials who continued to support Israel in the face of such attacks, he declared, "clearly committed treason against our country."

A number of far-right groups, however, applauded the attacks on the World Trade Center and the Pentagon, which they saw as targeting Jewish power, and praised the hijackers' courage and self-sacrifice. Bill Roper wrote: "The enemy of our enemy is, for now at least, our friends. We may not want them marrying our daughters, just as they would not want us marrying theirs. We may not want them in our societies, just as they would not want us in theirs. But anyone who is willing to drive a plane into a building to kill jews [sic] is alright by me. I wish our members had half as much testicular fortitude." Roper was deputy membership coordinator of the National Alliance, a leading neo-Nazi group that advocated the overthrow of the U.S. government and extermination of Jews, people of color, and White "race traitors."

Neo-Nazis' admiration for al Qaeda reflected more than momentary approval. Organizational ties between western fascists and Islamic rightists went back to the 1930s, based on shared hatred of Jews, communists, the British Empire and (later) the United States. By the 1990s, European neo-Nazis had built extensive links with both religious and secular Middle Eastern rightists. After the September 11 attacks, a number of Muslim newspapers published anti-Jewish hate pieces by American fascists such as David Duke and National Alliance head William Pierce.

In broader terms, sections of the U.S. Far Right sought to build alliances with militant right-wing anti-imperialists in Asia, Africa, and Latin America, as well as with rightist Black and Latino organizations within the United States. In the 1980s and 1990s, for example, both the Lyndon LaRouche network and Tom Metzger's White Aryan Resistance forged active ties with Louis Farrakhan's Nation of Islam. In conjunction with these efforts, some neo-Nazis moved from racial supremacist ideology toward a racial separatism that envisioned separate monocultural societies coexisting alongside each other. This trend was particularly notable among advocates of "Third Position," a neo-Nazi doctrine that denounced capitalism as well as communism and called for a revolutionary White working class movement to (in Metzger's words) "take the game away from the left." In the period after the September 11 attacks, some antifascists regarded Third Position as the most dangerous form of neo-Nazi politics in the long run, because of its potential to preempt egalitarian leftism as a voice of mass insurgency.

The September 11 crisis and the War on Terrorism highlighted and intensified the divisions within the U.S. right. On core questions of nationhood—foreign and military policy, domestic security and repression, and even fundamental loyalty—different factions of the right took diametrically opposing positions. Even when rightists agreed on specific questions, their motivations or underlying assumptions and priorities often differed. Christian rightists joined the neoconservatives in supporting the War on Terrorism and an interventionist foreign policy, but while many neocons described U.S. capitalist culture in rigidly upbeat terms, Christian rightists included materialism and consumerism in their critique of America's "sinfulness," and some criticized the Bush administration's growing power to repress U.S. citizens. Paleoconservatives and neo-Nazis opposed U.S. expansionism, vilified immigrants of color, and scapegoated Israeli Jews in terms that often sounded similar, but paleocons wanted to rebuild the American republic, while neo-Nazis wanted to dismantle or overthrow it.

Of the four factions, the neoconservatives most heavily influenced the federal government's response to September 11. True to their Cold War nationalist roots, the neocons saw a chance to rally Americans behind another global crusade against Evil, with "terrorism" or "radical Islam" replacing Soviet communism as the target. Their strident response gave voice to the fear and national pride that millions of Americans felt after September 11, and won favor with important sections of the political and economic elite.

Yet the neocons' lack of an organized popular base left them heavily dependent on elite backing. In addition, their program of open-ended, unilateral conquest in the name of spreading democracy was both expensive and risky. From a U.S. standpoint, the program's potential costs included skyrocketing military budgets, wrecked international alliances, crippled civil liberties, an open-ended stream of military casualties, a popular anti-American backlash across the Middle East, and more September 11–style attacks on U.S. civilians. Should such costs become too high, the neocons could rapidly lose their elite patronage, high-level appointments, and ability to shape U.S. nationalism.

The Christian Right, to the extent that it embraced the neocons' global crusade, shared some of the neocons' vulnerability. But the Christian Right was a mass movement, with millions of participants organized at all levels, from prayer groups to national mailing lists, and a broad funding stream largely beyond external control. Leading Christian Right groups were also skillful at borrowing populist rhetoric, such as denunciations of globalist elites, while working as a conventional power bloc within the Republican Party. The movement's ambivalence about U.S. culture spoke to many conservative Christians' sense of dissatisfaction with the existing order, but in a way that did not substantively challenge established power relations.

The Christian Right's internal disagreement about repressive measures such as the USA PATRIOT Act might weaken the movement if the debate became heated. But the split could also work to the movement's advantage, by enabling leading Christian Right groups to emphasize their loyalty to the government, while other sections of the movement kept their distance from domestic policies that could prove unpopular.

By contrast, far-rightists and paleoconservatives were shut out of power both before and after September 11. Both neo-Nazis and the more moderate racial nationalists associated with the paleocons benefited from the rise in ethnic scapegoating and violence that followed the World Trade Center attacks, but modest growth did not translate into significant political gains. That could change, however. Both paleo-conservatives and far-rightists tapped into political undercurrents that ran deep in sections of White America. The Patriot/militia movement's brief explosion in the 1990s indicated a broad reservoir of anger—anger at losing privilege and status over traditionally oppressed groups below, and at disempowerment by massive bureaucratic institutions, both public and private, above. The Patriot movement's own weaknesses led it to collapse quickly, but that collapse did not resolve any of the tensions that had brought it into being.

Paleoconservatives' mix of business nationalism and racial nationalism addressed that popular anger in a way that might still win broad support. The paleocons offered a telling critique of expansionist militarism and rising state repression, coupled with anti-immigrant scapegoating and a general celebration of traditional social hierarchies. If the neocons' global crusade ran into trouble—for example, if substantial numbers of U.S. troops began dying overseas—the paleocons (or others with comparable politics) could benefit.

The neo-Nazis' potential for broad support was more limited than that of the pa-leocons, because their anti-Semitic and White supremacist views were more explicit, they stood apart from the American patriotic consensus, and they called for more sweeping sociopolitical change. Only if the United States entered a much deeper social, political, or economic crisis were substantial numbers of people likely to embrace a right-wing (or left-wing) revolutionary alternative. However, far-rightists had a history of pioneering political slogans, tactics, and strategies that more moderate rightists then copied, and this pattern of indirect influence might well continue.

Right-wing nationalism did not speak with one voice either before or after September 11, 2001. The right's internal divisions and nationalism's multilayered history blocked the effort to restore the nationalist consensus of the Cold War era. Yet fragmented nationalism was also a mark of the U.S. right's strength. The ability to address hopes and fears, prejudices and grievances, in a shifting variety of ways has long contributed to the right's political success and durability.

Author's Note: Scholars have used many different terms to describe and label different branches of the political right. "Neoconservative" and "paleoconservative" are standard terms that are or have been widely used by members of these factions themselves. The Christian Right is often mislabeled the "Religious Right," a term which obscures the existence of completely separate right-wing movements among religious Jews, Muslims, Hindus, Buddhists, and others. What I call the Far Right is often termed the "Extreme Right" or sometimes the "Radical Right." I choose "Far Right" for the sake of consistency with my own earlier work.

Whiteness Is Not Inevitable!

Why the Emphasis on White-Skin Privilege Is White-Chauvinist and Why the Problematic of "Race" Needs to be Replaced with the Restoration of the National Question(s)

Fred Ho

In this insightful piece, radical artist Fred Ho reasserts the politics of revolutionary nationalism as a challenge for all "anti-racists." Suggesting that race itself is a misguided way of looking at the empire and the world, Ho reminds us that the question of national liberation and land is not just something for other people "over there."

This address shall vigorously critique the emphasis given to "white-skin privilege" as the dominant characteristic in the conceptualizing of the oppression of so-called "peoples of color" in the United States, and for its odious contribution to reinforcing white chauvinism within the U.S. left and working class by delimiting the struggle of "oppressed nationalities" (what I prefer to call so-called "peoples of color") to the goal of integration (with the white oppressor nation).

Indeed, ironically and paradoxically, I shall reveal the major problems of "white blind spot" in the "race" analysis framework that promotes a mistaken historical account of the development of the U.S. nation-state, the failure to apprehend how the genocide and conquest of the Native Indigenous nations, the importation of African and Asian laboring populations, the annexation of Mexico, Hawaii and transfer or purchase of colonial spoils has created the ascendancy of U.S. capitalism into the premiere global imperialist power by the mid-twentieth century, a process through which a white oppressor nation attains social, cultural and political supremacy, thereby "racializing" every aspect of American society.

I shall argue for the replacement of the "race" formulation and the overemphasis upon "white-skin privilege" with a "return" to the national question(s) framework and argue that no separate politics or forms of organizing that focus upon whites is correct or efficacious, but arguably harmful and hurtful to the cause of building working class unity and power within the United States.

A fresh and creative analysis of the stratification and division of the U.S. working class will be offered that rejects the dominance and leading role of "white workers," heretofore the assumed project of a white chauvinist–plagued U.S. labor and left. Rectifying political strategies and organizing approaches will be proposed which emphasize the central and essential importance of reconceptualizing the struggle to end white supremacy, white racism and inequality to be that one of building a multiplicity of national liberation struggles which require the leadership and organization of the multilingual, multicultural, multinational U.S. working class and allies.

The United States has a peculiar historical development. Founded by European settler colonization, the United States grew to its present borders through military force, the purchasing of vast land territories that were the spoils from former colonial powers (viz., the Louisiana purchase from France and the $45 million purchase of Alaska from Russia), the military annexation of northern Mexico and the Hawaiian islands, and the expansion of settlements and industries to the Pacific Ocean, and the acquisition of islands and territories throughout the Caribbean, central America (e.g., the Panama Canal) and the Pacific Islands (e.g., Guam, American Samoa, etc.). Concurrently, via the manipulation of immigration laws, a concerted campaign to repopulate the continent of North America in favor of European-descended peoples and disfavoring all others, continues to the present.

Before the consolidation of the United States of America could occur, the Native peoples who inhabited the land that we now call "the lower forty-eight," with a rough estimated population range at the beginning of the sixteenth century to be between 1 to 10 million, had to be driven off their lands to make way for the new settlers, and ultimately, given the resistance by the Natives, nearly annihilated.

At first, the early European settlers were at the mercy of Native benevolence and assistance. However, as settlers grew in number, their capitalist appetite for land and resources intensified. The Natives were unwilling to participate in the construction of a capitalist economic and social order, and worse, not able to be exploited either as indentured or enslaved labor since social stratification and private ownership of land and resources was completely alien to them, and once experiencing the cruelties of exploitation and oppression, resisted such incursions and assaults upon their way of life and homeland.

The Christians brought the Devil to the "New World" and the Devil was them. So-called primitive peoples did not subscribe to the monotheism and anthropocentrism of the Europeans. It was not possible for these societies to regard even their enemies as subhuman or without a soul. It was not possible for them to regard nature as not a living being for which they, as humans, came from and belonged to. The Europeans, however, slaughtered and enslaved them as if they were logs to be felled, and their land and ecology nothing more than objects from which money could be made.

Native Americans could not be coerced into American plantation society or indentured servitude. Their completely noncapitalist mode of production, which had proven to be self-sufficient and stable for eons, were devoid of highly developed state repression structures, which could not be appropriated by and made to service the formation, facilitation and social control needs of a capitalist economy. The capitalist mode of production was as inimical to Native peoples as the diseases that the Europeans brought. Not predicated upon or driven by profits and its concomitant social and cultural precepts of individualism, private ownership, monotheism, repressive state, patriarchy and the nuclear family, etc. large scale social production was both completely foreign and toxic. Never had the Native peoples experienced such pandemics on the order introduced by Europeans: both biological and sociological.

Once it became clear that Native submission wasn't going to happen, American settler-colonialism proceeded full force with genocide: the destruction of the native mode of production, a horrific "ethnic-ecological cleansing" that cleared natural and human life, which had existed and evolved for tens of thousands of years, an unprecedented ecocide, genocide and matricide waged for a few centuries, all for the purpose of the imposition of a new settler-colonial society that would become the United States.

Once the process of ecocide-genocide-matricide was underway, and settler-colonialist society expanded, endeavoring to build a capitalist mode of production foisted upon a continent that neither needed or engendered it, the newly expanding United States proceeded with the importation of a foreign-originated labor force, to at first supplement the already-existing indentured labor force of former Europeans, and then once the cotton gin revolutionized the instruments of mass production, for large scale agrarian labor.

Why were enslaved Africans more suitable? African feudalism and protocapitalism (the production of commodities for exchange and the social and class relations needed to facilitate that exchange) had similarities to European feudalism and emerging capitalism: Large scale social production, huge surpluses, huge repressive state apparatuses (often used to facilitate slave trading among other Africans, Arabs and Europeans), widespread use of precious metal currency and also nonmetal symbolic currency (e.g., cowry shells), development of large sectors of production for exchange (textiles and food production), rich resources for luxury items coveted by the European market (precious metals, ivory, etc.), elaborate infrastructure from centuries of intercontinental trade with Europe and Asia.

Imported Africans didn't arrive as a ready-amalgamated nationality or people. They were valued precisely because they were so disparate and ethnically-culturally-linguistically so varied, and with the forced splitting of kinship and family ties, made even more conducive to organized exploitation for capitalist plantations. Hence U.S. capitalism necessitated this ironic amalgamation of Africans in the United States erasing particular African national or tribal identities for the new, amalgamated oppressed nationality identity as African Americans.

During the entire nineteenth century, the expansion and consolidation of the U.S. nation-state included massive land acquisitions that included the 1803 Louisiana

Purchase from France battered by the loss of Haiti and strained from its foreign wars and domestic revolts; the military conquest of two-thirds of Mexico which became incorporated as the U.S. southwest; the ongoing pacification wars against the Native peoples; the acquisition of territorial spoils from the Spanish-American War; and the military annexation of the Hawaiian islands, 3,000 miles from the Pacific shores of the United States. In the early twentieth century, the vast territory of resource-rich Alaska would be purchased from a war-and-revolution-battered Russia for a measly $45 million, and two lands, completely disconnected from the other forty-eight states, would become the forty-ninth and fiftieth states of the United States (respectively, Alaska in 1904 and Hawaii in 1958).

From the eighteenth to mid-nineteenth centuries, during the consolidation process of the U.S. nation-state, the American bourgeoisie had constant external conflicts primarily from England and France, as well as a growing internal conflict between the southern agrarian capitalists with the northern industrial capitalists. The Civil War was the consolidation of a unified nation-state under the political and economic leadership of the northern industrial capitalists, who victorious, and in control over the surplus profits of the internationally traded southern-produced cash crops (cotton, tobacco, etc.) could now begin the formation of American finance capital and expand throughout the Americas and to the rest of the world (exporting either direct U.S. colonial rule and/or financial domination). As this unprecedented and exponential expansion of capital was occurring, huge labor needs had to be filled with the importation of labor from around the world and this period of the late nineteenth century is really the emergence of a U.S. multinational proletariat, though fitted into a constantly shifting racial matrix. This shift is primarily characterized by the increasing binary categorizing of "race" as "white" and "colored." The price of the ticket to settler-colonial Yankee American society was to become "white."

The myriad forms of national inequality cojoined with white supremacy to consolidate the United States as a racially defined nation-state in which an American or anything American became synonymously white.

(Today, as imperialism plunders and impoverishes the Third World, massive numbers of peoples flee those societies for the First World.)

Both for the purposes of social control, detailed in the important work of Ted Allen and others, and for what I've argued as the necessity of nation-state identity and structural formation and consolidation, the separation of peoples into "white" versus "others/foreigners/oppressed" in the United States was facilitated by the virus of "race" as a biosocial pseudoscientific/cultural construction, extended from its original applications by European colonization.

The privileges accorded to "whites" (i.e., those accorded the status/identity as Americans) were consequently rooted in the conquest and subjugation of entire peoples, and reproduced and consolidated by a matrix of ideological political and sociocultural privileges granted to those who were accorded the status and identity of being "American" (which meant white). Those deemed white/American had the benefits of glorification and "manifest destiny," whereas complete dehumanization was the condition for all those deemed "nonwhite" and excluded from consideration as Americans. White racism and white supremacy thus become normative. That which is American is equated as white. That which is or who is not "white" are NOT American.

Large influxes of Europeans to the United States including those who suffered national oppression in their homelands, such as the Irish, or faced harsh persecution, such as Jews and other religious-ethnic groups, were accorded the opportunity to join white American society, and share in the spoils of white-settler colonialism and expansionism. Though such European groups encountered initial discrimination, over-all, the access and possibility for white assimilation was far preferable as participants in the consolidation of the Yankee nation-state than the perpetual wretchedness of exclusion and oppression for nonwhites.

The unprecedented opportunities of settlerism, both real and hyped, included such privileges and enticements as the possibility for ownership of small plots of land, relative freedoms including voting rights for white males, small business ownership, and a host of other opportunities. What was required to access these real or propa-gandized privileges was a dedication to and support for the Yankee American way of life: kill off the Indians and take all of their land, disallow citizenship and competi-tion from formerly enslaved Africans, remove and exterminate the Asiatics, keep the Mexicans subjugated. All "white" immigrants were given relatively unrestricted access to American citizenship. With the Chinese exclusionary immigration laws, tantamount to genocide, the Chinese were the only immigrant group which steadily decreased in number for nearly a century. Racist immigration exclusion and persecution would extend to all Asian/pacific groups until 1964.

The formal history of the United States is the narrative of oppressor nation build-ing. The counternarrative is the history of the oppressed nations and nationalities. The American multinational proletariat emerges during this historical process, beginning after the Civil War with the unification of American capital, the integration of a com-mon national market (greatly facilitated by the transcontinental railroad for which super-exploited Chinese labor outperformed the higher paying Irish workforce, and for which the Chinese workers were both barred from the ranks of U.S. organized labor as well as the annals of American history), the promotion of a white supremacist American historico-cultural narrative and identity with a full repertoire of Yankee Doodle Dandy mythologies and grand master narratives from song to scholarship.

To conclude my analysis of the historical development of the American nation-state, I want to summarize the concomitant white oppressor nation building process and the process of national oppression as indelible to American society:

- White skin privileges both are byproducts of and contributors to white settler colonial national construction.

- White privileges, as partial, tenuous and minor as they may be for poor and exploited whites, exceed the condition of national oppression relegated to those not conferred as white: genocide, terror, extreme restrictions, exclusion and constant brutal oppression.
- In many cases whites have not been the majority population in "American history," but became dominant both numerically and socio-politically through genocide, unjust immigration laws, forced exodus, ghettoization and marginalization, all practices aimed at the repopulation of the continent to ensure the hegemony of white supremacy.

The problem of race is that it primarily juxtaposes the political question as one of integration, as one of learning how to get along with one another, and not dealing with the question of returning land and territory and the battle for national equality. So it is about how do we get rid of our racist ideas or how do we deal with white privilege. White privilege is only one phenomenon of national oppression. The privileges happen because of the inequality between peoples, of which the first basis was depriving people of their land, resources and control of the fruits of their labor and innovations. The process of Americanization was the seizure of land and territory and then absorption or assimilation of that territory and those peoples into this mythical white supremacist thing called America. African Americans become Black Yankees when they assimilate the imperialist history and values of the Unites States, as opposed to seeing themselves as oppressed nationalities. Malcolm X demarcated the difference between identifying as oppressed versus identifying with the oppressor values and narrative: "We [Africans in the United States] are not Americans, we are victims of America."

The political logic of "anti-racism" or "fighting white-skin privileges" ironically privileges the target of struggle upon the attitudes and behaviors of whites. It presumes white leadership, the apriori-ness of white numerical majority, the sanctity of the current borders and configuration of the fifty states, and even the presumption of white working class inclusion in the revolutionary struggle to end U.S. imperialism, viz., the domination of U.S. monopoly capital in the domestic aspect of such struggle. And hence, the U.S. left since its formal inception, with the exception of such notable energies as the African Blood Brotherhood, the CPUSA adoption of the Comintern position of the Black-belt Nation thesis, and the revolutionary oppressed nationality movements of the 1960s–early 1970s, has been plagued with the fundamental white chauvinist problem of centering and basing the U.S. multinational working class movement upon the white working class, i.e., the focus and concentration upon the workers of the oppressor nation, rather than centering, focusing and basing the leadership and development of forces among the workers of the oppressed nations/nationalities.

The U.S. multinational working class has erroneously been viewed as necessarily being a white majority (and the attendant chauvinist presumption, with majority white leadership). Rather, oppressed nationality workers are not only the numerical majority relative to their populations, but have, both respectively and collectively, it can be argued, greater political inclination towards radical and revolutionary positions due to the intrinsic nature of their contradiction with imperialism: super-exploitation combined with national oppression and external domination.

Only in the above cited notable exception of focus and concentration upon building the political leadership of the revolutionary national movements have any forces truly respected and grasped the objective reality that the national movements are objectively revolutionary, regardless of, and with or without, the approval, presence or support of whites and white workers.

Thus the white integrationist-white chauvinist plagued left has disregarded the importance of building and leading "nationality-in-form" formations, such as oppressed nationality student unions, militant community forces, independent cultural institutions, and the creative labor formations that elevate the role and leadership of oppressed nationality workers. The U.S. left has given scant emphasis upon the struggle to force the U.S. government to honor all treaties made with the Native nations, fighting for national rights, self-government, return of stolen lands and resources, reparations and the dismantling and eradication of all vestiges of white settler-colonialism, including the hegemony of classical music orchestras, white mythologies in education and scholarship, and even the notion of a white identity.

As part of upholding national self-determination, the U.S. left, in engendering the multiplicity of national liberation struggles, would support the dismantling and reconfiguration of the U.S. national borders should the struggle of oppressed nations culminate in forms of independence, autonomy or new federation relations. Asian Americans, for example, in the oppressed nation of Hawaii must choose between siding with the Yankee oppressor nation/identity or with being part of the oppressed Hawaiian nation: electing to identify as "I'm kanaka maoli (Hawaiian) of Japanese descent, for example. A white person must proclaim, "I am a new Afrikan of European descent" or a "Xicano of European descent," should they reside in what is now Mississippi or Texas, respectively.

Whites must recognize that they own no special allegiance to white anything, including even the privileged view that the primary role of white leftists or white anti-racists is to concentrate in white communities. Whites have no entitlement to monopolize anything, EVEN THE DRAGS OF ORGANIZING WORK! The best way to "unlearn" whiteness (and be a true race traitor!) is to for people of European descent in the United States to give their all in exactly the same way as oppressed nationality freedom fighters: liberate stolen and occupied lands, return of resources and wealth, reparations, and to build a new society that will certainly mean the destruction of the United States as it has historically been constructed and construed, and the coming-into-being of voluntarily associated liberated peoples and societies.

The Content of Our Character

An Interview with José López

Mike Staudenmaier with Matt Meyer and Dan Berger

One organization which grew out of the revolutionary nationalist movements of the 1960s and 1970s, along the lines discussed by Fred Ho, was the Movimiento Liberation Nacional (MLN)—a group of Puerto Rican and Mexican militants. Centered on fighting for independence for Puerto Rico and reunification of Mexico, the MLN eventually evolved into two separate entities, with the MLN-PR setting up Juan Antonio Corretjer Cultural Centers in U.S. cities with substantial Puerto Rican populations. With their central base in Chicago, the MLN-PR initiated some of the strongest, longest-lasting, and most dedicated community-based organizations in North America, including the award-winning Pedro Albizu Campos High School, a nursery school, an art space, legal and housing offices, and a bakery. One of the first national liberation movements to officially and formally acknowledge the importance of lesbian and gay liberation, they also helped set up an AIDS and health clinic, VIDA/SIDA, which has been seen as a model of patient-centered, grassroots health care. With some leading members of the broader MLN community arrested and charged in the early 1980s with participation in the Armed Forces of National Liberation (FALN), they have been involved in political prisoner support work—now under the leadership of the National Boricua Human Rights Network. But they have also been involved in local electoral work, closely connected to the offices of Congressman Luis Gutiérrez and working with the Latin Agenda. Throughout the 1980s and early 1990s, they also worked closely with a solidarity organization under their direct control, the Free Puerto Rico Committee (formerly the New Movement). Over these three decades of work, the consistent figure of inspiration, vision, and strategic direction has been José López, the director of the Cultural Center. The following interview, conducted for this book, begins to reveal how the late-1970s orientation toward revolutionary nationalism developed into the vibrant community empowerment model still growing in Chicago's Humboldt Park neighborhood.

Mike Staudenmaier: There's been a historic relationship, within the MLN and before that, between the Puerto Rican and the Chicano movements. What is the relationship between those movements and struggles today? What do you see as the strategic role of Puerto Ricans in shaping the strategic role of Latinos in the era of Obama? And also, how does the issue of immigration fit into this agenda?

José López: Well, I think that there has been a very long relationship between the Puerto Rican independence movement—it was before the MLN, and even after the MLN—in terms of the Puerto Rican independence movement and the Mexican and the Chicano movements. And we could date this obviously, here in Chicago, to the communities themselves. When the Puerto Ricans began to establish themselves in Chicago in the late 1940s and early 1950s, one of the places that they came to reside was in South Chicago, where there was a sizeable Mexican community already established in and around the steel mills. And that brought these two groups in the context of each other. But I would also say that there was a connection—a sort of cultural connection—of Puerto Rican people and Mexicans as far back as the 1930s. I say this because Mexican films begin to be introduced into Puerto Rico in the 1930s, and every small town that had a little theater were actually playing Mexican films. They were the only films that were, obviously, in Spanish. The films that were coming from the United States were—even the silent films—obviously dubbed and captioned in English.

In many ways, I would say that the Mexican film industry, and through it the introduction of Mexican music in Puerto Rico, created a climate that helped preserve Spanish in Puerto Rico. It was the popular thing. English had been imposed in the schools in Puerto Rico, and here you have now the beginnings of the mass media, particularly through radio and television, invading Puerto Ricans' popular space. All of a sudden, the Mexican films began to come in and through that also Mexican music.

So you have a very interesting intersection. Also with Puerto Rican, particularly Puerto Rican musicians going to Mexico, appearing in Mexican films (like Rafael Hernandez), and especially for Puerto Ricans who were migrating to the United States—there was already a cultural nexus with Mexico. While people now see that there is a disconnect between Mexicans and Puerto Ricans, I think that way before the migration, and even after the migration, this relationship existed. During the migration, it consolidated itself.

A lot of people don't see this connection, but in Chicago it is very important, particularly because there would be large numbers of Puerto Ricans and large numbers of Mexicans, coming together in this city. If we look at what happened here in the late 1960s, as a Puerto Rican movement—an authentic Puerto Rican movement that's organic to the United States—we have the Young Lords and other expressions of dissent and organization. And they were already a beginning to see some relationships between, say, the Chicano demands for bilingual education, the Puerto Rican demands for bilingual education; the intersection at the universities of opening up the universities to Puerto Rican and Mexican students. Obviously, in New York and then in Los Angeles too, you see these two communities rise up. But Chicago became a bridge between those two centers on each coast.

Mike: Because it had both populations?

José: It had both populations in large numbers. And already you would see, for example, in 1968 when Reverend King, before he died, had convened a Poor People's March, there were contingents of Puerto Ricans and Mexicans gathering in Washington and having discussions about Latino issues.

You begin to develop all those ties during that period. Mexicans in the Southwest already began talking about Puerto Rican independence and the need to support Puerto Rican independence. Puerto Ricans began talking about the land grabs and the urban struggles of Mexican people in Chicago and in other areas.

So there's a history to this that I think informs our relationship.

In the 1970s, with the wholesale U.S. attack on the Puerto Rican independence movement, particularly the armed sector, this relationship between Puerto Ricans and Mexicans deepened. At this time, some people had already been part of an organization that had been created by the Episcopal Church called the Episcopalian Commission on Latino Affairs. There was at attempt, particularly in New York at the central office of the Episcopal Church, to really hold the Episcopal Church responsible to the whole Latino community. The commission was made up of Puerto Ricans and Mexicans, grassroots leaders who came from New York and Chicago, from New Mexico and Colorado, from different parts of California, and so on.

Mike: Were the grassroots leaders all identified with the Episcopal Church? Or were they community leaders as well?

José: Some of them, like Grand Jury resister Maria Cueto, were directly involved in the Episcopal Church. Others were not as strongly linked. But the commission brought together this national encounter of Puerto Ricans and Mexicans, and the U.S. government, when it began to pursue the attacks on the FALN, saw the Commission as the bridge that connected what they thought to be an international conspiracy of armed struggle—linked from Mexico, to Cuba, to Puerto Rico and the United States. At that moment, they decided to come after Mexican activists and Puerto Rican activists. As a result of those attacks, that Mexicans and Puerto Ricans came together against the Grand Jury, and the MLN was formed as a result of the repression that we were facing at that time.

The MLN was formed as a way to put together a unified face against the political repression of both the Mexican struggle and the Puerto Rican struggle.

When you look at the present reality, one link is to the immigration issue Some Mexican leaders of the immigration struggle, particularly Rudy Lozano, worked with my brother Oscar López Rivera (who is one of the longest-held U.S. political prisoners), and many others. There was a Mexican leftist movement called CASA (Centro de Acción Social y Autónoma), and a whole series of Mexican organizations that emerged in this period. They became very important in Chicago around the struggle for Puerto Rican independence and Mexican human rights.

But many were also linked to community struggles. One of the most interesting acts of solidarity of Puerto Ricans was to actually house, support, and protect Elvira Arellano at Adalberto United Methodist Church. [Arellano is the president of La Familia Latina Unida, an advocacy group which focuses upon families that could be split up due to draconian deportation laws.] We have been told that the Immigration Naturalization Service (INS) had really almost made it a matter of policy that they were not going to arrest or got after Elvira as long as she was housed in this community. They were afraid of what the Puerto Rican community's reaction would be! I think that says a great deal about the importance of solidarity, and the importance of those historical nexuses that made that solidarity possible. Additionally I would say that solidarity, I believe, is both an ethical issue as well a political one. At the end of the day, we in the Puerto Rican movement have to clearly define the relationship to the sectors that are most oppressed in this society, and one of those sectors is obviously the undocumented.

On a political level, I also think that there is a special importance for a Latino dialogue, which would help to formulate a Latino agenda. But a dialogue has to be based on some concrete acts of solidarity. Solidarity, then, informs this political identity, which I believe "Latinidad" gives to us. I don't think Latinidad is necessarily an identity in which I subsume, or Mexicans (or any Latinos) subsume his or her national identity. It is, rather, the degree to which we link with one another, to work together on common issues and define a common agenda.

And I think that the formulation of a Latino agenda is perhaps one of the most important chapters in the future of the Americas. Many Latin American regimes are now emerging in ways that distance themselves from the practices of neoliberalism and globalization. I think that Latinos in this country have to be able to formulate a vision about what their role is in the body politics of the United States. Therefore, one of the most important demands that have to come out of a Latino agenda in the United States is if we are going to be able to redefine what globalization is. The reality is that we live in a global world that should not be a globalized world. By that I mean that if the United States and the vested interests of the United States want to pursue a politics of Free Trade, and a free flow of goods, then we have to demand that there be a policy and a practice that allows for the free flow of people with dignity. Ultimately, we have to begin to talk about redefining citizenship. And one way in which we have to redefine citizenship is by saying that the rights of people realizing and respecting themselves as human beings has to be seen as a human right—and not just a right that is given to people by governments or national states.

We have seen that the dislocation and the destruction of many of the dependent economies of Latin America has been the cause of a huge influx of immigrants from throughout the region. There is a clear responsibility that the U.S. government has had in creating those practices which have destroyed much of those economies, or that has engendered an economy of total dependence. I would say that we now have to think about a politics that says, "If you want these goods and the free flowing of goods, then how do you create a politics that's informed by the free flow of people with dignity?" You have the example of the Portuguese guest workers in Germany thirty years ago, who were literally treated as animals, totally ostracized in Germany. There were something like two million of them. But after the European Union was created, and created a European citizenship, today a Portuguese who goes to Germany enjoys the full rights of German citizenship. And this is accepted as a basic human rights. We have got to start to speak of a citizenship of the Americas, in which people throughout this continent can exist, can move freely, and can be entitled to full benefits of citizenship.

Mike: Probably more than either the Black liberation movement or the white new left, the armed struggle coming from Puerto Rican militants in the 1970s was more sustained and more ambitious. Over the past decade, the Puerto Rican community has relied on nonviolent action—from successful electoral campaigns and organizing within the church to civil disobedience—to push forward a progressive agenda. Comment on the reasons for the changes in tactics and strategy, and discuss the positive and negative aspects of both.

José: Well. I think that there is a politics that emerged in Latin America, which I don't believe has been studied very well. This was the politics of the theology of liberation. The politics of liberation theology proposed in many ways that people organically organize themselves and organically establish and meet their own needs. Through the institution of local churches, the idea was that if there was a problem of health care, or a problem regarding education, people should begin to address those things directly—often taking matters into their own hands.

At the same time, these movements were not going to let society or government get away with a politics of marginalization. I believe that today a lot of what's happening in Latin America was originally articulated as the politics of liberation theology. This is particularly true around the building of parallel institutions.

For example, in a country like Venezuela where you have had some interesting social experiments, at the same time that the government is trying to open up its commitment to social programs there is grassroots organizing that is formed around the concept of missions. Missions are created to meet people's immediate needs. If there's a problem of health, you create a mission *de salud*, or with teaching, you set us a *missiones de educación*. In the case of Venezuela, a lot of Cuban expertise has been brought in to train people to be able to take hold of their own destiny vis-à-vis health care, schooling, etc.

I believe that idea of dual, or parallel, institutions—in which government-sponsored programs are important but, at the same time, you create these organic people's institutions—are key in this current period. But I think that that's also a politics that has deep roots in Latin America, and that is in the practice of the Maroon societies.

I don't think we spend enough time discussing maroonage, which allowed for small group societies of resistance. Maroon societies, it must be remembered, were made up of more than simply runaway slaves. They also included Indian resistance movements, as well as runaway Europeans who didn't fit into the mold of the dominant colonial society. These communities of resistance met their own needs, created their own institutions, created their own language, created their own music; much of what the Latin Americans' identities that we would today call Mexican or Cuban or Dominican or Brazilian were informed by the practice of Maroon societies.

My contention is that there is a long history of this idea: one foot in and one foot out. How do you negotiate? Many of these Maroon societies would negotiate with the dominant system, and many times even became legal entities within the dominant societies—because they were able to negotiate their own existence. The Kilombos in Brazil, for example, or the Palenques in many parts of North and South America, were about to act in this way. These are all Maroon societies, and they never forgot that they had a commitment to ending slavery, to working with enslaved peoples to help them escape.

What we have tried to do—here in Chicago and in a few places in Puerto Rico—is to find innovative ways of thinking about struggle. We have said: "We can't wait till we create a system that's perfect. Let's look at models of how people self-determine, self-actualize themselves in practices of self-reliance." And I think that some of the things that we have tried to do, without becoming luddites or pretending to escape from the dominant society to form some ideal utopia, is to exist as a pocket of resistance that informs a great deal of anti-colonialist and anti-imperialist politics and practice. Whatever spaces are open for us we use to promote things that would help our community's identity, wellbeing, and independence.

This history, that's reflected both in the Maroon societies as well as in the Catholic theology of liberation, informs some of the things that we have done in what I would say is a practice of "one foot in, one foot out." And I think some of the successes that we've been able to build around creating the kinds of institutions that begin to directly serve people's needs are important.

At the same time, we don't believe this is the complete answer for people's problems. What we do believe is that if people could create examples like this in different areas, and people could begin to own their own process of liberation, then we wouldn't be waiting until we were through this whole system to say, "OK, now we've got the power to transform society." We say we can be transformative; we can bring transformative changes in the midst of the daily lives of our people right here, right now. We can bring about substantive changes, reflected around issues of gentrification and other colonial practices which still inform Third World communities within the United States and in Puerto Rico. The struggle against the U.S. Navy, and the island of Vieques, for example, or the various environmental struggles in Puerto Rico, all continue to inform the Puerto Rican reality. And while we can't expect to win victories in all of these cases, we can begin a liberating process.

Mike: The Puerto Rican independence movement continues to face considerable repression from the U.S. government. Describe what this repression now, looks like including the role of and response to Grand Juries. How does this repression differ for those on the island and those living within the United States?

José: Well, I think, obviously, the most horrific expression of the repression was the murder, the assassination some years ago, of Machetero leader Filiberto Ojeda Ríos. In a cynical way, the FBI murdered Filiberto on the day of the celebration of Puerto Rican 1968 independence from Spain, El Grito de Lares. In addition to that, there has been an obvious and continuous involvement of grand jury repression, since at least 1972. From arrest to assassination, the Puerto Rican people have been terrorized by the United States.

I think that the U.S. government, however, has also had to learn from the Puerto Ricans response. One of the first grand juries, which was convened against a Puerto Rican independentista, which was 1935, was met with widespread resistance. So we're looking at a very, very long and continuous period of resistance and noncollaboration.

Over the past years, we've seen massive uprisings in response to right-wing policies of privatization. There were 200,000 people on the streets in response to calls to privatize the phone company and other key industries. Though the government began to call people terrorists and subversives, the same language that it has used against the independence movement, people kept up the pressure. We also know that there is tremendous complicity between the Puerto Rican police and the FBI; there's always been a very interesting nexus between the two institutions. In the revelations about the murders at Cerro Maravilla—when the police and FBI created a fake independence group, then entrapped and killed young recruits who joined it—we saw clearly just how direct and deadly those repressive policies are.

Mike: What role do the remaining Puerto Rican political prisoners play in the overall agenda for social change? What is the significance of their continued imprisonment? And how will the campaigns to free them differ from the successful campaigns to free their now freed compatriots?

José: Well, I think the first thing is that we always have to look for new ways to reach people. The campaign of the 1970s to free the nationalists (Lolita Lebrón, Rafael Cancel Miranda and their compatriots) was different from the campaign to free the Puerto Rican political prisoners in the 1990s. We obviously have to talk about some differences in terms of what sectors are moving, and what sectors we can build alliances with to win hearts and minds. In general, though, there is a question about the symbolism of the prisoners. I was in San Sebastian, my hometown, this summer. The mayor of my town is a member of the Statehood Party—quite anti-independence. And yet he came to a special event to spotlight the case of my brother Oscar López

Rivera. Some years back, he spoke during one of the most important festivals of San Sebastian, which is El Festival de la Hamaca (the Hammock Festival). When he spoke, he made a very, very interesting observation. He said: "I didn't come here to demand the release of Oscar just because he has been in there for so many years and that's the right thing to do, or for humanitarian reasons, or for legal factors that show that they've been treated differently. I've come here because I believe that while we may differ in terms of our political ideology, the fact is that Puerto Rico needs leaders that have the moral imperative and show the moral leadership, the commitment to principles that Oscar and the other Puerto Rican political prisoners has shown."

In other words, for him, these prisoners stood out as beacons of hope. I found it really interesting that someone who is a member of a political party—the dominant political party—should make an observation like this. Historically I believe that when we speak about moral leadership—whether it's a shaman in an Indigenous society, or a Gandhi or Dr. Martin Luther King Jr., or even a figure like Che Guevara—these dominate the imagination of people across the world. It's a sign of the integrity that these men and women have displayed, the selflessness, which I believe inspires people. This ethical leadership has made and continues to make a tremendous contribution.

Mike: Finally, could you discuss the strategic alliances made between the Puerto Rican left and other radical movements in the United States? What role does solidarity and working with anti-imperialist North American whites and whites in the peace movement play at this time? And how have your thoughts about and work in coalition changed over the past three decades?

José: I believe that solidarity is probably the most human of human activities, because solidarity is not about what I will gain, but about what someone else will gain because they have been left out or marginalized. To the degree that I am in solidarity with those who are the most marginalized and downtrodden, is the degree that I believe that my humanity has become more evident.

If I were to say what ultimately was the most important thing that makes a human being different from an animal, it would be that human beings transcend simple survival. We transcend survival because we are willing to give up our lives, we are willing to give up everything for other human beings. I don't think any other living thing does that, unless it's a mother trying to protect its offspring. In the human sense, I believe it's a lot more than simple instinct to enable the species to survive. For me, the spirit that helps people beyond survival is the truest act of solidarity.

So solidarity, for me, is an ethical imperative. Over the years, I believe that we—at least those of us who continue to be active in the Puerto Rican independence movement and continue to be active in some of the social movements—have maintained a commitment to free humanity from all the shackles and things that bind us, and make us truly human.

I would also say, though, that for many years certain sectors of the left did political solidarity to the degree that they would also gain a foothold in trying to define the contours of the Puerto Rican independence movement. And I think that is not solidarity; that is opportunism. I believe that there are still sectors of the U.S. left which continue to exhibit that, and that's unfortunate because it's almost become a cliché: solidarity is not charity. It is not something you give to someone, and it is not something you can take from someone. It is something that you must make a commitment to which is independent from anything that you may benefit from.

There have been many people that I have met over the years who have shown that deep sense of solidarity, and continue to do so to this day. Many are not necessarily in organized groups, some serve as individuals, but they still have a strong sense of this moral imperative that they need to expose U.S. government imperial policies, racist policies, and colonial practices

My take on the Puerto Rican independence movement is that we're going through a major, major change. I don't really know where that change will take us, but I think there are some very interesting possibilities. One of them is that, just as it was in the nineteenth century, we have to go back to the Latin American roots, which defined our anti-colonial movements. I believe then we can begin to talk about an interdependent Puerto Rican world, or Puerto Rican people existing and being part of an interdependent world. I don't believe that nations declare their independence because they want to be isolated; I believe nations declare their independence because they want to be treated with dignity and respect. Just like any human being wants to be treated with dignity and respect, nations also want to be independent because they want to place themselves within the realm of people everywhere who have exercised their right to self-determination and self-actualization.

At the end of the day, there is a question for what this holds not only for Puerto Rico but for the entire world. I believe that we don't yet exist in a postcolonial world; we live in a very colonial world. Much of the world is still defined by neocolonial relationships, and much of it is defined by internal colonialism—as many countries have nationalities within their borders that are still colonial objects. All one has to do is look at is the western part of China, or what is happening in Afghanistan particularly with the Pashtuns. Nobody talks about the Kurds, and their right to self-determination.

I believe that the world is going to change. To the degree that we are able to create a system that ultimately will dignify people, we will live in a better balanced world. In such a world, we can create an interdependent system where the smallest identities of people can be preserved, languages that are disappearing will be encouraged to remain, and people will be able to practice their cultural expressions freely. We can create a world where people are not judged as inferior because of their racial or ethnic makeup. Ultimately, decolonizing efforts must take place all over the world, and Puerto Rico has to be part of that decolonizing effort. When we accomplish this, people will truly then be judged by the content of our character.

Truly Human

Spiritual Paths in the Struggle Against
Racism, Militarism, and Materialism

Gwendolyn Zoharah Simmons

As we celebrate and commemorate the great figures of the so-called civil rights and Black Power movements, we too often forget the thousands grassroots activists who made those movements possible—many of whom continue in our midst to carry on those struggles in new, creative forms. Zoharah Simmons is one such figure, and the lessons she reflects upon in this essay help to guide us in the direction we need to go in order to build stronger movements for human rights and dignity. Simmons's perspective is a unique one, as she was an active leader in both the nonviolent freedom campaigns of the early 1960s, and the Black Power initiatives that came to the fore later in the decade; she was also a member of the Nation of Islam. The moment when the Student Nonviolent Coordinating Committee (SNCC) suggested that white allies' most important role was to work against racism within the white community—allowing Black freedom fighters to work independently in the Black community—is still one of controversy and confusion. As a leader of SNCC at the time, Simmons explains some of the ethical and political basis of that decision. As a Muslim activist and professor of religion also affiliated with the Women's Studies Department at the University of Florida, Simmons reflects upon the role religion can play in maintaining as well as battling against the empire known as the United States of America. This paper, written especially for this book, was—in part—compiled from a series of talks given over several years, including a keynote address delivered for the annual Gandhi-King conference held in Memphis, Tennessee.

The situation facing people of color, poor people, people without power and influence in the United States and around the world is a deteriorating one that continues to grow worse—in spite of all the talk of progress and technological greatness that we are being bombarded with via the electronic media each and every day of our lives. We are facing in our nation tremendous forces of greed, avarice, racism, a disregard for people's lives, growing class disparities, and undisguised rampant militarism. We are facing a dire situation, the likes of which we may never have seen before. Since the beginning of this new century, with the events of 9/11 as the initial catalyst, our government and the transnational corporations have raided the U.S. treasury, taken away our civil liberties and civil rights, and bankrupted the nation in the name of "national security."

Even the election of the first Black president of the United States—Barack Hussein Obama—in 2008 has been a catalyst that has unleashed a virulent racism, which is a shield for the most draconian assault on the rights of middle and working-class people and the poor that is unprecedented. While embroiled in two unnecessary and unpaid for wars in the Middle East, our unregulated financial institutions launched an unbelievable assault on ordinary citizens that brought the U.S. economy to the brink of collapse. The government rescued the banks, Wall Street, and the large corporations responsible for the near collapse while, letting the people fend for themselves against these rapacious institutions and the individuals who lead them. This has led to millions losing their homes, their jobs, their savings, and their health insurance with no remedy in sight. Added to this has been the rise of the political Right—spearheaded by the Tea Party movement that has unabashedly sought to destroy unions and the right to collective bargaining for government employees and to roll back voting rights, especially for minorities and the poor. Last but certainly not least, these right-wing forces have set out to destroy Social Security, Medicare, and Medicaid in the name of fiscal austerity and reining in the U.S. Debt, so much of which is traceable directly to the unnecessary wars in Afghanistan and Iraq. They propose this while continuing to cut taxes on the rich and the corporations. It seems that the greed and avarice of the powerful and those that represent them in the state legislatures, governors' mansions, and the U.S. Congress know no bounds.

Our country is the largest arms manufacturer in the world, and the largest seller of weapons in the world. Since September 11, 2001, the U.S. government has spent more than a trillion dollars for operations in Afghanistan and Iraq and other places where we are engaged in the "War on Terror." Additionally the government has spent $7.6 trillion on defense. In order to maintain its imperial interest internationally, U.S. military bases, installations and personnel are deployed in more than 150 countries. In 2010, U.S. military spending accounted for 42.8 percent of the world's total in military spending, more than the next fifteen countries' military spending combined. Every year, a larger percent of the tax share falls on the people of the middle and lower income tax brackets, while service and benefits to these people are destroyed. No other "democratic" country takes as large a portion of its revenue from working people at the lower ends of the spectrum, and as little from persons who have property or high incomes as does the United States: 54 percent of the U.S. budget was spent on the military in 2009, a fact that is often camouflaged by the government and the media and hidden from the public. For what the U.S. government paid for the War in Iraq alone ($781.2 billion and counting) our government could have provided health care for all the children in the country for four years, provided renewable electricity for all homes in the United States for six years or provided four years' salary for every elementary school teacher in the country.

What is often hidden from the public's view here is the fact that the United States is an imperialist empire maintained by over 150 bases and military installations whose aims are not only military but are there to promote the economic and political objectives of U.S. capitalism. They are also in place to target countries where there are popular resistance movements directed against U.S. interests. The Pentagon owns 854,441 different buildings and equipment spread over thirty million acres, making it one of the largest landowners in the world. It takes 1, 332,300 persons to run all of the Pentagon's military bases and instillations. When we hear the phrase, "the U.S. is the sole superpower," we must understand what this means. Among other things it means that the United States has control over most UN member governments, and the conquest, control or supervision of the various regions of the world which fall under one of its several military command centers located both inside the United States and at several sites around the world. The United States has built fourteen new bases in seven countries in and around the Persian Gulf since 9/11. Additionally the government has constructed twenty installations in Iraq including the largest embassy in the world in Baghdad. Out of sight of most citizens, the government is expanding or building bases or installations in Algeria, Australia, Brazil, Czech Republic, Djibouti, France, Ghana, Italy, Kirghizstan, Mali, Morocco, Poland, Tajikistan, and Uzbekistan. Overall, the plan is to have a string of installations located in a west-to-east corridor extending from Colombia in South America to North Africa, the Near East, Central Asia to the Philippines. To pay for all this military might, our government spends more than $1.2 trillion a year.

From the facts cited above, we can see that Dr. Martin Luther King's statement that the United States has become the "greatest purveyor of violence in the world" has become more prophetic than ever. We are using our military technology to create more and more ways to kill and maim while "protecting" our own troops. While we are perfecting and using unmanned killer drones to kill more and more of the "enemy," we are still subjecting thousands of our own troops to death and serious injuries, from which many will never recover. As of the writing of this essay, over 6,000 U.S. military have been killed in Afghanistan and Iraq while some estimate that as many as 100,000 have suffered catastrophic injuries. Additionally, the numbers of veterans of these wars who have attempted to commit suicide or have done so are staggering. In 2005 alone, 6,200 veterans committed suicide and recent figures suggest that eighteen veterans commit suicide a day. While these numbers are horrific, the numbers of Iraqis and Afghanis killed are chilling. Iraqi deaths due to the U.S. invasion have a low estimate of 900,338 killed and 1,690,903 wounded. While the low estimate for the number of Afghanis killed is 19,629, the estimate of wounded Afghanis is 48,644. These combined totals equal 303 times as many as were killed on 9/11; to say that this is overkill is an understatement. This is not even to mention the number of refuges and internally displaced persons our invasion has caused in both Iraq and Afghanistan or the damage to the infrastructure in Iraq, particularly. These wars are costing the U.S. citizenry blood and treasure while creating enmity in these populations that will exist over many generations from members of the families of those we have slaughtered, maimed, and displaced. When we look at imperial adventures in historical terms, we find that as many U.S. veterans of the war in Vietnam took their own lives in suicide over the first ten years after that war ended than died in combat during the war itself.

It has become clearer than ever that those of us who oppose the role our government is playing in the world must work harder than ever before to change the course of this government. We must organize peace and justice movements stronger than any we have built in the past. In order to alter the path our country is now on, we must change our country and ourselves. We must affirm that we have no desire for this country to continue as the sole super power in the world at such a horrific cost to our citizens and others. We oppose using military might to bend the world to the dictates of the monied elites who are the beneficiaries of U.S. imperial projections of power. We must work for true peace, which requires both institutional justice and individual spiritual change. It is from this framework that I will explain some of my own journey, as a Muslim peace and justice activist and academic.

*

I first became involved in the student sit-in movement in 1962, as a freshman at Spelman College in Atlanta, Georgia. In 1964, I joined with a thousand other mostly college-aged volunteers who journeyed to Mississippi to participate in the Mississippi Summer Project. That summer finally put Mississippi on the nation's radar screen as one of the worst—if not the worst—state in the union for African American people. We volunteers, most of whom were white and middle class, made our country acknowledge what had been largely ignored by the politicians and business leaders in this, the mythical "land of the free and home of the brave." Our nation, that shining beacon of democracy, had some dirty little secrets that the Project exposed to the world during the summer of 1964. Those secrets included the denial of the franchise to Black Americans, the literal entrapment of thousands of Blacks in a sharecropping system (which was just a bit better than slavery), and the daily fear and terror under which Blacks lived (caused by lynching, beatings, cross burnings, false arrests and the like). As fate would have it, I became one of a very few female project directors that summer when I was unexpectedly appointed director of the Laurel, Mississippi Project. A veteran Student Nonviolent Coordinating Committee (SNCC) field worker, Lester McKinney, had been assigned the task but was arrested shortly after our small crew of three arrived in Laurel and set up the Project, leaving me and my first-time-in-the-South comrade, James Garrett, to continue our work.

Neither of us had ever set foot in Mississippi before, but at least I was from the South (Memphis, Tennessee), and there was a saying when I grew up: that the Mississippi Delta began on the main street in Memphis, Tennessee. Plus, SNCC folks in Atlanta knew me. I had been one of the student agitators from the Atlanta University complex, had served on SNCC's Coordinating Committee, and had been to jail a few times. But this was still hardly a resume for leading a project in Mississippi, where everyone's life was literally on the line twenty-four hours a day, seven days a week. Nonetheless, James Forman—the executive director of SNCC—didn't have anyone else to replace McKinney, so he told me to hold down the fort until he could send a more seasoned field worker to take over. Given that I was already scared to death by just being in Mississippi, I was none to happy to be given the assignment. By the grace of God, Garrett and I, along with the twenty-three other volunteers who joined us that summer, survived the summer alive and accomplished the Project goals in spite of the frequent attacks from the white establishment and the Ku Klux Klan types who dogged our steps at every turn. Six of us remained in Laurel for another thirteen months after the summer ended. We continued our Freedom Schools, as well as our organizing of the Laurel chapter of the Mississippi Freedom Democratic Party and holding mock voter registrations and mock elections in support of the Project's efforts to get the federal government to ensure the vote for Black Mississippians.

During my time in Laurel, some of the SNCC women from across the South began to challenge the authoritarian male leadership and rampant sexism in SNCC and the other civil rights organizations. I joined these women in several gatherings and was exposed for the first time to feminist thought. While the theory was new, the beliefs and actions were not. I realized that my grandmother, Rhoda Bell Douglass who raised me, and my closest aunts, Jessie Neal Hudson and Ollie B. Smith, were feminists—as were many of the strong women in the church of my upbringing, the Gospel Temple Missionary Baptist Church. It was from them that I had learned so many of the organizational and leadership skills that would be necessary in my future life. These women stood up for themselves against so many odds. They had respect for themselves and their abilities to make a way out of no way. They were the backbone of our churches and our communities; without them the Black community would not have survived.

After leaving my work as project director in Laurel, Mississippi, I became a participant in and architect of the Black Power wing of SNCC as a founding member of its Atlanta Project—the organization's first truly urban field project. The beginnings of a theory and rationale for Black Power were first developed in the Atlanta Project. We wrote "A Position Paper on Race," which we presented to the whole organization (and which appeared, in full, in the *New York Times*—labeled as SNCC's position paper for Black Power). The following is a brief excerpt from the position paper, in which we explained our Call for SNCC to become an all-Black organization. This was, one should remember, post–Mississippi Summer, when SNCC had become a much more racially integrated organization as a number of summer volunteers opted not to return home effectively becoming SNCC field staff. The Atlanta office staff was at least half white at the time we issued our paper.

> [We] believe that the form of white participation as practiced in the
> past is now obsolete.
> Some of our reasons are as follows:

- The inability of whites to relate to the cultural aspects of Black society;
- Attitudes that whites consciously or unconsciously bring to Black communities about themselves (Western superiority) and about Black people (paternalism);
- [White] inability to shatter white-sponsored community myths of Black inferiority and self-negation;
- The unwillingness of whites to deal with the roots of racism that lie within the white community;
- Whites, though individually liberal, are symbols of oppression to the Black community—due to the collective power that whites have over Black lives.

Because of these reasons…we advocate a conscious change in the role of whites, which will be in tune with the developing self-consciousness and self-assertion of the Afro-American people.

Many of our white colleagues saw this statement as a slap in the face; a number of the Black members also disagreed, thus causing the organization to practically split in two over the issue of the role of whites in SNCC. Tangential to this issue was the development of the Black power thrust within SNCC, which was enunciated by Stokely Carmichael while on a demonstration in Mississippi. The phrase caught on like wildfire and was later embraced as the future thrust and direction of the organization by a slim majority. This was announced to the press—and the rest is history. SNCC's embrace of Black Power caused it to lose much of its white liberal financial support, leading ultimately to its untimely and unfortunate demise.

My formal entry into the peace movement began when SNCC staff's consciousness about the injustice and immorality of the Vietnam War became a major topic of discussion within the organization. SNCC issued a bold statement against the war that all of us who worked in Atlanta took part in drafting. This is an excerpt from that statement:

We believe the United States government has been deceptive in claims of concern for the freedom of the Vietnamese people. …We know for the most part that elections in this country in the North as well as in the South, are not free. …We question then the ability and even the desire of the U.S. government to guarantee free elections abroad. We maintain that our country's cry of "preserve freedom in the world" is a hypocritical mask behind which it squashed liberation movements which are not bound and refuse to be bound by the expediency of the U.S. cold war policy.

The statement went even further and encouraged people of conscience to resist the draft and work instead to bring freedom and democracy to Black and poor people in this nation. SNCC was the first major civil rights organization to issue a public statement against the Vietnam War. After this statement was issued, I became very involved in the anti-war movement, and with my Atlanta Project co-workers began developing a Black anti-draft effort in Georgia.

SNCC began to falter for a number of reasons, including dwindling financial support due to its Black Power stance, its anti–Vietnam War position, and the growing tensions within the organization over the role of whites. During this period, several of the Atlanta Project members and I joined the Nation of Islam, under the leadership of the Honorable Elijah Muhammad. I did so out of my growing rage with white America and my evolving belief that white America would never give African Americans justice or equality no matter how much we marched and protested. I had seen so much white hatred, so much local government collusion with the Klan and other white supremacists; I had witnessed up close the federal government's stalling and reneging on promises made, as well as the racism and paternalism of my white liberal colleagues. My belief in Dr. King and his message of "love your enemy" and "turn the other cheek" had faltered. At that time, I thought that the only solution was the separation of the races and for America to give African Americans the economic reparations as called for by the Nation. These demands included five contiguous southern states and the necessary funds to build a viable and independent Black nation. I sadly thought at that time that reconciliation between Blacks and whites was an impossibility; the wounds were just too deep. I felt that whites would never admit their wrongs, much less make restitution for their past and current wrongdoings. I really believed at the time that it was only through the separation of the races with reparations could there ever be a just reconciliation between our two communities.

These were some of the major events that shaped my early years in the struggle for racial justice, women's rights, and an end to U.S. imperialism. These events have, of course, played a large part in shaping my current worldview. Much of my knowledge regarding social action and organizing was largely formed through my involvement in these great efforts to right the historic wrongs of our nation and to reshape our nation's collective consciousness of it true history, the good, the bad and the ugly of it. It had been my great fortune to know and work with human rights and peace luminaries as well as the largely unknown lieutenants and footsoldiers such as myself. These included Dr. Martin Luther King Jr., Mrs. Fannie Lou Hamer, Congressman John Louis, Miss Ella Baker, Stokely Carmichael, Howard Zinn, Staughton Lynn, Vincent Harding, Bob Moses, James Foreman, Ruby Doris Robinson, the Honorable Elijah Muhammad, and Minister Louis Farrakhan, to name just a few. The list of those who helped to shape and mold me in these crucibles of struggle is long, and I am grateful to have been touched by them all.

While I turned my back on the civil rights movement and the theories of nonviolent direct action that undergird it for a time, my post–civil rights experiences have led me back to the teachings of Mahatma Gandhi and Martin Luther King Jr. as the only way out of the cycles of violence and revenge fueling so much of the turmoil in our world today. It has taken me years to truly comprehend the importance of this movement and what it was able to do with a minimum amount of bloodshed and loss of life. It has only been since growing older and being exposed to the many struggles for justice in our world that I have been truly able to appreciate not only the gains but the methodology of the civil rights movement. This was a movement of our time, during the era of violent overthrows of governments, when a minority group that had been racially oppressed and stigmatized for centuries was able to change racist, sexist, anti-people policies and institutions in a region of the country steeped in prejudice, ignorance, tyranny, and violence. Through the use of nonviolent social protests and grassroots organizing, poor people—many of whom were illiterate—took on their state governments, the White Citizens Councils, the Ku Klux Klan, their employers on the plantations and in the mills, and ultimately the federal government. These poorest of the poor, these most despised ones, confronted the mighty institutions of entrenched hatred and oppression armed only with love and faith in God, with a conviction in the justice of their cause and a steadfast determination to change their own lives (and thereby the lives of their oppressors as well). Against all odds, these folks emerged victorious; they changed things and they changed themselves in the process. Most of us who were in that movement can never forget it, because—for a brief time—we experienced a Beloved Community in those towns and hamlets where we worked with people who loved God, loved themselves, and were determined to bring about a change in their own lives and the life of this nation.

It has taken years for me to really understand and appreciate the significance of this nonviolent revolution in which I was involved. I was blinded earlier by my rage and my impatience with the pace of change, and my lack of faith that fundamental change could occur through nonviolent means and the will of the people to overcome oppression. It has taken me many years to see the superiority of change brought about nonviolently versus change engendered through force and violence.

Most of the time, I am thankful to have been born a Black female in the Jim Crow South. Of course, it has taken me a long time to appreciate this fact and even now—given the persistence of racism and sexism in our world—I still feel sad to have to experience the prejudices that come to a person born Black and female in this, the twenty-first century. But when I am in my best mind, I can appreciate my life story because of what I have learned from my personal experiences. It is not the theory of nonviolent direct action that makes the difference for me. It is the practical lessons learned from the experiences of that time. I have seen incredible changes occur in the U.S. South, as well as in other parts of our nation. I teach a class in African American religious traditions, in which we focus on the liberatory role of religion in the African American sojourn from slavery to freedom. It amazes me that none of my students— who are Black, white, Latino, and Asian—can believe that less than forty years ago

African American people could not vote in many places in the South, could not eat in white restaurants, or go into the front door of theatres, visit museums, libraries, zoos, amusement parks, or art galleries (except on that one day of the week set aside for "Coloreds"). They cannot believe that there were white and colored toilets, white and colored water fountains, that Blacks sat in the backs of buses, with "colored only" and "white only" cars on trains, that there were segregated and unequal white and colored hospitals and that their beloved University of Florida was all-white by law, or that it was illegal for Blacks and whites to marry or date. It pleases me that they find this information so shocking, so awful, "so stupid," as they would say. This shows that the cataclysmic changes caused by the civil rights movement are now an ingrained part of this society, normalized for many if not most of us. It is unthinkable for most Southerners—Black or white—to advocate a return to the overt racism of the past. That would be as unthinkable as reinstituting slavery.

Now, I do not want to suggest in anyway that we have reached a racial nirvana in the South, or anywhere else here in the United States. A significant percentage of these same students, most expressly the white ones, oppose affirmative action—believing that it is "reverse discrimination." Most, if not all, oppose the idea of reparations for African Americans for past wrongs. But I wanted to point out the positives that grew out of the civil rights struggles, because there are many positives in my own life and in the collective life of our nation. We must hold onto these realities even as we confront the many negatives in our world today. There are huge issues confronting us, which threaten us individually and collectively. Especially since 9/11, for example, an anti-Muslim hysteria has been spreading in a way that harkens back to the bad old days—such that I myself thought long and hard before I informed my neighbors that I was a Muslim.

*

The second great influence on my own life, beyond my time in the Black-led freedom movement, has been my time as a student, a disciple, and a devotee of the contemporary Sufi Master Sheikh Muhammad Raheem Bawa Muhaiyadeen. It was Bawa (which means father) who initiated me into Sufism, the mystical path in Islam. My years with him radically altered my life—but in a different way than did my work in the civil rights movement. My social justice activist work—then and now—focuses on the needed external changes in the material world. My work on the Sufi path is directed at the internal changes that I need to address if my life is to reach its true destiny. This is the work of becoming a true human being. It took me a while to see the relationship between the needed internal changes and the external changes that I had focused upon in my youth. Initially, I even saw the two paths as being in conflict. How could I continue my social change work if I needed to focus all of my attention on spiritual development, and changing my inner self from that of an animal in human form to that of a spiritually enlightened person, as mysticism teaches? Sufism teaches us that the true destiny of the human being is to reach a highly exalted state of consciousness, which they refer to as becoming "God-man/man-God." My own teacher taught his students that to merge with God, so that one's base qualities are erased and only the qualities of God remain, is the destiny for all of us who have been born in human form. To become a purified human person is our true birthright; this is the belief that Bawa and all Sufis before him taught. It was my duty and the duty of everyone who receives "the inner call to become truly human" to achieve this state of spiritual consciousness in the time allotted us on this earth.

*

As we build for nonviolent revolution and the creation of beloved communities, if we are to understand how we can develop peace with justice, we must examine closely the process by which persons, groups, and even nations can become peaceful, harmonious, and restored to equanimity. We must understand how our religious and spiritual beliefs can help to guide us in this process. Of course we know that there are gruesome things being done by some people to others all the time in our world today. Most of these are the attacks of the powerful against the weak, and many of them invoke religion as the basis for inequity and hate. It's hard not to feel rage about these things.

In addition to the struggles with my government for justice here at home, I have been to some of the hot spots of our world, during or immediately after violent conflict over the last thirty years. I visited Vietnam, Cambodia, and Laos at the end of the Vietnam War and saw the horrific devastation caused by our bombs, our napalm, and our other weapons of destruction we rained down on the people and the infrastructure of those countries. I visited the Cambodian "killing fields" and saw the mountains of skulls and skeletons interspersed with the deceased's clothing dotted across that devastated and almost empty land—thanks to Pol Pot and his Khmer Rouge soldiers turned into killing machines, many of whom were children under the age of fifteen. I have traveled and lived in the Middle East, and have spent time in Israel and Palestine, and seen the fear and anxiety of the Israelis in Tel Aviv, Haifa, Jerusalem, and in the settlements in the West Bank and Gaza. I have traveled on the "Settlers Only" roads in an armor-plated Israeli bus, looked at the Israeli "apartheid wall" crisscrossing and swallowing up Palestinian farmland—built in the name of security, but bringing only more insecurity for the Israelis and hardships for the Palestinians. I have spent time in Palestinian towns and villages—Gaza, Ramallah, Hebron, Bethlehem, and others—waiting at the checkpoints and watching the humiliation of old Palestinian men and women at the hands of Israeli children in the military who police these checkpoints. I have scrambled over barricades made of huge concrete blocks, mounds of dirt and stones blocking vehicle and pedestrian entrances to Palestinian villages. I have waited for hours at the checkpoint in Ramallah trying to enter during the Israeli enforced curfew which locked the town down. I have been in Bethlehem just after the curfew of a week or more has been lifted and watched the men, women, and children dash around madly through the streets in the two or three hour window they had been given to do their shopping, run errands to the pharmacy, see the doctor, or visit a sick relative or friend before the curfew descended again and they are locked in their homes with no idea when they will be permitted to leave again. I have slept in Gaza while the Israeli military planes and helicopters flew overhead, shining menacing spotlights down on the people. I have seen the devastation and disruption of Palestinian life and lands at the hands of the Israeli military caused by brutal Occupation.

Given my own experiences in the United States with violence and oppression, alongside of the observations noted above, I am not interested in some sappy so-called reconciliation that does not change the power dynamics between the rich and poor, the oppressed and the oppressor. I am not interested in a "reconciliation" which enables the powerful to issue a verbal apology for what they have done, feel good about themselves for confessing without giving up any of their power or making social, political or economic restitution for their misdeeds. These so-called reconciliation processes let things continue pretty much as they did before the reconciliation process occurred and therefore the violence of the status quo is left intact—no fundamental change occurs and therefore no real healing occurs, and no real beloved community can be built on a sham.

The first thing that always comes to mind when I hear the people in power say that they long for or even demand peace from those challenging their power and the status quo is "if you want peace, you must work for justice." But what is peace; what is justice? As I wanted to share more than my own understanding on this matter, I consulted the words of Gandhi, Martin King, Howard Zinn, Elise Boulding, and others who have written perceptively about this issue to see what guidance they could give.

The inclusion of both parties to the conflict is a must. A peace agreement cannot be reached when one party has little or no respect for their opponent.

It was, after all, Gandhi himself who said: "I am a man of peace. I believe in peace. But I do not want peace at any price. I do not want the peace that you find in stone; I do not want the peace that you find in the grave; but I do want the peace which you find embedded in the human breast, which is exposed to the arrows of the whole world, but which is protected from all harm by the power of almighty God."

Physical violence often grows in a culture of sexual and emotional violence; it goes hand and hand with the abuse of alcohol or other drugs. There are violent up-heavals caused by industrial strife. Rape and pillage of the land continues unabated; racial prejudice and other forms of ethnic violence present another form of violence. What causes this violence, which is so ubiquitous in many places in the world today? Howard Zehr, the internationally known Mennonite writer whom some call a prophet of restorative justice has noted that "at the heart of most violence is disrespect." I certainly agree with this given my experiences with racial violence in the South. During the civil rights struggle, it was evident that those white officials and laypersons who attacked us not only hated us with a vengeance but also held us in contempt. They had no respect for us as fellow citizens or even as human beings. Any effort to enact a culture of peace and the building of beloved communities requires respect for other peoples, respect for their and our own forebears and future generations, respect for other ways of thinking, respect for creation, and self respect.

As we analyze the anti-justice and anti-peace forces in our world today, many of us feel like Karen Horst Cobb—who spoke out against the nurturance of revenge and vengeance, often promoted in the name of Christianity in our country. In her article "No Longer a Christian," Cobb cited Ephesians 6:12, saying, "We are not wrestling against flesh, but against powers and principalities and spiritual wickedness in high places." Bawa describes these powers and principalities in this way:

> These evil qualities are our only enemy if we truly understand things. Sufism teaches that one cannot find peace within until one engages in this war within. What I have learned is that while I am fighting the internal demons within I must also labor in my neighborhood, my community, my nation, and in my world to change the social and economic injustices and to work for peace and to build beloved communities in my neighborhood and lend to its building in our world. Our physical survival is at stake.

Dr. King would agree. He said in a sermon:

> I do not minimize the complexity of the problems that need to be faced in achieving disarmament and peace. But I am convinced that we shall not have the will, the courage, and the insight to deal with such matters unless in this field we are prepared to undergo a mental and spiritual reevaluation, a change of focus which will enable us to see that the things that seem most real and powerful are indeed unreal and have come under a sentence of death. It is not enough to say, "We must not wage war." It is necessary to love peace and sacrifice for it. We must concentrate not merely on the eradication of war but on the affirmation of peace.

My friend and colleague Dr. Farid Esack, a South African Qur'anic scholar and progressive Muslim, has written a wonderful book, On Being a Muslim. In it, Farid asks: "How does our faith manifest itself in socially relevant terms?" Is our religion a Sunday-only affair if you are a Christian, or a Friday-only religion if you are Muslim? He also asks, "How can we be witnesses for God in an unjust society? How do we join with others in our religious communities in a commitment to establish a just order on earth?" Esack believes that God's goal, according to the teachings of Islam, is nothing less than the creation of a nonracist, nonsexist, noneconomic exploitative society. And Dr.

King might add: "Any religion that professes to be concerned with the souls of men and is not concerned with the slums that damn them, the economic conditions that strangle them, and the social conditions that cripple them is a dry as dust religion. Such a religion is…an opiate of the people."

We people who seek peace and the building of beloved communities must intensify our actions right now. On February 4, 1968, only two months before King was gunned down by an assassin's bullets, he gave the sermon at Ebenezer Baptist Church titled *The Drum Major Instinct* in which he condemned racism, economic exploitation, and militarism as the interrelated triple evils that face all contemporary seekers of justice. Dr. King knew that in order to eliminate one of these triple evils, it was necessary to eliminate them all. We must remember that at the end of his life, King called for an economic Bill of Rights of the Disadvantaged; his final Poor People's Campaign would have united African American, Native American, Latinos, and poor Euro-Americans. Today, Farid Esack urges all people of faith to be committed to struggling against everything that works against the dignity of all people—including racism, sexism, homophobia, and poverty. If we truly believe that God created all human beings in his/her image, then we should be committed to eliminating those things that dehumanize. In Islam, there is the belief that men and women are vicegerents (deputies) of God who were given an *amanah* (trust) by God to care for ourselves and the entire creation. Each human and all of nature have been put into each of our trust by God to be the caretakers over this magnificent creation.

When we change ourselves, we change the world. Personal Transformation is a necessary element in our ability to fundamentally change the injustices in our world. As peace studies pioneer and Quaker Elise Boulding said, if we cannot imagine a peaceful world, then we cannot work to bring it into existence. Bawa, in his book *Islam and World Peace*, wrote on the prerequisites for establishing peace and ending conflict. He stated: "We must remove all the differences that separate us from God and our fellow humans. …We must fight against our tendencies toward separations of my race/your race, my country/your country/my religion/your religion. We must wage a holy war against our own evil qualities."

And what, then, must we work for? We have to stop the elites from using the race card against us. We have to struggle together for a just peace, which must include:

- Universal health care for all, which must include full medical and dental coverage;
- An end to homelessness by any means necessary, including massive construction programs for low-cost, decent housing, subsidized housing, housing vouchers, or other innovative ways of providing housing for all;
- A guaranteed living wage for all workers, with government-subsidized quality day care for all children, and an end to all unemployment; and

- Quality public education for all, not just the wealthy, including culturally competent curriculum, critical inquiry, skills-based learning environments with respect, and protected rights for students, teachers, parents, and community members;

These are the major issues that I would like to see a reinvigorated people's movement fight for and win!

Finally, it is clear that the best shield against war, terrorism, and violence in general is economic justice for all the peoples of the world. The United States, Europe, and all the multinational corporate fat cats everywhere must share the wealth and technology with the people of the global South. After all, the foundation for that wealth was built on the stealing of Indigenous land, the Atlantic Slave Trade, and the theft of the material resources of Africa, Asia and the Pacific, South America and the Caribbean, and the Middle Eastern world. Never have the armies of the North brought peace, prosperity or democracy to people of Africa, Asia, or Latin America. If, as Dr. King wrote, justice is really "love in application," then surely it is time to muster up the spiritual love we so easily talk about in our own religious and social inner circles, and forge a unified love-force powerful enough to end the triple evils of our era.

White Like Me

A Woman Rabbi Gazes into the Mirror of American Racism

Rabbi Lynn Gottlieb

Holiness, as the nineteenth-century Hasidic Rabbi Levi Yitzhak of Berdichev says, is a continual process of awakening. In our own time, a white person can only attain a state of holy awakening through ongoing attentiveness to our own racism. Developing an awareness of racism should be at the center of one's spiritual practice in America, whatever our particular form of faith.

For the past 500 years, racism has been denying people of color fundamental dignity and economic opportunity. Racism fuels the American caste system that perpetuates widespread oppression for the benefit of a few. It pits poor people of color and poor whites against each other and maintains the hold on power of a small elite. It allows us to carry forward brutal enforcement policies for economic gain here and abroad. It is the root of our spiritual sickness.

Within the North American construct of racism, I am Jewish and I am white. Like other white people, and especially those committed to social justice, identifying with my whiteness makes me squirm. Whiteness brings up feelings of embarrassment, rage, helplessness, and guilt for our shameful past and present.

As a Jew, my impulse is to emphasize the ways in which my whiteness is different. When people of color share their experience of racism, my first feeling is often, wait a minute, I'm not white, I'm Jewish! I belong in the "people of color circle."

This is a common response among Jews of European descent. We want to be in a category all our own. But when I mention to people of color that many Euro-Jews do not consider themselves white, most respond with looks of complete noncomprehension. We certainly look white to them. When I walk down an American street, no one assumes I am a person of color. When I look into America's racial mirror, America reflects back the color white.

That is why people of color question Euro-Jewish claims to be nonwhite. Jews in America enjoy the many benefits that accrue to whiteness. We, like other white people, are barely aware of the ways our white privilege has an impact on our relationships with people of color. We have certain expectations about the ways we are treated that emanate from our whiteness. Moreover, Jews have not suffered the brutalities of American racism. We did not come here as slaves. Jews of European descent were legal immigrants to this country who live on appropriated Native American lands. The majority of Jews in the South (like my distant relatives from West Virginia) identified with the Confederacy during the Civil War. Some Jews owned slaves and participated in the international slave trade. The foundation of American prosperity was built on the genocide of Indigenous Americans and African-Americans from which we have prospered.

This history separates us from the experience of people of color in the United States. Although Jews, like other European immigrants, were subject to the difficulties of first- and second-generation immigrant life, we nonetheless were able to advance economically in one or two generations. Although Jewish people have experienced discrimination based on Jewish identity, we never suffered the restrictions of legal segregation imposed upon people of color after the Civil War. We have not been lynched in the thousands. Jews have been able to enter most hotels, drink from most water fountains, eat at most lunch counters, work in most professions, live in most neighborhoods, buy goods in most stores, and go to the schools of our choice. We were not placed in segregated military units. Most Jewish people in America eventually move to the suburbs or all-white urban neighborhoods. We attend majority white schools and go to college. We are a very socially and economically privileged class of people.

Still, the temptation to deny whiteness is strong among Jews like myself. Like most of my peers, I have always lived with a sense of alienation from American society based on my Jewishness. Our disturbing history at the hands of the white Christian world includes the horrors of the Crusades, Inquisition, pogroms, and the Holocaust that murdered one-third of the entire world population of Jews less than eighty years ago. The story of the *St. Louis*, the ship of Jews turned away from American shores and returned to Germany during the most profound period of genocide in Jewish history, confirms the assumption that Jewish safety, even in America, is always conditional. Accusations of "Christ killer" and the oft-repeated stereotypes that Jews control the media, the world's money, and the world's government, coupled with the pressure to assimilate and convert, cause Jews to feel insecure about our status even in America. Moreover, whiteness is associated with Christianity. In the circles of the Klan, white supremacists, and other manifestations of racist Christianity, Jews are not white. We are viewed along with African-Americans and other people of color as the cause of racial impurity. These factors in Jewish life set us apart from other white people.

Even in good times, it is daunting to be Jewish in an America where four out of five people are Christian. For example, during one Christmas saturation period from Thanksgiving to the New Year, I took my son to the mall (a rare trip for us!) to see the Lubavitch Hasidim light a menorah in a public space. Nataniel commented, "Finally, someone remembered Chanukah!" It is hard for a Jewish child to grow up with the knowledge that he or she is not normative. Jewish children who seek acceptance and want to avoid the anti-Jewish slurs so commonly spoken in their schools, or to fit into the sports team that prays to Christ before every game, often choose to hide or leave behind the Jewish part of their identity in order to fit in. Given that children in school often divide themselves along racial lines, Jewish children are faced with the issue of how they place themselves in a world that does not allow them to be themselves. Many Jewish people grow up with negative feelings about being Jewish. Jews are very vulnerable to assimilation into normative whiteness. This is not a positive development.

Our appearance can add to our confusion. My fourth-generation American-German-Jewish grandmother had jet-black hair and dark skin and was often mistaken as a "foreigner from a Mediterranean country"—an identity she often cultivated without letting people know that she was, in fact, Jewish. Although she enjoyed being exotic in America, this same grandmother constantly nagged me to get my nose "fixed." Her efforts to "normalize" my looks caused me to feel embarrassed by my Jewish body and face. Big noses are not "white." Appearance confusion is often compounded by nonacceptance within one's own family for distinctive cultural expression. We don't want to stand out. When I was growing up, my father reacted angrily when I uttered "Oy vey!" or wanted to be associated with anything that he considered "too Jewish," such as keeping kosher. Jews are often pressured to lower their vocal output. I dated a white Christian man who was constantly telling me I spoke too loudly in public. These overt messages are about silencing distinctively Jewish traits. We internalize the message of our whiteness.

Another wrinkle in the effort of Jews confronting racism revolves around the issue of Israel. Jews committed to ending the Israeli occupation of Palestine sometimes come up against anti-Jewish feelings just under the surface of speech about Israel's occupation of the West Bank and Gaza, often framed in classic anti-Semitic rhetoric and innuendo. The widespread preaching and teaching of hatred of Jews is not a paranoid fantasy. The malevolent fiction known as *The Protocols of the Elders of Zion* is still one of the world's most popular books and, until recently, was on the Palestinian Authority's website. Interrupting anti-Semitism wherever it occurs is part and parcel of the struggle to end racism and injustice, yet our experience of anti-Semitism and genocide is often dismissed or denied. This makes some in the Jewish progressive community question our relationship to the progressive community as a whole.

However, we cannot ignore or justify the brutality of military occupation of Palestine in the name of a Jewish state. Noncritical American Jewish identification with the policies of the State of Israel is problematic. From a Jewish religious perspective, religion is viable only when it can speak truth to religious, government, and corporate elites that are all about the business of amassing privilege through either the manufacture of consent or the bald use of coercive force.

The prophetic tradition never identified itself with the state; instead, the prophets took the state and privileged classes to task for their preference for military might over human concerns. While we are told by the rabbinic tradition to honor the laws of the land, we also have to remember and practice rabbinic traditions of noncooperation with oppressive state policy throughout our history. And, most especially, when the state in question is a Jewish state.

The leadership of the American Jewish community has been unable to address the brutality of Israeli state policy for decades. This leadership constantly calls for a "balanced approach" and monitors speech about Israel. People who speak to human rights violations of the Israeli state are condemned by organizations such as the ADL, CAMERA, the Israeli consul, and local Jewish Federations as anti-Israel. This effort tends to silence voices that care deeply about Israel's future, just as they care deeply about the Jewish people, and are distressed by the havoc the occupation wreaks upon Jewish and Palestinian life. Those of us committed to human rights cannot countenance Israel's building a massive separation wall with American tax dollars, the ethnic cleansing of Palestinians through policies of internal and external transfer, the use of collective punishment, torture, administrative detention, targeted assassinations, land confiscation, daily humiliation at checkpoints, the lawless actions of settlers throughout the West Bank, and a whole host of policies perpetrated upon Palestinian society. We cannot talk reconciliation and peace without dealing with these dimensions of the conflict. The horror of suicide bombing, the corruption of the Palestinian Authority, and the anti-Semitism propagated by some in the Islamic world cannot justify these violations of Palestinian human rights.

In facing the nature of American racism, communities of color will inevitably hold Jews accountable for our racism toward Palestinians, especially since we identify so deeply with Israel. We must be consistent in our efforts on behalf of human rights for all people; otherwise we lose credibility and weaken the effort to liberate the human condition from injustice. We can only effectively challenge anti-Semitism while struggling in solidarity for Palestinian human rights, while supporting Jewish people wherever they live to be safe and secure in their societies, while forging solidarity with people of color in behalf of social justice, while confronting our own racism, while trying to delight in the beauty of this life as a single complex tapestry.

Trying to dismantle racism in America and confront anti-Semitism often places Jews in positions that reveal our place in the deadly system of white racism. For example, Jews often take Louis Farrakhan or Jesse Jackson to task, yet fail to hold Pat Buchanan, Jerry Falwell, or Rush Limbaugh equally accountable for their blatant preaching of anti-Semitism. We Jews should not allow ourselves to be positioned as the classical "middleman/fall guy," providing a distraction that permits the politically powerful to avoid responsibility for economic oppression. By focusing our ire on certain leaders in the African-American community, by joining the bandwagon against "illegal aliens," we unwittingly ally ourselves with white privilege. The effect is compounded by the decision of mainstream Jewish organizations to forge alliances with so-called "pro-Israel" white Christians who fuel the flames of division between Palestinians and Jews in order to bring about the evangelical vision of the Apocalypse. In the efforts of the mainstream Jewish community to create alliances with Christian

Zionism, we are lifting up some of the most racist elements of American society. The Jewish community's attempts to create respect and understanding between Christians and Jews must incorporate an evaluation of the way racism works in the context of that relationship.

What does an authentic relationship look like? I have learned from people of color that becoming authentic allies means taking direction and guidance from people of color who are struggling for justice in the context of their own communities. Agenda-setting should not be imposed from above, but arise from collaboration. Rather than focusing on the dispensing of charity (which allows us to maintain our privileged position as benefactors), we could choose to become more involved with people of color alliances around efforts to improve immigration policy; to provide affordable housing and better education and health care; to end police brutality in minority communities; to promote sustainable wages; to reform the criminal injustice system; and to uplift the possibilities for cultural creativity.

Finally, we cannot truly deconstruct racism in America without addressing the invisibility of the Native American community and its struggle to achieve historical justice. I believe our collective struggle to dismantle systems of injustice in America needs Native wisdom at the core. Native people are the bearers of the spirit of the American continent. Their cultural recovery is at the heart of transforming American society, because it will restore our memory and interrupt the vast wall of denial that most white people have about our history. We can't be satisfied by token efforts to involve them by asking them to be present in prayer, but no more. We need to seriously engage with their issues, on their terms.

Anti-racism work is fundamentally a spiritual task because it addresses the question of human dignity and wholeness. An authentic interfaith ethic must be at the center of our spirituality. The deepest self-examination by each of us, and the willingness to engage in a vibrant exchange of faith perspectives, is needed if we are to have any hope of accomplishing this task. We have a long way to go to truly heal the devastating impact of racism on the spiritual vitality of American life. May we accomplish this task quickly and in our time.

Dark Satanic Mills

William Blake and the Critique of War

Joel Kovel

This difficult, illuminating piece, written for this book by prolific author Joel Kovel, strikes at the heart of Judeo-Christian traditions, challenging a de-spiritualized society that allows the continuation of suicidal militarism. While focusing mainly on the crisis of capitalism and militarism, at the center of this essay is the position that all religions, and indeed all spiritual practices, cannot escape a turn to the "Satanic" without a clear and active check on, as Kovel puts it "dogmatism, sectarianism, fanaticism, a host of bad 'isms'—including militarism." By looking at Blake, and a radical spiritual path implied by his body of work, Kovel suggests a way by which we may arrive at and cultivate Revolutionary hope.

A "Colony of the Arts" Goes to War

Some time ago, I learned that Woodstock, the town in upstate New York I called home for almost three decades, occupies a small but very definite and enduring place in the satanic structure known as the "military-industrial complex," or MIC. Yes, Woodstock, self-proclaimed Colony of the Arts, the hippie capital of the world, the town of love, Rock and Roll, all-around mellowness, and also, of PEACE, with a fine-looking Peace Monument on its Village Green to prove the fact.

We have a firm in Woodstock called Rotron, which was founded in the 1950s by a Dutch gentleman named Constant van Rijn for the purpose of manufacturing fans. Rotron has grown to employ some 380 people, making it the largest employer in the area, no small thing in this time of economic woe. It sits at the end of a long driveway off a main road, and rather few people have actually seen it. The hundreds of cars who go by the entrance each day see the sign, and if they think about it at all, think according to the vague notion that there is good old Rotron, making fans and keeping local folk employed. As for the product, fans, well, they are useful devices. Everybody needs a fan now and then to cool down, and so do many machines. The whole automobile industry would not exist were there no fans. The same could be said for computers and much else in a world where industry, having extracted heat from nature, has to face the problem of disposing of heat when it becomes excessive. Weapons are machines, too, and every weapon larger than a rifle needs a fan to cool off some time or other. Multiple rocket launchers need fans; so do tanks, helicopters, fighter-bombers, destroyers, and heavy artillery all the way up to the heaviest. Thus thermonuclear-tipped missiles like the Minuteman, with its guidance systems and launching apparatus served by fancy computers, also needs fans.

It turns out that Rotron has been making fans for these weapon systems for more than a half-century. This has taken place in plain view, as a small group to which I belong discovered in an archive in the local library chock full of press clippings about the firm's contribution to America's Defense Effort, including its work on the Minuteman. Notwithstanding this and other polluting activities, the firm remains an esteemed member of the community, and essentially immune from criticism, as we discovered when we tried to call attention to its wrongdoings. This generated the expected outcry that we were threatening the most reliable employer in the area in hard times, despite our repeated assertion that we were talking about converting Rotron to production of fans that served peaceable ends, for example, wind turbines, rather than destroying the factory. We also heard what may be called the "widget" defense: after all, Rotron does not produce the actual death-dealing unit, but only a harmless component that keeps it cool. Then there was the patriotic line taken by middle management when we confronted them, that what kept them going was the challenge of making fans worthy of keeping our troops safe, not to mention cool and comfortable. Other members of the community went further to the right, to attack the critics of Rotron with accusations of communist sympathies, affections for terrorists, disloyalty, etc. But most of all there was the sense that in challenging the War Machine we had entered a zone into which the great majority of the town would not go. They didn't so much as disagree with us; they simply turned away, into a space of indifference.

How is this to be explained?

Woodstock is a place with certifiably left credentials dating back even before the 1930s, especially in the cultural sphere. As it made parts for weapons of supreme death, the town was poised to become a center of what came to be called the "counterculture." Yet the same Woodstock where musicians like Bob Dylan (he of "Masters of War" and "A Hard Rain's Gonna Fall") and Jimi Hendrix (remember his performance of "The Star Spangled Banner" at the 1969 festival) tore the assumptions of bourgeois society into shreds was the Woodstock that made fans for the Minuteman. Through it all, Rotron went about its business and Woodstock slept even as it celebrated its iconic artists. Today their images and replicas of their guitars delight the strollers who patronize the boutiques both trendy and funky where consumerism thrives on the manure spread by the counterculture. And Rotron keeps on making fans for weapons of mass and local destruction.

Consuming the '60s stands alongside weapon-making as the chief enterprise of the town. To this we can add the Healing and Wellness industries, and even, so it would seem, that religion much favored by the New Age enterprises, Buddhism, along with its numerous Eastern brethren. The largest center for Tibetan Buddhism outside of

Asia sits atop a small mountain to the North of Woodstock; a major community of Zen Buddhism occupies what used to be a Dominican monastery in the forest to the West; and a shop on the Village Green promotes the Auroville Community in South India. Did I mention that Mynheer van Rijn, founder of Rotron, was a Buddhist? No contradiction, there, any more than between the facts that Alfred Nobel gave the world dynamite and the Peace Prize. To put it another way, the contradiction is purely logical, not existential, which is to say, not a vital confronting of different portions of being. These tend, rather, to be split apart from each other, remaining mutually incommunicado in the classical way that a man spends his day programming drones to blow up an Afghani village, then comes home, plays with his kids, tucks them into bed, and sings them a lullaby.

Individuals stepped forth from the Woodstock community to support our anti-Rotron campaign—for example, the proprietor of the Auroville store was sympathetic—but they did so as essentially deviations from a social type, in this case, one of profound inertia.

Meanwhile the True North of the United States remains aligned with the growth of militarism. Thus the "good" people, who enjoy the benefits of a "high level of civilization," acquiesce in atrocity done in their name. The problem has been cited innumerably over the years since mass murder by states and the possible destruction of civilization itself by its own instruments of death emerged. It has appeared with increasing urgency since the Second World War exposed the "Good German" who went along with Nazi crimes, along with their mirrored brethren in the allied democracies, who acquiesced in mass murder of civilians up to and including the launching of nuclear weapons on Japan in August, 1945. The latter event signaled the emergence of the United States as the hegemony of global society, and the number one perpetrator of state violence and terror, responsible, to take just the instances of its major wars in Korea, Vietnam, and Iraq, for a violent end to perhaps eight to ten million human lives and the laying waste of whole societies.

The emergence of the Geneva Conventions concerning war crimes and crimes against humanity has been a salutary development in relation to augmented state violence. Notwithstanding Geneva and international law, the epoch known as the "American century" has shown no diminution of state-engineered destruction. The dreadful record is rooted in ever-growing militarization which invades many aspects of society, enabled by the gelatinous indifference we encountered when trying to confront Woodstock with its participation in the military-industrial complex. The growth of militarization depends in part, then, on the lack of such influences in the population as would inhibit it, or from another angle, the lack of traction in the popular mind of the anti-militarization message. Antiwar sensibility has risen impressively over the last century. Yet it has really achieved very little. Except for an ambivalent shift away from direct engagement by masses of troops and toward sophisticated and increasingly remote means of destruction, the overall rate of mayhem has remained roughly the same, while the cancer of military production continues to metastasize. The people, then, are perfectly capable of "putting an end to war" but have not wanted to do so strongly enough, despite all the death, suffering, waste, ecological devastation, corruption of society and economic ruination that goes with war. There is, in short, a kind of mentality, produced by militaristic society and reproducing militarism in turn. It is, one might say, a *state of being*, subjective, but not "psychologistic," that is, not internally generated by thoughts, fantasies, images, etc., and not really "in the head" at all. It is rather a kind of structure that represents and organizes the collectively lived life of a people over historical time. So let us set aside for now the vastness of war—its geostrategic aspect, its politics, the logic of combat and its psychology, the economics of the military-industrial complex, etc.—to focus on this territory both obscure and utterly familiar.

Dark Satanic Mills Revisited

> And was Jerusalem builded here
> Among these dark Satanic Mills?
> —William Blake, *Milton*, 1804

The "military-industrial complex" is identified as "satanic" in the opening sentence of this essay, perhaps jarring the reader unused to figures of speech that seem archaic to the contemporary mind. But surely the MIC is more than the sum of weapons, contracts, factories, military bases, political deals, and propagandistic manipulations of which it is ordinarily said to be composed. It must also be anchored in the mind, as part of the consent necessary for hegemony. However, mind, whether individual or collective, is fed by deep and archaic springs. These comprise that nightmare in which Marx recognized the tradition of all the dead generations weighing on the brain of the living. It is this context that frames an inquiry into the notion of the Satanic as developed by William Blake (1757–1827), poet and artist but also philosopher and student of war, and a unique interpreter of what it is to be a human being.

The kernel of Blake's worldview is this: that the fully realized imagination is the destiny of human existence. This was to him how we aspire toward God—not the God of traditional religion Blake dismissed as "Nobodaddy" (nobody's daddy), but the reaching toward infinity and eternity that is our supreme faculty. It is a potential never fully attained, and only approximated through intensive inner discipline and struggle, what Blake called "mental fight." We struggle, then, not merely against external evil, but a myriad of fallen states of being; these exist within the self and are organized collectively. Blake invests them with mythological import and tracks them through his works, especially the so-called Prophetic books, which he also called his "Bible of Hell. These are dramas on a cosmic scale in which the protagonists are not persons as such but organizations of states of being within and across human existence. They are immemorially human—gender, passion, intellect, creativity, mental paralysis, belief, doubt, rage, rebellion, etc., and they are personified, given names by Blake and made into the players in his cosmic drama. Thus emerge figures such as Los, Vala, Urizen ("your reason"), Orc, Tharmas, Rahab, etc., and, to be sure, Satan. They are at the same time recognizably human and utterly strange: they alter shape and identity, interpenetrate each other, are mutually constitutive; they converse with each other and have diverse sexual relations; they absorb, destroy and renew each other, form alliances, weep tears of blood, go to and return from "eternal death," that is, the falling away from eternity into ordinary life. They are hard to make sense of, but no harder than human existence itself, in its splendor and misery, is to the engaged mind; and anyone who is willing to recognize just what fantastic creatures we are and who has the patience to put up with a great deal of subtlety and complexity, is advised to read and study Blake—who also, you may recall, wrote gorgeous poetry and painted or engraved gorgeous images.

Blake was continually occupied as an engraver and water colorist, such being how he made his meager living. As a creator of poetic texts (some combined with his unique technique of engraving and coloring the plates individually, hence "Illuminated," while others appear in various notebooks and drafts), his activity tended to be phasic. One furious outburst occurred in context of the French Revolution and mainly dates from the early 1790s; another, more extended, began toward the close of that decade and continued for roughly twenty years. During this period he composed three large Prophetic works: *Vala, or the Four Zoas* (uncompleted and unengraved), *Milton* (1804), and *Jerusalem* (1814–1820) (finished and illuminated). They made practically no impact on the world, which dismissed their creator as a lunatic. They are to my eyes the most underappreciated and misunderstood writings in English literature. They also are unparalleled as a study of war.

The notion of "dark Satanic Mills" appears in the second verse of the famous opening hymn of *Milton*, which has become the best known of all Blake's work, thanks to its endorsement by the British socialists as an alternative national anthem for Britain. "Satanic Mills" have as consequently become symbolic of a critique of industrialism as a whole. This is a perfectly reasonable usage. It is, however, an abstraction from what Blake actually had in mind, and indeed, moved him to write *Milton* and his other prophetic works. For this account we are indebted to David Erdman, a superb researcher as well as editor of Blake's collected work.

Blake spent his entire life in London except for two miserable years at Felpham on Britain's Southern coast as the kept artist of his patron, William Hayley. He was appalled upon his return from exile in 1803 to see what had become of his native city. To convey the sense of this, he used the image of "dark Satanic Mills." Erdman observes that London had neither factories nor mills in any traditional sense at the beginning of the nineteenth century. There was, however, one exception: military production. For London "was a war arsenal and the hub of the machinery of war, and Blake uses the symbol [of dark Satanic Mills] in that sense." A transformation in Blake's thought was underway; for he had not simply encountered war-production, but the first instance of *modern war production*, the industrial systematization of death and the death-dealing of industry: "mills that produce dark metal, iron and steel, for diabolic [that is, Satanic] purposes." The London of 1803, writes Erdman, had become "fortified against French invasion, the Thames [was] filling with captured French ships…the Tower and numerous workshops [were] busy turning out small arms night and day…Blake did observe this daily cast of brazen cannon and hear ambassador and king call for war before the drying of their signatures for peace. These woes are in his prophecies."

War was building against Napoleonic France, and like all large-scale war it had large-scale effects, mostly very bad. Great numbers of British youth were being gang-pressed into wretched service with a high risk of death; public hangings took place at Tyburn, near Blake's home; intense political repression and jingoism prevailed everywhere. For Blake, this sorely tried the revolutionary hopes that had propelled the first wave of his Prophetic Books, and culminated in *The Marriage of Heaven and Hell* of 1793 (MHH), a kind of supernova stirred by the French Revolution and manifesting the radical imagination. We read MHH today amazed at its audacity and fervor. Blake felt then as did the countercultural radicals who took heart from him late in the twentieth century that Revolution was imminent and that it could take place, as it were, automatically, by the eruption of imaginative energy. He had not given serious thought to revolution as a process entailing not simply the release of energy but dialectically having to overcome the negative figurations of energy; nor had he appreciated that the release from the prison-house of repressive society ran great risks of violence and opened onto a difficult process of self- and social transformation. There was much to remind him of these defects a decade later when he encountered both the degeneration of France into Empire and the "dark Satanic Mills" of militaristic London. Through this dismal gloom he felt the decay of revolutionary hope with the rise of the war machine and its enabling henchman, the Police State. He must have felt then how naïve he had been, of how he had underestimated the repressive and murderous side within us, and of how much he needed to further radicalize his vision. The triad of late works, whose obscurity was as much based upon a well-founded fear of the authorities as it was the product of a radical refusal to go along with ordinary reason and religion, was primarily then, the rethinking of his earlier vision, not to abandon its goals but to advance them through a more profound understanding.

The reader will appreciate the parallels with our present circumstances, especially for those of us who acquired a similarly naïve hope during the 1960s, a time when it could seem that the system was ready to topple from the sheer force of countercultural imagination. Can we learn from Blake in re-visioning a better alternative?

Enter Satan

The Marriage of Heaven and Hell was grounded in the notion that what is commonly ascribed to the Devil and the fires of Hell is as essential to human existence as the notion of Angels and the reward of Heaven. What we call Evil, in other words, is not necessarily so, and the same holds for Good. Blake used the figure of John Milton, whom he revered, for some sharp criticism in MHH to make the point: Note: The reason Milton wrote in fetters when he wrote of Angels & God, and at liberty when of Devils & Hell, is because he was a true Poet and of the Devils party without knowing it.

But then, of whose party was Milton when he was fettered? And what were the fetters? For this Blake chose to differentiate a figure capable of representing the Devil so that the "evil" side could be brought forth and seen as distinct from the energetic and vital aspect while yet remaining connected to it. Such was Satan, an unimportant entity in MHH and scarcely appearing at all before it, who grows to enormous proportion in the larger work named after the great Puritan poet. Satan became the instrument Blake used to comprehend the rise of the War Party, the militarization of society, and the shadow cast over revolutionary hope.

Unimportant as he may have been in Blake's writings before *Milton*, Satan looms very large in the Judeo-Christian tradition; while the class of "*spirit-beings*" to which he belongs is ubiquitous throughout history and a transhistorical potential of human nature. This stems from the fact that it is evidently impossible for the human Self to remain undivided. A primal ambivalence seems to afflict our species, present in an enormous number of circumstances, refracted through notions of goodness, badness, and the like, and variously located within or without the Self. Bad aspects are experienced in a way that persecutes, misleads, torments, or leads to madness; from the other shore of ambivalence arises the source of creative activity—since agency of spirit-being is experienced as coming from beyond the self; thus a great artist like Blake would write that his work was like taking dictation from another source. Certain typologies can be sifted out of the great mass of these forms:

- Notions of the human Self as inherently plastic and polymorphous, going back to the aboriginal "Trickster," ancient Hindu representations such as Shiva, or the Greek deity, Hermes.
- Internal divisions within the Self that do not rise to the level of an externalized being but are considered as indwelling part-selves with various functions, generally speaking, malign. The Greek word for this may be transliterated as *daimone*, from which the term "demon" enters our language and spreads out from there into a great plenum of occurrences. Notably, the technocratic "psy" industries have de-spiritualized this notion and turned it into numerous complicated constructions, for example, "introjects," "subject-objects," and the like. To be de-spiritualized in this sense means to not reach beyond the socially defined boundaries of the self
- Certain figures that, so to speak, congeal from the inward/outward motion and represent more or less solidified figures, sometimes monstrous and bestial, sometimes in human form, who enter the *Agora* of events. Satan is

perhaps the leading member of this class, appearing throughout the Bible and as a major figure in the major works of England's two greatest exponents of freedom, John Milton and William Blake.

Originally a minor functionary, Satan becomes throughout Christian writings the prime antagonist to Christ and God's project. He appears in this guise as Lucifer, the superhuman Fallen Angel of *Paradise Lost*. Blake's notion, however, is subtler and more radical, for Satan's monstrosity is dressed in ordinary human form. The Satan who wanders through his *Milton* shows none of the grandeur of Lucifer; he is rather a mild-mannered conniver modeled upon Blake's erstwhile patron, Hayley, a guilt-tripping conformist who *accuses* the artist—bearer of the divine vision—with irresponsibility; and who *deceives* him and *tempts* him with careerist distractions and what Northrop Frye calls "the solid body of organized taste."

Accusation is paramount for Blake's notion of Satan, while other functions, like deception and temptation, are ancillary. It is through the Satanic complex drawn by Blake that the bureaucratic, pettifogging Satan succeeds where Milton's Lucifer, consumed by rebellion, cannot. Blake follows Paul in seeing this Confidence Man as "the god of this world [who] has blinded the minds of the unbelievers, to keep them from seeing the light of the glory of Christ, who is the image of God"—though needless to add, he has somewhat different goals in mind than the founder of Christianity. In any case, accusation is Satan's definitive intervention, but it can only achieve Satanic power when supported by material factors, that is, as long as it is backed up by Authority. And this in turn implies institutionalization, of Church or State. A Foucauldian ensemble, accusation-as-power devolves from these heights down to the numberless mediations of everyday life in family, workplace, team, and community group. Without a dense, confining network of codes, the Satanic complex would be no more prepossessing than a sand castle waiting for the next tide. With it—and above all, with the policing functions, the gendarmerie, courts, prisons; and standing behind them, the ranks of the soldiers and their hierarchical command structure, sergeants barking; and alongside that as well, the "Mills" with their manuals and codes, the impersonal weapon systems (yes, requiring fans, which require manuals and all), and the procedures of the technical elites, it becomes awe-inspiring. Through all this is the regime established, and moves to a drumbeat of accusation. It is this structure that Blake subtends with the figure of "dark Satanic mills," which for us becomes the "Military-Industrial Complex" and goes to War.

War is the health of the state, in Randolph Bourne's memorable phrase, and accusation is its plasma. To the degree that a state plans and executes aggression, so must it justify itself. Else the body politic, ever expanding and made robust for the task, would fall to pieces. To justify itself, the warrior state must incriminate others, and to do this requires signifiers of the Enemy (from the early twentieth century, Communist, type to the present day principle Satan, the Terrorist). Equally important, however, it requires a softened populace made ready to accept the order of things. This happens in part through the low-grade yet incessant application of accusation. Accusation must be pumped through the system of the warrior state, from its main vessels to its capillaries. Its instrument is surveillance. At one end, the great Spy and Terror cases and the spectacular violations of the Constitution, at the other, numberless reminders of Danger, each with its implicit subtext: *What are you, miserable citizen, doing to stanch the tide of Terror? Why are you not working hard enough? Just whose side are you on? Do you not remember the words of Bush the Second: Either you are with us or the terrorists?*

"If you see something, say something," says the sign in the Subway car; and each rider feels, at some corner of being, insufficiently militant in the common defense: for she *has seen something*, has she not; why, then, has she not spoken to the Authority about it? Then of course, there are the "Heightened security needs," intoned by the manufactured voice over the airport speaker; these require that the loyal traveler, "report all unattended luggage to the proper Authority." What, then, about that black object over there? A miasma of fear supervenes, spurring recruitment between the State and citizens eager to prove their fidelity, and the abyss for those who hold back. Ostensibly free, we become a society of snitches in a gigantic compound that is at the same time a prison and a zone of protection against a terroristic, terrifying outside.

Bear in mind: first, that these occurrences are generally speaking, minor in themselves, hence do not rise to the level of emergency, nor do they require full attention. Like the rituals at the airport security lines, each chipping away seems readily assimilate-able into the ranks of the ordinary and forgettable, and is remembered, if at all, as a nuisance. But this adaptation is also a danger, for by the same token these incidents become a kind of firmament and setting for the Satanic.

Second, that they bleed into a pattern highly familiar from normal life, spreading out spatially into everyday moments of domination and surveillance, and temporally into patterns inculcated from early childhood. Multiply every disembodied airport voice into scores of messages from the disembodied humanoid who ritually claims on the mechanized phone tree: "This call may be monitored for quality assurance." So somebody is snooping on your phone call—as on every bar code you enter into the supermarket checkout process. Add to these the surveillance cameras, brilliantly anticipated by Blake as "Satan's Watch-Fiends": thus surveillance, the inescapable accoutrement of accusation, springs up like toadstools in the advanced centers of the world, New York, London, Tel Aviv. There is an entire economy of accusation in the regime of Satanic Mills, watching, nagging, hemming in the masses, extracting power from them for the aggrandizement of the state. War is its matrix. And the system prepares for war in all its Mills, bringing the Satanic arts of surveillance to bear on the workers in advanced, monopoly capital, where *productivity* is the mode, and a century-old process of controlling and invading the bodies of workers are the norm: "quality control" is the fine structure of domination, the quiet, everyday humiliation of the worker, the control that does not speak its own name.

Third, how they radiate into patterns set going by the empire of capital, both political and ecological, headquartered in the United States. Much has been made since the middle of the last century of the so-called end of ideology, in other words, how no one interpretation can encompass the endless variety of life. No Pattern at all, say the ruling classes, as though their reign, aside from being disinterestedly benign, is random as well. This is of course standard bourgeois ideology, like adverts for HSBC (Honking Shanghai Banking Corporation, the "World's Local Bank," headquarters, London) which will typically show a triptych of the same image appended to various points of view, all presumed equivalent, viz., an automobile shown thrice and captioned "freedom," "status symbol," and "polluter." Anything goes under capitalism; or as National Public Radio calls their news program: "All things considered." "Things," by definition, have no qualities and no internal relationship with each other, and to string them out this way, aside from washing everything into the Sea of Exchange Value and thereby opening new paths of commoditization, leads to that de-territorialization at the heart of capital's regime, that transiently exhilarating, eventually soulless emptying out, the "all that is solid melting into air" that unmoors the self and leaves it empty and confused, a plaything of Satanic forces. Add to this the systematic destruction of the category of truth inherent in the late capitalist society of the commodity in which huckstering, public relations and advertising are dominant modalities, and we get a sense of how the transition from Satan as a coherently diabolic being to a "regular fellow" is achieved—and also of Blake's extraordinary vision, for he wrote well in advance of the emergence, much less maturation, of these tendencies and at a time when they were only dimly immanent.

Here I think we arrive at a partial answer to the question posed earlier, as to why the "good citizen" presents a gelatinous surface to the challenge of "putting an end to war." We might refer to Yeats's shockingly prescient poem of 1918, "The Second Coming," in which he calls attention to the looming epoch when "the best lack all conviction, while the worst are full of passionate intensity." It is not simply a matter for those who lack conviction of not caring—though we see this as well, just as we see plenty of folk, not at all the "worst," by the way, shouting with foolish or deluded passion at their Tea Party meetings. It is more a function of parts kept apart, of millions of people who lack the means of connection—to each other, to the knowing that can give coherence, to the deeper parts of themselves, to the universe of which they form a part—people beaten down by the steady beat of low-grade surveillance and accusation, made fearful by living, alone and separated, in the entrails of a monster whose laws grind on irrespective of life, a world where the great sweep of capital means that life can no longer be actively lived, but must be endured, rather, as the plaything of the System. No, it is not that the inert ones do not care. It is that they really do lack conviction, because their life is the life of the isolated Ego, produced by capital and reproducing capital. Ego: the product of Satan, the instrument of Satan, Satan himself.

Satan Goes to War

> And the Mills of Satan were separated into a moony Space
> Among the rocks of Albion's Temples and Satan's Druid Sons
> Offer the Human Victims throughout all the Earth, and Albions
> Dread Tomb immortal on his Rock, overshadow'd the whole Earth:
> Where Satan making to himself Laws from his own identity,
> Compell'd others to serve him in moral gratitude & submission
> Being call'd God: setting himself above all that is called God.
> And all the Spectres of the Dead calling themselves Sons of God
> In his Synagogues worship Satan under the Unutterable Name.

Who, finally, is Satan? The question is improper, as "who," implies some-body and Satan is nobody—though you would have a hard time convincing a lot of people in the backwater that is the United States of the fact. Better to ask, "what" or "how." As for the former, Satan is an epithet, to be hurled at anyone who brings forward the organized degree of evil-doing suggested by the ancient notion of the devil. Here, it is safe to say, we run into a great deal of variation depending upon one's moral universe. The United States (think of Bush's "Axis of Evil" or Reagan's "Evil Empire") freely uses this device, while being itself the Great Satan to a lot of its victims. Among recent politicians, snarling Dick Cheney perhaps takes the laurel for many, though Barack Obama, the mild-mannered deceiver, is perhaps the more perfect representative from Blake's perspective. (No wonder they quarrel so!)

Blake's perspective, however, resists any kind of narrow personification of Satan. For him, the "How," to be more exact, the way Satan is, becomes the leading question. Satan is not outside us and takes no particular form. He or it is rather a manifestation of our fallen being, and exists strictly because the fallibility of human being is as great as is its potential. This latter, the core of our being, is a gift of nature, for it is the birthright of every human creature as she or he enters the world: it is the universality of the human imagination. As such, we are set up for a fall—and fallen, create patterns to perpetuate the fall, which collectively take the name of Satan. Call it Original Sin, if you like, but if you think of original Sin as a kind of badness or essential evil to the human being, you are, in Blake's worldview, perpetuating the sin yourself. You have then become Satanic, you have become the Accuser, now of humanity in toto. For Blake, the original sin is error, and the path of redemption has a twofold aspect, consisting of awakening the creative imagination (which is in itself critical and truth-telling) and of pursuing the way of forgiveness. This latter path is given as Jesus, and it is explored in *Jerusalem*, though we set it aside for the present purpose.

Blake makes much of an enigmatic usage in which he asserts that Satan represents the "limit of opacity." An odd construction. Where have the red suit and pitchfork gone? Or the serpent in the garden, or Lucifer his rage, or Mephistopheles making his deal with Faust? Satan instead becomes something blocking the passage of light, something within the sphere of visualization, or perception. He is that part of us—internalized from normal and one should think, a follow-on to the famous passage of MHH: "if the doors of perception were cleansed every thing would appear to man as it is, infinite" Satan is the filth covering the doors of perception; though Blake uses another term in the next line: "narrow chinks of his cavern," that is, of the Self.

As that which blocks our reaching for ultimate being, the Satanic complex installs various barricades within the Self, and these, in their twistedness, comprise the internal regime of war, as a realm of delusive desire and alienated morality, "[w]here Satan making to himself Laws from his own identity,/Compell'd others to serve him in moral gratitude & submission/ Being call'd God: setting himself above all that is called God." War and aggression stem not from any particular biological instinct, but from what my mentor, Stanley Diamond, once called "unlived life." We can add that this unlived life is Satanic and points in the direction of war-making, which under a Satanic regime takes on a special value precisely because within it, life seems more authentic than under the conditions of "quiet desperation" lived under ordinary circumstance—even if such a life requires the sacrificing of the lives of innumerable others. War appears now as the higher truth and the more fully achieved existence; and "Human Victims throughout all the Earth" testify to its Satanic power, the familiar means of organized warfare and mass murder.

Satan's triumph is that of the isolated Ego, a form of the self in which the visionary dimension is closed off by a system of internal barriers and external manipulations. It is insufficiently appreciated just how tied is this form of being to the capitalist system. Ego-being may be said to be that original "fallen" state when the human becomes split-off from its original matrix, that is, when the capacity for visionary imagination loses its way. Capital exploits this just as much as it does the surplus value produced by the worker, and its realm may be seen from the triple perspective of generalized commodity production, generalized ego splitting, and generalized warfare under the aegis of the military-industrial complex. It is this Satanic Trinity that generates the ecological crisis, and blocks an aroused awareness of how to overcome it—a subject we cannot follow further at present, except to say that this approach converges with David Schwartzman's core notion that a "solar communism" beyond the ecological crisis cannot take place without thoroughgoing demilitarization.

Release from bondage to Satan is release from the Ego's power, and the resumption of the visionary imagination. It is essential to the struggle against war. Is this ever achievable? Not in any absolute sense, as neither the infinite, the eternal nor the notion of god can be an object of our knowing. These terms are, we might say, *naturally* opaque, in that no word can encompass the "is-ness" of the infinite—or of the eternal, or the meaning of God. Just so, all religions, and all spiritual practices however they may grasp at this truth, can go no further than to illuminate the lower reaches of the journey. But respecting these limits is necessary as a check to dogmatism, sectarianism, fanaticism, a host of bad "isms"—including militarism. More to the present point, the journey, however imperfect, releases us toward a goal illuminated by the recapture of a lost perspective. We do not reach the infinite, or god, but by seeking it, can achieve a matchless critique of the given war machine, its capitalist roots, and the alienated Satanic being that goes under the name of common sense. We generate, in other words, that kind of existentially alive engagement in which portions of being come into fruitful contact, in contrast to the pallid existence of those "best [who] lack all conviction,"—the mass of citizenry who acquiesce passively in the Satanic Mills.

There is a contemporary instance, unforeseeable by Blake and the society of his time, but entirely consistent with his vision. He concludes the extract quoted above from *Milton* with mention of the "Unutterable Name" directed toward Satan as he becomes the God of this world. It is clear that Blake means by this the Lord of the Israelites, YHWH. But the unutterable name has been recast in the age of modern war by the great Christian contemplative, Thomas Merton, and elaborated by his worthy successor, James Douglass: it becomes the "unspeakable."

The unspeakable, as Merton and Douglass conceive it, is a kind of shock produced in us by the overwhelming nature of modern-day militarism, from the world-ending weaponry down to the white phosphorus launched by Israel on Gaza. Douglass sees it as the Satanic congeries that converged on the lonely and brave figure of John F. Kennedy and eliminated him before he could reverse the war machine. It is, writes Merton, "the void that contradicts everything that is spoken even before the words are said, the void that gets into the language of public and official declarations at the very moment they are announced and makes them ring dead with the hollowness of the abyss. It is the void out of which Eichmann drew the punctilious exactitude of his obedience."

It is the void prepared by Satan, where the immortal vision is not to go, but must go. Blake had the last word for our adversary:

> To The Accuser who is
> The God of This World
>
> Truly My Satan thou art but a Dunce
> And dost not know the Garment from the man.
> Every Harlot was a Virgin once,
> Nor canst thou ever change Kate into Nan.
>
> Tho thou are Worshipd by the Names Divine
> Of Jesus & Jehovah: thou art still
> The Son of Morn in weary Night's decline
> The lost Travellers Dream under the Hill.

Draft Resistance and the Politics of Identity and Status

Edward Hasbrouck

This essay looks at the often forgotten issue of ageism, detailing how militarism and racism continue to have a particular effect on the youngest among us—and the responsibilities that implies for the building of future movements.

The most famous draft resister in American (or world?) history, Muhammed Ali, represented his refusal to submit to induction into the U.S. military in terms of his submission to Allah and his understanding of Islam. What non-Muslims mostly heard and responded to, however—regardless of whether the quote is apocryphal—was the explanation for his draft resistance variously attributed to the heavyweight boxing champion or to SNCC or other civil rights activists: "No Vietcong ever called me nigger." This was an explicitly anti-racist and anti-imperialist sentiment, but notably not an antiwar, much less a pacifist, one. More than anything else, it framed draft resistance in terms of identity politics.

To the world, it was a statement of self-emancipation: the world's best fighter wouldn't fight for "the Man" or the American empire (or their gods), but would instead make his own choices of what was worth fighting for (and what to believe in). As such, it epitomized victory in the struggle of colonized people and people of color to cast off internalized oppression.

Despite such historical examples, resistance to military conscription, in the United States and around the world, is typically assumed to be motivated primarily by opposition either to war in general or to a particular war for which soldiers are being drafted in that place and at that time. On the basis of this assumption, draft resistance movements are typically analyzed ideologically in the context primarily of pacifism, and organizationally in the context of antiwar movements.

There is substantial factual and historical basis for these assumptions. While draft resisters and their motives have usually been quite diverse, the basis of unity for most draft resistance movements and organizations has been opposition to a particular war. And with notable exceptions both religious (Jehovah's Witnesses and the traditional peace churches) and secular (the War Resisters International, the War Resisters League in the United States, other Gandhian pacifists, and some other libertarians and anarchists), draft resistance has rarely been able to maintain a sustained large-scale visibility or organizational expression in what is seen as "peacetime."

But as the case of Muhammed Ali makes clear, looking at draft resistance solely in relation to war and antiwar activism leaves important gaps in our understanding of the sources of draft resistance, and of its relationship to other issues and movements. Draft resistance has ideological elements, of course. But it also has connections to the politics of identity and status, in terms of age, gender, sexual preference, race, class, caste, citizenship, and nationality.

Military conscription isn't just about forcing people to fight. It also involves the enforcement of choices about who is conscripted to fight, and against whom they are conscripted to fight.

The labeling of the U.S. government's military conscription bureaucracy as the "Selective Service System" is a euphemistic evasion of any reference to the nature or purpose of military "service." Yet there's a fundamental truth to this terminology. An essential element of conscription is the system and the criteria by which draftees are selected and assigned to particular "service."

Around the world, even so-called "universal" service has invariably been limited to members of particular age cohorts. In most countries military conscription or national service is limited to males. In some countries such as the United States (at least during all past military drafts) it has been limited to heterosexuals. In many if not all countries it is limited to those residents holding particular citizenship or nationality. And in most apartheid states (including Israel today, and formerly including South Africa) it has been limited to members of preferred ethnic, racial, caste, or tribal status. Draft resistance thus can be, and has been at various times and places, an expression of opposition to status or identity-based discrimination on the basis of each of these distinctions.

How has this played out? A full answer would be far beyond the scope of this essay, but let's look at some examples of the relationship of draft resistance to struggles against ageism, patriarchy, sexism, homophobia, racism, and imperialism.

The most universal selection criterion for conscription is age, to the extent that symbols of conscription (such as draft registration or the issuance of a draft card) have often become key political coming-of-age rituals and totems. Draft resistance, as the deliberate rejection of submission to military service—one of, and often the most important, prerequisites of adult political and legal status—is thus correctly and literally regarded as "childish." It's a renunciation of adult status by those who have attained the age of eligibility for its privileges.

Draft resisters are commonly dismissed as "having issues" with their parents, especially their fathers. To those who see the claims of the state through the Selective Service System to authority over their newly adult bodies as resting on the same patriarchal ageist basis as their parents' prior claims over their bodies as children, that's precisely the point.

The "Solomon Amendments" in the United States, which impose lifetime ineligibility for Federal government jobs and funding for education on those who don't register for the draft by age twenty-six, can be seen as formal legal expression of this permanent "subadult" status of draft resisters.

The focus of the draft on just one or a few year-of-birth cohorts at a time, and the extremity of the burden it thus imposes on the basis of age, makes it one of the most overt expressions of ageism in government policy. As Phil Ochs famously sang, the reason why "I ain't marching any more" was the insight that, "It's always the old who lead us to the war; it's always the young who fall." In such circumstances, it's natural that awareness of the injustice of the draft has been central to consciousness-raising among young people about ageism, and that draft resisters have been in the forefront of many other struggles for youth liberation.

This was, of course, more true in the United States during the American War in Vietnam, when in general only the youngest of those deemed "adult" were being drafted. During periods of more total mobilization for war, such as World War II, when even middle-aged men were subject to at least some risk of being drafted, perception of the draft was much less closely linked to attitudes toward age and ageism.

The connections between draft resistance and youth liberation were perhaps clearest in the adoption of the 26th Amendment to the Constitution, by which those then of voting age (twenty-one and older in all but four states) extended voting rights to all citizens eighteen and older.

The 26th Amendment was a direct response to the argument that it was unfair to draft people too young to have a vote in whether to go to war or whether or how to conduct a draft. This was an argument purely about ageism, and quite distinct from any of the arguments against the war itself, or even against the draft *per se*. The argument about age discrimination was so persuasive, even to voters who wanted to continue the war and the draft, that they amended the Constitution with unprecedented rapidity. Purely antiwar and antidraft arguments failed to bring about any policy changes at a level remotely comparable to a Constitutional amendment.

The 26th Amendment was approved overwhelmingly by Congress after minimal debate, and ratified by the necessary three-fourths of the states in less than four months in 1970. That was far quicker than any Constitutional amendment before or since. By comparison, the Equal Rights Amendment for women was approved by Congress only after intense debate in 1972, and failed to get the necessary ratifications even after ten years of debate in state legislatures.

A similar argument to that about the draft and the voting—"How can you say we're too young to handle alcohol when we're old enough to be made to handle all manner of weapons and kill or be killed?"—led many states, during the same period, to lower the drinking age from twenty-one to eighteen, nineteen, or twenty. All of those state laws were overridden by a Federal law raising the drinking age in all states to twenty-one in 1984, almost a decade after the last inductions of draftees into the military. As with the voting age, the drinking age was lowered in an (unsuccessful) attempt to assuage not criticism of the draft in general, but criticism specifically of the ageism of the draft. Unlike the voting age, the drinking age was raised once the draft (and its ageism) was no longer seen as an issue.

The United States was willing amend the Constitutional provisions for eligibility to vote, and to change the drinking age (no small matter, considering the importance placed on alcohol policy in the twentieth century United States) to try to legitimate the draft in the face of public criticism of its ageism. That gives some indication of how closely the draft was linked in the public mind with broader issues of ageism and youth rights—not just issues of peace and war.

Historians, political scientists, and activists sometimes acknowledge the contribution of the draft to youth consciousness-raising, but less often recognize the converse role that youth liberation plays in draft resistance and through it in broader antiwar movements. So far as I know, a proper history of the relationship between the youth liberation and antiwar movements of the 1960s and 1970s in the United States has yet to be written, despite their obvious symbiosis and despite extensive study of other ideological, organizational, and identity-based aspects of the antiwar politics of the period. It's taken for granted, I think, that we have a better intuitive understanding of their interplay than we do.

Such an analysis would necessarily include the ideology of youth liberation, the objections to the draft as ageist (including the common arguments for the legitimacy of the draft derived from analogies to the presumed legitimacy of patriarchal/parental authority, and the basis for their rejection), and the connections (and divergences) between antiwar, antidraft, and youth organizations. It would need to consider the connections between apologia for the draft and apologia for patriarchy, and how objections to both have coincided or influenced each other. It would need to include the role of the draft in youth consciousness-raising, and the countercultural acceptance of overt draft resistance and norm of closeted or semicloseted draft avoidance (along with the illegality of drugs), in creating a countercultural meta-norm of outlawry and delegitimizing both governmental and patriarchal/parental authority in general.

Last but not least, it would need to look at the social dynamics of the antiwar movement in relation to youth culture and community. Starting points for such an inquiry would include Michael Useem's important but limited, near-contemporaneous, and largely forgotten sociology of the New England Resistance, *Conscription, Protest, and Social Conflict: The Dynamics of a Draft Resistance Movement* (1973), and David Harris's little-noticed (because published at exactly the ebb of interest in the topic) but classic memoir of the Resistance community, *Dreams Die Hard: Three Men's Journey Through the Sixties* (1982). But much remains to be written.

The second-most-universal basis of selection for military conscription has been gender, and there's been at least some recognition of draft resistance as a form of resistance to the sexism and heterosexism embodied by the military (and its choice of draftees). I won't go into this in detail, but will note that, at least in the case of straight men, this is a way in which members of a privileged group are opting out of one of the forms of straight male oppression of other groups. That parallels the ways discussed further below in which draft resistance has been a form of white anti-racist action as well as a form of resistance to imperialism by citizens and nationals of imperialist countries.

The treatment of women within and by the draft resistance movement of the Vietnam War era in the United States is often portrayed in purely sexist terms and equated with slogans of debatable interpretation like "Women say yes to men who say no." It's equally important, though, to realize that draft resistance then and since has also been, for some of its participants, an organized movement (and one of few such) of men opposing sexism and homophobia.

Gay men have been conspicuously overrepresented among draft resisters, especially given that even straight men in the United States could in the past, if they so chose, avoid the draft itself (if not the obligation to register and submit to its structures) by coming out as gay to military medical and psychological examiners—if they were willing to accept the consequences of having that reason for their exemption entered in their permanent military records.

Throughout history and around the world, class has played a key role in who is chosen for what roles in the making of war. The dilemma of sovereign or state has always been that those of the lowest class status, who might be deemed most expendable and thus most suited for front-line combat roles, are often those least trusted not to turn the guns around. The standard solution to this problem has been a complex class-based hierarchy of assignment of military roles, in and out of uniform, that mirrors the class structure of the larger society.

For feudal nobility, the grant from the monarch of a fiefdom of authority and revenue was conditioned on agreement to be on call to fight, at the king's command, whomever the king declared to be his enemy—at the knight's own expense, furnishing his own arms and equipment. The peasantry below them was subject to compulsory call-up for *corvée* labor, which might serve military purposes but didn't involve combat or carrying arms (or the risk of mutiny that might entail). At the bottom of the hierarchy, galley slaves were forced into some of the most dangerous jobs on the field of battle, but allowed neither weapons to defend themselves (whether against the "enemy" or their overseers) nor much opportunity to rebel or escape. In such a context, subjection to conscription or other forced labor in the service of war could be either an attribute of privileged class status or a symptom of inferior class status, depending on which group you are talking about. The same is true, if less obviously, in the modern world.

From the perspective of modern war-makers, military conscription is best understood as merely one component in a scientific scheme for the mobilization and optimal allocation of human resources for war. In the United States, the infamous 1965 Selective Service System memo entitled "Channeling" made explicit that the function of the SSS was not solely to select certain people for induction into uniformed military "service." Rather, the deferments, exemptions, and procedures were a deliberate system of carrots and sticks that would channel each young man into making his maximum contribution to the war effort and the other goals defined by the government, whether that could be done in or out of uniform.

The Channeling memo was widely reprinted by the alternative press and as a draft resistance recruiting tool. It made clear those who avoided induction by pursuing exempt or deferred occupations were not escaping the draft system but complying with its intent that they "serve" the military-industrial complex and the government in other ways that those institutions perceived to be more valuable and more appropriate to their class. That realization led more of those people to choose draft resistance instead, even when that entailed renouncing student, occupational, or other deferments or exemptions.

The leaked Channeling memo had more impact than almost any other involuntarily disclosed government policy document of the period. It was exceeded only by that of the Pentagon Papers, and that of the documents revealing the existence of the Cointelpro program which were "liberated" by the anonymous heroes of the "Citizens Commission to Investigate the FBI" and published by the WRL and draft-resistance-associated *WIN* magazine after mainstream media outlets to which they were sent declined to reprint or report them.

Class has always been one of the great taboos of U.S. political and social discourse. The 1960s and 1970s were a period of greatly expanded exploration of dissident ideas, when class was one of the largest factors in who was, and who wasn't, being sent to die in Vietnam. Class remained, however, a largely *sub rosa* issue even within the counterculture. So it's noteworthy that it was the classism of the draft, as exposed by the Channeling memo, that prompted one of the most open and widespread discussions of class in the United states—in both mainstream and alternative media and culture—of that era.

Now a less overtly militarist government channeling is carried out in the United States through a new channeling mechanism largely developed since the early 1980s— shortly after the draft ceased to play such a channeling role—when student aid shifted abruptly from primarily grants to primarily loans.

Through the 1960s, most young people left school or college largely debt-free and thus with a largely free range of life choices. Through the 1970s, average student loan burdens remained a fraction of what's since become typical. Today, the choices available to young people are shaped by the coercive power of the debt most students must incur as the effectively indenturing condition of higher education or postsecondary vocational training. Cost increases and debt burdens have been a concern for contemporary student activists. But they have been talked about as an entry barrier to higher education, and much less often as "the new channeling" or in terms of the constraints student debt places on postgraduate life choices.

In part because of greater access to the media by white people than people of color, the draft resistance movement has often been perceived as a movement of white people (Muhammed Ali excepted). But as an organized movement, draft resistance in the United States has long been multiracial and often explicitly anti-racist. That's partly due to the explicit anti-racism of the Communist and Gandhian ideologies and some of the religions (including Islam and Quakerism) that have been central to the values of some draft resisters. Perhaps more importantly, the particularly deep bonds of camaraderie felt by draft resisters across ideological, generational, and other lines—fostered by a sense of shared action, shared risk-taking, and in prison shared suffering, and leading to a sense of "The Resistance" as a community more than as an organization—have been a powerful counterpoise among draft resisters to the racism of the larger society.

For example, it was draft resisters' insistence on fraternizing across racial lines within their group, as long ago as World War II, even within prisons and against official prohibitions and punishments, that initiated the process of official desegregation of the Federal prison system.

Hawkish mainstream media typically equate draft resisters with "draft dodgers," and presumes that most opponents of the draft are privileged white college students. Even many progressives have been misled by this into a recent revisionist interpretation of draft resistance as an implicitly racist movement for the preservation of white skin privilege. If draft resisters are mainly just trying to avoid the risks of combat while people of color are economically coerced to "volunteer," the antidraft movement is partially to blame for the racist poverty draft.

Such a view ignores the reality that, while many people have, indeed, "evaded" the draft whenever it has been in operation, draft *resistance* has almost never been the most effective way for an individual to avoid being drafted. Additional motives much be taken into account to explain why people have chosen resistance, with its greater personal risks and costs, rather than more effective methods (from a purely selfish perspective, if that were their sole goal) of reducing the likelihood of personally being drafted.

Not all but some black and white draft resisters alike, both in the United States and other settler-colonial countries in particular, have framed their motives for draft resistance in terms of opposition to racism and imperialism and/or an unwillingness to participate personally in racist and imperialist wars, occupations, and invasions. Draft resistance among white people in such places has been, at times, one of the most visible forms of white anti-racist organizing. In the same vein, draft resistance and war tax resistance have long been (including repeatedly in the United States during a succession of imperial military ventures abroad) key forms of organizing against imperialism within the privileged populations of the imperial powers. Henry David Thoreau's and Mark Twain's opposition to the Spanish-American War and to taxes for it, it should be remembered, was not pacifist but anti-racist and anti-imperialist.

To the extent that wars are being fought to impose, expand, or perpetuate racist social, economic, and political structures, opting out of war by opting out of military conscription, even in ways that might be seen as "dodging" rather than confronting or resisting the draft, can be and often has been considered an inherently anti-racist act. That's been particularly true in Israel, as it used to be in South Africa. In both cases, draft resistance is or was directed primarily or exclusively at racial apartheid and territorial expansionism rather than at war or the draft in general.

Draft resistance is a Jewish movement in Israel, and was a white movement in South Africa. Neither Israeli Arabs nor nonwhite South Africans are or were drafted. Yet despite being movements organized within the privileged white community, the draft resistance movements in these countries were widely recognized among Palestinian Arabs and nonwhite South Africans as being movements not just of white consciousness-raising about race, and of renunciation of white-skin privilege, but of use of that privilege to subvert the structures that created and preserved it.

Many, perhaps most, organizers and supporters of groups like the Committee on South African War Resistance and the successive Jewish Israeli organizations of conscientious objectors and draft resisters have explicitly abjured pacifism, and many aren't even "antiwar" or "antidraft" in any general sense. They might support a draft in a fully inclusive, racially egalitarian, nonimperialist polity.

The same has been true, if less widely recognized even among progressives, for significant segments of the draft resistance movement in the United States. Most opponents of the American War in Vietnam weren't pacifists. Many draft resisters of the period said they could imagine other wars in which they would fight. Indeed, many of them were left with no other legal way to avoid being drafted, and ended up in the Resistance rather than doing alternative service as conscientious objectors, precisely because they weren't pacifists or opposed to war in general, but had more specific objections—often rooted in anti-imperialism or anti-racism—to the particular war they were being ordered to fight. "I Don't Fight for Conquerors," the title of a song by Dave Lippman, probably expresses the dominant motives of Vietnam-era and subsequent U.S. opposition to the draft at least as well as, if not better then, any pacifist ode.

Today in the United States, draft resistance has a different racial and class dynamic stemming from the different demographics of its participants. That's a consequence of the measures the U.S. government, unable to enforce draft registration, has taken since the 1980s to suppress the visibility of noncompliance with the draft registration laws.

The brief handful of show trials of publicly self-identified draft resisters in the 1980s taught subsequent cohorts of potential draftees an important and enduring lesson. Because the government must prove actual, individual knowledge of the registration requirement to convict you of "willful refusal to submit" to draft registration, the only real risk is in speaking out about your resistance—not in quiet noncompliance with draft registration. The result, a quarter of a century later, is that while noncompliance with the draft law is far higher than it ever was during any previous U.S. war, that resistance is almost entirely closeted.

That closeting in turn obscures the extent of the ongoing (albeit largely passive) draft registration resistance and the impossibility (even if a draft were enacted into law) of actually reinstating a draft in the face of such widespread noncompliance. By hiding the faces and voices of nonregistrants, it also obscures the contemporary racial and class demographics of nonregistration for the draft.

The Solomon Amendments make it impossible for men who haven't registered for the draft to get Federal money for postsecondary schooling or job training. That's widely but erroneously assumed to mean that only those whose families can afford to send them to college without financial aid can afford not to register for the draft, and thus that nonregistration is a tactic only available to rich college kids.

In reality, the pyramid of privilege is much larger at the bottom than at the top. There are far more people who can't afford, aren't academically or otherwise qualified for, or weren't brought up to consider college as an option than who can afford higher education without financial help from outside their families. As a result, nonregistration for the draft is concentrated, as the SSS itself has found, not among the rich but among the larger numbers of poor people, mostly people of color, who see no personal downside to nonregistration or the Solomon Amendments because they don't see college as a possibility regardless of whether they were eligible for Federal loan guarantees. That includes most obviously, but isn't limited to, undocumented U.S. residents who are supposed to register for the draft (and would be subject to induction were a draft reinstated) but who have nothing to lose from the Solomon Amendments because their undocumented status already disqualifies them from Federal jobs, grants, loan guarantees, or other funding.

Ironically, it's at a time when nonregistration for the draft has come to be predominantly a phenomenon of the underclass and of people of color that it is coming to be assumed in many circles, even some otherwise progressive ones, to be a movement of white racist privilege.

(All that's necessary to qualify for Federal student aid is to register once and be able to provide confirmation of having done so. Despite the legal requirement to keep a valid current address on file with the SSS until age twenty-six, registrants can still get Federal grants and loans if, as most registrants do, they effectively "unregister" by changing their address without notifying the SSS. But because this is currently the most widespread form of noncompliance with the Military Selective Service Act, the SSS publishes no estimates and has for decades avoided any investigation or audit of compliance with the address change notification law.)

I'm not trying to question the primacy of attitudes toward war in shaping attitudes toward, and motivating resistance to, military conscription. Draft resistance is *primarily* an antiwar phenomenon. Rather, my point is that other attitudes shaped not just by ideology (Marxism, anarchism, etc.) but also by identity and status, and linked to other forms of oppression on the basis of those distinctions—ageism, sexism, racism, and so forth—have been important influences on the politics and praxis of draft resistance, and have themselves been influenced—to a greater degree than is generally recognized—by anti-draft thought and action.

As long as any draft remains inevitably selective—on the basis of age, if nothing else, even when people blind to their own ageism call it "universal" national service—the criteria for that selection will continue to anchor the draft and the resistance to it firmly within the domains of identity and status-based politics.

War Resistance and Root Causes

A Strategic Exchange

Jim Haber and Matt Meyer

Reflecting on the root causes of war, Nevada Desert Experience coordinator and War Resisters League National Committee member Jim Haber wrote a short essay for this book, which he helped initiate. That piece grew into an exchange with coeditor Matt Meyer which we thought might be instructive in looking at some of the nuances needed in building this work "in real time."

On Resisting War and Racism (Jim Haber)

War is the ultimate failure of human society. Climate Change rivals it in scale, but war's impacts are also global and long-term. That is why I am first and foremost an anti-war activist. As a War Resisters League member, I have pledged to combat the root causes of wars, both "international and civil." That helps localize the issue, making individuals the focus, not just peoples and countries.

I need this book. Just when I think I have a handle on being anti-racist or a "good ally," a friend of color challenges what I say as dogmatic "anti-oppressionism." When organizing programs, I still struggle to ensure gender and different balances without resorting to tokenism. No one person can speak for a group, but then someone tries to or is asked to. Generalities can express understanding, but they also easily morph into stereotypes. It is dangerous to speak for a group one doesn't belong to, but sometimes it is necessary to try. People of a culture can lose the forest for the trees, or look beyond something that is otherwise glaringly obvious. Behaviors are rarely exclusive of one group or country, and exceptionalism continues to bedevil the world.

I'm Jewish by descent, and am aware that European Christians have oppressed many of my kin over generations. Even when going to fight and kill Muslims and Arabs in the various crusades, Jewish communities would be attacked en route. Still, I have white skin privilege, so I accept being lumped together with my historic oppressors. It is strange that most Jews in the United States don't fear Christians as much as Muslims even though so much more harm to our communities has been caused by white, European Christians. I'm not suggesting Jews should hate Christians, but rather that we all shouldn't hate Muslims!

When I march for or against something, the face I project is white. Marching against war in this country seems like a predominantly white endeavor. White males reportedly support wars more than others. I expect to meet people of color and women who oppose wars, but generally they have flag stickers on their cars, or ones that say "Marines" or something like that. Stopping at a high school car wash in New Mexico, I was sad that the Navajo youth were doing it for their JROTC unit. I guess economic hardship and the need for community youth programs trumps analysis and a sense of history.

At a candlelight vigil for Martin Luther King Jr.'s birthday here in Las Vegas, a ROTC cadet was honored at length by the organizers, and the color guard was from Nellis Air Force Base. During the audience participation time, I spoke in memory of the King who supported conscientious objectors and who decried the United States as the "greatest purveyor of violence in the world today." I tried to speak directly to the young honoree; I was politely received … and dismissed. The parade the next day had a competition for best JROTC drill team. The contingent of the "Peace Platoon" was well received by the people along the route, handing out his words rather than promoting a business or just partying, but sometimes it felt like we were intruding on a party by the Black community, as though King was only interested in them.

Going to Afghanistan for a week with a peace delegation in March 2011 sparked various thoughts. Racism, even genocide are not just the purview of western arrogance and militarism. Pacifism, nonviolence, "people power" have seen expression more widely in foreign lands than here, and among U.S.-based communities of color at least as much as among Euro-descended groups. Hatred, racism, genocidal intent aren't only the purview of white culture and history. But neither are generosity, compassion, and the rejection of violence. Exceptionalism, the belief in one's superiority, inferiority, or generalized difference tends to put people at odds with one another, and that I hope we can all find a way to be outstanding, but not with an attendant sense of superiority.

An Open Letter from Matt to Jim

Dear Jim,

There is so much good stuff in this short piece: many great images you bring to mind that I believe are common to so many of us these days. Yet there are also some assumptions, I think, which lead in a more confusing and difficult direction, toward a more subtle imbalance (if not superiority), which I know you are trying to struggle against. Let me try to explain.

You begin, powerfully, with the statement that war is the ultimate human failure; a statement sharp in its simple clarity. And yet, and yet … in reflection I wonder. War is almost always a collective endeavor, and when I think of the phrase "human failure," it is hard for me not to think in both individual and institutional terms. Surely both racism and sexism give war a run for its money in terms of failure, causing everything from personal self-hate to small scale street violence, from social injustice all the way up to the inter-state conflicts we recognize as war itself. You and I know that this book project was conceived as a means of looking at the links between war and racism—without favoring one ideological viewpoint, any single strategic remedy, or an answer to the chicken and egg questions of our time. I am certainly not advocating placing a hierarchy on human failure, debating which evil is the worst one, or even which (if any) causes the other. As far as scale is concerned, I am reminded of an initiative that a friend of mine, Jai Sen, put forward at the last gathering of the War Resisters International, in India. He suggested that we all rethink our understanding of climate change, finally recognizing it not simply as an environmental issue, but as an anti-war issue. Environmental degradation, after all, is individual and collective human war against the earth itself.

I also love the way you personalize things: yes, I too need this book, and I think that all of us defined by modern U.S. "standards" as "white" need it desperately as well, no matter how long we've worked against racism, or how studied or workshopped we've been in anti-racist methodology. But is it true that "sometimes it is necessary to try" to speak for a group one doesn't belong to? You admit that it is always difficult for any one person to speak on behalf of a group of people, but then imply that there is some anti-racist imperative to speak on behalf of people of color. This is a slippery slope, is it not—well beyond walking a mile in someone else's shoes? It seems especially so to me if the purpose is not, say, to help an oppressed people describe their realities to members of a group (i.e., straight white men) which one is a part of, but rather to help that group get a better perspective on themselves. While exceptionalism may be a universal human trait, it seems to me a special function of arrogance to suggest that, in general, white folks have something to teach Black folks (as a group, as a nation) about themselves.

I'm a history teacher, so I'm not saying that no single, individual white guy (me) never has anything to teach any single Black person (my students). But that is not the point, is it? We're talking about large group dynamics, and basic, guiding principles of solidarity and self-determination. And, in any case, the fact is that part of the reason I am an effective educator is that I take Paulo Freire's ideals to heart: my students must learn about *the* world by naming their own realities for their own selves and *their own* world—with the help of the members of their own communities. In this process I am, at best, a facilitator; a research assistant; an eager-though-older fellow student.

Like you, I am Jewish by descent. I enthusiastically agree with what you write about the ironies of Jewish-Muslim antagonism, while the Christians get off the hook! There is surely not enough talk in the anti- imperialist and peace movements about the growing anti-Semitism that affects us and our Arab sisters and brothers alike. Again, though, I wonder. Can we make any move, take any action, can we even profess to be anti-war or anti-racist, if we do not first and foremost work to end the colonialist, apartheid conditions which our own people inflict on the people of Palestine? Does a lack of consideration of this—an inability to make as priority an end to this shame which is carried out in our name—make all the rest moot?

I, too, was saddened by your story of the Navajo youth group raising money for their JROTC unit, but I think for different reasons. The "blanketing" of poverty-stricken communities of color throughout the United States with American flags and "We're Number One" slogans, the replacing of public school funds with an endless stream of corporate and military training "opportunities," the gutting of health care at a time when new prisons spring up at a literally unprecedented rate (with more African American men in prison in 2012 than were enslaved in 1850)—these are surely not all signs that economic hardship "trumps" analysis and a sense of history. I agree with you that racism and genocide might not be an exclusive feature of white supremacy, but it does seem to me that if we are to define racism as not just prejudicial behavior but prejudice plus institutional power, than we must recognize something more than individual agency in the alleged choices being offered at this time when the empire is in deep decline. "Hardship" may be something more than a small understatement here, after five hundred plus years of stolen land, two hundred plus years of broken treaties, and continued genocidal policies of COINTELPRO and cooptation.

One's "analysis and sense of history" within the quagmire can be so distorted and confused by the psychological operations inflicted upon us all. Our own (yours and mine) personal sense of power as white guys, our undeniable and uneasy feelings of superiority, are part of this distortion. Inability to see the forest for the trees is, sadly, a near universal condition.

And what about that King Birthday celebration in Vegas? I wonder why you were "dismissed," and whether you should be more surprised at this than at the fact that you were listened to politely, given what people who look like you might represent, on a very personal level, to the family of that young recruit. Might your dismissal have something to do with your race, or could it have been your gender? Was it merely your challenging politics, or could it also have been your tone of voice? Perhaps there was a hardly perceivable look on your face: a mild scowl, a sense of discomfort, something smug or dismissive on your part? Yes, we know that King was working for more than simply the advancement of Black people in the United States, and that his birthday must be much more than an annual party for the Black community if his vision is to even come close to fruition. And yet, I am reminded of the words of a young African American leader a decade or so ago—someone who worked quite closely with the War Resisters League, but left because of some unresolved issues of racist and ageist divisions: "Do you realize how often the names 'Gandhi' and 'King' are used as batons by white pacifists to strike down new ideas and initiatives by young people of color?"

I remember the smiling face of President Ronald Reagan as the National King Birthday holiday was signed into federal law, and know that these many years later have only seen even more callous use of King amongst white politicians who only interest in nonviolence is for the spreading of passivity and complacence amongst a potentially giant and riotous Black movement. To what degree have those of use with a truer belief in the militant and revolutionary potential of nonviolence, with a deeper and real appreciation of the radical legacy of Martin, taken just a tiny bit of cover in the massive and official sanction of this mandated holiday-party? Isn't that the ultimate personal sign of white skin privilege: to take a moment or two off from having to think about or worry about race? Perhaps we need to be a whole lot more worried about the "intrusions" we make within the Black community.

Like you, I remain a proud member of the War Resisters League, and I do not wish us to change our name to the Racism Resisters League or the Sexism Resisters League. I know that the WRL has a strong history of anti-racist action, from having some of the first and most vocal white freedom riders in our national leadership, such as Jim Peck, to having folks like Bayard Rustin on our very staff in the early days of the bus boycotts and sit-ins and so forth. And we've made major mistakes and made some recent advances as well, growing as any old institution must. But, while we keep our focus on resisting war—and sticking any and all gears into the war machinery through tax resistance, direct action against warheads, military mutiny, or noncompliance—we surely have got to, somewhere in our hearts and minds, begin to think and act like racism resisters and sexism resisters as well. We'll continue to make mistakes; that is inevitable if one takes the risks involved in struggling for radical change. But we'll be engaged in building an organization truly able to stand proud as an accountable ally in a movement which might finally force this nation-state to bend toward justice.

Forward Ever,
Matt M.

Jim Replies

Thank you for adding your thoughts to mine, Matt. You continue to help me refine my own thinking about racism and war whether I agree with your counterpoint or not, and so this book process has personally been a success. I hesitate to write on racism because people don't know me or my life, and the reader only can assume where I'm stuck and where I'm liberated based on a few hundred words and their own filter. I want to respond to specific points you make since, overall, we're in agreement about the issues.

1. About war being the greatest failure of human society: Much debate has ensued about which oppression is most foundational to war, but we reject such a construct. War IS the failure on a societal or global scale. Oppressions can manifest individually, but war is a collective failure, hence I placed it inherently on the larger scale of human failings. Certainly,

another view could be argued, that the -isms that seem endemic and ubiquitous, are pervasively more destructive than any war, and that they effect more people. All individuals can oppress, but we must oppress together to make war. Individuals can stop being racist or sexist, but it takes even greater unity to work together enough to overcome war.

2. About speaking for one another, and about representing for one's people: Maybe I was speaking at a simpler level than you gave me credit for. Like you, as a teacher, sometimes the best we can be is a facilitator, a different role, especially when striving to awaken self-awareness in others. Some people speak against speaking on someone else's behalf, even in situations when no one is around to speak for themselves (which is what I meant), and a sensitive person can help fill the gap…to a point, of course. I have to be clear about who I am and what I am or am not, but if I am humble, sincere and accurate in my presentation, my speaking is probably a plus, especially if I direct people to resources by the people in question. If someone is in the room, I am more likely to phrase my observations as questions, creating an opportunity to be corrected and educated from someone else in the group. If more "put yourself in the others' shoes" exercises were done throughout our lives, there would be more peace and understanding in the world.

3. As a Jewish-American active with Jewish Voice for Peace, I often share knowledge and background about the Palestinian struggle and about past and ongoing violence and injustice carried out by Israel and violent Zionists. Sometimes a Palestinian isn't present. Should I not share what I have learned, awaiting a Palestinian to speak for themselves? When I'm told, as a proponent of nonviolent resistance, that I shouldn't tell Palestinians (or others) how to resist their oppression, I respond that I am not telling anyone how to resist; I make clear that I am standing with Palestinians (or whomever) who reject the calls for violence and vengeance and who want help being visible and uplifted in their struggle.

4. About anti-Semitism, I want to say that much anti-Semitism is irrational, but since Israel has a symbol of Judaism on its flag and demands to be recognized as The Jewish State, its oppressive policies add a logical basis for people to hate Israel, and by extension, Jews (and Americans).

5. In my stories of struggle relating to the patriotic, prowar elements of society most often hurt by war—poor people, women, people of color—and least likely to be prowar in polls, I want to challenge the peace movement

not to treat communities of color and women as inherently anti-war. That strategy is destined to backfire. Sometimes it is pointed out that poverty and race make one less willing to defend a system that oppresses them, but they have historically been treated as cannon fodder. Nonetheless, we can't treat people who enlist as though they're just economic conscripts and not, in some cases, also true believers.

6. You raise questions for me to consider, regarding my demeanor at the MLK events. I don't think we just crashed a party with our politics, but I used to stay away, not wanting to put myself in that role. What else historically or in my delivery could have led people to listen and move on as most of them did? I still think I was sensitive to those questions at the time, but maybe not enough. On the other hand, we must listen to one another, knowing that they aren't the people from our past, and maybe they're not repeating some same, tired line. My point was that polls may suggest who supports or opposes wars, but we must never imagine that someone we meet in the streets will have those views.

7. Regarding the "iconification" or overuse of Gandhi and MLK: sadly, many white nonviolent activists in the United States are unclear about what risks come with activism. At a nonviolence training a few years ago, an exercise called for participants to name actions, which they considered violent. One person said that if it draws a violent response, then the act itself was violent. This view removes the risk of being injured, jailed, or worse from the purview of the nonviolent activist—and it would have removed much of the movements led by Gandhi and King. This view, the idea that one can work for radical social change without negative consequence or response from the powers that be, is a huge problem in the United States. Elsewhere, in lands largely populated by people of color, people suffering under brutally violent regimes are rising up and taking to the streets en masse, with their families, and without arms. They are risking everything, and many are suffering—but they are also making great strides and even succeeding. We all need to rise to the challenge presented by these historic and contemporary role models.

VI. Where Do We Go from Here? Organizing Against War and Racism

Perpetual Peace Matchboxes

Carrie Mae Weems

Before and After: The Struggle Continues

Malkia M'Buzi Moore

Even though I knew better,
I cheered when Barack Obama was elected
President of the United States of North America
I was very skeptical but became intrigued
With this man made of coffee and cream
Half King, half Kennedy
Malcolm's manner and Harriet's heart
Ancient wisdom in his soul
I was seduced by his African stride/glide
His ease in the company of all, a gift of his mother's skin privilege.
Knowledge gained by sitting at the feet of brilliant Black women and men
Surrounding himself with keenly intelligent people who span the range of
human geography
Made his candidacy compelling.

Even though I knew from my years of social movement work
And anti-war struggle that the dream was just that.
I allowed the soothing rumble of people's hope lull me to sleep
To dream in concert with the masses
This man called Obama gave the young,
The old, the disillusioned and the disaffected
A place to posit their hunger for justice

I cheered with the people as if we had won the lottery
And we hung on him like a sturdy branch
For help
For reconstruction and re-invention
Of this infected tree threatening to crush us all.
We looked forward to days of new promise
A balm on the wounds of our oppression.

Even though I knew better, after years of advanced political study
I had a progressive perspective and clear political analysis

Yet I was entranced by his promise
To recover this huge diseased organic structure by
Discovering the cure for this cancer called greed.
He made the unthinkable seem real
The apparently impossible
Inherently essential
And absolutely inevitable.

So... When the yes we can
Became maybe we will
When the right roared louder and longer than
They had in years
When racism fueled a rapid train of disfavor
That ran over reason
And crushed consensus

I watched the hopeful's dreams dissolve
As the racism fed the rage
Of the right
Bloated their positions
So much that their platform swayed
Under the weight of their morbid obesity.
Jefferson's descendants held on and
Stood firm and raised their voices
To drown out the sound of Capitalism collapsing
Trying to distract themselves
From economic decline and environmental decay
By focusing on destroying a symbol of progress
And diversity's victory.

Even though I understood how this system works
I joined the young, the old, the disillusioned and disaffected
Posit their/our hunger for justice
In Obama's promise of nourishing sustenance.

I was jarred back to awareness by
Conservatives who found a metaphor for their reactionary behavior
And created iconic figures from flamboyant, inane leaders
Who appealed to the ignorance of the racist poor and paid for them
To fight against their self interests
Used civil rights tactics to cover the streets with their slogans and their

sweet.

Even though I knew that the Presidency was an appendage to a diseased
democracy,
President Obama was a symbol of justice
Peace and liberation
Represented a new paradigm
Of power pride and love realized

Until the war machine kept
Diminishing funds for human needs and our dreams of peace
Were replaced by combat nightmares of oil spills.
While the left is so logical and deliberate that they are not heard
Above the deafening din of the rights racist assertions.

Even though I knew,
It hurt to see the contradictions and complicity of liberals
Help the right win (Did you see who replaced Ted?)
And even though I knew that America's history is a recurring refrain
A dirge of desperation
I watch Obama hide his tears and watch his gray head slump slightly on
stooped shoulders
I watch and mourn the good people dying at the hands of Capitalism
Even as I marvel at how greed makes the big C not only homicidal but
suicidal.

I knew better, but even the weary and wise become whimsical and wonder
"what if"

Sometimes.

A Reflection on Privilege

Chris Knestrick

The final section of the book is our most ambitious: a collection of commentaries on how—in concrete terms—to create the movement we all need if a just peace is to prevail. It contains personal anecdotes, frontline reports, a few pieces of contemporary analysis, and a manifesto for change. Together, we hope that these essays provide not a single road map, but several possible paths to take in building the beloved communities that a world free from violence and the root causes of violence will require.

It is Thursday night and I am sitting at the dinner table with the members of our house. The conversation turns to politics and the upcoming election in the United States. Everyone is eagerly discussing the topic—except me. I have only been in Colombia for two weeks and I do not know enough Spanish to contribute much to the conversation. I desperately want to be part of the discussion because I have not had an in-depth conversation in over two weeks. Back in the United States, these are conversations I had on a regular basis and my opinion always carried some weight. However, in this new land, I am unable to add anything of substance to the conversation and no one really seems to want to know what I have to say anyways. I attempt to mutter a couple words in my broken Spanish, but nothing of any substance comes out. I move into silence and finish my food, hoping dinner will end quickly and these feelings of vulnerability and powerlessness will go away, which they do.

These experiences are uncomfortable and humbling for a person of privilege. However, they offer us something important. Henry Nouwen, in his book *Gracias*, writes, "I, therefore, think that for those who are pulled in a strange land the Lord offers a unique chance."

What is this unique chance? Nouwen continues, "When our traditional defense systems no longer are available and we are not able to control our own world, we often find ourselves experiencing again the feelings of vulnerability. The inability to express ourselves in words as well as the realization that everyone around us seems to understand life much better than we do." This offered me a unique chance to think about hetero-patriarchy and white supremacy. Situations like this one are not something that people of privilege are use to. Generally, at home, the reality that has been created is one constructed for and by my race, class, gender, and sexual orientation. Everywhere I look, society reflects back to me the reality of people like me through television, books, and the newspaper. It is easy for me to understand reality and participate in it.

The experience at the dinner table is a new one for me because there have been very few times in my life when I have struggled to be heard. We live in a world dominated by the conversations by white heterosexual males. In a group setting if people seem not to be taking my opinion seriously, I can speak louder and with more force, and it is totally acceptable. I can force my voice to be heard and people don't wonder what is wrong with me. Society has told me that I have a right for my opinion to be heard and taken seriously all the time. When I speak about my reality people generally accept it to be true. In more simple words, the truth is that my voice holds more weight than others because of a system of hetero-patriarchy and white supremacy.

Unfortunately, it is the experiences of many people in the world. Over the past week I have begun to wonder: whose voice is excluded from my table? Do white heterosexual-male voices hold more weight in the conversations around the "dinner table?" Who is able to control my world—the spaces I participate in? Who has constructed our reality? Knowing the answers to these questions, what can I do to open room for other voices to be heard?

The experience at the dinner table taught me a great lesson. I know an important part of undoing oppressions is calling it out when I am able to see it. I need to say: "That's racism!" "That's sexism!" or any "-ism." But at the dinner table on this night, I learned a different lesson. As a person of privilege—a white male, I don't need to be part of every conversation. If I am serious about the work of undoing oppressions, sometimes I am going to have to learn to be silent. I am going to have to make room of other important voices to be heard. I am going to have to learn to listen deeply. Sometimes this may be necessary during times that I have strong opinions. Maybe, even when really important decisions are being made. This is not something that I am used too. Feelings of vulnerability and powerlessness will rise up within me and this will be uncomfortable. It will take practice to become comfortable in that silence. But hopefully after much time and practice these feelings will pass and soon make room for mutual liberation.

We Have Not Been Moved

How the Peace Movement Has Resisted

Dealing with Racism in Our Ranks

Matt Meyer

First written in 1998, this piece was not intended for publication and was subtitled "a partisan reflection of one white activist on the complexities of racism in the movement." Written for the War Resisters League's seventy-fifth birthday, for which Meyer served as national coordinator, the paper was handed out at the WRL national conference by Meyer, Jon Cohen, and members of Resistance in Brooklyn. Still prescient more than a decade later, it outlines some "insider" stories of missed opportunities as a means of suggesting how we can avoid some obvious mistakes in the future and "not get fooled again."

At the dawn of this century whose dusk speedily approaches, one of the greatest American intellectuals of our hundred years—W.E.B. Du Bois—put forth an assertion that has since caused considerable discussion and comment. "The problem of the twentieth century," Du Bois wrote, "is the problem of the color line." It seems appropriate now, all these years later, to review our progressive agendas with an eye toward building movements for social change more relevant to the current and upcoming period. With the peace program set around coalition efforts for "disarmament by the year 2000" and organizational efforts toward reassessment, with a growing number of academics raising questions about that very reassessment, and with a vocal number of left scholars and students raising questions about the very legitimacy of our definitions of racial categorization, the time seems right for a sober assessment of the state of Black and white and the rainbow of other nationalities contained within the U.S. empire.

As activists generally, we are in a unique position to make our assessment not simply of the nation as a whole, but of the degrees of change and continuity within our own integrated, segregated or separated organizations. It is the opinion of this writer that it is the particular and peculiar responsibility of white activists to examine the often hidden powers we hold within the institutions of which we are a part. My observation is that, as the left in the United States often experiences itself as small and disenfranchised, these examinations are particularly painful and hard to sustain. This paper attempts to break through these hardships, and present a brief and partisan review of institutional racism within peace and justice movements. In addition, assorted attempts at combating racism, and suggestions for the future, will be shared.

*

When Du Bois first published his famous quote, in the now classic *Souls of Black Folk*, he could no doubt barely imagine the uprisings he would witness in his own lifetime. By the end of the first third of the century, an integrated labor movement saw strikes throughout the country demanding economic justice for all in the shadow of the Great Depression. The white male leadership of most trade unions led to some terrible defeats due to racism—as in the case of the Colorado mine workers—but some models of successful multiracial organizing arose from this period. As Socialist, communist, and some anarchist organizing swept throughout Europe and much of the United States, the question of ethnic and national autonomy within the internationalist federations was raised time and time again—pushed especially by the great popularity of Pan-Africanist Marcus Garvey.

The so-called Black Belt thesis, proclaiming nationhood for African Americans on a Southern land base (and put forth primarily by the Communist Party, USA), dominated political discourse around issues of self-determination. Even as efforts to build "one big union" or organization were maintained by left groups up until the Second World War, this thesis and related programs became a major model for the organization of Black people. By 1953, however, on the fiftieth anniversary of the publication of Souls and on the cusp of the anti-Communist McCarthy and Cold War periods, Du Bois himself amended his previous appraisal of the primacy of racially based mobilization. He suggested that, in addition to the problem of race, there was another problem "which both obscures and implements it"—that of class divisions and the militarism which inevitably results from corporate capitalism. To maintain class privilege, Du Bois wrote, men wage war, "until war today tends to become universal and continuous, and the excuse for this war continues largely to be color and race."

The alliances between peace and justice advocates which led to the early freedom rides and summer educational efforts in the Deep South set into motion movements successful enough to contain within them diverse strategic and ideological approaches. The dominant position asserted then and since—that racist segregation might best be fought by creating multiracial community groups, churches, and neighborhoods— was later challenged by Black separatist and nationalist leaders who experienced the paternalism of most whites within the integrated groupings. The radical nationalists and some anti-imperialists still believed that only Black-controlled organizations could adequately represent their constituency. Though hindsight reveals that the two icons of these distinct philosophies—Martin Luther King Jr. and Malcolm X—were in fact moving toward a greater appreciation of one another's contributions on the complexities of organizing across the racial divide, these divisions still plague the generations that follow in their footsteps.

Beyond these divisions, however, lay other fundamental differences. Committed revolutionaries and uncommitted sell-outs could be found in both integrationist and separatist/nationalist camps. Some integrationists strove for the building of a new, anti-racist society—a beloved community in Martin's words. Others, however, had few concerns beyond seeing an end to the legal paper inequities—allowing a select few elite people of color to rise to some place close to the top of the world of big business. Similarly, though some separatists may have held simplistic beliefs that white people were "devils," most put forward a radical platform for social transformation—where an anti-imperialist program would support a Black-led nationalist movement with the gains of cultural recognition or the successes of a handful of Black-owned corporations. While a number of theoreticians on both sides of the integrationist-separatist split continue to argue that they are the only true revolutionaries (the other being "inherently" mere reformists), the truth is far from that simple. Like the dichotomy so often drawn between nonviolent activists and armed struggle advocates, there are in fact revolutionaries and reformists amongst both sets.

It seems reasonable to believe that one significant goal of a repressive state apparatus is to keep this fact obscured, to keep those with a revolutionary analysis and program (but differing tactics, strategies, or philosophical points) apart from and at odds with one another.

By the beginning of the 1970s, a political and racial divide was placed—in the form of a challenge to white activists—that is still most often misunderstood or simply ignored. In the leading activist group of that time, the militant pacifist-oriented Student Nonviolent Coordinating Committee (SNCC), came the figure of Stokely Carmichael. Perhaps—to this day—it is Stokely, later known by his chosen Pan-Africanist name of Kwame Ture, who best personifies the merger of ideals and strategies found in a dialectical understanding of the links between Martin and Malcolm, between nonviolence and armed self defense, between principled integration and revolutionary national liberation. Stokely Carmichael led SNCC in demanding that white comrades leave the organization and go, instead, to work against racism in their own communities, building anti-racist groups that could work in association with the burgeoning Black liberation movement.

Shock and dismay were the main reactions to this mandate, from the whites within SNCC and other civil rights groups as well as from leading African American activists who had worked for an integrated America. But a new generation, personified by the New Left, tried to heed this call in myriad ways—from new organizations and structures to personal attempts at consciousness-raising or trainings. As the organizations of the New Left have all but died out, and the older groups—rooted in the political experiences of an earlier period—now line up to celebrate their anniversaries, how much collectively, have we learned from the past? How far have we moved from the strategic debates of the 1930s, or the early 1950s, or the late 1960s and '70s?

It is difficult to begin an answer to those questions without drawing deeply upon my own personal experiences, subjective and partisan though they may be. Having worked at various times in multiracial white-majority groups, multiracial coalitions led by people of color, and white-only solidarity groups, my last twenty years of activist involvement has seen a range of tactical solutions to the color-line problem within our movements. Though the fury of any given moment causes me to swing between wanting to name names and tell all and wanting to maintain confidences and impartiality, perhaps the most honest way to deal with these questions is through a summarized and edited review of my circumstances.

*

When I first considered refusing to register for the draft in 1979 (eighteen months before my eighteenth birthday), there were already strong voices directing my generation to not make the same racist and sexist mistakes of the previous era. We could not be allowed to have "the resistance" dominated by a few white boys who might attract the bulk of the media's attention and the movement's attraction. By the time I "came out" as a public nonregistrant—one in a clear position to receive this attention because my hometown happened to be New York City—I took those critiques strongly to heart. Still, a photo of me burning a "registration" card in the pages of *Rolling Stone* magazine sent me on a tricky tight-rope path, even as I tried to use my new-found status on the left to build bridges between diverse peoples. These efforts were all-too-often fundamentally lost amidst the "more pressing" ideological bickering between the democratic socialists and the Trotskyists, the libertarians and some pacifists, taking place in the major anti-draft coalitions.

In one memorable instance, a grassroots group which had consistently engaged in these struggles—the Black Veterans for Social Justice (BVSJ)—rose to the top positions of leadership within the Committee Against Registration and the Draft (CARD)—the major national protest body at the time. It was noticeable and striking that around this same period, the rest of the major players in CARD—the more liberal and better-funded groups—had moved their resources and personnel on to other matters. It is not that the nuclear freeze or Central American solidarity campaigns were unimportant in any way; it just seemed that the "big players" were also loath to allow a Black-led association to direct "their" coalition. When BVSJ came to the organizing table around the 1982 United Nations Special Session on Disarmament, neither of the two major factions—together representing the entire organized peace movement—took them the least bit seriously. Leaders of each of these factions, fraught though they were in their own political and logistical battles, always had an assortment of excuses for their dismissive attitude in the face of serious BVSJ critiques. The concerns of BVSJ, and the recently founded National Black United Front, were wholeheartedly ignored.

Ultimately, a third, entirely separate coalition (of "Third World and Progressive Peoples" as they called themselves) was formed. Though few accounts of the antinuclear movement, and the largest demonstration in U.S. history, explain it this way, it was—in fact—the combined force of all three of these coalitions that brought one million people to New York City and the United Nations that year. I was the national student representative in the coalitions planning the UN actions, in attendance at some of the more combative meetings. And though it seemed harsh at the time, the words of one BVSJ leader at a particularly nasty moment has stuck with me to this day: "In my community," he said, "the dropping of the bomb might not be so bad...then, at least, there would be a level playing field!"

I watched as other coalitions and organizations of the 1980s debated and disintegrated over issues relating to race, inclusiveness, leadership, and the fair distribution of resources. At one point in the early history of the Mobilization for Survival (MFS or "the Mobe"), the group most responsible for the successes of 1982's UN mobilization, an African American national field organizer was traveling throughout the country telling folks how racist the Mobe was. Though many decried the indirectness and irresponsibility of this spokesperson's actions, few took notice when it was "discovered"—upon the closing of the Philadelphia-based office he had worked out of, that an African American secretary who had recently been laid off was also a leading member of the Black United Front (BUF). No one seemed to care to talk to her about anything other than her secretarial duties! To be honest, few in the MFS were probably aware of the significance (or even the existence) of the BUF. But had those lines of communication and political perspective been crossed, BUF and MFS would have been natural allies, with very similar broad progressive agendas.

Mobe, it should be noted, was still better than many leading groups, despite their shortcomings. For much of its life, MFS itself existed as a coalition of other national groups, enjoying the support and participation of at least two major organizations outside of the usual peace movement orbit: the Puerto Rican Socialist Party (PSP) and the All-African Peoples Revolutionary Party (AAPRP). After the national office reopened in New York City, representatives of both the PSP and AAPRP spent some time on staff, both prior to and following 1982. Still, despite the potential that these connections afforded, there always seemed to be a variety of reasons—largely administrative on the surface—which consistently came up as to why these staffing arrangements just didn't work out. No easily definitive "act" of overt racism can be pointed to as having caused these dis-connects. These relationships floundered due to a general insensitivity to cultural differences in work-style, coupled with political short-sightedness and inflexibility regarding the kind of movement we needed and need to build in order to be both radical and relevant.

When interpersonal insensitivity exists within progressive groups, it is a regrettable and sad thing in any case. When cultural insensitivity and political inflexibility exists, keeping individuals of a socially dominant group in positions of authority over individuals from historically oppressed or colonized groups, it is more than just regrettable. This is the heart of institutional and structural racism.

Ultimately, both the PSP and AAPRP dropped out of MFS, causing it to lose—in my view—much of its vitality and vibrancy. Eventually, the MFS coalition itself ceased to function, and it lived out its final years doing some good local campaigns but with little memory of its former movement-wide influence and multiracial possibility.

*

Clergy and Laity Concerned (CALC), one of the few groups in U.S. left history to truly remodel itself from a predominately white construct to a multiethnic and Black-led one, also went through its transformation in the 1980s. With great internal turmoil at first, CALC slowly shifted its political priorities to include a greater emphasis on economic justice and a special project focusing on an end to apartheid in South Africa. Separate meetings of whites and Blacks within CALC took place to provide personal consciousness-raising. A Third World Caucus lent legitimacy, empowerment, and a sense of ownership to those who had previously felt alienated. A strategic logistical and organizing shift took place, with eventual moving of the national office to Atlanta, Georgia; attempts were made to strengthen the Black church constituents who had always been a vocal minority within the group.

Throughout this process, however, as progressive groups all over the United States were losing members and funds, CALC was hit particularly hard. A vast number of CALC's large contributors who had been on board since the Vietnam war, and locals who were not committed to the "new direction" of the organization, were lost in a relatively short time period. There was little doubt amongst those Blacks and explicitly anti-racist whites who remained in CALC that the dried-up resources were at least in part due to unconscious white supremacy; the need to deal with issues relevant to the Black community was simply not a priority for many in the predominately white peace movement. With the ultimate demise of the organization several years after its move south, it is difficult to conclude what aspects of the CALC experiment might have been a success.

One might think that the various solidarity groups—most notably in the 1980s around Central American and Southern Africa—would serve as ideal opportunities for building anti-racist bridges. Nonetheless, at several strategic moments, the potent mix of covert and overt white supremacy combined with sectarianism to cause divisions and animosity. As early as 1981, when the call for United States out of El Salvador was beginning to gain momentum, a sectarian split sadly reminiscent of the Vietnam anti-war squabbles was repeated, as two coalitions called for Washington, D.C.–based demonstrations on two separate dates, one week apart. The People's Anti-War Mobilization (PAM) drew suspicion from the "mainstream" movement because they were founded by the Workers World Party, a small Leninist vanguard grouping that up till that time had not played a significant role in mass mobilizations. PAM, however, called for a linking of issues—especially trumpeting the need for African Americans to lead the coalition, and for one central demonstration demand to be an end to racism at home. The fact is that PAM out-organized the competing coalition by a margin of five-to-one, indicating that a new generation of progressive activists were less inclined toward single issue politics less concerned about red-baiting and name-calling. Would this generation also be less apt to deny that racism in the United States had to be boldly confronted?

To be sure, a fairly broad group of organizations—including the War Resisters League—eventually joined with PAM after a lengthy series of negotiations; the rival coalition, led by a loose, grouping united around the idea that only a single-issue demonstration dealing intervention but not its underlying causes or effects, and comprised of the Socialist Workers Party, the Democratic Socialist Organizing Committee, and others, eventually faded away. But the success of the 1981 multi-issue mobilization didn't prevent a continuation of sectarian splits and continued institutional racism, as solidarity groups went through bitter internal struggles over whether they should embrace the "rainbow" politics that would link the wars in Central America to injustices in the United States.

Some positive examples can be gleaned from the African solidarity and anti-apartheid movements, where a number of individuals and organizations came together across the racial and political divide. The fact of focusing on conditions in Africa did mean—at least—that the whites involved were taking up issues already of basic interest to at least a sector of the Black community. And Blacks focusing on this work, while often also involved in campaigns for racial and economic justice at home, at least gave some inclination toward the primacy of international issues. These two points should not be taken lightly, as one concrete problem of institutionalized racism is the common substitution, on the part of white progressives, of "outreach" activities for a true anti-racist politics. "If we could only just get a couple of people of color to work for us (on the issues which we define and feel are important)," the thinking goes, "then those people can reach out to their 'constituencies' and our problems of being perceived of as too white would be solved."

There is still, of course, another concrete problem inherent in the "safety" of any traditional solidarity work: working in support of peoples and struggles thousands of miles away when legitimate liberation struggles take place within the borders of the U.S. empire, in every state and region. The tacit agreement in making the anti-apartheid movement a priority enabled organizers to avoid splits along the above lines, but this did not lead to an avoidance of other aspects of white supremacy. Within a number of anti-apartheid groups, struggles for leadership resulted in some overtly racist incidents; an early divestment coalition initiated at Rutgers University by the Black Student Caucus saw an eventual vote whereby all Black student groups were removed from the leadership, ostensibly because their positions were "too radical." Even in the more established national organizations, white activists seem to make up a majority of staff and Board positions. With these examples in mind, a new generation of students set about to make some changes.

As a graduate student at Columbia University at the time of the well-publicized and nationally inspiring 1985 divestment blockade, I watched as my undergraduate comrades worked out a power-sharing arrangement such that the blockade leadership was made up of a multiracial array of students' groups, with Black groups always (and structurally) maintaining a sense of autonomy and power within the otherwise racist university system. The Black student organizations made up a guaranteed majority on the steering committee, and held a majority of leadership and spokesperson positions. Discussions about racist process or decision-making within the coalition of student groups, and amongst individuals on the front line of the blockade (which lasted over three weeks), were held openly—and people were held accountable for their actions to the steering committee. The students approach to the various African groups and others (including professors and nonstudent support groups), coming for an hour or a day or two to join with or speak to the blockade were consistently and carefully treated in a nonsectarian manner, even while the students themselves made sure to keep basic control of their own decision-making process. In this manner, though acts of racism within the massive and successful divestment campaign were hardly avoided, the fact that structures were created which watch-dogged and safeguarded against runaway institutional racism certainly helped make the Columbia model and inspiration for groups across the country.

Utilizing an entirely different political and structural approach to the question of solidarity, the John Brown Anti-Klan Network (JBAKN) and the Free Puerto Rico Committees (FPR)—also active throughout the 1980s—disallowed integrated, multiracial organization-building altogether, seeking instead to form direct alliances between groups of "north americans," or white people of European heritage, and specific organizations within the Black and Puerto Rican liberation movements within the United States. Based on the history of racism within white progressive groups, and heeding the call for whites to work together—countering racism in their own communities and lending support to the oppressed—these radicals espoused a form of revolutionary nationalism which, while recognizing the need for class struggle, analyzed U.S. socioeconomic and political systems as being—first and foremost—fundamentally racist. Having grown primarily out of struggles within the New African Independence Movement (forces within the Black nation calling for a separate land base, New Africa, in the five states of the Black Belt south), both JBAKN and FPR worked under the direction of their New Afrikan and Puerto Rican leadership groups. JBAKN was a solidarity arm of the New African Peoples Organization (NAPO), and FPR was created and directed by the Puerto Rican National Liberation Movement (MLN-PR).

Over time, varying degrees of autonomy existed within JBAKN and FPR, where campaigns focusing on police brutality, or militarism in Puerto Rico, or other projects of particular concern to white progressives would be taken up. The bulk of work, however, was focused on overall anti-colonial education and action, combined with steadfast support for political prisoners and, in the case of JBAKN, in active campaigns against the Klan and other racist groups. Fundamentally, the "parent" groups would determine political direction. Challenging the simplistic "majority rules" concept of democracy in a society and movement where tremendous resources, contacts, and access have been generally more "available" to one group (and state repression and poverty more available to the other), these structural separations sought to reconfigure the power dynamics of the society at large. Principled organization-to-organization links between people were built across the "color" line—and it didn't matter if, in a given city, there were ten JBAKN cadre and only three NAPO leaders.

By and large, these groups avoided guilt-tripping and finger-pointing to figure out who was the least or most racist, and discussions as well as actions were centered on practical solidarity and educational work. In building for accountability, frameworks were put into place for criticism and self-criticism of racism within the context of work or relationships. The structure of maintaining separate white and Black or Puerto Rican groups meant that occasional racist errors on the part of whites would not disrupt the functioning of the Black or Puerto Rican organizations. There was an understanding, along with study and struggle, that—as the liberation movements developed—solidarity activists of European descent would be primarily responsible for the disruption and ultimate destruction of the "white settler nation" or empire. The vision of this type of connection was meant to typify the definition of solidarity projected by Mozambican leader Samora Machel: "two fists coming together to strike a single blow." Even as organizational forms have changed over the years, the deep connections of mutual respect which built up amongst many of the people working within these groups carries on to this day.

Nevertheless, the pressures of this direct solidarity took its toll on many who were involved. In some early cases, criticism/self-criticism sessions turned into brutal personal attacks, where whites more in favor with the "leadership" at any given moment could vamp on their less experienced or well-connected colleagues. In addition, some FPR and JBAKN members felt stifled or dissatisfied with the sometimes bureaucratic, rigid, or formulaic nature of relationships, where one group remained permanently "under the leadership" of another. And leadership, in the occasional case of young activists from the liberation movements working with more experienced, older allies, could be inconsistent or ineffective. There can be little doubt that mistakes were made on both sides.

When both JBAKN and FPR folded in the early 1990s, questions remained regarding the nature of leadership between these groups and within the white left. In addition to the problems noted above, concerns were aired about the potentially "interventionist" nature of whites engaged in solidarity being linked directly in support of one and only organization within a larger nationalist struggle. Was the MLN-PR, for example, the only organization worthy of solidarity within the Puerto Rican movement? If FPR was to be building broad solidarity for the people of Puerto Rico, should we only have ties to the MLN-PR, even if all of FPRs members believe that the MLN-PR leaders have the best analysis of the Puerto Rican reality? What about nuanced differences—small but still significant, perhaps with no immediate right or wrong answers—between our comrades in the MLN and organizations on the island, or differences between individual leaders within the MLN? For the white left to take strong positions in these debates, or to shut off material aid or resources to one side of a given debate, can be "interventionist" and just as racist in practice as the paternalistic practices of less-self-conscious whites in multiracial integrationist groups. Despite the good intentions and more radical analysis of the anti-imperialist JBAKN and FPR, there was still work to be done to deal with some of these structural and political issues.

Also problematic was the sectarianism displayed by JBAKN and FPR members toward whites not in these solidarity groups; the "tendency" of the movement which produced most of the membership in these solidarity structures—supporters of the Weather Underground, Prairie Fire, and the May 19 Communist Organization—were particularly known for their sometimes ruthless competitiveness and disregard for the larger progressive and left movements. In undermining the ability for whites in general to build a broader, stronger, anti-racist struggle, a larger racist error occurred. Indeed, the need for multi-issue organizing which could attract a larger sector of progressive whites was not, for the most part, taken up by these narrower efforts. Important lessons must be learned, however, in the context of these new approaches. They have rarely been seriously examined by the rest of the peace and justice movement.

The coalition work which has grown out of this anti-imperialist sector, such as the various campaigns of amnesty for the more than one hundred U.S. political prisoners, prisoners of war, and prisoners of conscience, also provides an alternative to the all-too-typical white-dominated coalitions that have often built tremendous demonstrations while only exacerbating existing tensions between groupings from one or another national liberation or "racial" constituency. At their best, these structures and the projects they birthed were often exciting and dynamic, the personal and political relationships deeply respectful and highly productive. Led by revolutionary "people of color" who had their own organizations to report to and to represent, these efforts offered the opportunities to both learn and contribute, in a manner where real dialogues and exchanges took place. There is no doubt, for example, that the principle in support of lesbian and gay rights taken by the MLN-PR, the first such position held by any Latin American revolutionary political party, was influenced by the large number of strong lesbians and gay men who had worked in various coalition and solidarity groups with them (along with a number of gay folks in their own ranks). Similarly, it is no coincidence that some of the most perceptive and articulate white analysts of institutional racism in the United States today have come out of or been deeply influenced by this area of work.

*

412

Diversity, it should now be clear, refers to much more than a simplistic or ritualistic call for Black-white unity, or for us to all to "just get along." There is such diversity even in the tactics of groups that have continued to struggle for full social justice. There are examples of integrated organizing efforts in groups as different as the Committees of Correspondence and the Maoist-oriented Revolutionary Communist Party, each with strongly divergent ideological outlooks, with majority white memberships, but with a few key people of color in long-term positions of top leadership. The various formations of folks working for independent electoral action, for local third party campaigns, have a solid history of multiracial coalition-building. And many assorted workplace initiatives, from the push for multiculturalism in the field of education to various ongoing trade union efforts, suggest at least some short-term gains.

Why, then, some years ago, on the eve of its seventy-fifth anniversary, did the Fellowship of Reconciliation (FOR) find it necessary to concentrate some mediation efforts between its strong, well-intentioned Executive Director and its Racial and Economic Justice Coordinator? Why, in one of FOR's most consistently integrated and progressive programs—the Task Force on Latin America and the Caribbean— was it necessary to discuss how a colonial mentality creeps into our work, hindering relationships between staff of the dominant and subjected cultures, potentially weakening bonds between peoples from traditionally oppressor and oppressed groups? How, in good conscience, can it raise money touting the significance of its part in publishing a comic book fifty years ago relating to the Montgomery Bus Boycott and the influence that comic had—in turn—to the 2011 revolutionary events in Egypt's Tahrir Square, especially at a time when most staff people it had hired from leading positions within the Black community have left, in part due to the intractability of internal organizational racism? Is it inappropriate to ask, as an organization implies that it should be supported today for apparently helping to inspire massive people's movements in North Africa: what have you really done for us lately?

As the gay and lesbian-led National Black Justice Coalition celebrates the one-hundredth anniversary of the 1912 birth of civil rights icon Bayard Rustin, it is surely correct that many groups who worked with Rustin in his lifetime, or who he worked with and for, rally around to join the festivities. But is it little more than opportunism for the Quaker-based American Friends Service Committee to—in a very public and self-congratulatory manner—place Rustin's name back on the list of authors of the extremely influential 1955 pacifist pamphlet "Speak Truth to Power: A Quaker Search for an Alternative to Violence"? Rustin's name was omitted at the time of the initial publication because of the then-controversial nature of his sexual orientation (a fact which also got him fired from the FOR), despite the fact that he had a long history in nonviolence efforts and organizing in the Black community, including cofounding the first freedom ride (the 1947 Journey of Reconciliation) and ongoing work with Martin Luther King and other early civil rights leaders. Should it be especially disturbing to see the now-brightly-shone spotlight on the Rustin-Quaker connection, when—in the recent and ongoing economic crisis—the AFSC has chosen to especially target for firing many grassroots and national organizers of color, who had been at the core of their own Third World caucus and radical, anti-racist work?

Why, as the War Resisters League (WRL) celebrated our own seventy-fifth anniversary, was the unity that held together a diverse and hard-working national office and executive still, fundamentally, a precarious one? Looking back over decades in the national leadership, there were two broad goals which a number of us had hoped to achieve: to open the organization up to youth activists and a new generation of resisters, and to set the organization on a course where self-conscious white anti-racism and an acceptance of leadership from people of color would be a norm in an organization that actively included poverty, sexism, and the many manifestations of racial injustice in our definitions of and campaigns against the causes of war. The WRL, we felt, must understand that amongst the root causes of war were and are the economic and police wars which continue to take place daily on U.S. streets, manifestations of the internal colonial, neocolonial, and oppressed second-class citizen status which the empire requires to stay alive. Why is it so easy—with a world of experiences from the old, New and even-newer left, and with an incredible amalgam of wonderful and eccentric activists—to be able to say clearly that we have, indeed, achieved the first of those goals, but have, in fact, failed with regard to the second?

Why, as an organization committed to an end to violence, have no campaigns been developed centering upon the increasing violence against communities of color within the United States, a country and empire that is "at war" with so many of its own so-called citizens as much as it is at war in the Middle East? Why have we still not been moved?

There are, of course, at every point along the line, clear and apparently logical answers to why one or another project proposal or personal attempt at widening WRL's inclusiveness could not or would not work out. No white activist has ever said that they were against diversification, nor has anyone suggested that an anti-racist perspective was unimportant; the problem is a much subtler one that. It is true that, over twenty years ago, when several of us successfully proposed that WRL commit itself to looking at the links between racism and militarism in a campaign linking us with South Africa's End Conscription Campaign (ECC), a number of key leaders suggested that we were pointing the League in the wrong direction, that anti-apartheid work was being done by other groups and our own work—on disarmament or conscientious objection—would somehow be lost if we were to engage in even a little bit of connect-the-issues solidarity. Others, who supported those links at first but saw that they were in a small minority, were later quick to criticize every misstep taken during a national speaking tour.

It had seemed clear to some of us that these efforts, not designed simply to throw WRL as one of many into the existing solidarity movement (though there should be nothing wrong with playing an important, behind-the-scenes supporting role), could help to bring about some key changes in the way we looked at and did our work. We could, through spotlighting the links, which our fellow war resisters in the ECC made between resisting militarism and resisting racism, bridge constituencies and individuals within the United States who might be ready to work together but often not in contact. We could help get WRL's anti-war message to groups in diverse communities who are sometime unclear on those points, and on our secular, unilateralist approach to nonviolence. We could teach WRL organizers something about the new groups and peoples they were coming into contact with, groups already engaged in their own communities and local areas in African solidarity. In hindsight, one of the only consistent African American leaders within WRL over the past two decades joined us during this campaign; another was brought closer to us some years earlier, when we made part-time staff space for an organizer around Central America issues. These projects have come and gone, yet as an organization we still seem hesitant at times to learn any lessons, or even to remember the history.

Sometimes these hesitations grow out of little more than apparently aesthetic or cultural considerations, in something as simple as the modification of a logo. In 2005, a small group of SKA-influenced West Coast WRL designers and organizers came up with what they felt was a quirky change in WRL's traditional broken rifle trademark—something which would graphically demonstrate our commitment to greater diversity. The "integrated" broken rifle, though adopted for a time by some activists in the War Resisters International, was ultimately rejected by WRL's National Committee, with concerns that the image didn't adequately reflect what diversity should be about, or that the image suggested more violence on the part of people of color (a silly idea, as it is a Black hand *breaking*, not using the rifle), or simply that any change of the logo would be a bad idea. In any case, though a small example of resistance to change, it should be painfully clear that cultural considerations are never simple or insignificant. Cultural and political changes must surely go hand in hand.

At a time when police violence is at an all-time high (affecting mostly people of color), when the prison industrial complex has rivaled the military-industrial complex (with more African American men in jail in 2012 than enslaved in 1850 before the start of the civil war), when—in poor countries—high intensity (and often low intensity) traditional warfare has been partially replaced by economic recolonization, and when, domestically, economic conscription has been so successful that only the cream of poor communities can go into the armed forces while the rest are faced with the choice of dead-end, part-time, infrequent jobs and violent crime, at a time like this our own agenda, projects, and politics have only begun to see significant shifts in how we analyze the world. The content of our program work has barely changed, and our ability to become a broader organization by attempting to make these connections has barely begun.

Beyond programmatic priorities, what can we learn from the systematically unsuccessful struggles at fostering one-on-one working relationships across the racial divide?

Personnel committee reports, executive committee minutes and personal conversation will reveal a world of usually small items pertaining to the specific concerns of each of the revolving door of staff members and national committee members "of color" who have joined and left the organization since the early 1980s. Looking over the list, one finds people from different geographic, economic, and social backgrounds, with widely different politics from one another. It is hard, therefore, not to raise a question concerning what they all have in common. In addition to the fact that each worked in an office and organization where their race, culture, or ethnicity was far from dominant (or even a substantial minority), a common thread of critique can be traced from most of these individuals to a consistent concern over WRL's commitment to diversification and an anti-racist politics.

*

Conflicts and crisis in all of the institutions of the last hundred years of U.S. peace action must be seen in light of the left history described here. Individual administrative committees may complain about tardiness of some staff or Board member, or lack of cleanliness or clarity on the part of another. These are early signposts of our cultural divide. The air of often unspoken distrust around issues such as illness or disability issues, for example, are also often masks for deeper fears and feelings. Though it may seem like we speak the same language, the nature of what constitutes a supportive statement or confrontational accusation or neutral and appropriate query is reflected less in actual words spoken as in nuanced tones and what is left unsaid. Substantive political discussions could and should take place on issues such as the meaning of "the illusion of inclusion" or differences amongst how people and communities of color respond differently to the white peace movement, or how one-on-one, one-at-a-time outreach organizing compares to more radical shifts in mass organizing approaches, structural and institutional changes, and basic shifts in analysis and approach. So many of the peace movements problems in this past, "post-1960s and '70s" upsurge/backlash period, have, I believe, to do with a basic, deeply rooted, culturally focused, and unanswered question: are we, the leaders of these white, peace movement institutions, willing—after decades of diverse political perspectives but homogeneous cultural and racial leadership—to fundamentally shift or share power?

Several indicators, indirect though they may be, suggest that our general answer is "No." When we make decisions about whom our spokes people will be, we give indicators of our answer. When we deliberate on who's the boss in an office-based or executive-mandated question, choosing between titled administrative or titled programmatic leaders, we give indictors of our answer. When we nit-pick around financial issues or allow an easier flow of cash for one or another of our program areas, we give indicators. And when we give the necessary open space for the fluid development of a project, or raise consistent critiques and concerns of another even after it has been passed by our decision-making committees, we give indicators of what we are and are not ready for.

Looking back over the recent past, our indicators have been mixed; that "no" is neither a conclusive nor definitive one. And it is most definitely not the responsibility (though it would be easy to characterize it that way) of a few racist stalwarts who stand in the way of change. We—all of us—are responsible for our organizations political and cultural climates. We must all look at our individual and collective roles in maintaining unnecessary divisions and failing to fully embrace change. The struggles over our response to fundamental change are ultimately necessary and good, but struggles must have conclusions, and—I suspect—the "conclusion" to the struggle of old left peace institutions' ability to deal squarely with racism will have long-term effects on the ability of our groups to survive successfully into the twenty-first century.

As some folks know more clearly than others, survival is more than a passing concern. Just as the finishing touches were being put on the editing of the book that borrows its name from this essay, I was privileged to witness a round-table discussion between Wampanoag leader and educator Linda Jeffers Coombs and Pulitzer Prize–winning author Geraldine Brooks. The topic was Brooks's book *Caleb's Crossing*, a work of historical fiction based loosely on the real-life Wampanoag intellectual Caleb Cheeshahteaumauk—the first Native American to earn a degree from what was to become Harvard (way back in the late 1600s). The venue for the discussion was the Aquinnah Cultural Center, in the heart of Wampanoag territory in Massachusetts, so there were more than a few Wampanoag elders present—but the crowd was still majority non-Native. After an hour of insightful and intense dialogue between Coombs and Brooks, suggesting both that Brooks's process of developing the book had probably violated some basic principles of self-determination but also that Brooks was somewhat open to making some revisions in future editions, the conversation opened up to the "audience." One "white person" after another spent their entire talk-time directed angrily at Coombs, criticizing her for the audacity to confront Brooks about her work ("it was just a work of fiction, after all"). Though certainly a "progressive" community, there was no sense that the struggle for survival, self-definition, and dignified independence and interdependence was an ongoing issue for these "people of the first light" who saved the Pilgrims from starvation before colonialism had fully robbed them of their land and livelihoods.

One audience member non-self-consciously spoke of how historical memory is preserved in Auschwitz as a rationale for why Brooks should not modify her work ("the concentration camps are not 'annotated'; they are just left for people to see"); another praised Brooks for bringing to her attention this tribe of such interesting people. It occurred to me after the event that visiting this well-touristed part of Massachusetts without knowing about the ongoing existence of the Wampanoag is something akin to visiting modern-day Germany or Poland without a thought that large numbers of Jews had once lived there. Insensitivity here would be an understatement; what we fail to collectively take responsibility for are the small ways in which we continue to perpetuate, enable, or ignore genocidal policies and practices. As the title of a film on the ground-breaking Wôpanâak Language Reclamation Project (and the work of MacArthur awardee Jessie Little Doe Baird) states: *We Still Live Here*. But white folks, reactionary as well as progressive—right, center, and even left—live (and own) practically everything everywhere, right? The problem we white people face (even and maybe especially progressives) is our own lack of sense of agency and affect in given situations, and the ways in which we take survival, the commons, and humanity's collective future for granted.

This problem becomes compounded when we "discover" the ways in which real change about racism occurs. The recently published *Fire in the Heart: How White Activists Embrace Racial Justice* suggests that, unlike the overt racism more present 30 or forty years ago, the issue facing twenty-first century activists is largely one of "white passivity in the face of continued inequality." Author Mark R. Warren, a Harvard-based sociologist, conducted research on the ways in which white Americans embrace justice and change, finding evidence that the conventional wisdom about methods currently popular amongst anti-racist organizers may in fact be inherently unproductive. His summary of what now needs to be done combines engagement of the "heart, hand, and head." Only when people's values are actively confronted and engaged, especially through action in which we build relationships outside of our circles of comfort, and also when those actions align with our knowledge and interests, do we come to a place of lasting commitment. That the white left might have the power to organize and motivate people in this manner is too rarely understood, as we drift further away from the basics of neighbor-to-neighbor grassroots encounters.

Since the U.S. left as a whole does not self-reflectively understand the power we do hold in shaping society, we are poorly suited at understanding the personal and political ways in which we (individually or within one medium-sized organization) hold onto status quo power dynamics. Institutional racism, which all white folk in this society are exposed to and trained in, suggests that the privileges we accumulate alone or collectively are often barely visible, and are difficult to simply disavow or re-distribute. This brief review of a century of progressive struggle between the races has noted that no single "politically correct" formula, model, or solution exists. Certainly integrated organizations should not be seen as the be-all-and-end-all solutions to racism that they are often characterized as being. It is an open question as to whether any predominately white peace group has ever successfully evolved into a truly lasting, multiracial, integrated, power-sharing organizational arrangement. But the model of maintaining predominately white groups which are nonetheless anti-racist, working in dynamic collaboration with individuals and groups from other movements and constituencies, acting in direct and consistently accountable ways to the peoples most affected by the injustices of the empire is also, clearly, no easy model to build or follow.

*

One thing remains clear: one hundred years after Du Bois's initial pronouncement, that divisive subject that rears its head with great persistence has seen little progress, even amongst the most radical of organizers within white society. Some now proclaim themselves "race traitors," attempting to opt out of white skin nationalism by virtue of their noble proclamations. As far as this observer is concerned, though race may be little more than a social construct, and those who work in favor of radical power shifts across the color line are undoubtedly treated like traitors, the task of changing the politics of our country or our movement is far, far more complex than the proclaiming of opting out of white skin privilege. The logic of freeing oneself or one's group from the clutches of a deeply rooted social evil, even though the good and necessary taking of a strong anti-racist perspective (or participating in an action, or developing a program), does not bear out upon historical inspection. Whiteness is more than simply a privileged self-perception that can be removed with the proper consciousness-raising. White skin privilege cannot be simply given away; once one is understood to be "white," the process of sensitization to those oppressed in a racist system must be a twenty-four/seven, lifelong commitment. Our privileges—including the privilege to simply not think about the issue of race for even one minute of one day of the year—must be constantly challenged, not denied. We must commit and re-commit ourselves again and again; we must prove and re-prove ourselves until one hundred years after all oppression has ended. Only then can we say that we are free, able to live "colorblind" in a society with diverse peoples.

A self-confessed weakness of this very polemic is that it does not offer concrete programs for future work. In part, there are ideas which I believe would serve to address the problems of racism in the peace movement. A serious campaign targeting police brutality would go a long way in indicating a shift in analysis, especially one that would correctly conceptualize the police as an occupying force in a country moving steadily toward "friendly" fascism in the context of the right-wing war on poor people of color (the white poor is more often the target not of attack, but of outreach to those of the ultraright). Training in skills of interpersonal, cross-cultural sensitivity might still be necessary, but not those of the liberal, corporate variety, and not as an end in themselves. Institutionalized racism needs to be studied as a system, and should be addressed in facilitated trainings that have as a goal broader coalition work with our political allies across the divide (coalition work that doesn't simply call others to help shape our campaigns, but that requires us to listen carefully about their diverse priorities and how we can make those priorities meaningful and relevant to our own constituencies). We already know some of the types of issues that coalitions may easily be formed around; the far-from-leftist Amnesty International has now withstood enough pressure and gathered enough evidence to target the United States for our domestic human rights abuses, such as the holding of political prisoners and the maintenance of prisons which violate our own legal definitions of cruelty; issues of FBI repression and torture; colonialism and neocolonialism.

But this paper was never meant to be a program proposal, and there are other parts of this section of this book that will look more concretely at suggestions for change. I also believe that there are a number of potentially correct ways to move forward, and that different groups must engage in honest discussions if they/we are to find the ways and the programs most appropriate to them. A lack of movement, however, a lack of serious discussion and action, will do worse than simply keep us where we are. I do not believe that the peace movement can continue to ignore these issues, or—more fundamentally—can continue to attempt to deal partially with these issues on occasion while at the same time working to deflect or deny the immediacy and urgency in dealing with the divide. A strategy of trying to appease all positions at a given moment will not lead us to healthy organizations or to a movement that grows. It will lead us to further alienation, irrelevancy, and organizational death. Hard decisions must be made.

Mumia Abu-Jamal, a former Black Panther Party leader and current political prisoner/journalist who continues to languish on Pennsylvania's death row, wrote a response years ago to then-President William Clinton's Commission on Race. The Commission was, Mumia suggested, "a relatively cheap solution to an intractable problem; a talk-fest that barely satisfies; a rational discussion of that which is, at best irrational: race."

Let us plan for the future together, attempting to learn all of the lessons of our complicated past. Let us realize that it will take much more than a talk-fest, and more than a single event, position or platform, however rational. Real change is always costly. And, as we block the doors of the Pentagon, demanding a shift from military spending to economic conversion that meets human needs, as we sing out to the war-makers that "We Shall Not Be Moved," echoing the words of the Negro spiritual adopted and adapted by the civil rights movement, let us ponder why, as a peace movement, on the fundamental issue of race, we have still not yet been moved.

And then—carefully and strategically, and full of dynamic energy and a hopeful spirit for the movements we must build—let us plan our next steps.

CISPES in the 1980s

Solidarity and Racism in the Belly of the Beast

Suzanne Ross

This original paper is based on the very heated struggle which took place between 1981 and 1985 in the largest anti-war movement this country had seen since the end of the U.S. war in Vietnam. The challenges of how to build an anti-war movement, how to address the issue of white supremacy in the left, and what solidarity with an international struggle means in terms of maintaining both a sense of accountability to the country in struggle and to build-ing a movement in this country, were all critical questions back then; they remain so to this day. The Committee in Solidarity with the People of El Salvador (CISPES) was founded in 1980, in coordination with the founding of El Salvador's broad, leftist coalition of guerilla organizations, the Farabundo Martí National Liberation Front (FMLN). In this work, she is attempting to practice the kind of vision she espoused back in the 1980s about how to build a single-issue movement while also being committed to the larger struggle for peace and justice, thereby hopefully strengthening both.

Introduction

The Farabundo Martí National Liberation Front (FMLN), the revolutionary leadership of the Salvadoran struggle, consisted of five organizations, one of which, the Fuerzas Populares de Liberacion (FPL), was particularly involved in CISPES work. In 2009, the FMLN candidate, Mauricio Funes, won the presidency of El Salvador. The FMLN had shifted several years earlier toward active participation in electoral politics, and prior to the presidential elections won the majority of the mayoral elections throughout the country. But in the early 1980s, the FMLN was a revolutionary organization fighting the U.S.-backed puppet government and right-wing paramilitary forces that had free reign of the country. While engaged in international diplomacy and education of the people, the FMLN was primarily conducting a very effective armed struggle against the puppet government.

CISPES was the largest of the U.S.-based anti-war groups of that era and the only one working in close collaboration with the FMLN and openly supporting it. With Ronald Reagan's inauguration and his stated determination to defeat the Salvadoran resistance, in the aftermath of the 1979 Sandinista victory in neighboring Nicaragua, the struggle in El Salvador and the U.S. support quickly intensified. The FMLN, and the

FPL, in particular, saw CISPES and the U.S. anti-intervention movement as strategic in preventing a U.S. invasion of El Salvador. During this period, CISPES meetings in New York City regularly drew an attendance of between fifty to one hundred people, and a dominant slogan was "El Salvador: Another Vietnam." The focus of this article is on the early years of CISPES, from 1980 to 1985.

When founded and in its earliest years, the CISPES leadership maintained a very rigid definition of total accountability to the Salvadorans, even on the question of how and with whom to build the anti-war movement in *this country*. The National Office staff was young and relatively inexperienced and accepted this leadership, having little experience or commitment to building a movement in the United States. Staff members were often more familiar with what was happening in El Salvador than with what was going on in the United States or even in Washington, D.C., where the office was situated. Similarly, National Office staff and leadership were more familiar with the history of political struggles in El Salvador than the history of the progressive movement(s) in this country. Additionally, several of the National Office staff members were in personal relationships with FPL leaders, and that only strengthened the voice of the Salvadorans within the movement.

There was overwhelming agreement within CISPES that there should be total accountability to the FMLN on issues having to do with how the struggle was going to be waged in El Salvador—militarily, politically, and diplomatically. But disagreement gradually developed regarding who was responsible for developing the strategy for building the anti-war movement in this country, and what was the most effective way of doing that. Some argued, this writer among them, that building a strong anti-intervention movement required being engaged with the most active struggles in this country, particularly with the Black and Brown communities. The discussion also became one of principle: how much responsibility do solidarity activists supporting a revolutionary struggle in another country have to contributing, at the same time, to building an anti-imperialist movement or a movement for peace and justice in this country? Needless to say, the issue of white supremacy was totally intertwined with this discussion.

The issues of racism and how to build an anti-intervention movement began taking center stage in CISPES in 1983, as the Jesse Jackson Campaign and the Rainbow Coalition emerged as key phenomena in the African-American community in 1983. Because 1984 was a presidential election year, the progressive movement as a whole became preoccupied with the movement-building energy that the Rainbow Coalition generated.

In June of 1985, the first National CISPES Convention was held. Based on the lessons gained from CISPES' non-involvement with the Jackson Campaign, the New York City-based Mid-Atlantic Region, the Southern Region, and the Rocky Mountain Region (headed by a Mexican-American activist, Gonzalo Santos) came to that conference arguing for a different movement-building strategy than that of the CISPES National Office and Bay Area-based Northwest Region, the two centers in the organization most closely related to the FPL. Our argument was that our movement, while working in tandem with the struggles in El Salvador, also had to be more deeply rooted in the struggles going on in this country in order to build a strong anti-intervention movement.

The people involved in the Mid-Atlantic-led group had played significant roles in the solidarity movement. They included the late Lavaun Ishee, leader of the Southern Region of CISPES out of New Orleans. Lavaun, whose untimely death in 1996 left a significant void in the anti-racist movement in the South, was a remarkable young (but nonetheless experienced) activist who had previously worked closely with the Liberation Support Movement on the West Coast (a collective that produced and distributed revolutionary documents and booklets from the then-raging national liberation struggles in Asia, Africa, Latin America and the Caribbean). She was also the widow of the late Carlos Ishee, a North American revolutionary fighter who was killed in battle fighting alongside the FMLN in Morazán.

Another of the very creative and dedicated activists in CISPES who were struggling for a strategic shift was Bob Ostertag, now an accomplished and well-known musician. Bob had a history in the environmental movement and quickly became a key organizer within CISPES, a much sought after speaker, and later the editor of the national CISPES newspaper, *The Alert!* In the latter capacity he did some remarkable reporting from war-torn El Salvador. Bob also brought to the convention a proposal that CISPES do a caravan of material aid to El Salvador. This initiative was a harbinger of what has become one of the most powerful, multicultural, and internationally heralded solidarity projects in U.S. history: the Pastors for Peace material aid caravans to several Latin American countries (including Cuba, where it has played a major role in challenging the U.S. blockade).

With this background, it is worth examining how CISPES developed in those early years and the decisions and choices that were made by the organization in collaboration with the FPL.

CISPES as a "White" Organization

I had always thought of CISPES as an organization that was typical of the white left in this country in its refusal to seriously address the issue of how to build an organization that does not duplicate the racism or white supremacy of the larger society. Much has been said over the decades about racism in the peace and anti-war movements. The usual descriptions of white supremacy and privilege in the peace movement have focused on:

1. Access to resources, funders and foundations that individuals or organizations of color can't access nearly as easily;
2. The ease with which white people can "relate" to the suffering or needs of people thousands of miles from one's homes but show no comparable concern for the oppressed people of this country;

3. The all-white or nearly all-white composition of these organizations, even in cities or where it would seem a selective or exclusionary process would have been necessary to get such a homogenous racial composition.
4. The arrogance of relatively privileged white people in the imperial nation frequently trying to define what demands those they are supporting should be making: whether or not to engage in armed struggle, whether or not to take up negoatiations with the imperial or local power, etc.

Many of the phenomena described above applied to CISPES. At the point of its largest membership, there were certainly the big contributions that would regularly arrive in the NYC office, and certainly in the National Office (larger than any other group I've ever worked with), mostly from progressive individuals but also from progressive organizations and foundations. Most of the activists had little or no history in the struggles of the oppressed people of this country, certainly not with the Black or Brown movements, and saw no problem with all-white organizations or with CISPES having little or no relationship to the Black and Brown organizations (or even with people in the neighborhoods in which they lived or in which the National Office existed).

The National Office for years had an all-white staff in a city and neighborhood that was overwhelmingly Black. Yet the staff and leadership had no awareness of the Rainbow Coalition when it was formed and based in Washington, saying—when asked—that it did not exist in Washington! And while it surely would have been unrealistic to expect Black and Latino activists or supporters to join an all-white organization, relationships with these forces would be key to building a strong anti-intervention movement; yet these relationships were not pursued. In Washington there was no real attempt to link with the anti-apartheid forces and the Black organizations fighting in support of the liberation of South Africa, or with the D.C. Statehood movement, or with the All African People's Revolutionary Party (the late Kwame Ture's group)—let alone with the Rainbow Coalition.

It was not the "left" that was being avoided in some anti-communist concern or unconscious bias. Both the Communist Party USA (CPUSA) and the Socialist Workers Party (SWP) were present at the founding meeting of CISPES, and several left parties played roles throughout those years on the the local level. It was the blindness or avoidance of the Black movement that accounted for this pattern of omission. It was very significant that CISPES did not participate in the coalition of forces working to build the twentieth anniversary commemoration of the historic 1963 D.C.-based March for Jobs and Freedom. That 1983 march, which was organized out of Washington, D.C., where the CISPES National Office was located, brought together 300,000 progressive people. Participation in that could surely have won support for stopping U.S. intervention in El Salvador. Instead, CISPES leafleted at the demonstration, very much as an outsider and had a very minimal impact.

Following the founding of CISPES, there was similarly no attempt in its early stages to link with obvious potential allies in New York such as the Black United

Front, with the anti-police brutality forces, with progressive Black churches, with Black-led trade unions or anti-apartheid organizations. Even within the Latino movements, where there was a more organic connection of language and culture, there was at best a shallow attempt to build relationships. CISPES sought support, but offered little or nothing in return, when doing outreach to the Puerto Rican or Dominican struggles.

Yet, in one important aspect of the colonial white mentality that has sometimes affected the peace movement, CISPES was way ahead of other anti-war or even solidarity groups of the 1960s and '70s. There was a clear understanding that the Salvadorans had to define the strategy for *their* struggle—militarily and diplomatically—and that the U.S. solidarity movement had to support that leadership. There was almost unanimous agreement on this question. Occasionally, someone would raise the fact that we had to be independent and think for ourselves, and not fall into the historic error made by some on the left of blindly following a revolutionary struggle (whether in the Soviet Union, China, or elsewhere). But the strong principle of self-determination was considered almost inviolate in CISPES on the issue of how the FMLN chose to wage its struggle on the ground in El Salvador or diplomaticly around the world. When the FMLN, for example, decided that it was not timely to engage with the "puppet" government of José Napoleón Duarte, a Christian Democrat linked with the CIA or U.S. government representantives, according to former U.S. Ambassador Robert White, CISPES followed that position religiously. We did this even in the face of friends and allies such as the peace movement, Jesse Jackson, and even some in the more radical wing of the anti-intervention forces calling for negotiations.

This makes sense, of course, for an organization that was formed under the leadership of FMLN forces whose primary consideration was the building of a solidarity network. That same FMLN leadership, particularly the FPL, literally handpicked CISPES's national and even regional leadership. But there was also a sense among those of us who were not handpicked by the Salvadorans that self determination was a fundamental principle of all solidarity. Even when the divisions came up within CISPES about how to build an anti-intervention movement, they were not (contrary to some of the descriptions that those who remained in leadership argued) over CISPES's basic principles. CISPES, we all understood, would essentially need to be a single-issue, "solidarity" organization which recognized the leadership of the FMLN. The New York City papers for the 1985 National Conference and the papers I personally wrote (especially in the aftermath of my experiences with the Rainbow Campaign and the the Democratic Convention of 1984), all reiterated these core principles of solidarity. But, for us, that principle was restricted to the issues that had to do with the Salvadoran revolutionary struggle: armed struggle and negotiations, unity and struggle among the five organizations within the FMLN, etc. We all agreed that the basic politics, strategies, and tactics of the struggle in El Salvador was the sole domain of the Salvadorans.

Building the Anti-Intervention Movement

The real differences came up in the area of how to build an anti-intervention movement, and which anti-war or progressive coalitions we should participate in or build alliances with. Deciding who our strategic allies would be, and how to pursue those relationships, without weakening the primary focus of the organization, was the challenge. Here, the deadly combination of inexperienced white activists accepting leadership from Salvadorans who did not necessarily have a strong grasp of the progressive forces or the history of struggle in this country led to some serious errors. Many of these errors related directly to racial bias and a bourgeois view of power.

The New York City—led group, along with the South and the Rocky Mountain regions, felt that developing the anti-intervention strategy in this country was the challenge that U.S. activists had to take up and lead. Part of our conception was that relationships had to be reciprocal—that we were all in some way trying to build a progressive or anti-imperialist movement in this country together, even though we had particular areas of concentration, responsibility, and accountability. Some of the formulations of the Northwest Region in particular made it seem almost a betrayal if CISPES supported a broader movement with anything but an agenda that was 100 percent formulated by the FMLN. Any compromises made in such a movement, the Northwest argued, should only be made on the basis of their usefulness to the FMLN. In a paper called "CISPES and the Anti-intevention Movement," circulated by the Northwest Region at the time, the following was articulated: "A solidarity organization is defined by its basic agenda is [sic] serving the needs of the FMLN/FDR, of the Salvadoran people and their revolutionary process. Our agenda is no more and no less than this. Each decision we make should be based on fulfilling this function. It must be clearly emphasized, however, that this does not mean that this orientation is always put forward publicly."

It followed from this conception, that when CISPES and the Salvadorans did an about face after the 1984 Democratic Convention and decided that the Rainbow was a significant formation, the above guideline was practiced. CISPES wanted the Rainbow to endorse this or that initiative, but never felt it had to offer any reciprocal support. This was not perceived as opportunist but rather as "good solidarity practice."

Our group, on the other hand, saw a dynamic relationship between building an anti-intervention movement for El Salvador and Central America and building a movement in this country. We felt that building each movement in a principled way only contributed to the other, even though our primary task was to build solidarity for the revolutionary struggle in El Salvador. We saw it as the U.S. activists' responsibility to build an anti-intervention strategy that was truly effective, and that required not replicating the racism, sexism, and opportunism of this society. We could not rely on the Salvadorans to provide us with those strategic understandings, as the struggle in this country was not theirs. Building too narrow a definition of solidarity and anti-intervention politics, based on exclusive accountability to the FMLN, actually narrowed and weakened our ability to build a strong anti-intervention movement.

In late 1983 and through the Democratic Convention in July, a choice had to be made between two rather different paths toward building anti-interventionist momentum. We had to figure out, at the very least, how to balance two almost diametrically opposed paths. On the one hand, a coalition called the Central America Peace Campaign had been formed in Washington, D.C., which consisted of white liberal groups who were generally opposed to U.S. intervention in Central America but did not necessarily support the tactics of the FMLN. This Peace Campaign, which grew out of delegations which would go on to found Witness for Peace and the Pledge of Resistance, included the Coalition for a New Foreign and Military Policy, the American Friends Service Committee, SANE, and the Interfaith Task Force on Central America. One of this book's editors, Matt Meyer, represented the War Resisters League on the founding board of this grouping. While respected in congressional circles, most of these groups were primarily staff-centered rather than activist organizations. They moved slowly and cautiously and were willing to go a long way in order to gain congressional support for whatever limited "anti-intervention" position these congressional representatives would be willing to take. They paid little attention to the concerns or priorities of the FMLN.

The hope had been that the Central America Peace Campaign would make U.S. intervention in El Salvador and Central America an issue at the Democratic Convention, since some of its members had clout within the Democratic Party. The view was that Gary Hart, a senator relatively new to national politics, was "less" interventionist than Walter Mondale, a longtime mainstream Democrat. The plan was to use the Central America Peace Campaign to pressure Hart to take an anti-intervention position thus forcing Mondale leftward, and ultimately creating a Democratic Party platform more favorable to El Salvador's interests.

On the other hand, there was the formation of the Rainbow Coalition following the Twentieth Anniversary March on Washington. The 1983 March became the building base for the Jesse Jackson Campaign for president, conducted through 1988 both inside and outside the Democratic Party (though in the end, after the 1988 campaign was over and perhaps even earlier Jackson sadly chose to work only within the Democratic Party and refused to form a third party, as many in the Rainbow Coalition urged him to do). The Jackson Campaign provided a strong anti-intervention and justice-at-home challenge to the Democratic Party and its two leading contenders for the presidency, Mondale and Hart.

As we approached the Democratic Convention, the Rainbow Coalition became stronger and stronger following numerous regional and national meetings and rallies. It defined a clearer and stronger anti-intervention stance regarding South Africa, Central America, and even the Middle East. Thousands of people attended Rainbow meetings from all over the country with religious folks, elected officials, peace activists, members of organzied labor, and even white midwestern farmers joining. The Rainbow leadership (and the base of the Rainbow even more so), strongly supported anti-interventionist positions. As Sheila Collins described in her book on the Rainbow campaign and coalition, *The Rainbow Challenge,* a major part of what the Rainbow projected was an anti-nuclear, anti-war agenda with specific attention to Central America, South Africa, and the Middle East.

Despite the largely overlapping positions of both the Rainbow and CISPES on Central America hardly any interest was shown toward the Rainbow by the National Office or the Northwest Region. Almost exclusive attention was given to the Central America Peace Campaign. Perhaps the Salvadorans, coming out of a history of oppression and domination by the imperialist and capitalist forces, could not recognize power in a force such as the Rainbow. And the young CISPES activists, lacking (for the most part) experience with the Black movement, shied away from becoming involved with the Rainbow Coalition. Thus a huge amount of the organization's resources and personnel went into building the Central America Peace Campaign, hoping for that network to bring an anti-intervention agenda to the Democratic Convention. Much faith was placed in the Hart forces. The CISPES representative to the Central America Peace Campaign spoke of the impending Democratic Convention as though only two forces in the Democratic Party would be there: Hart and Mondale.

In a 1984 paper written by the CISPES National Program Coordinator on how to make U.S. intervention in El Salvador an issue at the Democratic Convention, Jesse Jackson was not even mentioned. In the end, the Central America Peace Campaign did not bring an anti-intevention campaign to the convention and little was gained from that effort toward building the anti-intevention agenda. Hart was neither clear nor strong enough to challenge Mondale's overwhelming support in the Democratic Party, and no challenge was mounted by the Central America Peace Campaign that in any way made visible anti-interventionist politics at the Convention.

In contrast, the Jesse Jackson Campaign/Rainbow Coalition, with its anti-intervention agenda for South Africa, Central America, and even for the Middle East, was very open to our specific campaigns, and included an extraordinarily diverse base of organizations and individuals. This writer, in her work with the Rainbow, developed relationships with people such as Anne Braden, the legendary white anti-racist organizer of the Southern Organizing Committee, as well as with longtime peace leader Dave Dellinger. She made connections for CISPES with Black United Front Chair Adayemi Bandele; Rev. Ben Chavis, Executive Director of the United Church of Christ's Commission on Racial Justice; Dominican Order Sister Marjorie Tuitt of Church Women United; and Jack O'Dell, former adviser to Martin Luther King and key adviser to Jackson. All of these individuals became important allies of ours, and were strategic people to include in the anti-intervention and solidarity movements. They all ended up supporting the FMLN, almost all were at the Democratic Party Convention, but none of them was seen as "key" by CISPES in the Democratic Convention strategy.

The idea that we could gain greater power by aligning ourselves with the more white centrist forces in staff-based organizations, rather than with the much more mass-based, Black-led movements such as the Rainbow reflected a one-sided, bourgeois conception of power. The Rainbow Coalition, which included the more radical and multiracial sectors of the progressive movement, was not only strategic in helping to build the anti-intervention movement, but also helped to consolidate a strong core of solidarity activists—those who would support the FMLN. Yet there was a fear of these people that there wasn't of the Central America Peace Campaign. Concerns were repeatedly raised that CISPES would be gobbled up by the Rainbow Coalition.

There is always the risk of losing one's primary focus when a solidarity organization or any single-issue group participates in a broader coalition. In NYC, those of us who argued for greater rootedness in the progressive movement had certainly made mistakes of our own—demanding too great a unity from other forces who were willing to participate in an anti-intervention agenda but not in a solidarity agenda. At times, in 1982, we would not work with folks who were not going to address the issue of white supremacy but who nonetheless were opposed to U.S. intervention in El Salvador. Yet why was the Central America Peace Campaign, which was not even sympathetic to the FMLN and had positions diametrically opposed to those of the FMLN, not seen as a similar "threat" to the independence and politics of CISPES? Why as only the Rainbow seen as so dangerous? In addition to a narrow definition of power which led the FMLN and those in CISPES who agreed with this strategy leading to an exaggeration of the Central America Peace Campaign's "power" and an underestimation of the power of the Jesse Jackson Campaign and the Rainbow, racist bias surely played some role.

There was no question, on the part of those of us pushing for greater involvement with the Rainbow, that the Rainbow or Jesse Jackson could or should replace CISPES' role as a solidarity organization. The concern on the part of the National Office and the Northwest region, that those of us who worked with the Rainbow would allow the Jackson agenda to deflect from the real challenge of building solidarity, was unfounded. We did not agree with Jackson's insistence that the FMLN should engage in negotiations with the reactionary government of El Salvador and the United States unless the *FMLN chose* that path. We understood, hearing Jackson's report back from his trip to Cuba, that he held what we considered "interventionist" conceptions of "helping" the Cubans. We certainly would never rely on Jackson's agenda for El Salvador; the Rainbow could never replace the solidarity agenda of CISPES. And yet Jackson and the Rainbow were absolutely strategic to building as broad and strong an anti-intervention movement as possible. Avoiding them out of an irrational and possibly race-based fear of their "taking over CISPES" prevented the building of the much-needed, broader movement.

It was clear to us that Jackson and the Rainbow Coalition were leading the largest anti-intervention force we had seen in years. It was they who were bringing that politics to the Democratic Convention. Only a distorted sense of U.S. politics would attribute greater power to the Central America Peace Campaign than to the Rainbow at that moment in history. And only white blinders would ignore the dynamism of the Rainbow.

It would be wrong to say that CISPES should have only been involved with the Rainbow and not at all with the Central America Peace Campaign. But the balance was distorted, based on a lack of recognition of people's power, and certainly based on a deep-seeded bias against Black leadership.

The 1985 CISPES national convention ended with a defeat of our proposal, and "victory" for the national office and the Northwest Region. At the end of the conference about one third of the locals affiliated with CISPES left the group, based on these differences about how to build the anti-intervention movement, and how to deal with racism. The three offices most directly involved in the struggle were decimated. The real story was never really told, because we were reluctant to make still more of a division in this key solidarity organization in the middle of a raging war in El Salvador with the U.S. so actively working on defeating the progressive, anti-imperialist forces. Our grouping did not disregard the importance of solidarity work—and in particular, material aid—as was claimed by those who remained in the organization. However, we did insist that racism within the solidarity movement be dealt with. Lavaun Ishee, for example, urged the organization to engage the People's Institute for Survival (a group that offers workshops and trainings in understanding and fighting white privilege), in an examination of white supremacy within CISPES. She eventually prevailed over the National Office's initial insistence that such a training and focus would deflect from the main task of CISPES.

After 1985, however, in the aftermath of the departure of so many CISPES members, some of the important questions which had been surfacing earlier in the decade were never fully addressed. Since these questions are undoubtedly still relevant, and could be useful to those engaged in building the current and future anti-war movement, this paper addresses those debates and experiences.

What Can We Learn?

It is regrettable that those who remained in the leadership of CISPES, and no doubt the Salvadorans who continued to lead them, did not draw some important lessons from that struggle or at least were not willing to share them. I understand from one of the current National Office staff members of CISPES, from an article that was written by Van Gosse many years ago, and from the current CISPES website, that the history being told is that there were those of us who wanted to submerge CISPES into the Rainbow Coalition, putting it all under Jesse Jackson's leadership! Others heard that we were trying to build a multi-issue organization in which support for El Salvador would be only one of many issues. At that divisive first National CISPES

Conference, Gus Newport, former mayor of Berkeley and a longtime member of the CPUSA-affiliated U.S. Peace Council, was brought in to castigate those of us who were arguing for a different way to build the anti-intervention movement. Newport ironically charged that our "secret agenda" was to build a political party! In these half-truths, mischaracterizations, or outright lies, important lessons were denied to subsequent CISPES activists. CISPES might have played a positive role in contributing to and gaining from an anti-intervention movement rooted in U.S. radical history, maybe even an anti-imperialist movement, had there been more serious thought and discussion.

CISPES, in any case, undoubtedly contributed significantly to the Salvadoran struggle over these three decades. Surely the Salvadoran revolution provided many lessons and inspirations to hundreds of U.S. activists—including this writer—who visited El Salvador in 1984 and met with heroic student and religious leaders, mothers of the "disappeared," labor activists, and workers in the refugee camps. But did CISPES contribute to building the kind of principled anti-war, anti-imperialist movement all progressive activists and organizations should be contributing to? Did CISPES even build the kind of anti-intervention movement it hoped to build or could have built? With the huge base it had, it had the opportunity to build both a solidarity organization and an anti-intervention movement. The example of the Pastors for Peace caravans to Cuba, led by the late Rev. Lucius Walker, provides one important model. With its multiracial composition, and its careful and principled development of the people it sends to Cuba for medical training, Pastors for Peace is widely respected for both its effectiveness in challenging the U.S. blockade of Cuba and for its political education of a new generation of young activists hoping to become doctors.

Those of us back in 1985 who left CISPES over the question of strategy were struggling for that kind of vision: an effective solidarity organization that would also have a major impact in contributing to the building of a principled U.S. anti-imperialist movement. We felt strongly that we did not simply support the anti-apartheid work or the struggle against police brutality in order to gain those movements' support for El Salvador, but because we were committed to those struggles in their own right. Even though they were not the priority work of CISPES, we understood them to be important efforts to support. We never felt we should simply gain as much support as possible from these other forces for solidarity with the FMLN without recognizing the challenges and needs these forces themselves faced. We thought movement groups could have separate priorities while also standing united to the extent possible in fighting the imperialist monster we all face. We understood that we must all work to the extent possible. We saw trying to build principled unity as a basic value of progressive or radical activism.

Such a conception of solidarity holds us all accountable to scrutiny on issues that transcend our political "specialities" or focus. It means that the issue of racism or white supremacy is not a "diversion" from anything, that dealing with sexism and homophobia is not irrelevant to anti-war organizing, and that class bias very much affects all political work. Solidarity activists need to be focused on their primary task, but that cannot mean ignoring the reactionary and destructive pulls of this society. This basically involves the issue of revolutionary morality. What are some of the principles that should guide all revolutionary or progressive work? Che and Fidel have talked and written about his subject at length, as have Amílcar Cabral and Samora Machel. The Salvadorans were so beset with fighting the United States and the various internal struggles within the FMLN that they never in my recollection raised this issue. This was true even when the leader of the FPL, Comandante Salvador Cayetano Carpio (known by his *nom de guerre*, "Marcial") reportedly assassinated his second in command, Comandante Melida Anaya Montes (known by her *nom de guerre*, "Ana Maria") presumably over a profound political difference regarding whether to continue the armed struggle or to engage in negotiations. There were surely internal discussions about this within the FPL but not with the North American activists. Such a tragic human and political development, even if the actual reports about culpability were not resolved, certainly called for some serious discussion.

We North Americans, on the other hand, skirted around the issue of morality. We knew it was not just a question of what was the most effective way of organizing an anti-war movement, but we focused on that and only hinted at the issue of principle. I think, in retrospect, that we felt we couldn't "win" by arguing morality. As it was, people trivialized our position by accusing us of calling those who disagreed with us "racists." Or perhaps we were afraid that people would accuse us of being idealists, not understanding the conditions the Salvadorans faced fighting U.S. imperialism and the neocolonial forces with a very divided revolutionary movement. We were not mature and secure enough politically to define revolutionary morality as a fundamental issue we had to address, but it was revolutionary morality which should have provided the compass to guide our work.

While we did not identify this issue head on, we did argue very clearly that it was essential to address the question of racism both on *principle* and for strategic reasons in building a more effective movement. Strategically, understanding and confronting white supremacy would lead to a more inclusive, more broadly based, and stronger movement. We could not agree to 100 percent accountability to the FMLN while leaving no space to the building of a progressive movement in this country. We could not relate to the definition of power that led to choosing the all-white, elitist Central America Peace Camapign over the Rainbow Coalition when the latter was so much more committed to and effective in promoting so many aspects of CISPES's own agenda.

Twenty-five years after all those struggles took place with such intensity, the challenges we faced then continue to embody critical challenges to our movements for peace and justice in the United States today.

Afterword

THE FPL: Because of the detailed discussion in this paper of the differences I/we had with the FPL on how to build an anti-intervention movement in this country, it may seem as though I am criticizing that organization more than the FMLN as a whole, or that I do not and did not appreciate the many positive and inspiring examples provided by the FPL particularly in their work in El Salvador. The fact is that I felt more closely identified with the politics and practice of the FPL than with the four other FMLN organizations. I will never forget running into their cadre in my short trip to El Salvador in 1984 at refugee camps, at the university, and at the human rights conference. The religious workers, the mothers of the disappeared, the labor leaders who visited the United States: their heroism and effectiveness were truly inspring. But that is not the focus of this paper.

COINTELPRO: CISPES was long surveilled by the FBI and police, in New Orleans, New York, and many other places. We know from the history of COINTELPRO with the Black Panther Party and many other progressive organizations, that the FBI and police often created havoc in the organizations they spotlighted for surveillance. I've often wondered what role those forces might have played in the "split" back in 1985 and in creating such an antogonistic atmosphere at the 1985 convention. That would require an entirely different paper and would still not erase the significance of the political differences that we struggled with at that time.

To Live Is to Resist

Greg Payton and Matt Meyer

When Greg Payton and Matt Meyer first met, it was practically "partnership at first sight." A clandestine plan was brewing among the young anti-militarists of South Africa's End Conscription Campaign (ECC): to defy the intensified repression of the racist apartheid regime, which was narrowing the subjects they could hold meetings about, the ECC would host forums on issues of international concern. "Worldwide War Resistance and the U.S. Movement Against the War in Vietnam" shouldn't be seen as too threatening to the South African authorities; so what if one of the speakers was an African American combat veteran who went AWOL because, as the saying went, "no Vietnamese ever called him nigger!" Meyer and Payton, both active members of the WRI Africa Working Group, wrote this short piece as a reflection on how their international work relates to their daily lives and struggles—and ours.

The connection between resistance and the struggles of daily survival, between war and the causes of war, is a necessary one to make if the peace movement is to be relevant in the twenty-first century. In our travels with War Resisters International (WRI)—throughout Africa, Europe, Asia, and the Americas—we have heard this theme repeatedly: one person's humanity is inseparably bound in another person's realities and only in united struggle can we hope to achieve a just peace. At a time when people's lives are being chopped apart, cheapened by a corporate mentality which attempts to break all of us into nothing more than products and commodities, acts of conscientious survival can become acts of struggle; to live is to resist.

This was clear even in the 1990s, when the two of us convened a theme group on racism, ethnicity and war at the twenty-first WRI triennial held in Porto Alegre, Brazil. With a long history of radical nonviolence, the Brazilian movement characterized their work as "firmeza permanente": relentless persistence. That phrase was originally associated with an incredible 150-month strike (from 1962 to 1974!), when a groups of "snarlers" (as they called themselves) formed the National Labor Front, ultimately succeeding in gaining laws protecting worker's rights, increased pay, and an end to the collusive corruption between the Brazilian judiciary and the industrial magnates. That struggle helped give rise to the ecumenical Servicio Paz y Justicia (SERPAJ), the Latin American nonviolence network committed to base-building and leadership development throughout the continent. SERPAJ-Brazil's own basic objective has been to "be an active service together with other groups, engaged in the construction of a communal, just, participative and nonviolent society where the oppressed class is the subject of its own history, controlling the means of production, and securing union, family, and religious autonomy."

With projects on peace education, Latin American integration, agrarian and urban land reform, and special initiatives on the role of the military in civilian society, the empowerment of women, the struggle for conscientious objection, and the illegality of the foreign debt, SERPAJ-Brazil played and plays a significant role in fostering the progressive changes which have swept through South and Central America over the past two decades. They have long understood that nonviolent philosophy and a desire for peace is meaningless without a program for and commitment to the basic human needs of people at the grassroots. Despite this, the work of the massive landless movement (MST), and the election of populist president Luiz Inacio Lula da Silva, over twenty million Brazilians still live in poverty, with twice that number living in only slightly better conditions. As one activist put it, "We are living in an unslept country: the poor can't sleep due to hunger and the rich can't sleep due to fear of the poor."

This was equally true when we travelled throughout South Africa in the last days of the racist regime—as apartheid laws were giving way to the massive organizing of the United Democratic Front and communities who would literally refuse to allow the old government to function. Sandile Thusi was just one of hundreds of those detained without charge, rounded up because he was a young upstart. His weeks-long fast, and the fasts of his colleagues, rivaled the drama of Gandhi, whose nonviolent soul-force resistance had gotten its start not far from Sandile's birthplace. The thousands of young whites who joined the End Conscription Campaign also understood that something was very wrong with the South African Defense Force, the army which was not only present in Namibia and southern Africa to uphold colonialism, but also was being deployed domestically in South African neighborhood townships. Their resistance to the military draft was made into a concrete and effective way to protest against the official and personal racism, which played a role in every South African's life. Our work with the UDF and the ECC was designed not only to show our support for the liberation movements, but to bring home to our U.S. comrades the connections between resisting racism and militarism. In this, we fulfilled Mozambican President Samora Machel's vision of the true meaning of solidarity: two fists coming together to strike a single blow.

This, of course, was years before the election (or even release) of unrepentant Nelson Mandela, before the amazing (and bloodless) democratic elections of 1994. It was before the much-regarded truth and reconciliation process—which hoped to both affirm the realities of mass injustice, to punish those who were responsible, and also to enable the society to move forward as a nonracial and interracial state. The judicial, political, or economic possibilities of making those high ideals into day-to-day practice may have been limited. But the process nevertheless helped bring to the fore some of the basic interpersonal characteristics which would be needed to build any new cultural or community. "Africans have this thing called Ubuntu which is the essence of being human," stated Nobel Peace Prize laureate Archbishop Desmond Tutu. "It is part of the gift that Africans will give the world ... that the solitary individual is a contradiction in terms. Therefore, you seek to work for the common good."

We, the People of the United States, have hardly begun to understand this gift, or to live in a way that suggests any large-scale understanding of democracy, humanity, justice, or peace. In order to reclaim a position of pride within the world and within ourselves, we must also reclaim the revolutionary roots of our work. Nothing short of a radical transformation of the United States will be sufficient to right the wrongs of a country which currently leads primarily in its racism, sexism, militarism, and materialism. Nothing short of a global network, collaborating in acts of militant resistance, will be able to usher in the "another world" which Arundhati Roy assures us is not only possible but on her way.

Argentine Nobel laureate and SERPAJ founder Adolfo Pérez Esquivel emphatically told us, while together with the WRI, that "we as a people—north and south—must walk together... Our people's work is a sign that, united, we can forge a new dawn." Esquivel suggested that there are three types of revolutionaries. One, he noted, carries a weapon in hand, looking to build everything anew. The second prefers to make revolution over a cup of coffee; but when the coffee is finished, so (too often) is the talk of social change. For the third type, revolution must be a daily act—one created by people committed to transforming our everyday activities as we work to transform the world around us. Only by taking up the personal and political challenges of this third option can we create the conditions needed for "solidarity for the liberation of all of our peoples."

Not Showing Up

Blacks, Military Recruitment and

the Anti-War Movement

Kenyon Farrow

When I was the Southern Region Coordinator for Critical Resistance I once spoke at an event in New Orleans titled "What Now: War, Occupation, and the Peace Movement." I was asked specifically to address why more people most adversely affected by systems of oppression were not involved in local antiwar work. Many of the white attendees were very concerned about how to bring Blacks into antiwar organizing work.

One white attendee from a local organizing project told a story of his organization's commitment to "connecting the war abroad to the war at home." The demonstration of that desire to connect with Blacks was to make the march route cut through one of the housing projects in New Orleans. I suggested this was a faulty strategy, since the march would draw additional police presence in an already overly policed community, in a city infamous for police brutality against Blacks.

This forum was not the first time I had heard this conversation, and nearly two years later, it has not been the last. In many organizations and activist circles, people can be found lamenting the same problem. More often than not, "most affected" means Blacks (and sometimes Latinos or immigrants, depending on the issue at hand). Even when the issue itself disproportionately affects Blacks, Blacks are not likely to be found in much of what the left considers to be valid forms of resistance—meetings, rallies, public forums, demonstrations, and the like.

The question that often underlies the discussion about getting people "most affected" involved is: "Why are Blacks these days so complacent or unwilling to stick their necks out for a 'good cause'?" Does their lack of involvement mean Blacks aren't doing their part to end the war in Iraq? What does their ambivalence about antiwar activism say about the left?

Even though the left is multiracial in many ways, the organizations that hold the seat of power, control much of the discourse, and shape what it means to be "left" are largely controlled by whites. This is true regardless of whether we're discussing liberal or radical organizations. Blacks (and other people of color) working in those organizations usually have to buy into the existing discourse as it is shaped by whites and/or are in constant negotiation to be able to shape the work as they see it. Therefore, if not actively challenging the status quo of these organizations' strategies, Blacks and other activists of color often help perpetuate problematic and narrow notions of what activism and organizing look like and should be.

Enlistment Plunge

In March 2005, Earl Ofari Hutchinson published an essay entitled "Where Are the Black Cindy Sheehans?" on HuffingtonPost.com, the blog for liberal pundit turned California gubernatorial candidate Arianna Huffington. He attempted to answer the question he posed in the title—why are Blacks not involved in the antiwar struggle?

Hutchinson's basic argument is that while Black people are opposed to the war in Iraq, they have historically not supported antiwar efforts—specifically during the Vietnam War—because they feel that the antiwar movement is disconnected from their day-to-day struggles around poverty and racism. Hutchinson goes onto say that Blacks also have too much invested in the Army to launch major opposition to it, since it is a primary source of employment.

Indeed, Blacks are about 13 percent of the total U.S. population and make up nearly a quarter of all Army enlistees. Black women are grossly overrepresented in the military, making up nearly a third of all women enlisted.

According to a 2003 Gallup poll taken near the beginning of the Iraq war, seven out of ten Blacks think the war in Iraq is an unjust one, compared to two out of ten whites. Hutchinson argues that because of overwhelming Black disapproval of the war, Blacks—and by using Sheehan as is a metaphor, specifically Black women—need to take up more action against a war that we clearly know is unjust.

But Hutchinson's contention, and one put forward by many on the left, that Blacks aren't actively opposing the war is simply not accurate. In March 2005, the U.S. Army reported that the enlistment of Black youth was at an all time low, dropping from 23 percent in 2001 to 14 percent by 2005. The report indicated that many youth were afraid of being killed in the conflict. However many also conveyed a lack of desire to serve in a war they felt was unjust. Additionally, the report showed that key role models—parents, ministers, and the like—who have traditionally encouraged military enlistment, are now actively discouraging Black youth from signing up. So the Black community has become actively involved in steering Black youth away from the military. Why is this not considered an act of radical defiance, especially considering the lack of options for Black youth?

Refusal Despite the Odds

It is important to think about what refusing military enlistment actually means for Black people materially. Black unemployment in the United States is usually twice the national average of whites at any given time. Unemployment rates for Black youth consistently fall between 30 and 40 percent. According to writer Dwight Kirk's February 24, 2005, article "Can Labor Go Beyond Diversity Light?" for The Black Commentator, 55 percent of all union jobs lost in 2004 were held by Black workers. Seventy percent of all women who lost union jobs were Black. With consistently high rates of unemployment and recent major job losses in stable union employment, enlisting is usually encouraged by Black parents as a means for their children to have steady employment.

Because of the highly promoted G.I. Bill that promises recruits money for college, many Black youth and their parents—unable to afford a four-year university—see the military as a way to pay for school. Since many attend underfunded, poorly staffed high schools with low expectations of students, Black youth often defer college education until they finish a term in the military, believing that veteran status will give them more leverage in the admissions process.

In addition, youth rates of imprisonment continue to rise nationally, and Blacks are 50 percent of the U.S. prison population. Some Black parents have encouraged joining the military as a means of providing structure and discipline to "troubled" teens that may be imprisoned thanks to the "three-strikes" laws, mandatory minimum sentencing, and the use of police and "zero tolerance" to solve school conflicts.

Oftentimes, young Black women who are perceived as promiscuous or who rebel against prescribed gender norms are encouraged to in the military as a means of "straightening them out." Black women also enroll in the military as a means to get skills in careers often unavailable to women, or to have stable employment to support their children.

Whose Resistance?

In the face of poverty, prison, and unemployment, why is Black communities' collective "NO" to the military not considered an act of bravery and resistance by much of the left? Part of the problem is that the white left wants Blacks to act on its terms, in forms it deems appropriate or recognizes as resistance. Why can't Blacks determine for themselves what their resistance will look like?"

Activists define resistance in a very narrow way," says Kai Lumumba Barrow, a longtime organizer and Northeast Regional Coordinator for Critical Resistance. Barrow says that while marches, rallies, and sit-ins are the most coherent forms of resistance for many whites, Blacks have also resisted through armed struggle, cultural production, and more subtle tactics.

During slavery, those more subtle acts took the forms of work slowdowns, poisonings, and other militancy that did not involve public displays of resistance—a dangerous way to show opposition. While some may debate whether or not Black people are in the same oppressive conditions where more subtle forms of resistance are necessary, the point is resistance is not a formula to be followed like a recipe. Those who are most affected by systems of oppression carry out daily acts of resistance that go unnoticed under the mainstream movement's radar.

Moreover, lest we forget, when Black people do in fact rise up en masse, it is immediately criminalized—usually by calling it a riot—and is violently put down. Whether in Los Angeles, Miami, Cincinnati, Toledo, or New Orleans in the days after hurricane Katrina, Black people have collectively taken action around political issues that affect them and have been consistently construed as violent and criminal. While there will be some show of force by police when whites organize, it will most likely not be labeled a riot. So while not legally enslaved, Black people are still are given the message that to publicly act against the state means to invite additional violence and oppression. Even the left, which sees itself as "allies" to Blacks, will often be the first to decry "violence" as a way to tell Blacks they do not support angry or militant resistance—whether actually violent or not. Many on the left fear Black militancy and discourage protests and forms of resistance that are "too angry."

Another way white organizations dictate their rules of engagement with Black and people of color organizers is through a kind of "safe" tokenization.

"On my campus, there has been a lack of engagement with students of color by the antiwar organizers," says Reginald Gossett, a Black activist and student at Columbia University. "There is a rush to produce a product, which means students of color, specifically Black students, only get asked to be visible at the events, but little is done to involve many of us in the actual planning and organizing."

Blacks are often showcased as part of the antiwar movement at marches or rallies, but their issues and political concerns are rarely allowed to shape the antiwar work in any meaningful way. Always following the traditional march or rally formula perpetuates this tokenization, as antiwar work is more of a dog-and-pony show than a grounded grassroots movement built on actual relationships. As in the case of the white antiwar group that wanted to march through a housing project, the left needs to develop strategies that are cognizant of the barriers to organizing that Black communities face. These include the militarization of Black communities via policing, public housing, and public schools.

With a growing refusal to join the military and the daily resistance to domestic warfare, perhaps Blacks have contributed more to ending the war in Iraq than the left realizes, or cares to admit. I don't know that Blacks need to join the antiwar movement as it currently exists. I am also unsure if we need to be engaged in more public, mass-mobilizing efforts that hearken to the days of the Civil Rights movement.

One thing is for sure, Black youth and Black parents today are exemplifying the old adage, "what if they gave a war and nobody showed up?"

A Challenge to Institutional Racism

Nada Khader

When someone mentions the phrase "the peace movement in the United States," I think of older white folk holding up anti-war signs, asking for troops to come home from Iraq or Afghanistan. I think of a movement that is more focused on what happens outside our borders than on what is happening right now inside our own communities.

The image I have is changing. For that, I and my colleagues at WESPAC, a peace and justice organization in Westchester County, New York, must thank the People's Institute for Survival and Beyond for sharing their powerful analysis of racism with us and for helping us transform the way we approach our work and our mission. We started our two and a half day "Undoing Racism" training with a discussion of why people are poor, including an analysis of power in our society. The training offers a crucial historical context of how race has been constructed in America and of how it is used to maintain and perpetuate a system that benefits people of European descent at the expense of other communities.

Shared Definitions

Two terms that now make sense to me as a result of this training are "internalized racial superiority" and "internalized racial oppression." Across generations, one group of people has been able to accumulate wealth and savings to pass on to their children, while other groups have had obstacles placed in their way to prevent and inhibit wealth and savings accumulation. The dominant group understands that society was meant to benefit them, receiving messages from birth that their group is entitled to the best that society has to offer, while other groups understand that they do not have the same access to power and resources necessary to meet their needs. In any social justice movement, it is crucial to understand the disorganizing impact that internalized racial oppression and superiority have on both our interpersonal relationships as well as on our institutional relationships in coalition-building.

Here, we are speaking about very well-intentioned white people who want the world to be a better, more peaceful place for everyone, but who have been socialized to accept that their community is "more efficient, more effective, better educated, more capable" of remaining in top leadership positions; often these same people include the top donors of the organization as well. As a result, this same group of people develops the agenda of an organization in a way that is safe for the white members of the group, but in a way that may not relate to the deepest aspirations of others.

The Global Is Local

How does this play out in a peace group? Peace groups chant for troops to come home and an end to the war in Iraq, but their movements are largely white and speak to a white agenda. People of color—Indigenous, African, Latino, Arab, Asian—are looking for justice, right here at home in our local communities. When we offer anti-oppression trainings in our offices, the majority of people who show up are people of color and women. Who decides the agenda of an organization? Is it the white members serving on a board of directors? Or is it communities who have to deal with systemic oppression on a daily basis?

Who holds the real power of an institution or a nonprofit? Is the board of directors accountable to the communities they serve or to their major donors? Do staff members figure out what solidarity looks like with oppressed communities by obtaining board permission or by checking in with those who deal with the brutality of our system on a daily basis? Is it easy for white folk to preach nonviolence because their communities are not the ones being targeted by capitalism, militarism, and war?

These are questions that we must grapple with if we decide that we would like to embark upon a truly multiethnic and anti-racist people's movement that is accountable to the communities that receive the brunt of the ongoing legacy of white supremacy in the United States.

How does this transform a peace group? With a deeper analysis, we can now see poverty as a form of economic violence that has been disproportionately devastating to communities of color in a society that was created to benefit people of European descent. Fighting poverty through an anti-racist lens becomes part of the agenda of an anti-racist institution.

WESPAC has been struggling with issues of power, race, internalized oppression, and identity politics for the past decade. Our agenda has shifted from a white liberal anti-war agenda to one that painfully explores the power dynamic involved with community organizing. We have not figured out how to keep everyone on board and happy while this process is occurring. Our institutional interest in racial disparities and profiling has attracted communities of color in a deeper and more meaningful way than our previous organizing. We continue to grapple with the ramifications of a shifting agenda and consciousness in our attempt to maintain our meeting space as a safe haven for all who wish to organize against injustice and oppression. In the end we feel it is the communities undergoing, experiencing and living the oppression who should guide the scope and content of our solidarity with them.

The challenge we have now is to develop a broad multiethnic, anti-racist people's movement that is clear in opposing all forms of oppression and that creates an honest space for difficult conversations about power, both within our organizations and in our society, while keeping our eyes on the goal of creating an equitable society that works for all.

Where's the Color in the Anti-War Movement?

Organizers Connect the War Abroad

to the War at Home

Momo Chang

Oakland-based writer Momo Chang's critique looks directly at the question posed by Elizabeth "Betita" Martínez some years earlier. Originally appearing in Color Lines *magazine in 2008, it reviews the basic question of agenda-setting for the peace movement.*

The occupation in Iraq is going on its sixth year and so are the antiwar demonstrations. While people of color can be seen at the demonstrations, it remains largely a white movement. But in a war where people of color and working class communities are impacted the most ($720 million dollars spent on the war each day) some activists are asking, as Betita Martínez did many years ago about the World Trade Organization (WTO) protests in Seattle: where is the color in the antiwar movement?

Organizers of color in the movement acknowledge that the movement itself does not have the broadest support in the United States. But they cite other reasons for the absence of people of color, specifically that many activists of color are already organizing on multiple fronts, from housing to education and jobs. And if they work for a nonprofit, then funding, time and energy are likely limited to specific issues. Still, organizers like Rama Kased with the Arab Resource and Organizing Center in San Francisco recognize other dynamics as well. "It's always been a challenge to get a Palestine-centered [agenda]" in the movement, said Kased, a Palestinian American who grew up in Brooklyn. "Because it's easy to be, 'I'm against the war. I'm against killing people.' But when it gets down to the nitty-gritty of human rights or Palestine or all this other stuff, they start stepping back."

Over the years, Kased has organized with other people of color in the antiwar movement in Brooklyn, New York, and in the San Francisco Bay Area. Palestine, education equity, Black liberation and queer rights are among the issues they've brought to the table. While many antiwar groups have been supportive, she said, they do little to actually work against the deep-rooted problems of racism and economic injustice.

Army veteran Eli Painted Crow is disillusioned with the war, the military and the antiwar movement. Coming back from Iraq, she recalls facing racism in antiwar organizations. "It's mostly run by white males [and] continues to oppress people of color and women," Painted Crow said, referring to the mainstream antiwar movement. "Because if they didn't, you'd see more people of color in the movement."

More organizers of color are trying now to connect the war abroad to the issues facing their members. This is especially visible in San Francisco, where opposition to the war has been more vocal than in other cities.

Steve Williams, executive director of People Organized to Win Employment Rights (a.k.a. POWER) cofounded the nonprofit eleven years ago to focus on welfare rights in the predominantly Black Bayview/Hunters Point neighborhood in San Francisco. There was some doubt at first about how they would connect antiwar work to their anti-gentrification agenda and to organizing Latina domestic workers. But they found many links. The kids of the approximately 600 members in the organization are constantly bombarded with messages of militarism. Corporations that are building the wall along the U.S.-Mexican border are some of the same ones profiting from the war in Iraq, Williams said.

The first goal of POWER's antiwar campaign is to kick the Junior Reserve Officer Training Corps out of San Francisco's public schools, which is an issue that members can get behind. The talk of the town in Black communities is not about how the military will give people better opportunities, but about how they can keep their kids from enlisting, Williams said. In the army alone, the percentage of Blacks has remained steady at about 21 percent since the mid-1980s, while the percentages of Asians and Latinos in the army have shot up.

"Increasingly, there's less tolerance in the [Black] community to allow the U.S. government to treat us as second-class citizens and to risk our lives at the same time," Williams said, noting the government's failure after Hurricane Katrina as a key turning point.

For some communities, joining the antiwar movement has been easier. The Filipino group BAYAN USA brings many Filipinos to antiwar demonstrations in major U.S. cities and is known for their colorful chants. The U.S. chapter is linked to the Philippines-based BAYAN, which calls for a true democracy there.

Since the United States declared the Philippines a second front in the War on Terror and targeted a Muslim group there, Filipinos have seemed more aware of how the war touches their community. BAYAN USA has also been pivotal in organizing people of color in antiwar marches such as Strength in Unity in San Francisco, an anti-imperialist, people of color contingent.

Following September 11, 2001, Professor Mari Matsuda at Georgetown University Law Center cofounded D.C. Asians for Peace and Justice, a group that is now inactive. She also started teaching a peacemaking course at the law school.

"Every single one of us has war in our genealogy as Asian Americans, and we can use that historical memory of what war did to our countries to oppose the war,"

Matsuda said. Japanese-American groups were among the first to reach out to the Muslim and Arab communities following September 11 because of the history of Japanese internment during World War II.

One of the reasons that soldiers were able to napalm and bayonet babies in Vietnam was because they didn't see Asians as human, Matsuda said. Similar things are happening in Iraq today.

The group Mujeres Unidas y Activas, a Latina organization in San Francisco and Oakland, is also trying to organize their members—mostly household workers—around the war. Claudia Reyes believes that the war abroad is linked to the onslaught of immigration raids. Militarism, war and poverty caused by wars are all root causes of migration, she said. Most of the women in their organization came to the country because of wars in Central America supported by the United States.

Organizers say it's crucial to link the war abroad to the domestic war against people of color and other disenfranchised communities here at home, but this alone might not bridge the gap with the larger movement.

"We need to see more organizations do outreach to people of color," said Kevin Ramirez of the Central Committee for Conscientious Objectors in Philadelphia, adding that antiwar activists need to start going to police brutality and death penalty rallies to link the issues of U.S. militarism abroad to the ones here at home. Founded by white peace activists shortly after the end of World War II, the Central Committee was one of the few white-led organizations to connect racism at home with the Vietnam War during the mass mobilizations of the 1960s and '70s. Today, the organization is led by people of color. Among their current publications is *AWOL!*, a countermilitary magazine that targets youth of color.

Some organizers say that while it is clear that the public face of the current antiwar movement is too pale and male, the deeper problem is that the antiwar movement hasn't been able to develop a broad base of support in any community.

"Even though the mobilizations are big, they have to be bigger," said Berna Ellorin of BAYAN USA. "In order for the U.S. antiwar movement to even break ground at this point, it needs to build the broadest and most uniform front here in the United States, and we're not at this stage."

Williams believes that mass appeal might come if the movement broadens its agenda. "The antiwar movement has missed an opportunity to say how much this war is based on racism," he said. "This war is just as much about race as it is about oil. We have a place as working class people and people of color to play a leadership role in this movement to end the war.

An Open Letter to Anti-Oppression/ Diversity Trainers

Daniel Hunter

Training for Change was created in 1992 as a center for strategic movement building, growing in part out of the work of George Lakey and Movement for a New Society. This classic Manifesto for Nonviolent Revolution echoes our own sentiments in asserting that "nonviolent revolution does not seek the liberation simply of a class or race or nation. It seeks the liberation of humankind."

Fellow trainers,

If you're like me, you're getting lots of requests for two-hour and one-hour workshops. Sometimes it's on very specific skill sets—like how to do a march or increasing facilitation skills. But I'm increasingly finding people asking for short workshops on topics that require deep work and thoughtful attention, like anti-oppression issues (race, class, gender, etc.).

Sometimes I've found situations in which doing short workshops helps make space for longer workshops to happen. But often I'm faced with groups that are cutting back on longer anti-oppression workshops (moving from three days to four hours); or I see groups using the workshops as cover for their organization ("See? We offered a workshop!").

And what most frightens me is that as trainers we're often agreeing to such constraints—knowing full well that we can't build the safety to do deep work in two hours.

I've been thinking about this especially since a recent conversation with folks who asked me to do a two-hour workshop on race, class, and gender differences (I thought it unlikely this workshop would lead to longer workshops; many of them had already undergone shorter trainings).

Rather than colluding with the minimal coverage approach to anti-oppression training—our own "race to the bottom"—I pushed back and found I could actually use that interaction as a teachable moment about structural injustices. (At the group's request, I've removed its name.)

THE REQUEST:

Hi Daniel,

We're looking to schedule a workshop on conflict and power dynamics in community living, particularly around race, class, and gender differences.

We thought you'd be a great facilitator and were wondering if you're interested. The date is still up in the air…both from 3–5pm.

If you are free one of those days and interested, I can tell you more.

I RESPOND:

Hiya! I'm open to doing a workshop with you—and the date you suggest is good for me. However, the idea of doing a two-hour workshop on—let me just repeat what you wrote—race, class, and gender differences.

Frankly, I wouldn't do that. I would consider one day barely enough time to really get in to the issues. So, to be honest, I think it would be short changing your time and my time to go with a two-hour workshop on such a deep and broad set of issues.

If people are open to devoting more time to working race, class, and gender and maybe have some more specific goals in mind, too, I'd be interested.

Warmly, Daniel

THE RESPONSE:

Daniel,

Yes, I understand your reaction, but that really is what we are looking for. Let me try to explain and maybe this will help.

This workshop is a part of a monthly series. The goal of the series is to have more intentional discussion and skill sharing about the best practices of living in intentional community. (We also hope that others besides just the community will benefit from this.) Around some aspects of community living, some communities have very good practices that can be passed on. Around other aspects, we have a lot to learn and talk about.

In planning the series we tried to alternate one month having a process-focused workshop and the other month having a hands-on focused one. So the process ones are deeper than you'd really think you could go into in 2 hours…like "income sharing" is one. And "consensus decision making." And this one: power and conflict around identity differences. The goal in each of these is not really to talk about these things in general—they are big topics and most community members probably address them from a broader perspective in general in other contexts—but more to talk about them from our experiences of living in community.

In terms of this workshop, it will be a challenging one and we do have some ideas about how to make it effective—mostly around creating an atmosphere where people feel welcome to share the good the bad and the ugly so to speak. There are a lot of conflicts that go on around these issues in our houses, and not too many areas to discuss them explicitly.

I hope what I wrote here helps to clarify a bit—what do you think? If you're interested, we could talk further about this, and you may well have suggestions for us…that would be awesome.

I RESPOND:

Thanks for giving me more context. I do understand more of where you are coming from. And I agree with you that it's often surprising how much can be done in two hours. I'm asked to do lots of two-hour workshops on a range of topics and often I'm willing to do them—consensus-building for example.

But consensus-building and race/class/gender work are very different. One is a skill set with high transferability—the other is doing deep work around issues of race and class and gender. The latter requires a strong container, people getting time to share vulnerably, and coaching and prodding in areas to take one's next steps. Doing relevant work on those issues requires working with entrenched attitudes and beliefs.

There are some trainers who will do two hour workshops on race/class/gender—and it's hard to say no since oftentimes groups structure themselves to not spend more time on such issues. But, in and of itself I think it's a structural injustice to give so little time to issues that need way more time. People simply don't grow from such entrenched positions in two hours.

And, I think it's a major disservice to suggest that it does or can. So that's why I'll have to say no again to your offer, even with the context you gave. Again, I'm open for something longer and I do understand the stretch your under.

And I hope I'm at least being clear that my saying no is part of me trying to be consistent in my attitude about growth: that surface level issues could be addressed around race/class/gender in two hours, but that deeper issues couldn't—and, rather than going in with "something is better than nothing" attitude, I'm holding on to the value of anti-privilege work as worthy of being deeply addressed, not merely glanced at.

Daniel

THE SHIFT IS REALIZED:

I agree. Perhaps this kind of workshop needs to be separate from the regular workshop series and a day-long or week-long activity for us, scheduled in the future. Perhaps later when folks are less summer busy and ready to really do the work that it takes and that we need (cause ya know we do need it). Thank you Daniel for pointing out the obvious, and we will definitely contact you later on if you are still interested.

And we're now picking that one-day date!

What became so clear to me in this conversation was:

1. We trainers need to offer clear thinking about what works for good training and stand up for the importance of taking the time do it!
2. If we devalue our work by accepting gigs that we know won't go anywhere, it's to be expected that others will begin to devalue our work, too—why not a 15-minute fast track version of anti-oppression?
3. I got reminded that doing surface level trainings on anti-oppression is likely to result in folks with surface level skills. Malcolm X called that the "liberal fox" and of any skin color they're worse than the wolf in wolf's clothing!

Hope others will join me in this push back!

New Orleans

A Choice Between Destruction and Reparations

David Billings

There is this monument to white supremacy in New Orleans. It is called the Liberty Monument. It commemorates the 1871 Battle of Liberty Place in which local white militia attempted to wrest control of the city from the Reconstruction forces after the Civil War. Thirty-three militia were killed. In their honor, this monument stood at the foot of Canal Street for over 125 years. It stood even as the city became majority African-American in population and even as successive Black mayors attempted to have it removed. It was finally moved—around the corner—in 1999 to a spot just outside the city's French Quarter and next to its waterfront. The Liberty Monument survived Hurricane Katrina.

Just about everything else in New Orleans was destroyed.

The Liberty Monument symbolizes New Orleans to me. During the thirty-four years I lived in the city, from 1971 to 2004, that monument reminded me of who really controls the city. White people do. We own it all.

Before Katrina, Black folks staffed New Orleans. Black folks worked it. But white folks ran it. The statistics are startling. Less than a third of the population of Orleans Parish was white (27 percent) and two-thirds was Black (66 percent), but according to local nonprofit agencies, almost all of the wealth in New Orleans has been held in the hands of whites—mostly the very rich white folks who have been there for generations and profit handsomely from its resources: the river, oil and gas, tourists. Theirs are the houses of the stately Garden District and St. Charles Avenue, and the tucked-away, hidden enclaves of the French Quarter. They survived Hurricane Katrina.

Just about everything else in New Orleans was destroyed.

Here are two scenarios for New Orleans.

SCENARIO I: New Orleans as a new Disney World

New Orleans will be a different city when it is rebuilt. Old money will stay wealthy. But new money will rebuild New Orleans and get even richer. The future of New Orleans will be Disney World: not the California or Florida version, but a raunchier version—more like Vegas or Rio. It will be replete with gambling casinos and restaurants galore. It will have music clubs and second-line parades. Bourbon Street will have strippers and Café du Monde will still sell beignets, but it will all be fake: "Faux New Orleans," if you will. Sanitized, commercialized, tourist-flavored New Orleans available to all at a price only a few will be able to afford.

It will have to import its funk.

Workers will have to be trained to dance in second-lines and flambeaux carriers will be outlawed as fire hazards. Mardi Gras parades will continue on St. Charles and down Canal Street, but the bands will be hired and brought into town and the crowds will be made up of people from the Midwest and points north. Few locals will remain.

Just about everything else in New Orleans will be destroyed.

In this scenario, there is no way all those poor folks are going to be allowed to return home. The poor folks you saw screaming for help on television. The people who were trapped on rooftops and nursing homes and hospitals and evacuation centers as the waters rose and the food and drinking water ran out. They will be dispersed across America. They are not the type of poor people likely to elicit this country's sympathies. Not for very long.

The United States likes poor people to be docile and compliant, certainly grateful and appreciative for the help given them. However late and however limited this help might be. But many of New Orleans flood victims were anything but grateful. They were angry and frustrated over years of neglect, injustice, and unfair treatment. While Katrina was the most recent example of institutional breakdown when it came to poor Black people in New Orleans, it was not the first.

In 1927, during the Great Mississippi River Flood so well chronicled in John Barry's book *Rising Tide*, the levees were bombed to save the French Quarter and the Central Business District at the expense of the poor and working class people of the city's Ninth Ward and the immediate areas adjacent to them, St. Bernard Parish. Hurricane Betsy in 1965 would breach the levees again and flood those same areas. One would be hard pressed to find any living resident of the Ninth Ward who does not believe those levees were again bombed to save the rich white parts of town.

Yet New Orleans has a long history of resisting white rule and control. The largest rebellion by enslaved Africans in the United States took place in 1811 right outside New Orleans. Forces led by Charles Deslondes marched on the city. They were called murderous savages and looters. They instilled deep fears in the white folk. Governor Claiborne called out the military. Deslondes was captured, his followers killed and hanged. They were beheaded and their skulls stuck on fence posts as a gruesome reminder of what happens in New Orleans to lawless thugs, looters, anarchists.

At the opening of the twentieth century, Robert Charles, a young Black man from Woodville, Mississippi, was so outraged when he witnessed everyday official brutality and murder of African-Americans in New Orleans that he set out to kill white people. Barricaded in a Central City house, he managed to shoot twenty-seven white people, including seven police officers. What he also struck was those deep fears buried in the psyches of white people of Black men with guns. Massive reprisals of whites against African-Americans resulted in scores of Black deaths.

In 1972, Mark Essex, a twenty-three-year-old Navy veteran from Emporia, Kansas, went on a shooting spree that ended on the top of a Howard Johnson's hotel across from the New Orleans City Hall. Essex, African-American, held off the entire police department and National Guard of New Orleans (at that time still almost totally white in an already Black-majority city). Essex killed five police officers, including the Deputy Chief Louis Sergo. Black people watched from chairs they set up across the street from the Howard Johnson's. They were not afraid since they knew Mark Essex was not shooting at them.

When Essex was finally killed, 200 bullets were found in his body.

So when Hurricane Katrina struck and the city flooded, the poor people who shoved and pushed, shouted and cried, knew what was happening. Alternating between being scared senseless and enraged, they knew this was not the first time the systems of the state had failed them. It was just the latest.

New Orleans's poorest people have been dealt with as nothing all their lives. Jobless for generations, they were ignored by the city's schools. At the time Katrina struck, 50 percent of New Orleans adults aged eighteen to sixty-five were virtually illiterate (sources: 1993 National Adult Literacy Survey and http://www.gnocdc.org). Before Katrina, 65 percent of New Orleanians were renters. Most public housing had already been gutted. Five years prior to Katrina's ravages, a federal policy of neglect and disinvestment we can call "Hurricane HOPE VI" had already destroyed four major public housing developments named Desire, Florida, Magnolia, and St. Thomas.

Poor Black people were in the way before Katrina and they would be in the way afterwards. They have no claim on the new New Orleans.

The new New Orleans will be filled with mixed-income developments, subsidized and guaranteed by the government. These mixed-income communities will be carefully monitored to control the percentages of poor people in any given neighborhood. As Congressman Richard Baker (R-LA; Sixth Congressional District, Baton Rouge) was overheard saying shortly after the storm waters wiped out huge swaths of the city: "Mother Nature accomplished what we couldn't. She emptied the housing projects of New Orleans."

The people in charge of New Orleans didn't give a damn about poor Black people. So some of the poor Black people didn't give a damn either. Somewhere deep in their psyche they knew they could all be locked up and forgotten and white folks would not shed a tear. So some of them broke into white folks' homes and businesses. One don't-give-a-damn deserves another.

In this scenario, a rebuilt New Orleans will be a free-market paradise rooted in unbridled capitalism and anti-public-sector values. Finally, in the heretofore most unlikely of American cities, public officials can hand out private school vouchers rather than reconstruct a failed public school system. Finally, they have an opportunity to put faith-based initiatives to work because Black preachers have lost their base. Because everything else in New Orleans has been destroyed.

Or has it?

Let's take a look at:

SCENARIO 2: Reparations for New Orleans now!

Why not rebuild New Orleans as the first major down payment of reparations for the descendants of Africa kidnapped and enslaved in the Americas? Instead of a New Orleans Disneyland built by riverfront developers for condo-buying real estate investors and pleasure seekers, let New Orleans represent a counter-diaspora. Let's rebuild the city with African-Americans and other peoples of color in the lead as a testimony to this nation's efforts to destroy white supremacy once and for all. Let's guarantee that those families spread so far afield by Katrina will design and lead the reconstruction. Let's implement a Second Reconstruction. And this time we will get it right.

Let's rebuild New Orleans with equity in mind, rooted in the strengths that made it America's most unique city. Let's use government resources to invest in and preserve some of America's greatest cultural heritages.

Let's rebuild City Hall in Louis Armstrong Park—in the heart of Tremé, the oldest African settlement in the United States. Build it around Congo Square, the one location that Africans were allowed to gather for celebration, dance, and (unbeknownst to white people) organizing—not as a neglected artifact of slavery past, but as the cultural rooting of a liberated future. Far-fetched notion? Well, Congo Square survived Katrina.

Not everything in New Orleans has been destroyed.

There are thousands ready to rebuild and who have a plan.

Community Labor United (CLU) is one. CLU is organizing evacuees to actively participate in the rebuilding of New Orleans. In their call to action, just four days after the storm, CLU stated, "We will not go quietly into the night, scattering across this country to become homeless in countless other cities while federal relief funds are funneled into rebuilding casinos, hotels, chemical plants and the wealthy white districts of New Orleans… We will not stand idly by while the disaster is used as an opportunity to replace our homes with newly built mansions and condos in a gentrified New Orleans."

The People's Institute for Survival and Beyond is another. It has called for an investigation by the United Nations. "This calamity demonstrates how racism manifests itself in every institution in this country," said Ron Chisom, cofounder of the twenty-five-year-old organization headquartered in New Orleans. Core trainer Daniel Buford said from the West Coast office of the Institute, "We need the United Nations to oversee an international public works campaign similar to the post-tsunami rebuilding efforts in South Asia and the Pacific. We can't allow this tragedy to become a 'cash cow' for those who always benefit from war and crisis… Only an international body can guarantee that."

There are many others steeled for resistance. Many of us who love New Orleans, despite its racist history, are looking toward building its future with anti-racist fervor.

Not everything in New Orleans has been destroyed.

Alas, the Liberty Monument still stands. Protected by its proximity to the huge concrete barriers that hold the Mississippi at bay, it is a constant reminder of the axiom that regardless of how much things change, some things remain the same.

Why Not Freedom for Puerto Rico?

Building Solidarity in the United States:

An Interview with Jean Zwickel

Meg Starr

For some anti-racist activists in the United States, the question of colonialism and neo-colonialism are fundamental both to challenging white supremacy and to dismantling the Empire. In this analysis, Puerto Rico is much more than simply another nation or peoples who have to deal with U.S. economic, political, cultural, or military interventions. It is the last major remaining direct colony in the world, and a potential Achilles' heel to imperialist design. With the "special" status of Puerto Ricans living in the United States while disenfranchised when they travel back to the island, with a military draft, military bases, and widespread repression coexisting on lands where "taxation without representation" is very much a daily reality, solidarity with Puerto Rico becomes an urgent task from both strategic and humanistic perspectives. Ruth Reynolds's best friend and cohort Jean Zwickel explains, in this interview with Free Puerto Rico and Resistance in Brooklyn activist Meg Starr, her own experiences with the freedom movement. Conducted for Puerto Rico The Cost of Colonialism, *a primer on Puerto Rico produced by the Fellowship of Reconciliation's Task Force on Latin America and the Caribbean, this interview from 1994 was an early example of direct support for decolonization from the "mainstream" peace movement.*

Meg: I will never forget meeting solidarity activist Ruth Reynolds in 1984. The Free Puerto Rico Committee (FPR) was reeling from a Grand Jury investigation of the independence movement, to which one of our members had been subpoenaed. Our member had refused to cooperate and, like the Independentistas who had also been subpoenaed, she had been sent to jail. When we spoke of this to Ruth, she looked at us sternly and said, "Just another sacrifice for the struggle!" Then she looked away and fell silent. Perhaps she was remembering her own experience as the first European-American to be jailed for supporting Puerto Rican independence, or she might have been remembering Pedro Albizu Campos and the other Nationalist Party leaders she had known—some jailed, some disappeared, others beaten or shot—all in a long history of resistance to colonialism. Without offering us consolation, she had put our trouble in perspective.

There is an old saying in Africa that "as long as the hunters write the history, we will never learn about the lion's perspective." The other view we won't be told about is that of those hunters who refuse to hunt. We need to learn the real history of Puerto Rico from the Puerto Rican's perspective, but we also need to hear from those European-Americans who have said "NO" to colonialism. The majority of white citizens, middle-class and working class, have swallowed the lies of jingoism and accepted the benefits of stolen land or higher wages based on the exploitation of foreign or Native Peoples. Who refused?

Before Ruth Reynolds, Jean Zwickel and their colleagues "discovered" the Puerto Rican movement, progressive organizations in the United States had done very little work on issues of Puerto Rican colonialism. After the Spanish-American War of 1898, an American Anti-Imperialist League did form, protesting the U.S. military takeover of Guam, the Philippines, Puerto Rico, and Cuba. The League numbered 40,000 members at its height, and the political reasons for opposing imperialism were varied. Some expressed genuine humanitarian concerns, while others offered a racist isolationist perspective and feared an influx of "uncivilized colored people" to the United States.

A progressive Italian-American congressman, Vito Marcantonio, spoke out in Congress during the late 1930s and 1940s, supporting Puerto Rican independence and a process of decolonization. After the infamous Ponce Massacre in 1937, when the United States directed Puerto Rican police to open fire on unarmed demonstrators, killing twenty-one and wounding 150, the American Civil Liberties Union wrote a report condemning the event.

When Jean and Ruth founded the American League For Puerto Rican Independence in 1946, it became the first progressive U.S. group to specifically dedicate itself to Puerto Rican solidarity. The American League leaders challenged their fellow pacifists by supporting the Nationalist Party, which was not a pacifist organization. After the 1950 Jayuya rebellion on the island, when 5,000 Nationalists were jailed or shot, Ruth Reynolds spent seventeen months in prison for "advocating the overthrow of the U.S. government in Puerto Rico." Rather than increasing support in this time of repression, the American League and the Nationalist Party were isolated from other progressive peace and justice groups. The American League dissolved shortly after Ruth's release from jail.

During the 1960s, the Independence movement recovered from the repression of the previous decade. Within the United States, the Puerto Rican Young Lords exposed the colonialism that existed in our inner cities as well as abroad. The national liberation and resistance movements in Vietnam taught a generation of "new leftists" the possibilities for new forms of solidarity and support. Out of these lessons, renewed activity focusing on Puerto Rico seemed possible. In 1974, the Puerto Rican Solidarity Committee (PRSC) had twelve chapters throughout the United States and hundreds of members. Though PRSC split after only a few years, with differences over support of Grand Jury resisters and the imprisoned Nationalists, the Free Puerto Rico Committee was formed in 1977 (under the name "New Movement") and has continued to educate North Americans about the realities of Puerto Rican colonialism—both in Puerto Rico and here at home.

The following interview with Jean was conducted to bridge the gap between our generations of activism and to understand the continuity of our work and the work that still needs to be done.

Meg: How did you first become a supporter of Puerto Rican Independence?

Jean: It seemed a tragedy at the time. But it turned my life around in the direction of world concerns. I lost my job as a French teacher along with an easy, conventional life. As luck would have it, no other teaching job turned up. I retreated to a religious, pacifist community in New York City, the Harlem Ashram. Founded by Jay Holmes Smith, former missionary to India deported because of his support for Gandhi, the Ashram was involved not only in interracial and peace work but in active support of "Free India!"

Pedro Albizu Campos, Nationalist Party leader who was bedridden in a New York hospital, heard of our concern for India and invited us to visit him. If freedom for India, who not freedom for Puerto Rico, the responsibility of our own government?

At first, our group seemed isolated in its support of independence. Pacifists were not only disinterested, but regarded us as "out of the fold" because of our association with the "revolutionary" Albizi Campos. A. Philip Randolph, international president of the Brotherhood of Sleeping Car Porters, was supporter of the Ashram, but not of Puerto Rico. The one contact we had with a Socialist was unfortunate. We had formed an American Committee for Independence and were delighted when a Socialist friend joined in. Much to our dismay, however, he presented a set of bylaws that did not clearly support a process of decolonization. We turned in distress to Pearl Buck, who advised us to dissolve and start over again.

I recall the incident in which Vito Marcantonio, New York congressional representative and member of the American Labor Party, ripped out a bug from Don Pedro's hospital wall after venting his outrage over the intrusion into Don Pedro's privacy. The American Friends Service Committee published selected speeches by Marcantonio, including once in which he introduced his first bill for the independence of Puerto Rico.

Lydia Collazo speakers of sympathetic support by members of the Catholic Worker movement during the imprisonment of her parents. The Women's International League for Peace and Freedom has supported Puerto Rican Independence since the days of its founder, Jane Addams, an outspoken anti-imperialist. In general, however, we found ourselves in a wilderness of ignorance about Puerto Rico and the whole issue of colonialism.

Meg: How do you think that has changed over the years?

Jean: This interview could never have occurred when I first joined the Fellowship of Reconciliation forty-eight years ago. Recently, Fellowship has ventured a few articles on Puerto Rico. I struck a wall of silence whenever I visited the War Resisters League office, until its National Conference of 1990 included Puerto Rico in its agenda.

Meg: You are constantly lobbying within the pacifist community for more support for the Puerto Rican independence movement. Why do you think, with so many other issues to address, that the peace movement should do more work around Puerto Rico?

The formation of the United Nations Decolonization Committee proclaimed "the necessity of bringing a speedy and unconditional end to colonialism in all its forms and manifestations." It declared that "subjection of peoples to alien domination and exploitation constitutes a denial of fundamental human rights, and its contrary to the charter of the United Nations and an impediment to promotion of world peace and cooperation." As a longtime pacifist, I have tried for years to bring this realization to peace organization. There are many facets to the creation of a peaceful world. I expect that at one time or another I have given support to practically all issues comprising peace. But colonial oppression is an issue that has been widely ignored and is only beginning to receive recognition.

In the past, peacemaker Ralph Templin fasted in Puerto Rico in his concern for the imprisonment of Nationalist. Quakers succeeded in ousting the U.S. Navy from Culebra. Ruth Reynolds led peace marches. But then the peace movement seemed to lose interest, when it should be giving encouragement to nonviolent solutions.

President Wilson once remarked that it was embarrassing for our country to have a colony. As pacifists, we must be aware of the injustice of subjugating Puerto Rico to our own benefit. In these days, declared by the united Nations as the decade for decolonization, at a time when our government proposed a plebiscite on the political status of Puerto Rico, at a time when many celebrate the "invasion" of Columbus and the Spanish forces, at a time when states throughout the world are declaring themselves free and independent, it is high time for pacifists to become informed about Puerto Rico and the moral necessity for self-determination.

Meg: One of the Puerto Rican independence movement's current campaigns is a unified demand from the major organizations to free the Puerto Rican political prisoners. As a pacifist, how do you support the release of someone accused of armed activities against U.S. government, government property, who take the position that they are anti-colonial combatants and should be tried under international law?

Jean: A Nationalist friend, art teacher and daughter of Oscar Collazo once teased me about how I, as a pacifist, could associate with "terrorists." A publisher once refused help with my book, Voices of Independence, asserting that I could not possibly call myself a pacifist and write about Puerto Ricans who have been involved in violence.

Don Pedro knew that I was a pacifist when he had me prepare a speech about non-violence. My independentista friends know that I am a pacifist. But we respect each other in the realization that we are all working for the same cause, each in our own way. Independentista friends appreciate the fact that pacifists have an important role to play in their liberation.

As for destruction of government property, some of our pacifists have done a good job at it, though armed only with hammers! Actually, most of the violence has been on the part of our government and Puerto Rican violence has occurred only in retaliation.

I know a number of the Puerto Rican political prisoners and prisoners of war. Some have not committed any act of violence, but are accused of belonging to the militant Armed Forces of National Liberation (FALN), drawing a sentence of thirty-five years. Juan Segarra Palmer, accused of participating in the Wells Fargo robbery in which no lives were taken, drew a sentence of sixty-five years—way out of proportion to sentencing of nonpolitical prisoners. Alejandrina Torres was subjected to almost two years in the control unit of [the federal prison in] Lexington, Kentucky. She was held in a small cubicle with no windows, twenty-three-hours-per-day lock-up, and video camera focused on her at all times. National indignation forced the closing of the unit.

At the International Tribunal held in New York during December 1990, the issue of political prisoners and POWs was addressed. Charges against the government of the United States, and those involved, are stated as follows: "The above named defendants are charged with forced colonization and enslavement of Sovereign peoples, genocide, illegal declarations of war against people seeking national liberation, failure to comply with fundamental laws and principles of international law and human rights and conspiracy to commit the above acts. The indictment also charges the defendants with illegal and arbitrary arrests and detentions, denial of fair trials, denial of habeas corpus, cruel, degrading and inhuman treatment of prisoners." The judges, of international prestige, dealt with the over one hundred political prisoners, including not only Puerto Ricans but Blacks, Mexicans, Native Americans, as well as a few Caucasians. Whether or not they committed acts of violence did not obscure the fact that human rights are being denied to people struggling for liberation. Prisoners of war declare that, since the United States invaded Puerto Rico and is still carrying out acts of violence against independentistas, war still exists between Puerto Rico and the United States. I have been visiting with three of the Puerto Rican political prisoners and POWs at Pleasanton FCI. They are beautiful, deeply committed young women. They are gentle but firm in dedication to the cause of independence. One of my friends, Lolita Lebrón, is a deeply spiritual woman, who spent her last years writing religious poetry. I'm not about to tell her that she should not have attached our Congress, after she has suffered twenty-five years of imprisonment. I do not condone her violence, but I can understand the frustration and bitterness over continual harassment by our government, her patriotic fervor no less than that of Patrick Henry.

Meg: Describe an experience, in your years of involvement with the Puerto Rican independence movement, that, more than any other, exemplifies the spirit of the movement.

Jean: There are several experiences I could elaborate on: the little fishing boats of Viennese encircling U.S. battleships; vigilant with a dentist and his wife whose son was twice incarcerated for refusing to answer to the federal grand jury; walking with Nationalists to the cemetery in commemoration of the twenty-one killed in the Ponce-Massacre; marching with thousands on a Fourth of July celebration in demand of independence for Puerto Rico. These have all been moving experiences.

But one personal experience that impressed me most deeply was the 1981 destruction of the squatter community, Villa Sin Miedo (Town Without Fear). We had been camping with the community, which declared itself a "land rescue" of territory the government had set aside for housing and had refused to release to the community. They established through hard work a beautiful settlement of some 250 families, digging out roads by hand, laying water pipes, building homes and a small chapel, planting gardens. The last picture I took of the community, just two days before the invasion, was of a man on his knees sowing seed. It typified the hope of the community for survival.

Troops moved in, drove the people from their homes, set fire to the houses and all their belongings, bulldozed the gardens—a typical search-and-destroy tactic. Some of the families moved onto the five acres provided by the Episcopal Church. Previously self-sufficient, they now depended on the provision of tents, food and clothing. A poignant scene was that of a family planting a geranium in front of their tent.

In time, they were able to purchase their own land, rebuild their homes, and plant their gardens. Unfortunately, Hurricane Hugo destroyed again the simple shacks, and once again the people were forced to rebuild.

I see in this community the hope for economic independence. Muñoz Marín, first governor elected by the people, renounced his efforts toward independence with the conviction that there must first be economic self-sufficiency. Here we have a community growing its own food, developing home industries as well as a clothing factory, freeing themselves from external dependency. We know that governing a colony requires a docile and dependent people, hence the efforts of our government to destroy Villa Sin Miedo.

There are other "land rescue" communities cooperating to develop democratic procedures and learning from each other. I see this as a necessary preparation for nonviolent achievement of economic and eventually political independence.

"National Security" and the Violation of Women

Militarized Border Rape at the U.S.-Mexico Border

Sylvanna Falcón

This piece on the militarized border, and its racist and gendered implications, originally appeared in The Color of Violence: The INCITE! Anthology.

The U.S.-Mexico border represents an uneasy "union" of the First and Third Worlds. Due to disparaging levels of nation-state power, it is a contentious region that has been militarized to violently reinforce the territory of the United States. In this region, daily attacks occur against border crossers in the form of brutal beatings and assaults—including rape and harassment—by the state and by racist vigilantes. Due to the hypermasculine nature of war and militarism, the use of rape as a tactic against women is well documented.

In this article, I explore documented rape cases involving Immigration and Naturalization Service (INS) officials or Border Patrol agents at the U.S.-Mexico border by accessing data from nongovernmental organizations, government committees, and U.S. newspapers. Each of the women in the case studies took some action against the INS, with some of them using an advocate to move their cases forward through an investigation. (Data indicate that some men report being raped at the border, but the vast majority of rapes involve women victims/survivors, at this border and throughout the world.) In this article, I argue that rape is routinely and systematically used by the state in militarization efforts at the United States–Mexico border, and provoked by certain factors and dynamics in the region, such as the influence of military culture on Border Patrol agents.

U.S.-Mexico border militarization rests on two key elements: the introduction and integration of military units in the border region (the war on drugs and national security concerns provide primary justification for involving military units); and the modification of the Border Patrol to resemble the military via its equipment, structure, and tactics. At one time, domestic duties were not part of the U.S. military's mandate. But this regulation changed with the approval of numerous Department of Defense (DOD) authorization acts that facilitated the integration of military units in the border region and loosened restrictions placed on the military for domestic duties.

The 1982 DOD Authorization Act nullified a hundred-year statute prohibiting cooperation between the army and civilian law enforcement, and changing the role of the military in domestic affairs. This act encouraged an alliance between civilian law enforcement and the military, and subsequent DOD Authorization Acts advanced and expanded this cooperation. Ideological and institutional shifts have also had a role in border militarization. Transferring the INS from the Department of Labor to the jurisdiction of the Department of Justice in 1940 altered the classification of immigration as an issue of labor to one of national security. And more recently, by moving the INS to the Department of Homeland Security (the INS has been renamed "U.S. Citizenship and Immigration Services"), the link between immigration and national security issues has intensified.

Sociologist Timothy Dunn draws on low-intensity conflict (LIC) military doctrine to contextualize the militarization of the U.S.-Mexico border. LIC doctrine advocates for "unconventional, multifaceted, and relatively subtle forms of militarization" and emphasizes "controlling targeted civilian populations." The U.S. military-security establishment drafted this doctrine to target Third World uprisings and revolutions, particularly in Central America. LIC doctrine is characterized by the following: an emphasis on the internal defense of a nation; an emphasis on controlling targeted civilian populations rather than territory; and the assumption by the military of police-like and other unconventional, typically nonmilitary roles, along with the adoption by the police of military characteristics.

Dunn's study demonstrates that these aspects of LIC doctrine have been actualized in the border region, indicating that a form of "war" exists there. And in every war, in every military conflict, rapes occur because sexual assault is in the arsenal of military strategies; it is a weapon of war, used to dominate women and psychologically debilitate people viewed as the "enemy."

In the context of mass war rape in the former Yugoslavia, Susan Brownmiller likens female bodies to territory. "Rape of a doubly dehumanized object—as woman, as enemy—carries its own terrible logic. In one act of aggression, the collective spirit of women *and* of the nation is broken, leaving a reminder long after the troops depart." Beverly Allen extends this analogy to the imperialist practice of colonization.

Acts of sexual violence which target undocumented (primarily Mexican) women at the U.S.-Mexico border are certainly informed by a legacy of colonialism, which dates back to the forced imposition of a border in 1848. More than 150 years later, migrant women's bodies continue to denote an "alien" or "threatening" presence subject to colonial domination by U.S. officials. Many women who cross the border report that being raped was the "price" of not being apprehended, deported, or of having their confiscated documents returned. This price is unique to border regions in general; while militarized rapes are part of a continuum of violence against women, I call these violations militarized *border* rapes because of the "power" associated with the border itself. In this setting, even legal documentation can provide a false sense of security, because militarization efforts have socially constructed an "enemy" and Mexican women and other migrants fit that particular profile.

My goal in this article is to make visible a form of military rape which has not been previously considered in the range of military rapes by feminist scholars. Militarized border rape is overlooked because many of the world's border regions are not considered war zones. For example, the U.S.-Mexico border conflict is not typically thought of as a "war," because opposing military forces (or insurgents) are not trying to kill each other. But a war is underway at the U.S.-Mexico border, facilitated by cooperating military and civilian units, and the adoption of a militaristic identity in border patrolling efforts. Furthermore, the stance of the U.S. government on immigration suggests that the United States views itself in some form of war with undocumented migrants. Calls to "shut down" the border, or to build an entire wall along the two-thousand-mile border, are frequently reported in the news and supported by members of Congress as a way to "protect" the United States. And when engaged in any form of war, women are always disproportionately affected.

Feminist scholar Cynthia Enloe explores three conditions under which rape has been militarized. Observes Enloe, "'recreational rape' is the alleged outcome of not supplying male soldiers with 'adequately accessible' militarized prostitution; 'national security rape' as an instrument for bolstering a nervous state; and 'systematic mass rape' as an instrument of open warfare." She also contends that certain conditions that allow militarized rapes are in place on the U.S.-Mexico border:

A regime is preoccupied with national security; a majority of civilians believe that security is best understood as a military problem; national security policymaking is left to a largely masculinized policy elite; and the police and military security apparatuses are male-dominated.

In my view, a variation of national security rape and systematic rape characterize the reality in this border region. First, national security entails the control of labor, migration, and women. In the 1990s, the U.S. government expanded the definition of national security to include "domestic political concerns and perceived threats to culture, social stability, environmental degradation, and population growth." During this time, immigrants and refugees became top national security issues. And in the aftermath of 9/11, the U.S.-Mexico border was completely shut down for several days due to national security reasons, reifying the classification of the U.S.-Mexico border as an area of national security. With a masculinized elite emphasizing the normalcy and role of militarism with regards "national security," broader definitions of security have become marginalized.

For example, the provision of basic necessities—such as shelter, health care, and food—is not seen as a "security issue" by the U.S. government, though international human rights standards and laws do characterize the meeting of basic human needs in this way.

The cases of militarized border rape discussed here can be categorized as a form of "national security rape" for two reasons: first, the absence of legal documents positions undocumented women as "illegal" and as having committed a crime. Thus, law-abiding citizens need "protection" from these criminals; the existence of undocumented women causes national *in*security, and they are so criminalized that their bodily integrity does not matter to the state. Second, national security rape privileges certain interests; in other words, Arizona ranchers who rick up arms to "protect" their property, or recently formed "Minutemen patrols" along the U.S.-Mexico border (specifically in Arizona and California) are seen as legitimate because they are protecting their property, land, and families. Their actions are supported by the state because they are literally taking the issue of national security into their own hands.

Occurrences of rape are systematic if they fall into a pattern, suggesting that they have not been left to chance, according to Enloe. "They have been the subject of prior planning. Systematic rapes are *administered* rapes." In the cases highlighted here, the planning involved is palpable. These were not random acts of violence against women; they were violent crimes that involved planning and efforts to avoid being caught. Additionally, the rapists capitalized on the institutional power over undocumented women, and each man followed their own "script" in attacking these women. These individual patterns became clear during court testimonials by victims/survivors.

Notably, because of the prevalence of sexual violence at the border, a Mexican immigrant woman told the National Network for Immigrant and Refugee Rights in Oakland, California, that women heading north routinely use birth control pills because they anticipate possible sexual assaults. This suggests border rapes are neither random, nor isolated.

From Bases to Bars

The Military & Prison Industrial Complexes Go "Boom"

Mumia Abu-Jamal

This piece, which originally appeared in the Fall 2009 issue of WIN *magazine, connects the dots between the military and the prison industrial complexes.*

Looking back to the halcyon days of the movement against the Vietnam War, one sees the birth of what seemed to be a new world. Every day, one could almost see and touch giant boulders crumbling off the edifice of repression: students protesting from coast to coast—even as some students at Kent State (Ohio) and Jackson State (Mississippi) Universities were being shot to death by National Guardsmen and police, for demonstrating!—a president resigning in disgrace; soldiers returning from war join the protests, many in their battle fatigues.

Few could have envisioned a future some two generations hence, when the nation would not only be involved in two wars simultaneously (also begun under false, misleading pretexts) but would rival Rome in its bases in virtually every region of the world, a vast, armed archipelago of empire erected by the permanent government—the corporate government, on behalf of corporate interests.

As Chalmers Johnson, author of *Nemesis*, has observed, the post-Vietnam military resolved to erect a system immune from the popular and democratic will that spelled the end to that war. In part, they did this by abolishing the draft. Johnson explains: it takes a lot of people to garrison the globe. Service in our armed forces is no longer a short-term obligation of citizenship, as it was back in 1953 when I served in the navy. Since 1993, it has been a career choice, one often made by citizens trying to escape from the poverty and racism that afflict our society. That is why African-Americans are twice as well represented in the army as they are in our population, even though the numbers have been falling as the war in Iraq worsens, and why 50 percent of the women in the armed forces are minorities. That is why the young people in our colleges and universities today remain, by and large, indifferent to America's wars and covert operations: without the draft, such events do not affect them personally and therefore need not distract them from their studies and civilian pursuits.

Johnson, writing of the U.S. "increasingly powerful military legions," states that over 700 U.S. military bases cover the world, acquired through threat, subterfuge, sleight of hand, or questionable payment of host states.

These hundreds of bases, regardless of how they were acquired or are retained, constitute an imperial presence abroad and a none-too-subtle check on a "host" nation's political (and military) options.

In Bushian parlance, the presence of these bases is the essence of "force projection"—the ability of the U.S. imperial military to project its forces around the globe at whim.

Even Rome would envy such a capability.

Was force projection not the essence of the (latest) Iraq war? While a United States traumatized by the events of September 11 was force-fed fears of weapons of mass destruction (via a supine media and a compliant Congress), U.S. military thinkers knew better.

Chalmers Johnson cites retired Air Force Colonel Karen Kwiatkowski, a former strategist in the Near East division of the Secretary of Defense. When asked, "What are the real reasons for invasion of Iraq?" she responded: "one reason has to do with enhancing our military-basing posture in the region. We had been very dissatisfied with our relations with Saudi Arabia, particularly the restrictions on our basing. . . . So we were looking for alternate strategic locations beyond Kuwait, beyond Qatar, to secure something we had been searching for since the days of Carter—to secure the energy lines to the region. Bases in Iraq, then, were very important."

The unstated question, "Why?" is answered by the obvious. As long ago as 1945, the U.S. State Department was eying the Persian Gulf region with something akin to lust.

U.S. anti-imperialist critic, author, and linguist Noam Chomsky noted in his 2007 work *Interventions* that the events of September 11 opened wide the door to a long-coveted "prize": The September 11 atrocities also provided an opportunity and pretext to implement long-standing plans to take control of Iraq's immense oil wealth, a central component of the Persian Gulf resources that the State Department, in 1945, described as a "stupendous source of strategic power, and one of the greatest material prizes in world history."

This prize is at the very core of why the current Iraq War is being waged and why almost all wars are fought: for resources. For wealth. For power.

Fighting Terror, Fighting Crime

Perhaps it is not too surprising to find a similar trajectory, from big to bloated, from massive to vast, in the prison industrial complex (PIC) as in the military-industrial complex (MIC). The similarity is not coincidence. They are two sides of the same coin.

Linda Evans, a former anti-imperialist political prisoner, and Eve Goldberg, a prison activist, have penned a pamphlet, *The Prison Industrial Complex and the Global Economy*, that conclusively shows not just the correlation between the MIC and the PIC but the interrelationship with the emerging global economy. They write: "like the military/industrial complex, the prison/industrial complex is an interweaving of private business and government interests. Its twofold purpose is profit and social control. Its public rationale is the fight against crime."

Not so long ago, communism was "the enemy" and communists were demonized as a way of justifying gargantuan military expenditures. Now, fear of crime and the demonization of criminals serve a similar ideological purpose: to justify the use of tax dollars for the repression and incarceration of a growing percentage of our population. . . . Most of the "criminals" we lock up are poor people who commit nonviolent crimes out of economic need. Violence occurs in less than 14 percent of all reported crime, and injuries occur in just 3 percent. In California, the top three charges for those entering prison are: possession of a controlled substance, possession of a controlled substance for sale, and robbery. Violent crimes like murder, rape, manslaughter, and kidnapping don't even make the top ten.

Remember the Reagan administration's "war on drugs"? It has led to the largest prison binge on earth, and if it were indeed a war rather than a poor metaphor, then the massacres erupting from Mexico would signal the Tet Offensive that spelled the end of the Vietnam War. The only thing missing from the war on drugs is a signature on a piece of paper pleading surrender.

Whole communities have been shattered, and where once hundreds of thousands were cast into U.S. dungeons, prisons now hold millions, with millions more under lifetime voting bans and career blockages—in virtual prison while ostensibly free.

Just as cynicism led to wars abroad, similar social forces waged war on Americans, as, in many states and jurisdictions, the only growth industry could be found in construction, jobs, and services in the PIC.

How much has it grown?

The United States, the abode of some 6 percent of the world's population, today imprisons nearly 25 percent of all the prisoners on earth.

In her book *Is the Prison Obsolete?* scholar-activist and prison abolitionist Dr. Angela Y. Davis, herself a political prisoner during the Black Liberation movement of the 1960s, brings her unique lived and learned perspective to the question:

> When I became involved in anti-prison activism during the late 1960s, I was astounded to learn that there were then close to two hundred thousand people in prison. Had anyone told me that in three decades ten times as many people would be locked away in cages, I would have been absolutely incredulous. I imagine that I would have responded something like this: "As racist and undemocratic as this country may be [remember, during that period the demands of the Civil Rights movement had not yet been consolidated], I do not believe that the U.S. government will be able to lock up so many people without producing powerful public resistance. No, this will never happen, not unless this country plunges into fascism."

Captive Markets

Along with the immense and unprecedented explosion in the U.S. prison population has come the expansion in business for corporations trading behind bars.

Prisons today, although islands separated by brick and steel from "free" society, are captive markets where merchants make billions.

From Dial soap to Famous Amos cookies, there's enormous profit to be made. In 1995 alone, Dial sold more than $100,000 worth of its products to the New York City jail system. VitaPro Foods, a Montreal-based maker of soybean meat substitutes, sold $34 million worth of its products to Texas state prisons.

Dismantling Peace Movement Myths

Frida Berrigan

This moment in time contains so much hope and possibility and so much death and destruction. These are not easy times and they are not getting easier—and so I thought that I would take on some of the myths that burden, complicate, and undermine our peace movements. We have internalized some of these myths pretty deeply. We even reinforce them with one another. So, I thought it might be a valuable exercise to spend some time together dismantling a few of them.

What follows is my highly subjective (and certainly incomplete) compilation of the myths of the peace movement.

In the 1960s, the peace movement was so much more powerful and so much cooler than we are. There are no young people active in the peace movement. Don't they care? We are marginalized and we are not having an impact. We're not smart enough to oppose the war. All we need to do is get the right person in the White House and then they'll enact our solutions.

Does any of this sound familiar? This is what I hear from brothers and sisters over and over again. Now, these myths are not equal—some are bigger than others. And some have a kernel of truth (which is why they are myths and not lies) but cumulatively this constant bombardment is a real bummer.

So, I'm saying they are not true—I'm saying that there are young people, and we are having an impact, and that no one person in any position of power is going to offer any answer automatically or just because they promised they would. I'm saying we are the ones we have been waiting for, that we are creating the alternative. If that is what we are doing, not just going through some exercise of opposition, some knee-jerk resistance or recalcitrance, then we have a lot of work ahead of us—and need to take the work more seriously, and ourselves less so.

And that starts with dismantling myths.

Myth One: In the 1960s, the peace movement was so much more powerful and so much cooler than we are today.

I want to start with the 1960s one: 2008 is a big year for revivals and recollections and reunions for the historians and the academics and the activists. Forty years since: the police riot in Chicago, the assassination of Martin Luther King and of Bobby Kennedy, Tommie Smith and John Carlos giving the Black power salute as they received their

Olympic medals, since Catonsville. And those are just a few of the things that happened in the United States that year. Around the world there was Prague Spring, the massacre at Tlatelolco, the Paris uprising, the Biafran war. Here we are forty years later, and it is a potent moment for reflection.

The demonstrations at the Democratic National Convention in Denver this summer (2008) are happening under the slogan "Recreate Sixty-Eight." Disclaimer: Now, I don't mean to undermine or disparage the work of activists and organizers in Denver and all of the friends who will go to Colorado this summer to demonstrate, and at the same time implore the Democratic Party to be the party of the people.

I like the rhythm of language a lot. And I love alliteration. In that way—"Recreate Sixty-Eight" is AWESOME. I love how it sounds. The organizers have their reasons for choosing it beyond how cool it sounds. There are a lot of lessons to learn from that era, and a lot of good things that happened that year.

But "Recreate Sixty-Eight"? We cannot and should not recreate sixty-eight. The parallels between today and forty years ago are clear and compelling, and as I said there is a lot to learn from that period. Here we are in 2008 and we need to be building a movement and building bridges between movements (because we are not a monolith) that is rooted in an analysis and understanding of this moment, this place, this context.

I was struck to read recently that at the beginning of 1968, less than half the American people believed the war in Vietnam was wrong, 45 percent, and that more than 15,000 U.S. soldiers had been killed and nearly 100,000 wounded. So the Vietnam War was both more bloody and more popular than the war and occupations in Iraq and Afghanistan were in 2008.

In every way, this nation is less homogeneous than it was forty years ago: we are racially, ethnically, religiously more diverse and more stratified. We are so much poorer, and so much richer than we were forty years ago. We are less innocent. We are less naïve. In short—we are different. And this war is different. And so our movements must also be different.

The media compares 1968 and 2008—the peace movement then and now. Some activists then and now compare us; some leaders (those who survived) compare that time to now as they seek new relevance. But, we must not fall sway to this comparison.

We live in the United States of America—a deeply nostalgic and deeply ahistorical nation saddled with a case of amnesia that approaches pathology. My SAT prep teacher would be so proud of that sentence. This is a dangerous and counterproductive combination—nostalgic amnesia. And it infects our peace movements. We are tempted to fetishize the past instead of learn from it. The past is constantly being rewritten and repackaged and then sold to us as a distorted reflection in a house of mirrors. So, we don't want to recreate sixty-eight; we want to harness some of that energy, that sense of power and possibility and apply it to our very different context today.

Myth Two: There are no young people active in the peace movement. Don't they care?

And that leads to an interconnected myth: "Where are the young people?"

I was at a college in Connecticut a few years ago and I think I was talking about war profiteering. It was a Friday afternoon and one of those early spring, warm days where the flip-flops get dragged out of the back of the closet. Needless to say, there were not a lot of students there—but those who were there were active, engaged and very, very earnest. The dialogue was going great until a professor stood up and asked me: "Where are the students? Where are the young people? They don't care. In my day, we were so radical. If there was a draft, man, then they'd know."

"If there was a draft…" It struck me as so spiteful. That would teach 'em. They'd be sorry they never paid attention in my class. I did not hear from him a sense of responsibility as a professor. No understanding of who these young people are he has made it his career to teach. And, no sense of agency, that he could help them do or be anything different.

So, I responded in a few ways:

1. There is a draft. It is a whole series of backdoor drafts; the people who are fighting these wars don't want to be there and they cannot easily and legally leave. They are drafted.
2. There will not be another draft—so hoping that instituting a draft will catalyze a new generation of resistance is a nonstarter (as Cheney would say).
3. The draft during the Vietnam War turned out lots of people against the war, but organizing under the banner "bring our boys home" meant that when Nixon "Vietnamized" the war, the mass anti-war movement packed up and went home—long before the war was over, long before the killing stopped.

It was for many people a movement based on self-interest—which may be bigger, but is in many ways less powerful than one built on principle and solidarity. The average "lifespan" of a '60s activist was about six months—from tuning on at their first protest to tuning out and going back to Middle America. You don't end war in six-month increments, no matter how much you rage during that period.

Can we see ourselves today building an anti-war movement founded on the idea that war is a failure of the imagination, that war is wrong, and that it must be resisted and opposed even if it is not affecting one personally? I think we can.

This question—where are the young people?—is heartbreaking. It misses all the incredible and courageous work that young people are doing all over this country. It says that young people are not doing peace and justice work because they are not doing it with us.

And it misses the fact that young people today have so much more to lose—unless they are from very poor or very wealthy backgrounds, young people graduate from college saddled with tens of thousands of dollars in debt and no guarantee of a job. That debt is a kind of draft—college grads are drafted into a lifecycle of taking on more debt, working two jobs, having little time for friendships or community. And all the time the culture whispers: go ahead and buy it—you deserve it—and a little more debt doesn't matter. But, step out of line, miss one payment, and the house of cards collapses. We need to understand our young people and what they are up against.

We are at war and young people are at the forefront—not just of the college-educated, debt-burdened variety. But urban and rural high school students are finding the new Students for a Democratic Society and creating a new legacy for that '60s-era organization. And there is something else that is missed by that "where are the young people?" question. More and more young people are in uniform. And they are calling cadence of the anti-war movement. And the war is not an abstraction for them: they know what 138-degree heat under Kevlar feels like. They see the lies up close. They have tasted fear and witnessed and participated in war crimes. They are paying the price for this administration's hubris and imperial designs with part of their bodies. They come home haunted and broken and hopping mad.

So, there are young people. And they need support and guidance, not condescension. One of the best things the War Resisters League has done in the last ten years or so is to sublet space to Iraq Veterans Against the War in New York City. And over coffee and at the copy machine a dialogue between principled pacifists and people who volunteered for military service begins. It is a dialogue that will need to continue for years. It is a dialogue that makes us stronger, and it ensures that the next generation of peace activists will be more powerful and more sophisticated than the last—understanding the past, but looking and moving forward, never back.

Myth Three: We are marginalized and we are not having an impact.

At the War Resisters League, we have had to relearn the fine art of the press release, because a few years back we realized that not only was the media coming out to our demonstrations, but they were lifting whole sections from our press releases—warts and all, and we had better write better ones if we wanted better coverage.

We were so used to being marginalized and written off and now there we were on the front page. It took some adjustment. Starting in 2003, just about every demo we've organized has gotten great press coverage. Sometimes the tone is snarky, and reporters always ask why we did not have more people—but we got covered.

Eventually, I realized we were getting press coverage not just because of our cutting edge, awesome demonstrations, but because we were manifestations of popular sentiment against the war. At a time when the administration is desperately trying to distract the American people from the war and the economy those two things are becoming fused in people's minds, and we are part of triggering, directing and sustaining that discussion.

And that discussion turns the wheel of action.

We are still small. But, we speak for the majority of Americans every time we go into the streets. And it leads to this interesting sense of accountability. I am not just here for me. I am here for many people who cannot be here because they are working or they are afraid or they don't know this is happening—but would be happy if they did.

We are having an impact. So let's use it while we have it—because it will not always be that way. Whenever I am at a protest and it is all thumbs up and honking horns, I think about World War II, and what it would have been like to be a peace activist then.

Two of the peace activists I most admire—my mother and father—both supported the war in their own way. My mom was just a girl then, and talks about collecting cigarette and gum wrappers that they turned in. They were told that the wrappers would be made into ammunition. Everyone was part of the war effort. People planted victory gardens—and at one point during the war, 40 percent of people's food came from those gardens, even in urban areas. I am staying at a friend's house and they have a sign from that era that says: "Save waste fats for explosives. Take them to your meat dealer."

My dad served in the Army in World War II. He was a field-decorated lieutenant. My uncles Jerry, Tom and Jim all served in World War II and my Uncle John was in the army, but did not go overseas. Of six brothers, only one—my Uncle Dan who had already entered the Jesuits—did not enlist.

People in the United States suffered because of World War II. Sacrificed was demanded and expected. Food and gas were rationed and Americans were called on to buy war bonds. At the height of the war, 40 percent of gross domestic product went to fund war. Ralph DiGia, Bill Sutherland, the others who refused to serve in the military during World War II had to withstand that propaganda, and I cannot imagine how difficult that was.

So, today we are not opposing a popular total war. We are resisting a war that barely registers on many peoples' radar screens. But—when it registers—the war is profoundly unpopular. The latest polls about the war have more than 70 percent of Americans opposed to the war, and when the question gets more general. Eightysomething percent of Americans are dissatisfied with the direction this country is going.

But, we risk falling into a Mobius strip logic trap: the war is unpopular; people oppose the war, war ends. But, it has not ended. It has ground on for five long years in Iraq, for seven for the long global war on terrorism.

Myth Four: We are not smart enough to end the war.

We have to dismantle the myth that only experts can get us out of Iraq, and unless we can formulate a rock solid plan for withdrawal from Iraq, we cannot really oppose the war.

Why? Why? Why does the war go on if the American people don't want it? There are many answers to this question and I don't have all of them—but the one I see most often and most clearly is this: even good people who would like there not to be a war don't see a clear way out. And they don't understand the complexities—you start talking Sunni, Shiite, Awakening, Badr Brigades, Nouri al-Maliki, Sadr City, phased redeployment and you have lost them one, two, three, seven times over. And not seeing a clear way out, and not being completely fluent in the language of deadly quagmire on an epic scale, they tune out.

We have a role and a task here as peace activists and organizers. And our role is not to teach them the grammatical nuances of the language of deadly quagmire on an epic scale. Our role is to say: you do not need to have a PhD in foreign affairs to say that the war is wrong, to say that withdrawal needs to be immediate and complete, to say that we should not be spending our blood and treasure on wars of preemptive aggression based on lies. In fact, it is the PhDs and the experts, the armchair warriors who got us into this war.

It takes courage, and moral and political clarity to reject the "pottery barn" maxim of foreign policy: we broke it, we bought it. No, we need to say: Iraq is not a vase or a candelabra. We need to say to Washington: you broke it. And we did not buy it. And, at the same time acknowledge that we will be paying for Iraq forever—$3 trillion and counting is the estimate that Stiglitz and Bilmes are using these days.

But we cannot occupy that country forever. The U.S. occupation is a catalyst and cause of violence, not the deterrent. The immediate and complete withdrawal is not a process; it is an executive order.

Myth Five: We can elect our way to an end to war.

If we can't stand up for all of that, we fall back on another myth—the myth that we can express our anti-war sentiments through candidates. That the Democratic majority in Congress—the so-called revolution of 2006—or an Obama or Clinton in the White House—will fulfill our anti-war agenda. The myth is that the right politician will say the right thing at the right time. Those magical incantations will part the quagmire like Moses parted the Red Sea and allow a new administration to do right what Bush did so wrong. It is a myth.

It is a myth. And I am not just saying this because I have found the last two years of campaigning emotionally and physically exhausting. And I'm not even running. Just watching it is irritating at this point.

Politicians will not save us. Democracy is not lever pulling or chad punching. It is not branding and messaging and framing and divining the new micro-interest group. It is not one day every two or four years. And it certainly is not the elaborate and vicarious puppetry spectacle and pageantry of the last eight years. It is hard, sustained, incremental, engaged work.

The nameplate on the desk in the Oval Office is a very, very small part of what we need to be working for. And yet the election sucks all the oxygen out of the room—especially this one when there are racial and gender milestones at stake. And it sucks all the money out of the room. And it sharpens the lines that divide us.

When we cede the answers to some politician, we invest in other people and in other systems what we really need to be investing in ourselves, in one another and in our movements. It puts our hope and our energy in the hands of people with other agendas and other masters.

That brings me to my stirring conclusion: It is Us. It is you and I. It is Peace Action's platform to Reclaim Maine (a great—and meaningful—name). We are the alternative. This movement is full of good people who work so hard—war tax resisters making a principled decision not to pay for war and philanthropists who are generous and dependable, carpenters and green thumbs, computer whizzes and luddites, visionaries and implementers.

We are the alternative. We are the answer. And if you are looking around thinking "uh-oh," that's a good thing. Because coming to grip with this truth in the midst of all these myths means we need to be self-critical and challenge each other. It means we should do more—be more. Reach out more and welcome more in.

We cannot wait. We cannot wait for a leader. We cannot wait for "the plan." We cannot wait for things to get worse. We cannot wait for the answers.

We have the answers, and it is us.

What is the alternative to depression and recession? Sharing.

What is the alternative to subprime mortgages crisis? Collective ownership.

What is the alternative to hunger? Farms and gardens.

What is the alternative to war and terrorism? International cooperation, universally accepted and enforced norms for nation-states, development that meets peoples' needs.

What is the alternative to prison, to soulless schools, to militarized borders? to capitalism and market driven globalization? to cluster bombs? We answer these questions together and we create the alternatives together. We enact news truths that replace the myths.

Structural Racism and the Obama Presidency

john a. powell

The racial landscape of America changed dramatically on November 4, 2008. Early that evening it became clear Senator Barack Obama would be the next president of the United States. What was not clear and may take some time to unfold is what this means in terms of racial justice in the United States and the world. Some rush to claim that the election means the United States has moved past race and more particularly racism. Others argue that nothing has really changed and nonwhites continue to face deep racial barriers. Both of these positions are much too simplistic and represent a naïve view of race. Racialization is not simply an event, but a complicated process that reflects a social history and set of structural arrangements. There is a reason that we are likely to make the mistake that either nothing has changed or that everything has changed. Only a few years ago, it was all but impossible to imagine the U.S. populace electing a black person to the highest position in the country. However, race still largely determines where we live, who we live with and how we live.

There is an increasing understanding that racialization is largely a historically rooted social project. But we fail to take this insight seriously and continue to think of it in concrete terms. This failure does not help us to understand or anticipate how race has changed and continues to change based on social and cultural conditions. It is clear that the conditions and meaning of racialization were very different before and after the Civil War, for example. For those who associated racialization only with slavery, there were reasons to suggest that ending slavery would necessarily end racialization and hierarchy. Most people did not anticipate the Jim Crow laws that mandated segregation and the rise of anti-black racism, which reached its zenith following the end of slavery from the late 1800s to the beginning of the twentieth century.

During that time, the state-sponsored racial arrangement helped create what author Douglas Blackmon calls "slavery by another name." Racialization became different but essentially unfinished. The language of racism became part of the American lexicon during the 1930s when the word "racism" first became popularized in the United States and explicit white supremacy was called into question. Events in the United States, Germany, Africa and Latin America and the rest of the world helped to usher in a new racial consciousness and set of practices. In the United States, the poster child for racism was the southern segregationist explicitly holding on to claims of white supremacy and Jim Crow. This also became the challenge as the U.S. fight against racism was a fight against Jim Crow in addition to the conscious expression of racial animus and hierarchy.

When lawyer Thurgood Marshall won the landmark decision in Brown v. Board of Education, which effectively outlawed racial segregation in education, he and millions of other Americans believed that racism was on its deathbed. Marshall and others thought that ending segregation would necessarily end racism. Judge Robert Carter, who worked with Marshall on the Brown case, would later lament that he was mistaken in thinking segregation was coterminous with racial hierarchy. He further stated that segregation was not the cause of white supremacy but an expression of white supremacy. Thurgood Marshall would go on to serve on the U.S. Supreme Court, but he died with a deep sense of regret that much of his work to integrate schools was undone by de facto segregation. The failure to understand the mutating and multiple expressions of racialization was also made by many whites. They feared that ending segregation and laws limiting interracial marriage would not only end racial hierarchy but would also destroy the white race.

It is important to note that around the time of the Brown decision, the housing market was being restructured so that whites were more likely to end up in suburbs. The Federal Housing Administration subsidized migration to suburbs and the Federal Highway Act of 1956 further facilitated the process of so-called white flight and disinvestment from urban areas. The segregation that resulted had a fundamental effect on the quality of education available to minorities living in low-income neighborhoods. This connection between housing and education is one component of a broader reality that where you live determines your access to opportunity structures and your life chances.

By the 1960s, we began to understand that racialization was not just an expression of conscious individual prejudice, but also an expression of institutional norms and practices. America was introduced to something called institutional racism. However, this insight never completely penetrated the heart of American discourse, partly because the United States is a country obsessed with an ideology of extreme individualism. This ideology is largely fiction, but it frames how people make sense of the world. It makes the work done by structures all but invisible. If there is racialization, this position holds that it must be located in the conscious mind of the individual. There are a number of counter examples, but they simply do not stick within this narrative. For example, if nonwhites are doing worse than whites and there is no conscious racist to blame, the failure must rest with the nonwhites themselves.

American attitudes toward race have certainly changed, and it would not have been possible for a black person even of Barack Obama's stature to be elected president even ten years ago. Today, much of the work that produces and reproduces racial hierarchy is done through institutional arrangement and structures. This is called structural racialization. It does not mean that other racial dynamics no longer exist; they continue to play the same central role as before. There are still some people screaming about the demise of the white race and about losing control over the country, who are consciously hostile to nonwhites. While these attitudes persist, they are not dominant, and as the election of Obama suggests, they do not represent majority opinion even among whites.

This suggests a change in racial attitudes in America, but not an end to racialization. The meaning of race has changed, but change should not be confused with the end. In order to better understand this new racial dynamic, we must reject views of society and membership prevalent in the 1940s. As we travel further into the twenty-first century, we are likely to see another kind of racialization that will be informed by a different understanding of society and people.

So what does racialization in the United States look like today? First, we are talking about a process that is too unsettled to define with exactitude, but one in which some contours are clear. We as a society are more socially conscious and racially egalitarian than at any time in our short history. However, this improvement in the societal position on race is not reflected in either our conscious attitudes or our interinstitutional practices and policies. Recognizing this gap, scholars have pointed to a phenomenon called implicit bias. There is a growing body of work that documents that Americans have implicit, unconscious biases which can be tested. These attitudes can shift to be more salient in some situations rather than others. One cannot identify implicit racial bias by simply asking an interviewee, because the individual will not be aware of it. In spite of this, implicit attitudes can impact behavior and choices. It is interesting to note that implicit bias is a social phenomenon reflecting the collective social culture. This means that even nonwhites are likely to carry some level of implicit bias, but generally not to the same extent as whites.

The second insight is that structures interact to produce outcomes that are not dependent on conscious or even unconscious intent. Consider the problem of climate change. It is not something that anyone intended, but rather a result of several interactive institutions and practices that have produced disturbing results. So why do institutions produce racialized outcomes? One reason is that people are situated differently in relation to institutional practices and arrangements. For instance, there is some indication that creating universal health insurance would likely make doctors less available in rural areas and to people of color. This is because a system based solely on insurance would likely drive doctors away from areas where blacks are overrepresented.

Also, the current subprime lending problem has powerful racial overtones that continue to be largely ignored. A history of racially discriminatory housing and lending practices contributed to economic segregation and concentrated poverty of low income minorities. Discrimination was achieved through redlining which limited the availability of mortgage loans for minorities and through racial covenants that prevented minorities from living in certain areas. In the absence of traditional lending institutions, the practice of reverse redlining or predatory lending became prevalent as subprime lenders targeted these isolated communities. These subprime loans are high risk, and have much higher interest rates, fees and penalties. The racial impact of predatory lending is evident as subprime loans are three times more prevalent in low-income areas and five times more likely in African-American neighborhoods than in predominately white neighborhoods. As a result of the crisis, it is estimated that African-American borrowers will lose between $71–$122 billion dollars in wealth, while Latino borrowers will lose $76–$129 billion. The unwillingness to consider the racial component of the subprime crisis will lead many to continue blaming these communities for the problem and inevitably result in further marginalization.

Structural racialization as an analytical tool is a particular example of a systems approach. This approach recognizes that causes are not linear or unidirectional, but cumulative, mutual and interactive. This model has been well developed in the areas of health and the environment. Recently, the economist Jeffrey Sachs in his work on poverty mentions a similar, albeit narrower systems approach which he calls clinical economics. His approach marks a shift away from the IMF's structural adjustment programs which adopted false universalism and promoted static economic solutions while neglecting the particularities of specific developing countries. Clinical economics partially corrects this, but it does not however pay enough attention to Western normative assumptions about culture that too easily dismiss and misinterpret cultural complexities. This does not suggest we adopt simplistic relativism that asserts our inability to understand one another, but rather the need to reject the hubris of racial objectivity based on underlying notions of superiority. Instead, we should recognize that our interconnectedness is based not only on our material situatedness, but also our interactions with others and others' cultures, and the broader social and physical environment within which these interactions take place.

One important point Sachs makes is that two people with a fever may experience very different symptoms and each require a different diagnosis. Similarly, two people or groups of people who are poor may be experiencing very different situations. This point was made by Swedish economist Gunnar Myrdal over sixty years ago in a study entitled "The America Dilemma." According to Myrdal, there was a qualitative difference between black and white poverty in the United States. He asserted that blacks suffered from a cumulative causation or mutually reinforcing constraint—a set of interconnected structures, institutions and norms that operate simultaneously to produce a negative cumulative impact.

A seemingly race-neutral approach to issues of social and economic inequality and exclusion will not only fail to address the situatedness of particular groups, but may make disparities worse. This was the consequence of many race-neutral programs adopted in the United States under the New Deal and after World War II. For example, the National Labor Relations Act protected the right of unions to organize, but excluded occupations such as "farm worker" and "maid" typically open to African-Americans. Also, the Social Security Act which claimed to provide a universal social insurance plan excluded domestic and agricultural workers in acquiescence to demands from southern politicians. In addition, there was the G.I. Bill, which appeared to be race-neutral but proved to be problematic in two ways. Blacks had a more difficult time getting into the military in part as a result of a poor, racially segregated educational system. For those who did get into the military, the G.I. Bill gave them the same federal money for education, but they had to use it in a deeply racialized education system that locked blacks out of higher education. This further contributed to disparities between blacks and whites.

Universal programs that are likely to be pushed using a colorblind, postracial frame are not likely be effective in disrupting entrenched and structured racial inequality. This is not because of racial animus, but because these programs will be mapped onto other circumstances and conditions that will translate these efforts into new racial disparities. When this happens, the public discourse seeks to explain the continued inequality. Unfortunately, instead of seeing structures and systems at work, the rationalization is more likely to default to a personal or culture explanation that locates the failure in the marginalized group. A universal approach will only be effective if it is sensitive to the situatedness of particular groups and to the operation of institutions and policies. We call this "targeted universalism."

The failure to develop a structural understanding will not only exacerbate racial inequality, but will likely usher in a new type of racialization. This suggests that plans which fail to understand how people are positioned in relation to institutional prac-tices are likely to have racial impacts. For example, a plan in New Jersey assumed that making affordable housing available in a race-neutral way would still address race because blacks and Latinos were more likely to be poor. However, while poverty was the major constraint holding back poor whites, there were a number of constraints operating simultaneously against blacks and Latinos. This untargeted plan benefited whites, but only marginally impacted Latinos and did not benefit blacks at all. The end result was a racially stratified housing market with blacks becoming more isolated from opportunity. It is necessary then to take an approach that is sensitive to the work of interactive institutions on the situatedness of particular populations and to the intersectionality of issues such as race, gender class, and sexuality.

Neglecting the role of structures and systems will allow weak structures to impede the life chances of all and limit the ability for people to contribute to society economi-cally and politically. The structures in place impact all groups but operate unevenly. The identification of structures should not be seen as a rejection of personal responsibility or autonomy. In the United States, we are too often inclined to see social structures and social responsibility in direct tension with the responsibility of the individual, but this is misguided. A healthy society requires both structures and social footing to support healthy individual expression. Also, individual responsibility requires individuals to collectively call the appropriate structures and institutional arrangements into being. Political science professor Iris Marion Young made the observation that the greater the complexity of a society and its interactions across distances, the more likely relations and opportunity within that society will be mediated by institutional arrangements.

Barack Obama's ascendancy to the U.S. presidency has radically changed the world. However, if we are to avoid a kind of incipient individualism that allows structures to reproduce and creates new forms of racial hierarchy, we must participate in developing an understanding of situatedness and propose remedies along the lines of targeted universalism. While it is certain that the role of structural racialization will become more important under the Obama administration, it is not clear that this is on the radar of the new administration. It remains to be seen whether the election of President Obama will move us to a type of false transcendence of race and particularity, or if it will allow us to more robustly examine the work that structures and institutions are doing to promote or hinder inclusion for racially marginalized populations.

Notes on an Orientation to the Obama Presidency

Linda Burnham

Obama is clear—and we should be too—about what he was elected to do. The bottom line of his job description has become increasingly evident as the economic crisis deepens. Obama's job is to salvage and stabilize the U.S. capitalist system and to perform whatever triage is necessary to restore the core institutions of finance and industry to profitability.

Obama's second bottom line is also clear to him—and should also be to us: to salvage the reputation of the United States in the world; repair the international ties shredded by eight years of cowboy unilateralism; and adjust U.S. positioning on the world stage on the basis of a rational assessment of the strengths and weaknesses of the changed and changing centers of global political, economic and military power—rather than on the basis of a simple-minded ideological commitment to unchallenged world dominance.

Obama has been on the job for only a month but has not wasted a moment in going after his double bottom line with gusto, panache and high intelligence. In point of fact, the capitalists of the world—or at least the U.S. branch—ought to be building altars to the man and lighting candles. They have chosen an uncommonly steady hand to pull their sizzling fat from the fire.

For some on the left this is the beginning and the end of the story. Having established conclusively that Obama's fundamental task is to govern in the interests of capital, there's no point in adjusting one's stance, regardless of how skillful and popular he may be. For the anti-capitalist left that is grounded in Trotskyism, anarcho-horizontalism, or various forms of third-party-as-a-point-of-principleism, the only change worthy of the name is change that hits directly at the kneecaps of capitalism and cripples it decisively. All else is trifling with minor reforms or, even worse, capitulating to the power elite. From this point of view the stance towards Obama is self-evident: criticize relentlessly, disabuse others of their presidential infatuation, and denounce anything that remotely smacks of mainstream politics. Though this may seem an extreme and marginal point of view, it has a surprising degree of currency in many quarters.

The effective-steward-of-capitalism is only one part of the Obama story. Obama did what the center would not do and what a fragmented and debilitated left could not do. He broke the death grip of the reactionary right by inspiring and mobilizing millions as agents of change. If Obama doesn't manage to do even one more progressive thing, he has already opened up far more promising political terrain. His campaign:

- Revealed the contours, composition and potential of a broad democratic coalition, demographically grounded in the (overlapping) constituencies of African-Americans, Latinos, Asians, youth across the racial groups, LGBT voters, unionized workers, urban professionals, and women of color and single white women, and in the sectors of organized labor, peace, civil rights, civil liberties, feminism, and environmentalism. Obama did not create this broadly democratic electoral coalition single-handedly or out of whole cloth, but he did move it from latency to potency and from dispirited, amorphous and unorganized to goal oriented, enthusiastic and organized.
- Busted up the Republicans' southern strategy, the foundation of their rule for most of the last forty years, and the Democrats' ignominious concession to this legacy of slavery.
- Wrenched the Democratic Party out of the clammy grip of Clintonian centrism. (Although he himself often leads from the center, Obama's center is a couple of notches to the left of the Clinton administration's triangulation strategies).
- Rescued political dialogue from its monopolization by hate-filled, xenophobic, ultranationalistic ideologues.

This is not change of the anti-capitalist variety, but certainly it is change of major consequence. In this period, then, the left has three tasks.

Our first job is to defend the democratic opening. This is a job we share with broader progressive forces and with centrists. Obama won big and retains the favorable regard of a sizeable majority. And meanwhile the Republican Party is in glorious disarray. But in no way should we take this situation for granted.

Our second job is to contribute to building more united, effective, combative and influential progressive popular movements. This places the highest premium on strengthening and extending our ties with broader progressive forces, both inside and outside the Democratic Party, with an eye towards building long-term relationships and alliances among individuals, organizations and sectors. Anything that thickens and enriches the relationships among left and progressive actors in labor, religious institutions, policy think tanks, grassroots organizations, academia etc. is to be supported in the interests of strengthening the capacity of the left-progressive alliance to influence policy, to encourage and shore up whatever progressive inclinations might emerge from within the administration, and to resist administration tendencies to accommodation and capitulation to center-right forces. After Obama's election, we exited a period of collective psychic depression only to enter one of global economic depression. Each day, as the institutions of finance capital collapse, the corruption, greed and mismanagement of the nation's economic system are further revealed. Broad sectors of the population have been shocked into a more skeptical and critical stance towards capitalism, and the need for some measure of structural change wins near-universal acceptance. In this political environment, alliance building will be complicated, messy and filled with political tensions and tactical differences. It is imperative nonetheless.

Our third job, and perhaps the trickiest, is to build the left. First let it be said that unless we are able to demonstrate a genuine commitment and growing capacity to take on the first two jobs, the third is a nonstarter, and a prescription for political isolation. In other words, defending the democratic opening in conjunction with the center and building long-term relationships between the anti-capitalist left and broad progressive sectors in the context of the struggle over administration policy must be understood as critical tasks in their own right, not simply as arenas in which to advance an independent left line or to recruit new adherents to an anti-capitalist perspective.

In these circumstances, among our biggest challenges is how to attend to building the capacity of the left without succumbing to the siren songs of dogma, the old addictions of premature platform erection, or the self-limiting pleasures of building parties in miniature. For the anti-capitalist left, this is a period of experimentation. There is no roadmap; there are no recipes. Those organizational forms and initiatives that enable us to synthesize experience, share lessons and develop broad orientations and approaches to seriously undertaking our first two tasks should be encouraged. Those that would entrap us in the hermetic enclosures of doctrinal belief should be avoided at all cost.

There is no way to predict how things will unfold over the next years. But this much we can foresee: if the opportunity at hand is mangled or missed, the takeaway for the left will be deepened isolation and fragmentation. If, on the other hand, the left engages with this political opening skillfully and creatively, it will emerge as a broader, more vibrant force on the U.S. political spectrum, better able to confront whatever the post-Obama world will bring.

Where Was the White in Phoenix?

A Ten-Year Movement Update

B. Loewe

In 1999, following the massive demonstrations in Seattle against the World Trade Organization, Betita Martínez shook things up with the simple question, "Why were most of the demonstrators white?"

After the state of Washington ran out of tear gas, after the echoes of bucket drums faded, after the teamsters and the "turtles" (environmentalists) parted ways, and global capital appeared momentarily derailed by a city full of barricades, her short article circulated list-servs and e-mail inboxes with penetrating questions for the debut showing of the newly born "anti-globalization movement." Martínez highlighted the ways in which people of color did participate but asked us to reconcile the apparent divide. If "we are to make Seattle's promise of a new, international movement against imperialist globalization come true," she wrote, we must understand and learn from the low-level of participation from people of color.

In dry Arizona one decade later, on July 28, 2010, sweat evaporated before it hit the ground. Nervous eyes avoided one another and watched their clocks on the eve of the International Day of Non-Compliance, called for by the Puente Movement in Phoenix. At 4:10 pm, wheels were set in motion and a countdown began. But five minutes later, the action was officially in question as the Phoenix skies filled with unusual clouds and burst open in a freak and sudden summer rainstorm.

Those in the know cursed under their breath as others danced outside enjoying a respite from the 110 degrees that caused the secret climbers to second-guess their plan of ascending a metal structure that's been soaking up the sun all-day. The puddles dried. The skies cleared. The steel divinely cooled. A ladder lay against the base of a downtown crane. A construction worker yelled into his phone. And minutes later, four small dots—230 feet in the air—methodically emerged to unfurl a banner by dropping themselves into the sky live on Telemundo and NBC. The message was sent to the world, and to the signatories of Arizona's recently passed racial profiling law, as the stage was sent for further militancy: "We Will Not Comply."

In the first decade of the new millennium, we've been presented with a new image of defiance, a new face of what courageous direct action and democracy looks like. Indeed, in the past ten years, many took Martínez's challenge seriously. Challenging White Supremacy Workshops emerged to train dozens of young primarily white organizers in principled racial justice work. The Ruckus Society, after being called out at the Los Angeles Democratic National Convention in 2000, redefined itself from a culture ripe with white male chauvinism to an organization rooting in long-term relationship building with front line communities of color. Serious capacity building was done, with direct action skillsets and sensibilities at the fore.

Racial, gender, and economic justice formations have sought to internationalize their relationships through networks like Grassroots Global Justice; both work and networks have been consolidated through the U.S. Social Forum process. A new world of low-wage and contingent-worker organizations, like the National Day Laborer Organizing Network and the National Domestic Workers Alliance, have broken open the labor movement and taken their rightful place at the table. The movement landscape we operate in today is far different, and more diverse, than a decade ago.

By the time anti-globalization mobilizations landed in Miami for the Free Trade Agreement of the Americas summit in 2003, it considered itself the "global justice movement" and had the Miami Worker Center, Coalition for Immokalee Workers, Power U and others leading Root Cause marches addressing the links of global and domestic inequity.

The work was led by those who had come out of the fights of the early and mid-1990s, like the Proposition 187 battle in California or housing fights in New York. It was led by those who had recently arrived in the United States after civil wars or displacement from their home countries, and from those who found no reason to celebrate the quincentenary anniversary of Columbus's arrival on the continent. The efforts of all those who had turned their attention to the shovel-work of relationship and institution building was now bearing fruit on a mass scale.

Llegaron los Jornaleros (The Day Laborers Have Arrived)

No one saw them coming. Most men looked away when the volunteer doctors, providing free blood tests to the workers while visiting street corner hiring sites, plunged needles into their taut arms resting on folding card tables. When one shouted "Migra!" as three white vans eased into the parking lot, tables toppled. Syringes hit the ground. Men who were patients seconds ago barreled past stunned medics from UCLA.

When Omar returned to the same spot the next day to look for work, he brought his guitar and sang in Spanish:

> The raids are now in style / They search for us everywhere. All afternoon and morning / All they know how to say to us is / "We're taking you to Tijuana" / But the people are amazing / They know everything there is to know / If they kick us out in the evening / We'll be back first thing in the morning.

With that, the band Los Jornaleros del Norte was born, and alongside them, a national network of corner day laborer organizations now forty-two members strong. Within five years, they would sing the same song to a throng of one million people in Los Angeles as part of the migrant rights movement that was reborn in 2006. Day laborers previously considered scabs by labor unions were now forming national partnerships and, with the emergence of the National Domestic Workers Alliance (whose members altered centuries of second-tier labor law with the passage of a Bill of Rights in 2010), represented a vibrant new hope for the continually stagnant U.S. labor movement.

Arizona: A Testing Ground

While the nation debated immigration reform on a national level, a Sheriff who made his name with juvenile chain gangs and dressing his inmates in his decertified prison with pink underwear, teamed up with the federal government to enforce immigration on a local level. Sheriff Joseph Arpaio signed up for the federal 287(g) program and started equipping his deputies with the tools of law enforcement for a new America; ski masks and teddy bears. The ski masks to hide their identities in their pursuit of undocumented residents and the teddy bears to replace the parents the volunteer posses just stole away from children left behind.

Salvador Reza of the Puente Movement in Phoenix would tell us that giants like these lose their power when lured into an alley fight. The new flagship federal program and the "toughest sheriff in America" became questionable when Arpaio rolled into a day laborer hiring site atop a tank to defend the property of a complaining furniture store owner. In that moment in 2007, the seed of 2010's dilemma between criminalization and legalization, security and community, human rights and hate was sown.

The Puente Movement continued to fan the local flames, using Arpaio as a piñata to beat at the federal administration and the larger logic of enforcement. In February 2009 they responded to the segregation of Arpaio's jails by documentation status with what was billed as a megamarch of 8,000 that now pales in comparison to the 100,000 that marched through the same streets two years later. As the rest of the country got turned on to the outrages passing for law in Arizona many asked about civil disobedience, direct action, and militant tactics. Reza was criticized for his lack of militancy but explains, "You can only be as radical as the conditions allow." In January 2010 the marches grew to 20,000; a prelude to what the state was about to see after the appointed Governor Jan Brewer signed Russell Pearce's SB 1070 into law, codifying racial profiling, criminalizing day laborers, and prohibiting the housing or transportation of anyone undocumented in the state.

Nine students arrived at the Nahuacalli, an Indigenous embassy of the Americas and hub for local organizing, to consult and pray before blocking the entrances to the Capitol building in protest. On the day of their action, they announced:

> We are chained to the state capital the way this legislation is chained to our people. … We have done everything under the law to have our voices heard, only to be met with more hostile laws. …That is why today we are doing a massive call out for civil disobedience because we are reclaiming our democracy…because this state capital is acting in a violent way and we will not continue to allow this to happen.

Days later, the 20,000 who marched on May 1 arrived at the Capital and, instead of hearing speakers from a platform, broke up into small groups to discuss and plan. The event signified the biggest departure from the legislative strategy governed by Washington, D.C., and gave birth to the Barrio Defense Committees that now populate each side of town with self-organized groups of residents exchanging skills and knowledge, developing detention preparedness plans, monitoring the police, and planning on-going actions.

Puente called for the Arizona Summer of Human Rights and invited the world to participate in the International Day of Non-Compliance on July 29, the day that SB 1070 was to go into effect.

> Today we announce the beginning of Arizona Human Rights Summer. Two days ago, we met veterans of the Mississippi Freedom Summer from 1964 who took the Civil Rights movement to a new level through their work. They encouraged us to carry on that legacy and pledged to participate deeply in the Arizona struggle.
>
> In the coming months, we will peacefully escalate resistance… to strengthen a migrant rights movement from the bottom up, a movement uncompromisingly against the criminalization of our communities. We will make this summer a Human Rights summer everywhere. Wherever the Diamondbacks play, protest. Wherever there are new police/ICE collaborations, push back. Wherever Arizona companies do business, boycott. Wherever there is injustice, we must shut it down.

The summer of 2010 showed that the relationship-building and exchange Martínez had called for a decade earlier had occurred and paid off—and not just for the migrant rights movement. 18,000 people from grassroots movements gathered in Detroit for the second U.S. Social Forum, consolidating the trend of transformative organizing, lifting up Detroit as a symbol of capital's failure and communities' solutions, and integrating themselves into an international movement led by the rising left in the Global South under the banner, "Another World is Possible."

Young people declared themselves "Undocumented and Un-Afraid" and fearlessly challenged lawmakers to deport them in their acts of civil disobedience. The seeds of a shanty town in Miami called the Umoja Village sprouted into a national movement called Take Back the Land with people refusing to leave their foreclosed homes or vowing to move back in to those the banks held on the market. Indigenous organizers from across the hemisphere attended the World People's Conference on Climate Change and the Rights of Mother Earth hosted by the Bolivian Government in Cochabamba. And on July 29, joined notably by hundreds of Unitarian Universalists acting in solidarity, residents of Phoenix blocked the entrance to Sheriff Arpaio's office and locked down his jail, effectively stopping the celebration raids he planned for SB 1070's inaugural day.

One can look at the early decades of this twenty-first century as marked by the rise of right, the gutting of the social safety net, entrenchment of war, and the worsening of conditions. But a careful eye can see an entirely different picture. While conditions decline, movements' strength is ascending. Institutions are maturing. And the challenges are mounting. As Nuh Washington, the former Black Panther who died in jail, suggested: Victory isn't necessarily bringing your enemy to their knees. It is "passing it on" from one generation to the next. We're the ones without power. Our survival in these times is a sure sign of our inevitable victory.

If one looks at the past decade and incorporates the lessons from the big moments of fight back after Katrina in New Orleans, after the Jena 6 trials and the assassination of Oscar Grant, after the Siege on Gaza, the Dream Act, the struggles around health care and against the privatization of education, one can begin to imagine a brighter future. The ongoing work in Arizona, ten years beyond Seattle and the lessons Betita Martínez guided us towards, shows both some areas of work we need to improve as well as some exciting prospects around us. As we also struggle daily to keep our homes and our hearts intact, one can see, as Arundhati Roy points out: "Another world is not only possible; she is *on her way.*"

Moving Forward

Ideas for Solidarity and Strategy to Strengthen

Multiracial Peace Movements

Clare Bayard and Francesca Fiorentini

These days, it isn't difficult to envision what a multi-racial, anti-racist peace movement might look like. As the country faces the economic burdens of cost-heavy foreign wars, corporate abuses, environmental crisis, and a resurgent radical right, the points of contact between antiwar work and racial and economic justice grow stronger by the day.

Follow any young working class soldier from their de-industrialized hometown to the horror of war and occupation in Iraq or Afghanistan, and back home again as they face mental trauma and unemployment. Talk to the residents of the Gulf Coast, dependent on jobs from the oil and weapons industries, whose livelihoods were devastated by the BP oil spill and subsequent layoffs, about the sustainability of an economy driven by war and oil. Ask immigrants forced to migrate to the United States in search of work and political asylum how they have experienced the "War on Terror's" increased criminalization and racial and cultural demonization.

We don't need to look far to see that the task of ending wars on people abroad and the economic and racialized war on people at home are deeply intertwined. As we work to unravel one end, we inevitably begin to loosen the other end of this noose that strangles our country and the countries we prey upon. Under these conditions, the past few years have been ripe with opportunities for the peace movement to build lasting cross-class and cross-race alliances; these could ultimately be the foundation for halting militarism in the coming decade.

Despite successfully turning the tide of public opinion against the war on Iraq, the peace movement has ebbed since its heights of 2001–2005. In the midst of a new political landscape—the candidacy and presidency of Barack Obama, and the economy eclipsing issues of war—the peace movement has struggled to "find itself." As the protracted withdrawals from Iraq and Afghanistan slip from American consciousness, antiwar work faces political limitations. The question becomes: how can the peace movement adapt to this shifted terrain and use this moment to further the critical alliances that can fortify future movements against both domestic and foreign war?

In addition to these alliances, another major piece of developing a forward-thinking antiwar strategy is recognizing the need for day in and day out "base-building" and infrastructural capacity. Major mobilizations are fundamental short-term tactics to mounting resistance to specific wars, but what are the medium and long-term strategies that take a wider view of militarism? How might we better integrate healing from militarization's violence into work to end wars? How can the peace movement equip people with the knowledge and skills to both sustain their local organizing and become directly involved with antiwar work, thereby nurturing future generations of war resisters?

Much has been discussed about the peace movement falling short of incorporating an anti-racist analysis into its politics and work. Whether by hiring people of color onto staff in tokenizing ways, or going through a one-off anti-racist training, many white middle class-led peace groups have gone about anti-racist work in a compartmentalized fashion without altering their programs or strategies. Yet many anti-racist critiques of the peace movement, while important, often focus on individualized behavior and fail to offer constructive anti-racist strategies.

Antiwar sentiment has historically been stronger in working class people of color communities than among those richer and whiter. The question therefore is not how to get these communities "active in peace work," but rather to adapt antiwar strategy toward key and commonly shared issues that lie at the intersections of our organizing. To begin with, this approach of "intersectionality"—to borrow a frame from women of color feminist organizing—expands our notions of peace work to include things like the economy and immigrant rights and allows us to understand how war and militarization affect different communities in different ways. But beyond this, this approach is a strategic shift that could infuse peace work both with new bases and concrete campaigns and campaign goals.

This essay will therefore focus on action-based anti-racist work surrounding four points of struggle that we believe are critical to building a sustainable antiwar/anti-militarist movement but that are perhaps outside of the traditional and predominately white peace movement: the war economy, GI and veterans organizing, Immigrant rights and countering anti-Arab racism, and healing justice work. Together with long-term strategies that prioritize a kind of "antiwar base-building," we believe a focus on these areas of work can light a path for the future of a peace movement that is both multi-racial and effectively anti-racist. More than transforming peace organizing, it is work that, over time, may have the political power to transform the country and our communities. (took out "and the nation")

Putting It into Practice: Four Points of Struggle

1. Tackling the War Economy

As federal and state governments slash budgets for social spending, a red flag for all antiwar and social justice organizers should be going up: the people are being handed the bill for Washington's wars. When half of every tax dollar goes to the Pentagon, and military spending is preserved while public education and healthcare are defunded, it is clearer than ever that the United States is running on a war economy. Those who most severely bear the brunt of these cuts are the poor and working classes, predominantly made up of African American, Latino, Indigenous and immigrant communities.

Given this, though peace and economic justice initiatives haven't always intersected, they have increasingly needed each other to face the current political climate.

"Working poor people clearly can't get the jobs and services they need without challenging military spending," says Christine Ahn of *War Times* and the Global Fund for Women. "Likewise, peace groups can't end wars without a broad movement challenging the military-industrial complex."

A number of efforts have gained steam in the past few years that have challenged this war economy, and in doing so, have begun to build bridges between peace and economic and racial justice organizers. Alliances like antiwar Military Families Speak Out teaming up with the budget transparency organization National Priorities Project to launch a "True Costs of War" campaign could be considered strategic movement milestones. Other projects such as the American Friends Service Committee and partners in Greensboro, North Carolina, created alternative job fairs that both educated and encouraged youth to steer away from enlistment, as well as provided viable alternatives that improve their ability to do so. Veterans Green Jobs in Colorado has sought to train veterans and connect them with jobs in "green" industries, connecting issues of veteran unemployment with oil wars/dependency and climate justice.

In October of 2010, about thirty peace and labor groups came together to form the New Priorities Network (NPN), an organization specifically dedicated to ending the wars in Iraq and Afghanistan by cutting the Pentagon budget and restoring domestic public services. Including traditional peace organizations like Veterans for Peace and the American Friends Service Committee, the network is a heartening sign that the antiwar movement is stepping out of its single-issue focus on war abroad and building cross-sector alliances.

Since its creation, NPN has sparked new and coordinated existing local campaigns across the country to pass city council and state resolutions calling for a redirection of funds from war to jobs. Though a handful of these have had success around such resolutions, the work is not easy and results don't appear overnight. NPN member Michael Eisenscher, also with U.S. Labor Against the War, says that a more serious commitment must be made by "recognized leaders who will nurture this process to assure its success."

Other national actions calling for redistribution of funds from war into jobs have been coordinated under the Move The Money umbrella, with the American Friends Service Committee providing infrastructural support. Massachusetts economic justice organizers' "25 percent Solution," that has worked to reduce military spending by a quarter and redirect funds into social services, provides an example of localized, streamlined war economy campaigning. This campaign was able to build upon years of intentional multiracial alliance building by NPN member group Dorchester People for Peace, who had in 2002 centralized relationships with local economic and racial justice and spent years laying the foundation for a war economy campaign to emerge from a rooted coalition.

Bridging the Gap

Many union leaders and prominent racial and economic justice organizations have been working together to carve out their own campaigns around the economy. From 2010–2012, these new liberal/progressive alliances have been seen in nationally co-ordinated events and actions such as We Are One and One Nation Working Together made up of unions like the SEIU and other AFL-CIO affiliates, and racial and economic justice groups like the NAACP and Latin@ civil rights organization National Council of La Raza. Groups like U.S. Uncut and the community organization-based anti-gentrification network Right to the City Alliance have also organized around the budget, both locally and nationally.

U.S. Labor Against War, and efforts by the International Longshore Workers' Union (ILWU), run counter to Cold War tendencies for more mainstream labor to rubber stamp U.S. military policy. We look to examples of militant labor solidarity like the ILWU, who continue their tradition of organizing explicitly as working class people in the United States in solidarity with global struggles and an international working class. The ILWU has shut down ports along the West Coast to support struggles against the Iraq War, as well as against the World Trade Organization, just as they refused to offload boycotted cargo from South Africa.

While these economic justice efforts make up an important challenge to a right-wing corporate order in the United States, they are often separate from antiwar organizing and most have not stressed an end to the wars in Iraq and Afghanistan as a part of their vision and strategy to realign the country's economic priorities. October 2010's One Nation Working together mobilization in D.C. focused on "jobs, justice, and education" but made little mention of the war abroad and its toll on the domestic economy and people.

As Michael Eisenscher recounts:

> One Nation initially sought to avoid any discussion of peace issues or involvement of antiwar forces, but ultimately did establish a Peace Table under the leadership of United for Peace and Justice (UFPJ) that brought together more than 90 organizations. But One Nation continued to resist giving any publicity to peace issues in promoting the event. After much lobbying by the Peace Table, the organizers ultimately included two antiwar speakers: Harry Belafonte and Bob King. This might be described as an uneasy partnership in which the antiwar movement was most certainly a junior partner. All

this notwithstanding, hundreds and possibly thousands of people brought homemade signs with antiwar themes.

Eisenscher's reflections on the One Nation mobilization reveal that while shared interests exist, there are many political challenges in building national alliances between liberal institutions like mainstream labor and the peace movement. Hesitation from unions, and from some racial and economic justice groups, to include issues of war stem from a fear of diluting their focus or being labeled as "radical" and alienating liberal support from elected Democrats.

By a similar token, as mentioned above, the peace movement tends to see domestic issues as secondary (or sometimes unrelated) to war, and is generally removed from the day-to-day local organizing in which racial and economic justice groups are immersed.

Therefore Eisencher's comments about the peace movement playing a "junior partner" are poignant. Playing this role could, in fact, be necessary for antiwar forces in certain political spaces—while simultaneously pushing the envelope to include issues of war and its domestic ramifications. The peace movement isn't used to assuming a political back seat, accustomed as it is centers itself on short-term emergency mobilizations in which an end to war is the central demand. Yet as the Peace Table at the One Nation mobilization proves, while war may not be at the forefront of a given agenda, it could be more effective to engage these large liberal organizations than to dismiss or organize separately from them. Though it has yet to be seen, the hope is that at some point the two poles, despite their political differences, will partner more regularly around these shared interests of changing the nation's priorities.

Dreaming big, one might imagine a coherent set of New Deal–style demands emerging from such a mass national movement. Or a movement that could throw its weight behind and build momentum around initiatives like The People's Budget, proposed by the Progressive Congressional Congress in 2011, that addressed the deficit and job creation and through a fair corporate tax, end to the current wars of the United States, and a reduction in military expenditures. Lacking media coverage and without a movement of popular support, these proposals do not even make their way into the national discussion and remain a long way off from being passed. But articulating such an agenda—which comes both from the progressive wing of Congress and from organized communities around the country—is fundamental to charting a course toward a peaceful and green economy.

Tea Party Antidote?

Another area where the peace movement could begin making inroads when addressing the war economy is in postindustrial and formerly agricultural regions suffering severe job loss. Many working class communities continue to watch their job options narrowed to sectors serving social control, like prisons, or in industries tied to war and resource control including weapons manufacturing and oil production. These aren't exactly the industries investing in a sustainable future for anyone. The 2010 BP oil disaster in the Gulf South revealed the chokehold that oil and weapons corporations have on survival interests of many Louisiana communities. Even though oil workers had just been killed and Gulf residents were experiencing immediate health impacts and tremendous economic losses, residents were also mobilized to speak up in support of BP and Big Oil's role in the region despite its role in devastating it.

At the same time, Northrup Grumman, the world's fourth largest defense contractor and one of the major industrial employers in southern Louisiana, announced major job cuts due to a shipyard closure, and warned of cutting aircraft maintenance jobs if some of their contracts with the military weren't renewed. This brings to mind the struggle in Appalachia and other regions of the Southeast to create jobs outside the mining/prison guard/Wal-Mart chokehold that has been devastating impoverished areas. Both urban and rural youth without opportunities are more vulnerable to recruiters if we don't invest in more viable alternatives for them.

As oil resources dwindle and U.S. empire and influence crumbles, so will these industries and the last sectors of work for many. It is a wake-up call to a reenvisioned peace movement that could connect the dots and assert a different future for U.S. working class communities based on green and human values. To organize local workers to withhold their labor—and their consent—from these industries would be difficult, but could deal a huge blow to U.S. empire. Historically, many working class people in the United States often haven't directed their anger at the military, often clinging to the shreds of U.S. privilege that are becoming more and more of an illusion.

Meanwhile right-wing, Republican, and corporate forces have been quick to capitalize on the economic frustrations of particularly the white working class, leaning on ingrained tropes of white supremacy and winning them over on cultural issues (gay marriage, abortion, etc.), rather than economic ones. Yet despite appearances, polls have consistently shown that continuing war is low on Americans' list of economic priorities. To "out-organize" the likes of Tea Party and related groups and build alliances with working class organizations in middle America, particularly in more rural areas, would be a powerful move by the peace movement. Part of such an effort would have to come from a clear commitment to end racism, and an overt willingness to counter the hate bubbling up from what often begins as legitimate discontent about the economy.

If the peace movement wishes to activate the dormant majority that prefers healthcare to bombs, it cannot rely solely on arguments of morality to motivate a mass base. Instead it must insert itself into these realities of growing unemployment, job loss, and limited opportunities, and set its sights on taking down the "war economy." It isn't easy work that will bear results overnight. It will require a change in how the peace movement relates to the already ongoing struggles for economic justice in the United States. As Eisenscher puts it, "it will require a long-term commitment to influencing not only political decisions but to change the political culture."

2. Choking the War Machine: G.I. Resistance

Wars still require bodies for the frontlines, as well for as the innumerable layers of maintenance of military forces and a global network of bases. Cutting off the supply of labor to each node of the military is a clear, materialist strategy to end wars. In the past decade, some of the most effective grassroots peace and antiwar energy has come from veterans' organizing and counter-recruitment work.

Though small and limited by a lack of resources, this ongoing G.I. and veteran work has concretely served to expose the military as a force of violence and dishonor, and to reclaim some of the lives it has destroyed. Equipped with clear organizing goals and a focus on building a tight membership base, it is work that other peace organizing cannot only support but also learn from.

A Way Forward: Iraq Veterans Against the War

Iraq Veterans Against the War, founded in 2004 for post-9/11 veterans and active duty troops opposing the Iraq War (later expanding its mission to explicitly include opposition to the Afghanistan War), adopted a clear strategy of withdrawing troops' consent in order to end war. IVAW and other G.I. resistance efforts aim at where the military-industrial complex is vulnerable: anywhere it depends on the compliance of its workers. IVAW draws on the powerful legacy of G.I. resistance during the Vietnam War, where mounting rebellion in the ranks, combined with the fierce resistance of the Vietnamese people and a domestic movement for peace and justice, forced the war's end.

IVAW offers the peace movement one model of what grassroots antiwar work can look like, and have committed to reenvisioning/reinventing their work as they develop their politics. The organization spent its first years functioning primarily as a speakers' bureau before experimenting with more of a community organizing model; their current work focuses on outreach to active duty troops, within a campaign framework.

The dominant model used by the mainstream peace movement, a combination of public witness and unfocused mass education, influenced IVAW and many other organizations who placed a lot of hope in "speaking truth to power." This strategy was the most visible thread that survived the short couple years of mass antiwar mobilizations leading up to the invasion of Iraq in 2003. The Winter Soldier public testimonials, organized in the legacy of the Vietnam-era Winter Soldier hearings, were the most significant national example. When it became clear that no amount of speaking out would end the occupations (although it plays an important role in shifting public discourse as well as empowering antiwar veterans to step forward), IVAW dug deeper into studying how to organize, develop, and mobilize a base.

IVAW is beginning a significant organizational transformation process. Concurrent with this exploration of organizing strategy, the group is taking steps to more seriously address its internal obstacles of racism, sexism, and homophobia that have contributed to many members' burnout. In addition to committing itself to a leadership development model, and attempting for the first time to lead a campaign with winnable elements, the organization is exploring how to strengthen its collective liberation politics.

In 2010, IVAW launched a campaign called "Operation Recovery: Stop the Deployment of Traumatized Troops." The campaign has tiered short and long-term goals, all within IVAW's strategy to withdraw troops' consent as a way to end war. By organizing for and within active duty communities to stop re-deployment of the estimated third of service members suffering from post-traumatic stress disorder, military sexual trauma, or traumatic brain injury, this campaign has the potential to hamstring the military's ability to fight these wars. In the meantime, it meets immediate needs, exposes more of the military's damage, provides leadership development opportunities for emerging antiwar leaders, and creates opportunities for collective action toward healing instead of harm. Operation Recovery is also developing a survival networks program—to better coordinate resources that active duty troops need to access in order to resist while in the military, and to take care of people afterwards.

Solidarity with War's "Most Affected"

Within G.I. Resistance, there is a frequent tension about which communities are centralized as "most affected" by the wars. Veterans who have experienced years of tokenization by nonveteran peace organizations sometimes choose to limit their organizing, wanting to channel their energies into military communities rather than focus on alliances with other non-veteran impacted communities. More challenging is the occasional depiction of U.S. military personnel and their families as being the "most impacted" by U.S. wars abroad. However, many antiwar veterans are providing consistent leadership in keeping Iraqi and Afghan experiences of occupation at the center of the withdrawal movement.

Direct connections with Iraqi and Afghan voices and resistance forces have been difficult given the political conditions on the ground in the occupied countries, but links do exist. Since 2001, there have been only a few projects that have attempted to cut through the "us" and "them" framework by linking communities in the United States to communities of Afghans and Iraqis. One of IVAW's original points of unity is reparations to the Iraqi people. The organization has been a leader on the issue of reparations in the peace movement. Members have discussed how the impulse to create reparations initiatives comes from wanting to make direct amends to people they specifically harmed. In partnership with U.S. Labor Against War, the organization is working with Iraqi trade union leaders to support their sovereignty initiatives. Two members have also spearheaded a direct reparations initiative working with Basra and Milwaukee-based aid organization Iraqi Health Now.

Another example comes from alliance-building efforts of the IVAW chapter in Champaign-Urbana, Illinois, described by Sarah Lazare of Civilian-Soldier Alliance who discusses possibilities coming from this work: "Members of IVAW reaching out to Iraqi student organizations is one direct way to start conversations about what shapes reparations work might take, and about struggles within different communities that are affected and traumatized by war. It can be a stepping stone for what it looks like for people to be organizing partners, and also to take responsibility for how they've affected the lives of Iraqis and Afghans."

For non-veteran peace organizations, supporting and facilitating these relationships could be vital roles. An anti-racist peace movement must maintain our focus on the effects of U.S. wars on the targeted populations in occupied countries, and on supporting their progressive resistance movements. Civilian organizers, including Arab-American activists and non-Arab demilitarization organizers, have been supporting veteran organizers to develop and navigate several different alliance/reparations initiatives.

Every reparations project carries complications and challenges of how to most effectively support left elements within the occupied countries—those responding accountably to peoples' needs within a larger goal of rebuilding peoples' power and restoring political and economic sovereignty. Navigating the complexity of building working relationships with Iraqis, Afghans, and other left forces opposing U.S. militarism globally is a key challenge for our generation. While there is no sure outcome that such projects will automatically result in building trust with people whose lives our country has devastated, we have to commit ourselves to reaching out regardless.

Another side of the antiwar equation is: what we are doing with our folks here at home? We need to take all these people who are polling at ever higher numbers in favor of withdrawing troops from Afghanistan as well as Iraq, and create opportunities for them to take action that places them in real relationship with the people we're at war with. Non-veteran groups could also facilitate the support of this large majority of the country. Via fundraising efforts or other means, peace groups might begin plugging in these unorganized masses who oppose the wars but are not connected with any means of turning that sentiment into anything concrete or substantial.

The strategy of building financial support (which implicitly embodies a level of political support) for Iraqi and Afghan grassroots efforts also challenges the racist narratives that people resisting U.S. occupation can't be trusted with the resources to rebuild their own democracy, that they are not sufficiently evolved to take hold of their own fate. Afghanistan, in particular, has proven confusing for many unorganized people in the United States. Many people don't fully support the U.S. occupation and its effects on Afghan civilians, but still express confusion about whether Afghans "need or want us (U.S. military presence)" there for safety. It's therefore crucial to have both the information coming directly from progressive democratic Afghan voices, as well as to have next steps available to provide direct support to those forces. Veteran organizers are particularly well positioned to anchor this work; supporting their initiatives is another important element of civilian work in the G.I. Resistance movement—where it overlaps with broader antiwar work.

Civilian Solidarity and Alliance-Building

The stronger the peace movement's ability is to hold and support war resisters—who often have families or dependents they must consider when resisting—the bigger the G.I. Resistance movement can grow. Though much support happens through informal networks, one organization that has done a large share of solidarity work is Courage to Resist. Providing direct political and material support for public and private resisters, Courage to Resist offers opportunities for antiwar-oriented individuals to contribute directly to building this movement's capacity.

Another nonmilitary G.I. Resistance organization is Civilian Solider Alliance (CivSol), a collective of nonmilitary personnel that has worked to support G.I. resistance within the ranks. CivSol has helped to build the antiwar leadership of veterans and service members, as well as to coordinate greater involvement by nonmilitary activists. It came together in 2010, formalizing preexisting working relationships between its core organizers and IVAW organizers, and has focused since its inception on helping develop IVAW's Operation Recovery campaign. In 2010, members of CivSol and the anti-racist/anti-imperialist organization Catalyst Project helped coordinate the release of the open "Letter of Reconciliation and Responsibility to the Iraqi People "from members of Bravo Company 2-16; it was this company which was responsible for the Wiki-leaked incident in 2007 that included shootings of unarmed civilians outside of Baghdad.

The efforts of groups like Courage to Resist and CivSol are often under the radar—not just of the mainstream media, but of progressive movements as well. Small and underresourced, their work offers examples of G.I. and veteran solidarity organizing whose efforts could be reinforced by the broader peace movement.

Overall, the G.I. Resistance movement is fertile ground for alliance-building in multiple directions. One example is in work countering military recruitment. As economic opportunities wane and the prison system expands, the military inevitably becomes a funnel for many working class youth looking for a way out of poverty and toward educational opportunities. Through counter-recruitment efforts, G.I.s and vets have built alliances between themselves and these heavily targeted youth. Addressing issues like criminalization and the prison system, counter-recruitment work ranges from helping youth defend themselves against recruitment tactics and dispelling recruiters' lies, to developing alternatives to the military and plugging youth into other job and educational opportunities.

IVAW members involved in this work have often partnered with youth or peace groups to talk to high school students about the realities of war. Many veterans of color describe their particular stories around joining the military, having experienced family pressure against enlistment, or family conversations acknowledging that occupied people in Iraq and Afghanistan have much in common with communities of color in the United States. This community awareness could be the basis for more partnership with peace groups doing real work around employment and education alternatives.

The most successful counter-recruitment work continues to be that which is led by youth themselves, partnered with more experienced activists who can provide resources, knowledge and mentorship. Many peace organizations, on both a local and national level, have often done this kind of partnering around counter-recruitment work with a good amount of success. Still, a more coordinated national project has yet to form and become a solid and lasting anti-militarist force.

G.I. Resistance, veteran and service member organizing, and counter-recruitment work constitutes a very broad umbrella. Individuals and organizations represent a range of politics, theories of change, and visions. Demilitarization is one thread woven throughout this movement, but not a dominant theme. The challenge, then, is to continue incorporating a wide range of people and approaches, while also increasing its consistent opposition to the underpinnings of war, rather than focusing just on its trappings. Clear and principled work against racism and imperialism is visible in this movement, but must continue to grow through its strategies and partnerships. Beyond just language or rhetoric, the broader peace movement must increase its support of these efforts.

3. Immigrant Rights, Solidarity, and Countering Anti-Arab Racism

The domestic side of the "War on Terror" and of all war has always included the further policing and imprisonment of immigrant communities, founded on racist and xenophobic notions of the United States. As militarization of immigration has increased, the two-pronged imperial strategy of domestic control and foreign expansion has become harder to disguise. On the heels of 9/11 came the rehousing of the Immigration and Naturalization Services Department under the Department of Homeland Security, which escalated this trajectory of militarization.

With the new attacks also came some of the first and fiercest post-9/11 antiwar work spearheaded by immigrant justice groups like Desis Rising Up and Moving (DRUM), which spoke to the connections between escalated attacks on their families and communities and the subsequent invasions of Afghanistan and Iraq.

A few national projects—like the Racial Justice 9/11 Network made up of people of color-led groups such as CAAAV Organizing Asian Communities of the Bronx, New York, the Indigenous Environmental Network, and the Labor/Community Strategy Center of Los Angeles—were able to provide a brief period of coordination for antiwar actions with an explicit anti-racist and immigrant justice lens, one which also drew links to the movement for the liberation of Palestine.

Despite the activity of these groups, the majority white peace movement didn't readily prioritize supporting migrant-led anti-militarist work. Nor did it directly challenge the attacks on Arabs, South Asians, and other targeted migrants of color. United for Peace and Justice, the central coordinating coalition of the antiwar demonstrations at the time, did eventually incorporate immigrant justice into its political scope.

However, challenges continued, especially in moving beyond cosponsoring single days of action to longer-term work. The Bay Area's direct action coordinating spokes council, Direct Action to Stop the War, faced a similar challenge when transitioning from 2003's focus on street mobilizations into a strategic plan in 2004 to explore longer-term work more rooted in local communities. An Immigrant Rights Working Group was developed, anchored by nonimmigrant direct action antiwar activists who were able to draw upon long-term relationships with immigrant justice organizations they had been doing solidarity work with since before 9/11. But the efforts of this working group drew a significantly smaller number of demonstrators, and momentum was hard to maintain.

Some of the strongest support for immigrant justice came from Japanese immigrants and first-generation activists. Older Japanese survivors of the World War II internment camps and children of survivors spoke out against the "special registrations" imposed in 2002, and provided historical context for the U.S. government's tactic of demonizing immigrants at home. Asian-Pacific Islander organizations and coalitions provided leadership within broader antiwar coalitions, and contributed to creating broader space for communities of color to feel ownership in antiwar actions.

In 2006, hundreds of thousands of immigrants and supporters came out in every major city across the country in massive May Day mobilizations in protest of the national Border Protection and Anti-terrorism bill (HR4437). But beyond broad endorsement, there was no large peace presence backing the day's actions. Again in 2010, there was no coordinated solidarity work from antiwar forces in response to Arizona's passage of the SB1070 bill that promoted the further criminalization and policing of immigrants in that state. As SB1070-like bills are already being passed throughout the country, the antiwar movement will continue to have opportunities to connect the dots between domestic and international militarism, and mobilize alongside targeted immigrant communities.

Though antiwar organizations may never be integral to immigrant justice work, building relationships with such groups whose central issue may not be war is a critical piece to creating a mutually supportive and broad-based peace movement. From the alliances mentioned above that began to form in the wake of 9/11, more sustained work could be built that doesn't solely come about in times of crisis. With investment and continuity, work between the antiwar and immigrant rights movement has the potential to fortify both struggles and allow for better preparation to resist the next wave of raids and deportations, and the next sounding of the drums of war.

Internationalism and Solidarity

Beyond its overall strategic importance, alliance-building with immigrant justice groups is also an opportunity for mutual learning. Migrant-led organizations cull rich local and global politics that come from working with people continually facing displacement—from economic and military policies in their home countries, to the policing and gentrification of immigrant neighborhoods in the United States. Though they are working within the United States, they maintain powerful connections and solidarity with their counterpart communities abroad. These cross-border models of working would be a potent approach for the peace movement's work with Iraqis and Afghans abroad and those displaced and migrated to the United States.

The War Resisters League has been involved in several such projects. WRL field organizer Ali Issa has been building ties with Iraqi youth on the East Coast, developing WRL's Iraqi Education Project to provide political education and leadership development to young refugees. Along with the South Asia Solidarity Initiative, WRL and IVAW came together in 2009 to hold joint events and plan work to bring together their different constituencies. Events pivoted on anniversary dates like the invasion of Afghanistan on October 7, national days of action in protest against budget cuts, and special opportunities like the U.S. book tour of Afghan human rights leader Malalai Joya.

These events have included local Iranian, Afghani, and Sudanese activists and groups, as well as other leaders from the street vendors' movement, from youth counter-recruitment organizers; groups like the Malcolm X Grassroots Movement were also involved. Malalai Joya's tour included meetings with anti-imperialist activists from Palestine, South Asia, the Philippines, and elsewhere in the Arab world—all struggling against U.S. militarism. These activists spoke of how important it felt to be sitting down together building toward more active global solidarity.

As described by Issa, organizers see the potential for their efforts to bear longer-term fruit. This could mean that the broader memberships of these groups move toward collaborative work challenging the Afghanistan War, and linking their economic justice work with antiwar demands. One project emerging from these meetings has been the development of a workshop focused on linking the war economy with the impacts of the war itself, especially spotlighting Afghani voices. The workshop curriculum includes case studies of common potential targets for antiwar political action. For example, research is presented explaining Verizon's role as both primary supplier for U.S. military bases, as well as a major target of the Communications Workers of America's fight for domestic labor rights. The strategy behind developing such workshops is to offer a framework for the development of concrete, grassroots-initiated campaigns that make the links vital to lasting change.

There are also national networks connected to global organizing that peace organizations might well pay greater attention to. Some groups, like Grassroots Global Justice (GGJ), already have a clear analysis of U.S. imperialism and would be a logical partner to antiwar groups. GGJ was initiated to facilitate the participation of base-building community organizations in low-income communities of color in international left arenas, such as the World Social Forum process.

Internationalism was crucial to Central America solidarity work of the 1980s and beyond, as well as to the global justice movement of 1990s and early 2000s.

By looking at organizations like the Committee in Solidarity with the Peoples of El Salvador (CISPES), peace organizations can glean some valuable lessons. While CISPES fortified relationships with the Salvadoran movement through its connection to their united front, the FMLN, it also worked to defund the U.S.-supported war in El Salvador by pressuring Congress each time a vote came up. Given the lack of a clear united front with democratic aims in Iraq and Afghanistan, U.S. anti-war organizers have had a tougher time pursing such a solidarity model. Only a handful of antiwar organizations have been able to do so, and have connected with NGOS, unions, or individuals in these countries.

Turning to the global justice movement in the United States, solidarity with people of the Global South was part and parcel of a politics of fair international trade, and a rejection of the exploitation of transnational capitalism largely controlled by First World/Western powers through the International Monetary Fund, the World Bank, and the World Trade Organization. Much of the initial structure, energy, and experience that helped launch the anti-Iraq antiwar movement came from the networks and people who had, up until 9/11, been focused on challenging economic imperialism, neoliberalism, and recolonization. The "Seattle Generation" therefore deeply informed and shaped peace mobilizations in the 2000s.

However, the massive and bold street mobilizations of 2002 and 2003 burned brightly but did not sustain. The global justice movement neither continued with its central work against transnational capitalism, nor got on board with longer-term antiwar movement building.

There are many nuanced lessons to explore there. One important question for peace workers is how to recapture or recreate a spirit and practice of international solidarity when it comes to confronting war.

Countering Anti-Arab Racism

In a post 9/11 world, we have seen the return to a high level of acceptance for blatantly racist policy and discourse, and the development of Islamophobia as a new "red scare."

This culture of devaluing certain lives (not a new tune for the United States) has reinforced the wedge of cultural and material superiority between average folks in the United States and the world's people we invade and undermine.

Under these conditions, a peace movement dedicated to anti-racism is one dedicated to ending the dehumanization and racism against Muslims and Arabs. Taking it a step further, much of Washington's ability to move forward with its wars of resource control and regional domination in the Middle East requires the notion that Muslims and Arabs are "not like us." Ending anti-Arab racism and "rehumanizing" the peoples of the region is key to ending war. The peace movement has not, over the last ten years, managed to develop a significant national counterweight to this dominant racist narrative.

To do this, we must confront our own collective ignorance when it comes to things like left/progressive movements in the Middle East and Islam in general. As Rami El-Amine, activist and cofounder of *Left Turn* magazine, told the War Resisters League in their 2008 Listening Process, there is a lack of understanding of Islam in the movement. El-Amine suggested:

> People have a very static view of Islamist activists. They're not all right wing. Some might even be considered progressive. When we consider liberation theology in Latin America or the role of the church in the Black civil rights movement, there are parallels to the role Islam may play in liberation movements in the Middle East. …If people's misunderstanding of Islam and wholesale dismissal of all Islamist politics is not addressed, it sets us up for the next war. Islamophobia exists to dehumanize Muslims (and by extension, all people in the Middle East), to make killing them easier. Activists have to work to change these attitudes in the culture.

As movements for democracy in the Middle East and North Africa continue to develop in the coming decades, the need is great for a counter-narrative to the "angry Arab" and "fundamentalist Islamist" discourses. The peace movement has a role of national leadership to play in countering these racist notions and supporting the peoples trying to wrestle free from undemocratic regimes backed and armed by the United States.

To do this, majority white peace organizations need to build transnational alliances as well as domestic ties with progressive Arab and Islamic groups within the United States, such as the Council on American Islamic Relations, the Arab Resource and Organizing Center in the Bay Area, and even local mosques that have suffered the brunt of anti-Muslim hate crimes.

"Make a symbolic chain around a mosque," suggests El-Amine, "Hold a rally, a meeting, something to break down the sense of isolation and attack that Muslims feel, particularly in light of the rise of the tea party and far right."

State repression, legitimized against Arabs, has also begun to bleed into peace work in communities usually more protected through race and class privilege. The 2010 FBI raids on the homes of twenty-three antiwar activists, particularly those associated with work around Palestine and Colombia, was a wakeup call to the peace movement that a climate of unchecked racism affects us all. The opportunities for campaigns and political education work around anti-Arab racism abound.

4. Trauma, Healing, and Cultural Transformation

In strategic discussions, we often talk about combating, fighting, or mounting an offensive to the war machine. Yet much of the work to be done to end war and its root causes has a lot to do with healing internally. Working against the clock to organize against Washington's imminent and "endless" wars, the peace movement tends to overlook this fundamental area of work: how to transform ourselves and our militarist culture.

War produces enormous amounts of trauma, whether for its direct victims, or for those who are or have been in combat and their families. We also must not discount the trauma and sorrow felt while seeing one's country wage war on another, with all the horrors that entails—from murder to torture to environmental destruction. We are all impacted, to whatever extent, both by the accumulation of trauma, and by the interrelated effects of racism, heightened gender-based violence, and the economic savagery of the war budget. The results are injured people and communities in desperate need of repair: emotionally and psychologically as well as physically and economically.

Learning from Veterans' Organizing

There are many lessons about healing to draw from the antiwar veterans'/G.I. Resistance movements, which have been forced to address the importance of integrating mental health care into all organizing work because its community is in ongoing crisis.

According to the military's public figures, eighteen veterans commit suicide every day (though the military does not acknowledge the legitimacy of many more suicides). Studies show that up to eighty percent of people partnered to a veteran with post-traumatic stress disorder experience physical abuse. At least one third of active duty service members are denied adequate mental health care, and crushing taboos pressure vets against talking about their experiences or seeking care for trauma. Military psychologists are more accountable to the command structure, and work much harder to maintain good press relations around the war than they do to care for individual soldiers suffering from trauma or stress. Many veterans experience pressure from families and friends to keep it all inside. Where these pressures intersect with the internal crises of trauma and the external crises of a failing economy and a society that fails to reintegrate its military veterans on many levels, we have a storm of violence that is rocking our communities amid very little discussion or collective response.

Veteran organizing has therefore needed to experiment with creating support structures for mental and emotional health, and build those into campaign development, chapter-building, and leadership development of members. After years of hard work by veterans and allies, the discussion of combat trauma has begun to enter mainstream discourse, decades into overt wartime. IVAW's Operation Recovery campaign is one example of this "dual power" strategy that integrates a healing justice into a plan oriented toward forcing troop withdrawal. For people with severe post-traumatic stress disorder, care is nonnegotiable.

Vets also use "politically neutral" peer support spaces that allow them to share traumas and begin to heal from them. Talking with fellow veterans in safe nonjudgmental spaces can be a powerful and transformative experience. This also happens through public speaking, in the forms of testimonials or sharing military/combat experiences with event or rally audiences or at a school, something antiwar veteran activists are frequently asked to do.

Arts-based work also helps veterans grapple with their direct experiences of war. Combat Paper holds workshops where veterans pulp their uniforms, make them into paper, and use this paper for art and storytelling. Fatigues Clothesline invites veterans to draw or paint their stories onto their uniforms, and has provided a platform for veterans who survived sexual assault within the military to bring their stories out into the community through art exhibits. Warrior Writers, developed initially as a project within IVAW and now an independent vehicle, teaches writing workshops by and for veterans and publishes their work. These creative and powerful exposures of the costs of militarism could be brought to a national scale by the broader peace movement.

Part of restoring the damage done by war is addressing the physical, emotional, and psychological wounds that veterans carry themselves and also inflict on their families and communities. Violence is cyclical, and traumatized people perpetuate these cycles even when it is contrary to their own values, sense of self, or how they want to be with other people. An empathetic, patient, and present peace movement is needed nourish the small-scale projects working to break these cycles of violence.

Because veterans' organizing takes supporting one another seriously, in many ways they are laying the foundation for stronger movements, with less burnout and deeper and more powerful relationships. Though many in the peace movement overlook this support and healing work or see it as separate from organizing, it is in fact integral to the health and sustainability of the antiwar movement.

Healing and Transformative Justice

Outside of veterans, many groups working around the prison industrial complex, sexual abuse and domestic violence, homelessness, gender/sexuality justice and disability rights have also incorporated healing and transformative justice into their organizing.

Healing justice centralizes two important concepts. One is recognizing that people experience both state and interpersonal trauma and oppression, and that those who deal with multiple layers of structural violence in their lives have a tremendous amount of insight and resiliency to offer. The other is that we have no other choice than to acknowledge and engage with this trauma, including trauma that is passed on generationally, if we desire a more functional and sustainable society.

Transformative justice is a concept that Generation Five, an organization which works to end child sexual abuse, describes as a "response to the lack of a liberatory approach to violence…that seeks safety and accountability without relying on alienation, punishment, or State or systemic violence." As people advocating an end to wars and the use of violence to solve international and civil conflicts, we would do well to join the conversations around transformative justice and ally ourselves with these politics.

Just as organizations like Generation Five work to envision and implement alternatives to prisons or the police as a means of punishment, so must peace workers seek alternatives to military force and assassination as a means of global problem-solving.

Imagine the peace movement synthesizing practices learned from our comrades in Rwanda, who are rebuilding their postgenocide society on the foundations of Indigenous cultural practices like *gacaca*—a community-based people's court which is based on reconciliation and not retribution. There are so many lessons from to be learned from women of color in the southern United States, like the work of the Ubuntu and Kindred collectives. The peace movement needs to build its experience with and fluency in different forms of community healing. It is an immediate and practical need. But it is also a very strategic one, if we ever hope to contribute to a serious reshaping of society.

Cultural Shifts: Alternatives and Joyful Resistance

Doing peace work inside the United States holds many contradictions. As those living within the global superpower, we experience benefits from the same systems of exploitation that we are working to end, even while those benefits are whittled down to crumbs. Living inside the empire even as we work to undo its dominance and change its priorities is a complicated project. Through peace work, we affirm our connection to people around the world who have been bombed, occupied, and exploited by the U.S. government—but many of us are removed from their unthinkable realities.

Our complicity as taxpayers, as the beneficiaries to some extent of this plunder, and especially those of us more closely connected to the military itself, creates yet another layer of distress.

Added to this is a pervasive culture of aggression, a long resume of military intervention, and the fact that the nation was formed by, and continues to benefit from, Indigenous genocide, land theft, and the enslavement of Africans (now through widespread policies of imprisonment). Our nation's elected officials enshrine military solutions and "American exceptionalism"—whereby what the United States does militarily is warranted despite being illegal or immoral. Too often these ways of thinking are widely accepted even by those who may oppose a particular war. There has been, particularly over the past couple of generations, a broad manufactured consensus that fundamentally affirms empire-building, critiquing only details but not the project. In this atmosphere, even for those opposed to war, there is also a collective sense of responsibility (yet helplessness) that prevents many from joining organizing initiatives.

Heavy with the grimness of war, our organizing and mobilizing often takes on a similar somber tone. Reacting to quickly executed war plans, the antiwar movement tends to be in "emergency mode," working quickly and with a ubiquitous "NO." And while that "NO" is vital, the peace movement has yet to popularize nonviolent alternatives to aggression, or to spread a culture of joy which offers visions and examples of how interdependence actually creates more sustainable futures for everyone. We need to meet the density of hate in U.S. popular culture, which is mobilized so easily into war and racist attacks, with more compelling and positive paths.

In developing and asserting alternatives to war, we must not only present workable alternatives to violence, but also offer different people and Earth-based priorities to shape our foreign policy. Instead of protesting death, we can be celebrating life—our richness and diversity, our creativity, our common threads—in ways that are appealing to masses of people and can capture their imaginations about the change that is possible. We must transform the image of the didactic peace activist who's always on a Christian-toned "mission" to educate other people about The Truth and the Right Thing to Do. This overserious emphasis doesn't represent the heart of demilitarization work. We do this work out of love, commitment, and a belief that the future can be different than what's prescribed for us by the politicians and war-makers: that we deserve a different, joyous future and that we are capable of creating it together.

Changing Internal Culture

Within our movements, we are not immune to the impact of militarism, racism, sexism, and class oppression; we all absorb the culture we live in. Against our best intentions, we carry it with us into our work for justice. These traumas aren't merely challenges to our movements, they are opportunities to radically transform our lives and our work.

Yet we must be careful how we approach this internal work. If we demonize one another and certain behaviors and label them as being bad, we risk alienating one another and creating internally antagonistic organizations. We must understand the traumatic culture which has come to surround us as a reality which must be worked with and transformed over time. We've got to invest in the hard stuff: talk about internal racism, sexism, classism, and homophobia with intention and with love for ourselves and each other.

In order to forge the alliances that we've discussed above, the wide array of groups and individuals involved in peace and militarism work must approach one another with this openness and acceptance. Additionally we must be ready and willing to step outside of our comfort zones and usual political circles to build these relationships, perhaps the most fundamental element of social movements.

For the peace movement, that means getting the white, middle-class pacifist to sit, respectfully, at the same table with the high school student organizing for immigrant rights; bringing together the Iraq War veteran with the prison abolition activist. We mustn't shy away from building these bridges because they don't appear strategic (i.e. don't immediately advance our particular campaigns), or because we don't all share tactics. Only by taking risks can we navigate potential joint struggle, develop collective vision, and practice cooperative rather than competitive efforts.

As our external attitude could use an injection of joy, so could our internal one. The more vibrancy, joy, and nourishment that we as organizers gain from the peace movement, the more we will be able to stick around for the long haul and attract new people to the work. Developing our resiliency and reweaving our fragmented movements is a key piece of how we are building peace work that has the potential to grow exponentially.

Base and Infrastructure-Building for Peace

To help form the alliances mentioned in these four spheres of work, peace work could use a certain strategic realignment: developing medium and long-term strategies that focus on winnable goals for a movement that usually swells within short-term periods of urgency. Medium-term strategy could be campaign-based and locally rooted—such as antiwar or military spending referendums in local government, counter-recruitment work, or specific divestment campaigns. A long-term strategy could be capacity and infrastructure building, to enable a movement known for major mobilizations (but not for ongoing, winning campaigns), to have a visionary project of peace that can withstand the comings and goings of Washington's wars.

Antiwar Base-Building

While the antiwar movement has historically been a point of entry for many into social change work, it does not make up the bulk of political organizing in the country. Many who became involved in social justice organizing between 2001 and 2005 did so through attending large-scale antiwar demonstrations or becoming active in local peace work. However, many of these people returned to or were drawn into other areas of political activity such as union work, racial justice work, or environmental organizing, where work either felt more relevant to their everyday lives or offered paying jobs. Additionally, during this antiwar upsurge, organizers from these various sectors perhaps came out to demonstrations or dedicated a portion of staff and resources to peace work, but have since returned to focusing on their primary issues.

Peace and antiwar work also tend to be outside of the nonprofit political arena. Its politics of de-militarization and ending all wars don't win it favor with foundations, and when comparing peace work to environmental or economic justice work, the amount of paid organizers or staff is minimal. This can be seen as a strength—pushing organizers to seek grassroots strategies and avoid the pitfalls of "professionalization" of the left—at the same time that it drastically affects capacity and the movement's ability to sustain its organizers.

Given these realities, in a sense, what the peace movement lacks is kind of antiwar "base-building," a term that many people of color–led grassroots organizations use to describe increasing membership numbers and participation, doing community outreach, and developing the future leaders of their organizations. A peace movement that works on "antiwar base-building," is therefore a peace movement that can provide a home for organizers and look beyond the empire's next move. Such a movement will invest in its future leaders, and build the capacity for communities to resist militarism.

To grow a base however, a movement must have seeds to begin with. In the last couple of generations, the antiwar movement has been made up of predominately white and middle-class youth or middle-aged folks—those not necessarily targeted by the state's domestic clampdowns. A solid base might be harder to come by as the issues being addressed may be farther removed from organizers' everyday realities. The G.I. and veteran antiwar groups perhaps come the closest to doing this kind of "base-building," as they do have a community commonly affected by war. Religious peace communities such as the Catholic Worker movement, and occasional local collectives or grassroots groups, are also places to find antiwar bases. But by and large, those that make up the broader movement don't always share much more than their opposition of war.

Base-building for the antiwar movement might therefore look a little different than "bases" traditionally conceived of for many membership-driven grassroots organizations. It might not only entail sustaining the existing sectors of peacemakers—those who see antiwar work as their primary work—but a strengthening of analysis and organizational power of other communities around issues of war, militarism, and methods of protest such as nonviolent direct action.

As the horrors and costs of war are not currently motivating large numbers of people to join their local antiwar groups, the peace movement must meet people where they are at. We must both offer information, as well as communicate a sense that the antiwar movement has a long, rich history full of bravery and successful work. These facts and perspectives are not read about in history textbooks or given voice to in the mainstream media. But they can provide vision for alternative futures as well as structure for resisting empire.

The older membership of the traditional peace movement possesses an enormous wealth of knowledge—not just about global militarism, but about past antiwar struggles and lessons learned. With resisters from WWII to the Vietnam War and beyond, from the anti-nuclear movement to the feminist movements, to those who have been working against global bases and U.S. puppet regimes—these organizations and their long-standing members are an invaluable resource to young and newer activists in every sector of struggle. Those of us who have had the privilege to be immersed in this hub of political history, and the opportunity to participate in bridge-building with community-based racial and economic justice work, see tremendous potential in getting more younger-generation organizers involved in this type of alliance-building.

There is also a new core of organizers in this country—made up predominately of people of color—with similar historical and political knowledge that come from other sectors of social justice work. Whether working in the labor movement, civil and human rights, international solidarity work, or immigrant justice, these movement leaders are well-versed on issues of militarism and war, though they may not place these issues at the center of their day-to-day organizing. Their knowledge could also be tapped to form collaborative educational efforts that move beyond an inner circle and out to local groups, community centers, churches and other religious or spiritual institutions, and schools. This collaboration would be an inarguable mechanism for antiwar base-building.

Developing popular peace education programs and trainings that could equip communities with intellectual and practical organizing skills could go a long way in nurturing the future of the antiwar movement. Nonviolent trainings and teach-ins on militarism abound, but this generation hasn't had a coherent program coordinated by the peace movement that invests in its participants on a long-term basis. Elements of this program could include local conflict resolution, job training, basic organizing skills, counter-recruitment, know-your-rights and other workshops that can be useful on a community level.

In previous eras of the antiwar movement, opportunities like organizer trainings helped many feel that they belonged to the movement, dedicating themselves as lifelong members. That political appeal (the stuff makes one want to stick around) and sense of belonging can't be cultivated by large mobilizations. If partnered with racial and economic work, these kinds of programs could be a form of solidarity, which planted seeds for future alliances and joint work.

Fortifying for the Future

As we have detailed in this chapter, the future of peace and antiwar work may not be primarily contained in the traditional predominately white peace groups and their action-based "strategy" consisting of little more than seasonal mass marches and demonstrations. Rather, we hope that both long-standing antiwar organizations and their well-studied and developed tactics will continue to evolve, but with more creativity and a broader base of support, building alliances which hail from different movements and sectors.

Through strategic shifts in focus—to points of struggle such as the war economy, immigrant rights, anti-Arab racism, G.I. and veteran collaborative organizing, and healing work—the anti-war movement can put an anti-racist politics of solidarity with those most affected by war into practice. By staking out not just short but medium- and long-term goals—from passing local antiwar resolutions to political peace education and "base-building"—anti-war organizations can concretize their work, making it more politically accessible, positive, and empowering. As wars "wind down" in Iraq and Afghanistan and troops are withdrawn, peace workers know well that our work is nowhere near over. The decades ahead will undoubtedly hold more imperial projects of war and resource control, once again challenging the anti-militarist movement's strength and breadth.

We hope that this chapter has highlighted some of the areas in which the peace movement can and must build the alliances needed to rise to these challenges. We hope that with the dedication of individuals and groups, working both in their communities and on a national level, a multiracial and antiracist peace movement will blossom into a broad-based movement that can truly move forward.

An Anti-Racist Gandhi Manifesto

Sachio Ko-Yin

This manifesto is surely not meant to be the final word on the connections between racism, militarism, and the struggle to end both. Nor is it a summary of all that has come before. But it seems a fine way to close this book, in review of the meeting points between beauty, and thought, and action.

Mutiny against injustice and the methods of fighting without violence or hatred are now, as always, fundamentally important. But the movement that self-consciously spreads the nonviolent method is beset with certain stumbling blocks that keep us from the beloved community. If pacifism is to move forward, the development of an anti-racist pacifism is indispensable. I address these points to certain friends in the Caucasian pacifist movement in the hope of dialogue and mutual growth.

1. In renouncing violence, the violence of racism must be fully identified. In growing to understand white privilege, privilege must be renounced. (What could be more Gandhian?) The injustice of a white supremacist culture has an impact on every aspect of our lives (as does sexism, classism, and homophobia). Oppression is not an issue separate from war. Anti-war activity must expose the racism of the war machine.

2. The American history of slavery and genocide shapes this nation today. As we open our mouths, this history must always be before our eyes.

3. The existence of the Caucasian bubble must be recognized. White activists tend to form and maintain relationships with other white activists. When white pacifists think of the political landscape, they are usually only aware of white pacifist groups, and the landscape of African American pacifism is below the radar. When the bubble is recognized, change can begin.

4. Over and over again, white activists initiate projects with other white activists, and reach out to people of color as an afterthought. Planning committees are almost exclusively Caucasian, even if the program planned is multicultural. If the means contain the ends, then multicultural outreach should be the beginning.

5. Work initiated by communities of color should be supported and amplified.

6. Beware of styles of nonviolence that come exclusively from the disaffected Caucasian experience, for example long lists of Caucasian heroes and priority of Caucasian music and food. The peace movement must be self-consciously multicultural in all things, bending over backwards to end old habits, and to welcome other cultures. Be conscious of political issues that are far from the day-to-day reality of people of color. Be mindful of expectations of time and funds that only certain people can afford.

7. Do not condemn or condescend to groups in oppressed communities that do not advocate nonviolence.

8. Be careful not to be pacifist isolationists. Distinguish between "kindred spirits" and "coalition partners." Caucasian pacifists should have a special kinship to nonviolent activists in communities of color. This relationship must begin in earnest. But this should not preclude them from being in coalition with groups that are not nonviolent—this is also an important part of the work.

9. Often, King is invoked, implying that his "'real' message was anti-war, as if his work for racial freedom was not radical.

10. In thinking of pacifists of color, Gandhi and King are invariably invoked, but it's essential to honor the living pacifists of color!

11. At the opposite pole of anti-racist pacifism is "color blind' pacifism. King is quoted out of the context of his work to imply that thinking about race is racism, which leads to a laissez-faire approach. "We'll keep doing what we're doing; if people of color want to join us, they are welcome to." This approach in every instance leads back to the Caucasian bubble. Anti-racist pacifism must replace this paradigm with a radical multiculturalism at every stage of the work.

AfterPoems

Why War Is Never a Good Idea

Alice Walker

Poet/activist Grace Paley often spoke of how she considered herself a "combative pacifist"—a challenge to all those around her, to not sit too comfortably in rigid definitions or dogmatic ideologies. With deceptive simplicity and unflinching honesty, Paley put her body in the way of the war machines, and shared her passion and love with people of all races, religions, and nationalities. In a style reminiscent of Paley, Alice Walker wrote the following poem, about the nature of war, as a children's book (though we believe that people of all ages would do well to heed her words). Also like Paley, Walker has often put herself "on the line," most recently on several trips to Palestine, delivering messages of hope and solidarity. In writings about one of her visits, Walker poignantly noted the connections between nonviolence and liberation, and between the U.S. civil rights movement, international movements for independence and justice, and the nature of peace. She said:

> When I was in Cairo en route to Gaza in 2009, I met the then U.S. Ambassador to Egypt Margaret Scobey, and struck up an interesting conversation about the use of nonviolence. She—a white woman with a Southern accent—mentioned the success of "our" civil rights movement and asked why couldn't the Palestinians be more like us. It was a remarkable comment from a perspective of unimaginable safety and privilege; I was moved to tell her of the effort it took, even for someone so inherently nonviolent as me, to contain myself during seven years in Mississippi when it often appeared there were only a handful of white Mississippians who could talk to a person of color without delivering injury or insult. If we had not been able to change our situation through nonviolent suffering, we would have most certainly, like the African National Congress (ANC), like the Palestine Liberation Organization (PLO), like Hamas, turned to violence. I told her how dishonest it seemed to me that people claim not to understand the desperate, last-ditch resistance involved in suicide bombings, blaming the oppressed for using their bodies where the Israeli army uses armored tanks.

In 2011, en route to Gaza as a member of a peace flotilla, Walker wrote about "the peace of nonviolent revolt which entails a radical dedication to nonabandonment of the peaceful self." She likened the Palestinian people to the red poppy—that tenacious wild flower,

517

waving bright hope in the smallest wind. Walker again reminded us of our connectedness, noting that "Each of Earth's peoples teaches the rest of us something: You demonstrate steadfastness: how to hold on, through lies, murder, brutal repression, breathtaking theft, unbearable despair, until at last, singing our own outraged and wild poppy song, we come to join you."

We are honored to have Alice Walker's poem conclude this book about making connections. It is our best hope, as Walker implores, that we come and join together to build a better tomorrow.

Though War speaks
Every language
It never knows
What to say
To Frogs.

Picture frogs
Beside a pond
Holding their annual
Pre-rainy-season
Convention.

They do not see War
Huge tires
Of a
Camouflaged
Vehicle
About to
Squash
Them flat.

Though War has a mind of its own
War never knows
Who
It is going
To hit.

Picture a donkey
Peacefully
Sniffing a pile
Of Straw
A small boy

Holds
The end
Of its
Frayed
Rope
Bridle.

They do not see it
They are both thinking
Of dinner
The boy
Is hoping for
Polenta & eggs
Maybe a carrot
Or apple
For
Dessert.

Just above
Them
Something dark
Big as
A car
Is
Dropping.

Though War has eyes
Of its own
& can see oil
&
Gas
& mahogany trees
& every shing thing
Under
The earth

When it comes
To nursing
Mothers
It is blind;
Milk, especially

Human,
It cannot
See.

Picture a woman
Beside a window
She is blissful
Singing
A lullaby
A baby twirls
A lock of her
Dark Hair
Suckles
For all
It is
Worth.

They do not smell War
Dressed in
Green & brown
Imitating
Their fields
Marching slowly
Towards them
Up
The steep
Hill.

Though War is Old
It has not
Become wise
It will not hesitate
To destroy
Things that
Do not
Belong to it
Things very
Much older
Than itself.

Picture the forest

With its
Rivers
& rocks
Its pumas
&
Its
Parakeets
Its turtles
Leopards
&
Snakes.

High above them War
Has turned itself
Into a white cloud
Trailing
An
Airplane
That
Dusts
Everything
Below
With
A powder
That
Kills.

War has bad manners
War eats everything
In its path
& what
It doesn't
Eat
It
Dribbles
On:

Here
War is
Munching on
A village

Its missiles
Taking chunks
Big bites out
Of it.

War's
Leftover
Gunk
Seeps
Like
Saliva
Into
The
Ground.
It
Is finding
Its
Way
Into the
Village
Well.

War tastes terrible
& smells
Bad. It never
Considers
Body
Odor
Or
Weird
Side
Effects.
When added
To water
It makes
You sick
Sip by sip.

You could die
While
Choking

&
Holding
Your Nose.

Now suppose You
Become War
It happens
To some of
The nicest
People
On earth:
& one day
You have
To drink
The
Water
In this place.

Reflections after the June 12th March for Disarmament

Sonia Sanchez

When Marilyn Buck died just weeks after her early parole, granted because it was clear that terminal cancer had spread through her body, many felt that we had lost our latter-day John Brown: an uncompromising, radical freedom fighter whose love of Black people and liberation transcended race, gender, class, and time. Writing for a Resistance in Brooklyn conference and booklet put together for the two-hundredth birthday of abolitionist Brown, Buck imagined a modern-day Johnetta Brown, an indefatigable woman who would make solidarity her clarion call. And though she was not (like Brown) hung at the gallows just before a civil war, Buck's decades of political imprisonment—a diseased state of inherent abuse and negligent treatment—undoubtedly had a similar physical effect. As "John Brown's Body" stirred generations to greater consciousness and militant action, so too might we expect and hope that Marilyn Buck's life and example will not have been in vain.

We may be, as Gil Scott-Heron wrote, facing "Winter in America." But, unlike the words of the song or the fate faced by so many of our imprisoned peace and freedom fighters, not all of the leaders and heroes have "been killed or sent away." Sonia Sanchez, in a major talk given late in 2010, spoke of the upcoming generation's duty to preserve our world through peace, resistance, and compassion.

"'Resist' is a holy word," Sanchez said,

> It's a political word, a word to teach ourselves and our children. …Unless this generation walks in peace, there won't be a twenty-second century. I know we can't afford to have another generation die on us. This world has given us too many warnings. We must resist going to war and being placed against each other. If you still think like that, you're still a slave. Do we have the courage to be resistant—to be peaceful?"
>
> Let us decide what it is we will die for, what it is we will live for. Let us decide to harmonize. We must position ourselves in the world, with all kinds of people. Power belongs to a group, not an individual. From Gandhi to Tupac, from Einstein to Bob Marley, many people have done things in this century to make us think about who we are and who we must be. Now we must change the direction of our country

and the world—as African Americans, as Native Americans, as Asian Americans, as Whites, as gays, as lesbians. We need to understand why we are here. We need to understand what we should be.

A true people's poet, author, and activist, Sanchez has noted that the idea of race has always been used to separate people. And though America was built on lies, with land rights placed above human rights, the only way to resist such manipulation, in Sanchez's estimate, is by cultivating a sense of "community, nonviolence and caring." Another theme in U.S. history has been struggle, and in collective struggle, generations have realized that "We are not alone; we've found that we are one."

Though Sonia Sanchez correctly calls on us to look to the next generation for new leadership, heroes, and sheroes, we are humbled to have her own leading voice help us conclude this book with a poetic afterward. Versions of these poems were published in the February 2004 edition of the Women's Review of Books.

> I have come to you tonite out of the depths
>   of slavery
>   from white hands peeling black skins over
>   america;
>
> I have come out to you from reconstruction eyes
>   that closed on black humanity
>   that reduced black hope to the dark
>   huts of america;
>
> I have come to you from the lynching years,
>   the exploitation of black men and women by
>   a country that allowed the swinging of
>   strange fruits from southern trees;
>
> I have come to you tonite thru the
>   delaney years, the du bois years, the
>   b.t. washington years, the robeson
>   years, the garvey years, the
>   depression years, the you can't eat
>   or sit of live just die here years,
>   the civil rights years, the black power
>   years, the black nationalist years, the
>   affirmative action years, the liberal
>   years, the neo-conservative years;

I have come to say that those years
  were not in vain; the ghosts of our
  ancestors searching this american dust for
  rest were not in vain, black women
  walking their lives in clots were not
  in vain, the years walked
  sideways in a forsaken land were not
  in vain;

I have come to you tonite as ah equal,
  as a comrade, as a black woman
  walking down a corridor of tears,
  looking neither to the left or the right,
  pulling my history with bruised
  heels,
  beckoning to the illusion of america
  daring you to look me in the eyes to
  see these faces, the exploitation of a
  people because of skin pigmentation;

I have come to you tonite because no people
  have been asked to be modern day people
  with the history of slavery, and still
  we walk, and still we talk, and
  still we plan, and still we hope and
  still we sing;

I have come to you tonite because there are
  inhumanitarians in the world, they are not
  new. they are old. they go back into history.
  they were called explorers, soldiers, mercenaries,
  imperialists, missionaries, adventurers,
  but they looked at the world for what
  it would give up to them and they violated
  the land and the people, they looked
  at the land and sectioned it up for
  private ownership, they looked at the
  people and decided how to manipulate
  them thru fear and ignorance, they looked
  at the gold and began to hoard and
  worship it;

I have come to you because it is time
  for us all to purge imperialism from
  our dreams, to purge materialism
  from our eyes, from the planet earth
  to deliver the earth again into the hands
  of the humanitarians;

I have come to you tonite not just for the stoppage
  of nuclear proliferation, nuclear
  plants, nuclear bombs, nuclear
  waste, but to stop the proliferation
  of nuclear minds, of nuclear generals
  of nuclear presidents, of nuclear scientists,
  who spread human and nuclear waste
  over the world;

I come to you because the world needs to be
  saved for the future generations who must
  return the earth to peace, who will not
  be startled by a man's/woman's skin color;
I come to you because the world needs sanity
  now, needs men and women who will
  not work to produce nuclear weapons,
  who will give up their need for excess
  wealth and learn how to share the
  world's resources, who will never
  again as scientists invent again just
  for the sake of inventing;

I come to you because we need to turn our
  eyes to the beauty of this planet, to the
  bright green laughter of trees, to the beautiful
  human animals waiting to smile their unprostituted smiles;

I have come to you to talk about our inexperience
  at living as human beings, thru death marches and camps,
  thru middle passages and slavery
  and thundering countries raining hungry faces;

I am here to more against
  leaving our shadows implanted on the

earth while our bodies disintegrate in
nuclear lightning;

I am here between the voices of our ancestors
and the noise of the planet,
between the surprise of death and life;

I am here because I shall not give the
earth up to non-dreamers and earth molesters;

I am here to say to you:
my body is full of veins
like the bombs waiting to burst
with blood.
we must learn to suckle life not
bombs and rhetoric
rising up in redwhiteandblue patriotism;

I am here. and my breath/our breaths
must thunder across this land
arousing new breaths, new life.
new people, who will live in peace
and honor one day.

Peace (a poem for Maxine Green)

Sonia Sanchez

1. Peace. What is it?
   Is it an animal? A bird? A plane?
   A mineral? A color? A drumbeat?
   (doowop doowop doo doo dee doo doo dee)

2. Is it a verb? A noun? An adjective?
   A prophet with no pockets?
   Circling our paragraphed lives?
   (dwoodop bopbop dwowaa doo bop bop doo bop bop bop)

3. DuBois said: The cause of war
   is the preparation of war.
   DuBois said: The cause of war
   is the preparation of war.
   I say the cause of peace
   must be the preparation of peace,
   I say the cause of peace
   must be the preparation of peace.
   (Blaablablabaaaa blue blueblay blueblay)

4. Shall I prepare a table of peace
   before you in the presence of mine enemies?
   Shall I prepare a table for peace
   will you know how to eat at this table?
   (skee dee dee dah dah doo dah bop dah bop bop dah boo)

5. Where are the forks of peace?
   Where are the knives of peace?
   Where are the spoons of peace?
   Where are the eyes of peace?
   Where are the hands of peace?
   Where are the tongues of peace?

Where are the children of peace?
(Peace, peace, ting ting tee tee peeeeace ting ting tee)

6. Is peace an action? A way of life?
   Is it a tension in our earth body?
   Is peace you and I seeing beyond
   bombs and babies roasting on a country road?
   (bop bop bop bop bop bop bop bop bopooooooooueeeeeee)

7. Peace must not be still we have to
   take it on the road, marching against
   pentagon doors lurking in obscenity.
   Peace must not find us on our knees
   while a country holds hostage
   the hearts and penises of the workers.
   (bleep bleep bleep blueee bleep bleep blueee doo da boom doo da boom)

8. Can you say peace?
   Can you resurrect peace?
   Can you house the language of peace?
   Can you write a sermon of peace?
   Can you populate the chords of peace?
   (dee dee dadum peace la la la la dum peace)

9. A long time ago someone said: I think, therefore I am.
   A long time ago someone said: I think, therefore I am."
   Now we say preemptive strikes therefore we are.
   Now we say preemptive strikes therefore we are.
   (boom boom boom ay ay ay ay ay boom ay boom ay ayaay)

10. Can you rise up at the sound of peace?
    Can you make peace lighter than air?
    Can you make peace sing like butterflies?
    Until peace becomes the noise of the planet
    Until Peace becomes the noise of the planet
    (PeaceeEeeeeEeeeeEeeeEeeeeEeeEeeEeeeEE)

11. I know as MLK knew that the universe
    is curved ultimately toward justice and peace.
    I know as MLK knew that the universe
    is curved ultimately toward justice and peace.

for "war is the sanction of failure"
for "war is the sanction of failure"
(dobam doom-doooobam dooooood doooom)

12. Martin said a riot is the language of the unheard
    and I say a terrorist's bomb is the language of the unheard
    how to make the unheard heard?
    without blowing themselves and the world up?
    how to make the unheard heard?
    without blowing themselves and the world up?
    (BOOOM BOOM BOOM BOOOMM BOOOOMMM)

13. Mos Def said: Speech is my hammer
    bang my world into shape
    now let it fall.
    I say peace is my hammer
    bang my world into peace
    and let it fall on the eyes of the children.
    (frère Jacques dooodoodoo frère Jacques dooooo doooo
    dormez-vous vous vous vous ding dong ding ding dong ding)

14. Where are the forks of peace?
    Where are the knives of peace?
    Where are the spoons of peace?
    Where are the eyes of peace?
    Where are the hands of peace?
    Where are the tongues of peace?
    Where are the children of peace?

15. Where are you—you—youuuuuuu (click)
    Where are you you you youuuu (click)
    you you where are you you
    where you where are youuu (click)
    click—click—you—youuu (click)

Stop the Violence Matchbox Fishbowl

Carrie Mae Weems

Acknowledgments

On behalf of the editors:

This book project, as mentioned in the introduction, came about in part following an article written by coeditor Elizabeth "Betita" Martínez, followed up by a forum based in New York City, sponsored by the War Resisters League (WRL). Those responsible for making that forum happen include Judith Mahoney Pasternack, John Miller, Ruth Benn, and others. After that point, the initial ideas to put the issues discussed into book form were generated by the WRL Anti-Racism Task Force. Those playing an early role in this process included Ellen Barfield and Jim Haber, and—at a somewhat later point—Jackie Battise. More recently, Kimber Heinz, Isabell Moore, Ali Issa, Oskar Castro, Sam Diener, Liz Roberts, Linda Thurston, and Joanne Sheehan have played invaluable roles in shaping the end product.

All books require a fair amount of logistical arranging, and this one could not have been completed without the able assistance of Denise Rodgers Vosburgh. That her dad, the wonderful Rodge Rodgers is a lifelong Air Force man may not be as ironic a contradiction as it initially appears to be. Captain Rodgers was one of the original Tuskegee Airmen, a World War II hero who returned home to support the work of his wife, Suzanne Rodgers, who led the local Colorado chapter of the NAACP.

Also deserving of special thanks is Tessa Koning-Martinez, a San Francisco-based actress and the daughter of Elizabeth "Betita" Martínez and Hans Koning; and Meg Starr, a Brooklyn-based activist, educator, and author.

We would like to take this opportunity to thank all of the authors of pieces in this collection; as their names appear in the table of contents, on the pieces themselves, and in the contributors list, we will not repeat them a fourth time here. However, certain pieces came through the special support of relatives, estate executives, and others connected to authors long past. In this regards, we give thanks to Walter Neagle, to Noelle Ghoussaini, to John Stoltenberg, and to Phyllis Chester. Thanks also to Sunny Birdstone, Alejandro Molina, Amy Shuster, Soffiyah Ellijah, and Kai Lumumba Barrow.

Many WRL colleagues over many years of struggle have fought the good fight with what appeared to be only fleeting results at the time. On good days, we like to think that those battles have helped to pave the way for some of the positive possibilities we imagine today. They include: Ralph DiGia, Grace Paley, Jim Peck, Ed Hedemann, Iris Marie Bloom, Greg Payton, Bob Lepley, Bob Henschen, Mavis Bellisle, asif ullah,

Malkia M'Buzi Moore, Chris Ney, Michael Marsh, Yeidy Rosa, Sarah Husein, Jesse Heiwa, Ibrahim Abdil-Mu'id Ramey, Susan Kingsland, and so many others.

Finally, we are pleased with the support we have received from the world of publishing. We are first indebted to and appreciative of the inimitable Frances Goldin, who helped us along early in our process. We are pleased to be working with the good folks at PM Press, with special thanks to the always-encouraging Ramsey Kanaan, to the indefatigable Craig O'Hara, and to Romy Ruukel, Gregory Nipper, and Jonathan Rowland for their careful eyes; Josh MacPhee, working under impossibly difficult conditions, is a true artist in all the connotations of that word, as well as a brother and dear comrade. It is also with great pleasure that we note the expert indexing of this volume by Elliot Linzer. His work with us helps bring this history full circle and underscores the commitment of so many anti-racist war resisters over the decades; Linzer served for years as indexer for WRL-related *WIN* magazine and *The Nonviolent Activist* (where some of the pieces were originally published).

On a personal note:

Elizabeth "Betita" Martínez would like to extend a special tribute to Roberto Maestas, a founder of El Centro de La Raza in Seattle, and an inspiring fighter for social justice. He is and will be missed. She is also thankful for the friendship and assistance of Bill Knowles.

Mandy Carter would like to acknowledge some of those she has been most inspired by, both colleagues and mentors. These include: Bayard Rustin; Barbara Smith, co-founder Kitchen Table Press; Joan Baez, Ira Sandperl, and the Institute for the Study of Nonviolence; the American Friends Service Committee; the War Resisters League and the former WRL/West and WRL/Southeast offices; the National Black Justice Coalition; the National Black Lesbian and Gay Leadership Forum; and her own Southerners On New Ground (SONG)—especially Mandy's cofounders Suzanne Pharr, Mab Segrest, Pam McMichael, Joan Garner, and Pat Hussain.

Matt Meyer would like to add some thanks to those who helped provide him with early foundations for this work, including: Freedom singers Matt Jones and Cordell Reagon; Jim Haughton of Harlem Fightback; Norma Becker and Vivian Stromberg of the New York Mobilization for Survival (and so much more); Mustaffa Randolph of the Black Vets for Social Justice; Clarence Fitch of Vietnam Veterans Against War; Connie Hogarth of WESPAC; Abigail Fuller, and Mark Lance; Standing Deer; Grace Paley, and Abbie Hoffman; Bettina Washington and Chief Ryan Malonson; Sonia Sanchez; and Rev. Jew Don Boney of the Black United Front (who went on to become a prominent Houston City Councilman and Mayor Pro Tem). The major mentors of his political life—Mawina Sowa Kouyate of the All-African People's Revolutionary Party, Pan-African pacifist Bill Sutherland, and dean of the Puerto Rican movement

Dr. Luis Nieves Falcón—also deserve special mention, as do his mentors on the "other side of the wall"—especially David Gilbert, Marilyn Buck, Sundiata Acoli, Herman Bell, Leonard Peltier, Oscar López Rivera, and so many of the now-released or exiled comrades from the Puerto Rican, American Indian, and Black liberation movements. They remind us that giving up, even for one minute, is not an option.

Matt would also like to acknowledge his own family—Marilyn, Sylvia, Mollie, and Simon—who prepared him in their own ways for the work he does now; may they rest in peace (with justice). William P. Starr III of Colorado continues in their tradition of support and hospitality. Matt's chosen family—Resistance in Brooklyn comrades Elspeth, Betsy, Bobby, gabriel, Liz, Dan, Meg, Jessica, Colin, John, Jess and others along the way—provide the context and orientation to view the world and this work from a critical and strategic vantage point. His partner Meg continues to indulge him with her patience, challenge him with her insights, and fortify him with her love. Matt's buddy and brother Jon Cohen travelled so many of these roads with him that it is still inconceivable, ten years since his passing, that he is not just in the other room, ready to help figure out the next steps.

Finally, Matt's "truest teachers"—his son Michael Del and his daughter Molly Soo—live their lives in-between our traditional definitions of race and biology, challenging our everyday definitions of nonviolence and oppression and justice. They give him, and with their generation may well give all of us, concrete cause for the hope that must carry us forward.

Contributors

Mumia Abu-Jamal is a noted print and radio journalist who has been on Pennsylvania's Death Row since the early 1980s, convicted of the murder of a Philadelphia police officer. A leading member of the Black Panther Party, and former President of the Philadelphia Association of Black Journalists, Abu-Jamal's trial was obviously prejudicial, making him one of the world's best-known political prisoners (despite the U.S. government's continued refusal to admit the existence of holding anyone on political grounds). He is the author of numerous books, including *Life on Death Row* (1995), *Death Blossoms: Reflections of a Prisoner of Conscience* (South End Press, 2003), *Faith of our Fathers* (Africa World Press, 2003), and *We Want Freedom: A Life in the Black Panther Party* (South End Press, 2008). In April of 2011, the Third Circuit Court of Appeals reaffirmed its prior decision to commute the death sentence on the grounds that the instructions to the jury were "ambiguous and confusing."

Ellen Barfield is a leader of Veterans for Peace and has served as its vice president. She is also a United Nations NGO representative of Women's International League for Peace and Freedom, and a board member of the School of Americas Watch. An active member of the War Resisters League for many years, Barfield continues to serve on its National Committee, and on the WRL Anti-Racism Task Force which helped initiate this book project.

Clare Bayard is a core member, organizer and trainer with the Catalyst Project, and a member of the anti-imperialist Heads Up Collective in the Bay Area. She is also a member of the War Resisters League National Committee and WRL's Anti-Racist Task Force, and writes for *War Times/Tiempo de Guerras.*

Dan Berger is coeditor (with Chesa Boudin and Kenyon Farrow) of The Nation Book's *Letters from Young Activists* (2005). Berger is also author of *Outlaws of America: The Weather Underground and the Politics of Solidarity* (AK Press, 2006) and editor of *The Hidden 1970s: Histories of Radicalism* (Rutgers, 2010). The George Gerbner Postdoctoral Fellow at the University of Pennsylvania, Berger is a member of Resistance in Brooklyn and of the Wild Poppies Collective.

Frida Berrigan, former research associate with the World Policy Institute and senior program associate of the Arms and Security Institute of the New American Foundation, has been a lifelong member of the Catholic Worker and Plowshares communities. Berrigan is a columnist for Foreign Policy in Focus and a contributing editor for *In These Times*. She also serves on the War Resisters League National Committee, and is a leader of Witness Against Torture.

Rev. David Billings has been an anti-racist trainer and core organizer with the People's Institute for Survival and Beyond since 1983, and is a member of its national staff and Community Organizing Strategy Team. An historian with roots in Mississippi and close to four decades in New Orleans, Billings helped found the anti-racist collective European Dissent.

Karl Bissinger was a lifelong peace and justice activist, serving on the staff of the War Resisters League for many decades. As a founder and key staff person of the Greenwich Village Peace Center during the height of the Vietnam War, he served as a draft counselor and underground railroad conductor for thousands of Vietnam-era resisters. Bissinger was also a world-renowned photographer, primarily known for his iconic portraits of the post–World War II literary and art world. He worked as a photographer for Condé Nast Publications, *Harper's Bazaar, Theater Arts, Town & Country*, and *Vogue*; his first photographic subjects were Richard Avedon's wife and author James Baldwin. A retrospective of his work was published in 2003 by Harry Abrams; *The Luminous Years: Portraits at Mid-Century* is introduced by Gore Vidal, who cites Bissinger as the key photographer for "our brief golden age."

Iris Marie Bloom is founder and director of Philadelphia-based Protecting Our Waters, a key environmental group working to protect the waters of the Delaware River Watershed and beyond. Founder of Women's Anti-Violence Education, Bloom is also a safety/self-defense expert and instructor, and has worked as a professional massage therapist. Bloom's prolific work as a writer and poet has appeared in *University City Review*, Philadelphia's *Weekly Press, Positive Psychology News Daily*, and elsewhere; a cover story on Bloom and her work was featured in March 2011's *Grid Magazine*. Bloom is a lifelong peace and social justice activist who has served on the staff of the American Friends Service Committee, New Society Press, Training for Change, and the War Resisters League. She is happiest when she is out sailing, or just hanging out with loved ones, both human and canine.

Anne Braden was a Kentucky-based pioneer of Southern anti-racism, campaigning for equality and human rights from the 1940s onward. Blacklisted for sedition during the 1950s, she remained active in regional work—eventually helping found the Southern Organizing Committee for Economic and Social Justice. She and her husband Carl Braden authored a popular book based on their work, *The Wall Between* (1958), which was praised by Dr. Martin Luther King Jr. and Eleanor Roosevelt. An annual anti-racist training institute has been set up in her name, coordinated by the Catalyst Project.

Bob Brown, a lifelong friend and comrade of Kwame Ture (a.k.a. Stokely Carmichael), was a leader of the Congress of Racial Equality and the Student Nonviolent Coordinating Committee, founder of Illinois's Black Panther Party, mentor to Fred Hampton, and a key architect of the All-African People's Revolutionary Party (the international Pan-Africanist organization which Ture founded under the direct leadership of Ghana's Kwame Nkrumah and Guinea's Sékou Touré). Brown played key roles in helping to elect Harold Washington, first Black Mayor of Chicago (1983), and Carol Moseley-Braun, the first Black woman U.S. Senator (1993); he was a staff member of Jesse Jackson's 1984 presidential campaign (1984). Brown has been at the center of most historic coalition and mobilization efforts of the past half-century, including as a national staff member of Mobilization for Survival prior to the June 12, 1982, million-person disarmament and anti-nuclear march in New York City, and as the national coordinator for logistics and operations of the 1995 Million Man March in Washington, D.C. Brown has done prison time in conjunction with his solidarity with Libya in the 1980s, he has lived in Conakry as a coordinator of the Kwame Ture Work-Study Institute and Library, and served as the national campaign manager for the Pan-Africanist Congress of Azania (South Africa)'s presidential and local government election campaigns in both 2000 and 2004. Brown was a co-plaintiff, with the City of Chicago, in a multi-billion-dollar qui tam (whistle blower) lawsuit against 102 defendants who committed perjury and fraud on their Economic Disclosure Statements and Certificates of Slavery Era Business. He is the author of *Slavery and the Slave-Trade Were and Are Crimes against Humanity* and editor of the new edition of *Stokely Speaks: From Black Power Back to Pan-Africanism*. A much-demanded public speaker, Brown is also the founder and editor of the Pan-African Roots website http://www.paroots.org.

Marilyn Buck was an American revolutionary: an early feminist student activist, she was imprisoned for her participation in the 1979 prison escape of Assata Shakur, the 1981 Brinks robbery, and the 1983 U.S. Senate bombing. Buck received an eighty-year sentence, which she served in Federal prison, and was released in 2010 less than a month before her death from cancer at age sixty-two. Buck received a PEN American Center prize for poetry in 2001; her poems appeared in the anthologies *Hauling Up the Morning, Wall Tappings, Igniting a Revolution: Voices in Defense of the Earth, Seeds of Fire*, and in her chapbook, *Rescue the Word*. Her poems also appear on the audio CD *Wild Poppies* (Freedom Archives, 2004). Her translations and introduction to Cristina Peri Rossi's poetry appeared in *State of Exile* (58) in the City Lights Pocket Poets Series.

Linda Burnham is a cofounder and former executive director of the Women of Color Resource Center, a community-based organization that links activists with scholars and provides information and analysis on the social, political and economic issues that most affect women of color. She was a leader in the Third World Women's Alliance, an organization that grew out of a women's caucus in the Student Nonviolent Coordinating Committee (SNCC), and that, early on, challenged the women's movement to incorporate issues of race and class into the feminist agenda.

Mandy Carter began her long career as a human rights and nonviolent activist working with the War Resister's League (WRL) in San Francisco, beginning in 1969. A veteran of Rev. Dr. Martin Luther King Jr.'s Poor People Campaign, Carter has been called "one of the nation's leading African American lesbian activists" by the National Organization of Women. She has served on countless planning committees for national and regional lesbian and gay pride marches—including the steering committee for the historic 1987 March on Washington for Lesbians and Gays. As a staff member of the WRL's Southeast regional office throughout the late 1970s and 1980s, Carter worked on the boards of the National Stonewall Democratic Federation, the Triangle Foundation, Equal Partners in Faith, and Ladyslipper Music. In 1992, Carter joined the staff of the Human Rights Campaign in Washington, D.C., serving as Public Policy Advocate with a particular focus on the religious and radical right's attacks on gays and lesbians through exploitation of the black community. In 1995, she returned to the south and founded North Carolina Mobilization '96, an electoral campaign organizing against longtime Senator Jesse Helms. She also has served as the national field director and board member of the National Black Gay and Lesbian Leadership Forum. Carter is a cofounder of Southerners on New Ground (SONG). In 2010, the National Black Justice Coalition featured Mandy in their "Jewel" column, noting that she is "a legend in the LGBT community, the Black community, and to all of us concerned about peace." She is a coeditor of this book.

Momo Chang is an Oakland-based writer and activist.

Janet Charles is a documentary and public relations photographer. In the early 1970s, she spent a summer working for Women Strike for Peace and after graduating from college worked for the Fellowship of Reconciliation on the Seeds of Life project. While at the FOR, she documented demonstrations in New York City and Washington, D.C., including the end of the Continental Walk. She now resides and works in New York City and Kingston, New York. Her website is http://www.janetcharlesphoto.com.

Chrystos is the pen name of an Indigenous Two Spirit activist who first began fighting for justice at age thirteen, marching to desegregate schools in San Francisco, where she was born on November 7, 1946. She has been a part of struggles for Native Treaty Rights, prisoner rights, Palestinian land rights as well the movements against war and sexist violence. Racism and sexism have been her greatest teachers, as well as obstacles.

She travels internationally to perform her poetry; her books are: *Not Vanishing, Dream On, In Her I Am, Wilder Reis* (German translations), *Red Rollercoaster, Fugitive Colors,* and *Fire Power* (the latter two are still in print). Her work also appears in many anthologies and textbooks, most notably *This Bridge Called My Back,* and *Reinventing the Enemy's Language.*

Jon Cohen was a staunch freedom fighter for the liberation of all people. A member of the War Resisters League's National Committee for twenty years (which he joined as a young, public draft registration resister), Cohen became a lifelong activist in the intersecting struggles against racism, homophobia, patriarchy, capitalism, and empire while a student at Washington University in St. Louis. An active member of RAVEN, one of the oldest batterer intervention programs in the United States, Cohen served as co-chair of the National Association of Men Against Sexism, editor of the *Activist Men's Journal,* and a founder of BrotherPeace. Cohen was assistant director of the Community Change Project at Volunteer Counseling Services of Rockland County, New York. He was a member of the Resistance in Brooklyn anti-imperialist collective, and a developing alternative health activist when he succumbed to cancer at the age of forty in 2003.

Dorothy Cotton was the chief student organizer of the 1963 Birmingham campaign and its Children's Crusade. As educational director of the Southern Christian Leadership Conference (founded by Dr. Marin Luther King Jr., Bayard Rustin, and Ella Baker), Cotton was part of the inner circle of strategic thinking throughout the 1960s, an iconic figure of the civil rights movement. A vice president of the MLK Center for Nonviolent Social Change, Cotton has also served as student activities director at Cornell University, and as a board member of the Fellowship of Reconciliation.

Chris Crass is an anarchist organizer and writer from San Francisco, California, now living in Tennessee. Crass was a founder of the California-based Catalyst Project, which is a center for political education and host of an annual Anne Braden anti-racist training program. Crass also worked with the Challenging White Supremacy program after the 1999 World Trade Organization mass actions in Seattle, Washington, and was involved with the Heads Up Collective.

Dorothy Day was the founder of the Catholic Worker movement.

Dave Dellinger was a World War II conscientious objector, who—with Ralph DiGia, Bill Sutherland, and Art Emory—formed the Peacemakers project to bicycle across Europe in early opposition to the Cold War. As editor of *Liberation* magazine, he became central to the peace and justice movements of the 1950s, eventually serving as the central coalition-builder and architect of the movement against the war in

Vietnam. Indicted for the 1968 demonstrations at the Chicago Democratic National Convention, Dellinger gained international prominence as a member of the Chicago 8. He authored *Revolutionary Nonviolence, More Power than We Know,* and the memoir *From Yale to Jail.*

Barbara Deming was a prominent author and one of the editors of *Liberation* magazine. An early lesbian feminist and pacifist, her essays—collected in the *Barbara Demining Reader*—have inspired generations of activists and scholars as she helped define the concept "revolutionary nonviolence"—especially in the ground-breaking essay "On Revolution and Equilibrium," excerpted in this collection. She is a subject of recent popular biography *A Saving Remnant: The Radical Lives of Barbara Deming and David McReynolds.*

Often reviled and attacked for her criticism of pornography—in both the mainstream media as well as progressive circles—**Andrea Dworkin** was an internationally recognized radical feminist who dedicated her life to the fight against violence against women. Lesser known for her passionate work in nonviolence movements, Dworkin was an anti-war activist and anarchist in the late 1960s, and authored ten books on feminist theory and practice. She gained prominence for *Pornography: Men Possessing Women* (1981) and *Intercourse* (1987), which remain her two most widely known books. The excerpts and essays in this collection represent a small sampling of her work focusing on the militarized aspects of what Dworkin termed "the war against women."

Sylvanna Falcón is assistant professor at the Latin American and Latino Studies Department of the University of California, Santa Cruz, and author of *From Apartheid to Intersections at the United Nations: Antiracisms, Feminisms, and Human Rights.*

Kenyon Farrow has served as a leader of countless community groups, including the National Gay and Lesbian Task Force, the Center for Gay and Lesbian Studies, Queers for Economic Justice, and Critical Resistance. He was a founder of FIERCE!, New York's LGBTQ youth empowerment group, and coeditor of *Letters from Young Activists: Today's Rebels Speak Out.*

Francesca Fiorentini is an independent journalist based in Argentina, and an editor of *Left Turn* magazine. A former editor of WRL's magazine *WIN: Through Revolutionary Nonviolence,* she was also the coordinator of the 2004 Life After Capitalism conference, held in New York City. She is a writer for *War Times/Tiempo de Guerras.*

Bill Fletcher is a Senior Scholar for the Institute for Policy Studies in Washington, D.C. He is the immediate past president of TransAfrica Forum, a founder of the Black Radical Congress, and has served as educational director and in other positions for the AFL-CIO. Fletcher is an Editorial Board member and columnist for BlackCommentator.com.

Political prisoner **David Gilbert** was a founding member of the Columbia University chapter of Students for a Democratic Society, and served as a negotiator for the strike team during the 1968 student take-over. A writer and activist, Gilbert was part of the SDS faction which became the Weather Underground, and he remained in clandestinity through much of the 1970s, working in solidarity with the Black Panther Party and other groups. Arrested in 1981, Gilbert has continued his work inside prison, founding one of the first and most successful prison-based HIV/AIDS peer intervention programs in the nation. He has been a prolific writer and reviewer, with essays collected in the 2004 anthology *No Surrender*. His memoir, *Love and Struggle: My Life in SDS, the Weather Underground, and Beyond*, was published by PM Press in 2011.

Ruth Wilson Gilmore, radical prison abolitionist, is a cofounder of Critical Resistance. She is author of *Golden Gulag: Prisons, Surplus, Crisis, and Opposition in Globalizing California*, professor at the Graduate Center of the City University of New York, and President of the American Studies Association.

Ted Glick is cofounder of the Climate Crisis Coalition and national coordinator of the U.S. Climate Emergency Council. He is currently Policy Director for the Chesapeake Climate Action Network. A draft resister during the Vietnam War, Glick has been a lifelong coalition builder, serving as a founder and national coordinator of the Independent Progressive Politics Network from 1995 until 2005. He is the chair of the Essex County Green Party and writes a regular column entitled "Future Hope."

Susan B. Goldberg is a member of the Alliance of White Anti-Racists Everywhere (AWARE), a Los Angeles–based collective.

Rabbi Lynn Gottlieb was a leader of New York's Temple Beth Or of the Deaf, becoming the first woman ordained in the Jewish Renewal movement and one of the first ten women rabbis in the United States. Based now in the west, Gottlieb has been a founder of the Bat Kol national Jewish feminist theater troupe, and of the Muslim-Jewish Peace Walk Pilgrimages; she helped lead a 2008 interfaith peace delegation to Iran.

Jim Haber is the coordinator of the Nevada Desert Experience and a member of the War Resisters League National Committee, leading its Organizing Task Force and the Anti-Racist Task Force that initiated this book.

Vincent Harding is an activist, historian, and former professor of religion and social transformation at the Iliff School of Theology. A close associate of Dr. Martin Luther

King Jr., he is author of numerous works including *There Is a River: The Black Struggle for Freedom in America* (1993), and *Hope and History: Why We Must Share the Story of the Movement* (Orbis, 2010). Harding is currently chairperson of the Veterans of Hope Project: A Center for the Study of Religion and Democratic Renewal.

Edward Hasbrouck was imprisoned for six months in 1983–1984 for organizing resistance to draft registration after being personally selected for prosecution by FBI Director Robert Mueller as one of the "most vocal" nonregistrants in the country. A former coeditor of *Resistance News*, the national journal of the draft resistance movement of the 1980s, Hasbrouck today maintains the website www.Resisters.info, and writes books and a blog of consumer advice for travelers. He identifies himself as an atheist, an anarchist, a pacifist, and as a no-longer-young supporter of youth liberation; he is a member of the War Resisters League.

Fred Ho, a world-renowned baritone saxophonist, is also an organizer and the author of numerous political works, including *AFRO/ASIA: Revolutionary Political and Cultural Connections between African and Asian Americans*, edited with Bill Mullen.

Daniel Hunter is an associate of Training For Change and its former director. He has years of experience leading diversity, nonviolence, and strategy workshops for grassroots transformation on five continents.

Sarah Husein, born in New York City, grew up in Hong Kong, Sudan, and Pakistan. Her writing is concerned with memory, nation, violence, bioterrorism, and the female body. As an activist and artist, she has worked with communities of color on issues of immigrant rights, access to public higher education, and grassroots anti-violence projects in the Muslim, Arab, and South Asian communities. Her work makes active interventions in the current discourses on gender, sexuality, and violence as it relates to Muslim women. She began her poetry career on the spoken word stages of Staten Island and Manhattan, and her work continues to render across the country. She is the editor of *Voices of Resistance: Muslim Women on War, Faith and Sexuality* (Avalon, 2006). She is currently living and teaching in Pakistan.

Dean Johnson is assistant professor of religious studies, and peace studies advisor for the International and Global Studies program, at Defiance College in Ohio. Johnson was director of the Goshen College Plowshares Peace Studies Project, and has served as a board member of the Peace and Justice Studies Association.

Nada Khader has served as the executive director of WESPAC in New York's Westchester County since 2001. A leading anti-racist educator, Khader was also a United Nations Development Program consultant in Gaza, Palestine.

Rev. Dr. Martin Luther King Jr. was the founding president of the Southern Christian Leadership Conference, a leading clergyman and civil rights organizer, and recipient of the 1964 Nobel Peace Prize.

Chris Knestrick has been living in Colombia since 2008 as a member of the Christian Peacemakers Team. He maintains a blog, El Rio De La Vida—The River of Life.

Joel Kovel was a noted psychiatrist and professor at the Albert Einstein School of Medicine and the author of such profound writings as *White Racism: A Psychohistory Against the State of Nuclear Terror*, and *The Age of Desire*. Disillusioned with the limits of the psychoanalytic field, Kovel shifted his work in the mid-1980s, eventually becoming Alger Hiss Professor of Social Studies at Bard College in 1988. Active in anti-war and solidarity work, Kovel also became a leader of the Green Party, running as its New York candidate for Senate in 1998, and its Presidential candidate in 2000. An avowed socialist, he wrote *Red Hunting in the Promised Land* in 1994, and *The Enemy of Nature: The End of Capitalism or the End of the World* in 2002. His outspoken critiques of Israel, including his 2007 book *Overcoming Zionism*, have been the cause of much public controversy. Current editor-in-chief of the eco-socialist journal *Capitalism, Nature, Socialism*, Kovel has also served as a member of the executive committee of the War Resisters League.

Sachio Ko-Yin was born in 1972, the only child of poet Adrianna St. John and Confucian philosopher Hideo Takashima. Though his driving mission in life is poetry, Ko-Yin entered the anti-war movement at age nineteen, demonstrating his commitment to nonviolence and anarchism. He founded the Anarchist League (which publishes the periodical *Anarchia*) and cofounded the Root and Branch Collective. Ko-Yin was also affiliated with the Society of Friends as a distinctly non-Christian pacifist, and worked on the National Committee of (and as a local activist with) the War Resisters League. In 1998, he and a fellow pacifist enacted a "ploughshares" action at a nuclear missile silo by cutting through the gates, setting off the alarms, painting a mural on the blast cap and symbolically hammering on the lid and tracks so as to beat "swords into ploughshares." Convicted of sabotage and conspiracy, Ko-Yin was sentenced to a two-and-a-half-year sentence.

Cameron Levin is a member of the Alliance of White Anti-Racists Everywhere (AWARE), a Los Angeles–based collective.

Victor Lewis, seen by many as the quintessential "angry Black man" in the classic film *The Color of Fear*, is an internationally sought-after diversity trainer and alliance builder. Along with fellow film participant Hugh Vasques, Lewis is the author of the four-volume anthology *Lessons from the Color of Fear*, and a leader of the Oakland-based SpeakOut! National network.

B. Loewe was the national student organizer for the Service International Employees Union, and served as the planning director for the Latino Union in Chicago from 2003 to 2009. Since that time, B. has worked as a key field organizer for the Detroit-based U.S. Social Forum, and has been a leading immigrant rights activist in Arizona.

José López is the founder and Executive Director of the Puerto Rican Cultural Center in Chicago. A longtime community and Puerto Rican independence leader, López has been at the center of countless organizing efforts and ongoing projects, including the award-winning HIV/AIDS program VIDA/SIDA, the award-winning alternative school Dr. Pedro Albizu Campos High School, the National Boricua Human Rights Network, and the Borinquen Bakery. A leading member of the Movimiento Liberacion Nacional, López is also a professor at Northeastern University and Columbia College.

Audre Lorde was a leading writer, and activist, serving as a key critic of racism in the burgeoning feminist movement of the 1960s and '70s. A self-described "Black feminist lesbian mother poet," her books include *The Black Unicorn* (1978), and *The Cancer Journals* (1980). Along with Barbara Smith and Cherrie Moraga, Lorde was a cofounder of Kitchen Table Women of Color Press. Her classic essay included in this volume and originally printed in her 1984 collection *Sister-Outsider*, recounts some of her basic concerns about strategy and tactics.

Matthew Lyons is a researcher and writer specializing in contemporary right-wing movements. He has worked with Political Research Associate's Chip Berlet in coauthoring the groundbreaking *Right-Wing Populism in America: Too Close for Comfort*. A former member of Resistance in Brooklyn, Lyons's recent writings can be found on the radical anti-fascist blog Three Way Fight.

Elizabeth McAlister is a founder of Baltimore-based Jonah House, a center based on nonviolence, resistance, and community. A former nun, she has been a central figure in the Plowshares disarmament movement, and many other movements for justice and peace.

Elizabeth "Betita" Martínez is a Chicana feminist and a longtime community organizer, activist, author, and educator. She has written numerous books and articles, including the bilingual *500 Years of Chicano History in Pictures*, which later formed the basis for the educational video ¡*Viva la Causa! 500 Years of Chicano History*. Her work has been hailed by Angela Y. Davis as comprising "one of the most important living histories of progressive activism in the contemporary era … [Martínez is] inimitable . . . irrepressible … indefatigable." Martínez began her political work in the early 1950s, and served full-time in the civil rights movement with the Student Nonviolent Coordinating Committee (SNCC). In 1968, she moved to New Mexico to start a newspaper to support the Alianza Federal de Mercedes. Along with lawyer Beverly Axelrod, Martínez founded the bilingual movement newspaper *El Grito del Norte,* and cofounded and directed the Chicano Communications Center, a barrio-based organizing and education project. Since moving to the Bay Area in 1976, Martínez has organized around Latino community issues, taught women's studies, conducted anti-racist training workshops, and worked with youth groups. She ran for governor of California on the Peace & Freedom Party ticket in 1982 and has received many awards from student, community, and academic organizations, including Scholar of the Year 2000 by the National Association for Chicana and Chicano Studies. She is the author of *De Colores Means All of Us: Latina Views for a Multi-Colored Century* (1998), and editor of SNCC's *Letters From Mississippi* (1964). In 1997, she and Phil Hutchings cofounded the Institute for Multiracial Justice, which "aims to strengthen the struggle against white supremacy by serving as a resource center to help build alliances among peoples of color and combat divisions." She is a coeditor of this book.

Kitty Mattes is an environmental activist from upstate New York.

David McReynolds is a widely respected writer and public speaker, serving close to forty years on the staff of the War Resisters League. A leading member of the Socialist Party, USA, he ran as Socialist candidate for president in both 1980 and 2000. While he did not win, he received widespread press in part because he was the first openly gay person to run for that executive office. A candidate for Congress with the Peace and Freedom Party in 1968, and for Senate with the Green Party in 2004, McReynolds is also no stranger to nonviolent direct action, having been among the first five draft card burners in 1965 (just after it became a federal felony to do so). A former chairperson of the War Resisters International and leader of the International Peace Bureau, McReynolds has long advocated a theoretical and practical convergence of Gandhi and Marx. He is the author of *We Have Been Invaded by the Twenty-First Century,* and is the subject of the recent Martin Duberman biography *A Saving Remnant: The Radical Lives of Barbara Deming and David McReynolds.*

Matt Meyer is a New York City based educator-activist. Founding co-chair of the Peace and Justice Studies Association, and former Chair of the Consortium on Peace Research, Education and Development (COPRED), Meyer has long worked to bring together academics and activists for lasting social change. A former public draft registration resister and chair of the War Resisters League, he continues to serve as convener of the War Resisters International Africa Working Group. With Bill Sutherland, Meyer authored *Guns and Gandhi in Africa: Pan-African Insights on Nonviolence, Armed Struggle and Liberation* (2000), of which Archbishop Desmond Tutu wrote, "Sutherland and Meyer have begun to develop a language which looks at the roots of our humanness."

Meyer is author of *Time is Tight: Transformative Education in Eritrea, South Africa, and the USA* (2007), based in part on his experiences as Multicultural Coordinator for the NYC Board of Education's Alternative High Schools and Programs. He has edited the Fellowship of Reconciliation's *Puerto Rico: The Cost of Colonialism*; guest edited numerous special issues of Blackwell/Sage Press's professional journal *Peace & Change*; and—with Elavie Ndura-Ouedraogo—coedited the two-volume series *Seeds of New Hope: Pan-African Peace Studies for the Twenty-First Century* (2009) and *Seeds Bearing Fruit: Pan-African Peace Action for the Twenty-First Century* (2010). Meyer is also a founder of the local anti-imperialist collective Resistance in Brooklyn, and editor of *Let Freedom Ring: A Collection of Documents From the Movements to Free U.S. Political Prisoners* (2008). Argentine Nobel Peace laureate Adolfo Pérez Esquivel has commented that "Meyer is a coalition-builder," one who "provides tools for today's activists" in his writings and work. He is a coeditor of this book.

Andrea Modica lives in Philadelphia, Pennsylvania, and works as a photographer and associate professor at Drexel University's Antoinette Westphal College of Media Arts and Design. Her work is included in the permanent collections of the Metropolitan Museum of Art, the Whitney Museum of American Art, the International Center of Photography, the Brooklyn Museum, the George Eastman House, the National Museum of American Art, Smithsonian Institution, the San Francisco Museum of Modern Art, the San Diego Museum of Photographic Arts, the Biblioteque Nationale and others. Her published work includes *Real Indians: Portraits of Contemporary Native Americans and America's Tribal Colleges* (2003).

Malkia M'Buzi Moore is an Atlanta-based activist, poet, author, and codirector of Creative Resources consulting service. A former program director of the War Resisters League, and educational coordinator of the Alliance for Justice, Moore is also a noted leader of the Black Arts Movement. Her poems have been published in several notable anthologies, including *Bum Rush the Page*, a Def Poetry Jam publication edited by Tony Medina and Louis Reyes Rivera.

Dylcia Pagán is a Puerto Rican warrior-poet-artist, one of eleven Puerto Rican former political prisoner/POWs who were released in 1999 after a massive international campaign. A founder of the Puerto Rican Students Union at Brooklyn College, she was involved in cinematography and reporting, forming a film school in East Harlem before her arrest in 1980. While incarcerated, she continued her writing and video work, featured in several anthologies and films including the publication *Have You Seen La Nueva Mujer Puertoriquena?* and the award-winning movie *The Double Life of Ernesto Gomez-Gomez* (about her son). Since her release from prison, Págan has continued her art and activism in Puerto Rico.

Greg Payton has long been a key leader of Vietnam Veterans Against War, and has served on the Boards of the War Resisters League and the New Jersey American Friends Service Committee. He is an Executive Vice President of the Communication Workers of America, and an active leader of Labor Against War. He has appeared on countless television and radio shows, and in numerous films including *Another Brother* about the life of his friend and fellow VVAW member Clarence Fitch.

Professor **john a. powell** is an internationally recognized authority in the areas of civil rights and civil liberties, and a wide range of issues including race, structural racism, ethnicity, housing, poverty and democracy. He is executive director of the Kirwan Institute for the Study of Race and Ethnicity at The Ohio State University and holds the Gregory H. Williams Chair in Civil Rights & Civil Liberties at the Moritz College of Law. Previously, powell founded and directed the Institute on Race and Poverty at the University of Minnesota, served as Director of Legal Services in Miami, Florida, and was National Legal Director of the American Civil Liberties Union. He is also one of the cofounders of the Poverty & Race Research Action Council.

Before his work in Washington, D.C., **Ibrahim Abdil-Mu'id Ramey** served on the national staffs of both the Fellowship of Reconciliation and the War Resisters League, and was a leader of the Pan-African Skills Project. His "Voice of Reason" column continues to inspire and educate broad groupings of progressive people around the world. Ramey is the Vice President of the Steering Committees of the Religious NGO Community at the United Nations.

Ruth Reynolds was a member of the Harlem Ashram of the 1940s, set up to emulate and work in solidarity with the Gandhian independence movement of India. She and her friend Jean Zwickel came into contact with Puerto Ricans living in El Barrio, New York's Latino neighborhood adjacent to Harlem on the Upper East side, who implored her and other members of the Ashram to pay a hospital visit to Harvard-educated lawyer and leader of the Puerto Rican Nationalist Party Pedro, Albizu Campos, serving out the end of a ten-year prison sentence for "seditious conspiracy" against U.S. occupation of his homeland. Transferring to Columbia Hospital after becoming critically ill, Albizu Campos began teaching Reynolds about the realities of the U.S. colonial conquest of his island, urging her to make solidarity work with those seeking independence from the United States a more significant priority. Reynolds took these urgings to heart, committing the rest of her life from 1943 to 1989 to the Puerto Rican cause. She is generally considered the most consistent North American supporter of the Puerto Rican anti-colonial cause.

Liz Roberts is the development and membership coordinator of the War Resisters League and has been a part of Resistance in Brooklyn—an anti-racist, anti-imperialist collective—since 1998. From 2000 to 2006, Roberts was the Outreach Coordinator for the Brecht Forum. She has a BA degree in Politics and Women's Studies from Mount Holyoke College and an MA in Anti-Racist Education from Vermont College. Her poetry has been included in small zines and several *We'Moon* publications, and will appear in the forthcoming *The Widow's Handbook*. She organizes locally with a Boycott, Divestment, Sanctions group in support of Palestinian liberation.

Suzanne Ross was CISPES Mid-Atlantic Regional Coordinator, later serving as the group's National Organizational Relations Coordinator. Ross also participated in the Jesse Jackson Campaign and in the Rainbow Coalition, and was one of the speakers who introduced Jackson at the 1984 Democratic Party national convention. She was a board member of Clergy and Laity Concerned, and is now a key organizer in the movement to free Mumia Abu-Jamal, including its New York City–based Coalition to Free Mumia Abu-Jamal. She also supports the other U.S.-held political prisoners and prisoners of war and is a frequent speaker at special prison events addressing the general prison population.

Bayard Rustin, a World War II conscientious objector, staff member of the Fellowship of Reconciliation, and executive secretary of the War Resisters League, was the chief architect of the historic 1963 March on Washington for Jobs and Freedom. A chief advisor to Dr. Martin Luther King, Rustin was an openly gay man—stating toward the end of his life that the modern LGBT movement was the new Civil Rights movement of the current time. Rustin was the director of the A. Philip Randolph Institute, author of *Down the Line* (1971) and *Time on Two Crosses* (2003), and subject of the movie *Brother Outsider*. He was a figure of enduring controversy in the 1950s (for arrests due to "sex perversion"), the late 1960s, and beyond (for "selling out" the movement to mainstream trade union and Democratic Party politics). The year 2012 marks the centennial of Rustin's birth, commemorated by many organizations, including the National Black Justice Coalition.

Sonia Sanchez is a poet, mother, professor, and an internationally revered lecturer on Black culture and literature, women's liberation, peace and racial justice. A sponsor of the Women's International League for Peace and Freedom. Sanchez is also a Board Member of MADRE, and a supporter of countless other groups. She is the author of over sixteen books including *Homecoming, We a BaddDDD People, Love Poems, I've Been a Woman, A Sound Investment and Other Stories, Homegirls and Handgrenades, Under a Soprano Sky, Wounded in the House of a Friend* (Beacon Press, 1995), *Does Your House Have Lions?* (Beacon Press, 1997), *Like the Singing Coming off the Drums* (Beacon Press, 1998), *Shake Loose My Skin* (Beacon Press, 1999), and most recently, *Morning Haiku* (Beacon Press, 2010). In addition to being a contributing editor to *Black Scholar* and *The Journal of African Studies*, she has edited an anthology, *We Be Word*

Sorcerers: 25 Stories by Black Americans. BMA: The Sonia Sanchez Literary Review is the first African American Journal that discusses the work of Sonia Sanchez and the Black Arts Movement. Sanchez is a recipient of a National Endowment for the Arts citation, the Lucretia Mott Award for 1984, the Outstanding Arts Award from the Pennsylvania Coalition of 100 Black Women, the Community Service Award from the National Black Caucus of State Legislators, and the 1985 American Book Award *for Homegirls and Handgrenades.* She was the first Presidential Fellow at Temple University, where she also held the Laura Carnell Chair in English. Currently, Sanchez is one of twenty African American women featured in "Freedom Sisters," an interactive exhibition created by the Cincinnati Museum Center and Smithsonian Institution traveling exhibition.

An inspiring writer and activist, **Mab Segrest** is widely recognized as the central figure ridding North Caroline of the Ku Klux Klan in the 1980s. A founder of North Carolinians Against Racist and Religious Violence, she also worked for the World Council of Churches Urban-Rural Mission, and countless other grassroots groups. Chair of the Women's Studies Department, and Fuller-Maathai Professor at Connecticut College, Segrest is author of the groundbreaking *Memoir of a Race Traitor* (South End Press, 1994).

Gwendolyn Zoharah Simmons is professor of religion at the University of Florida, where she is affiliated with the Women's Studies Department. A leader of the Student Nonviolent Coordinating Committee, she represented the National Council of Negro Women, joined the Nation of Islam, and was involved in every major aspect of the Black-led freedom movements of the 1960s and 1970s.

Andrea Smith, a cofounder of the national network INCITE! Women of Color Against Violence, is a Cherokee intellectual and activist who was also one of the founders of Women of All Red Nations. Now based at the University of California, Riverside, Smith is the author and editor of numerous books, including *The Color of Violence: The INCITE! Anthology* (South End Press, 2006), from which the essay in this collection is excerpted.

Starhawk is a well-known global justice activist and organizer and one of the most respected voices in modern earth-based spirituality. She is the author or coauthor of ten books, including *The Spiral Dance: A Rebirth of the Ancient Religion of the Great Goddess,* long considered the essential text for the neo-Pagan movement, and the now-classic ecotopian novel *The Fifth Sacred Thing.* Starhawk's newest book (winner of the 2010 Nautilus Award) is *The Last Wild Witch,* an eco-fable for kids and adults alike.

Meg Starr was a leader of the Free Puerto Rico committee and its predecessors, and is a founder of the anti-imperialist collective Resistance in Brooklyn. An educator and author, she wrote about the modern Puerto Rican independence movement in *The Hidden 1970s: Histories of Radicalism* (2010), and about life in El Barrio in the noted children's book *Alicia's Happy Day* (Star Bright, 2001).

William P. Starr is a photographer, writer, archivist, and dramaturge. Named "best photographer" by Colorado's *The Independent* newsweekly, his photographic images—which focus on movement, dance, and the human form—have been described as "simple, elegant, fluid, sexy, witty, reflective, and a little strange." Living with rheumatoid arthritis since the age of nine, Starr, in the words of *The Independent*, "seems to have a deeply intuitive understanding of the body, of the way that we move, and of the nature of our physical frame." He studied chemistry at Colorado College, dropped out to have bilateral complete hip and knee replacements, returned to study Comparative Literature, then inherited a 1959 twin-lens Rollei Flex camera. An occasional instructor at the University of Colorado, Colorado Springs and premier photographer for Colorado College's arts festivals, Starr's teaching work has focused upon the historical photographic process. His images have appeared in many solo shows, as well as in *Dance Magazine, Pointe Magazine, The Dance Insider & Arts Voyager, TimeOut New York,* and the *National Arts Magazine* of Taiwan. He has performed as a dancer/mover in works choreographed by Domenico Giustino and Peggy Berg; has worked as visual collaborator/dramaturge with Thaddeus Phillips and Tea Alagic; and has performed in both devised and text-based theater. His over twenty years of collaboration with the Minneapolis-based dance group HIJACK resulted in a 2011 residency at the Maggie Allesee National Center for Choreography at Florida State University. Starr's work can be purchased through http://www.Phototroph.com. Starr would like to note that the specific photograph used in this book is from a theater production based on Franz Kafka's unfinished novel *Amerika*, in which the author, who had never been to the United States, describes the travails of a Czech-Bohemian boy fleeing his family's displeasure by immigrating to the United States. Much of *Amerika* concerns the displacement and alienation of the new immigrant who also encounters the violence of capitalism.

John Stoltenberg is a profeminist activist and author of *Refusing to Be a Man: Essays on Sex and Justice* (1990), and *The End of Manhood: A Book for Men of Conscience* (1994). A founder of the groups Men Can Stop Rape, Men Against Pornography, and New York Men Against Sexism, Stoltenberg has also served as a creative director of the U.S. Department of Defense's Sexual Assault Prevention and Response Office.

Mary Jane Sullivan is a poet, documentarian, and instructor of philosophy at the University of Colorado at Colorado Springs, where she also teaches cross-platform classes in poetry and social justice, and women and war. Before relocating to Colorado, Sullivan was an early producer with the Manhattan based Paper Tiger Television, a founder of Now and Then Productions, an editor of *WIN* magazine, an Executive Committee member of the War Resisters League, and a participant in the Women's Pentagon Action. She is associate producer of *Maria's Story*, an award-winning 1991 documentary on life in El Salvador, and producer of *Are Cruise Missiles Good for New York City?* (1987), *What's the Difference Between a Country and a Home?* (1986), and *Signals from the Empire City* (2002). Currently, she is working on *Stitching Rites*, a feature-length documentary on cultural land rights issues in the San Luis Valley in Colorado. Her book *Engaged Embodiment*, an investigation into poetic thinking, will be published by Atropos Press in 2012.

Alejandra Cecilia Tobar Alatriz is a Chilean-born nonviolence trainer who was active with the Fellowship of Reconciliation's Peacemakers Program. She remains an activist and performing artist based in Minneapolis.

Alice Walker is a prolific poet, short story writer, novelist, essayist, anthologist, teacher, editor, publisher, womanist, and activist. As a self-described "daughter of the rural peasantry," Walker grew up in Georgia, studied at Spelman and Sarah Lawrence colleges, and began work at the Legal Defense Fund of the National Association for the Advancement of Colored People, in Jackson, Mississippi in 1965. Her fiction has established her as a canonical figure in American letters, as well as a major figure in what scholars term the renaissance in African American women's writings of the 1970s. Her 1982 book, *The Color Purple*, earned her the Pulitzer Prize for fiction (the first African American woman writer to receive this award) and the National Book Award. Walker has written several other novels, including *The Temple of My Familiar*, *Possessing the Secret of Joy* (which featured several characters and descendants of characters from *The Color Purple*), and *Now Is the Time to Open Your Heart*. She has published a number of collections of short stories, poetry, and other work, including *In Search of Our Mothers Gardens*. Walker's most recent collection of essays is *We Are the Ones We Have Been Waiting For* (2006). As an anthologist, Walker lifted from obscurity and honored the writer Zora Neale Hurston, who has served as an important model in her own artistic development. Her activism has, in recent years, been focused upon anti-war work with groups such as Code Pink, and work in solidarity with the people of Palestine. In 2010, she published her book-length essay, *Overcoming Speechlessness: A Poet Encounters the Horror in Rwanda, Eastern Congo and Palestine/Israel*. Walker's awards and fellowships include a Guggenheim Fellowship, a residency at Yaddo, and the 2010 Lennon/Ono Grant for Peace.

Liz Walz is an active nonviolence trainer and practitioner.

Carrie Mae Weems is a world-renowned photographer and artist. Her photographs, films, and videos have been displayed in over fifty exhibitions in the United States and abroad and focus on racism, gender relations, politics, violence, and personal identity. Storytelling is fundamental to her work, as has been evident in her *Family Pictures and Stories, Ain't Jokin'* (1987–1988), *And 22 Million Very Tired and Very Angry People, Colored People* (1989–1990), and the *Kitchen Table* series (1990). She has explored issues relating to Africa, and the African Diaspora beginning in America, with the *Sea Islands* series (1991–1992), *Africa, Slave Coast* (1993), and *From Here I Saw What Happened and I Cried* (2005). Weems created a trilogy of large-scale fabric installations that resulted in *Ritual & Revolution* (1998)—commissioned by the Whitney Museum of American Art; *The Jefferson Suite* (1999)—commissioned by the Santa Barbara Museum of Art; and *The Hampton Project* (2000). Her recent *The Louisiana Project* was part of the bicentennial celebrations surrounding the commemoration of the Louisiana Purchase, commissioned by Tulane University's Newcomb Art Gallery. *Coming Up for Air* (2004) was her first video endeavor, first screened at the Museum of Modern Art in New York City. In her own explanation, Weems has "worked toward developing a complex body of art that has at various times employed photographs, text, fabric, audio, digital images, installation, and, most recently, video. ...Despite the variety of my explorations, throughout it all it has been my contention that my responsibility as an artist is to work, to sing for my supper, to make art, beautiful and powerful, that adds and reveals; to beautify the mess of a messy world, to heal the sick and feed the helpless; to shout bravely from the roof-tops and storm barricaded doors and voice the specifics of our historic moment." Recognition of Weems's work includes the Distinguished Photographers Award (Women in Photography International, 2005); the Alpert Award for Visual Arts (1996); a Visual Arts Fellowship (National Endowment for the Arts, 1994); the Photographer of the Year award (Friends of Photography, 1994), and selected one person exhibitions at Museum of Modern Art in New York, the International Center of Photography, the J. Paul Getty Museum, and the Museum of Modern Art in San Francisco. A major retrospective of her work will be touring throughout 2012–2014, including a season at the Guggenheim.

Cornel West is an American philosopher, author, critic, actor, and civil rights activist; he is the Class of 1943 University Professor at Princeton University, where he teaches in the Center for African American Studies and in the Department of Religion. West has worked as assistant professor at Union Theological Seminary in the City of New York; Yale University and Yale Divinity School; and as professor of African-American studies at Harvard University, with a joint appointment at the Harvard Divinity School. The recipient of more than twenty honorary degrees and an American Book Award, he is a longtime member of the Democratic Socialists of America, for which he now serves as honorary chair. He is also a co-chair of the Tikkun Community and the Network of Spiritual Progressives. West has appeared on numerous musical and spoken word recordings, and in film, including a recurring role in *The Matrix* movies.

Robert Franklin Williams was the president of the National Association for the Advancement of Colored People of Monroe County, North Carolina for much of the 1950s. After publically advocating the right to armed self-defense in a case that gained national prominence, Williams was eventually forced into exile, taking residence in the early days of revolutionary Cuba. From Havana, he published the newsletter *Black Crusader*, which he struggled to get into the United States as often as possible. After disagreements with the leadership of the Cuban Communist Party, Williams relocated to Beijing, China, where he and his family became guests of Chairman Mao. Continuing to write and produce the *Crusader*, Williams was elected first president of the Republic of New Afrika (Provisional Government), and eventually moved to Tanzania and back to the United States (as Nixon was brokering a rapprochement with communist China). Williams authored the popular "underground" book *Negroes with Guns* (Third World Press, 1973).

Tim Wise is among the most well-known anti-racist writers and educators in the United States. Recently named one of "25 Visionaries Who Are Changing Your World" by *Utne Reader,* Wise is the author of numerous books and articles, including *White Like Me: Reflections on Race from a Privileged Son; Affirmative Action: Racial Preference in Black and White; Speaking Treason Fluently: Anti-Racist Reflections From an Angry White Male; Between Barack and a Hard Place: Racism and White Denial in the Age of Obama,* and *Colorblind: The Rise of Post-Racial Politics and the Retreat from Racial Equity.*

Conrad Worrill is a noted activist and columnist, and served for several decades as the national chairman of the National Black United Front. His essay in this volume suggests not only NBUF's position on the connections between racism and war, but also the economic underpinnings of what justice might begin to look like.

Jean Zwickel was, along with Ruth Reynolds, a member of the Harlem Ashram who befriended Don Pedro Albizu Campos and continued to work in solidarity with the people of Puerto Rico for the rest of her life. A member of the War Resisters League, the Fellowship of Reconciliation, and the Unitarian Universalist Service Committee, she is author of *Voice for Independence*, a series of remembrances from her work with Puerto Rican leaders.

Index

ABOUT PM PRESS

PM Press was founded at the end of 2007 by a small collection of folks with decades of publishing, media, and organizing experience. PM Press co-conspirators have published and distributed hundreds of books, pamphlets, CDs, and DVDs. Members of PM have founded enduring book fairs, spearheaded victorious tenant organizing campaigns, and worked closely with bookstores, academic conferences, and even rock bands to deliver political and challenging ideas to all walks of life. We're old enough to know what we're doing and young enough to know what's at stake.

We seek to create radical and stimulating fiction and non-fiction books, pamphlets, T-shirts, visual and audio materials to entertain, educate and inspire you. We aim to distribute these through every available channel with every available technology — whether that means you are seeing anarchist classics at our bookfair stalls; reading our latest vegan cookbook at the café; downloading geeky fiction e-books; or digging new music and timely videos from our website.

PM Press is always on the lookout for talented and skilled volunteers, artists, activists and writers to work with. If you have a great idea for a project or can contribute in some way, please get in touch.

PM Press
PO Box 23912
Oakland, CA 94623
www.pmpress.org

FRIENDS OF PM PRESS

These are indisputably momentous times—the financial system is melting down globally and the Empire is stumbling. Now more than ever there is a vital need for radical ideas.

In the four years since its founding—and on a mere shoestring—PM Press has risen to the formidable challenge of publishing and distributing knowledge and entertainment for the struggles ahead. With over 175 releases to date, we have published an impressive and stimulating array of literature, art, music, politics, and culture. Using every available medium, we've succeeded in connecting those hungry for ideas and information to those putting them into practice.

Friends of PM allows you to directly help impact, amplify, and revitalize the discourse and actions of radical writers, filmmakers, and artists. It provides us with a stable foundation from which we can build upon our early successes and provides a much-needed subsidy for the materials that can't necessarily pay their own way. You can help make that happen—and receive every new title automatically delivered to your door once a month—by joining as a Friend of PM Press. And, we'll throw in a free T-shirt when you sign up.

Here are your options:
- **$25 a month** Get all books and pamphlets plus 50% discount on all webstore purchases
- **$40 a month** Get all PM Press releases (including CDs and DVDs) plus 50% discount on all webstore purchases
- **$100 a month** Superstar—Everything plus PM merchandise, free downloads, and 50% discount on all webstore purchases

For those who can't afford $25 or more a month, we're introducing **Sustainer Rates** at $15, $10 and $5. Sustainers get a free PM Press T-shirt and a 50% discount on all purchases from our website.

Your Visa or Mastercard will be billed once a month, until you tell us to stop. Or until our efforts succeed in bringing the revolution around. Or the financial meltdown of Capital makes plastic redundant. Whichever comes first.

War Resisters League

War Resisters League, a national organization with chapters and affiliates throughout the United States, has been resisting war at home and war abroad since 1923. Today, as one of the leading radical voices in the antiwar movement, WRL supports GI resisters, produces counter-military recruitment materials, provides trainings in non-violent direct action and creates resources and curricula on war profiteering, war tax resistance, and movement building. We organize campaigns against war and militarism, focusing on connections between and among the struggles for peace and justice.

War Resisters League affirms that all war is a crime against humanity and works for the removal of the causes of war, including racism, sexism and all forms of human exploitation.

Join WRL or find out more about our programs and campaigns at:
warresisters.org and on:
Twitter: @resistwar
Facebook: www.facebook.com/pages/War-Resisters-League/171910856163140
Blog: warresisters.wordpress.com/about
Tumblr: warresistersleague.tumblr.com

War Resisters League
339 Lafayette Street
New York, NY 10012
(212) 228-0450
wrl@warresisters.org

Let Freedom Ring

A Collection of Documents from the Movements to Free U.S. Political Prisoners

Edited by Matt Meyer
Foreword by Nobel Peace Laureate Adolfo Perez Esquivel
Afterwords by Ashanti Alston and Lynne Stewart
$37.95 • ISBN: 978-1-60486-035-1

Let Freedom Ring presents a two-decade sweep of essays, analyses, histories, interviews, resolutions, People's Tribunal verdicts, and poems by and about the scores of U.S. political prisoners and the campaigns to safeguard their rights and secure their freedom. In addition to an extensive section on the campaign to free death-row journalist Mumia Abu-Jamal, represented here are the radical movements that have most challenged the U.S. empire from within: Black Panthers and other Black liberation fighters, Puerto Rican independentistas, Indigenous sovereignty activists, white anti-imperialists, environmental, and animal rights militants, Arab and Muslim activists, Iraq war resisters, and others. Contributors in and out of prison detail the repressive methods from long-term isolation to sensory deprivation to politically inspired parole denial—used to attack these freedom fighters, some still caged after 30 plus years. This invaluable resource guide offers inspiring stories of the creative, and sometimes winning, strategies to bring them home.

Contributors include: Mumia Abu-Jamal, Dan Berger, Dhoruba Bin-Wahad, Bob Lederer, Terry Bisson, Laura Whitehorn, Safiya Bukhari, The San Francisco 8, Angela Davis, Bo Brown, Bill Dunne, Jalil Muntaqim, Susie Day, Luis Nieves Falcón, Ninotchka Rosca, Meg Starr, Assata Shakur, Jill Soffiyah Elijah, Jan Susler, Chrystos, Jose Lopez, Leonard Peltier, Marilyn Buck, Oscar López Rivera, Sundiata Acoli, Ramona Africa, Linda Thurston, Desmond Tutu, Mairead Corrigan Maguire, and many more.

> "As a convicted felon, I have been prevented from visiting many people in prison today. But none of us should be stopped from the vital work of prison abolition and freeing the many who the U.S. holds for political reasons. *Let Freedom Ring* helps make their voices heard, and presents strategies to help win their release."
> —Daniel Berrigan SJ, former Plowshares political prisoner and member of the FBI Top Ten Wanted List.

TOWARDS COLLECTIVE
LIBERATION
★
ANTI-RACIST ORGANIZING, FEMINIST PRAXIS,
AND MOVEMENT BUILDING STRATEGY

CHRIS CRASS
FOREWORD BY ROXANNE DUNBAR-ORTIZ
INTRODUCTION BY CHRIS DIXON
"These are words from the heart, overflowing onto the streets."
VIJAY PRASHAD

Towards Collective Liberation
Anti-Racist Organizing, Feminist Praxis, and Movement Building Strategy

Chris Crass • Introduction by Chris Dixon
Foreword by Roxanne Dunbar-Ortiz
ISBN: 978-1-60486-654-4 • $20.00

Towards Collective Liberation: Anti-Racist Organizing, Feminist Praxis, and Movement Building Strategy is for activists engaging with dynamic questions of how to create and support effective movements for visionary systemic change. Chris Crass's collection of essays and interviews presents us with powerful lessons for transformative organizing through offering a firsthand look at the challenges and the opportunities of antiracist work in white communities, feminist work with men, and bringing women of color feminism into the heart of social movements. Drawing on two decades of personal activist experience and case studies of antiracist social justice organizations, Crass insightfully explores ways of transforming divisions of race, class, and gender into catalysts for powerful vision, strategy, and movement building in the United States today.

Over the last two decades, activists in the United States have been experimenting with new politics and organizational approaches that stem from a fusion of radical political traditions and liberation struggles. Drawing inspiration from women of color feminism, justice struggles in communities of color, anarchist and socialist movements, the broad upsurges of the 1960s and '70s, and social movements in the Global South, a new generation of activists has sought to understand the past while building a movement for today's world. Towards Collective Liberation contributes to this project by examining two primary dynamic trends in these efforts: the anarchist movement of the 1990s and 2000s, through which tens of thousands of activists were introduced to radical politics, direct action organizing, democratic decision making, and the profound challenges of taking on systems of oppression, privilege, and power in society at large and in the movement itself; and white anti-racist organizing efforts from the 2000s to the present as part of a larger strategy to build broad-based, effective multiracial movements in the United States.

> "In his writing and organizing, Chris Crass has been at the forefront of building the grassroots, multi-racial, feminist movements for justice we need. Towards Collective Liberation takes on questions of leadership, building democratic organizations, and movement strategy, on a very personal level that invites us all to experiment and practice the way we live our values while struggling for systemic change."
> —Elizabeth 'Betita' Martinez, founder of the Institute for Multiracial Justice and author of *De Colores Means All of Us: Latina Views for a Multi-Colored Century*

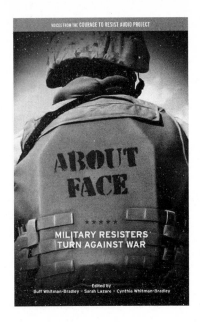

About Face
Military Resisters Turn Against War

Edited by: Buff Whitman-Bradley, Sarah Lazare, and Cynthia Whitman-Bradley
ISBN: 978-1-60486-440-3 • $20.00

How does a young person who volunteers to serve in the U.S. military become a war-resister who risks ostracism, humiliation, and prison rather than fight? Although it is not well publicized, the long tradition of refusing to fight in unjust wars continues today within the American military.

In this book, resisters describe in their own words the process they went through, from raw recruits to brave refusers. They speak about the brutality and appalling violence of war; the constant dehumanizing of the enemy—and of our own soldiers—that begins in Basic Training; the demands that they ignore their own consciences and simply follow orders. They describe how their ideas about the justification for the current wars changed and how they came to oppose the policies and practices of the U.S. empire, and even war itself. Some of the refusers in this book served one or more tours of duty in Iraq and Afghanistan, and returned with serious problems resulting from Post-Traumatic Stress Disorder. Others heard such disturbing stories of violence from returning vets that they vowed not to go themselves. Still others were mistreated in one way or another and decided they'd had enough. Every one of them had the courage to say a resounding "NO!" The stories in this book provide an intimate, honest look at the personal transformation of each of these young people and at the same time constitute a powerful argument against militarization and endless war.

Also featured are exclusive interviews with Noam Chomsky and Daniel Ellsberg. Chomsky looks at the U.S.-led wars in Iraq and Afghanistan and the potential of GI resistance to play a role in bringing the troops home. Ellsberg relates his own act of resistance in leaking the Pentagon Papers in 1971 to the current WikiLeaks revelations of U.S. military secrets.

> "*About Face* gives us important insights into the consciences of women and men who volunteer for the military but find they cannot obey orders to fight in illegal wars. These are brave and loyal Americans who are willing to challenge the U.S. government and perhaps go to jail rather than betray their inner voices that say NO to these wars!"
> —Ann Wright, retired U.S. Army colonel and diplomat who resigned in protest of the invasion of Iraq, author of *DISSENT: Voices of Conscience*

Blood on the Tracks
The Life And Times of S. Brian Willson

S. Brian Willson
Introduction by Daniel Ellsberg
ISBN: 978-1-60486-421-2 • $20.00

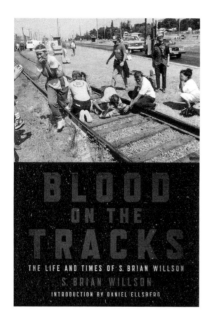

"We are not worth more, they are not worth less." This is the mantra of S. Brian Willson and the theme that runs throughout his compelling psycho-historical memoir. Willson's story begins in small-town, rural America, where he grew up as a "Commie-hating, baseball-loving Baptist," moves through life-changing experiences in Viet Nam, Nicaragua and elsewhere, and culminates with his commitment to a localized, sustainable lifestyle.

In telling his story, Willson provides numerous examples of the types of personal, risk-taking, nonviolent actions he and others have taken in attempts to educate and effect political change: tax refusal, fasting, and obstruction tactics. It was such actions that thrust Brian Willson into the public eye, first as a participant in a high-profile, water-only "Veterans Fast for Life" against the Contra war. Then, on a fateful day in September 1987, the world watched in horror as Willson was run over by a U.S. government munitions train during a nonviolent blocking action in which he expected to be removed from the tracks and arrested.

Losing his legs only strengthened Willson's identity with millions of unnamed victims of U.S. policy around the world. He provides details of his travels to countries in Latin America and the Middle East and bears witness to the harm done to poor people as well as to the environment by the steamroller of U.S. imperialism. These heart-rending accounts are offered side by side with inspirational stories of nonviolent struggle and the survival of resilient communities.

Throughout his personal journey Willson struggles with the question, "Why was it so easy for me, a 'good' man, to follow orders to travel 9,000 miles from home to participate in killing people who clearly were not a threat to me or any of my fellow citizens?" He eventually comes to the realization that the "American Way of Life" is AWOL from humanity, and that the only way to recover our humanity is by changing our consciousness, one individual at a time, while striving for collective cultural changes toward "less and local." Thus, Willson offers up his personal story as a metaphorical map for anyone who feels the need to be liberated from the American Way of Life—a guidebook for anyone called by conscience to question continued obedience to vertical power structures while longing to reconnect with the human archetypes of cooperation, equity, mutual respect, and empathy.

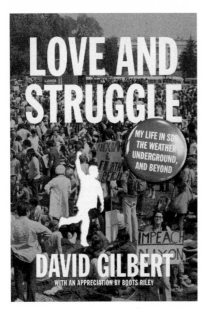

Love and Struggle
My Life in SDS, the Weather Underground, and Beyond

David Gilbert • Foreword by Boots Riley
ISBN: 978-1-60486-319-2 • $22.00

A nice Jewish boy from suburban Boston—hell, an Eagle Scout!—David Gilbert arrived at Columbia University just in time for the explosive Sixties. From the early anti-Vietnam War protests to the founding of SDS, from the Columbia Strike to the tragedy of the Townhouse, Gilbert was on the scene: as organizer, theoretician, and above all, activist. He was among the first militants who went underground to build the clandestine resistance to war and racism known as "Weatherman."

And he was among the last to emerge, in captivity, after the disaster of the 1981 Brink's robbery, an attempted expropriation that resulted in four deaths and long prison terms. In this extraordinary memoir, written from the maximum-security prison where he has lived for almost thirty years, Gilbert tells the intensely personal story of his own Long March from liberal to radical to revolutionary.

Today a beloved and admired mentor to a new generation of activists, he assesses with rare humor, with an understanding stripped of illusions, and with uncommon candor the errors and advances, terrors and triumphs of the Sixties and beyond. It's a battle that was far from won, but is still not lost: the struggle to build a new world, and the love that drives that effort. A cautionary tale and a how-to as well, *Love and Struggle* is a book as candid, as uncompromising, and as humane as its author.

"David's is a unique and necessary voice forged in the growing American gulag, the underbelly of the 'land of the free,' offering a focused and unassailable critique as well as a vision of a world that could be but is not yet—a place of peace and love, joy and justice."
—Bill Ayers, author of *Fugitive Days* and *Teaching Toward Freedom*

"Like many of his contemporaries, David Gilbert gambled his life on a vision of a more just and generous world. His particular bet cost him the last three decades in prison, and whether or not you agree with his youthful decision, you can be the beneficiary of his years of deep thought, reflection, and analysis on the reality we all share. If there is any benefit to prison, what some refer to as 'the involuntary monastery,' it may well look like this book. I urge you to read it."
—Peter Coyote, actor, author of *Sleeping Where I Fall*

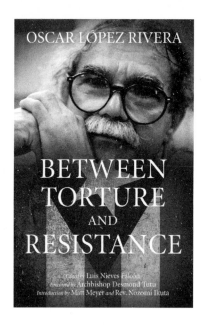

Oscar Lopez Rivera
Between Torture and Resistance

Oscar López Rivera
Edited by Luis Nieves Falcón
Foreword by Archbishop Desmond Tutu
Introduction by Matt Meyer
ISBN: 978-1-60486-685-8 • $15.95

"In spite of the fact that here the silence from outside is more painful than the solitude inside the cave, the song of a bird or the sound of a cicada always reaches me to awaken my faith and keep me going."
—Oscar López Rivera

The story of Puerto Rican leader Oscar López Rivera is one of courage, valor, and sacrifice. A decorated Viet Nam veteran and well-respected community activist, López Rivera now holds the distinction of being one of the longest held political prisoners in the world. Behind bars since 1981, López Rivera was convicted of the thought-crime of "seditious conspiracy," and never accused of causing anyone harm or of taking a life. This book is a unique introduction to his story and struggle, based on letters between him and the renowned lawyer, sociologist, educator, and activist Luis Nieves Falcón.

In photographs, reproductions of his paintings, and graphic content, Oscar's life is made strikingly accessible—so all can understand why this man has been deemed dangerous to the U.S. government. His ongoing fight for freedom, for his people and for himself (his release date is 2027, when he will be 84 years old), is detailed in chapters which share the life of a Latino child growing up in the small towns of Puerto Rico and the big cities of the U.S. It tells of his emergence as a community activist, of his life underground, and of his years in prison. Most importantly, it points the way forward.

With a vivid assessment of the ongoing colonial relationship between the U.S. and Puerto Rico, it provides tools for working for López Rivera's release—an essential ingredient if U.S.-Latin American relations, both domestically and internationally, have any chance of improvement. Between Torture and Resistance tells a sad tale of human rights abuses in the U.S. which are largely unreported. But it is also a story of hope—that there is beauty and strength in resistance.